Percentage of Muslims in the Member States of the U.N. General Assembly

1) Canada 1%
2) United States of America 2.2%
3) Mexico N/A
4) Cuba N/A
5) Jamaica N/A
6) Haiti N/A
7) Dominican Republic N/A
8) Bahamas N/A
9) Saint Kitts and Nevis N/A
10) Antigua and Barbuda N/A
11) Dominica N/A
12) Saint Lucia 0%
13) Saint Vincent and the Grenadines N/A
14) Barbados N/A
15) Grenada N/A
16) Trinidad and Tobago 5.8%
17) Guatemala N/A
18) El Salvador N/A
19) Costa Rica N/A
20) Panama N/A
21) Belize N/A
22) Honduras N/A
23) Nicaragua N/A
24) Ecuador N/A
25) Colombia N/A
26) Venezuela N/A
27) Suriname 19.6%
28) Guyana 10%
29) Brazil N/A
30) Peru N/A
31) Bolivia N/A
32) Paraguay N/A
33) Argentina N/A
34) Uruguay N/A
35) Chile 0%
36) South Africa 2%
37) Lesotho 0%
38) Swaziland 10%
39) Namibia N/A
40) Botswana N/A
41) Zimbabwe 1%
42) Malawi 20%

43) Madagascar 7%
44) Mauritius 16.6%
45) Comoros 98%
46) Mozambique 20%
47) Zambia 1%
48) Angola N/A
49) Democratic Republic of the Congo 10%
50) Burundi 10%
51) Rwanda 4.6%
52) United Republic of Tanzania 35%
53) Kenya 10%
54) Uganda 16%
55) Congo 2%
56) Gabon 1%
57) Equatorial Guinea N/A
58) Sao Tome and Principe N/A
59) Benin 20%
60) Togo 20%
61) Ghana 16%
62) Côte d'Ivoire 60%
63) Liberia 20%
64) Sierra Leone 60%
65) Guinea 85%
66) Guinea-Bissau 45%
67) Gambia 90%
68) Cape Verde 2.8%
69) Senegal 94%
70) Western Sahara[1] 100%
71) Mauritania 100%
72) Mali 90%
73) Burkina Faso 50%
74) Niger 80%
75) Nigeria 50%
76) Cameroon 20%
77) Central African Republic 15%
78) Chad 51%
79) Sudan 70%
80) Djibouti 94%
81) Ethiopia 35%
82) Somalia 99.9%
83) Eritrea 47.7%

84) Egypt 94%
85) Libyan Arab Jamahiriya 97%
86) Tunisia 98%
87) Algeria 99%
88) Morocco 98%
89) Seychelles N/A
90) Russian Federation 7%
91) Kazakhstan 47%
92) Uzbekistan 88%
93) Turkmenistan 89%
94) Afghanistan 99%
95) Pakistan 97%
96) Tajikistan 90%
97) Kyrgyzstan 75%
98) India 12%
99) Sri Lanka 7%
100) Maldives 100%
101) Nepal 3.8%
102) Bhutan 0%
103) Bangladesh 83%
104) China 1.5%
105) Mongolia 4%
106) Democratic People's Republic of Korea N/A
107) Republic of Korea N/A
108) Japan N/A
109) Philippines 5%
110) Palau N/A
111) Malaysia 53%
112) Brunei Darussalam 67%
113) Indonesia 88%
114) Timor-Leste 4%
115) Australia N/A
116) New Zealand N/A
117) Papua New Guinea N/A
118) Federated States of Micronesia N/A
119) Marshall Islands N/A
120) Nauru N/A
121) Kiribati N/A
122) Solomon Islands N/A
123) Tuvalu N/A
124) Samoa N/A

125) Vanuatu N/A
126) Fiji 8%
127) Tonga N/A
128) Turkey 99%
129) Cyprus 18%
130) Lebanon 59.7%
131) Israel 14.6%
132) Syrian Arab Republic 90%
133) Jordan 94%
134) Iraq 97%
135) Islamic Republic of Iran 98%
136) Kuwait 85%
137) Bahrain 85%
138) Qatar 95%
139) Saudi Arabia 96%
140) Yemen 100%
141) United Arab Emirates 96%
142) Oman 88%
143) Iceland N/A
144) Ireland N/A
145) United Kingdom of Great Britain and Northern Ireland 2%
146) Norway N/A
147) Sweden N/A
148) Finland N/A
149) Estonia N/A
150) Latvia N/A
151) Lithuania N/A
152) Belarus N/A
153) Ukraine 0%
154) Republic of Moldova 5.5%
155) Romania <1%
156) Serbia and Montenegro 19%
157) Bulgaria 12.2%
158) Greece 1.3%
159) The former Yugoslav Republic of Macedonia 29%
160) Albania 70%
161) Bosnia and Herzegovina 40%

162) Croatia 1.3%
163) Slovenia 1%
164) Austria 4.2%
165) Hungary N/A
166) Slovakia N/A
167) Czech Republic N/A
168) Poland N/A
169) Germany 3.7%
170) Denmark 2%
171) Netherlands 4.4%
172) Belgium N/A
173) Luxembourg N/A
174) Switzerland 2.2%
175) Italy 1.2%
176) Malta N/A
177) San Marino N/A
178) Liechtenstein N/A
179) Monaco N/A
180) France 10%
181) Andorra N/A
182) Spain 0.5%
183) Portugal 0.1%
184) Georgia 11%
185) Armenia N/A
186) Azerbaijan 93%
187) Myanmar 4%
188) Thailand 3.8%
189) Lao People's Democratic Republic N/A
190) Vietnam N/A
191) Cambodia 2.3%
192) Singapore 14.9%

[1] Western Sahara is not a U.N. Member and not universally recognized.

GLOBAL STUDIES

ISLAM AND THE MUSLIM WORLD

Mir Zohair Husain
University of South Alabama

OTHER BOOKS IN THE GLOBAL STUDIES SERIES
- Africa
- China
- India and South Asia
- Japan and the Pacific Rim
- Latin America
- The Middle East
- Russia, the Eurasian Republics, and
  Central/Eastern Europe

McGraw-Hill/Contemporary Learning Series
2460 Kerper Boulevard, Dubuque, Iowa 52001
Visit us on the Internet—http://www.mhcls.com

Staff

Larry Loeppke	*Managing Editor*
Jill Peter	*Senior Developmental Editor*
Lori Church	*Permissions Assistant*
Maggie Lytle	*Cover*
Tara McDermott	*Designer*
Kari Voss	*Typesetting Supervisor/Co-designer*
Jean Smith	*Typesetter*
Sandy Wille	*Typesetter*
Karen Spring	*Typesetter*
Julie Keck	*Senior Marketing Manager*
Mary Klein	*Marketing Communications Specialist*
Alice Link	*Marketing Coordinator*
Tracie Kammerude	*Senior Marketing Assistant*

Sources for Statistical Reports

U.S. State Department *Background Notes* (2003)

C.I.A. *World Factbook* (2002)

World Bank *World Development Reports* (2002/2003)

UN *Population and Vital Statistics Reports* (2002/2003)

World Statistics in Brief (2002)

The Statesman's Yearbook (2003)

Population Reference Bureau *World Population Data Sheet* (2002)

The World Almanac (2003)

The Economist Intelligence Unit (2003)

Copyright

Cataloging in Publication Data
Main entry under title: Global Studies: Islam and the Muslim World
ISBN 0–07–352772–6   ISSN 1556-8911

Printed in the United States of America   1234567890BAHBAH54   Printed on Recycled Paper

Islam and the Muslim World

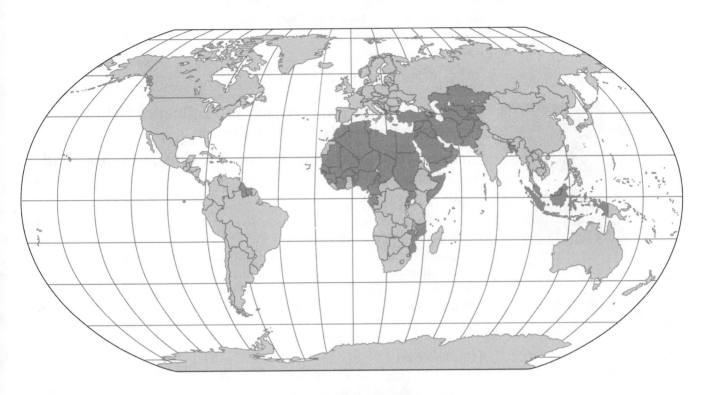

AUTHOR/EDITOR

Mir Zohair Husain

University of South Alabama

The author/editor of *Global Studies: Islam and the Muslim World* is an Associate Professor in the Department of Political Science and Criminal Justice at the University of South Alabama. He teaches International Relations, Comparative Politics, the Muslim World, Middle East Politics, and South Asian Politics. In 2003, Longman Publishers published the second edition of his book, Global Islamic Politics. He has presented many papers at professional conferences and lectured on a broad spectrum of global events, issues, and problems in Philadelphia and Mobile. He has been nominated twice for the University of South Alabama Alumni Association's Outstanding Teacher Award (1993 and 1999). Also, he has received the Best Faculty Member Award for Outstanding Service to International Students at the University of South Alabama (1994 and 2002), and the University of South Alabama's Student Government Association's Outstanding Advisor Award for Dedication and Service (2003–2004).

Contents

Chapter 1: Momentous Events and Influencial Muslims That Have Shaped Islamic Civilzation   1

Chapter 2: Understanding Islam, Muslims, Islamism, and Anti-Americanism   10

Country Reports

Articles from the World Press 287

Using *Global Studies: Islam and the Muslim World*

THE GLOBAL STUDIES SERIES

The Global Studies series was created to help readers acquire a basic knowledge and understanding of the regions and countries in the world. Each volume provides a foundation of information—geographic, cultural, economic, political, historical, artistic, and religious—that will allow readers to better assess the current and future problems within these countries and regions and to comprehend how events there might affect their own well-being. In short, these volumes present the background information necessary to respond to the realities of our global age. Each of the volumes in the Global Studies series is crafted under the careful direction of an author/editor—an expert in the area under study. The author/editors teach and conduct research and have traveled extensively through the regions about which they are writing. In *Global Studies: Islam and the Muslim World,* the author/editor has written several regional essays and country reports for each of the countries included.

MAJOR FEATURES OF THE GLOBAL STUDIES SERIES

The Global Studies volumes are organized to provide concise information on the regions and countries within those areas under study. The major sections and features of the books are described here.

Regional Essays

For *Global Studies: Islam and the Muslim World*, the author/editor has written several essays focusing on the religious, cultural, sociopolitical, and economic differences and similarities of the countries and peoples in 57 Organization of the Islamic Conference (OIC) states. Regional maps accompany the essays.

Country Reports

Concise reports are written for each of the countries within the region under study. These reports are the heart of each Global Studies volume. *Global Studies: Islam and the Muslim World* contains 57 country reports.

The country reports are composed of five standard elements. Each report contains a detailed map visually positioning the country among its neighboring states; a summary of statistical information; a current essay providing important historical, geographical, political, cultural, and economic information; a historical timeline, offering a convenient visual survey of a few key historical events; and four "graphic indicators," with summary statements about the country in terms of development, freedom, health/welfare, and achievements.

A Note on the Statistical Reports

The statistical information provided for each country has been drawn from a wide range of sources. (The most frequently referenced are listed on page iv.) Every effort has been made to provide the most current and accurate information available. However, sometimes the information cited by these sources differs to some extent; and, all too often, the most current information available for some countries is somewhat dated. Aside from these occasional difficulties, the statistical summary of each country is generally quite complete and up to date. Care should be taken, however, in using these statistics (or, for that matter, any published statistics) in making hard comparisons among countries. We have also provided comparable statistics for the United States and Canada, which can be found on pages xiv and xv.

World Press Articles

Within each Global Studies volume is reprinted a number of articles carefully selected by our editorial staff and the author/editor from a broad range of international periodicals and newspapers. The articles have been chosen for currency, interest, and their differing perspectives on the subject countries. There are 14 articles in *Global Studies: Islam and the Muslim World*. The articles section is preceded by an annotated table of contents. This resource offers a brief summary of each article.

WWW Sites

An extensive annotated list of selected World Wide Web sites can be found on the facing page (x) in this edition of *Global Studies: Islam and the Muslim World*. In addition, the URL addresses for country-specific Web sites are provided on the statistics page of most countries. All of the Web site addresses were correct and operational at press time. Instructors and students alike are urged to refer to those sites often to enhance their understanding of the region and to keep up with current events.

Glossary, Bibliography, Index

At the back of each Global Studies volume, readers will find a glossary of terms and abbreviations, which provides a quick reference to the specialized vocabulary of the area under study and to the standard abbreviations used throughout the volume. Following the glossary is a bibliography that lists general works, national histories, and current-events publications and periodicals that provide regular coverage on Islam, Muslims, and Muslim countries. The index at the end of the volume is an accurate reference to the contents of the volume. Readers seeking specific information and citations should consult this standard index.

Currency and Usefulness

Global Studies: Islam and the Muslim World, like the other Global Studies volumes, is intended to provide the most current and useful information available necessary to understand the events that are shaping the cultures of the region today. This volume is revised on a regular basis. The statistics are updated, regional essays and country reports revised, and world press articles replaced. In order to accomplish this task, we turn to our author/editor, our advisory boards, and—hopefully—to you, the users of this volume. Your comments are more than welcome. If you have an idea that you think will make the next edition more useful; an article or bit of information that will make it more current; or a general comment on its organization, content; or features that you would like to share with us, please send it in for serious consideration.

Selected World Wide Web Sites for Islam and the Muslim World

(Note: Some Web sites continually change their structure and content, so the information listed here may not always be available. Check our Web site at: http://www.mhcls.com/online/ —Ed.)

GENERAL SITES

BBC News
http://news.bbc.co.uk/hi/english/world/middle_east/default.stm
Access current Middle East news from this BBC site.

CNN Interactive—World Regions: Middle East
http://www.cnn. com/WORLD/#mideast
This 24-hour news channel often focuses on the Middle East and is updated every few hours.

C-SPAN Online
http://www.c-span.org
See especially C-SPAN International on the Web for International Programming Highlights and archived C-SPAN programs.

Library of Congress
http://www.loc.gov
An invaluable resource for facts and analysis of 100 countries' political, economic, social, and national-security systems and installations.

ReliefWeb
http://www.reliefweb.int/w/rwb.nsf
UN's Department of Humanitarian Affairs clearinghouse for international humanitarian emergencies. It has daily updates, including Reuters and Voice of America.

United Nations
http://www.unsystem.org
The official Web site for the United Nations system of organizations. Everything is listed alphabetically, and data on UNICC and Food and Agriculture Organization are available.

UN Development Programme (UNDP)
http://www.undp.org
Publications and current information on world poverty, Mission Statement, UN Development Fund for Women, and much more. Be sure to see the Poverty Clock.

UN Environmental Programme (UNEP)
http://www.unep.org
Official site of UNEP with information on UN environmental programs, products, services, events, and a search engine.

U.S. Central Intelligence Agency Home Page
http://www.cia. gov/ index.htm
This site includes publications of the CIA, such as the World Factbook, Factbook on Intelligence, Handbook of International Economic Statistics, CIA Maps and Publications, and much more.

U.S. Department of State Home Page
http://www.state.gov/ www/ind.html
Organized alphabetically (i.e., Country Reports, Human Rights, International Organizations, and more).

World Health Organization (WHO)
http://www.who.ch
Maintained by WHO's headquarters in Geneva, Switzerland, the site uses the Excite search engine to conduct keyword searches.

ISLAM AND MUSLIM WORLD

The Abraham Fund
http://www.coexistence.org
The goal of peaceful coexistence between Jews and Arabs is the theme of this site. Information about various projects and links to related sites are offered.

Al-Jazeera News Online
http://www.aljazeera.net
This Web site features Al-Jazeera news articles online and is offered in English and Arabic.

America's War Against Terrorism
http://www.lib.umich.edu/govdocs/usterror.html
This Web site, by the University of Michigan, provides a news chronicle of the September 11, 2001, attacks and the war against terrorism.

Arab.Net
http://www.arab.net/sections/contents.html
This Web site is an extensive online resource for the Arab world in the Middle East (Southwest Asia and North Africa). It presents links to 22 Arab countries ranging alphabetically from Algeria to Yemen. Each country's Web page classifies information using a standardized system of categories. The site includes a search engine.

ASEAN Web
http://www.asean.or.id
This official site of the Association of Southeast Asian Nations (ASEAN) provides an overview of Asia: Web resources, Asian summits, economic affairs, political foundations, and regional cooperation.

The Avalon Project at Yale Law School
http://www.yale.edu/lawweb/avalon/terrorism/terror.htm
Yale Law School has undertaken to collect and house digital documents relevant to the fields of law, history, government, economics, politics, diplomacy, and terrorism. This particular site provides documents relating to terrorism.

Bosnia Home Page
http://www.cco.caltech.edu/~bosnia/bosnia.html
Data about past and present Bosnia history of war, war criminals, U.S. and NATO involvement, culture, and daily life are available here. The site also offers an information resources list for further exploring.

Carnegie Endowment for International Peace (CEIP)
http://www.ceip.org
One of the most important goals of the CEIP is to stimulate discussion and learning among both experts and the public on a wide range of international issues. The site provides links to the *Foreign Policy* journal, the Moscow Center, and descriptions of various programs.

The Carter Center
http://www.cartercenter.org
The Carter Center is dedicated to fighting disease, hunger, poverty, conflict, and oppression through collaborative initiatives in the areas of democratization and development, global health, and urban revitalization.

Center for Conflict Resolution
http://www.conflict-resolution.org/
This site is the Center for Conflict Resolution, located at Salisbury University in Maryland. It features information on the programs offered on the campuses and provides access to some lectures. In the future the site will provide access to student reports.

Center for Middle Eastern Studies
http://w3.arizona.edu/~cmesua/
This Web site is maintained by the University of Arizona Center for Middle Eastern Studies. The Center's mission is to further understanding and knowledge of the Middle East through education.

The Center for Middle Eastern Studies
http://menic.utexas.edu/menic/
The Middle East Network Information Center at the University of Texas at Austin is an inclusive source for general as well as country-specific information. Read about the history, culture, business, energy resources, and government of each country; view maps and scan newspapers of the region; familiarize yourself with Islam, Judaism, and Christianity and how these religions interact in the region; and click the News and Media link in order to hear Arabic spoken on radio stations in the Middle East.

Coalition for International Justice
http://www.cij.org/index.cfm?fuseaction=homepage
This site provides all kinds of information about the investigation and prosecution of war crimes in the former Yugoslavia and in Rwanda, including some audio and video files.

Columbia International Affairs Online
http://www.ciaonet.org/cbr/cbr00/video/cbr_v/cbr_v.html
This site provides excerpts from al-Qaeda's two-hour videotape used to recruit young Muslims to fight in a holy war. The tape demonstrates al-Qaeda's use of the Internet and media outlets for propaganda and persuasion purposes.

Conflict Resolution and Ethnicity
http://www.incore.ulst.ac.uk/cds/countries/index.html
The University of Ulster has developed an Internet Guide for the Initiative on Conflict Resolution and Ethnicity that examines the most recent international conflicts and nationalist movements in detail. Arranged by geographic location, this site offers information about conflicts from Kosovo to Ethiopia and

Eritrea. There are links to research sources, news sources, maps, nongovernmental organizations, and email lists and newsgroups. Information can be gathered according to themes as well as "Children and Conflict."

A Conflict Resolution Page
http://www.geocities.com/Athens/8945/

This is a privately sponsored Web site that offers links to search engines, biographies and books on conflict resolution, ethnic and minority-majority relations, and other conflict resolution Web sites.

Country Indicators for Foreign Policy
http://www.carleton.ca/cifp/

This site features statistical risk assessment data on nation-states, compiled by Carlton University in Ottowa, Ontario, Canada.

Data on the Net
http://odwin.ucsd.edu/idata/

The University of California at San Diego has created a gateway Web site from which one can browse the collection of several hundred Internet sites of numerous social science statistical data.

The Duncan Black Macdonald Center for the Study of Islam & Christian-Muslim Relations
http://macdonald.hartsem.edu/muslimworld.htm

This Web site is dedicated to the promotion and dissemination of scholarly research on Islam and Muslim societies and on historical and current aspects of Christian-Muslim relations. The journal for this site includes research articles, book reviews, notices, and surveys of periodicals.

The Economist Online
http://www.economist.com/index.html

This Web site provides access to *The Economist* magazine articles online.

EI: Electronic Intifada
http://electronicintifada.net/new.shtml

EI is a major Palestinian portal for information about the Palestinian-Israeli conflict from a Palestinian perspective.

Foreign Policy in Focus (FPIF): Progressive Response Index
http://fpif.org/progresp/index_body.html

This index is produced weekly by FPIF, a "think tank without walls," which is an international network of analysts and activists dedicated to "making the United States a more responsible global leader and partner by advancing citizen movements and agendas." This index lists volume and issue numbers, dates, and topics covered by the articles.

Foreign Policy in Focus: Asia and Pacific Rim
http://fpif.org/indices/regions/asia_body.html

This site offers papers, reports, and policy briefs on nuclear proliferation, women's issues, environment, self-determination, and economic development for Asia and Pacific Rim countries.

Fourth Freedom Forum
http://www.fourthfreedom.org/

This Fourth Freedom Forum's goal is "a more civilized world based on the force of law rather than the law of force." This Web site gives a prosanctions point of view. It contends that the effective use of economic incentives and sanctions offers the greatest hope for creating a more secure and peaceful future. The "Sanctions and Incentives" link on the homepage will provide an extensive collection of articles related to international sanctions and case studies.

Freedom House
http://www.freedomhouse.org/

This nonprofit organization focuses on threats to peace, democracy, and human rights around the world. Each year since 1972, Freedom House has published comparative ratings for countries and territories around the world, evaluating levels of political rights and civil liberties.

Graphs Comparing Countries
http://humandevelopment.bu.edu/use_exsisting_index/start_comp_graph.cfm

This site allows you to compare various countries and nation-states with statistics using a visual tool.

Human Rights Watch (HRW)
http://www.hrw.org/

HRW is an independent, nongovernmental organization dedicated to protecting the human rights of people around the world. To this end, the organization investigates and exposes human rights violations and holds abusers accountable. HRW challenges governments to respect the laws drafted by the international organizations. Its Web site provides stories on breaking news concerning human rights around the world. The site delivers HRW reports on specific countries' human-rights abuses.

Institute for War and Peace Reporting (IWPR)
http://www.iwpr.net/

The main goal of the IWPR is to bring unbiased information on international conflicts to Internet users. An independent media source, IWPR informs readers on international conflicts and supports media development in war-torn areas. Special reports provide in-depth analysis of conflict, media, and human rights issues in regions across the globe. There is also a list of Internet links for those who want more information on the conflicts.

International Conflict Resolution: Information Sources
http://www.columbia.edu/cu/lweb/indiv/lehman/guides/icr.html

This Web site is sponsored by the Lehman Social Sciences Library and possesses features that aid one in finding journal articles and books, background information, United States government agencies, intergovernmental agencies, and research and policy centers.

International Court of Justice (ICJ) Considers Genocide
http://oz.uc.edu/thro/genocide/index.html

Professor Howard Tolley of the University of Cincinnati has created an interactive Web site on which you can role-play the judge at the ICJ when Bosnia brought charges against Yugoslavia in 1993. You can explore the facts, research the law, and consider opposing arguments, and then make your judgment.

International Criminal Tribunal for the Former Yugoslavia (ICTY)
http://www.un.org/icty/

Established by the UN Security Council in 1993, the ICTY is mandated to prosecute persons responsible for serious violations of international humanitarian law committed on the territory of the former Yugoslavia since 1991. This Web site also informs about who was indicted for war crimes and what judgment was rendered.

International Crisis Group (ICG)
http://www.intl-crisis-group.org/

The ICG is a private, multinational organization dedicated to understanding and responding to international crises. The organization's analysts conduct field research and prepare reports about ongoing conflicts that are used to make recommendations to states' decision makers. Currently, ICG has projects in northern and central Africa, the Balkans, and Southeast Asia. Those interested in conflicts in these regions will find useful overviews of specific countries, reports on developments, and maps.

International Information Programs
http://usinfo.state.gov

This wide-ranging Web page offered by the State Department provides definitions, related documentation, and a discussion of topics of concern to students of foreign policy and foreign affairs. It addresses current and ongoing issues that form the foundation of the field. Many Web links are provided.

International Network Information Center at University of Texas
http://inic.utexas.edu

This gateway has many pointers to international sites, organized into African, Asian, Latin American, Middle Eastern, Russian, and East European subsections.

The International Policy Institute for Counter-Terrorism (ICT)
http://www.ict.org.il

ICT is a research institute and think tank dedicated to developing innovative public policy solutions to international terrorism. The Policy Institute applies an integrated, solutions-oriented approach built on a foundation of real-world and practical experience.

IRIN
http://www.irinnews.org

The United Nations Office for the Coordination of Humanitarian Affairs provides free analytical reports, fact sheets, interviews, daily country updates, and weekly summaries through this site and e-mail distribution service. The site is a good source of news for crisis situations as they occur.

Islam Denounces Terrorism
http://www.islamdenouncesterrorism.com

This Web site was launched to reveal that Islam does not endorse any kind of terror or barbarism and that Muslims share the sorrows of the victims of terrorism. It includes many references to the Qur'an and preach tolerance and peace.

IslamiCity
http://islamicity.com

This is one of the largest Islamic sites on the Web, reaching 50 million people a month. Based in California, it includes public opinion polls, links to television and radio broadcasts, and religious guidance.

ISN International Relations and Security Network
http://www.isn.ethz.ch

This site, maintained by the Center for Security Studies and Conflict Research, is a clearinghouse for extensive information on international relations and security policy. Topics are listed by category (Traditional Dimensions of Security, New Dimensions of Security, and Related Fields) and by major world regions.

The Jaffe Center for Strategic Studies (JCSS) at Tel-Aviv University
http://www.tau.ac.il/jcss/lmas.html

The JCSS at Tel-Aviv University lists five different groups of Web site directories on low-intensity warfare and terrorism.

Middle East Policy Council
http://www.mepc.org

The purpose of the Middle East Policy Council's Web site is to expand public discussion and understanding of issues affecting U.S. policy in the Middle East.

Middle East Studies Association
http://w3fp.arizona.edu/mesassoc/

This Web site is sponsored by a nonpolitical association to further understanding of the Middle East and related issues. It includes information about its organization and programs, and it provides links to other useful Web sites.

Middle East Times
http://metimes.com

The Middle East Times is a source for independent analysis of politics, business, religion, and culture in the Middle East.

The New York Times on the Web
http://www.nytimes.com/

This Web site provides access to The New York Times newspaper articles online.

NewsDirectory.com
http://www.newsd.com

This site, a Guide to English Language Media Online, lists over 7,000 actively updated papers and magazines.

Oneworld.net
http://www.oneworld.net/article/frontpage/

Search this Web site for information and news about issues related to human sustainable development throughout the world. Information can be accessed by topic or country.

Political Science Quarterly
http://www.psqonline.org/

This Web site features articles from the Political Science Quarterly journal and is published by the Academy of Political Science. The journal features articles concerning public and international affairs.

Political Science Resources
http://www.lib.uci.edu/online/subject/subpage.php?subject=poli

This University of California/Irvine Web site features a list of links on such topics as online references, data sources, intelligence sources, international organizations, and think tanks.

Richard Kimber's Political Science Resources
http://www.psr.keele.ac.uk/

This is a privately run Web site that features a wealth of information and links on the major dimensions and branches of political science.

Social Science Information Gateway (SOSIG)
http://sosig.esrc.bris.ac.uk

A project of the Economic and Social Research Council (ESRC), this is an online catalog of thousands of Internet resources relevant to political education and research. It catalogs 22 subjects and lists developing countries' URLs.

South Asia Resources
http://www.lib.berkeley.edu/SSEAL/SouthAsia/

From this University of Berkeley Library site, there is quick access to online resources in Asian studies as well as to South Asian specialists and other special features.

South Asian History
http://www.stockton.edu/~gilmorew/consorti/1aindia.htm

As part of Stockton's Word Wide Web Global History Research Institute, the history of the Indian subcontinent has been arranged chronologically at this Web site. This excellent resource contains maps, pictures, short writings, and scholarly writings.

Southeast Asia Information
http://sunsite.nus.edu.sg/asiasvc.html

A gateway for country-specific research is presented here. Information on Internet Providers and Universities in Southeast Asia is available as well as links to Asian online services.

Terrorism Files
http://www.terrorismfiles.org

This is an up-to-date Web source for news and editorial covering terrorism and current events.

The United Nations
http://www.un.org

The United Nations (UN) is an intergovernmental organization with global membership that performs multiple purposes. This Web site is the gateway to information about the UN. It is organized according to the organization's primary concerns: peace and security, international law, humanitarian affairs, economic and social development, and human rights. Also see http://www.undp.org/missions/usa/usna/htm for the U.S. Mission at the UN.

UNAIDS
http://www.unaids.org/

UNAIDS is a joint program of the UN and a leading advocate for worldwide action against HIV/AIDS. Its mission is to support and strengthen an expanded response to the global AIDS epidemic. UNAIDS devises programs that will prevent the spread of HIV, provide care and support for those affected by the diseases, and alleviate the socioeconomic and human impact of the epidemic. This site provides access to those interested in exploring the HIV/AIDS epidemic by country and finding out about the World AIDS Campaign.

United Nations Children's Emergency Fund (UNICEF)
http://www.unicef.org

UNICEF, founded in 1946 and headquartered in Paris, is the only truly global organization devoted exclusively to children and to the protection of children's rights. You can learn about the terrible impact that HIV/AIDS is having on children in several countries by going to the UNICEF link: http://www.unicef.org/pon99/.

United Nations High Commissioner for Refugees (UNHCR)
http://www.unhcr.ch/

The UNHCR leads and coordinates international action for the worldwide protection of refugees and the resolution of refugee problems. This Web site offers a wealth of information on refugees. The "Protecting Refugees" link describes one of the fundamental aspects of the UNHCR; the "Statistics" link gives the current numbers on refugees worldwide as well as by country; and the current "News" link examines important current topics.

United Nations Peacekeeping Operations
http://www.un.org/Depts/dpko/dpko/home.shtml

The United Nations has deployed numerous international military and civilian personnel to conflict areas to stop or contain hostilities and supervise the carrying out of peace agreements. Click on an ongoing mission and read about the profile, background, and facts and figures concerning the mission. Do the same thing for an older mission. Are there any similarities and differences?

United States Census Bureau: International Summary Demographic Data
http://www.census.gov/ipc/www/idbnew.html

The U.S. Census Bureau offers the chance to use its computerized bank of demographic data for all countries of the world. From the homepage, one can look at the "Summary Demographic Data" to see totals in population and rates of growth for each country. The U.S. Census Bureau's World Population Clock can be accessed by going to http://www.census.gov/cgi-bin/ipc/popclockw. The latter projects the world population every second of every day. Look at the number of people in the world. Then, hit the Reload button at the top of your Web browser. How many more people were born in the time that it took to read the number of people in the world?

United States Department of State
http://www.state.gov/index.html

This is the homepage of the U.S. State Department. Organized alphabetically, this Web site presents country reports and information on human rights and international organizations, etc.

The U.S. Federal Bureau of Investigation (FBI) Homepage
http://www.fbi.gov

The homepage for the FBI includes up-to-date news and information and a section on terrorism.

United States Information Agency (USIA)
http://usinfo.state.gov/

This USIA page provides definitions, related documentation, and discussion of topics on global issues. Many Web links are provided.

United States Institute of Peace (USIP)
http://www.usip.org

USIP, which was created by the U.S. Congress to promote peaceful resolution of international conflict, seeks to educate people and to disseminate information on how to achieve peace. Click on Highlights, Publications, Events, Research Areas, and Library and Links.

GLOBAL STUDIES

United States International Affairs
http://www.state.gov/www/regions/internat.html
Data on U.S. foreign policy around the world are available here. Some of the areas covered are arms control, economics and trade, and international organizations.

U.S. Library of Congress
http://lcweb.loc.gov/rr/
This massive research and reference Web site of the Library of Congress leads to invaluable information on the former Soviet Union and other countries attempting the transition to democracy. It provides links to numerous publications, bibliographies, and guides in area studies.
http://lcweb2.loc.gov/frd/cs/cshome.html#toc
An invaluable resource for facts and analysis of 100 countries' political, economic, social, and national security systems and installations.

University of Pennsylvania Library: Resources by Subject
http://www.library.upenn.edu/cgi-bin/res/sr.cgi
This site is rich in links to information about subjects of interest to students of global issues. Its extensive population and demography resources address such concerns as migration, family planning, and health and nutrition in various world regions.

Virtual Library on International Development
http://w3.acdi-cida.gc.ca/Virtual.nsf/
This Canadian site outlines international development issues by topic, region, country, and organization. You can click on the outlines to discover links to organizations, news, and resources. The reference desk announces upcoming conferences and events related to international development and provides links to libraries, periodicals, and reports of value in the study of international development.

The Washington Post on the Web
http://www.washingtonpost.com/
This Web site provides access to *The Washington Post* newspaper articles online.

World Bank
http://www.worldbank.org
News (press releases, summary of new projects, speeches) and coverage of numerous topics with regard to development, countries, and regions are available on this Web site. This site also provides links to other global financial organizations.

World Citizen Foundation
http://www.worldcitizen.org
The World Citizen Foundation believes that the Internet can help serve as a communication tool whereby the citizens of the world can vote on common global issues. This Web site leads people to think about their world citizenship and ask how they, as sovereign world citizens, can collectively govern the world—perhaps one in which a world government is possible and in which people in the future will be able to vote on world issues like they do now on national issues.

World Health Organization (WHO)
http://www.who.int/en
The main goal of the WHO is the attainment by all peoples of the highest possible level of health. Health is defined in the WHO's constitution as the "state of complete physical, mental, and social well-being and not merely the absence of disease or infirmity." This homepage of the World Health Organization provides links to a wealth of statistical and analytical information about health and the environment in the developing world.

World Resources Institute
http://www.wri.org
The World Resources Institute provides information and practical proposals for policy and institutional change that will foster environmentally sound, socially equitable development.

The World Trade Organization (WTO)
http://www.wto.org/
The WTO is an intergovernmental organization with 145 member-states and multiple purposes. Its mission is to ensure that trade flows between states as freely, smoothly, and predictably as possible. Topics include a foundation of world trade systems, data on textiles, intellectual property rights, legal frameworks, trade, and environmental policies, recent agreements, and other data.

The Worldwatch Institute
http://www.worldwatch.org
The Worldwatch Institute advocates environmental protection and sustainable development.

World Wide Web Virtual Library:
International Affairs Resources
http://www.etown.edu/vl/
Surf this Web site and its links to learn about specific countries and regions; to research think tanks and international organizations; and to study such vital topics as international law, development, the international economy, human rights, and peacekeeping.

WWW Virtual Library: Demography & Population Studies
http://demography.anu.edu.au/VirtualLibrary/
A definitive guide to demography and population studies can be found at this site. It contains a multitude of important links to information about global poverty and hunger.

See individual country statistics pages for additional Web sites.

The United States (United States of America)

GEOGRAPHY

Area in Square Miles (Kilometers):
3,717,792 (9,629,091) (about 1/2 the size
of Russia)

Capital (Population): Washington, DC
(3,997,000)

Environmental Concerns: air and water
pollution; limited freshwater resources,
desertification; loss of habitat; waste
disposal; acid rain

Geographical Features: vast central plain,
mountains in the west, hills and low
mountains in the east; rugged mountains
and broad river valleys in Alaska; volcanic
topography in Hawaii

Climate: mostly temperate, but ranging from
tropical to arctic

PEOPLE

Population

Total: 280,563,000

Annual Growth Rate: 0.89%

Rural/Urban Population Ratio: 24/76

Major Languages: predominantly English; a
sizable Spanish-speaking minority; many
others

Ethnic Makeup: 77% white; 13% black; 4%
Asian; 6% Amerindian and others

Religions: 56% Protestant; 28% Roman
Catholic; 2% Jewish; 4% others; 10% none
or unaffiliated

Health

Life Expectancy at Birth: 74 years (male); 80
years (female)

Infant Mortality: 6.69/1,000 live births

Physicians Available: 1/365 people

HIV/AIDS Rate in Adults: 0.61%

Education

Adult Literacy Rate: 97% (official)

Compulsory (Ages): 7–16; free

COMMUNICATION

Telephones: 194,000,000 main lines

Daily Newspaper Circulation: 238/1,000
people

Televisions: 776/1,000 people

Internet Users: 165,750,000 (2002)

TRANSPORTATION

Highways in Miles (Kilometers): 3,906,960
(6,261,154)

Railroads in Miles (Kilometers): 149,161
(240,000)

Usable Airfields: 14,695

Motor Vehicles in Use: 206,000,000

GOVERNMENT

Type: federal republic

Independence Date: July 4, 1776

Head of State/Government: President
George W. Bush is both head of state and
head of government

Political Parties: Democratic Party;
Republican Party; others of relatively
minor political significance

Suffrage: universal at 18

MILITARY

Military Expenditures (% of GDP): 3.2%

Current Disputes: various boundary and
territorial disputes; "war on terrorism"

ECONOMY

Per Capita Income/GDP: $36,300/$10.082
trillion

GDP Growth Rate: 0%

Inflation Rate: 3%

Unemployment Rate: 5.8%

Population Below Poverty Line: 13%

Natural Resources: many minerals and
metals; petroleum; natural gas; timber;
arable land

Agriculture: food grains; feed crops; fruits
and vegetables; oil-bearing crops;
livestock; dairy products

Industry: diversified in both capital and
consumer-goods industries

Exports: $723 billion (primary partners
Canada, Mexico, Japan)

Imports: $1.148 trillion (primary partners
Canada, Mexico, Japan)

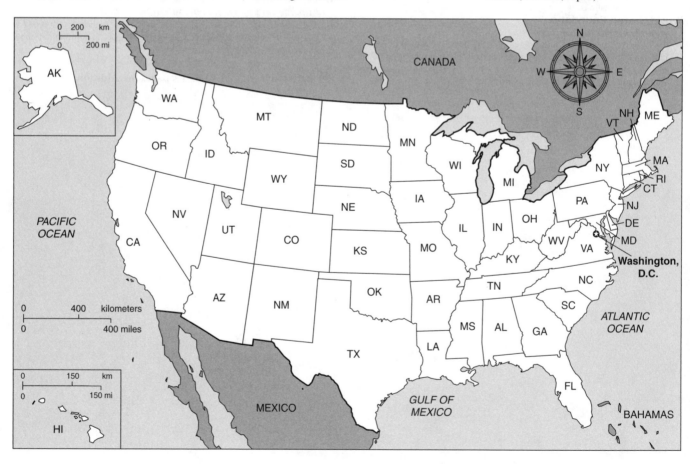

Canada

GEOGRAPHY

Area in Square Miles (Kilometers):
3,850,790 (9,976,140) (slightly larger than the United States)
Capital (Population): Ottawa (1,094,000)
Environmental Concerns: air and water pollution; acid rain; industrial damage to agriculture and forest productivity
Geographical Features: permafrost in the north; mountains in the west; central plains; lowlands in the southeast
Climate: varies from temperate to arctic

PEOPLE
Population
Total: 31,903,000
Annual Growth Rate: 0.96%
Rural/Urban Population Ratio: 23/77
Major Languages: both English and French are official
Ethnic Makeup: 28% British Isles origin; 23% French origin; 15% other European; 6% others; 2% indigenous; 26% mixed
Religions: 46% Roman Catholic; 36% Protestant; 18% others

Health
Life Expectancy at Birth: 76 years (male); 83 years (female)
Infant Mortality: 4.95/1,000 live births
Physicians Available: 1/534 people

HIV/AIDS Rate in Adults: 0.3%

Education
Adult Literacy Rate: 97%
Compulsory (Ages): primary school

COMMUNICATION
Telephones: 20,803,000 main lines
Daily Newspaper Circulation: 215/1,000 people
Televisions: 647/1,000 people
Internet Users: 16,840,000 (2002)

TRANSPORTATION
Highways in Miles (Kilometers): 559,240 (902,000)
Railroads in Miles (Kilometers): 22,320 (36,000)
Usable Airfields: 1,419
Motor Vehicles in Use: 16,800,000

GOVERNMENT
Type: confederation with parliamentary democracy
Independence Date: July 1, 1867
Head of State/Government: Queen Elizabeth II; Prime Minister Jean Chrétien
Political Parties: Progressive Conservative Party; Liberal Party; New Democratic Party; Bloc Québécois; Canadian Alliance
Suffrage: universal at 18

MILITARY
Military Expenditures (% of GDP): 1.1%
Current Disputes: maritime boundary disputes with the United States

ECONOMY
Currency ($U.S. equivalent): 1.39 Canadian dollars = $1
Per Capita Income/GDP: $27,700/$875 billion
GDP Growth Rate: 2%
Inflation Rate: 3%
Unemployment Rate: 7%
Labor Force by Occupation: 74% services; 15% manufacturing; 6% agriculture and others
Natural Resources: petroleum; natural gas; fish; minerals; cement; forestry products; wildlife; hydropower
Agriculture: grains; livestock; dairy products; potatoes; hogs; poultry and eggs; tobacco; fruits and vegetables
Industry: oil production and refining; natural-gas development; fish products; wood and paper products; chemicals; transportation equipment
Exports: $273.8 billion (primary partners United States, Japan, United Kingdom)
Imports: $238.3 billion (primary partners United States, European Union, Japan)

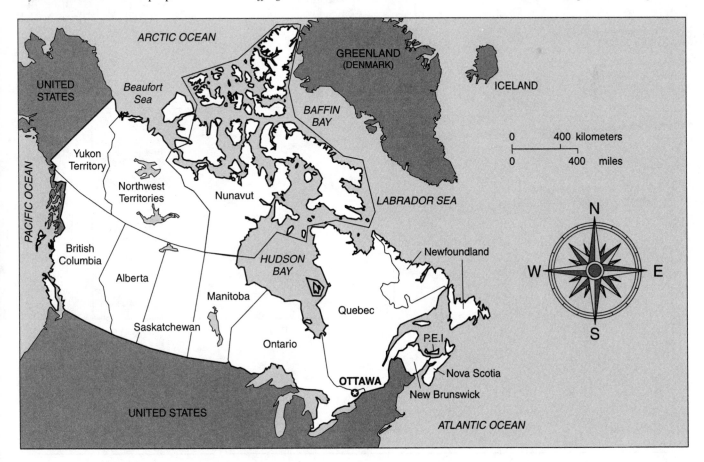

GLOBAL STUDIES

This map is provided to give you a graphic picture of where the countries of the world are located, the relationship they have with their region and neighbors, and their positions relative to major trade and power blocs. We have focused on certain areas to illustrate these crowded regions more clearly. The European region covered in this volume is shaded for emphasis.

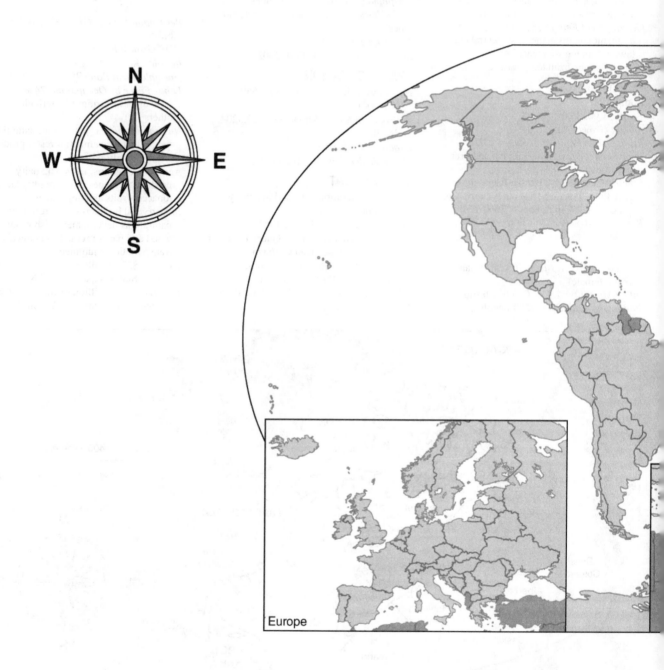

Europe

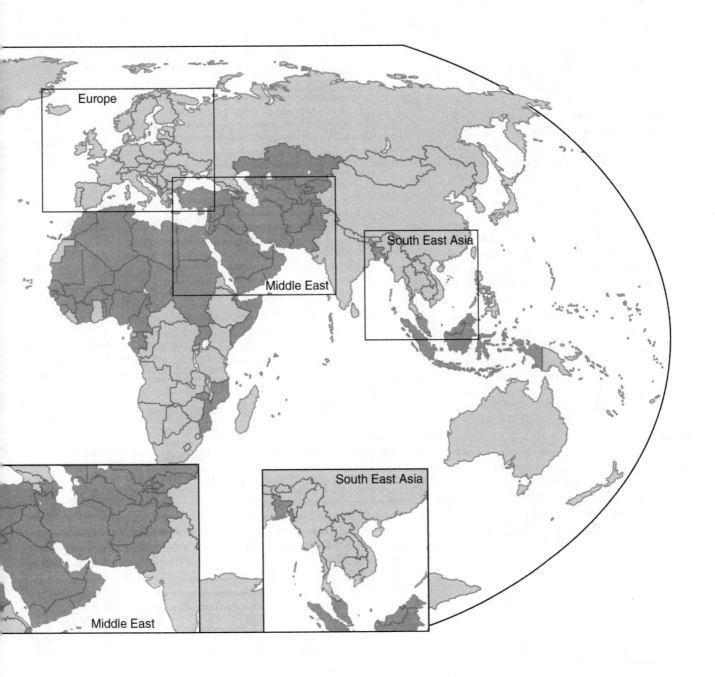

Preface

Islam is one of the fastest growing and most influential religions today, with Muslims numbering over one-fifth of the world's population (1.3 billion). In fact, Islam is the world's second largest religion after Christianity, which has 2.2 billion followers.

Although Islam shares much in common with Judaism and Christianity, most Jews and Christians unfamiliar with Islam consider it to be an alien, intolerant, and violent religion based on the frequent mass media's portrayal of misguided Muslim extremists engaging in violence and terrorism.

Muslims are most heavily concentrated in Asia and Africa, constituting more than two-thirds of Asia's population and a little less than one-half the population of Africa. However, the Muslim presence is not restricted to only these two continents. There are over 7 million Muslims in the United States and over 20 million Muslims in Europe who are making a positive contribution to the Western world. Indeed, Islam has emerged as the second largest religion in the United States, France, Britain, and Germany. Muslim communities are not only on every continent, but also in most countries around the world; therefore, it is incumbent on non-Muslims to understand Islam because Muslims will increasingly be their fellow citizens, neighbors, and coworkers.

Moreover, Muslims and their institutions play an increasing role in world affairs. Perhaps the most obvious example is the Organization of the Islamic Conference (OIC), established in 1969, which comprises 57 member-states stretching from Morocco in Northwest Africa to Indonesia in Southeast Asia and from Somalia in Southeast Africa to Albania in southern Europe. Moreover, 50 of the 57 OIC countries have majority Muslim populations, and there are significant and/or influential minorities in the other 7 OIC countries as well as in many non-OIC countries. Muslim countries are also active participants in other international organizations that influence the lives of millions of people, most notably the Organization of Arab Petroleum Exporting Countries (OAPEC), the Organization of Petroleum Exporting Countries (OPEC), the Arab League (AL), the African Union (AU), the Association of Southeast Asian Nations (ASEAN), the Group of 77, the Non-Aligned Movement (NAM), and the United Nations (UN).

An examination of Islam, Muslims, and the Muslim world is further merited because

- We are living in an interdependent world. In this age of globalization, faraway events affect us in a smaller or bigger way either now or later. This new global reality makes it imperative for non-Muslims to understand the 1.3 billion Muslims that live all over the world.
- The Muslim world, including all the 57 OIC member-states, is a microcosm of the developing world—a region mainly in the southern hemisphere, comprising over 140 countries and 80 percent of the world's population. Therefore, studying the Muslim world will give readers a much better understanding of the political and socioeconomic ills plaguing the entire developing world.

Muslim countries are located in close proximity to six geostrategic seas: the Mediterranean Sea, the Black Sea, the Caspian Sea, the Arabian Sea, the Red Sea, and the Sea of Marmara. The Muslim world also contains five gulfs: the Gulf of Aqaba, the Gulf of Suez, the Gulf of Aden, the Gulf of Oman, and the Persian Gulf. In spite of the ease of travel across these seas and gulfs, there are seven easily blocked straits—where the passage of water narrows significantly—called "chokepoints," which could potentially disrupt the entering or leaving of the region via water. For example, the Strait of Gibraltar, the Bosphorus, the Dardanelles, the Bab al-Mandeb Strait, the Strait of Tiran, the Strait of Hormuz, and the Strait of Malacca could easily be blocked.

Muslim countries produce over half the petroleum and petroleum products consumed in the West, and they control as much as two-thirds of the world's known petroleum reserves. Petroleum products are used in a myriad of ways all over the globe, especially in highly developed societies. Besides fueling automobiles and airplanes and generating electricity, petroleum is used to make plastics, fertilizers, polyester fiber, insecticides and pesticides, and tar, among other items.

Muslim countries also possess substantial reserves of natural gas, iron ore, phosphate rock, cotton, and many other resources. Approximately 60 percent of the world's phosphate rock (from which fertilizer, soap, and detergents are made) is found in Morocco and the Western Sahara, which is under Moroccan control.

The Muslim world possesses a substantial pool of inexpensive and hard-working workers. Therefore, many Western multinational corporations already have many of their operations in these countries.

Most of the OIC countries provide lucrative markets for Western goods and services, including arms and technical military training, as well as nonmilitary services, machinery, and food.

Muslims all over the world are important consumers of American goods and services.

At its zenith, Islamic civilization contributed to other civilizations (including Western civilization) in the fields of astronomy, medicine, optics, mathematics, engineering and technology, geography, history, philosophy, literature, art, and architecture. This historical reality is little known to many non-Muslims. Chapter 1: "Momentous Events and Influential Muslims That Have Shaped Islamic Civilization (570–1605 CE)", will not only enlighten non-Muslims about the formative period of Islamic history but also the contributions of Muslims to world civilization.

With the end of the Cold War, the dismemberment of the Soviet Union, the demise of communism in the former Soviet bloc, the September 11, 2001, terrorist attacks on America, and terrorist incidents in several European countries, the religiopolitical ideology of "Islamism" is now a potent force in international relations. However, the violent strain of revolutionary

Islamism is only one ugly face of a multifaceted phenomenon. Misunderstanding the rich diversity of Islamism and its many manifestations (most of them peaceful), disregarding the root causes of Islamism, and making the "war on terrorism" or "the struggle against violent extremism" (as it is now being called) into a "war against Islamism" could lead down the slippery slope to the catastrophic and impending "clash of civilizations" that Harvard professor Samuel Huntington warned about in 1993. Indeed we are already witnessing not only a major intra-civilizational clash within the World of Islam—between the Revolutionary Islamists, Progressive Islamists, and Muslim secularists—but also an intercivilizational clash between the Islamic civilization and Western civilization, as well as the Islamic civilization and non-Western civilizations (such as the Israeli, Russian, Indian, Chinese, and Black African civilizations). These intercivilizational clashes, heavily sensationalized by the mass media, are already generating an enormous amount of "Islamophobia" (distrust and fear of Islam and Muslims). The principal concern is that if the suicide bombings by misguided Muslim extremists continue into the future, the twenty-first century could end up being the "century of Islam" as well as a much more traumatic century than the twentieth century.

Anti-Americanism seems to be rapidly growing and spreading across the Muslim world. Understanding the root causes of anti-Americanism and developing peaceful, multilateral, and medium- to long-term strategies for dealing with it will help the United States remain a superpower in the twenty-first century. Misunderstanding and aggravating this phenomenon could result in more terrorism against Americans and American interests in the world by misguided Muslim extremists; more anti-American revolutions (like the Islamic Revolution in Iran) in Muslim countries; Muslims buying fewer American goods and services; fewer American multinational corporations locating in Muslim countries; higher prices of goods from Muslim countries due to the instability there; Muslim countries ganging up against the United States; increases in the cost of living and a decline in the U.S. standard of living; and eventually the possible decline of America's current hyperpower status and civilization because of invaluable resources being diverted into fighting a longer, bloodier, and economically debilitating "Crusade."

Global Studies: Islam and the Muslim World comprises three principal parts. Part I comprises two chapters. The first chapter provides a timeline of "Momentous Events and Influential Muslims That Have Shaped Islamic Civilization (570–1605 CE)." The second chapter, "Understanding Islam, Muslims, and the Muslim World," introduces the reader to the fundamentals of Islam and compares Sunnis and Shi'as. This section features two boxes: the first box focuses on the 99 names/attributes of Allah (who is paramount in the Islamic belief system); the second box covers the sensational highlights about Islam, Muslims, and Muslim countries in the mass media. In this section the reader is encouraged to look at three important tables: the first table compares Sunnis and Shi'as the second table compares Islam to Judaism and Christianity, and the third table compares Jesus to Muhammad.

The next section of Chapter 2 elaborates on "Islamism" and how this religiopolitical ideology, which is in vogue today, is different from the religion of Islam. In this section, there are two tables: the first table compares Revolutionary Islamists (Islamic fundamentalists) to Muslim secularists (who are the elite in most Muslim societies); the second table compares Revolutionary Islamists and Progressive Islamists, who are fighting for the hearts and minds of Muslims around the world.

The third section focuses on the genesis of "Islamophobia" in the Western world and discusses and offers a causal analysis for anti-Americanism.

The fourth section gives readers eight major myths and misconceptions about Islam and Muslims. One of these myths pertains to Islam and the Nation of Islam being similar and is accompanied by a table comparing the two markedly different religions.

Part II comprises 57 country reports profiling the member-states of the Organization of Islamic Conference (OIC). Each country report contains vital facts and figures, along with a historical background, timeline, and thumbnail sketch of the country's current leader.

Part III provides readers with informative world press articles by well-known scholars and journalists who present Islam from different perspectives.

The reference section at the end of the book has a comprehensive bibliography with an annotated list of Internet sites, articles, and books on Islam, Muslims, and Muslim countries. To aid the reader's comprehension, a glossary includes essential Islamic terms, geographical areas, political concepts, and Islamic organizations.

Acknowledgments

First and foremost, I would like to express my immense gratitude to Renee Harper, the University of South Alabama's Writing Center director, and Carla Saint-Paul, who is an instructor in both the English as a Second Language (ESL) and the Developmental Studies programs at the University of South Alabama, for their invaluable assistance in editing my manuscript.

Second, I would like to express my deepest appreciation to the research assistance provided by my former student, Stephen Shumock. If Stephen had not given me his invaluable assistance (including his wonderful feedback and insights), this manuscript would never have been completed on time.

Third, I am indebted to the following gentlemen for giving me feedback and insights on Chapters 1 and 2: William Turnage, an instructor in the Department of English at the University of South Alabama; Syed Mohsin Naquvi, a computer programmer and a close family friend; Husain Abdullah, a former student of mine; Dr. Moiez A. Tapia, chairman of the Institute of Islamic Education and Research and professor at the University of Miami/Coral Gables, Florida; and Dr. Farukh Khambaty, a close family friend.

Finally, I owe a debt of thanks to Jill Peter, the senior developmental editor at McGraw-Hill, for her patient and diligent editing of my manuscript.

Chapter 1: Momentous Events and Influential Muslims That Have Shaped Islamic Civilization (570–1605 CE)

This timeline focuses on the genesis, growth, and development of Islamic civilization from 570 CE to 1605 CE. This thousand-year period or millennium of Islamic history has been selected because

- It is the source for most Islamic doctrine and practice, including commentaries on the *Qur'an*, works on Prophet Muhammad's *hadith* (sayings) and *seerah* (life), the *shariah* (Islamic law), and several schools of Islamic jurisprudence.
- This was the era when Islam was the fastest spreading and most dynamic religion in the world.
- During this era, Muslims made great strides in the Sciences and Humanities, and took Islamic civilization to its zenith. Ironically, while Islamic civilization was flourishing, Europe was languishing in the "Dark Ages." As a result of the Crusades and trade, ideas, discoveries, inventions, and goods spread from Islamdom to Europe. It is no wonder that Muslims have been credited with having sparked the European Renaissance (1350–1650 CE).

570 CE Muhammad ibn Abdullah is born in Makkah (present-day Saudi Arabia) into the Qureish tribe. Muslims believe he was the last of 124,000 prophets sent by God to guide mankind.

Death of Muhammad's father, Abdullah bin Abd al-Muttalib

The Qur'an mentions this blessed year as the "Year of the Elephant" in which Abraha, the Viceroy of Yemen, failed to conquer the city despite his powerful army because God sent birds to drop stones on the elephants that panicked and began to trample Abraha's army.

576 Death of Muhammad's mother, Aminah bint Wahhab; Muhammad's father died before Aminah gave birth to him.

578 Death of Muhammad's grandfather, Abdul Mutalib ibn Hashim, who looked after Muhammad for the first eight years of his life.

595 Muhammad marries Khadijah bint Khuwaylid, a successful and influential businesswoman.

610 Muhammad experiences his first divine revelation from the Archangel Gabriel in a cave at Mount Hira outside Makkah.

613 Muhammad propagates Islam and is persecuted by the wealthy and influential tribal leaders who are threatened by his monotheistic and egalitarian message.

615 When the Muslim converts face ostracism and persecution, Muhammad encourages them to emigrate to the neighboring kingdom of Axum/Abyssinia (later renamed Ethiopia) where Negus, Abyssinia's Christian Coptic king gives them asylum.

618–619 Muhammad is exposed to increased persecution and death threats after the deaths of his wife, Khadijah (618), and his uncle, Abu Talib (619), a Banu Hashim clan leader.

620 Archangel Gabriel transports Muhammad from Makkah to the Al-Aqsa Mosque, and then to the Rock of Foundation (Dome of the Rock since 691 CE) in Jerusalem, where he ascended to Heaven for a meeting with God and His prophets (Moses, Jesus, Abraham, and Adam), which led to the institution of the five daily liturgical prayers as an integral part of the Islamic faith.

621 Muhammad's followers in Yathrib become concerned about the Prophet's safety in Makkah and invite him to assume the leadership of their strife-ridden multi-ethnic community.

622 Muhammad, accompanied by a few close companions, migrates from Makkah to Yathrib (renamed *Madinat an-Nabi* or City of the Prophet; henceforth Madina), a pivotal event because Muhammad not only survives, but goes on to establish the first Islamic state, undertake major socioeconomic reforms, and complete his religious mission in this world. The Islamic lunar calendar is dated from this event, leading to the After *Hijra* (AH) system.

623 Muhammad promulgates Madina's Constitution, which guarantees tolerance, civil liberty, and justice to citizens of all religions.

624 Muhammad, on God's command, changes the direction of daily ritual prayers from Jerusalem to Makkah. In Islam, Jerusalem is associated with God's Judeo-Christian-Islamic prophets, but Makkah was chosen as the new spiritual center of the Muslim world because this is the site where Abraham built the first house of worship (the *Ka`abah*) dedicated to the one true God, and this is also where he went to obey God's command to sacrifice his son.

Although significantly outnumbered, Muslims defeat the non-Muslim Makkan force in the Battle of Badr. Muhammad promises the Makkan soldiers/prisoners their freedom if they would each teach ten Muslim children to read and write. This was the first school in Islamic history where Muslim students were taught by non-Muslims.

625 Makkans defeat Muhammad's army in the Battle of Uhud, outside Madina, but fail to conquer Madina.

627 Madina is besieged by Makkah's Qureish tribe. Muhammad has trenches built around Madina. The Makkans are unable to use their cavalry charge to vanquish the Muslims because of the trenches. The Makkans send Amr bin Abd al Wad, their best warrior, to fight against the best warrior from the Muslim side. Ali ibn Abi Talib, Muhammad's cousin and son-in-law, accepts the challenge to fight the legendary Makkan warrior and kills him. The Makkan army withdraws after al-Wad's death and their inability to put their battle plans into effect. Muhammad orders the execution of the Jewish men of Madina's Banu Qureiza tribe for conspiring with the Makkan Qureish to attack the Muslims from the rear.

628 After the Makkans are defeated in a few more battles, they sign the Treaty of Hudaybiyyah, which would allow the Muslims to make the *hajj* (pilgrimage) to the *Ka`abah* if the ceasefire prevails for one year.

Muhammad dispatches emissaries to invite the rulers of Egypt, Persia, Byzantium, and Yemen, to Islam. Only the ruler of Yemen accepts Islam.

629

The Makkans attack the Muslims, thereby violating the Treaty of Hudaybiyyah. When the Makkans are defeated, their preeiminent leader, Abu Sufyan, and many of his followers surrender and convert to Islam. Some of these conversions were undertaken for mere convenience.

Muhammad leads Muslims in the first pilgrimage to Makkah.

630

Muslims peacefully take control of Makkah and end the era of *jahiliyyah* (barbarism). Muhammad destroys over 360 idols in the Ka`abah (house that Abraham built with his son) and rededicates it to the worship of one God, and requests Bilal, a former black Abyssinian slave and an early convert to Islam, to call people to prayer. The oral call to ritual prayer distinguished Islam's invitation to congregational prayer services from that of Christian and Jewish congregational worship, wherein bells and the shofar (ram's horn) are used respectively.

630–632

Muslims subjugate the tribes of the Arabian Peninsula; tribal delegations from all over Arabia come to Madina to accept Muhammad as their religiopolitical leader and to convert to Islam.

632

Muhammad makes his last pilgrimage to Makkah and delivers his last sermon atop Mount Arafat. In this "Farewell Pilgrimage," Muhammad urges his followers to remain united. He receives Allah's final revelation, which completes the verses of the *Qur'an* (Holy Book of the Muslims). These revelations are memorized and written down by his comparnions to be compiled later on.

Muhammad dies in Madina at 62 in 11 A.H. (After *Hijri*). He is buried in *Masjid al-Nabawi* (The Prophet's Mosque) in Madina—the first *masjid* (mosque) and one which he contributed to building.

Perceiving a power vacuum, several Arab tribes in the Arabian Peninsula rebel.

Soon after Muhammad dies, and two days before he is buried, a dozen influential Muslim leaders of Makkah (including the tribal chieftains of Qureish) meet in a conclave called Saqeefa of Banu Sa`eda, and nominate the 60-year old Abu Bakr to succeed Muhammad as the *Khalifah* (Caliph) or religiopolitical leader of Islam's *ummah* (community of believers).

Shi`at-i-Ali (Ali ibn Abi Talib's followers) are incensed that Ali is not chosen as Islam's first caliph despite the fact that Prophet Muhammad had groomed him for just such a role. However, Ali strongly discourages his followers from challenging the authority of Caliph Abu Bakr in order to maintain harmony within the *ummah*. This disagreement over the succession to Prophet Muhammad's leadership of the *ummah*, is the inception of the Sunni-Shi`a split.

632–634

Caliph Abu Bakr suppresses the rebellious bedouins (633) and consolidates his caliphate over the Arabian Peninsula.

633

Muslims conquer Iraq and Syria, and begin the invasion of the Persian Sassinian Empire.

634

Just before his death, Caliph Abu Bakr nominates Umar ibn al-Khattab (Umar I) as his successor, again by-passing Ali.

634–644

Caliph Umar I significantly expands the Islamic empire. In 635, Arab Muslims defeat the Persian Sassanians at the Battle of Qadisiyya (in present-day Iraq). In 636, they conquer Lebanon and defeat a powerful Byzantine army at the Battle of Yarmuk and conquer Syria, going on to conquer Jerusalem (637), Mesopotamia (639), and Persia, as well as much of North Africa (including Egypt) in 642.

Arab Muslims take 300,000 papyrus scrolls from Alexandria's library in Egypt, representing centuries of accumulated knowledge back to Baghdad.

Caliph Umar creates a number of new departments, including the police department, a welfare service to assist the poor and needy, and an education department. He also organizes a sound financial system, constructs several forts and new cities throughout the Islamic empire, and establishes a *shura* (consultative body) that deliberates on public policy and guides him in its implementation.

642

Death of Khalid Bin Waleed—a courageous and talented army commander during the early years of Islam. His military leadership contributed to the conquest of the Arabian Peninsula and a signifant part of Persia. His victory over the Byzantine army paved the way for future Muslim conquests in Europe, Africa, and Southeast Asia. Prophet Muhammad called him *Saifullah* (the Sword of Allah).

644

A non-Muslim Persian slave assassinates Caliph Umar.

A small group of the most influential Muslim tribal and business leaders select Uthman ibn-Affan, a wealthy merchant and close companion of Prophet Muhammad, as Islam's third caliph.

644–656

Caliph Uthman continues the Islamic empire's expansion into northern and eastern Persia as well as North Africa. In 645, he begins developing the Islamic empire's sea-power and directs it against the Eastern Orthodox Byzantine Empire. In 650, he introduces the first organized news service and calls on Islamic scholars to collate and codify the Qur'an. In 653, a standard edition of the Qur'an is established and distributed throughout the Islamic empire. In 656, Caliph Uthman is murdered in Madina, igniting the first civil war in the *ummah*.

656–661

The influential leaders of Arabia select Ali ibn Abi Talib to be the Islam's fourth caliph. Shi`as believe that Prophet Muhammad nominated Ali to succeed him as the first Imam (religiopolitical leader) of the *ummah*. Ali contributed many *Qur'anic* revelations and *Hadith* to the compilers. He was also a prolific writer and wrote the *Nahjul Balagha* (The Path of Eloquence), which provides sage advice to Muslim rulers and citizens alike.

656

Talhah and Zubair, along with Prophet Muhammad's widow, Aiysha, challenge Ali's authority in the Battle of the Camel. Talhah and Zubair are killed, while Aiysha is freed and sent back to Madina.

657

Muwiyyah, the powerful governor of Syria, leads his army against Ali's forces in the Battle of Siffin. To avoid fratricide and peacefully end Muawiyyah's challenge to his caliphate, Ali accepts Muawiyyah's suggestion of arbitrating their conflict using several prominent individuals of Muawiyyah's choosing. Some of Caliph Ali's followers perceive his concession to Muawiyyah as appeasement and revolt. These rebels, called *Kharajites* (the seceders) because of their act of secession, are the first group of misguided and violent Muslim extremists in Islamic history. Ali leads Muslim troops to vanquish the Kharajites' main military force at the Battle of Nahrawan.

661

Avenging the Battle of Nahrawan, a Kharajite by the name of ibn Muljim assassinates Ali, while he is praying at a central mosque in Kufa (since then referred to as the Ali Mosque in Iraq). His death marks the end of what Sunnis refer to as the era of the *Khulafah-e-Rashidun* (the Righteous Caliphs).

In Kufa, Hasan bin Ali—Caliph Ali's eldest son and grandson of Prophet Muhammad—is proclaimed caliph. However, Hasan's religiopolitical leadership of the *ummah* is immediately challenged by Muawiyyah ibn Abu Sufyan, Syria's governor. To prevent fratricide within the *ummah*, Hasan agrees to abdicate his authority as the political leader of the *ummah* and permit the militarily powerful Muawiyyah to assume the title of caliph provided the Syrian governor would pledge to allow Hussein bin Ali, Hasan's younger brother, to succeed him as the caliph of a popular republic. Muawiyyah agrees.

661–680 Muawiyyah rules the Islamic empire from Damascus, Syria. He develops an autocratic, monarchical, and hedonistic style of rule, ruthlessly suppresses internal dissent, and develops a powerful naval fleet in the Mediterranean. He also undertakes the expansion of the Islamic empire from North Africa in the West (which had been controlled by the Orthodox Christian Byzantine Empire) to the Indus River in the East.

679 Abdul Aswad ad-Du-ali, a protege of Ali ibn Abi Talib, initiates the famous Basra school of Arabic grammar and philology by documenting the rules of basic Arabic grammar.

680 Just before his death, Muawiyyah reneges on his pledge that Hussein bin Ali will succeed him as Islam's caliph and designates his son, Yazid, as his successor. By this strategy Muawiyyah prevents the formation of an Islamic republic and instead establishes the first hereditary monarchy in Islamic history—the Umayyad Dynasty.

When Yazid bin Muawiyyah assumes the title of caliph, he orders Hussein bin Ali to pledge allegiance to him as the religiopolitical leader of the *ummah*. Hussein refuses to recognize Yazid, who was unenlightened and morally unfit to govern the Islamic empire.

Yazid dispatches a powerful army to force Hussein and his followers to concede and kill them if they refuse.

At Karbala in southeastern Iraq (61 A.H.), Hussein bin Ali and his small group of 71 male Shi`a followers are massacred by Yazid's army after being deprived of food and water for three days. This ruthless massacre, followed by Yazid's disgraceful treatment of the surviving women and children of Prophet Muhammad's extended family, deepens the split between the Sunnis and Shi`as, and makes Yazid unpopular among the *ummah*.

685–691 Umayyad ruler Abd al-Malik bin Marwan constructs the Dome of the Rock on the Temple Mount in Jerusalem. Built to enclose the Rock of Foundation (from which Muhammad is believed to have ascended to Heaven for his meeting with God), this beautiful and imposing architectural monument is the oldest in Islamic civilization. He also completes the construction of the Al-Aqsa Mosque, the largest mosque in Jerusalem, which Muslims believe Prophet Muhammad came to in his miraculous night journey from Makkah.

693 Umayyad ruler Abd al-Malik issues the first Arab-Islamic currency, replacing the Byzantine and Persian currency used in the empire until this date. The gold and silver coins (dinars and dirhams) minted in Damascus bear no facsimile of the ruler, but are instead inscribed with words from the Qur'an and glorify Arab-Islamic legends.

698 Arabic is recognized as the Islamic empire's official administrative language.

710 Tariq ibn Ziyad, a Berber convert to Islam, leads his Berber and Arab army from North Africa to the southern Iberia to invade the Christian Visigoth kingdom of Hispania (Spain). He defeats the Christian Visigoth King Roderick at Rio Barbate (711), and then with the conquest of Cordoba (712) brings Islam into Europe. The Visigoth cities of Seville and Toledo fall to the Muslims conquerors soon thereafter.

As a result of Tariq ibn Ziyad's conquests, the gigantic rock at the mouth of the Mediterranean Sea between North Africa and Europe is called *Jabel al-Tareq* (Gibralter).

712 Arab Muslims introduce Islam to the people of Central Asia and Afghanistan

Muhammad bin-Qasim leads an Arab-Muslim force to conquer Sind (current-day Pakistan) in the Indian subcontinent. His military victory helps spread Islam in the region, lays the foundation of a future Muslim empire in India, and helps Arabs to understand and draw from the rich Indian civilization.

718–719 Umayyad Caliph Umar bin Abdul Azeez orders Zuhri, his court scholar to start systematically recording Prophet Muhammad's *Hadith*, which until then had been carried by oral tradition. This becomes the source for later *Hadith* scholars such as Muhammad Ismail al-Bukhari and Al-Hajjaj Abul Husain al-Kushairi al-Nishapuri (popularly known as "Bukhari" and "Muslim" respectively).

728 Death of Hasan al-Basri—a teacher and preacher whose religious and political views influenced the generation after Prophet Muhammad's. His ideas profoundly influenced Islamic mysticism.

732 The European Christian armies led by the Frankish King Charles "Martel" ("The Hammer") defeat Abd-ar-Rahman's Moorish (Spanish Muslim) armies in a decisive battle between Tours and Poitiers in France, stopping the further advance of Muslims into Europe.

749–750 The Umayyads are overthrown and massacred by the *Abbasids* (family members of Abbas, Muhammad's uncle). Only the Umayyad Prince Abd-Rahman escapes to North Africa.

751 Muslims capture Chinese paper-makers during their conquest of Central Asia and establish the first paper mill in the Islamic empire. Paper, which is easier and cheaper to produce than papyrus, becomes the medium of scholarship and accelerates the dissemination of information and learning in the Islamic empire. Papermaking technology spreads to Europe through Andalusia (Islamic Spain).

756 Umayyad Prince Abd al-Rahman—survivor of the Abbasid massacre—establishes a Muslim dynasty in Cordoba, Spain, which rules the Iberian Peninsula for 300 years.

785 The Great Mosque of Cordoba, Abd al-Rahman's cherished project, is completed three years before his death.

762 Abbasid Caliph Al-Mansur establishes Baghdad as the capital of the Islamic empire.

765 Death of Ja'afar-e-Sadiq, Shi`a Islam's sixth Apostolic Imam, credited with compiling and codifying Shi`a jurisprudence, which contains the major hallmarks of Islam's minority Shi`a sect.

767 Death of Al-Numan ibn Thabit ibn Zuta "Abu Hanifa," Iraqi-born theologian and jurist, whose religious and legal views were adopted by the majority of Sunnis in Turkey, Afghanistan, Egypt, Central Asia, China and South Asia.

768 Death of Abu Mikhnaf, the first major scholar to write a history of Islam.

Death of Muhammad ibn Ishaq, the first authoritative biographer of Prophet Muhammad's *seerah* (life), whose seminal biography was fist published in Arabic by his student, Ibn Hisham. Alfred Guillaume translated this biography into English, *The Life of Muhammad, A Translation of Ishaq's "Sirat Rasul Allah"* (1970)

777 Death of Muhammad ibn Ibrahim al-Fazari, who along with Yaqub ibn Tariq, translated an eighth century Indian astronomical handbook with tables known as Zij al-Sindhind.

786–809 Arabic literature and science flourish in Harun al-Rashid's Abbasid Empire. His death results in the division of the Abbasid Empire between his two power-hungry sons: al-Amin and al-Mamun.

795 Death of Imam Abu Abd Allah Malik ibn-Anas, a companion of Prophet Muhammad, one of the most learned Islamic scholars, and the founder of the Maliki Sunni sect. Among his writings is a treatise on the *Hadith* entitled *Kitab al-Muwatta* (The Book of the Trodden Path), which codified Islamic common law. The Maliki sect spread in Muslim Spain as well as North and East Africa.

800 A paper factory is established in Baghdad, the capital of the Islamic empire. Within a few years, paper is used to record documents for the growing Islamic empire's bureaucracy. Paper also greatly facilitates the creation of the world's first credit system based on the *sakk* ("check" in Farsi/Persian). Merchants and traders are able to write checks in one town, which could be cashed in another town in the Islamic empire thousands of miles away. This new paper economy not only facilitates international banking, but international trade and commerce as well.

801 Death of Rabiah al-Adawiyah, female Sufi mystic, who synthesized asceticism with love of God.

813 Abbasid Caliph Abdallah al-Mamun defeats his brother al-Amin (r. 809–813 CE) and reunites the Abbasid Empire.

815 Death of Iraqi-born Jabir ibn Hayyan (known as "Geber" in the West), whom many in the East and West regard as the father of modern chemistry and alchemy. Some scholars even credit him with the introduction of the scientific method. He is most famous for *The Book of Mercy, On Poisons and Their Antidotes*, and his brilliant revision of Aristotle's theory of the constituents of metals, which survived until the beginning of modern chemistry in the eighteenth century.

820 Death of Imam Muhammad ibn-Idris ash-Shafi, founder of the Shafi'i Sunni sect. He studied Islam in depth; traveled widely in Middle East and taught for some time in Baghdad, Egypt, and Makkah; and investigated the principles of jurisprudence. He promoted a moderate and eclectic brand of Islam that stood for the continuity of tradition as well as change through *ijtihad* (independent reasoning). The Shafi`i school is prevalent in southern Egypt, Yemen, East Africa, Indonesia and parts of Southeast Asia.

830 Abbasid Caliph Al-Mamun establishes and generously supports the *Bait al-Hikmah* (House of Wisdom) in Baghdad. He assembles the best scholars from different parts of the world to transcribe and translate books from foreign languages (such as Greek, Persian, and Sanskrit) into Arabic. He also establishes an observatory at which Muslim scholars study astronomy. The transcription and translation of numerous ancient works as well as the publication of numerous scholarly works in the sciences and humanities contributed to a plethora of articles and books as well as the democratization of knowledge in the Islamic empire and beyond.

The Mu`tazilite school of Islamic theologians and jurists, which advocates rationalism, and free-will gains favor under Abbasid Caliph al-Ma'mun.

833–842 Abbasid Caliph Al-Mu`tasim continues al-Ma`mun's enlightened policies and programs. Al-Mu`tasim creates an elite bodyguard of Turkish and Arab troops.

842–847 Abbasid Caliph al-Wathiq continues al-Mu`tasim's and al-Ma`mun's enlightened policies.

847–861 Abbasid Caliph al-Mutawakkil rules over the Islamic empire. He disapproves of the liberal Mutazilite school, favors the conservative Asharite movement, and persecutes Shi`as for their religious beliefs. He is murdered by his Turkish bodyguards.

850 Death of Ibn Musa al-Khwarizmi (known as Alghorismus in the West), the founder of "Algebra." He was the first Arab to use numerals, the number zero, and the decimal system developed in India to find new methods of solving complex mathematical problems. Author of *Kitab al-Jabr wal-Muqabala* (The Book of Compulsion and Comparison). His book proved invaluable for future advanced research in the field. He was also the first to reexamine and build on Greek knowledge of Geometry (especially Euclid's works). He also conducted numerous geographic experiments, measured the height of the earth's atmosphere, and authored the *Shape of the Earth* in which there was a world map and a list of coordinates for the important locations of his era. He translated and revised Indian-Hindu "astronomical tables" and came up with tables for the movements of the sun, the moon, and five planets. His tables were used for keeping "time," and determining the direction of Makkah. Many of his works were translated into Latin and read by European scholars and scientists. Many Muslim and Western scholars also credit al-Khwarizmi's mathematical contributions with facilitating the scientific revolution in Europe

Death of Ahmad al-Farghani, an astronomer working at the House of Wisdom, who wrote *Kitab fi Jawami Ilm al-Nujum* (A Compendium of the Science of the Stars) in which he not only provided a concise and simple overview of Ptolemy's astronomy, but also corrected the latter's work based on the critical analysis and findings of earlier Arab astronomers.

855 Death of Ahmad ibn Muhammad bin Hanbal, Iraqi-born Islamic theologian-jurist, who was the author of *Al-Masnad* (The Authentic Hadith) a collection of 28,000 of Prophet Muhammad's *Hadith* (sayings). His religious doctrine was based on a literal interpretation of the *Qur'an* and *Hadith*. In the 18th century, Muhammad ibn Abdul al-Wahhab, the Hanbali *qazi* (Islamic judge), converted Muhammad ibn Saud to Hanbali Islam. When the Al-Saudi dynasty came to govern Saudi Arabia in 1930, the Hanbali sect, because of its puritanism and the efforts of Ottoman rulers to crush it, was the smallest of the three Sunni sects. However, the Al-Saud family has used its petrodollars and missionary zeal since the early 1970s to spread Hanbali Islam all over the world.

856 Death of Muhammad Ismail Al-Bukhari, author of the Sahih *Bukhari*—regarded by Sunnis as the most authentic canonical collection of Prophet Muhammad's *Hadith*. According to one report, Imam Bukhari gathered some 200,000 *Hadith* reports, out of which he chose 7,000 as being authentic for his final compilation.

868 Death of ibn Mahbub al-Jahiz, a Muslim intellectual and literateur who contributed significantly to the Arabic language. In his Arabic prose, he employed an innovative style and creativity to free the language from the limitations of religious themes. His intellectual capability was far reaching, and he touched a wide variety of subjects such as theology, politics, and natural sciences. His writings, addressing the low and high aspects of human nature, were presented in an eloquent style and manner.

873 Disappearance of the twelfth Shi`a Imam Al-Mahdi, who is awaited by Shi`as as Islam's Savior, towards the end of the world. Shi`as also believe that the Mahdi will reappear accompanied by Jesus in order to end inequity and corruption in the world.

Death of Abu Yusuf Yaqub ibn Ishaq al-Kindi (Europeans referred to him as Alchendius and "the philosopher of the Arabs"), an Iraqi Arab philosopher who translated, interpreted, and developed the works of Indian and Greek philosophers while working in the courts of Caliph al-Mamun (r. 813–833) and Caliph al-Mutasim (r. 833–842). He tried to combine the views of Plato and Aristotle and attempted to harmonize Greek philosophy with Islam. Its Latin translation, *Deaspectibus*, greatly influenced Roger Bacon. He discussed the nature of the universe, God, and the soul, which set a pattern for subsequent work. He regarded the neo-Pythagorean mathematics as the basis of all science. Al-Kindi was also an astrologer, alchemist, optician, and music theorist. His pioneering work in the field of Optics (based on the optics of Euclid) was widely used in medical schools and hospitals in both the East and the West. His works exerted great influence on the philosophy and intellectual development of Europe in the thirteenth century.

875 Death of Al-Hajjaj Abul Husain al Kushairi al-Nishapuri—better known as Imam Muslim. He traveled widely in the Arabian Peninsula, Egypt, Syria, and Iraq consulting outstanding authorities of the Prophet Muhammad's *Hadith* before compiling over 300,000 *Hadith*. He also wrote a scholarly introduction to the Science of Traditions in his outstanding work entitled *Sahih Muslim*, which cover the major subjects in Islamic traditions—the five pillars of Islam, marriage, barter, slavery, hereditary law, war, sacrifice, manners and customs of Prophet Muhammad and the Companions and other theological subjects.

892 Death of Muhammad al-Tirmidhi, *hadith* scholar who formulated rules for assessing the reliability of isnads (chains of transmission of Prophet Muhammad's sayings).

900 Paper manufacture starts in Cairo, Egypt, assisting in the dissemination of scholarly literature in the Islamic empire and beyond.

910 Death of Ibn Muhammad al-Junayd—known as Sultan or Syed (lord) of the Sufis for his development of early Sufi doctrine and of "sober" mysticism as compared to "God-intoxicated" mysticism.

923 Death of Abu Ja`afar Muhammad ibn Jarir al-Tabari, Persian historian and Qur'an commentator. He labored for forty years to produce his monumental compendium, *History of Prophets and Kings*, which starts with the creation of the world and ends at 915 CE. This detailed work of history has been a great source of information for later writers and historians. He was a prolific in theology and literature. His work, *The Full Exposition of Qur`anic Commentary*, has been a major reference source.

925 Death of Abu Bakr Muhammad ibn Zakariyya al-Razi (known as Rhazes in the West), Persian physician and philospher whose best works were in the field of scientific alchemy, pharmacy, and medicine. His research and treatise on smallpox and measles was the earliest of its kind on the subject. His comprehensive medical encyclopedia not only summarized the knowledge of Greek, Persian and Hindu medicine, but greatly added to that knoweldge. His principal work in alchemy, *The Book of Secrets*, became the main source of chemical knowledge until superseded in the fourteenth century by Jabir's works. Many of his scholarly works were translated into Latin and influenced Europeans for several centuries.

929 Death of Ibn Sinan al-Battani (known as Albatenius in the West), Arab mathematician and astronomer, who significantly contributed to the development of trigonometry. He determined the slanting/sloping direction of the eliptic and corrected the astronomical theories of Ptolemy. His calculations of planetary motion proved remarkably accurate.

Emir Abd al-Rahman III of Cordoba, Spain, is the first to take the title of Caliph in Spain (r. 912–961). As a result, the Emirate of Cordoba becomes the third Caliphate (after Umayyads and Abbasids) and a seat of Arab learning, science, commerce, and industry. Through his enlightened, competent, and tolerant policies, he brings prosperity to his people, consolidates Muslim power in Spain, and takes Islamic civilization in the Iberian Peninsula to its zenith. During this era, Jews enjoyed religious freedom and prominent positions in Islamic Spain.

935 Death of Abu Hasan al-Ashari, Arab theologian and jurist who posited that reason can only help the reader understand the *Qur'an* up to a point, beyond which the *Qur'anic* verses must be accepted on faith. He was responsible for Islam's conservative Asharite movement, with its emphasis on the traditionalist dogma of the *ahl al-hadith* and its methods of *kalam* (science of theology). His writings heavily influenced Al-Ghazali and Ibn Khaldun.

950 Death of Abu Nasr Muhammad bin Tarkhan al-Farabi (known as Alfarabius or Avennasar in the West), Turkish philosopher who made significant contributions to logic, metaphysics, ethics, mathematics, political science and music. He not only translated Aristotle's philosophical works into Arabic, but also made extensive comments on them. He also interpreted Islamic prophecy and theocracy using concepts of Greek philosophy, thus synthesizing Platonism, Aristotelianism, and Sufism.

956 Death of Arab Muslim Abu al-Hussain al-Masudi (known as the "Herodotus of the Arabs"), Arab historian who travelled widely and wrote detailed reports about his travels. His encyclopaedic work helped correct old geographical views of Ptolemy and other Hellenistic writers.

969 Fatimids wrest Egypt from the Ikhshidids and soon emerge as a major Mediterranean power. The town of al-Fustat is renamed al-Qahira (Cairo).

970 Fatimid Caliph Al-Muizz orders the construction of al-Azhar mosque in Cairo. Completed in 972 CE, it becomes the spiritual center of the Ismaili Shi'a sect. In 988 CE, it becomes an Islamic university and probably the oldest and most respected institution of higher education in the world.

975 Ali ibn-Abbas, an Arab physician, publishes a twenty-volume reference book on the theory and practice of medicine. It is translated into Latin in 1227, and printed in Lyons (France) in 1523.

998 Death of Abu al-Wefa al-Buzajani, Arab astronomer and mathematician, whose improvements to trigonometry helped him correct errors in astronomical calculations.

1000 Death of al-Muqaddisi, author of a manuscript on the cultural geography of the world.

1013 Death of Abul Qasim Khalef ibn Al-Zahrawi (known as Albucasis, or Abucasis, or Alsabaravius in the West), a competent surgeon. Even European surgeons of his time came to regard him as more erudite than Galen, the ancient world's acknowledged master. He wrote a 30-volume medical encyclopedia entitled *The Method of Medicine*. It included over 200 drawings and explanations of surgical instruments, most invented by Al-Zahrawi himself. He also covered an amazing number of operations performed while treating accident victims and war casualties.

1020 Death of Abul Qasim Firdowsi, Persian poet who wrote *Shahnama*. This work transformed the Persian language, which then became the court language and the language of many scholars in significant parts of the Muslim world.

1021 Death of al-Sulami, who wrote a mystical commentary on the *Qur'an* and a biographical dictionary of the Sufi teaching tradition.

1025 Ibn al-Razzaz al-Jazari publishes *The Book of Knowledge of Ingenious Mechanical Devices.*

1037 Death of Abu Ali al-Husain bin Abdullah ibn-Sina (known as Avicenna and "The Prince of Physicians and Philosophers" in the West and the "leading wise man" in the East)—an immensely versatile and influential Persian philosopher and physician. He diagnosed and described the causes of, and proposed remedies for, many illnesses. Among his famous books are: *Kitab al-Shifa* (Book of Healing)—a philosophical and scientific encyclopedia which deals with logic, physiology, geometry, astronomy, arithmetic, and metaphysics; and *The Canon of Medicine*—a medical encyclopedia that was used in European medical schools until the seventeeth century. He interpreted the writings of Plato and Aristotle in the Islamic framework. He wrote on history, physics, chemistry, mathematics, astronomy, geology, economics, politics, religious/spiritual issues, Qur`anic exegesis, poetry, and music. Avicenna's influence on medieval European philosophers such as Michael Scot, Albertus, Magnus, Roger Bacon, Duns Scotus, and Thomas Aquinas is undeniable.

1039 Death of Abu Ali al-Hasan ibn al-Haitham (known as Alhazen in the West), Arab astronomer, physicist, mathematician, physiologist and optician. His *Book on Optics* is a masterpiece. He was the first scholar to accurately describe the parts of the eye and the process of vision. He discovered the laws of refraction and reflection, conducted the first experiments on the dispersion of light into its constituent colors, and wrote about various physical phenomena (such as shadows, eclipses, rainbows, and the physical nature of light). He also discussed the theories of attraction between solid bodies, and their acceleration due to gravity, and pointed to the first law of mechanics. He authored many scholarly books and monographs in the fields of mathematics, astronomy, optics, medicine, and anatomy as well as wrote commentaries on the works of Aristotle and Galen (Greek physician). He explained the apparent increase in the size of heavenly bodies when present near the horizon based on physics rather than on Ptolemy's abstract astronomical system as well as the thickness of the atmosphere. As a mathematician, his fame lies in deriving the geometrical solutions of various optical problems. His works were widely studied in the West and had profound influence on the thinking of such greats as Roger Bacon and Johannes Kepler.

1048 Death of Abu ar-Rayhan Muhammad Ben Ahmad al-Biruni, Arab physician, astronomer, mathematician, physicist, chemist, geographer, historian, and philosopher. Among his many scholarly works are lists of the latitude and longitude of the world's principal towns.

1058 Death of Ali ibn Muhammad ibn Habib Abul Hasan al-Mawardi, Arab author of *The Ordinances of Government,* a legal theory of Sunni Islam's political institutions.

1067 Seljuk Turkish Sultan Nizam al-Mulk establishes the *Nizamiyyah Madrassah* (Governor's Seminary) in Baghdad and patronizes Muslim scholarship. He openly favors the conservative Asharite school of thought, and the liberal Mu`tazilite school loses favor among the elite.

1087 Muslims establish Timbuktu in Africa as a center of commerce and learning.

1090–1124 Hassan ibn al-Sabbah, leader of the Nizari sect of the Ismailis (a subsect of Shi'a Islam) in Persia, is alleged to have trained and sent an elite group of *fida'is* (sacrificers) to kill the Sunni princes and religious leaders in Arabia who were responsible for persecuting the minority Nizaris as heretics. The medieval Muslim majority portrayed the Nizari *fida'is* as *hashishiyya* or "users of hashish," to discredit them as "evildoers" (as Islam condemns both the taking of drugs and murder). Since these *fida'is* also targeted a few Europeans in Europe, writings of the Crusaders embellished earlier medieval Muslim writings in portraying the *fida'is* as a group of immoral, sadistic, and heretical "assassins."

1092 Death of Nizam al-Mulk Tusi, a competent and visionary vizier who served under two Seljuk Sultans. His *Seyasat-Namah* (Political Handbook) is a practical guide on statecraft for rulers. He established institutions of higher learning in Persia and the Arab world.

1095 Pope Urban at Clermont calls on Christians to engage in a Crusade to rid the Holy Land of the "wicked Heathens" (Muslims), marking the start of the First Crusade.

1096 The Christian Crusaders launch their First Crusade against Muslims.

1099 The Crusaders conquer Jerusalem, killing numerous inhabitants and destroying part of the city.

1106 Death of Yusuf ibn Tashfin, a capable and valiant spiritual and political leader of the Almoravides, a religious sect that ruled over a large territory of North-Western Africa. In 1062, he made Marakesh the capital of his empire. He was invited by King Mutamid of Seville to protect and defend Muslim rule in Spain against the Christians, whom he vanquished in 1086, returning to Africa as he had promised. However, he returns to Spain a few years later to conquer and govern its southern and central regions and incorporating them into the Almoravide Empire. The religious leaders, especially the *Faqihs* (Islamic jurists) exercised great influence under the Almoravide sovereigns.

1111 Death of Abu Hamid Muhammad al-Ghazali (known as Algazel in the West), Persian theologian, jurist, and mystic, whose works in the fields of Islamic jurisprudence and theology were so highly regarded by conservative Muslims that he was considered a *mujaddid* (Renewer of Islam)—a role enjoyed by one figure in each century.

1123 Death of Ghayasuddin Abulfazl Omar Khayyam, Persian poet, philosopher, astronomer and mathematician. While his work in algebra was recognized and praised during his time, he is more famous today for his eloquent and moving poetry. With Abdur Rahman Haseni, he also revised the calendar several centuries ahead of the Gregorian reform.

1130 Death of Muhammad ibn Tumart, the celebrated North African religious reformer, known as the Mahdi of the Almohads. He founded the Almohad movement which ended Almoravid rule in North Africa, then organized and unified the Berber tribes of North Africa who ruled over Morocco and Spain for almost 140 years.

1138 Death of Abu Bakr Muhammad ibn Bajja (known as Avempace in the West), philosopher and vazier at Saragossa in Muslim Spain, who represented the Arab Aristotelian-Neo-Platonist philosophical tradition. His seminal works survive in Arabic and in Hebrew translations. He was also a talented poet, musician, and composer of popular songs.

1160–1206 Reign of Muhammad Ghauri of Gaur in northwestern Afghanistan. His armies vanquish the Ghaznavids in the Punjab (currently in Pakistan) and take over their domains in eastern Afghanistan (1187), then conquer Delhi in India (1193), and finally bring much of Northern India under Muslim rule (1199). His Islamization of India, however, provokes Hindu resistance and results in his assassination (1206).

1162 Death of Abd al-Malik ibn Zuhr, physician/surgeon in Moorish Spain who worked against superstitious remedies. Paravicius translated his book, *Teisir* into Latin. He described the surgical procedures for removing kidney stones and for the excision of cataracts. He also developed a procedure known as tracheotomy to relieve obstructed breathing.

1165 Death of Al-Hammudi al-Idrisi, Arab geographer who entered into the service of Sicily's Norman King Roger II, and became a leading map maker and scientific consultant to the royal court of Palermo. He designed the first world map that was similar to those later made by modern geographers. His work served for several centuries as a model in geography.

1166 Death of Abd al-Qadr al-Jilani, a famous Sufi.

1171 Salah al-Din Yusuf ibn Ayyubi—the Kurdish Muslim governor of Egypt who is popularly known as Saladin in the West—ends the Fatimid Caliphate and establishes the Ayyubid Dynasty in Egypt. During his twenty-year reign, he expands and promotes Sunni institutions of learning, rapidly strengthens Egypt's naval fleet, greatly expands trade between Egypt and India, excludes Europeans from passage through the Red Sea, restores Abbasid authority in the Islamic empire, and makes Cairo an influential center of Islam, which it remains to this day.

1187 Saladin defeats the Crusaders at the Battle of Hattin thereby causing the downfall of the Frankish Kingdom of Jerusalem. His conquest of the Levant and Palestine (especially Jerusalem), leaves the Crusaders with only the coastal fortress cities of Antioch, Tripoli, and Tyre.

1193 Saladin dies and his Ayyubid Empire is soon divided. His major legacy is that he made Cairo an Islamic center of influence and he successfully defended and expanded the Islamic empire. His military victories against the Crusaders and Mongols have given him a prominent place in not only Islamic history, but in world military history as well.

1198 Death of Abu al-Waleed Muhammad ibn-Ahmad ibn-Rushd (known in the Muslim world as Ibn Rushd and in the West as Averroes), North African Arab who wrote books on philosophy, medicine, Islamic law, and astronomy. He attempted to reconcile faith with philosophy and logic. His Arabic translation of and commentary on Aristotle and Plato had a significant impact on the development of Latin scholastic philosophy and the Renaissance philosophers of Europe.

The Mongol tribal chieftain, Temugin—better known as Chenghez Khan (literally, "The Lord of the World")—embarks on his conquests of Muslim lands with his invasion of Turkestan.

1206 Qutb-ud-din Aibak, a politically savy Afghan general in Muhammad Gauri's army, becomes Sultan of India and establishes the Delhi *Sultanate* that lasts until 1526.

1220 Chenghiz Khan's Mongol armies conquer the Abbasid Empire's eastern region.

1235 Death of Ibn al-Farid, the most prominent Sufi poet in the Arabic language.

1240 Death of Muhammad Ibn al-Arabi, Arab philosopher renowned for his works on Islamic mysticism and esoteric speculation. His writings presented a synthesis of astrological signs, alphabetical and numerical symbolism, and the science of mysticism.

1248 Death of Abu Muhammad Abdullah ibn Ahmad ibn Al-Baitar, botanist and pharmacist of Moorish Spain, who made a detailed study of plants growing in Spain, along the Mediterranean coast, in North Africa, Egypt, Syria, Palestine, Iraq, and the Arabian Peninsula. His encyclopedic works not only discuss plants and vegetables (some not known up to that time), but also focus on pharmacological remedies for all sorts of ailments.

1250 Mamluks, descendents of Turkish slave troops, begin to control the Ayyubid Sultan. This marks the beginning of the end of the Ayyubian Empire. The Mamluk state in Egypt and Syria is founded and lasts until 1517.

1258 The Mongols, led by Halagu Khan—the grandson of Chenghez Khan—destroy Baghdad's infrastructure and burn its famous libraries. At this time, the Mongol empire covers the Eurasian continent from the Caucasus Mountains to the China Sea. They also control the Muslim lands of Iran, Iraq, and parts of Syria and Anatolia. With the death of the Caliph, the Abbasid Empire comes to an end.

1273 Death of Jalaluddin Rumi, the Sufi poet who wrote the *Masnavi*, a lengthy Persian poem which is an anthology of proverbs, folk stories, and sufi instructional work. Through his Persian lyrics and spiritual couplets, he exerted enormous influence on Sufi doctrine and practice. He also inspired the formation of the Mevlavi Sufi order. The Mevlavis have come to be known in the West as "the whirling dervishes" due to their whirling devotional dance.

1274 Death of Nasir al-Din Toosi—a versatile Persian scholar whose works included astronomy, mathematics, sciences, optics, geography, medicine, philosophy, logic, music, mineralogy, theology, and ethics.

1277 Death of Rukhunuddin Baybars I—the fourth and most famous of the Mamluk Sultans of Egypt and Syria. He rose from slavery to become the most eminent ruler of the Mamluk dynasty. A capable military commander and administrator, he defeated the Mongols, starting the decline of their military might.

1288 Death of Ala al-Din Ibn al-Nafis, who was not only a practicing physician, but also learned in Islamic theology and jurisprudence, philosophy, and linguistics. Besides making original contributions to medical articles and textbooks, he made some pioneering and accurate discoveries about blood circulation in the human body. His scholarly output was voluminous and so varied that he was referred to as the "Second Ibn Sina."

1295 The Mongol ruler of Persia, Oljaitu—great-grandson of Chengez Khan—converts to Islam and changes his name to Ghazan Khan. Mongols begin to promote the Persian language, culture, and Islamic faith in their vast empire.

1301 Beginning of the Ottoman Empire. A Turkish tribal chieftain with the Muslim Arabic name "Uthman"—but pronounced "Osman" in Turkish and Ottoman by the Europeans—defeats the Byzantine army at Baphaeon and creates a kingdom near the present city of Eskisehir (Turkey). Osman becomes a major power in Anatolia, and his successors expand the Ottoman Empire to encompass not only Anatolia, but much of the present-day Middle East, Greece, Albania, Bulgaria, and Yugoslavia as well. The Empire rapidly disintegrates after World War I (1918) and the Dynasty comes to an end (1922) after nearly 620 years in existence.

1326–1334 Islam spreads in Central Asia through conquest, trade, and Sufis.

1328 Death of Taqi ad-Din ibn-Taymiyyah, a Syrian-born Hanbali theologian-jurist. His criticism of Muslim rulers and the influential traditionalist *ulama* (Islamic scholars), results in his periodic imprisonment (during which he does most of his writing). He insists on the literal interpretation of the Qur'an and *Sunnah*; condemns *bid`a* (innovations in Islam), the influences of Greek philosophy, and Sufism; and denounces the excessive adulation of Prophet Muhammad, and the practice of what he considers to be saint-worship. For many Sunni Muslims, he is the prototypical revolutionary Islamist (popularly known as an "Islamic fundamentalist" in the non-Muslim mass media and scholarly literature). It is his puritanical version of Islam that was adopted by Muhammad ibn-Abdul al-Wahhab and Muhammad ibn-Saud. In the last three decades, this religiopolitical ideology has spread from Saudi Arabia and Qatar to influence Sunni Muslims in many part of the world.

1337 Death of Mansa Musa, the king of Mali who developed Saharan trade, introduced brick buildings, founded Timbuktu as an important center of learning and culture, promoted Islamic civilization in the West African region, and brought peace and prosperity.

1368 Death of Muhammad ibn Battuta, Arab who traveled from Tangiers in present-day Morocco to the Arabian Peninsula, India, China, and even to Spain and Timbaktu, Mali. The narrative of his travels, *The Adventures of Ibn Battuta*, was written with an assistant, Ibn Juzayy, and has been translated into many languages.

1370–1405 Muslim Mongol tribal chieftain, Timur-e-Lang (Timur the Lame), famous as Tamerlane, conquers eastern Persia (1379–1385), western Persia and Mesopotamia (1395–1400), northern India (1398–1399), Syria (1400) and Anatolia (1402) before returning to his capital in Samarkand, Turkmenistan. At the time of his death (1405), Timur was planning to invade and incorporate China into his vast empire. He is succeeded by a series of weak leaders who cannot hold on to the over-extended Mongol empire. As a result, the empire rapidly disintegrates and Timur's descendants are eventually left with only Central Asia.

1405–1417 Timur's son, Shahrukh, becomes ruler in Khurasan (1405), and later also in Transoxiana, western Persia, and Iraq. The Muslim Timurid dynasty in Herat (1405–1506), in present-day western Afghanistan, spark a "renaissance" in the fields of architecture, art, and Persian poetry.

1406 Death of Abd al-Rahman ibn-Khaldun, Arab philosopher, historian, jurist, and politician. He wrote *Muqaddima* (Introduction to the Science of History), a monumental history of the Arabs in which he explains the rise and fall of states by the waxing and waning of the spirit of *asabiya* (solidarity). His art of history writing exerted a great influence among historians worldwide.

1453 Ottoman Turks, led by Sultan Mehmed II, conquer Constantinople, put an end to the Christian Byzantine Empire, and make Constantinople (which they rename Istanbul) the capital of the Ottoman Empire and the spiritual center of the Muslim world.

1492 King Ferdinand and Queen Isabella take the Muslim kingdom of Granada from the Moors. Muslim rule of Spain ends and the Christianization of Spain starts. This date also marks the beginning of the Inquisition when many Muslims and Jews are persecuted and expelled from Spain.

1493–1529 Under Askia Muhammad, the Songhoy Empire in Western Africa absorbs most of the Manding Empire and expands east of the Niger River.

1500 Muslim sultanates replace Hindu regimes in Sumatra and Java (in present-day Indonesia).

1501 Ismail I establishes the Safavid dynasty. The Safavid shahs ruling Persia, impose Twelver version of Shi'ism as the state religion, recruit a large number of Shi'a *ulama* from Arab nations, and govern Persia until 1730.

1502 The Funj Sultanate at Sennar (present-day Sudan) is established and lasts for more than three centuries until Muhammad Ali, Viceroy of Egypt under the Ottoman Empire, conquers Sudan in 1820.

1502 Death of Jalal al-Din al-Dawani, Persian philosopher and theologian, who elaborates on the philosophic theory of the Islamic state according to al-Farabi and Nasir al-Din al-Tusi.

1517 Ottoman Turks complete the conquest of much of the current day Middle East. Ottomans armies take hundreds of thousands of public and private documents on public administration from the Mamluk archives to the Ottoman Empire's capital in Istanbul (formerly known as Constantinople). They also coopt and take many prominent Egyptian and Syrian *ulama* to Istanbul in order to support the Ottoman Dynasty's imperial claims.

1520–1566 Ottoman Sultan Suleiman I—also known as Suleiman "the Magnificent" and "the Law-Giver"—rules the Ottoman Empire at the height of its power. The governmental system is reformed; profound and lasting political, economic, and social changes are made throughout the Ottoman Empire.

1526 Zahiruddin Muhammad Babar (r. 1526–1530), descendant of the Turko-Mongol conqueror Timur, invades India. After defeating the last Lodhi Sultan of Delhi at the Battle Panipat, Barbar (literally, "Panther"), who comes from the Persianized city of Ferghana in Central Asia, establishes the Moghul dynasty that rules with capitals in Delhi and Agra for the next 332 years.

1526–1707 Modern Afghanistan is divided between the Shi`a Muslim Saffavid Empire of Iran and the Sunni Muslim Moghul Empire of India.

1605 Death of Moghul Emperor Jalal ud-Din Muhammad Akbar, who after coming to power in 1556, extended the Moghul Empire throughout northern and central India. In order to become the supreme ruler of the Indian subcontinent, "Akbar the Great" adopts a policy of religious and cultural tolerance, founds a new religion called *Din-e-Elahi* (Religion of God) comprising elements of a number of religions prevalent in India, and fosters a new "golden age" of Indian civilization (with a heavy influence of Persian culture).

After reading about these momentous events and the role of influential Muslims that have shaped Islamic civilization, the question on everyone's mind is what contributed to the decline of Islamic civilization. In my opinion, there were at least eight principal causes for the decline of Islamic civilization:

- The Crusades—comprising a series of military battles with European Christians—that preoccupied the Islamic empire for nearly 200 years (1097–1291 CE)
- The Mongol invasion in 1258 CE destroyed the Abbasid Empire's centers of learning and infrastructure in what is present-day Iraq and Iran. Many thousands of intellectuals were killed in the reign of terror that ensued.
- The European military reconquest of Andalusia/ Spain (1400–1492) ended a flourishing Islamic civilization.

- The rapid spread of the Islamic empire created intra-civilizational conflicts within Islamdom.
- The rise of orthodox *ulama* (Islamic clerics) who emphasized dogmatic and doctrinaire Islam instead of progressive Islam, which was based on independent reasoning and judgment (*ijtihad*).
- The resurgence of the West between the 14th and 19th centuries (the Renaissance between the 14th and 16th centuries, the Reformation in the 16th century, the Age of Enlightenment in the 18th and 19th centuries, and the Industrial Revolution, which began in the last quarter of the 18th century in Britain and then spread to the rest of Europe).
- European colonialism, which resulted in the conquest of much of the Muslim world during the 18th and 19th centuries and the first half of the 20th century.
- The rise and spread of secular nationalism: the division of the Muslim world into nation-states ruled by many autocratic, incompetent, and corrupt secular leaders fixated on the parochial interests of their own nation-states rather than thinking about the well-being of the global *ummah* (community of believers/Muslims).

SOURCES:

Engress, Gerhard. *An Introduction to Islam*. Translated by Carole Hillenbrand, New York: Columbia University Press, 1988, pp. 164–215.

Esposito, John L., ed. *The Oxford History of Islam*. Oxford and New York: Oxford University Press. 1999.

_____ *The Oxford Encyclopedia of the Modern Islamic World*. 4 Volumes. Oxford and New York: Oxford University Press, 1995.

_____ *The Oxford Dictionary of Islam*. Oxford and New York: Oxford University Press, 2003

Gibb, H. A. R. and J. H. Kramers. *The Shorter Encyclopedia of Islam*, Netherlands: E. J. Brille, 1974.

Glasse, Cyril. *The Concise Encyclopedia of Islam* (New York: Harper & Row), 1989, pp. 454–467.

Martin, Richard C., ed. *Encyclopedia of Islam and the Muslim World*. 2 Volumes. New York: Macmillan Reference USA. 2004

Nicholson, Reynold A. *A Literary History of the Arabs*, Cambridge University Press, 1979 print (originally published by Unwin in 1964).

Robinson, Francis. *Atlas of the Islamic World Since 1500*. New York: Facts on File, Inc., 1982, pp. 8–9.

Wintle, Justin. The Rough Guide History of Islam. New York: Penguin Putnam, Inc. 2003.

Chapter 2: Understanding Islam, Muslims, Islamism, and Anti-Americanism

This chapter will concisely introduce readers to "the fundamentals of Islam"; the life and a few sayings of Prophet Muhammad; the *Shariah* (Islamic law); and Sunnis and Shi'as. The chapter will then discuss Islamism, clearly showing the difference between Islam, the faith of 1.3 billion Muslims, and the religiopolitical ideology of Islamism. Next, readers will be introduced to the eight most common myths and misconceptions about Islam. This Chapter will then focus on the genesis and development of Islamophobia in the Western world and anti-Westernism in the World of Islam and then examine a subset of anti-Westernism, namely, anti-Americanism. The Chapter will end with "What Muslims Want."[1]

THE FUNDAMENTALS OF ISLAM

Iman: Islam's Foundational Principles

Iman literally means "faith," "belief," or "spiritual convictions." The Qur'an refers to the five articles of faith, or the basic foundations of the Islamic belief system:

O ye who believe! Believe in God and His Apostle and the scripture which He hath sent to His Apostle and the scripture which he sent to those before (him). Any who denieth God, His angels, His Books, His Apostles, and the Day of Judgment, hath gone far, far astray

[4:136].

Thus the five articles are: (a) belief in Allah (God); (b) belief in angels; (c) belief in God's prophets, with Adam as the first prophet and Muhammad as the last; (d) belief in the holy books revealed by God—the Torah, the Bible, and the Qur'an—and (e) belief in the Day of Judgment. Each article of faith can be further defined as follows:

- The first and most important foundational tenet on which Islam rests is **tawhid** (the absolute oneness and uniqueness of Allah). Allah is the Islamic term for the one omnipotent, omnipresent, omniscient, eternal, perfect, just, and merciful God or Supreme Being. Muslims believe that God is the sole Creator, Sustainer, Provider, and Controller of the universe; that He, and He alone, ought to be worshiped; and that He has neither feminine nor plural attributes. Although the mention of Allah is prevalent throughout the Qur'an (which Muslims believe is God's final Message revealed to Prophet Muhammad), it is concisely, cogently, and lucidly demonstrated in a Qur'anic chapter entitled *Al-Ikhlas* (Sincerity). *Al-Ikhlas* is so important and central to Islam that it is recited during each prayer performed by Muslims five times a day. *Al-Ikhlas* has been translated from the classical Arabic in the Qur'an to English as follows:

In the name of the merciful and compassionate God.
Say: (O Muhammad) He is God, The One and Only!

God is Eternal.

He did not give birth (to anyone),

Nor did anyone give birth to Him.

And there is no one equal to (or similar to) Him [Qur'an: Surah 112, Verses 1-4].[2]

- The second doctrine of Islam is belief in God's angels. Unlike human beings, these celestial creatures are made not of dust but of light; have no physical desires nor material needs of any kind; do not eat, drink, or sleep; have no capacity for reasoning; have no free will; are immortal; and obediently carry out God's orders during the day or night. Some of these angels have been assigned special duties. Archangel Gabriel is believed to have brought God's messages to all His prophets; two angels, one on each side, accompany every individual and record his or her deeds for the Day of Judgment; and some angels help true believers when the latter call out to God to help them.

- The third foundational principle of Islam is the belief in God's prophets. Muslims believe that every known nation has had a warner or messenger from God. God chose these messengers to teach humankind and deliver His divine messengers. Although the Qur'an alludes to 124,000 prophets since the time of Creation (with Adam as the very first prophet), it specifically mentions the name of only 25 of them. Among them, Muhammad stands as the last and most important of God's prophets.

- The fourth basic premise of Islam is to believe in God's Holy Books. Muslims believe that God revealed the *Suhuf* (Scrolls) to Ibrahim (Abraham), the *Zabur* (Psalms) to *Dawud* (David), the *Tawrah* (Torah) to *Musa* (Moses), the *Injil* (Gospels) to *Isa* (Jesus), and the Qur'an to Muhammad. Each of these Holy Books mentioned in the Qur'an showed their respective people the straight path to God. However, according to Islam, the original scriptures given to prophets Abraham, David, Moses, Jesus, and others were lost or corrupted (tampered with by fallible human beings) over the centuries, while the only authentic and complete book with God's final message to humankind that is in existence today is embodied in the Qur'an.

- The fifth and final article of the Islamic faith is belief in **Yaum al-Akhira** (the Day of Judgment). The Qur'an clearly informs Muslims that the world will come to an end someday. On that Day of Judgment, the dead will be resurrected to be judged by an all-knowing, totally just, and immensely merciful God. Righteous human beings who have done good deeds in this world will be rewarded with an eternal life of happiness in Heaven/Paradise, while those who have refused to follow God's guidance, hurt their fellow human beings, and commit evil deeds in this world will be sent to Hell to suffer.

AL-ASMA AL-HUSNA

Allah's Nine: Nine Beautiful Names or Attributes Mentioned in the Qur'an

1. Al-Adl: The Just
God is absolutely, totally, and perfectly fair and equitable.

2. Al-Afuw: The Pardoner
God will forgive someone if that person sincerely atones for his/her sins and implores God for His forgiveness.

3. Al-Ahad: The One
God is absolutely unique and exceptional; there can be no one like Him.

4. Al-Aakhir: The Last (With No End)
God will remain forever, even after the demise of all living things in the universe.

5. Al-Ali: The Exalted
Nothing can be superior to God in the universe.

6. Al-Aalim: The Omniscient
God is all-knowing and [most] wise

7. Al-Awwal: The First (With No Beginning)
God always existed even before He created the universe.

8. Al-Azeem: The Greatest
Nothing can be greater than God Almighty.

9. Al-Aziz: The Almighty
God, the most powerful force in the universe, cannot be defeated.

10. Al-Ba'adi: The Unique
God is exceptional and incomparable.

11. Al-Baari: The Originator
God has created the universe and all living things in it without any previous model.

12. Al-Baasit: The Giver
God is most generous in bestowing favors to His true believers.

13. Al-Ba'atin: The Hidden
God knows what is within people's hearts and minds as well as the secrets and mysteries of the universe.

14. Al-Ba'ith: The Resurrector
God will resurrect all human beings on judgment day.

15. Al-Baaqi: The Everlasting
While every living thing dies, God is eternal.

16. Al-Barr: The [Most] Beneficent and [Most] Dutiful
God is the source of all goodness and is faithful to His creation.

17. Al-Baseer: The All-Seeing
God sees everything.

18. Ad-Daarr: The Afflictor
God will bring distress, adversity, and harm to evildoers.

19. Al-Fattaah: The Decider
God can tell the difference between true believers, hypocrites, and disbelievers.

20. Al-Ghaffaar: The Forgiver
God's compassion, mercy, and forgiveness is unlimited and unending.

21. Al-Ghaffoor: The [Most] Forgiving
No one can be more merciful and forgiving than God.

22. Al-Ghanee: The [Absolutely] Independent and Self-Sufficient One
God is totally self-sustaining; He doesn't need anyone or anything.

23. Al-Haafiz: The Preserver
God is the supreme protector and guardian of His message and His true believers.

24. Al-Haadee: The [Best] Guide
God is the supreme and perfect guide for human beings.

25. Al-Hakeem Al-Mootlaq: The [Most] Wise
God is infinitely wise and judicious.

26. Al-Hakkaam: The Judge
God is the ultimate, just, and perfect judge of all human beings.

27. Al-Haleem: The [Most] Clement
God is most gentle, calm, patient, and merciful (even when provoked and angered).

28. Al-Hameed: The Praiseworthy
God is worthy of admiration and glorification.

29. Al-Haqq: The Only True and Just God
He is the only authentic God; He is the source of ultimate truth and justice.

30. Al-Haseeb: The [Supreme] Reckoner
God knows everything that people do throughout their lives.

31. Al-Hay'y: The Alive and Eternal
God is everlasting, with no beginning and no end.

32. Aj-Ja'amay: The Assembler
On the Day of Judgment, God will assemble all human beings in one place.

33. Al-Jabbaar: The Compeller
Those who disregard God's message of righteousness will suffer in this world and the hereafter.

34. Al-Jaleel: The Sublime
God possesses awesome grandeur and splendid majesty; He is the only true God worthy of worship.

35. Al-Kabeer: The Greatest Force
God is the biggest, greatest, and most powerful force in the universe.

36. Al-Kareem: The Most Generous One
God is most kind, considerate, compassionate, and generous towards His creation.

37. Al-Khaaliq: The Creator
God is the only creator of the universe; no one can duplicate His creation.

38. Al-Khabeer: The Most Acquainted
God has infinite awareness, understanding, and insight into all things.

39. Al-Khafudh: The Abaser
God humbles, disgraces, and humiliates those who disobey Him and do evil deeds.

40. Al-Lateef: The [Most] Gracious One
God knows the nuanced meaning of everything and bestows His blessings in subtle ways.

41. Al-Maajid: The Glorious One
God's grandeur and majesty are most exalted.

42. Al-Ma'ani: The Depriver
God will support His true believers and deprive the evildoers.

43. Al-Majeed: The Most Glorious
God is the most exalted and majestic.

44. Al-Malik: The Ruler
God is the supreme ruler of the universe.

45. Maalik Al-Mulk: The Sovereign Lord
God is the supreme ruler of the universe.

46. Al-Mateen: The Firm
God is determined, resolute, and steadfast.

47. Al-Mu'akhkhir: The Deferrer
God can delay whatever He wills.

48. Al-Mubdi: The Creator
God created everything in the universe from nothing, without any model to emulate.

49. Al-Mu'eed: The Resurrector
God will resurrect the dead on Judgment Day and reward the righteous with Heaven.

50. Al-Mughnee: The Enricher
God is overwhelmingly generous and will provide His true believers with abundant favors.

51. Al-Muhaymin: The Protector
God is the ultimate protector of the truly faithful and righteous.

52. Al-Muhsee: The Reckoner
God knows what everyone has done; He will decide their fate on Judgment Day (Day of Reckoning) after accounting for their deeds.

53. Al-Muhyee: The Life-Giver
God is the supreme and miraculous giver of life.

54. Al-Mu'izz: The Honorer
God rewards His true believers with respect and glory in this world and in Paradise.

55. Al-Mujeeb: The [Most] Responsive
God responds to the needs of the faithful when they sincerely pray for His help.

56. Al-Mumeet: The One Who Ends Life
God determines the length of our earthly life.

57. Al-Mu'min: The Preserver of Security
God is the ultimate guardian of the faithful.

58. Al-Muntaqim: The Avenger
No evildoer escapes God's punishment.

59. Al-Muqaddim: The Advancer
God advances the truly deserving.

60. Al-Muqeet: The Sustainer
God is the ultimate nourisher and nurturer of all life in the universe.

61. Al-Muqsit: The [Most] Equitable
There can be none more objective, fair, and just than God.

AL-ASMA AL-HUSNA, cont'd

62. Al-Muqtadir: The Prevailer
God is the most powerful force in the universe and will always prevail.

63. Al-Musawwir: The Designer
God designs, fashions, and organizes all things in the universe.

64. Al-Muta'ali: The [Most] Exalted
God is most high, irreproachable, impeccable, and flawless.

65. Al-Mutakabbir: The Majestic and Glorious One
God demonstrates His supremacy, glory, majesty, splendor, and grandeur in all things.

66. Al-Muzil: The Humiliator
God will punish the evildoers with dishonor and humiliation in this world and in the hereafter.

67. An-Naafih: The Benefactor
God has created many beneficial things for all living creatures.

68. An-Noor: The [Glorious] Light
God enlightens His creation with divine guidance.

69. Al-Qaabidd: The Withholder
God withholds His favors from those who don't worship Him and follow His righteous guidance.

70. Al-Qaadir: The [Most] Able and Capable
God posseses supreme resourcefulness and competence.

71. Al-Qahhaar: The Destroyer
God has absolute power and control, can subdue one and all, and can do anything He wills.

72. Al-Qawwee: The All-Powerful
God is most powerful; No one can oppose Him and prevail.

73. Al-Qayyoom: The [Totally] Self-Sufficient
God is totally independent, self-sustaining, and eternal.

74. Al-Quddoos: The [Most] Holy
God is most pure, perfect, and incorruptible.

75. Ar-Ra'afi: The [Supreme] Exalter
God rewards and honors His true believers in this world and in Paradise.

76. Ar-Raheem: The [Most] Compassionate
God is the most munificent, kind, generous, and forgiving.

77. Ar-Rahmaan: The [Most] Merciful
God is most kind and compassionate.

78. Ar-Raqeeb: The [Most] Observant
God is eternally vigilant and watchful; No human action goes unnoticed.

79. Ar-Rasheed: The [Most] Righteous, Wise, and Persuasive Guide.

80. Ar-Ra'oof: The [Most] Compassionate
God is the most loving, kind, helpful, and merciful.

81. Ar-Razzaaq: The [Supreme] Provider and Sustainer
God is the ultimate source of all of man's needs

82. As-Saboor: The [Most] Patient and Steadfast One
God is long-suffering and supportive of His righteous followers.

83. As-Salaam: The [Most] Peace Loving
God, who loves peace, will reward those who strive for peace in this world.

84. As-Samad: The Eternal Refuge
Humankind has and will always look up to God for help.

85. As-Sami: The All-Hearing
God hears everything.

86. Ash-Shaahid: The Witness
God is omnipresent and observes/witnesses everything everywhere.

87. Ash-Shakoor: The [Most] Appreciative
God always appreciates and rewards His true believers.

88. At-Tawwaab: The [Greatest] Forgiver
If someone atones for his/her sins, God accepts his/her repentance and is most forgiving.

89. Al-Waahid: The One True God
There is no God but God.

90. Al-Waajid: The Founder
God established the universe and created everything in it.

91. Al-Waalee: The [Supreme] Ruler
God is the only supreme ruler of the universe.

92. Al-Waaris: The [Ultimate] Inheritor
While human beings have temporary ownership of their possessions, God has supreme and eternal ownership over everything in the universe.

93. Al-Waasih: The All-Encompassing and All-Embracing
God has limitless capacity and super-abundance of good will to help His followers.

94. Al-Wadood: The [Most] Loving
No one can be more loving and generous than God.

95. Al-Wahhaab: The [Supreme] Bestower
God generously showers His blessings and favors on all living things.

96. Al-Wakeel: The Trustee
God provides the means to solve all problems in the best way.

97. Al-Walee: The [Ideal] Ally and Supporter
God will protect and support His righteous followers.

98. Az-Zaahir: The [Most] Manifest
God, who is above all, is apparent, evident, and obvious to His true believers.

99. Zul-Jalaali wal-Ikram: The Lord of Glory, Majesty, and Splendor
God is the most magnificent and majestic.

Faraidh: The Five Pillars of Islam

Faraidh literally means "compulsory duties" or "obligations." Muslims believe that neglect of the five fundamental *faraidh* (ritual obligations), also known as the five **arkan ad-din** (pillars of the faith), will be punished in the next world, while their fulfillment will be rewarded. The five *faraidh* enjoined on all Muslims are the *shahadah, salat, zakat, sawm,* and *hajj.*

Shahadah is Arabic for witnessing, professing, or declaring. In Islam *La ilaha illa 'llah, Muhammad ar Rasul Allah* (I bear witness that there is no God but Allah, and Muhammad is His [last] Prophet) is the first and most important pillar of Islam. This declaration of faith in God and in Muhammad as His last Prophet implies that there is none worthy of worship except God and that Muhammad is His messenger to all human beings till the Day of Judgment. It marks a person's entry into Islam and the worldwide **ummah** (brotherhood of believers); it is the first statement that Muslim parents (often the father) utters into

the ears of a newborn; and it is the last words a Muslim should utter before death.

Salat or *salah,* the ritual of daily prayers to worship God, is the second pillar of Islam. The Qur'an expects Muslims to establish a direct relationship with God and be conscious of His presence from the time they rise in the morning till the time they go to bed at night. However, although the Qur'an mentions prayer many times, the obligation for adult Muslims to pray five times a day derives from Prophet Muhammad's *hadith* rather than the Qur'an. Each prayer is offered in a fixed pattern of recitation of Qur'anic verses coupled with prostrations. The times of prayer, with their Arabic terms, are as follows: (1) the morning prayer before dawn/sunrise (*salat al-subh* or *salat al-fajr*); (2) the midday/noon prayer (*salat al-zuhr*); (3) the afternoon prayer before dusk/sunset (*salat al-asr*); (4) the evening prayer, just after sunset (*salat al-maghrib*); and the night prayer before midnight (*salat al-ishah*), thereby consecrating the entire day.[3] The Qur'an instructs Muslims to offer their Friday prayers: "O ye who believe! When the call is proclaimed for prayer on Friday, hasten earnestly to the remembrance of God, and leave off business; that is best for you if you but knew" (62:9). Prophet Muhammad recommended that Muslims perform their Friday Zohar prayers along with their brethren at a mosque. These congregational prayer services often include a sermon by a respected Islamic cleric in the community called *Imam-i-Jum'ah wa Jama'at* (Friday congregational prayer leader).

Zakat, or *zakah*, almsgiving, is the third pillar of Islam. A Muslim's service to humanity is considered an essential part of his or her service to God; the obligatory humanitarian duty of *zakat* epitomizes and illustrates this most vividly. Muslims with the financial means to do so are enjoined by the Qur'an and *sunnah* to donate at least 2.5 percent of their net worth—not just their annual income—to the welfare of the poor and needy, to charitable institutions, and/or to orphanages every year. *Zakat* literally means "purification" in Arabic. This is because, when a Muslim contributes a small portion of his or her wealth to the welfare of the poorest and neediest members of the ummah, he or she pleases the beneficiaries of this generosity and earns their heartfelt prayers; plays a small role in reducing poverty and bridging the gap between the rich and poor; pleases God, who loves to see human beings helping one another; and feels a sense of emotional and psychological gratification by reaffirming his or her humanity and goodness.

Sawm is the fourth pillar of Islam. The Qur'an clearly states: "O ye who believe! Fasting is prescribed to you as it was prescribed to those before you, that ye may (learn) self-restraint." (11:183). *Sawm* represents the obligation of all adult Muslims to fast from dawn to dusk during the ninth Islamic calendar month of **Ramadan** when the revelations of God started coming down to Prophet Muhammad to guide humankind to "the straight path." The word *Ramadan* is derived from the Arabic root *ramz*, which literally means "to burn." Ideally, fasting during Ramadan should metaphorically "burn away one's sins." During the month of Ramadan, adult Muslims are expected to abstain from food, liquids, and sexual intercourse from sunrise till sunset. When one fasts, all the sense organs—eyes, ears, tongue, hands, and feet—ought to do the right thing. The eyes should see no evil; the ears should abstain from hearing music, lies, and gossip; the tongue should not tell lies or spread rumors; the hand should not physically hurt anyone or steal; and the feet should not walk toward forbidden places. Fasting was also enjoined to build good character traits, such as a social conscience, patience, tolerance, willpower, and altruism. Just before the end of Ramadan, Muslims are enjoined to donate *zakat al-fitr* (donations to the poor).

Hajj, the fifth pillar of Islam, is an obligation on only those adult Muslims whose health and resources permit them to fulfill the religious journey to Makkah at least once in their lifetime. The focal point of the pilgrimage is a shrine in Makkah that Muslims believe was established by Abraham for the worship of one God. The pilgrimage must take place between the seventh and tenth days of the Islamic month of *Dhul-Hijjah*, which is the twelfth and last month in the Islamic calendar. On the tenth and last day of the pilgrimage, Muslims (who can afford it) have been enjoined to slaughter an animal commemorating Prophet Abrahams' obedience to God's command that he should sacrifice his son (Ishmael). Of course, when Abraham was about to carry out God's command, He sent a ram (through the agency of Archangel Gabriel) to be sacrificed instead of his son. Such total obedience to God vividly illustrates the very essence of true Islam, which entails a mu'min, or true believer, surrendering his or her entire self to God (Qur'an 2:131).

The *hajj* brings together—physically, spiritually, and emotionally—over two million Muslims from all over the world. All the Muslim pilgrims have been enjoined to wear an unstitched white cotton cloth to cover their bodies in order to signify the equality of all Muslims before God. The pilgrim who completes the *hajj* during the annual *hajj* season can carry the honorific title of *hajji* for the remainder of his life.

Muhammad: A Brief Profile of Islam's Last Prophet

The name Muhammad comes from the Arabic verb *hamada*, to praise, to laud, and to glorify. Thus, Muhammad means the praised one or the one who is glorified. Muhammad was born in the oasis town of Makkah in the Arabian Peninsula (present-day Saudi Arabia) in 570 CE. His father, Abdullah, died before his birth and his mother, Aminah bint Wahab, died when he was six. His grandfather, Abd al-Muttalib, died when he was eight and Muhammad's upbringing was assumed by his uncle, Abu Talib, his guardian for the next forty years.

Muhammad was deeply disturbed by the ignorance, polytheism, and primitive customs prevalent in Arabia. The practice of female infanticide was common; slavery, alcoholism, and gambling were widespread; wealthy and influential men kept large harems; widows and orphans suffered poverty and terrible indignities; and tribal wars were frequent. Although Muhammad quietly sought spiritual answers to these social ills, he earned his living as a merchant-trader. By his mid-twenties, Muhammad had acquired a reputation in Makkah for honesty and integrity, earning the titles *Al-Sadiq* (honest and truthful) and *Al-Amin* (the trustworthy). Muhammad was employed by Khadijah bint Khuwaylid, a wealthy and influential woman in Makkah. Muhammad's exceptional character, personality, and work habits were so impressive that Khadijah proposed marriage based on love and respect, as opposed to the more common arranged marriages of the day.

In his thirties, Muhammad meditated regularly in the Makkan cave of Hira. Muslims believe Muhammad was visited in the cave by the Archangel Gabriel in 610 CE, who told him he should announce his prophethood and preach the message of Islam. His wife, Khadijah, and a few relatives converted immediately to Islam.

The first Muslims suffered extremely brutal persecution by corrupt pagan leaders of Makkah. Responding to this persecution in 622 CE, Muhammad led his followers to the nearby town of Yathrib, renamed *Madinat un-Nabi* (the Prophet's city) or Madina, where a small band of converts had invited him. This migration from Makkah to Madina, called the *Hijrah*, marks the beginning of the Islamic lunar calendar. The year 622 CE is thus designated as 1st *Hijri* and all subsequent years are referred to as "After *Hijrah*" (abbreviated "A.H."). The establishment of the first Islamic state in Madina, illustrates the centrality of the *ummah* (community of believers/Muslims) and the fusion of religion and politics in Islam.

Once in Madina, Muhammad established and governed the Islamic state. However, the Makkans gave the Prophet no

S.M. Amin/Saudi Aramco World/PADIA (3511_024)

The Ka'abah, Islamdom's holiest shrine, situated in the middle of *Masjid al-Haram* (The Holy Mosque or The Grand Mosque) in Makkah, Saudi Arabia.

peace, and a series of wars between the Makkans and the Muslims ensued for nine years. When Muhammad conquered Makkah, most of his former enemies converted to Islam. Muhammad died in 632 CE, at the age of sixty-two, leaving behind a young and dynamic faith.

The Qur'an

According to Muslims, Prophet Muhammad's greatest miracle was the Qur'an or Koran (as it is popularly known in the West), from the Arabic *Al-Qur'an*, which literally means "The Recitation." Some of the other names given to the Qur'an are *Al-Furqan* (The Discernment) for it contains the principles of both intellectual and moral insights and understandings; *Umm al-Kitab* (The Mother Book) for it is the ultimate source of all knowledge and wisdom; *Al-Huda* (The Guide) for it is the supreme guide for a person's journey through life.

Muslims believe that the Qur'an, which resembles a book of poetry rather than essays, is a collection of God(s revelations sent down to Prophet Muhammad through the agency of Archangel Gabriel. Most often, these revelations (which were the verbatim Word of God) were communicated to Muhammad in classical and eloquent Arabic prose. Muhammad, who could not write, recited these revelations to his companions, who wrote them down, memorized them, and recited them to others. The name Qur'an was later given to the sacred book containing all these revelations and provides guidance for almost every aspect of a believer's life.

Muslims also believe the Qur'an is the last of the sacred books containing the authoritative "Word of God." Approximately as long as the New Testament, the Qur'an comprises 114 *surahs* (chapters), each one further divided into *ayats* (verses).

The chapters in the Qur'an are not based in the order that Prophet Muhammad received the revelations, but in the sequence that Prophet Muhammad recommended that they should be placed. Of course, Muslims believe that it was on God's command that Prophet Muhammad decided to place the longer chapters in the Qur'an before the shorter ones.

The chapters of the Qur'an can be divided into two principal categories. The first thirteen years of Muhammad's prophethood were in Makkah (610–622 CE) and the Makkan revelations focus on two principal themes: condemning primitive and barbaric tribal customs in Arabia (such as female infanticide, superstitions, witchcraft, and men inheriting their widowed mothers as wives of their own) as well as enlightening people about the stupidity of idolatry and the rationality of believing in one God. Most of the remaining period of Muhammad's life was spent in Madina (622-632 CE) and the Madinan revelations focused on Islam law (marriage, divorce, inheritance, statecraft, and criminal punishments) as well as relations with non-Muslims.

Nearly one-third of the Qur'anic verses focus on Old Testament prophets, interfaith issues, and the human experience. Another third of the Qur'an covers subjects pertaining to legal, ethical, and moral issues as well as the accountability of human beings for their deeds in this world. The final third of the Qur'an relates to issues concerning the next life and what people will find after death.

Most Muslims all over the world learn to recite the Qur'an in Arabic, whatever their native language, believing that it is God's final guidance to humankind until the Day of Judgment. Qur'anic verses are the first words that the newborn child hears and the last words recited before the dead are lowered into their graves.

Prophet Muhammad's *Sunnah*

Sunnah is an Arabic term that refers to a path, road, or way. In Islam, Prophet Muhammad's *sunnah* is understood as Prophet Muhammad's trodden path, way, custom, or tradition. It comprises all the reliable reports about his sayings as well as his *sirah* (stories about his life, behavior, and deeds). The *sunnah* provides a valuable source of information and guidance for Muslims about how to behave. In this respect, the *sunnah* complements the Qur'an as the major source of Islamic faith and practice.

Prophet Muhammad's Hadith

Hadith is an Arabic term for an eyewitness account, narrative, report, or record. Unlike the Qur'an, which are a direct recitation of God's words, the Prophet Muhammad's *Hadith* are sayings attributed to him (that were passed along through a chain of reliable oral transmitters), albeit informed by the Prophet's divine inspiration. They deal with the contents of the Qur'an, religious as well as socioeconomic affairs, and the conduct of everyday life from the time one awakes to the time one goes to bed at night.

The most famous collections of *Hadith* for all Sunnis are the *Sahih* (Authentic) of Muhammad ibn Ismail al-Bukhari (died 870 CE) and *Sahih* of Abul Hussein Muslim ibn al-Hajjaj (popularly called "Muslim," died 875 CE). The other four highly respected collections of Prophet Muhammad's *Hadith* are those of Abu Dawood (died 875 CE), Ibn Maja (died 886 CE), at-Tirmizi (died 892 CE), an-Nasa'ee (died 915 CE). These make up the *al-kuttub as-sahah sitta* (the six authentic books): Sahih Bukhari, Sahih Muslim, Abu Dawood , Ibn Maja, Tirmizi, and Nasa'ee. However, Malik ibn Anas' *Muwatta* (the first collection of Hadith ever written down) and Ibn Hanbal's *Masnad* are also highly respected Hadith collections.

While respecting Prophet Muhammad's *Hadith* found in *Sahah Sitta*, Shi'as consider the *Hadith* transmitted by Ali ibn Abi Talib (Prophet Muhammad's cousin and son-in-law), and their infallible Imams as being most authentic. In this regard, they find beyond reproach the Prophet *Hadith* found in *Kulayni's Usool al-Kafi*, Sheikh Sadooq's *Man La Yahdharahul-Faqeeh*, Shaykh Toosi's *Tahzeeb* as well as *Al-Istebsaar*, and Majlisi's *Bihar-ul-Anwar*.

Prophet Muhammad's *Hadith* are Islam's second most important textual source after the Qur'an, an essential part of Prophet Muhammad's Sunnah (sayings and deeds), and a major source after the Qur'an for the development of the *shariah* (Islamic law).

Shariah

Shariah is the comprehensive, eternal, immutable, and divine law of Islam that governs all aspects of the public and private, social and economic, religious and political life of every Muslim. The *shariah's* provisions were compiled by the *ulama* (Islamic scholars) during the middle ages using the discipline of *fiqh* (Islamic jurisprudence), *hadith* (Prophet Muhammad's sayings), *ijma* (consultation and consensus), and *qiyas* (analogy). Shi'as commonly substitute *ijtihad* (independent reasoning) for *qiyas*, and interpret *ijma* as the consensus of the Imams or the Grand Ayatollahs. For a Muslim country to be called an Islamic state, it must impose the *shariah* as the law of the land. No wonder all Islamists call for the imposition of the *shariah*.

SUNNIS AND SHI'AS

In addition to the *shahadah* (profession of the faith), "There is no God but God, and Muhammad is His Messenger," Shi'as often add the phrase "Ali is the beloved of God." Although Ali did become Islam's fourth caliph, he was preceded by Abu Bakr, Umar, and Uthman. Therefore, while Sunnis revere the first four "rightly guided" or "pious" caliphs, many orthodox Shi'ahs usually reject the legitimacy of Ali's three predecessors and all his successors. This difference in belief is an obstacle to Shi'a and Sunni reconciliation and reunification.

In addition, Sunnis insist that Prophet Muhammad was a mere human being through whom God revealed his message (as recorded in the Qur'an), whereas Shi'as contend that the Prophet was close to infallible and possessed some semidivine attributes because of the *Nur-i-Elahi* (Divine Light) shared by all of God's prophets. Moreover, Shi'as assert, elements of the *Nur-i-Elahi* were bestowed upon Muhammad's daughter Fatimah, her husband, Imam Ali, and their descendants through their male progeny. While Sunnis respect Ali and his descendants, they do not revere them to the extent that Shi'as do. Indeed, the Sunnis reject the Shi'a contention that Muhammad selected Ali to be the first *Imam* of the Islamic state and thus repudiate the Shi'a institution of the Imamate (the divine right of Ali and his male descendants to lead the *ummah*). These differences in doctrine have contributed to Shi'ah-Sunni conflict.

Closely connected to the institution of the Imamate is the doctrine of the *Ithna Ashari* Shi'a sect regarding the disappearance of the twelfth apostolic Imam in 873 CE and his expected reappearance as the *Mahdi* (the divinely guided one or messianic savior), who will usher in a golden age of Islamic justice, equality, and unity of the *ummah*. So powerful is the idea of the *Mahdi* in Islam that many Sunnis have accepted it, as well.

Another major difference between Shi'as and Sunnis is in the realm of *fiqh* (Islamic jurisprudence). While Sunnis recognize four schools or rites of *fiqh* (the Hanafi, Hanbali, Maliki, and Shafi'i sects), the Shi'a have only one major *madhab* (sect), *Fiqh-i-Jafariyyah*, which was compiled and codified by the sixth Shi'a Imam, Jafar-i-Sadiq (died 765 CE). Shi'ahs promote the exercise of *ijtihad* (independent reasoning and judgment) by experienced *mujtahids* (learned theologians, or *ulama*, entitled to exercise *ijtihad*) and reject the Sunni concept of *qiyas* (deduction by analogy) as the fourth source of Islamic law after the Qur'an, the *sunnah*, and *ijma* (consensus). Furthermore, differences exist between Shi'as and Sunnis in the laws of marriage, divorce, and inheritance. Twelver Shi'as, for example, permit temporary marriage, or *mut'ah*. For Sunnis, any marriage contract that sets a limit to the duration of marriage is sinful. Shi'as, by contrast, place greater restrictions than do Sunnis on the husband's right to divorce his wife. In addition, in matters of inheritance, female heiresses often are treated far more generously in the Shi'ah *Fiqh-i-Jafariyyah* than under the Hanafi, Hanbali, Maliki, or Shafi'i schools of Sunni *fiqh*. Further differentiating Shi'as from Sunnis is the exclusively Shi'a practice of *taqiyyah* (concealment), which permits an individual to conceal his true religious, ideological, or political beliefs to avoid persecution or death at the hands of enemies. This practice evolved in response to fifteen hundred years of persecution of Shi'as throughout the Muslim world.

The two major sects of Islam likewise differ with respect to religious tradition. The Shi'as engage in more rituals than do the Sunnis. Indeed, Sunni Revolutionary Islamists (especially the Wahhabis) often denounce Shi'as for their adulation of saints, especially the most prominent members of the *Ahl al-Bayt* (Prophet Muhammad's extended family), and their pilgrimages to the mausoleums of saints in Iraq, Iran, and Syria. Portraits of Prophet Muhammad, *Imam* Ali, *Imam* Hussein, and the battle of Karbala are publicly displayed and sold in Iran. Such pictures would never be displayed in predominantly Sunni societies where there is a much greater concern that people would start venerating, idolizing, and even worshiping Prophet Muhammad and prominent members of his family.

The practice of daily liturgical prayers also differs between Sunnis and Shi'as. Shi'as are permitted to perform their five daily prayers three times a day (between dawn and sunrise, between midday and sunset, and between sunset and midnight) instead of the five times practiced by Sunnis (before sunrise, around midday, in the late afternoon, at dusk, and before midnight). The two sects' calls to prayer also differ, as do their manners of praying: Shi'as stand with their arms hanging straight down, while Sunnis fold their arms in front of themselves. Shi'as and Sunnis differ greatly in their commemoration of Muharram, the first month in the Islamic lunar calendar and the month in 680 CE in which Prophet Muhammad's grandson Hussein ibn Ali and his male followers were martyred on the battlefield of Karbala by Umayyad caliph Yazid's army. While Sunnis revere Hussein and lament his martyrdom, the *Ithna Ashari* (Twelver) Shi'as attend *majlises* (meetings) where Islamic scholars deliver sermons recounting the lives, deeds, and sayings of the twelve Imams as well as portraying vivid and powerful stories about the significance of Karbala. After all *majlises*, Shi'as engage in *ma'atam* (breast beating) and deeply mourn the massacre of Imam Hussein and his small band of followers and the deplorable treatment of the female members of the *Ahl al-Bayt* (family of the Prophet). Through these *majlises*, Shi'ahs educate the younger generation in the lessons of true Islam. Sunnis, however, feel that Shi'as have created an inappropriate cult around the personalities of Hussein and his father, Ali, and strongly criticize the manifest masochism of some Shi'as during Muharram.

Although Shi'as and Sunnis have their differences, as do adherents of the four Sunni sects, Muslims of both sects agree that they have much in common. Not only do they share most fundamental religious beliefs, but the devout members of all Islamic sects express their conviction that Islam provides answers and guidance in all endeavors, even political.

ISLAMISM

Many non-Muslim tends to confuse Islam and Islamism. Islamism has its roots in mainstream Islam, but is distinct from the Abrahamic faith of Islam. Islamism is a comprehensive religio-political ideology in world affairs. Islamism is promoted by Islamists who seek to reintroduce the comprehensive body of Islamic law (shariah) and the fundamentals of Islam, in Muslim societies; for Islamists, religion and politics ("church and state") should be fused. Non-Muslims are also under the erroneous impression that all Islamists are terrorists. In reality, only a infinitesimally small fraction of Islamists are misguided Muslim extremists or terrorists. Most Islamists are enlightened teachers, preachers, and scholars as well as progressive reformers and religiopolitical revolutionaries. Islamism can also be defined as the ideologization or politicization of Islam. This phenomenon has been referred to in the scholarly literature and popular mass media as Islamic revivalism, Islamic reassertion, Islamic resurgence, political Islam, and Islamic fundamentalism.

Prominent Features of Islamism

The Islamism we have witnessed since the late 1960s encompasses at least five prominent features. First, the spread of Islam from homes, mosques, and *madrassahs* (Islamic schools) into the mainstream of not only the sociocultural life of Muslim societies, but the legal, economic and political spheres of the modern-day Muslim countries as well. Islamists stress the observance of the five *faraidh*, or the five pillars of Islam: *shahadah* (belief in one God), *salat* (prayers), *sawm* (fasting during Ramadan), zakat (charity), and *hajj* (the pilgrimage to Makkah). They emphasize modesty in dress for men and women and the *hijab* (veil) for women. They also exert considerable pressure on their respective governments to ban alcohol, gambling, night clubs, prostitution, pornography and a number of other corrupting influences. They further demand the implementation of the *shariah*, which includes severe penalties for a

TABLE 1: Sunnis and Shi'as: A Comparison of Islam's Two Major Sects

	Sunnis	Shi'as
Historical Background		
Origin of the Terms Sunni and Shi`a	*Sunni* has been derived from the Arabic term *Sunnah* that means "those who follow the sayings and deeds of Prophet Muhammad ibn Abdullah" (570–632 CE, hereafter referred to as "the Prophet").	• *Shi`a* has been derived from the Arabic term *Shi'at-i-Ali*, which means "followers of Ali ibn Abi Talib (henceforth referred to as "Ali")—the Prophets first cousin and son-in-law through Alis marriage to Fatimah, the Prophets daughter). • Also believe in the Prophets *Sunnah*.
Transfer of Religiopolitical Authority	• Claim that Prophet Muhammad did not designate a religiopolitical leader of the *ummah* (community of believers), whether *Khalifah* (caliph) or *Imam*, before he died. • On the death of Prophet Muhammad (632 CE), the most influential leaders of Arabia met at Saqifah and chose Abu Bakr to be the first *Khalifah* (caliph). Abu Bakr was one of Prophet Muhammads closest *sahabis* (companions) who even accompanied him on the *Hijra* (migration from Makkah to Madina in 622 CE), the Prophets father-in-law (through his daughter Aysha, who was one of the Prophets wives), and one of the most respected elderly gentlemen in the meeting (in a society that respects the elderly for their wisdom).	• Claim that the Prophet, after completing his last *hajj*, stopped at a place between Makkah and Madina called Ghadeer-i-Khum and designated Ali as the first *Imam* on divine command because Ali was the most righteous, knowledgeable, wise, and courageous Muslim. The Prophet was also close to Ali because the two had grown up together in the same household, and the Prophet chose Ali out of all the suitors who wanted to marry Fatimah (the Prophets only daughter). • On the death of Prophet Muhammad, Ali, who had been designated as the *Imam* by Islams last prophet, was not present at the conclave to choose the religiopolitical leader of the *ummah* because Ali and his family were burying Prophet Muhammad.
The Size of the Two Islamic *Madhabs* (Sects or Branches)	• The majority *madhab*, comprising 80% of the global *ummah* (over 1 billion Muslims) • Claim they are the majority sect because they are following "the straight path."	• The minority sect, comprising 20% of the global *ummah* (over 260 million Muslims) • Claim they are the minority sect in Islam because (1) Sunnis governed most Islamic empires and discriminated against the Shi`as; (2) the majority of *sufis* (pious Muslim mystics) and traders/merchants who engaged in proselytizing non-Muslims were Sunnis; and (3) and much of the Islamic literature studied in schools and colleges was written by Sunnis.
Major Commonalities		
Allah (God)	• Believe in one, transcendent, omnipotent, omnipresent, omniscient, eternal, just, and merciful God called Allah. • Believe that Allah is indivisible, has no equals, no partner, no parents, and no offspring. • Believe in the story of Creation (that Allah created the universe as well as Adam and Eve at a definite point in time).	
Iman (Islams Foundational Principles)	• Allah • Allahs angels • Allahs Prophets (Adam to Muhammad, including those in the Old Testament) • Allahs Holy Books (the Scrolls revealed to Abraham, the Psalms to David, the Torah to Moses, the Ingil to Jesus, and the Qur'an to Muhammad) • Judgment Day (when Allah will determine whether individual human beings will go to Heaven or Hell)	
Faraidh (Compulsory Duties), Also Known as *Arkan ad-Din* (Pillars of Islam)	1) the *shahadah* (declaration of the Islamic faith): *Ash hadu an La ilaha illa 'llah, Muhammad ar rasul Allah* (I bear witness that there is no God but Allah, and Muhammad is His [last] messenger.) 2) *salat* (liturgical prayers five times a day) 3) *zakat* (almsgiving of 2.5% of ones net worth annually to the poor, needy, charitable institutions, and/or orphanages) 4) *sawm* (fasting during the ninth Islamic calendar month of Ramadan) 5) *hajj*: pilgrimage to the *Ka`abah* (the first house built by Prophet Abraham to worship Allah) in Makkah (present-day Saudi Arabia) during the twelfth Islamic calendar month	
Qur'an (Allah's Final Message to Humankind)	• Believe Allahs final message was revealed to Muhammad (610–632 CE) and is preserved in its original form in the Qur'an.	
Prophet Muhammad	• Believe that Muhammad ibn Abdullah was Allah's last Prophet. • Believe that Archangel Gabriel revealed to Muhammad Allah's final message in the Qur'an, which was the continuation of the same message He had given to Abraham, David, Moses, and Jesus. • Believe that Prophet Muhammads receiving and then revealing God's final message to humankind (embodied in classical Arabic in the Qur'an) was his greatest miracle. • Consider Prophet Muhammad to be *insan-e-kamil* (perfect human being) and the ideal role model. • Believe Prophet Muhammad's Islamic state in Madina (622–630 CE) and then in Makkah (630–632 CE) was the ideal that Islamists should aspire to emulate.	

TABLE 1: Cont'd

Major Commonalities, continued

Islams Holy Cities	• Makkah is the location of the Ka'abah; Muslims turn in Makkahs direction when offering their liturgical prayers and visit that holy city once in their lifetime to perform the *hajj*.
	• Madinah (present-day Saudi Arabia) or *Madinat-un-Nabi* (City of Allahs Messenger) was the city that welcomed the Prophet when he was being persecuted in Makkah; it is where the Prophet established the first Islamic state and where he is buried.
	• Jerusalem (present-day Israel/Palestine) is the third holiest city, reverentially called *Al-Quds* or "The Holy" because of its association with the biblical prophets: Abraham, Jacob, David, Soloman, Moses, Jesus, and Muhammad. For the first 13 years of his prophethood (610–623 CE), Prophet Muhammad enjoined Muslims to turn toward Jerusalem to say their liturgical prayers. After 623 CE, the Prophet instructed Muslims to turn toward the *Ka`aba* in Makkah.
Shariah (Islamic Law)	Most Islamists believe that the *shariah* should be implemented in Muslim societies.
Religion and Politics	Islamists believe there is a fusion of religion and politics in Islam and that no laws can be legislated if they contradict the *shariah*.
Ijtihad (Reasoning and Judgment)	Believe that learned and revered *ulama* (Islamic scholars) have the religious authority to engage in *ijtihad* and issue *fatwas* (religious edicts).
Angels	Believe in angels who act as Allahs agents and operate throughout the universe to carry out His divine scheme.
Iblis/Shaytan (Satan or the Devil)	• Believe in the Qur'anic view that Satan, who was a *jinn* (made of fire), felt superior to Adam (made of dust), and therefore refused to bow to Adam when Allah asked him to (Qur'an 18:50).
	• Believe that Satan resolved to turn human beings against Allah.
Mahdi (The Messianic Savior)	Believe that when the world is filled with corruption, oppression, and anarchy (and the world is coming to an end), the *Mahdi* will appear in order to unite the *ummah* and usher in the "golden age" of Islamic piety, equality, and justice.
View of Humanity	Believe that human beings are the highest of Gods creation
Humanity's Problem	Not following "the straight path" revealed in the Qur'an
Original Sin	• Believe that human beings are sinless at birth.
	• Believe in the Qur'anic view that Satan's disobedience and arrogance made him the first sinner.
	• Disagree with the Christian concept of "Original Sin" (the theory that God condemned the whole human race until the Day of Judgment as sinners because Adam and Eve sinned when they disobeyed Allah and ate from the Tree of Knowledge in the Garden of Eden). Believe that Eve did not tempt Adam to eat from the Tree of Knowledge; thus both Adam and Eve sinned. However, they both repented for their sin and God forgave them.
Solution for Humanity or Basis for Salvation	• Devout Muslims of both sects believe that "the straight path" revealed in the Qur'an and Prophet Muhammads *sunnah* provides answers and guidance in all endeavors.
	• Believe in doing "good works."
Sanctity of Life	Believe in the sanctity of life and condemn suicide, murder, and terrorism because only God has the right to create and take life.
Jihad	• Believe in *jihad al-nafs*—a perpetual, non-violent, spiritual struggle against ones baser instincts/impulses—which Prophet Muhammad called *jihad-e-akbar* (the greatest *jihad* or sacred struggle in the way of Allah).
	• Believe in engaging in a *jihad-e-asghar* (the lesser *jihad*), which entails a military engagement in self-defense and defending ones home/family, homeland, religion, or fellow coreligionists against aggressors/invaders and tyrants. When ones homeland is invaded, the political leaders of the invaded country often call on a revered *alim* (Islamic scholar, preferably a *mufti* in the case of Sunnis or a grand *ayatollah* in the case of Shi`as) to formally declare a *jihad*.
	• Believe that Muslims who engage in a *jihad* (declared by a revered *mufti* or grand *ayatollah*) are called *mujahidin* (holy warriors fighting to defend Islam and the *ummah*), and if they die, they are referred to as *shaheed* (martyrs) who are destined to go to *Jannah* (Heaven).
Masjids (Mosques)	Frequent mosques to perform their liturgical prayers, especially *Salat al-Jumah* (the Friday afternoon congregational prayer) that was recommended by Prophet Muhammad (Qur'an, Chapter 62, Verse 9).
Madrassahs (Islamic schools)	Go to *madrassahs* to learn Arabic, the Qur'an, Prophet Muhammads *Hadith*, and *seerah* (the life of Prophet Muhammad) while also attending pre- kindergarten, kindergarten, and primary and/or secondary school.
Main Holidays	*Eid al-Fitr* (festival of fast-breaking) at the end of *Ramadan* and *Eid al-Azha* (festival of the sacrifice) at the close of the four-day ritual of *Hajj* commemorating Abrahams willingness to sacrifice his son, Ishmael, as commanded by God in dream to test his faith, during *Dhul-Hijjah* or the twelfth month in the Islamic calendar
Circumcision	Circumcise their baby boys.
"Unclean" Foods	Do not drink alcohol or consume pork, and try their best to eat *halal* (ritually slaughtered) meat
Greetings among the Faithful	Frequently say *as-salaam alaykum wa `rahmat allah wa barakatu* (peace be on/with you) and *wa`alaykum as-salaam wa `rahmat allah wa barakatu* (peace be on/with you too).

TABLE 1: Cont'd

	Sunnis	Shi'as
Major Differences		
Muhammad	• Believe Prophet Muhammad was *ummi* (illiterate). • Believe Prophet Muhammad was a fallible human being except when he was revealing Allahs message and dealing with religious/spiritual matters.	• Accept the idea that Prophet Muhammad was referred to as an *ummi* because he did not receive any "formal" schooling and never learned to read and write. • Categorically reject the notion that he was "illiterate" (which often implies "ignorance") due to his God-given intelligence, intuition, and enlightenment; extensive travels; interactions with people; and serious contemplation. • Believe Prophet Muhammad was an infallible human being and possessed divine attributes because of the *Nur-e-Elahi* (Divine Light) shared by all Allah's prophets.
The First Four Caliphs (Abu Bakr, Umar, Uthman, and Ali)	Revere the first four caliphs as *Khulafah-e-Rashidun* (the first four righteous caliphs)	• Most revere only the fourth caliph, Ali, and consider his writings and deeds (especially the Islamic state he established—656–661 CE) worthy of emulation. • Conservative and revolutionary Shi`as consider the first three caliphs as usurpers, and thus illegitimate religiopolitical rulers of the *ummah*, while progressive Shi`as respect the first three caliphs as well.
Qur'ans Interpretation	Accept interpretation by *sahaba* (Prophet Muhammads companions), first four caliphs (Abu Bakr, Umar, Uthman, and Ali), and Prophet Muhammads wives.	Accept interpretation by 14 *masumeen* (infallible human beings), including Prophet Muhammads daughter, Fatimah, and the 12 Imams, starting with Ali ibn Abi Talib.
Ahl al-Bayt (Prophet Muhammads Extended Family)	• Respect *ahl al-bayt* • Most do not follow the *hadith* and *sunnah* of the Shi`a Imams. • Do not commemorate birth and death of Fatimah and Shi`a Imams. In fact, adherents of the Hanbali sect are strongly against the practice.	• Reverence and love for ahl *al-bayt* is the cornerstone of Shi`ism. • Follow the *hadith* and *sunnah* of their infallible Imams. • Twelver Shi`as commemorate the birth and death of the 14 *masumeen* (Prophet Muhammad, Fatimah, and the 12 Shi`a Imams). Ismailis (Khojas and Aghakhanis) and Bohras commemorate the birth and death of their *imams*.
Sahaba (Prophet Muhammads Companions)	Respect all the *sahaba*.	Respect most of the *sahaba*; critical of those *sahaba* who harmed the *ahl al-bayt*.
Khilafat/Imamat (Caliphate/Imamate)	• Believe in *Khilafat* (Caliphate) or the idea that the *Khalifah* is the supreme religiopolitical leader of the Islamic state after Prophet Muhammad. In Al-Mawardis *Ahkam as-Sultaniyya* (The Rule of Governance) and in Mawlana Sayyid Abul Ala Mawdoodis *Khilafat-o-Mulookiyyat* (Caliphate and Kingship) Muslims have been discouraged from rebelling against any pious Muslim ruler who establishes an Islamic state (where the *shariah* is implemented). • Revere the *Khulafah-e-Rashidun*—the first four "rightly guided" *Khalifahs* (caliphs): Abu Bakr, Umar ibn al-Khattab, Uthman ibn Affan, and Ali ibn Abi Talib. • Reject the Shi`a institution of *Imamat* or the idea that Prophet Muhammad nominated Ali ibn Abi Talib—and thereafter his male descendants—on Gods command to be the first *Imam* of the Islamic state and the global *Imamate*.	• Reject the concept of the *Khilafat* and believe instead in the institution of *Imamat* or the divine right only of Ali and his 11 male descendants to lead the *ummah* (Shaykh Mufeed, who wrote *Kitab al-Irshad*, translated into English by I. K. A. Howard, has collected Prophet Muhammad's *Hadith*, which validate the legitimacy of the 12 Imams). • Most reject the legitimacy of all *Khalifahs* except Ali ibn Abi Talib, who Shi`as believe was publicly nominated by Prophet Muhammad on Gods instructions at a place called *Ghadir-e-Khom*, which was between Makkah and Madinah. • Prophet Muhammad's *Nur-i-Elahi* was passed on to his daughter Fatimah, her husband, Imam Ali, and their male descendants. • While definitely *not* part of the *shahadah*, Shi`as often add *Ali un wali Allah* (Ali is the beloved of God)—a tradition that began during the rule of the first Umayyad caliph, Muawiyyah (661–680 CE), who had ordered all mosque *imams* to curse Ali during their sermons.
Prophet Muhammads *Hadith* (Sayings)	• Follow Prophet Muhammad's *Hadith*, especially those found in the Sahah Sitta (the six authentic books): *Sahih Bukhari, Sahih Muslim, Tirmizi, Abu Dawood, Ibn Maja,* and *Nasa'ee*. • In recent times, Sunni scholars (particularly from Al-Azhar seminary in Cairo, Egypt) have engaged in the science of evaluating the Prophets *Hadith* in the Sahah Sitta, and pointed out discrepancies in some of the *Hadith* found even in Sahih Bukhari and Sahih Muslim.	• While respecting Prophet Muhammad's *Hadith* found in Sahah Sitta, Shi`as consider beyond reproach the *Hadith* of the Prophet found in Kulaynis *Usool al-Kafi,* Sheikh Sadooqs *Man La Yahdharahul-Faqeeh,* Shaykh Toosi's *Tahzeeb* as well as Al-Istebsaar, and Majlisis *Bihar-ul-Anwar*. • Learned *ayatollahs*, especially in the Islamic seminaries in Qom, Iran, carefully evaluate and validate each *Hadith*.

TABLE 1: Cont'd

	Sunnis	Shi'as
Major Differences, continued		
Major Schools of *Fiqh* (Islamic Jurisprudence)	Adhere to one of the four major schools of Sunni *fiqh*—Hanafi, Maliki, Shafi`i, and Hanbali—each named after the learned *alim* (Islamic scholar) that developed it.	• Most adhere to *Fiqh-i-Jafariyyah*, compiled and codified by Jafar-e-Sadiq, who was the sixth Shi`a Imam. • The erudite Jafar-e-Sadiq tutored Imams Abu Hanifah al-Numan ibn-Thabit and Abu Abd Allah Malik ibn Anas, who were the founders of the first two Sunni *madhabs*. • Comprise three major subsects: Ithna Asharis (Twelvers), Bohris, and Ismaelis.
Ijtihad	Most follow *fatwas* (religious edicts) issued by *muftis*.	Most follow the *fatwas* of the *marja` al-taqlid* (sources of emulation) or grand *ayatollahs*.
Salat (Liturgical Prayers)	• Practice five times a day: before sunrise, around midday, in the late afternoon, at dusk, and before midnight. • Fold their arms in front of themselves in prayer (except Malikis, who stand with their arms hanging straight down). • In the azan for the morning prayers, Sunnis say: *salat al-khair al minan naum* (prayers are better than sleep).	• Can perform their five daily prayers three times a day: between dawn and sunrise, between midday and sunset, and between sunset and midnight (but in the right order). • Stand with their arms hanging straight down. • In the *azan*, Shi'as say: *hayya la khair-ul-amal* (let us perform the most righteous duty) and Ali un-Waliullah (beloved of God).
Khums (Donations Given to *Marja al-Taqlid* to Distribute among Needy Shi`as)	Do not give any *khums*, but give 2.5 percent of their wealth annually in *zakat*.	Give *khums* (20% of annual savings after expenses) in addition to giving 2.5 percent of their wealth annually in *zakat*.
Fasting in *Ramadan*	Start fast at dawn and end it at sunset.	Start the fast approximately 10 minutes earlier and end it approximately 10 minutes later than Sunnis.
Mahdi	Believe that the Mahdi or savior—who will eventually come at the end of time—is yet to be born.	*Ithna Asharis* believe the Mahdi is the twelfth Imam, who was born in 873 CE (256 A.H. or after Prophet Muhammads *hijra* from Makkah to Madinah in 622 CE), went into occultation (hiding) in 877 CE, and will reappear on earth on Gods command to usher in the era of peace and justice.
Qiyas (Deduction and Analogy)	Support the concept of *qiyas* as the fifth source of Islamic law after the Qur'an, the Prophets *sunnah*, *ijtihad*, and *ijma* (consensus).	Reject the concept of *qiyas*.
Mut`ah (Temporary Marriage)	Consider *mut`ah* to be sinful.	• *Ithna Asharis* accept the idea of *mut`ah*.
Divorce	• Few restrictions on the husbands right to divorce his wife. • More restrictions on the wife's right to divorce her husband.	• Greater restrictions on the husband's right to divorce his wife. • Fewer restrictions for the wife to divorce her husband. • In fact, a woman can ask to include in the marriage contract her exclusive right to ask for a divorce, as and when she wishes.
Inheritance	Female heiresses are treated less generously under the Hanafi, Hanbali, Maliki, or Shafi'i schools of *fiqh*.	Female heiresses are often treated far more generously in *Fiqh-i-Jafariyyah*.
Taqiyyah (Concealment)	Reject *taqiyyah*, which permits an individual to conceal his/her true religious, ideological, or political beliefs to avoid persecution or death.	Permit *taqiyyah*—a practice that evolved due to the minority Shi`a sects persecution.
Commemoration of *Muharram* (The First Islamic Calendar Month in 680 CE when *Umayyad* Caliph Yazid ibn-e-Muawiyyah ordered his army to kill Prophet Muhammad's grandson, Hussein ibn Ali, and his 72 male followers on the battlefield of Karbala in present-day Iraq)	• Many lament the martyrdom of Hussein ibn Ali. However, most believe that Shi`as have created a cult around the personality of Hussein ibn Ali, and criticize the manifest masochism of some Shi`as during Muharram. This criticism has become much more pronounced through Saudi Arabias promotion of the puritanical Hanbali worldview, and particularly Wahhabism, since 1973. • The majority respect Muawiyyah, and a few even respect Yazid.	• During *Muharram*, the *Ithna Asharis* attend *majlises* (religious meetings) where Islamic scholars deliver sermons on the extraordinary deeds and sayings of the 12 Imams as well as relate vivid stories about Hussein ibn Ali and his martyrdom the Battle of Karbala (680 CE/61 AH). • Following the *majlises*, Ithna Asharis engage in *ma`atam* (breast beating) and mourn the massacre of Imam Hussein and his small band of followers and the abuse of the female members of the *ahl al-bayt*. • Critical of Muawiyyah and Yazid for their tyranny, corruption, and injustice.

20

TABLE 1: Cont'd

	Sunnis	Shi'as
Major Differences, continued		
The Iraqi Cities of Najaf and Karbala	Do not make pilgrimages to Najaf (from where Ali ibn Abi Talib governed the *ummah* and where he is buried in a mausoleum) and Karbala (where Hussein ibn Abi Talib was martyred and where he is buried in a mausoleum).	Try their best to make pilgrimages to Karbala and Najaf once in their lifetime.
Religious Tradition	• Many (especially the Wahhabis or adherents of the Hanbali *madhab*) denounce Shi`as for their many rituals, like holding *majlises* for their Imams; wearing *taweezes* (amulets with the Qur'an or passages from it) around their necks; lighting candles and giving *tabaruk* (offering of food to people) after visiting the graves of their relatives; making pilgrimages to the tombs of the *ahl al-bayt* in Iraq, Iran, and Syria; and displaying pictures of Ali ibn Abi Talib and Hussein ibn Ali (the martyr of the Battle of Karbala).	• Often denounce Hanbalis (especially Wahhabis/Salafis) for their puritanism and intolerance. • In predominantly Ithna Ashari Shi`a countries of Iran, Iraq, Lebanon, and Bahrain, portraits of *Imam Ali*, *Imam Hussein*, and the Battle of Karbala are available. However, wherever Shi`as are in a minority in a predominantly Sunni country, those portraits are not displayed.
Imambaras—religious centers frequented by Shi`as to pray to God; hold *majlises* (religious meetings) remembering their 14 *masumeen*; and calling on the *masumeen* to intercede with God on their behalf	Do not visit *Imambaras* and many are critical of the practice.	Besides frequenting mosques, Twelver Shi`as also frequent *imambaras*, where they say their prayers to God and hold *majlises* (meetings) commemorating the lives, deeds, sayings, suffering, and death of their 14 *masumeen*.
Clerical Establishment	• Not hierarchically organized • Most do not believe in *taqlid* (rigid and unquestioning adherence to one or more Islamic schools of jurisprudence).	• Hierarchically and tightly organized with grand *ayatollahs* at the very apex (like the Catholic clerical establishment). • Have a *marj'a* system in which every Shi`a in the laity is encouraged to choose and follow a revered Shi`a *alim* (often a grand *ayatollah*) on religious matters.

broad spectrum of crimes. There is also an increased attendance of Muslims of all walks of life at *Jum'ah* (Friday) congregational prayer services and during the annual hajj to Makkah in the twelfth Islamic calendar month of *Dhul-Hijj*. In response to the Islamists, many regimes in Muslim countries, even those run by Muslim secularists, display their Islamic credentials by stepping up their funding of *masjids* and *madrassahs*.

Second, Islamism engenders the widespread discussion and debate of Islamic issues in the mass media, leading to a proliferation of books and articles on Islamic theology, history, jurisprudence, culture, and civilization. Indeed, besides engaging in a critique of the dominant secular and materialist values imported from the West or the Socialist-Communist world, these periods of intense debate could very well lead to a revision of Islamic theory and practice in light of contemporary times and yield an Islamic approach to solving current problems of Muslim societies. In this respect, Islamism could well represent the beginning of an "Islamic renaissance" or "Islamic reformation" that is urgently needed in the Muslim world.

Third, Islamism has resonance among the Muslim masses because the Muslim secularists, who have governed Muslim countries since independence, are guilty of "bad governance." Islam emphasizes honesty as well as socioeconomic equity and justice, while Muslim countries are trapped in grinding poverty, inequality, and corruption. In fact, the growing disparity of wealth between a small privileged elite and the impoverished majority in Muslim countries infuriates the religious masses. Islamists win support among these masses when they pledge to

institute the *shariah* and push an Islamization program that will break the dominance of capitalists, industrialists, landlords, tribal leaders, generals, and bureaucrats.

Fourth, Islamists often point out that all the imported secular "isms" (nationalism, capitalism, socialism, communism, Ataturkism, pan-Arabism, Ba'athism, and Nasserism) have failed to end the problems of poverty, unemployment, disease, illiteracy, inequality, injustice, corruption, and nepotism plaguing Muslim societies. Islamists believe that their version of Islamism will alleviate these problems plaguing Muslim societies.

Fifth, Islamist movements have strong anti-imperialist and anti-colonialist undercurrents. Muslims are constantly reminded in educational institutions (in *madrassahs*, secular K-12 public schools, and colleges/universities) about their glorious Islamic civilization and the thousand-year long conflict with the Western Christian world. Islamists would like Muslim countries to end their dependence on the Big Western Powers and Russia (pertaining to the five Central Asian countries and Azerbaijan), which they perceive as dividing the *ummah* (between the elites and the masses, between the secular and devout Muslims, between the older and younger generations, between sects within Islam, and between Muslim countries) and stealing their resources in the Muslim world. These Islamists champion the development of a united Islamic bloc of fraternal Muslim states based on pan-Islamism, which in turn could become an influential force in international relations for the good of the global *ummah*.

Sixth, Islamists are alarmed about the westernization and corruption of Islamic culture. They despise the values of excessive freedom, individualism, and hedonism promoted by Western music, movies, magazines, and over the Internet. They frown on the decadent culture advance by the likes of Elvis Presley, Michael Jackson, Madonna, and Britney Spears. They believe that with the spread of Western culture, the generation gap between the older and younger generations will grow; sexual permissiveness, divorce, drugs, and violence will increase; and a new era of jahiliyyah (uncivilized culture) will spread in the Muslim world.

Besides the six major hallmarks of Islamism, there are four noteworthy manifestations of Islamism. The most dramatic and revolutionary manifestation of Islamism is an Islamic resurgence—involving the groundswell of a broad spectrum of the Muslim society for a Islamic political system or an Islamic state. This has been referred to in the literature on Islam as an "Islamic resurgence" and as "populist Islam." The world witnessed an Islamic resurgence in Iran in the late 1970s; in Afghanistan, Sudan, the Israeli-controlled West Bank and Gaza during the 1980s; and in Algeria, Tajikistan, the Indian state of Kashmir, and Chechnya (in Russia) during the 1990s.

The second major manifestation of Islamism is when Islamic movements, parties, and interest groups attempt assertively, though peacefully, to establish an Islamic political system. Examples of such organizations include the Ikhwan al-Muslimin (Muslim Brotherhood) in Egypt, Jama'at-e-Islami (the Islamic Association) in Pakistan, India, and Bangladesh; and the Islamic Salvation Front (FIS) in Algeria.

The third major manifestation of Islamism is when misguided Muslim zealots—individually, as part of a cell or a small tightly knit group, or as part of large Islamist organizations—engage in a campaign of violence and terrorism against those they perceive as the enemies of Islam and Muslims (namely imperialistic powers and their Muslim collaborators who are exploiting the resources of the Muslim world and contributing the poverty, inequality, and humiliation of the ummah). Examples of such organizations are Al-Qaeda (The Base); Takfir wal-Hijra (Repentence and Flight) and al-Gamaa al-Islamiya (the Islamic Group) in Egypt; and Harkat al-Muqawama al-Islamiya (Islamic Resistance Movement or HAMAS/Zeal) and Islamic Jihad in the Gaza Strip and the West Bank.

The fourth major manifestation of Islamism is in the form of government-sponsored Islamic policies and programs. The most prominent examples of political Islam being imposed from above are the theocratic regime of Iran; the House of Saud in Saudi Arabia, which emphasizes Islam to appease the influential Wahhabi establishment; the Taliban in Afghanistan (1996–2001); General Omar Hassan al-Bashir's National Democratic Alliance in Sudan; and General Muhammad Zia-ul-Haq's military regime in Pakistan (1977–1988). Islamism is also employed by regimes in Muslim countries to appease influential domestic movements, parties and interest groups; enhance governmental legitimacy; assist in the integration of a fragmented society; and/or acquire funds from rich Muslim countries. The most vivid examples of the latter were the regimes of Muhammad Ja'far al-Numayri in Sudan (1969–1985), Prime Minister Zulfikar Ali Bhutto (1971–1977), and President Muhammad Anwar al-Sadat (1970–1981).

Historically, Islamism has occurred in cycles followed by periods of relative dormancy. The current phase of Islamism started with Israel's humiliating defeat of the Arabs in the 1967 Arab-Israeli war. It gathered momentum after the 1973 Arab-Israeli war and OPEC's oil-price increases. Islamism fueled Iran's Islamic Revolution (1978–1979) and the concurrent "Islamization" campaigns in Pakistan and Sudan. It was responsible for the 444-day long "hostage crisis" in the U.S. Embassy in Tehran, the assassination of Egypt's President Muhammad Anwar al-Sadat, and it contributed to turmoil in Lebanon. It was responsible for the humiliating defeat and expulsion of the well-equipped Soviet imperialists from Afghanistan and is an important element in the civil strife in many countries around the world, including Algeria, India, Russia, Tajikistan, Egypt, Tunisia, Sudan, and the two intifadahs in Israeli-controlled West Bank and Gaza to mention but a few.

However, today's Islamism differs markedly from Islamism in the past. First, the current reassertion of political Islam is not merely a localized or even regional phenomenon, but is global in scope. This universality of Islamism has been a significant development in international relations and can be explained by numerous links that bind the world together in ways unknown in the past. The revolutions in mass communications, mass transportation, and computerization as well as the roles played by multinational corporations and international banking and finance have drastically shrunk the world in time and space. Significant occurrences anywhere in the world may be communicated through CNN almost instantaneously. Furthermore, the establishment of non-governmental and transnational Islamic organizations, like the Organization of the Islamic Conference (OIC) or the Ikhwan al-Muslimun, have spread Islam's populist message to Muslims the world over.

Ironically, while globalization heightens the probability of Islamism spreading all over the world, it also insures that Islamism is neither monolithic nor homogeneous, but polycentric, pluralistic, heterogeneous, and multifaceted, with as many aspects as there are Islamic groups. For instance, the current Islamism, unlike the past, is a product of the interaction of at least three categories of Islamists—namely, the Revolutionary, Traditionalist, and Progressive Islamists—and the Muslim secularists, who are non-practicing Muslim elites governing Muslim societies (see comparisons of the Revolutionary Islamists and Progressive Islamists who are in the vanguard of most Islamist movements on p. 29 and see p. 26 for a comparison of Revolutionary Islamists and Muslim secularists. The latter have dominated Muslim countries since these societies gained their independence from European colonial rule in the twentieth century). In this respect, the reassertion of political Islam is hardly conducive to the creation of a unified Muslim ummah (brotherhood of Muslims) or united Islamic bloc. Nevertheless, Islamism progresses daily with greater vigor and vitality than the day before. While the violent facets of Islamism are unpopular and bring disrepute to Islam, the many peaceful facets of Islamism are immensely popular and have prevented it from being discredited. Thus, any action taken by secular and corrupt Muslim despots or non-Muslims to contain or suppress Islamism, will only serve to strengthen Islamism among the frustrated and angry Muslims all over the world.

Islam: A Vehicle of Political Action

Islam is a vehicle for political change in the Muslim societies because it is a "historical religion," an "organic religion," a religion that emphasizes socioeconomic equity and justice, and a faith that stresses *jihad* (holy struggle). As a "historical religion," Muslims consider history as divinely ordained, and Islam explains the beginning and end of human history and the direction it will take. Islamists therefore interpret success and failure in the recent, even immediate, past as indicative of divine grace or anger respectively. Islamists have also always tried to build a political and socioeconomic order based on principles laid down not only in Islamic theology, jurisprudence, and the *shariah* (Islamic law), but in specific historical precedents set by Prophet Muhammad and his first four "rightly-guided caliphs."

Islam is an "organic religion" possessing a comprehensive belief system because the divine and immutable shariah incorporates the temporal within the all-encompassing spiritual realm and has something to say about every aspect of a Muslim's life. Islam is a holistic religion in which no distinctions exist between the realms of individual worship and community government, or between the realms of religion and politics. The Qur'an enjoins Muslims to get involved in politics because politics determines the shape of society. Moreover, Islamists believe that only politics based on robust Islamic foundations can be honest, just, and beneficial to the majority. Islam sets forth universal principles of human behavior in all its aspects. These principles are binding on Muslims and provide for them an answer in all areas of human endeavor. Therefore, for Islamists, when secular ideologies and systems cannot answer the gigantic political, economic, social, and cultural grievances of Muslims, there is always recourse to Islamism.

Socioeconomic equity and justice enjoy paramount importance in Islam. There are frequent references in the Qur'an to justice, fairness, truth, and piety, as well as economic and social equality. Prophet Muhammad repeatedly emphasized the importance of justice and frequently stated that all are equal before Allah and His divine laws on earth, whatever their race, color, sex, creed, and social, economic, or political status. This emphasis is in marked contrast to secular political ideologies that in the Muslim world have led to the increasing misery of the population and the growing gulf between the elite that keeps getting richer and the masses that keep getting poorer. In Islam, all are equal in the eyes of God and none goes unpunished for a crime. Furthermore, Islam provides for specific measures to ensure socioeconomic equity and justice, which has greatly enhanced the attraction of political Islam in a Muslim world where such equity and justice are notably absent.

Central to an understanding of Islamism is the pivotal importance of *jihad*, which literally means "to exert oneself to the utmost" or "to struggle in the way of God." Indeed, the achievement of justice is possible in Islam through the application of *jihad*, a term much maligned and misunderstood. Two principal categories of *jihad* exist in Islamic theology: personal and martial. Personal *jihad, jihad an-nafs* (self-discipline, will-power, or the control of self) or *jihad-e-akbar* (the greater *jihad*) is the non-violent spiritual struggle waged by Muslims to purge themselves of their base desires and evil impulses. Martial *jihad* or *jihad-e-asghar* (the lesser *jihad*), the less favored in the eyes of God and the last resort of Muslims according to the Qur'an, is an armed struggle fought to protect, defend, and promote the integrity of Islam and the *ummah* against hostile unbelievers, whether they are invading armies or "un-Islamic" internal despots. Nevertheless, martial *jihad* gains proponents in proportion to the oppression of political Islam in the Muslim world. *Jihad* is popular among Muslims because of the Qur'anic promise that a *mujahid* (the devout Muslim who fights in a *jihad*) who dies while fighting a *jihad* will earn the title of *shaheed* (martyr) and be rewarded with *al-Jannah* (Paradise). Unfortunately, the misapplication of martial jihad has maligned this term as well as Islam and Muslims. For instance, since September 11, 2001, terrorists who belong to the Islamic faith are being called *jihadis, jihadists*, and Islamic terrorists in the non-Islamic mass media.

These characteristics of Islam are the keys to understanding why Islam lends itself to politicization. It is no wonder that in every Muslim community there exists, always has existed, and always will exist, an individual or a group of Muslims who will ideologize and politicize Islam. Those in power will make Islam an instrument to enhance their interests and those in the opposition will make Islam an idiom of dissent against shared injustice and inequity. Political Islam, however, need not be violent or revolutionary. For example, it has operated well within a democratic context and many Islamists have worked and continue to work within that context with mixed results. In many cases, however, it is the war waged by secular Muslim regimes and non-Muslim governments against Islamists that has tended to radicalize Islamists, Islamic organizations, and political Islam.

Three Major Types of Islamists

The ideologization of Islam is not merely the work of Revolutionary Islamists, as the mass media and scholarly preoccupation with Islamic fundamentalism suggests, but the compound effect of the dynamic interaction and crude synthesis of the ideas and ideals of three types of Islamists, namely, the Revolutionary Islamists, Traditionalist Islamists, and Progressive Islamists, as well as the influential Muslim secularists who are part of the elite and the middle class. All three types of Islamists propagate their perception of the "true" Islam and attempt to win over the hearts and minds of the Muslim masses. However, it is the cooperation, competition, and conflict between the three different types of Islamists as well as the Muslim secularists that contributes to the revitalization and reassertion of political Islam. The first three types of individuals and groups are called "Islamists" because they are devout Muslims and frequently, but not necessarily, promote the creation of an Islamic state by teaching, preaching, and/or writing, and on rare occasions even by the force of arms. The fourth category, namely, the Muslim secularists, are not called Islamists because they are not practicing Muslims, but merely expoit Islam from time to time to further their interests.

Revolutionary Islamists

Revolutionary Islamists constitute the largest and most conspicuous category of Islamic revivalists or Islamists. They are referred to as "scripturalists," "legalists," "literalists," and "fundamentalists" in the Western mass media because they advocate rigid adherence to the fundamentals of Islam, as literally interpreted from the Qur'an and the sunnah (Prophet Muhammad's sayings and deeds). They often strive to establish an Islamic state based on the rigorous implementation of the *shariah* and insist that the five *faraidh* (duties) be scrupulously adhered to by all their coreligionists.

Revolutionary Islamists strongly object to being called "fundamentalists" because they believe the term fundamentalism has its origins in Christianity and does not transfer well to Islam; all Muslims believe in the fundamentals of Islam and, therefore, all Muslim should be called "fundamentalists"; the term fundamentalists has been much maligned and has come to mean "extremists," "zealots," and even "terrorists."

Some scholars have called Revolutionary Islamists, "puritans," because many of them would like to purify their religion of all the "unholy," "impure," and "permissive" values, traditions, and institutions that have become part of the faith since Islam's classical period (that of Prophet Muhammad and his close companions). For instance, Revolutionary Islamists: zealously crusade against secularism and secularization; are extremely critical of *taqlid* (unquestioning conformity to legal rulings that developed during the middle ages); consider the veneration of saints, holy men, Imams, and the glorification of Prophet Muhammad and members of his extended family as shirk (polytheism) that violates their strict interpretation of *tawhid* (Allah's Oneness). Indeed, this is why the Revolutionary Sunni Islamist Wahhabis of the Hanbali school of Islamic jurisprudence invaded Shi'a Islam's holiest cities in 1801 and demolished a number of tombs, mausoleums, and shrines built in the memory of Islam's heroes; killed Shi'as in Afghanistan under Taliban rule; and have been killing Shi'as in Pakistan and Iraq.

Revolutionary Islamists have also been called "restorationists" and "restitutionists" because they constantly strive to recreate an Islamic state founded on the same fundamental principles as the first Islamic state established in 622 CE by Prophet Muhammad in Madina and then continued by the Khulafah-i-Rashidin (the first four rightly-guided caliphs—Abu Bakr, Umar, Uthman, and Ali). They try to closely emulate Prophet Muhammad and the pious *aslaf* (Prophet Muhammad's Companions). They even place any and all Muslims who doubt the finality of Prophet Muhammad (such as Ahmadis and Bahais) outside the pale of Islam.

Moderate Revolutionary Islamists in the late twentieth-century (such as Iran's former presidents Hashemi Rafsanjani and Muhammad Khatami), unlike other Revolutionary Islamists (such as Muhammad Ahmad Abdallah al-Mahdi or the Mahdi of Sudan in the 1880s), are willing to embrace what they perceive as beneficial modern values that conform to the basic tenets of Islam. For example, although they wish to follow the revered body of *shariah*, they are willing to interpret it more broadly than in the past. Many, though certainly not all, Revolutionary Islamists in the modern period have come to accept Western notions of democracy such as periodic elections on the basis of one vote for every adult person, a multiparty political system, secret balloting, a national assembly or parliament to pass laws for the entire nation, and good relations with non-Western countries provided those relations are based on mutual respect and non-interference in each other's internal affairs.

Some of the most prominent Revolutionary Islamists in Islamic history are the Syrian-born theologian-jurist, Taqi al-Din ibn Taimiyyah (1263–1328 CE), who spent much of his life elaborating on the ideas of Iraqi-born theologian and jurist Ahmad ibn Hanbal (780–855 CE) in his own puritanical writings and sermons. Muhammad ibn Abd al-Wahhab, who together with Muhammad ibn Saud, launched the Wahhabi movement in the Arabian peninsula in the late eighteenth century; Sudan's Muhammad Ahmad Abdallah al-Mahdi who established an Islamic state in Sudan in 1885; Egypt's Hasan al-Banna who established one of the first populist, urban-oriented, and transnational religiopolitical organizations in the Muslim world in 1928; and Ayatollah Ruhollah Khomeini, who influenced Iran's Islamic Revolution (1978–1979) and established the first Islamic state in modern times. Unfortunately, some Revolutionary Islamists, like the activists of Al-Qaeda, the Palestinian Hamas and Islamic Jihad, or the Egyptian Islamic Jihad and *Gama'a al-Islamiyyah* (The Islamic Group) resort to terrorism. However, most God-fearing Revolutionary Islamists, not to mention Islamists and Muslims in general, shun this kind of violent and ugly manifestation of Revolutionary Islamism and terrorism. Yet, it is often this very violent, ugly, and rare manifestation of Islamism that receives overwhelming mass media exposure with little or no mention of the fact that most Muslims are honorable, peaceful, law-abiding, hardworking, and family-oriented people.

Traditionalist Islamists

Traditionalist Islamists constitute the second category of Islamic revivalists or Islamists. The products of traditional *madrassah* (Islamic schools) education, Traditionalists are often drawn from the ranks of the devout and learned *ulama* (Islamic scholars).

Traditionalist Islamists and Revolutionary Islamists have much in common. They are both devoutly religious and strong opponents of increasing secularization of the educational, legal, economic, and social realms of Muslim societies. In the educational sphere, the Traditionalist Islamists, like the Revolutionary Islamists, demand the generous funding of *madrassahs*; advocate syllabi that contain mainly Islamic disciplines; and promote the segregation of the sexes and extreme modesty in dress in educational institutions. In the legal sphere, both Traditionalist Islamists and Revolutionary Islamists demand an Islamic constitution drawing heavily upon the Qur'an, the *sunnah*, and the *shariah*, and the establishment of Islamic law courts presided over by *qadhis* (Islamic judges) and based on the *shariah*. In the social realm, the Traditionalists, like the Fundamentalists, encourage monogamy while at the same time allowing Muslims who meet certain criteria to have up to four wives; and enjoin women to adopt the *hijab* (veiling, segregation and seclusion). In the economic sphere, both advocate the institution of the *zakat* and *ushr* taxes, as well as the prohibition of *riba* (usury).

An open air *madrassah* (Islamic school) in Djenne, Mali, where a teacher in native dress and white cap teaches children how to read, write, recite, and understand the Qur'an. It is in such schools that children all over the Muslim world are socialized into Islam while also acquiring a basic education.

However, Traditionalist Islamists and Revolutionary Islamists also have major differences. While Revolutionary Islamists ceaselessly crusade for these beliefs and are often in the vanguard of the ideologization of Islam, Traditionalist Islamists disdain political activism and are generally detached, nonviolent, apolitical Islamic scholars, teachers, and preachers. Thus, Traditionalist Islamists are perceived by many Muslims as having been co-opted by Muslim regimes to support the status quo. But when Islam or the *ummah*—whether at local, regional, or global levels—appear to be in imminent danger, Traditionalist Islamists have temporarily abandoned their passivity and vigorously asserted themselves in the political arena.

Furthermore, unlike the Revolutionary Islamists, the Traditionalist Islamists conserve and preserve not only the Islamic beliefs, customs, and traditions practiced in the classical period of Islam but also those of subsequent Islamic periods. They are tolerant of Sufism and numerous local and regional customs and traditions commonly referred to in the aggregate as "folk Islam" or "popular Islam." Traditionalist Islamists believe that Islam is not merely a set of abstract and utopian principles, but

a comprehensive and living belief system that interacts with the historical and cultural traditions of devout Muslims. To suppress these traditions, therefore, would be to weaken the popular form of devotion of the Muslim majority. The Revolutionary Islamists, in contrast, oppose "folk Islam" in all its manifestations and discourage its practice as essentially un-Islamic.

One other difference with Revolutionary Islamists is that most Sunni Traditionalist Islamists are staunch opponents of *ijtihad* (which encourages independent thought in legal matters) and committed proponents of the dogma of *taqlid*. For the Traditionalist *ijtihad* represents an attack on traditional values and practices and therefore undermines Islam.

While Traditionalist Islamists are respectable Islamic scholars, they are often naive, if not ignorant, of modern natural and social sciences. If they read modern scientific theories at all, they either accept or reject them according to the Qur'an and the *sunnah*. Traditionalist Islamists are generally oblivious to the complexities, institutions, and processes of modern governments and international relations in an interdependent world— although they do not perceive this ignorance as a shortcoming. They are convinced that the perfect religion of Islam, in which they are well versed, reveals all truths and can help to resolve all internal crises and external threats facing Muslim societies around the world. For Muslim Traditionalists, Islam has not, cannot, and should never change, for it is founded on God's immutable words and laws. Consequently, they argue that immutability is not the cause of the Muslim world's decline, but on the contrary its decline results from the Muslim world's inherent imperfections, and because Muslims have not steadfastly followed the letter and spirit of the religion.

One of the most prominent Traditionalist Islamists was Iran's Ayatollah Sayyid Kazem Shariatmadari (d. 1986). Another is Iraq's Grand Ayatollah Ali Hussein Sistani who has played a big role behind the scenes in the post-Saddam Iraq. Many of the muftis (Islamic theologian-jurists who issue *fatwas* or authoritative decrees) and *shaykhs* (Islamic scholars) of Al-Azhar in Cairo could also fall into this category, for example, Shaykh Ali Gadd el-Haqq, the 79 year old Traditionalist *alim of al-Azhar* who died in Cairo on March 15, 1996.

Progressive Islamists

The third category of Islamists are the Progressive Islamists, also known as "adaptationists," "apologists," "syncretists," and "revisionists." Progressive Islamists are devout and knowledgeable Muslims whose mission is to redefine and reinterpret Islam in a rational and liberal manner; to emphasize the basic ideals of Islamic brotherhood, tolerance, socioeconomic equity, and political justice; and to interpret the teaching of Islam in such a way as to bring out its dynamic character in the context of the intellectual and scientific progress of the modern world.

Progressive Islamists, like Revolutionary Islamists, vehemently disagree with the Sunni Traditionalist Islamists' belief in the dogma of *taqlid*, which requires the unquestioning and rigid adherence to one of the four schools of Sunni *fiqh* (Islamic jurisprudence) developed in the postclassical period. The Progressive Islamists feel the primary causes of the decline of Islamic culture and power are the inhibition of independent, creative, and critical thought, and the lack of vigorous discus-

TABLE 2: Revolutionary Islamists and Muslim Secularists: A Succinct Comparison

	Revolutionary Islamists	Muslim Secularists
Belief in the Fundamentals of Islam	Both believe in (1) *Tawhid* (oneness of God); (2) Omnipotence, Omnipresence, Justice, and Infinite Mercy of God; (3) Prophet Muhammad as the last in a long line of Gods prophets starting with Adam and including Abraham, Moses, and Jesus; (4) The Scrolls as revealed to Abraham, the Psalms to David, the Torah as revealed to Moses, the Gospels to Jesus, and the Holy Qur'an as revealed to Prophet Muhammad; and (5) The Last Day of Judgment.	
Degree of Devoutness	• Practicing Muslims • Extremely devout, austere, and often puritanical	• Often non-practicing, nominal, and very liberal Muslims • Moderately devout at best
Education and Learning	• Formal education acquired in Islamic educational institutions. Informal learning also primarily, but not exclusively, religious. • Minor influence of some non-Islamic (e.g., Western) ideas, ideals, and practices among fundamentalists in the modern period	• Secular formal and informal education for the most part. Relatively knowledgeable about Islam and Muslims • Heavily influenced by non-Islamic (e.g., Western) ideas, ideals, and practices
Clerical Affiliation	Not exclusively from the ranks of the *ulama* (Islamic scholars); many non-clerics among them	Never come from the ranks of the *ulama*
Normative Periods	• Look primarily to classical periods of Islam for inspiration and emulation; secondary emphasis on medieval Islamic era. • Consider true Islams immutability and perfection to transcend time and space. Determined to prove that many popular and beneficial ideas, ideals, and practices across cultures, ideological systems, and time are Islamic in essence or have Islamic roots or influences.	• Look to broad spectrum of philosophies and ages for models of political and socioeconomic development. • Often adapt concepts and practices from Western capitalist and socialist countries to their indigenous environments, deriving syntheses that are often nominally Islamic, but so labeled to legitimize and popularize their use.
Respect for Tradition and Openness Toward Change	• Zealous crusaders against doctrine of *taqlid* (whereby legal rulings of one or more schools of Islamic jurisprudence are blindly and unquestioningly followed) and all accretions and innovations in Islam from post-classical period. • Vigorously advocate *ijtihad* (independent reasoning that creatively and insightfully interprets the Qu`ran and Prophet Muhammads *sunnah*, in solving modern-day problems. • Extremely opposed to modern secular (especially Western or socialist) ideas, practices, and institutions that are contrary to Islam • Extremely particular about compatibility of policies and programs with the letter and spirit of Islam.	• Against *taqlid* and all those Islamic concepts, customs, and traditions that they regard as inhibiting the progress of Muslim societies. • Advocate *ijtihad*, which they interpret broadly as using the general spirit of Islam (in the light of the Qur'an and *sunnah*) in solving contemporary problems. • Have no qualms about accepting modern secular ideas, practices and institutions that revolutionary Islamists oppose. • Not concerned about compatibility of programs with Islam unless heavily pressured by the other three groups of Islamists.
Tolerance of Secularization	Vociferously and virulently against secularization. Often launch a *jihad* (crusade) to stop and reverse secularization processes. Their active political involvement is often taken into account by regimes in power.	Strong advocates of secularization. Only when Islamists concertedly challenge Muslim secularists do the latter pay lip service to Islam and engage in Islamic rhetoric and symbolism.
Principal Reasons for the Muslim Worlds Decline	Ascribe decline of Muslim world (including its poverty and impotence) to two commonly shared reasons: (1) colonialism and neo-colonialism (especially by Western powers) and (2) disunity within the "House of Islam."	
	• Believe that decline is also due to (a) failure on the part of Muslims to adhere to letter and spirit of Islam; and (b) "corrupt," "incompetent," and often "dictatorial" leadership of "secular" (and thus "un-Islamic") secularists. • Also believe that it is due to the lackluster leadership and inhibiting influences of the detached and apolitical traditionalist Islamists and Muslim secularists.	• Also believe that decline is due to rigid, doctrinaire, and dogmatic orthodoxies promulgated by the Islamists. • Mention (often in passing) lack of *ijtihad* as a contributory cause.

TABLE 2: Cont'd

	Revolutionary Islamists	Muslim Secularists
Manifestation of an Islamic State		
Type of Islamic State	• Advocate an Islamic state, though its character differs significantly in each case • Prefer one with puritanical manifestations	• Although on a few occasions call for a liberal democratic "Islamic state," often opposed in practice to the creation of a genuine Islamic state (where mosque and state—or religion and politics—are fused). • Often prefer a secular state
Who Should Govern?	Convinced that enlightened, sincere, and dedicated revolutionary Islamists would do the best job of governing the truly Islamic state. Often very critical of non-revolutionary Islamists and Muslim secularists.	Believe that lay Muslim politicians instead of the *ulama* or Islamists should govern modern-day nation-states.
Nature of Constitution and Laws	• Would like to formulate and implement a Constitution that is Islamic in both letter and spirit. • Would like the Islamic state to be governed by the Islamic *shariah*, which for them is sacrosanct, immutable, and capable of successful application to all given situations regardless of time and place.	• Would like to formulate and implement a primarily secular Constitution, but sometimes pressured to concede a number of Islamic provisions and clauses to devoutly religious interest groups. • Very reluctant to implement the *shariah* (even if revised) at the national level. Feel much more comfortable relying primarily on secular laws.
Basis of Sovereignty	Believe that sovereignty primarily rests with God. Believe all devout Muslims should reject sovereignty of man. With few exceptions, have come to accept (Western) liberal democracy in the modern period, implying that they do give importance to "popular sovereignty" (especially in the post—World War II period) after sovereignty of God.	Often talk about establishing (Western) liberal democracy and giving their citizenry popular sovereignty, but only concede it reluctantly for fear of losing power.
Integration of Society	Believe in integrating a predominantly Muslim countrys citizenry on the basis of puritanical Islam	Most often based on secular nationalism; in a few instances, Islamic nationalism is used, although Islamic component is largely rhetorical and symbolic
Degree of Fatalism and Activism	Vary in their fatalism, believing in such notions as kismet, *taqdir* (fate), predestination, and preordination	
	Very fatalistic, but also very active religiopolitical crusaders for Islamization (Islamic puritanism)	Minimally fatalistic; active modernizers and secularizers of Muslim societies. A few are perceptive and astute politicians and statesmen imbued with the vestiges of the "spirit of Islam."
Major Foreign Policy Orientation	Ardent exponents of a united Muslim world/Islamic bloc	
	• Often extremely insular and parochial • Believe in *dar al-Islam* (abode of Islam) and *dar al-harb* (abode of the infidel) dichotomy of the world. Thus, end up with a we-they, us-them, and good-evil dichotomous orientation toward the outside world.	• Often cosmopolitan, broad-minded, liberal, and pragmatic • Not at all concerned about *dar al-Islam* and *dar al-harb* dichotomy. Considered by the devout as well as by non-Muslim observers as having made controversial alliances with non-Muslim (even atheistic-communist) states in their preoccupation with promoting their countrys national interests.
Common Stereotypes		
Critics	Fundamentalists; puritans; iconoclasts; Islamic militants; Islamic zealots; Islamic fanatics	Westernizers; opportunists; manipulators; puppets of the Big Powers
Defenders	Purists; literalists; scripturalists; religious ideologues/revolutionaries; restorationists; restitutionists	Reformers; modernizers; realists; liberals; pragmatists

TABLE 2: Cont'd

	Revolutionary Islamists	Muslim Secularists
Common Stereotypes, continued		
The Most Prominent Figures	Shaikh Ahmad Sirhindi (1564–1624) Shah Waliullah (1702–1762) Muhammad Ibn Abd Al-Wahhab (1703–1792) Sayyid Ahmad Shahid (1786–1831) Mir Nisar Ali (1782–1831) Haji Shariatullah (1781–1840) Mohsenuddin Ahmad (1819–1860) Muhammad Ibn Ali Al-Sanusi (1787–1859) Hassan Al-Banna (1906–1949) Sayyid Qutb (1906–1966) Muhammad Ahmad Abdullah Al-Mahdi (1844–1885) Sayyid Abul A'la Maududi (1903–1979) Ayatollah Ruhollah Khomeini (1902–1989) Gulbuddin Hekmatyar (b. 1947) Osama bin Laden (b. 1957) Ayman Zawahiri (b. 1951) Mullah Muhammad Omar (b. 1959) Muqtada al-Sadr (1974–)	Mustafa Kemal Ataturk (1881–1938) Reza Shah Pahlavi I (1877–1944) Muhammad Reza Shah Pahlavi II (1919–1980) Gamal Abdel Nasser (1918–1970) Muhammad Anwar al-Sadat (1918–1981) Saddam Hussein (b. 1937) Muhammad Ali Jinnah (1875–1948) Zulfikar Ali Bhutto (1928–1979) Ja'afar Muhammad Al-Numeiri (b. 1930)

sion about Islamic laws and issues that resulted from the closure of "the gates of *ijtihad*" a millennium earlier. Convinced that Islam is a progressive, dynamic, and rational religion, the Progressive Islamists denounce the inhibiting dogma of *taqlid* and advocate an unconditional reopening of "the gates of *ijtihad*" to facilitate the reinterpretation and reformulation of Islamic laws in the light of modern thought. Indeed, they feel dynamic change in Islam is not only possible, but desirable. Therefore, according to most Progressive Islamists, Islamic laws must be carefully revised to be flexible and adaptable enough to incorporate modern political, economic, social, cultural, and legal conditions.

In addition to being devout Muslims, who are enlightened about Islam, Progressive Islamists are also knowledgeable about modern non-Islamic (especially Western) ideas, to which they are exposed in their formal and/or informal education, either in their homelands or abroad. Most Progressive Islamists have been filled with new ideas and insights after exposure to the West, and have been eager to introduce them into their own societies.

Consequently, unlike the Revolutionary Islamists and Traditionalist Islamists, Progressive Islamists do not fear or dislike Western ideas and practices. On the contrary, they welcome those non-Islamic ideas and practices that they consider beneficial to the progress and prosperity of Muslim societies. Thus, Progressive Islamists are constantly endeavoring to reconcile differences between traditional religious doctrine and secular scientific rationalism, between unquestioning faith and reasoned logic, and between the continuity of Islamic tradition and modernity. Their imaginative synthesis of Islamic and Western ideas tends to produce a reasonable and relevant reinterpretation of Islamic thought with enlightened cosmopolitan, liberal, and realistic perspectives. Their tolerance for diversity and their willingness to adjust rapidly to a changing environment contributes to the emancipation of the individual Muslim and to the progress of Muslim societies.

Progressive Islamists are generally saddened by the discrepancy between the improved status of women during Islam's classical period and their second-class status in the Muslim world of the nineteenth and twentieth centuries. They are also profoundly concerned about the divisions and frictions between the various *madhabs* (sects). In fact, they spend considerable time and effort advocating Muslim reconciliation and unity.

Some of the most prominent Progressive Islamists are Jamal ad-Din al-Afghani (1838–1897) of Persia/Iran; pre-partition India's Sir Sayyid Ahmad Khan (1817–1898); Egypt's Muhammad Abduh (1849-1905), who became the grand mufti of al-Azhar; pre-partition India's Muhammad Iqbal who conceived of Pakistan and encouraged the Muslim League leadership to pursue the establishment of such a homeland; Iran's Ali Shariati (1933–1977), the intellectual father of modern revolutionary Shi'ism, who contributed significantly to the Islamic Revolution (1978–1979); Mahdi Bazargan, the first interim president of Iran under Ayatollah Khomeini; and Abulhassan Banisadr, the first popularly elected president in Ayatollah Khomeini's Islamic Republic of Iran.

Muslim Secularists

Although Muslim secularists are not Islamists, they cannot be overlooked in any discussion of Islamism or global Islamic politics because they are a significant part of the political, economic, and cultural elite that governs most Muslim societies, and in most cases it is the vigorous opposition to them that is contributing to Islamism. Sometimes these Muslim secularists themselves cynically engage in the politics of Islam and speed up Islamism.

Muslim secularists are Muslims by name and birth, and are nominal Muslims with a veneer of a liberal and eclectic version of Islam. They are influenced by their formal and informal secular Western education and experiences at home and/or in the West, and consequently are more knowledgeable about Western

TABLE 3: A Comparison of Revolutionary and Progressive Islamists

	Revolutionary Islamists	Progressive Islamists
Belief in the Fundamentals of Islam	Both believe in (1) *Tawhid* (oneness of God); (2) the omnipotence, omnipresence, justice, and infinite mercy of God; (3) Prophet Muhammad as the last in a long line of Gods Prophets starting with Adam and including Abraham, Moses, and Jesus; (4) the Holy Qur'an as revealed to Prophet Muhammad as the last of Gods Holy Books along with the Torah as given to Moses and the Bible to Jesus; and (5) the Last Day of Judgment.	
Degree of Devoutness	• Practicing Muslims who closely follow the five *faraidh* (compulsory duties/obligations) or *arkan ad-din* (pillars of the faith): the *shahadah* (proclamation of the faith), *salat* (liturgical prayers), *zakat* (alms to the poor), *sawm* (fasting during the ninth Islamic month of Ramadan), and *hajj* (pilgrimage to Makkah in present-day Saudi Arabia). • Believe that God will reward them for performing the five *faraidh* and punish them for neglecting the *arkan ad-din*. • Follow Prophet Muhammads hadith (sayings) that are found in Sahih Bukhari and Sahih Muslim. • Follow the *shariah* (Islamic law) and would like to improve it on predominantly Muslim societies.	
	• Extremely devout, austere, and often puritanical.	• Devout to very devout, eclectic, and not rigid or puritanical.
Education and Learning	• Formal education acquired in Islamic educational institutions. Informal learning also primarily, but not exclusively, religious. • Minor influence of some non-Islamic (e.g., Western) ideas, ideals, and practices among revolutionary Islamists in the modern period.	• Formal and informal education not confined to religious learning. • Significantly influenced by non-Islamic (especially Western) ideas, ideals, and practices.
Respect for Tradition and Openness Toward Change	• Opposed to doctrine of *taqlid* (whereby legal rulings of one or more schools of Islamic jurisprudence are blindly and unquestioningly followed) and all accretions and innovations in Islam from post-classical period. • Advocate *ijtihad* (independent reasoning, especially in matters of Islamic law). • Opposed to modern secular (especially Western or socialist) ideas, practices, and institutions that are contrary to Islam. • Seek compatibility of policies and programs with the letter and "spirit of Islam."	• Against *taqlid* and all those traditions that they consider to inhibit the progress of Muslim societies. Believe in the continuity of essential, useful, and popular traditions along with comprehensive progress (including structural change) that they deem compatible with the spirit of Islam. • Advocate *ijtihad*. Often believe that *ijtihad* should be exercised by all devout, enlightened, and progressive Muslims who are knowledgeable about Islamic thought and practice. • Opposed to modern secular (especially Western or socialist) ideas, practices, and institutions that are contrary to Islam. However, in practice, often tolerate them in varying degrees. • Seek compatibility of policies and programs with the "spirit of Islam."
Degree of Fatalism and Activism	Vary in their fatalism, believing in such notions as *kismet, taqdir* (fate), predestination, and preordination.	
	Very fatalistic, but extremely active religiopolitical crusaders for revolutionary Islamism, piety, and puritanism.	Moderately to very fatalistic, though extremely dynamic reformers of Islam and Muslim societies. Imbued with and desirous of promoting the spirit of Islam.
Tolerance of Secularization	Opposed to secularization. Often launch a *jihad* (crusade) to stop and reverse it. Their active political involvement is often taken into account by regimes in power.	Opposed to secularization in principle, theory, and rhetoric, but tolerate secularization with either benign neglect or as a necessary evil that must be accommodated in contemporary times.
Normative Periods	• Look primarily to classical period of Islam for inspiration and emulation; secondary emphasis on medieval Islamic era. • Consider true Islams immutability and perfection to transcend time and space. Determined to prove that many popular and beneficial ideas, ideals, and practices across cultures, ideological systems, and time are Islamic in essence or have Islamic roots or influences.	• Look to classical period of Islam as well as to Western capitalist and socialist worlds for their ideas, ideals, and practices. • Place all adopted popular and beneficial non-Islamic/foreign concepts, practices, and institutions within Islamic framework.
Principal Reasons for the Muslim Worlds Decline	Ascribe decline of Muslim world (including its poverty and impotence) to (1) colonialism and neo-colonialism (especially by Western powers), and (2) disunity within the "House of Islam."	
	• Believe that decline is also due to (1) failure on the part of Muslims to adhere to letter and spirit of Islam; and (2) "corrupt," "incompetent," and often "dictatorial" leadership of secularists (and thus wayward Muslims). • Also believe that it is due to the lackluster leadership and inhibiting influences of the detached traditionalist Islamists.	• Believe that decline is also due to rigid, doctrinaire, and dogmatic orthodoxies promulgated by revolutionary and traditionalist Islamists. • Emphasize inhibiting of *ijtihad* and banning of *bidah* (innovation in Islamic beliefs, practices, and laws) as counterproductive practices.

TABLE 3: Cont'd

	Revolutionary Islamists	Progressive Islamists
Manifestation of an Islamic State		
Type of Islamic State	Advocate an Islamic state, though its character differs significantly in each case.	
	Prefer one with puritanical manifestations.	Prefer one with liberal democratic manifestations.
Who Should Govern?	Convinced that enlightened, sincere, and dedicated revolutionary Islamists would do the best job of governing the truly Islamic state. Often very critical of non-revolutionary Islamists.	Believe that enlightened and competent progressive Islamists would do the best job of governing the modern-day Islamic state. In practice are very tolerant of and even support competent secularists in leadership positions.
Nature of Constitution and Laws	• Would like to formulate and implement a constitution that is Islamic in both letter and spirit. • Would like the Islamic state to be governed by the *shariah*, which for them is sacrosanct, immutable, and capable of successful application to all given situations regardless of time and place.	• Would like to formulate and implement a constitution consonant with the letter and especially the spirit of Islam. • Believe in revision of Islamic legal system in order to cope with contemporary problems. Would not remove many secular laws already implemented.
Basis of Sovereignty	Believe that sovereignty primarily rests with God. Believe all devout Muslims should reject sovereignty of man. With few exceptions, have come to accept (Western) parliamentary democracy in the modern period, implying that they do give importance to "popular sovereignty" (especially in the post-World War II period) after sovereignty of God.	Believe above all in Gods ultimate sovereignty but next in "popular sovereignty." The latter is manifested in a form of (Western) parliamentary democracy legitimized as essentially Islamic.
Integration of Society	Believe in integrating a predominantly Muslim country's citizenry on the basis of Islam, although the character of that Islam differs markedly in each case.	
	Based on revolutionary Islamism.	Based on progressive Islamism and/or Islamic nationalism.
Major Foreign Policy Orientation	Exponents of a united Muslim world/Islamic bloc.	
	• Often extremely insular and parochial. • Believe in *dar al-Islam* (abode of Islam) versus *dar al-Harb* (abode of the Infidel) dichotomy of the world. Thus, end up with an Us-Them, Good-Evil dichotomous orientation toward outside world.	• Often relatively cosmopolitan, broad-minded, and highly principled pragmatists. • Hardly preoccupied with *dar al-Islam* and *dar al-harb* dichotomy.
Common Terms		
Critics	Fundamentalists, fanatics, militants, religious zealots, puritans, and iconoclasts	Apologists, revisionists, and syncretists
Defenders	Purists, literalists, scripturalists, religious ideologues/revolutionaries, restorationists, and restitutionists	Progressives, reformers, modernizers, adaptationists, realists, liberals, and pragmatically oriented islamists
Prominent Islamists	Shaikh Ahmad Sirhindi (1564–1624) Shah Waliullah (1702–1762) Muhammad ibn Abd al-Wahhab (1703–1792) Sayyid Ahmad Shahid (1786–1831) Mir Nisar Ali (1782–1831) Haji Shariatullah (1781–1840) Mohsenuddin Ahmad (1819–1860) Muhammad ibn Ali al-Sanusi (1787–1859) Hassan al-Banna (1906–1949) Muhammad Ahmad Abdullah al-Mahdi (1844–1885) Sayyid Abul Ala Maududi (1903–1979) Sayyid Qutb (1906–1966) Ayatullah Ruhollah Khomeini (1902–1989) Ayatollah Sayyid Ali Khamenei (1939–) Muhammad Zia-ul-Haq (1924–1988) Hasan al-Turabi (1932–) Muammar al-Qaddafi (1942–) Omar Hasan al-Bashir (1935–) Gulbuddin Hekmatyar (1947–) Shaykh Ahmad Yassin (1938–) Mullah Muhammad Omar (1962–) Shaykh Omar Abdel Rahman (1938–) Aiyman Zawahiri (1951–) Osama bin Laden (1957–)	Jamal ad-Din al-Afghani (1838–1897) Sir Sayyid Ahmad Khan (1817–1898) Muhammad Abduh (1849–1905) Muhammad Rashid Rida (1865–1935) Muhammad Iqbal (1873–1938) Ali Shariati (1933–1977) Mehdi Badar Bazargan (1905–) Abdul Hasan Bani-Sadr (1933–) Ali Akbar Hashemi Rafsanjani (1934–) Abdul Karim Saroush (1945–) Muhammad Khatami (1942–) Burhanuddin Rabbani (1940–) Ahmad Shah Massoud (1956–2001)

intellectual thought than Islamic thought. This background makes them view classical and medieval Islamic doctrines and practices as anachronistic, reactionary, and impractical for contemporary purposes. They look to a broad spectrum of ages and philosophies for models of political and socioeconomic progress. In their search for the ideal system, they adopt concepts and ideologies from both capitalist and socialist countries, but unlike the Progressive Islamists, fail to adapt them to their own indigenous environments. They concern themselves with the dynamic modernization of their societies and display an interest in addressing practical realities in a rational manner. Though at times pressured by the Revolutionary Islamists and Traditionalist Islamists to promote and defend the faith, they often prefer a state whose guiding principle is secularism and believe that the secularization process is part of modernization, and therefore not only inevitable, but desirable.

Though a minority in all Muslim societies, the Muslim secularists wield a disproportionate degree of wealth and power. They are in the upper echelons of their governments' civil service and armed forces. They are heavily represented in the mass media, educational institutions, business community, among the landlords and throughout a broad spectrum of other professions. They are aware of events in their country and in the world at large, and comprise the most assertive and vocal segment of their societies.

Muslim secularists are pleased that Islam does not give a privileged status to the *ulama* in the governance of Muslim societies and iterate the view that there is no institutionalized clergy in Islam, but that all Muslims are responsible to Allah for their thoughts and deeds. While Muslim secularists comprise the privileged class, they shrewdly and hypocritically point to Islam's emphasis on equality, and aversion to the formation of any privileged class (including a priestly one) which fosters elitism and encourages differentiation between men. According to the Muslim secularists, the *ulama* are experts in the Islamic religion only, and are therefore fully entitled to their invaluable religious guidance in the affairs of the state. However, in economic, political, technical, international, and non-Islamic legal matters, the *ulama* cannot claim the right to impose their viewpoint on the nation.

Ironically, some Muslim secularists find it expedient to use Islamic rhetoric and symbolism to capture the support of the Muslim masses despite their essentially secular worldview and their firm conviction that religion is a personal affair between man and God. In the short run, their use of Islamic rhetoric and symbolism allows them to gain or enhance their legitimacy, integrate and unite their fragmented Muslim societies, and inspire and mobilze the Muslim masses. But in the long run, the politics of Islam in which they so astutely engage to win over the masses and consolidate their power leaves them exposed and vulnerable to the whirlwind of the mass-based Islamic movement.

The six most prominent Muslim secularists who contributed to Islamic revivals where Pakistan's founding father, Muhammad Ali Jinnah, in the 1940s; Sudan's President Jafar al-Numeiri in the first half of the 1980s; Pakistan's Prime Minister Zulfikar Ali Bhutto during the 1970s; Egyptian President Muhammad Anwar al-Sadat during the decade of the 1970s; and

Iraqi President Saddam Hussein during Operations Desert Shield and Desert Storm (August 1990–March 1991).

Failure of Secular Ideologies

Following the independence of Muslim societies from colonial rule, Muslim secularists were the first to fill the power vacuum. Muslim secularists have promoted secularism and thereby strictly adhered to the religious neutrality of the state; pushed secularization which is the institutional separation of Islam from politics and the governmental system; refused to give in to the temptation of assuming the role of promoters and defenders of Islam; and rejected Islamic ideas and ideals as framing the basis of their political legitimacy.

Initially, Muslim secularists considered Islam as an impediment to progress and actively pursued modernization policies and programs to transform their traditional societies into modern nation-states. Wedded to such ideologies as secular territorial nationalism, socialism, capitalism, secularism, pan-Arabism, Nasserism, and/or Ba'athism, the Muslim secularists promised the masses everything, but delivered little. State-imposed secularization undermined Islam. Elite-mandated modernization benefited the elites at the expense of the masses. In fact, the applications of Western and pseudo-Western secular ideologies have utterly failed to achieve holistic and equitable development in much of the Muslim world and end the dependency of Muslim countries on the Big Powers. Moreover, the imported "un-Islamic" secular ideologies mentioned earlier are no longer seriously discussed as solutions to endemic socioeconomic and political dysfunction in the Muslim world. Such ideologies are now equated with the causes of such dysfunction. Islamism stands ready to fill the developmental void unscathed by the failures of the past. Therefore, by default, Muslims look to the Islam alternative as the answer to their socioeconomic and political ills and Muslim secularists turn to exploiting Islam when they need to shore up wavering internal support. This effort seems to have backfired in most cases, however. Far from undermining or co-opting the Islamists and their Islamic agendas, some Muslim secularists have legitimized political Islam as an idiom of anti-government dissent and have strengthened the Islamic revival.

The Simultaneous Occurrence of Several Developmental Crises

Rapid modernization policies and programs, ill-suited to the realities of the developing societies of the Muslim world, have occasioned five developmental crises, namely, those of identity, legitimacy, participation, penetration, and distribution. These crises have profoundly destabilized Muslim societies and overwhelmed Muslim governments.

Identity Crisis

The identity crisis is the failure of Muslim regimes to successfully cultivate a common "national" identity that transcends the traditional religious and other rival primordial claims to the loyalty of their country's citizens. Devout Muslims, however, place their loyalties in Islam and have not fully embraced the alien, secular notion of territorial nationalism. Those Muslims who left their extended families and the familiar surroundings of their villages to look for jobs in the towns and cities have experienced a terrible "culture shock" in the form of selfishness, materialism, depersonalization, alienation, and crime. The "urban jungle" has disillusioned them and threatened their security and identity. For Muslims, this identity crisis often draws them closer to the religion into which they were socialized as children. Their religion acts as an anchor in times of uncertainty, a security blanket that alleviates their fears, and gives them a sense of stability, direction, hope that things will turn out well in the future.

The apparent primacy of the identity crisis suggests a failure of nation-building and political development. Unlike Europe and America, the Muslim world was initially conceived as a single political and religious unit. The creation of nation-states from the dismemberment of this unit was an artificial and arbitrary contrivance of the colonial powers; it was not wholly consensual. Consequently, the resulting false borders were rejected as truly legitimate among Muslims. This rejection has been exacerbated by the oppressive, but otherwise ineffectual, leadership of Muslim secularists who worship the secular nation-state as though it were a god and want their countrymen to do likewise. Sincere Islamists, particularly the Revolutionary Islamists, Traditionalist Islamists, and even many Progressive Islamists, wish to unify Muslims under the universal law of the *shariah* and the banner of the universal *ummah* or pan-Islamism. At the other extreme, community units smaller than the nation-state are more likely to arise—units based on family, a religious sect, a tribe, a village, etc.... But whether the pull is toward utopian Islamic universalism or toward narrow Islamic parochialism, the pull is decidedly away from the nation-state. As an appropriate and acknowledged unit of community, the nation-state, like the Muslim secularist leadership advocating it, is discredited.

Legitimacy Crisis

The greater the public's perception that their regime is honest, fair, and doing their best to improve the quality of life in the country, the more popular and effective it can be. A political system that does enjoy the trust and goodwill of the governed, enjoys no legitimacy, and is forced to resort to increasing degrees of coercion to maintain itself in power.

The chronic legitimacy crisis in the Muslim world is the result of immense differences in values between the rulers and the ruled. The governing secularists and Pragmatists are often educated, Westernized, and secularized. In contrast, the masses are far less educated, far more steeped in Islam, and thus not on the same wave length as their elitist leaders. The culture of the masses is permeated with the religious tradition of Islam which conflicts with secularism and the secular society that their leaders are creating. Hence the secularlists are unable to legitimize their rule, mobilize their populations behind their policies and programs, or integrate their profoundly fragmented multi-ethnic citizenry. Lacking mass support, they are ever vulnerable to overthrow. Thus, to stay in power they have resorted to a mixture of secular indoctrination, co-optation, and coercion. However, oppression only further polarizes the power elite from the governed.

Penetration Crisis

The penetration crisis refers to the chronic problem faced by central governments of all Muslim countries to enforce their decisions at the grass roots level. This process of state-building is associated with the emergence of a centralized bureaucracy with increased coercive capacity to effectively enforce national authority, secure public compliance and govern the society.

All political systems are created and controlled by the governing elite. The problem of penetration, then, is one of identity and legitimacy. The penetration crisis can be resolved only by bridging the conspicuously wide gulf between the governed and the governing so that the developmental needs of the country can be met. This task in the developing Muslim world is particularly formidable as the ambitious modernization programs of the governing elite far exceed the comprehension of people accustomed to old parochial ways. The wide "cultural gap" or "cultural cleavage" which impedes any resolution of the legitimacy crisis, is also impeding leaders from developing a rapport with the people they govern, from legitimizing their rule, or from reaching down to the grass roots level to change old values and behaviors. Hence, the secularists and Pragmatists are unable to motivate and mobilize the masses behind their essentially secular modernization programs.

Distribution Crisis

The ultimate gauge of a government's political performance is its management of the distribution crisis in terms of national security, general socioeconomic welfare, and individual liberties. The distribution crisis is the most difficult of the developmental crises to resolve because the power elite lacks the vision, political will, and in most cases even the resources to resolve it.

The distribution crisis is compounded in the Muslim world by the population explosion which contributes to a chronic shortage of resources (such as food, drinking water, clothing, housing, education, health care, consumer goods, electricity), leads to the chronic overcrowding of cities and towns, contributes to inflation and the sharp rise in the cost of living, greatly reduces the opportunities that job seekers will have obtaining relevant job training programs and jobs, and accelerates ecological degradation. A shortage of food, consumer goods, and services creates inflationary pressures that make the attainment of goods and services more expensive, and thus less accessible to the needy majority more of whom are slipping into the category of the "absolute poor."

Likewise, the distribution crisis is accentuated by the problem of "relative deprivation" which causes sociopolitical instability. After all, people act aggressively, and even violently, not only because they are poor and deprived in an absolute sense, but because they feel deprived relative to others, or relative to their own expectations. Rebellions and revolutions may also occur when a society, having enjoyed a prolonged period of rising expectations and rising gratifications, suddenly experiences a sharp reversal. A period of rapid growth may have heightened people's expectations of continuing improvement in their lives. Thus, when a sudden reversal occurs, the gap between the accelerating expectations and the realities of plummeting gratifications is far more distressing and intolerable than if the reversal had followed a period of relative stag-

Tor Eigeland/Saudi Aramco World/PADIA (1124-043)

The Great Mosque of Cordoba in Spain that was completed in 966 CE under Umayyad Caliph al-Hakim II (961–976 CE). It was built during the high point of Moorish Muslim rule in Andalusia's capital, which was a major center of Islamic civilization at that time.

nation. These accumulated and intolerable frustrations eventually seek violent outlets. If frustration and bitterness have been festering for a long time and are sufficiently widespread, intense, and focused on the established regime in power, violence may explode into revolution that displaces the ruling regime, undermines the old and discredited power structure, and radically transforms the entire society through coercion and attendant bloodshed. If the outbreak of violence is not focused, intense, or widespread enough, the result may merely be a coup at the apex of power, or government oppression. In the latter case, potential rebels may choose to live with their frustrations than endure job loss, long prison terms, torture, or execution. Just as often, the government partially or completely addresses the grievances of the discontented masses.

In Muslim societies today, the distribution crisis is particularly acute because the gap separating the rich and powerful few from the poor and powerless majority has grown wider. Since Islam emphasizes socioeconomic equity and justice, and enjoins devout Muslims to play an active role in politics, Islamism has become a powerful revolutionary ideology used by the poor, disenfranchised, exploited, frustrated and alienated masses (socialized in the Islamic faith) to challenge the governing elite.

The Participation Crisis

Relative political deprivation, or the participation crisis, occurs when the governing elite does not accommodate the aspirations and expectations of citizens to participate in the political system's decision-making process. The participation crisis acute because the Muslim masses today are politically conscious of numerous benefits of democracy in the Western world and democratization occurring in the non-Muslim Third World.

The grass roots pressure for increased participation in the Muslim world is contributing to Muslim regimes becoming more authoritarian as they struggle to stay in power. Sometimes the participation crisis will cause a military coup d'etat or, more rarely, a broad-based revolution.

The participation crisis is often related to the legitimacy and penetration crises. Legitimacy often becomes untenable either under conditions of severely limited participation, which is common in the Muslim world, or under conditions of widespread participation occurring outside existing political institutions. Excepting controlled forms of pluralism and democracy in Bangladesh, Malaysia, Turkey, Jordan, Lebanon, Indonesia, and Iran, there are no other functioning democracies among the remaining forty-four predominantly Muslim countries.

33

In contrast to the West where modernization, secularization, and democratization occurred gradually over several centuries, the Muslim world is beset by all five developmental crises simultaneously. These five unresolved crises have bred dissatisfaction with present governments, widespread unrest, and renewed faith in political Islam as the last viable alternative. The frustrated, disappointed and alienated Muslim masses have turned away from the neo-Western ideologies of the secularists and have returned to Islam as an anchor in a turbulent and unpredictable world. Although some Muslim secularists began employing Islamic symbolism to garner support, they have been perceived as hypocrites and their cynical use of Islam has only further legitimized the Islamic "backlash" to their rule.

The Influential Role of Mosques

Since few democratic institutions exist in Muslim societies through which the masses can vent their grievances or from which they can expect justice, the *masjids* seem to be filling this institutional void. Prophet Muhammad is believed to have strongly recommended congregational prayers, especially on Friday afternoons (the Muslim sabbath). Disallowing Friday congregational prayers would cause a furor among worshipers. Moreover, *masjids* in the Muslim world often require no government license to operate and authoritarian Muslim governments refrain from closing even politically objectionable *masjids*. Because *masjids* are, to a certain degree, immune from blatant government repression, the *masjid* has become the focal point of antigovernment opinion in many Muslim countries. Numerous Muslim clerics, following the example of Muhammad, utilize the sacred premises of the masjid not only to worship God, but as a political platform from which to enlighten, influence, and mobilize the faithful to political action. Some clerics deliver sermons sharply critical of government policies, programs, and leadership. Thus, the clerics in the Muslim world have risen to positions of leadership in opposition to unpopular and tyrannical secularist regimes and their corrupt and unrepresentative political institutions. This clerical class largely has not imbibed Western intellectual thought, has not traveled abroad, and can speak no Western languages. Therefore, when the clerics communicate with the people in the Islamic idiom, they are seen as sincere, unlike the Muslim Secularists. These Islamic revivalists have risen repeatedly throughout Islamic history leading mass movements against foreign imperialists and domestic despots perpetuating injustice. The last two decades represent a cyclical renewal of this Islamic revivalism. The Revolutionary and the Traditional Islamists, often insulated from direct government control in the *masjids*, have effectively used potent Islamic concepts of khurooj (the right to revolt against an unjust and tyrannical ruler), of *jihad*, and of *shahadat* (martyrdom attained in a *jihad)* to agitate and mobilize the Muslim masses against regimes throughout Islamic history.

Aware of the lessons of this history, the Muslim Secularists have not stood idly by in the face of *masjid*-instigated antigovernment activity. Possible spontaneous demonstrations following congregational prayer are thwarted by the ubiquitous presence of government troops within sight of the *masjid* entrance. Many Muslim regimes have taken this strategy a step further and have attempted to exercise direct control over urban *masjids* by appointing the imams who deliver the *khutbahs* (sermons). Despite these efforts, the dynamism of political Islam is undiminished, the clerics undeterred, and the *madrassahs* remain a safe haven for antigovernment opposition.

The Influential Role of Madrassahs

Madrassahs have been around since 969/970 CE, when the Fatimid dynasty established the Islamic seminary of Al-Azhar in Cairo, Egypt, to train students in the Qur'an, Prophet Muhammad's *Hadith*, Islamic law, Islamic jurisprudence, and the sciences. In 1067 CE, Seljuk Vizier Nizam al-Mulk Hassan bin Ali Tusi founded an Islamic seminary in Baghdad to train students in the Shafi'i school of Islamic law. Nizam al-Mulk intended to create a class of *ulama, muftis*, and *qazis* (Islamic judges) who would legitimize the Abbasid Empire's Sunni rulers as righteous, promote a conservative version of Islam, and create obedient subjects.

For over a thousand years, Muslim children and teenagers have frequented *madrassahs* (Islamic schools) in order to learn how to read the Qur'an in Arabic, along with its translation and commentary; learn about the lives and achievements of Old Testament prophets that are also in the Qur'an; appreciate Prophet Muhammad's *hadeeth* and *sunnah*; familiarize themselves with Islamic history; and learn to be ethical, moral, spiritual, and righteous human beings. Most of these *madrassahs* are part of mosques and Islamic centers. And most of these *madrassahs* have done and continue to do a good job in informing the younger generation of Muslims about Islam and inculcating good moral and ethical values in them.

In the realm of politics, it was *madrassah* students that played a big role in the growth and influence of the Muslim Brotherhood in Egypt and the *Jama'at-e-Islami* in Pakistan. In fact, it was the Muslim Brotherhood that assisted Colonel Gamal Abdel Nasser overthrow Egypt's King Farouk and establish military rule in Egypt that exists under President Hosni Mubarak to this day.

It is noteworthy that since the oil price increases of October 1973, Saudi Arabia's royal family has appeased the influential Wahhabi/Salafi religious establishment in their country by spending billions of petrodollars in building thousands of mosques and *madrassahs* around the world. Most of these new *madrassahs* as well as those that have been in existence for a long time have been supplied with Saudi-funded Hanbali Sunni Islamic literature. More importantly, many of the mosque *imams*, principals, teachers, and/or preachers in the numerous mosques and *madrassahs* who are responsible for ordering Islamic literature for the *madrassahs* have studied Islam or worked in Saudi Arabia for a time, are supported with Saudi funding, or have themselves been significantly influenced by the Wahhabi/Salafi version of Islam. Furthermore, this Hanbali/Wahhabi/Salafi literature on Islam is free or very reasonably priced because it has been heavily subsidized by Saudi petrodollars. This makes it easily accessible and widely prevalent. In this way, Saudi Arabia has managed to spread its revolutionary and puritanical religiopolitical version of the Hanbali Sunni sect which was the smallest of the four Sunni sects until 1973.

Although all segments of Iranian society were involved in the success of the Islamic revolution in Iran in 1978–1979, it was *madrassah* students who started the revolution in January 1978 to overthrow the Shah and sustained it until the Shah was forced to give up Iran's Peacock Throne and go into exile in mid January 1979. When Ayatollah Ruhollah Khomeini came to power in Iran in February 1979, he called on the Muslim masses in the Gulf kingdoms to overthrow their corrupt monarchies, supported Islamic movements around the world, and his government organized conferences for teachers from *madrassahs* in several Muslim countries.

In response to the threat Khomeini posed to the rule, the Arab monarchs gave Saddam Hussein the green light to invade Iran; supported him financially and diplomatically; established the Gulf Cooperation Council (comprising Saudi Arabia, Bahrain, Kuwait, Oman, Qatar, and the United Arab Emirates, headquartered in Riyadh, Saudi Arabia; dramatically increased their funding of Sunni *madrassahs* with blatantly anti-Shi'a literature to counter the revolutionary Shi'a religiopolitical ideology and funding to Shi'a *madrassahs*; called for a *jihad* against the spread of Western cultural decadence rather than a struggle against Muslim rulers; and after 1983, Saudi Arabia significantly increased its oil exports in order to drive oil prices down and make it more difficult for Iran to finance its war effort against Iraq.

It is also the Iranian *madrassah* students that constitute the backbone of the elaborate security apparatus that has kept the Shi'a clerical establishment in power since the overthrow of the Shah in January 1979. When the Iraqi armed forces invaded the Islamic Republic of Iran in September 1980, it was primarily Iranian *madrassah* students that fought the Iraqi troops for eight long years.

After the Israeli invasion of Lebanon in 1982 and the negotiated evacuation of the Palestine Liberation Organization (PLO) fighters to six Arab countries, it was mainly Shi'a *madrassah* students (of the Iranian-backed Islamic Amal and Hezbollah organizations) that harassed the powerful Israeli Defense Forces (IDF) and the Israeli-supported Christian Southern Lebanese Army troops in guerrilla attacks that finally drove the Israelis out of Southern Lebanon in May 2000.

During the decades of the 1980s, it was also *madrassah* students who made up the bulk of the Afghan *mujahideen* that fought against the Afghan Communist regime and the Soviet occupation of Afghanistan. After expelling the Soviets in Spring 1989 and overthrowing the Afghan Communist regime in 1992, it was another group of *madrassah*-students called the Taliban that came to power in Afghanistan, gave sanctuary to Osama bin Laden and his Arab Afghans (1996–2001), and were overthrown by the American-led "coalition of the willing" in November 2001 in retaliation for September 11, 2001.

Of course, one cannot exclude the role of the Big Powers and their *realpolitik* or benign neglect of Muslim suffering around the world. As a result, Muslim students in many *madrassahs* all over the world have come to perceive or misperceive the *ummah* as pawns and victims of the Big Powers on the world stage and Islam and the *ummah* to be in serious danger. Therefore, it is not surprising that some of these impressionable, utopian, and restless young men are not content to just focus on engaging in the peaceful, spiritual, and defensive *jihad* enjoined by Islam. Out of a sense of deep-seated frustration, alienation, and desperation, some of these militant Muslims in their late teens and twenties, overreact and adopt an extremist and distorted version of *jihad* to call attention to the callous victimization and suffering of Muslims around the world. It must also be pointed out that these revolutionary Islamists are overly alarmed at the globalization of Western culture that is undermining Islamic values and corrupting the Muslim youth with excessive secularism, freedom, individualism, greedy capitalism, materialism, consumerism, and hedonism. Some of these revolutionary Islamists in their zeal to end the unjust status quo only stir-up the "power that be" into a military overreaction. After all, Muslim secularists fearing an overthrow of their regimes, also tend to overreact, label these revolutionary Islamists as "terrorists," and callously crush the Islamist challenge to their authority. Sometimes, even Big Powers perceiving a threat to their national interests overreact, and engage in military and economic wars (such Operation Desert Storm, comprehensive sanctions against Iraq, overthrowing the Taliban in Afghanistan, and Operation Iraqi Freedom to bring about regime change in Iraq).

Thus, *madrassahs* are at the center of the struggle for hearts and minds of Muslims all over the world. Educated Muslim secularists eager to modernize their countries are facing stiff resistance from the *madrassah* school teachers. The latter, marginalized by modernization (and Westernization) of their societies, are indoctrinating their *madrassah* students about the glories of Islam's past, and the pressing need for an Islamic revolution and Islamic states. Since private schools are too expensive and the public schools are full, the rapidly multiplying student population is attending *madrassahs*, which are generally free. Poor students in the villages and the slums attending *madrassahs* find it easy to believe that the West, which assists tyrannical, corrupt, and incompetent leaders, is responsible for their misery and that Islam as practiced during the classical and even medieval periods of Islamic history can deliver them from tyranny, poverty, and hopelessness.

It is not surprising, therefore, that the leaders of Muslim countries are calling on affluent and powerful Western governments to give generous economic assistance for education, and the reform of *madrassah* school curriculums. In this regard, *madrassahs* will have more natural science, mathematics, social studies, and humanities in addition to traditional Islamic education.

The Arab-Israeli Conflict

The Arab-Israeli conflict has contributed significantly to Islamism. The failure of Arab regimes and secular Palestinians led by the PLO to defeat Israel and repair even a small part of the former Palestine has reinforced a sense of humiliation among Arab Muslims, has discredited secular Arab regimes, and has contributed to an Islamic backlash to perceived Western neocolonialism through the Israeli "surrogate." Thus, the conflict, still unresolved since 1948, is fueling Islamism by playing upon anti-imperialist feelings among Muslims and by underscoring the incompetence of the secular regimes in the region.

Israel's swift humiliating defeat of Arab armies in the June 1967 War was a watershed for the global revival of Islamic. After much boasting and bravado, the Arab world's political giant, Egyptian President Gamal Abdul Nasser, in the space of a week discredited himself and his secular and pseudo-Western ideology of Nasserism. Islamic groups throughout the world were quick to ascribe the defeat of the Arabs to the emphasis on the fashionable secular ideologies of the Muslim world's political and economic elites. Political Islam, it was increasingly claimed, could defeat the Israelis; a conclusion bolstered by the improved showing of the Arabs against the Israelis in the 1973 War when Islamic rhetoric and symbolism was used.

It is also rather ironic that both explosive conflicting events and dramatic peace agreements between the Arabs and Israelis have contributed to furthering Islamism on the world stage. This was especially true after the Six-Day War in June 1967 when the Islamic revival in Egypt began. After growing and spreading throughout the Middle East for the next six years, the revival of political Islam got much media attention during the 1973 Yom Kippur/Ramadan War. Then, the Israeli invasion of Lebanon in the summer of 1982 inflamed the reassertion of political Islam, particularly in Lebanon, but more generally in the entire Muslim world, as television pictures of that invasion were broadcast all over the world. Israel's periodic bombing of Southern Lebanese villages and towns by air, sea, and land for much of the 1980s and the 1990s has kept the ideologization of Islam in Lebanon simmering and continues to strengthen political Islam in the Muslim world.

One would think that Arab-Israeli peace agreements would dampen the rise of Islamism, but they seem to have had the opposite affect. Egyptian President Muhammad Anwar al-Sadat's trip to Jerusalem in November 1977 and the 1979 Camp David Peace Treaty between Sadat and Israeli Prime Minister Menachem Begin were widely condemned by the *ummah* as a sell-out and a betrayal of the Arab and Muslim cause. Thus, Sadat's efforts at peace with Israel may have actually reinforced the reassertion of political Islam, not only in Egypt but in the Middle East at large. Just as Sadat lost his leadership of the Arab world and then his life to Revolutionary Islamists, a result of the Declaration of Principles for limited Palestinian self-rule in Gaza and parts of the West Bank. Many Palestinians in the Israeli-occupied territories and in the *diaspora* (wilderness) see the Arafat-Rabin handshake on the White House lawn in September 1993 as a "raw deal" for the Palestinians. Thus, the Arafat-Rabin "land for peace agreement" has greatly swollen the ranks of radical Palestinian Islamic organizations such as Hamas and Islamic Jihad. With the Hebron massacre of Palestinian worshippers in Ibrahimi Mosque, the Islamic revival in the West Bank and the Gaza Strip gathered greater momentum. But that Islamic momentum was slowed by the assassination of Prime Minister Yitzhak Rabin in November 1995 and the assumption to power of Shimon Peres. However, suicide bombings launched by the Qassam Brigades of Hamas resulted in nearly 60 Israeli civilian casualties during Peres' tenure in office resulted in the government of Israel engaging in a war against Hamas. Hizbullah attacks against the Israeli security zone in Southern Lebanon and katusha rockets into Israel resulted in massive Israeli retaliation against Southern Lebanese villages. Peres' desire to create the impression that he was tough against Arab terrorism did not help him in the May 28, 1996 elections. With Benjamin Netanyahu and the conservative Likud party victory in Israel, the peace process may have come to an impasse. This is bound to lead to a restart of the *intifadah*

and some more Hamas attacks against Israelis. This is bound to bring on a disproportionate Israeli response, which in turn will undermine Yasser Arafat's Palestine National Authority, give Hamas and Islamic Jihad many more recruits, and the Islamic resurgence in the Gaza Strip and West Bank will be back in full swing. The major question is: Can the Israeli Defense Force (IDF) and Zionist and Jewish Fundamentalist settlers crush the Islamic resurgence sweeping the Israeli-occupied West Bank or will the Jewish-Muslim crusade make the West Bank ungovernable and therefore an unbearable liability for Israel?

The West's creation of Israel in predominantly Arab Muslim Palestine in 1948 infuriated Muslims the world over. Most Muslims are further incessed by

- the generous economic, military, political, and diplomatic support that the West (especially the U.S. since 1973) has given to Israel in both war and peace
- the systematic usurpation of Palestinian lands and the loss of Palestinian lives and livelihoods
- the building of Jewish settlements with as many as 300,000 Jewish settlers in the disputed West Bank and 8,000 in the Gaza Strip that Israel conquered in the 1967 War
- the Israeli annexation of Jerusalem (with its many Islamic shrines)

Additionally, the Palestinians have been maligned as "terrorists" for their struggle to regain even a small part of their homeland. This has all taken place while the West paid lip-service to international law, human rights, and democracy.

OPEC's Impact

The predominantly Muslim Organization of Petroleum Exporting Countries (OPEC) established in 1960 did not flex its muscles until the early 1970s. It was Libya's leader Colonel Mu'ammar Qaddafi's success in demanding larger revenues and higher taxes from foreign oil companies operating in Libya that was soon repeated by other members of OPEC. Then came the 1973 Yom Kippur/Ramadan War, which was soon coupled with the Organization of Arab Petroleum Exporting Countries (OAPEC) oil embargo against Israel's allies in the West. The resulting oil shortage put an upward pressure on oil prices.

The oil price explosion that the world witnessed from 1974 to 1982 when OPEC flexed its economic muscle in the aftermath of the 1973 Arab-Israeli war, fueled the fires of political Islam on several levels. First, OPEC was perceived by Muslims the world over as having broken the bonds of prostrate dependency on the West. Second, OPEC's rapid modernization resulted in rapidly escalating expectations, unprecedented socioeconomic dislocation, and immense uncertainty. Third, the Muslim member governments of OPEC (especially, Saudi Arabia, Libya, Kuwait, the United Arab Emirates, and Iran) donated much aid to poverty-stricken Muslim countries, gave a number of financially-strapped Muslim countries a discount on oil, purchased food and had it distributed among starving Muslims around the world, financed a number of Islamic organizations (movements, parties, and interest groups) both at the grass roots level and in the corridors of power in the Muslim world; built *masjids* and *madrassahs*, and distributed Qur'ans and other Islamic literature to the *madrassahs*. The worldwide *ummah* interpreted OPEC's success during the "oil boom" years as Allah coming to the assistance of His "chosen people."

However, initial satisfaction, indeed euphoria, in the Muslim world for the apparent successes of OPEC were short-lived and tempered by the realization that OPEC, with the exception of Iran and Libya, represented status quo powers uninterested in revolutionary Islam. The governments of many Muslim countries complained that they were promised far more by their oil-rich brethren than they received. Moreover, OPEC's dramatic oil price increases contributed to increased inflation, followed by higher interest rates and recession. All three of the aforementioned economic problems plagued the oil-poor Muslim countries many times more than the developed Western world and resulted in the Third World being far worse off than before the oil price explosion. Furthermore, the glut of oil and decline of oil prices in 1982, the effort by OPEC member-states to sell more oil than their OPEC-allotted quota, the Iran-Iraq War, Operations Desert Shield and Desert Storm, and division of OPEC ranks between pro- and anti-Western member states led to the decline of OPEC's decade-long influence on the world stage.

OIC's Role

The 1969 burning of the Al-Aqsa Mosque in Israeli-occupied Jerusalem infuriated Muslims around the world and led to the establishment of the Organization of the Islamic Conference (OIC) in the same year. Dedicated to principles of Islamic solidarity, the OIC has contributed to the Islamic revival by institutionalizing the lost but never forgotten Islamic dream of the universal *ummah*.

Like OPEC, however, the promise of the OIC has not yet been realized. There is a widespread perception in the Muslim world that the OIC has failed to protect and defend the rights of the *ummah*. Among other things, they have failed to achieve their principal objective of getting Israel to withdraw from all the Arab territories captured in the 1967 war and restoring the legitimate rights of the Palestinian people; they have done nothing to stop the periodic Israeli aggression in Lebanon or the rapid growth of Israeli settlements in the West Bank; they have failed to prevent two disastrous Persian Gulf wars; they have been impotent to prevent the starvation of Muslims in Somalia or the massacres of Muslims in Bosnia-Herzegovina, Chechnya, India, Algeria, Israel, Burma, and other parts of the Muslim world; and, they have failed to unite the Muslim world and improve the lot of the *ummah*.

Despite its shortcomings, the very existence of the OIC is both the result of and a contribution to the global Islamic revival and Islamism. Its affiliated institutions, like the Islamic Development Bank, have shown Muslims around the world the potential power of an Islamic bloc dedicated to Islamic politics. Nevertheless, Islamists are encouraged to fulfill the potential inherent in pan-Islamism and institutionalized by the OIC.

The Islamic Revolution in Iran

In 1978 the people of Iran, led by Iran's Shi'a clerical establishment and their theological students, rose up en masse throughout the country to challenge the thirty-seven year long autocracy of the Shah. A little more than a year later the Shah, overwhelmed by the revolutionary Islamic tide, fled Iran on an "extended vacation"; his secular, pro-Western monarchical regime, long considered by Western analysts to be an anchor of stability in the stormy Middle East, collapsed as a result of the people power movement, catching the whole world by surprise. Suddenly, a political void opened in Iran, and the Shi'a *ulama* stepped into the vacuum, assuming total power, setting up an Islamic model of government and development, breaking Iran's ties of dependency with the West, forging a sovereign and non-aligned Islamic Republic on the anvil of past Iranian grievances against despot and imperialist alike.

The events leading to the Islamic Revolution are now well known. The Shah of Iran pursued very rapid modernization policies incompatible with the traditional Islamic way of life. In turn, the Shah aggravated the five crises of development. He permitted no political participation in the system and thus delegitimized himself and his government. The Shah failed to insure the just and equitable distribution of resources and goods to all Iranians; the Shah's policies and programs benefited the upper middle class far more than it did the masses. The rapidity of the Shah's modernization programs also caused incredible dislocation in the countryside. The cities were suddenly filled with a growing population of job-seeking ex-farmers. This dislocation and the consequent frustration and alienation felt by most Iranians engendered a crisis of identity that left Iranians unsatisfied with the government of the Shah and more interested in returning to traditions in the countryside, traditions centered around Islam. Moreover, the Shah's reign was further undermined by the singular place in Iranian society of the Shi'a clerical establishment. Their ability to solve, at least to a greater degree than had the Pahlavi monarchy, the developmental crises besetting the nation, and the popular leadership of a charismatic Ayatollah made the transition of power from the secular government of the Shah to the Islamic Republic both possible and, in Iranian eyes, desirable.

The implications of the Iranian Revolution extend far beyond Iran's borders. It is a classic case study illuminating the causes of Islamic resurgence. The new Islamic regime under the leadership of the Ayatollah Khomeini signified a watershed in world history, its repercussions shaking both West and East. Seizing the attention of all Muslims, the Iranian Revolution became the "source of emulation" for Islamists and Islamic organizations throughout the world. Inspired by its success, stirred by its utopian appeal to pan-Islam and against both the capitalist West and the communist East, Islamists were emboldened to bring about Islamic revolutions in their countries. On the other hand, Muslim secularists trembled at the triumph of the Islamic Revolution. Western analysts, in turn, perceived a new threat to Western hegemony in the "crescent of crisis": the specter not of fascism or communism, but of revolutionary political Islam.

The significance of Iran's Islamic Revolution for Islamism throughout the Muslim world is simple: the Iranian Revolution was the Islamic movement that toppled a secular, Western-looking government purely "in the name of Islamic purification." For Muslims around the world, and especially for Islamists and Islamic organizations that continue to endure the heavy hand of governmental oppression, the success of Iran's Islamic Revolution in the face of palpable Western hostility, was an inspiring and heartening experience that greatly accelerated and fortified the global Islamic revival and Islamism.

The Soviet Invasion of Afghanistan and Its Repercussions

On April 27, 1978, the Afghan Communists came to power for the first time in Afghanistan's history. Afghanistan's clerics and conservative tribal leaders encouraged the devoutly Muslim Afghans to rise up and overthrow their new Communist rulers. Concerned about losing power and their lives, the pro-Soviet Afghan Communist leaders implored the Soviet leaders to help them crush the nascent Afghan revolt. The Soviet leadership complied because they feared the spread of revolutionary Sunni Islamism from Afghanistan spilling-over into their predominantly Sunni Muslim Central Asian republics—Iran was a predominantly Shi'a country that had been totally preoccupied with the war against Iraq (1980–1988) and debilitated after that war to export its brand of Shi'a Islam to Central Asia—that were susceptible to revolutionary Sunni Islamism after nearly sixty years of totalitarian Soviet and secular and atheistic Communism. Moreover, the Soviet leadership expected their highly organized and disciplined, expertly-led, well-equipped, rigorously trained, and powerful armed forces to easily liquidate the poorly-led, primitively armed, ill-trained, badly fragmented, and terribly weak Afghan Islamic groups. Indeed, the Soviet leadership expected something on the scale of their interventions in Hungary and Czechoslovakia in 1956 or Czechoslovakia in 1968. They definitely did not expect the U.S. playing a central role in organizing, arming, and training the Afghan *mujahideen* and making the Russian occupation of Afghanistan, a "Soviet Vietnam." In 1988, the Russian leadership under Mikhail Gorbachev began pulling out its troops from Afghanistan. The Russian troop pullout was completed in February 1989 and the Afghan Communist regime clung to power until 1992, when it was completely overpowered by the Afghan *mujahideen*.

However, the Afghan *mujahideen* after coming to power began fighting amongst themselves. At least seven different Afghan tribal and ethnic warlords fought a bloody civil war for the control over post-Communist Afghanistan for four years. This anarchic period of warlordism came to an end when the Taliban ("seekers of religious truth," or *madrassah* students), who had been attending Islamic schools in refugee camps along the Pakistani border, came to power. In fact, in these Pakistani *madrassahs*, the leaders as well as the foot soldiers of the Taliban were taught a particularly revolutionary and puritanical religio-political brand of Wahhabism/Salafi'ism imported from Saudi Arabia. The Pakistani government assisted the Taliban in taking over the predominantly Pashtun southeastern Kandahar region of Afghanistan in 1994. Law and order came to Kandahar under the Taliban leadership; and the Taliban gained a regional reputation for incorruptibility and religious piety. This reputation made it relatively easy for the Taliban to conquer Kabul in 1996. Osama bin Laden and Al-Qaeda (made up of Arab Afghans, also called Afghan Arabs—Arabs who had come to Afghanistan from all over the Arab world to fight against the Soviet invaders, but later came to include all foreign fighters who came to fight in the *jihad* against the Soviets) returned to Afghanistan in Summer 1996 after they were expelled from the Sudan and established their headquarters in Kandahar where the Taliban leader, Mullah Muhammad Omar, also maintained his headquarters. It was invaluable assistance of fanatical and battle-hardened Arab Afghans as well as the massive quantity of weapons that had flooded into Afghanistan during the Soviet occupation that helped the Taliban take over as much as ninety percent of the country by 1998. However, the Taliban's literalist and intolerant application of the *shariah*, sexism, and harsh Wahhabi interpretation of Islamic law made them unpopular at home and their inexperience in international affairs and xenophobia resulted in their isolation in world affairs (only three Muslim countries had diplomatic relations with them). The U.S.-led "coalition of the willing" overthrew the Taliban and uprooted Al-Qaeda from the country in retaliation for September 11, 2001. However, much of the Muslim world felt it was a case of "overkill."

The U.S Invasion of Iraq

In February 2003, a few weeks before "Operation Iraqi Freedom" to bring about regime change in Iraq, millions of people protested in the streets of the world to influence George W. Bush not to invade Iraq with the "Coalition of the Willing." However, President Bush had already made the fateful decision to send American troops into Iraq and establish a base in that country. After all, President Bush and Vice President Cheney, being intimately familiar with the world of "black liquid gold" (petroleum) knew that Iraq had the second largest known peteroleum reserves in the world; significantly large reserves of natural gas; intelligence that showed that the Shi'a majority (60 percent) and a Kurdish Sunni minority (20 percent) that had been harshly persecuted by the Saddam Hussein's minority Sunni Arab Ba'athist regime since 1968, would welcome the U.S.-led "liberators" with flowers, hugs, and dancing in the streets; American could help the educated and talented Iraqis rebuild their country with a more enlightened leadership; a bonanza for American and British corporations and banks that would win most of the contracts to rebuild Iraq's devastated and dilapidated infrastructure; a country that was geostrategically-located close to 66 percent of the world's known petroleum and natural gas reserves in Persian Gulf and Caspian Sea regions; the comprehensive economic sanctions and isolation of Iraq since August 6, 1990, had taken a terrible toll on the Iraqi people (resulting in over a million innocent Iraqis dying of hunger and the ill health), while the oil for food deal with the United Nations to feed and provide medicines to the Iraqi people was not helping the truly needy. Instead, Saddam Hussein and the high level members of his regime siphoned off billions of dollars into their private bank accounts and supported only their loyalists among the Sunni minority (who got the food and medicines and other necessities). It is also noteworthy that Iraq shares borders with two countries that are high on America's enemy list, namely, Iran and Syria. Moreover, the U.S. decision makers may also have felt that once Iraq had been stabilized, American resources could be used to first undermine and then overthrow the Iranian and Syrian regimes at an opportune time.

The key U.S. decision-makers saw Iran as a big prize (after Iraq) because it is another geostrategically-located country (in the Persian Gulf and just south of the Caspian Sea) with the third largest known petroleum reserves and huge natural gas reserves; with Iran back in America's sphere of influence, the U.S. petroleum companies could build a pipeline from the Caspian Sea to the Iran's ports on the Persian Gulf for the supertankers transporting petroleum from the Iranian ports to the rest of the world;

Iran also has over 70 million people and could be a good market for U.S. goods and services; Iran's rapidly growing younger generation in the urban areas seem to be discontented with, and alienated from, the conservative theocratic regime and there are constant complaints about inflation, unemployment, and underemployment due to Iran's isolation on the world stage. The U.S. also perceives Iran as a threat to its national interests in the Persian Gulf since the pro-American Shah's overthrow, the rise of Khomeini's theocratic regime, the Tehran "hostage crisis," and spread of revolutionary Islamism all over the world.

Bush's inner circle also felt that Syria was ripe for the picking because of its unpopular and dictatorial minority Shi'a Alawite Ba'athist regime that has been in power since 1970. A more pliable, pro-American democratic regime in a country neighboring Israel, could result in a breakthrough in the Israeli-Syrian peace process and the Syrian masses would be grateful to the U.S. for the democratization and economic development of their country.

So, the Bush administration was prepared to invade Iraq, and bring about "regime change" in that country with or without another United Nations Security Council resolution giving the U.S. permission to do so. No international institution had the courage, conscience, or clout to stand up to the U.S. and British governments and stop them from invading Iraq in March 2003. The war that Bush started against Iraq was a war of choice, a violation of the sovereignty of an independent country, and a violation of international law. What is more, the war has not gone well for the U.S.-led "Coalition of the Willing" or Iraqis. As many as 2,000 Americans have been killed and thousands more have been wounded. There is talk abroad and even in the United States of the "Vietnam syndrome" and the "Iraqi quagmire."

Unfortunately for the U.S., those rosy scenarios have not been realized. The invasion and occupation of Iraq is seen by the majority of the world as illegal. The reasons given by the US and UK governments for the invasion and occupation of Iraq starting on March 20, 2003 have proven to be false. Much evidence supports the conclusion that a major motive for the war was to control and dominate the Middle East and its vast reserves of oil as a part of the US drive for global hegemony. Blatant falsehoods about the presence of weapons of mass destruction in Iraq and a link between Al Qaeda terrorism and the Saddam Hussein regime were manufactured in order to create public support for a "preemptive" assault upon a sovereign independent nation. The imposition of severe inhumane economic sanctions on August 6, 1990, the establishment of no-fly zones in the Northern and Southern parts of Iraq, and the concomitant bombing of the country were all aimed at degrading and weakening Iraq's human and material resources and capacities in order to facilitate its subsequent invasion and occupation. In this enterprise the US and British leaderships had the benefit of a complicit UN Security Council.

The American-led occupation of Iraq has led to the breakdown of the Iraqi state and the pervasive lack of security. After three major wars—the Iran-Iraq War (1980–1988), Operation Desert Storm (1991), and Operation Iraqi Freedom (2003–present), and 13 years of economic sanctions, the country's physical infrastructure is in shambles; the health care delivery system is in poor condition; the education system has virtually ceased to function; there is massive environmental and ecolog-ical devastation; and the archaeological heritage of the Iraqi people has been desecrated.

The American and British occupation has exacerbated ethnic and sectarian tensions in Iraqi society. According to some reports, as many as 100,000 Iraqis have been killed and thousands have been held in US custody, without charges.

There is widespread opposition on the part of the minority Sunni Arab population to the occupation. It is the occupation as well as America's inability to provide security, sufficient electricity, water, and jobs that has provoked a strong armed resistance and suicide bombings never seen before in Iraq.

EIGHT MYTHS AND MISCONCEPTIONS ABOUT ISLAM AND MUSLIMS

1) Islam is another name for Muhammadanism.

It is absolutely wrong to call the religion of Islam "Muhammad-anism" and totally inappropriate to call Muslims, who are the adherents of Islam, "Muhammadans." However, the terms Muhammadanism and Muhammadans were used for centuries in the West by Western scholars and journalists, who in turn, popularized these terms in the rest of the world.

The Arabic terms Islam (submission), salaam (peace), and Muslim (one who submits to Allah) are derived from the Arabic root consonants "s, l, and m." The word Islam stems from the fourth verbal form of the root "s, l, m": aslama, which literally means "to submit" or "to surrender." Thus, the term Islam actually means the complete submission, surrender, resignation, and obedience to Allah (God) and His guidance. Islam's emphasis on tawhid (the absolute oneness and uniqueness of God Almighty) though prevalent throughout the Qur'an—which Muslims believe is God's last message to humankind, revealed to Muhammad ibn Abdullah (Prophet Muhammad) by Archangel Gabriel between 610 CE and 632 CE—is concisely, cogently, and lucidly illustrated in a Qur'anic chapter entitled Al-Ikhlas (Sincerity). Al-Ikhlas is so important and central to Islam that Muslims recite it during each ritual prayer, five times a day:

> In the name of the Merciful and Compassionate God.
> Say (O Muhammad): He is God, the One and Only!
> God is Eternal.
> He did not give birth (to anyone),
> Nor did anyone give birth to Him.
> And there is no one equal to (or similar to) Him
>   (112: 1–4).

The following Qur'anic verses are just as eloquent in God's (not Prophet Muhammad's) praise:

- "God (Allah) is He, than Whom there is no other god who knows all things both secret and open; He Most Gracious, Most Merciful. God (Allah) is He, than Whom there is no other god—the Sovereign, the Holy One, the Source of Peace and Perfection, the Guardian of Faith, the Preserve of Safety, the Exalted in Might, the Irresistible, the Supreme: Glory to God (Allah)! (High is He) Above the Partners they Attribute to Him. He is God (Allah) the Creator, the Evolver, the Bestower of forms or colors. To Him belong the most beautiful names: Whatever is in the heavens and on earth

TABLE 4: A Comparison of Islam, Judaism, and Christianity

Key Topics	Islam	Judaism	Christianity
General Information			
Symbol of the Religion	The Crescent	Menorah; the Star of David	Cross; Crucifix
Holy City(ies)	• Makkah and Madina (in present-day Saudi Arabia) • Jerusalem (in present-day Israel/Palestine)	Jerusalem	• Jerusalem (for all Christians) • Vatican City in Rome, Italy (for Roman Catholics)

Number of Believers Worldwide	• 1.3 billion Muslims in the world (one-fifth of the worlds population):
	  – 58% in South and Southeast Asia
	  – 28% in Africa
	  – 9% in Southwest Asia
	  – 4.4% in Russia and the former Soviet Republics
	• Arab Muslims comprise 25% of the Muslim world.
	• 35% of the Muslim world resides in the Middle East (Southwest Asia and North Africa).
		• 18 million Jews in the world:
		  • 48% in North America (most in the U.S.)
		  • 27% in Israel
		  • 18% in Europe, Russia, and former Soviet Republics
		  • 4.5% in the Middle East (minus Israel)
		  • 1% in Africa
		  • 0.5% in South America
			• 2.2 billion Christians in the world (one-third of the worlds population):
			  • 37% in North and South America
			  • 22% in Europe
			  • 18% in Africa
			  • 16% in Asia

Major Sects and Subsects	Two major sects/branches (Sunnis and Shi'as) and several subsects/denominations	Three major groups (Orthodox, Conservative, and Reform)	Three major sects: Catholic, Orthodox, and Protestant, with several subdivisions or denominations in each.
House of Worship	*Masjid* (mosque)	Synagogue	Church
Veneration of Images	Forbidden		Eastern Orthodox Church and Catholicism condone it; most Protestant churches do not permit it.
Religious Schools	Send their children to religious school at least once a week.		
	Madrassahs (Islamic schools), often in *masjids* (mosques)	Synagogues and Jewish community centers have Sunday and day Jewish schools, and Jewish community programs for adult education.	Sunday schools at church and parochial primary and secondary schools during weekdays.
Religious Leaders	*Ulama* (Islamic scholars), especially *Muftis*, who are the ultimate religious authorities in Sunni Islam, and *Marja-e-Taqlid* (source of emulation) or Grand *Ayatollahs*, who are the ultimate authority in Shi`a Islam.	Rabbis	Ministers/reverends in Protestant denominations; bishops and priests in Catholicism
Training for Religious Leadership	Islamic seminaries for aspiring teachers and *ulama* (Islamic scholars)	Yeshiva and/or rabbinical seminaries for the training of rabbis	Christian seminaries and theological institutes for aspiring ministers, bishops, and priests
Religious Leaders and Marriage	The religious/spiritual ministers of Islam, Judaism, and the Protestant sects of Christianity can marry and have children		
			Catholic priests and nuns practice celibacy.
Calendar	• Muslims and Jews follow lunar calendars to commemorate their holy days. • Both lunar calendars are 12 lunar months or 354 days long.		Christians follow the Gregorian (solar) calendar, which is made up of 12 months or 365 days.
	The Islamic lunar calendar began with Prophet Muhammads *hijrah* (migration) from Makkah to Madina in 622 CE.	The Jewish lunar calendar began at least 2,200 years ago.	The Gregorian calendar was introduced in 1582 CE by Pope Gregory XIII. It is based on zero being the birth of Jesus Christ.

TABLE 4: Cont'd

Key Topics	Islam	Judaism	Christianity
General Information, continued			
Main Holy Days	• *Eid al-Fitr* (Festival of the Fast Breaking) at the end of the ninth Islamic calendar month of Ramadan • *Eid al-Azha* (Festival of Sacrifice) at the close of the ritual of *hajj* in the twelfth Islamic calendar month of *Dhul Hijjah*, commemorating Abrahams willingness to sacrifice his son Ishmael, as commanded in a dream by God to test his faith	• *Rosh Hashanah* (Jewish New Year) • Yom Kippur (Day of Atonement) • *Sakkot* (commemorating 40 years of wandering); Passover (commemorating redemption from Egyptian slavery) • *Shavuoth* (Anniversary of the Ten Commandments) • *Purim* (Jews saved from Persian genocide) • Hanukkah (commemorating victory of Maccabees over Syrian armies of Antiochus Epiphanes)	• Christmas (celebrating the birth of Jesus on December 25) is based on the solar calendar. • Easter (commemorating the death of Jesus on Good Friday and his resurrection on Easter Sunday) is calculated on the basis of the lunar calendar. Thus Easter is not the same day every year.
Obligatory Duties	Belief in one God and Muhammad as His last prophet, ritual prayers (five times a day), fasting during the month of Ramadan, giving alms to the poor and needy, and making a pilgrimage to Makkah once in ones lifetime in the twelfth Islamic calendar month.	Belief in one God and in the Hebrew Bible prophets, observe the Sabbath and all Jewish holidays, pray thrice daily, and give alms to the poor and needy.	Belief in God, the Father; Jesus Christ as Lord and Savior; and the work of the Holy Spirit. Also attend church on Sundays and give alms to the poor and needy.
Greetings Among the Faithful	*As-Salaam Alaykum wa rahmat Allah-e-wa `barakatu* (Peace be on/with you) and *Wa`Alaykum as-Salaam* (peace be on/with you too)	Shalom (Peace)	No widely used public greeting of equivalence.
Circumcision	The Qur'an and the Hebrew Bible enjoin Muslims and Jews, respectively, to circumcise their baby boys.		The New Testament does not require Christians to circumcise their baby boys.
"Unclean Foods"	The Qur'an enjoins Muslims to avoid consuming pork or alcohol, and to eat *halal* (ritually slaughtered) meat.	• The Hebrew Bible enjoins Jews to avoid consuming pork and to eat kosher (ritually slaughtered) meat. • There are no injunctions in the Hebrew Bible against consuming alcohol.	• The New Testament does not have any food taboos. • Drinking alcohol in moderation is permitted.
Male Role Model(s)	Prophet Muhammad	Abraham, Moses, David, and Solomon	Jesus Christ
Female Role Model(s)	Maryam (mother of Jesus); Khadijah (Prophet Muhammads first wife); Fatimah (Prophet Muhammad's daughter)	Sarah (Abraham's first wife); Rebbeca (Abraham's daughter-in-law/Isaacs wife); Leah and Rachel (Jacobs wives)	Mary (mother of Jesus Christ)
Major Commonalities			
Religious Origin	Have their origins in the Middle East and are faiths first practiced by Semites.		
Monotheism	Monotheistic faiths:		
Monotheism	• Believe that God is indivisible, has no equals, no partner, no parents, and no offspring. • Do *not* believe in the Christian doctrine of the Holy Trinity.		Believe in the Holy Trinity: God the Father, the Son (Jesus Christ), and Holy Spirit, three entities coexisting within one Godhead.
Monotheism	• Muslims refer to God as *Allah*. • Uncompromising monotheism present throughout the Qur'an and encapsulated in *Al-Akhlas* (the Purity of Faith): "Say (O Muhammad) He is Allah, The One and Only! Allah, the Eternal, Absolute; He did not give birth (to anyone), Nor did anyone give birth to Him And there is no one equal (similar) to Him" (Chapter 112, Verses 1–4).	• Jews refer to God as *Adonai* (my Lord/Master). • Monotheism present throughout the Hebrew Bible: "Hear O Israel, the Lord our God, the Lord is one," is often repeated in synagogues (Hebrew Shema).	Christians refer to him as God (the Heavenly Father)

TABLE 4: Cont'd

Key Topics	Islam	Judaism	Christianity
Major Commonalities, continued			
Concept of God	Believe in the one, transcendent, omnipotent, omnipresent, omniscient, eternal, perfect, just, compassionate, and merciful God, who is the provider and protector of humanity and the universe.		
The Creation	Believe that God created the universe (all things visible and invisible) and all life at a definite point in time.		
Angels	Believe in angels who act as Gods agents and operate throughout the universe to carry out His purpose.		
Satan (The Devil)	• Believe Satan fell from Heaven when he did not conform to Gods Will by refusing to acknowledge Adams place of honor. Satans fall from his position in heaven among the angels is explained by his refusal to worship Adam on Gods command. • Satan's chief activity, corroborated in the Torah, Bible, and Qur'an, is to mislead human beings and beguile them away from God.		
	In the Qur'an, Satan was expelled from the Garden of Eden when he refused to obey God and bow to Adam. After that, Satan resolved to turn human beings against God and His will.	In Hebrew references, the Satan is a role rather than a being. The role is one of adversary to God and tempter of human beings rather than a cosmic force for evil.	Christian scriptures mention Satan as the fallen angel. They also discuss the evil role that Satan/the Devil/the Evil One plays in the world. In the New Testament, the Devil is regarded as the great cosmic force for evil.
Purpose of Humanity	Agree the chief purpose of humankind is to serve God and obey His will as expressed in the divinely revealed books.		
View of Humanity	Regard human beings as God's highest creation because they are endowed with a higher intellect and free will.		
View of History	Are "historical religions"—that is, God cares about history and expects people to be involved in shaping it. Many in all three faiths also believe that there is a beginning and an end to human history.		
Concept of Time	Hold a linear concept of time, unlike Hinduism's and Buddhism's cyclical concept of time and rebirth.		
End of Time	Believe that God is testing them in this world, and that at the end of time, God will announce the Day of Judgment and the world will end.		
Day of Judgment	Believe all human beings will be judged on the Day of Judgment and rewarded or punished according to the deeds they have performed in their lives.		
The Afterlife	• Unlike Hinduism's and Buddhism's belief in reincarnation (rebirth of the soul in successive life forms in this world), Muslims, Jews, and Christians believe there is only one life in this finite world. • Believe in the Hereafter and in the realms of Heaven and Hell in that Hereafter. Those who have done good deeds will be rewarded for their good deeds in Heaven or Paradise, while those who have committed sinful deeds will be punished for their sins in Hell.		
	Believe that after death, individuals await Judgment Day, when all will be resurrected, judged, and sent to Paradise for doing good deeds or to Hell for doing evil deeds.	Diverse Jewish beliefs include judgment by God, eternal afterlife, messianic redemption for everyone, and individual death as lasting and complete.	The New Testament mentions the resurrection of the dead at the end of time and a final judgment made then. Most Christians also believe in an individual judgment that takes place at the time of death.
Adam	Believe that Adam was the first human whom God created.		
	Regards Adam as the first of God's prophets.	Do not regard Adam as God's first prophet.	
Eve	• According to the Qur'an, God created Adam, and then Eve. • In the Qur'an, God forbade Adam and Eve to eat the fruit from The Tree in the Garden of Eden; however, Iblis/Shaytan (Satan) encouraged Adam and Eve to eat the forbidden fruit, which both did at the same time. Thus, in Islam, Eve was not the temptress who persuaded Adam to disobey Gods command.	• In the Torah and Old Testament, God first created Adam. Then, while Adam slept, He created Eve from the side of Adams body or from his rib. • Believe that the Devil (in the guise of a serpent) tempted Eve to disobey God and eat the fruit from the Tree of Knowledge. Eve, in turn, tempted Adam to eat the forbidden fruit.	

TABLE 4: Cont'd

Key Topics	Islam	Judaism	Christianity
Major Commonalities, continued			
	Abraham is revered as the "father of the faith" or "patriarch" because he was the first promoter of the monotheistic creed shared by the three faiths.		
Abraham (lived after ca. 1800 BCE)	• Abraham and his eldest son, Ishmael, built the first house of worship dedicated to one God 4,000 years ago. Muslims believe Muhammad rid this house (which is in present-day Makkah, Saudi Arabia) of over 360 idols had been placed there since Abrahams death. • Abraham was going to sacrifice Ishmael because in a dream God commanded him to. • In the Qur'an, there is no mention of God promising Canaan/biblical Israel to Abraham to pass on to his descendents through his first wife Sara.	• Abraham and his youngest son, Isaac, built altars at Bethel (north of Jerusalem) and at Shechem (Nablus) upon which to worship God. • Abraham was going to sacrifice Isaac because in a dream God commanded him to. • God promised Canaan/biblical Israel to Abraham to pass on to his son Isaac, by his first wife, Sara.	
Moses (ca. 1450–1300 BCE)	A great prophet in all three religions. Adherents of all three faiths believe that God gave Moses the Torah (the Five Books of Moses: Genesis, Exodus, Leviticus, Numbers, and Deuteronomy). These books include the Mosaic Law, which governed the conduct of the Jews in biblical times and which include the Ten Commandments/Ten Statements, followed by the adherents of all three faiths (Exodus 12:1-17 and Deuteronomy 5: 6-21, with confirmation in the Qur'an): • "I am the Lord, thy God, thou shalt have no God before me"; In the Qur'an, "There is only One God" (47:19). • "Thou shall make no image of God, there is nothing whatsoever like unto Him" (Qur'an 42:11) • "Thou shall not take the name of the Lord, thy God, in vain"; In the Qur'an, "Thou shall not use Gods name in vain, make not Gods name an excuse to your oaths (2:224). • "Thou shall honor thy Father and thy Mother"; In the Qur'an, "Thou shall honor thy mother and father, be kind to your parents if one or both of them attain old age in thy life, say not a word of contempt nor repel them but address them in terms of honor (17:23). • "Thou shalt not kill/murder"; In the Qur'an, "Thou shall not kill/murder; If anyone has killed/murdered one person, it is as if he had killed/murdered the whole of humankind (5:32). • "Thou shalt not commit adultery"; In the Qur'an, "Thou shall not commit adultery, do not come near adultery. It is an indecent deed and a way for other evils" (17:32) • "Thou shalt not steal"; In the Qur'an, "Thou shall not steal" (5:38-39). • "Thou shalt not bear false witness against thy neighbor"; In the Qur'an, "Thou shall not lie or give false testimony" (24:7). • "Thou shalt not covet thy neighbor's wife or possessions" (Qur'an 4:36). • "Thou shall establish a holy day"; In the Qur'an, "Thou shall keep the Sabbath holy" (62:9).		
David (died c. 970 BCE)	Regard David as one of Gods great prophets; a just, competent, and successful king of Biblical Israel; and the young man who, with Gods help, killed Goliath, the Philistine giant.		
	God revealed the Psalms to David. In their original form, they were the Word of God. However, human revisions over 3,000 years have corrupted them.	Many Jews believe that David wrote the Psalms.	The Book of Psalms in the Old Testament is attributed to David, but scholars of religion do not believe that he wrote all of them.
		In the Hebrew Bible/Old Testament, God makes the promise to David that his house and kingdom will endure forever. Once there is no Jewish kingdom, the expectation of a future descendent of David develops, who will come to rule again, as the "Messiah."	
		For Jews, the Messiah has not yet come.	For Christians, the Messiah has come, as Jesus Christ.
Solomon (died ca. 931 BCE)	• Regard Davids son, Solomon, to be one of Gods great prophets, one of the greatest kings of biblical Israel, and the one renowned for his wisdom and justice. • Believe that Solomon had the temple in Jerusalem constructed, only one wall of which remains today.		
		Jews called this the "Wailing Wall" until the creation of Israel on May 14, 1948. Since then, it has been called the "Western Wall."	

TABLE 4: Cont'd

Key Topics	Islam	Judaism	Christianity
Major Commonalities, continued			
Faith	Believe that humans can never completely know God or discern His purposes; therefore, humans must have faith in Him and be content to take one step at a time in fulfilment of the service He has appointed for us.		
Family, Work, and Religion	Expect their followers to balance worship with work and family life.		
Sabbath Day	Enjoin their adherents to attend their holy places of worship for congregational prayer at least once a week.		
	No sabbath day; the *ummah* (brotherhood of believers) has been encouraged to go to the *masjid* for noontime congregational prayers on Fridays.	Saturday	Sunday
Sinfulness of Humanity	• Encourage their adherents to engage in constant self-scrutiny. • Encourage peace and tolerance and strongly condemn a long list of ills, including suicide, abortion, homosexuality, terrorism, tyranny, pornography, and alcoholism.		
Sanctity of Life	• Believe in the sanctity of life. The Qur'an states: "Whosoever killeth a human being for other than manslaughter or corruption on earth, it shall be as if he had killed all humankind, and whosoever saveth the life of one, it shall be as if he had saved the life of all mankind" (5:32). Judaism has a similar verse in the Sanhedrin (laws of jurisprudence) in Chapter 4, *Mishnah* 5. Christianity has a similar thought mentioned in *Genesis*, 9:5–6. • Strongly condemn suicide and state that only God has the right to create and take life.		

The Golden Rule	Enjoin their followers to follow the "Golden Rule."
	  • Jesus Christ said: "Do unto others as you would want others to do unto you."
	  • Prophet Muhammad said: "None of you truly believes until he wishes for his brother what he wishes for himself."
	  • Rabbi Hillel said: "Do not do to others what you would not have them do to you."		

Birth Control	Protestantism, Islam, and Judaism permit artificial means of birth control; Catholicism discourages artificial means of birth control and permits only the rhythm method of family planning.		
In-Vitro Fertilization	Allowed between husband and wife, but borrowing sperm or ovum is not allowed.		
Homosexual lifestyle and Gay/Lesbian Marriage	Not allowed		
Nudity, Pre-Marital Sex, Adultery, and Divorce	• Nudity, pre-marital sex, and adultery are not allowed • Divorce (annullment in Roman Catholicism) condoned as a last resort; however, divorce is much more common in the developed and relatively secularized countries of the Christian West than in the developing and much more religious Muslim countries.		
Abortion	Early or late abortion is not allowed in all three religions; however, early abortions are relatively common in the secularized Western world and among non-practicing Jews in Israel.		
Burial Rites	Enjoin their believers to bury their dead.		
	Very specifically and categorically disallow cremation.		• Does not specifically disallow cremation. • Roman Catholicism strongly discourages it
Secularization and Secularism	In theory, against "secularization" (gradual transformation of peoples values from adherence to religious beliefs and practices to an increasingly secular, rational, and pragmatic orientation in the political, economic, legal, and educational realms of society) and against "secularism" (separation of mosque/synagogue/church from the state as well as separation of religion from politics).		
Religious Revivalism	The world is witnessing a resurgence of Islam, Judaism, and Christianity. The adherents of all three faiths are returning to their religion for identity, security, meaning, and happiness in their lives.		

TABLE 4: Cont'd

Key Topics	Islam	Judaism	Christianity
Major Commonalities, continued			
	Many aspects of all three religions are misunderstood by people outside the religion.		
Most Misunderstood Aspect of the Religion	• Islam is not Muhammadanism, and Muslims are not Muhammadans. • *Jihad* means "to struggle," primarily against ones baser instincts and against invaders or aggressors. Islam never intended *jihad* to be an aggressive "holy war" against infidels.	Judaism and Zionism are not synonymous—the former is a 4,000-year-old religion; the latter is a century-old political ideology.	"The Trinity" is the most misunderstood concept. Most non-Christians incorrectly think that Christians believe in three Gods: the Father; His Son, Jesus Christ; and the Holy Spirit.
Major Differences			
"Original Sin"	• Reject the concept of "Original Sin" and believe that each person is only responsible for his/her own sin(s). If no one is responsible for anothers sins, the whole human race could not be condemned by God because of Adams disobedience/sin. The Old Testament states: "The fathers shall not be put to death for the children, nor shall the children be put to death for the fathers; every man shall be put to death for his own sin" (Deuteronomy 24:16). The Qur'an states: "My behavior is my own concern, while your behavior is your own concern. You are innocent of anything I do, while I am innocent of what you are doing (10:41). • Believe that Adam and Eve sinned when they disobeyed God and ate the fruit from the Tree. • Believe that an absolutely just God would not hold future generations responsible for the sin of Adam and Eve. Thus, God did not have to send Jesus Christ to take away our sins. We have to overcome our own sins by believing in God, following His guidance, living a righteous life, and doing noble deeds. • Believe that human beings are born "sinless" and only by their disobedience of Gods guidance (as set forth in the Qur'an and Hebrew Bible, respectively) do they become sinful.		• Christian sects have several different interpretations of "Original Sin." • Adam and Eve sinned when they disobeyed God and ate the fruit from the Tree of Knowledge in the Garden of Eden. • Most believe that the sin of Adam and Eve was passed on to succeeding generations.
Humanitys Problem	Not following "the straight path" revealed in the Qur'an	Disobeying Gods guidance as revealed in the Hebrew Bible.	Unable to follow God's law without accepting Jesus Christ because of the sinful nature of humanity.
Humanitys Salvation	Follow "the straight path" as revealed in the Qur'an and found in Prophet Muhammad's *sunnah* (sayings and deeds). Good works and charitable deeds are also strongly recommended.	Follow the Torah and do good works in society to earn salvation.	To attain God's forgiveness and to be reconciled with Him, one needs to trust in the saving work of Jesus Christ. God has completed the work of salvation on humankinds behalf by allowing His son, Jesus Christ, to be crucified. Christs blood has washed away the sins of those who believe in him. Salvation cannot be earned by good works alone; one must accept Jesus Christ as Lord and Savior.
The World to Come	Unlike this world, the world to come will last forever; after the Day of Judgment, human beings will either enjoy their lives in Heaven or suffer in Hell.	The world to come is inextricably bound up with the restoration of Israel to the land, the reconstruction of the Temple and of the holy city of Jerusalem, and the inauguration of the Messianic age that would end the rule of pagans over the "people of God" and restore peace and justice.	Christ will come again triumphant at the end of the world as judge of all human beings and all angels. This second coming will manifest the mercy and the justice of God. There will be a general resurrection of the dead, followed by the Last Judgment, which will determine the destiny of each person in heaven or hell. Finally, the "kingdom of God" will be established by the creation of a new heaven and a new earth.

TABLE 4: Cont'd

Key Topics	Islam	Judaism	Christianity
Major Commonalities, continued			
Jesus Christ (ca. 6 BCE–30 CE)	• The Qur'an mentions Jesus as one of Allahs great prophets and messengers (one who brought a message for humankind). • The Qur'an states that Jesus performed several miracles, such as speaking from the crib to silence those who doubted his mothers virginity, curing lepers and giving sight to the blind, feeding the multitude who came to hear him talk with abundant food provided by God, giving life to a bird of clay, and raising Lazarus from the dead. • The Qur'an states: "They did not really slay him [Jesus], neither crucified him; only a likeness of him was shown unto them" (4:157). • The Qur'an states that Jesus ascended to Heaven alive and will return at the end of time or before the Day of Judgment.	• Jews do not believe that Jesus was the prophet or Son of God, but he was a rabbi and/or teacher. • Jews question the many miracles that Jesus performed. • Adherents believe that Jesus Christ was crucified because the Romans saw him as a threat to their rule and the Jews were not responsible for his crucifixion.	• Believes that Jesus Christ was the Son of God, was the unique demonstration of Gods love for humankind, and was sinless. • Believes Jesus Christ performed many miracles, such as curing lepers and gaving sight to the blind: with abundant food, feeding the multitude who came to hear him talk; raising Lazarus from the dead; changing water into wine; exorcizing demons from the possessed; and walking on water. • Believes that Jewish leaders handed Jesus over to the Romans to be crucified. • Believes in the Resurrection (God raised Jesus Christ after his crucifixion and burial), and ascension to Heaven, to return at end of time or on/before the Day of Judgment..
Muhammad (570–632 CE)	Muslims believe that Prophet Muhammad is God's last Prophet; that Archangel Gabriel revealed Gods final message to him; and that Gods final message, embodied in the Qur'an, was the continuation of the same message that God sent to Abraham, David, Moses, and Jesus earlier in history.	Jews and Christians do not believe that Muhammad was Gods prophet.	
Mary, Mother of Jesus (born ca. 25 BCE)	Maryam (Arabic name for Mary) is a revered figure in Islam. The Qur'an devotes Chapter 19, comprising 98 verses, to her.	An unimportant figure in Jewish theology and history	A revered figure in Christian theology and history. The New Testament presents the story of the virginal conception of Jesus. Orthodox Christians and Catholic Christians give her the title "Mother of God." "The Blessed Virgin Mary" is a saintly figure in Catholicism.
Paul (ca. 4 BCE–64 CE)	Viewed negatively because Saul of Tarsus, who converted from Judaism to Christianity, was responsible for the following controversial ideas/myths: Jesus was divine; Christ died for humankinds sins; his crucifixion and suffering on the cross can redeem us; and, a person who does not accept Jesus Christ as the Lord and Savior cannot be "saved" and go to Heaven.		• Paul taught that denying Jesus Christs Crucifixion (physical death) and Resurrection is to deny the very means of atonement and salvation for which God sent Jesus into the world. • Christians revere him (many even consider him to be a saint) because he played a critically important role in the development of Christian theology. His writings constitute a considerable portion of the New Testament, and he was the main proselytizing force for Christianity during the first century CE.
Original Languages of the Scriptures	Arabic	Mainly Hebrew (however, some Aramaic in the third section of the Hebrew Bible)	Aramaic, Hebrew, and Greek
Divine Trinity	Muslims and Jews reject the doctrine of the Holy Trinity because it implies the association of the human Jesus with God. Any confusion of the Creator and a mere creature of God is a sin in both Islam and Judaism. Many Muslims consider the Holy Spirit to be the divine instrument of God, but consider the concept of Trinity as polytheistic.		Most Christians believe in the Divine Trinity (God considered to be three entities): God the Father, the Son (Jesus Christ), and the Holy Spirit.

TABLE 4: Cont'd

Key Topics	Islam	Judaism	Christianity
Major Commonalities, continued			
Evangelism/ Proselytization	Believes in evangelism, propagation of the faith, and proselytization of the disbelievers to the "right/true path."	Does not believe in evangelism, propagation of the faith, and proselytization of disbelievers to the "right/true path."	Believes in evangelism, propagation of the faith, and proselytization of the disbelievers to the "right/true path."
Organic Religion	Islam and Judaism are "organic religions" because they have a comprehensive body of sacred laws governing every aspect of society.		Catholicism and Eastern Orthodox Christianity are "church religions," with a well-established and highly structured clerical organization having a separate identity from both government and society. Most forms of Protestantism are neither an "organic" nor a "church" religion.
Sacred Texts	• Believe that the Qur'an is God's last message to humankind and has been preserved in its original form to this day; was revealed to Prophet Muhammad by Archangel Gabriel; that God's revelations embodied in the Qur'an came to Muhammad over a period of 22 years (610–632 CE); and that in Prophet Muhammad's case, the Qur'an was his greatest miracle. • Believe that the Psalms of David, the Torah (Hebrew Bible), Old Testament, and the Injil (Gospels of Jesus Christ) are not in their original form, and therefore do not contain the original Word of God.	Do not believe that the Qur'an was the Word of God. Believe in the Hebrew Bible, comprising the Torah (the Five Books Of Moses: Genesis, Exodus, Leviticus, Numbers, and Deuteronomy), the Prophets, and the Writings.	Believe that both the Old Testament and the New Testament (Bible) are the Word of God. The Old Testament comprises the Pentateuch (the Five Books of Moses), the Historical Books, the Wisdom Books, and the Prophets.
Gambling and Lotteries	Not allowed	Allowed in moderation	
Religion and Politics	There is a fusion of religion and politics. Many Muslim countries have Islamists actively lobbying for an Islamic system and some actively trying to come to power and establish an Islamic state. Likewise, in Israel, many Jewish political parties are lobbying the Israeli government to make Israel a truly Jewish state.		Most Christians believe that religion has an important role to play in politics (although Protestants favor the separation of church and state). In practice, much of the Western world has effectively separated religion and politics.
	In Islam, religion and politics are fused and inseparable.	In Judaism, religion and politics were fused before the modern era, but they are much less so today.	

doth declare His Praises and Glory and He is the Exalted in Might, the Wise" (59:22-24).

• "O Mankind, keep your duty to your Lord who created you from a single person and from it created its mate (of same kind), and from the two of them spread men and women in multitudes; so fear God in whose name you importune one another, and be mindful of kinship; verily, God keeps watch over you" (4: 1).

In fact, devout Muslims constantly use such expressions as *Bismillah* (I start this in the name of Allah), *Inshallah* (If Allah Wills), and *Al-hamdu lillah* (Thanks and Glory be to Allah). Muslims never call on Prophet Muhammad to help them when they start an endeavor, nor thank Prophet Muhammad when they complete a task, and above all, never say if "Prophet Muhammad wills it." For to make such statements would be considered *shirk* (associating someone with God), and thus a cardinal sin.

The term "Islam" also comes from the same root as *salaam* (literally, "peace"), and therefore peace is an integral part of Islam. *As-Salaam* is one of the ninety-nine attributes or names of God, as well as the name given to the blissful abode of Heaven/Paradise. Muslims believe that if true Islam is rigorously followed, it will instill "peace" and serenity in the true believer in this world, lead to harmony and cooperation between fellow Muslims, and will result in earning a blissful life and eternal life in the peaceful abode of Heaven. In fact, "peace" is such an important idea in Islam that Muslims have been recommended to say *As-salaam alaykum* (peace be upon you) when they greet another Muslim (6:54), and are given the response of *Wa alaykum as-salaam* (peace be upon you, too).

TABLE 5: Jesus and Muhammad: Founders of Worlds Two Largest Religions

	Jesus	Muhammad
Personal Background		
Names Meaning and Significance	"Jesus" literally means "The Lord is Salvation"; Muslims refer to him as *Isa*.	"Muhammad" literally means one who is highly praised, celebrated, or lauded.
Honorific Titles	• Christians refer to him as Jesus Christ, Son of God (Christ or Messiah means "the anointed one"). • Muslims consider him one of Gods major Prophets, call him "messiah" "Seal of Sanctity," and *Ruhallah* or Spirit of God (Qur'an 4:157; 9:31; 19:31; 4:171).	• Muslims refer to him as Gods last and most significant prophet. • Because he was Islams last prophet, Muslims call him the "Seal of the Prophets." • Also called *Al-Sadiq* (The Truthful) and *Al-Amin* (The Trustworthy).
Circumstances of Birth	• Christians and Muslims believe that his imminent birth was announced by Archangel Gabriel to Mary (Luke 1:34; Qur'an 3:45). • Both Christians and Muslims believe God miraculously conceived Jesus in the Virgin Mary, although she was engaged to Joseph (Luke 1:34; Qur'an 3:47). • Popular tradition places his birth in Bethlehem (around 5 BCE) and upbringing in Nazareth. • Christians celebrate his birth annually on December 25, although scholars have not determined precisely when he was born. • His birth marks the transition from "Before Christ" (BC) or "Before Christian Era" (BCE) to "Anno Domini" (In the year of our Lord or AD) or CE (Common Era).	• Muslims believe his birth was alluded to in the Old Testament. Many Muslims also believe that Jesus Christ alluded to Muhammads coming in the future, when referring to Muhammad as "The Comforter" (John, 16:7) • Both Christians and Muslims believe Muhammads mother, Amina bint Wahhab, conceived him through natural means, and that his father, Abdullah ibn Abdul Muttalib, died before his birth. • Popular tradition places his birth in Makkah (present day Saudi Arabia) in April 570/571 C.E. • Sunni Muslims celebrate his birth on the 12th Rabi al-Awwal (the third Islamic lunar month) and Shi`as celebrate his birth on the 17th Rabi al-Awwal. He spent the first 52 years of his life in Makkah. • His *hijra* (migration) from Makkah to Madina in 622 CE marks the beginning of the Islamic lunar calendar and is dated 1st *Hijri* (subsequent dates are followed by A.H.).
Ancestry and Religion	• Descended from Abraham and Sarahs son, Isaac. • Born into a Hebrew/Jewish Semitic family, which practiced monotheism. • Practiced Judaism in his formative years; objected to the elaborate laws governing the lives of practicing Jews.	• Descended from Abraham and Hagars son, Ishmael • Born into an Arab Semitic family • Most Sunnis believe that some members of Muhammads extended family (such as his grandfather, Abdul Mutalib and his uncle, Abu Talib) practiced polytheism before Muhammad invited them to Islam in 610 CE; Shi`as believe that Abdul Mutalib and Abu Talib practiced monotheism from birth.
Social Class	His family was lower middle class.	His grandfather, Abdul Mutalib, and uncle, Abu Talib, were influential middle class members of the Quraysh tribe; Muhammad himself was a person of modest means.
Formative Years	• His "earthly" father, Joseph, raised him, and likely taught him his own trade of carpentry. However, no details of his childhood and early adulthood are available.	• Spent his early years as a shepherd, and his late teens and early twenties as a trader in his uncle, Abu Talibs trading company. • Spent his late twenties and thirties in Khadijah's much larger international trading company that took him to other lands.
Language	Most scholars believe he spoke Aramaic and/or Hebrew.	Arabic.
Marriage	No documentation of his being married.	First marriage to an Arab Semite named Khadijah; married several Arab Semites after her death, primarily with the intention of uniting feuding tribes in the Arabian Peninsula.
Beginning of Mission	Discussed religious issues at the temple as a boy; some refer to him as a rabbi, although he didnt go to rabbinical school. Became an itinerant teacher/preacher at around 30.	Muslims believe he was visited by Archangel Gabriel in the cave of Hira (on the outskirts of Makkah) when he was 40, informed of his prophethood, and asked to start reciting Gods revelations.

TABLE 5: Cont'd

	Jesus	Muhammad
Personal Background, continued		
Miracles	• Christians and Muslims believe he provided sight to the blind, raised Lazarus from the dead, healed the sick, provided a banquet of fish and bread to the multitude that came to listen to him, and ascended miraculously to Heaven (Matthew 4:24; Qur'an 5:110). • Muslims also believe he spoke from his crib to defend his mothers honor and breathed life into a clay bird (Qur'an 5:110).	• Muslims believe that the highly refined classical Arabic embodied in the *Qur'an* is in itself a miracle underscoring the prophethood of Muhammad • Muslims believe he journeyed from Makkah to Jerusalem in one night and ascended to Heaven for a meeting with God and several prophets before returning back to earth. • Some Muslims even believe he temporarily split the full moon into two parts one night to show his people a sign that he was Gods prophet.
Personal Characteristics	• Courageous, honest, revolutionary, honorable, humane, humble, and compassionate. • Charismatic personalities.	
Lifestyle	Lived humbly in an undistinguished home, dressed modestly, ate abstemiously, spent several waking hours in contemplation, and preached constantly (Jesus from 30-33 and Muhammad from 40-62).	
Offspring	Never married, and hence had no children.	Possibly four: a daughter, Fatimah, with first wife, Khadijah; three from the women he married after Khadijahs death; and an adopted son, Zaid, whom he treated like his own son.
Migration	No major migration from one town to another (like Muhammads) was reported; but traveled extensively throughout present-day Israel.	According to Muslims, God commanded him to undertake the *hijra*—migration from Makkah to Yathrib (renamed Madina on his arrival)—in 622 CE.
Events Surrounding Death	• Christians believe the Romans crucified him on a Friday when he was 33; then God resurrected him the following Sunday, and he ascended to Heaven. • The Qur'an states that Jesus was not crucified (rather the Romans crucified someone who looked just like him) and that he miraculously ascended to Heaven. • Some Islamic scholars believe he will return before the Day of Judgment.	• Died at age 62 in 632 CE/10 A.H. (10 years "After *Hijri*") after receiving and announcing a premonition of his death.
Burial Place	Christians believe after his crucifixion, he was entombed in Jerusalem for two days, then resurrected, and ascended to Heaven; Muslims believe that he ascended to Heaven (Qur'an 3:55).	Muslims and Christians believe he was buried in Madina, which is in present day Saudi Arabia.
The Political and Socioeconomic Environment		
Geography	Worked primarily in an agrarian area of Palestine (Biblical Israel in the pre-Roman period), which was less than five-hundred miles northwest of where Muhammad was born and died.	Worked primarily in Makkah, in the western Arabian region of Hejaz.
Political Background	King Herrod ruled Judea as a vassal of the pagan and autocratic Roman empire. The Jews suffered oppression under Roman rule, but patiently awaited the coming of their messiah, who would be their king and liberator.	The Arabian Peninsula at the advent of Islam had no central authority, and comprised many tribes governed by power-hungry, avaricious, and incompetent tribal chieftains, constantly fighting one another.
Sociocultural Climate	The polytheistic Roman Empire dominated the region and relegated the Semites to second-class status.	Polytheism, disorder, tribal warfare, female infanticide, slavery, alcoholism, prostitution, unemployment, underemployment, hunger, and beggary were prevalent.
Religious Persecution	In the last three years of his life, Jesus suffered persecution after proclaiming his ethical, moral, and spiritual message.	Muslims believe Muhammad propagated Islam among family and friends for the first three years of his prophethood (610–613 CE); but once he began publicly propagating Islam, the Makkans persecuted him and his followers (613 to 622 CE).

TABLE 5: Cont'd

	Jesus	Muhammad
Beliefs and Teachings		
Overview	• Besides Mosaic Law (Ten Commandments), he did not believe that people should be governed by a comprehensive body of religious laws. • Christians and Muslims believe that his message was entirely spiritual and ethical, summarized by the commandment "Love God and love your neighbor." • Most Christians believe that only those who believe in Jesus Christ as Lord and Savior will go to Heaven.	• Besides Mosaic Law and a message emphasizing ethical behavior, he did promote a comprehensive body of religious laws enumerated in the *Qur'an*. • Encouraged his followers to establish and maintain a strong relationship with God and help humankind. • Only those who follow the *Qur'an*, the original Jewish and Christian scriptures, and the scriptures emphasizing monotheism will go to Heaven (2:62).
Attitude Towards Polytheism	• Strongly opposed; both constantly advised their followers to worship only God and have faith in Him. • Muslims do not attribute divinity to any mortals, including Gods Prophets. Most Christians see no conflict between considering Jesus divine and their belief in monotheism.	
Fairness and Justice	Emphasized this virtue. Muhammad left behind extensive laws and guidelines to develop a just society.	
Almsgiving and Charity	Urged their followers to give alms to the poor and do volunteer work for the betterment of society. Islam requires its followers to give a stipulated portion of their assets to charity.	
Marital Institution	Marriage encouraged, and men were expected to be the head of the household. In Islam, monogamous marriage is strongly encouraged (even for clerics); under certain special circumstances, polygamy was permitted. Roman Catholicism prohibited priests from marrying.	
Divorce	Divorce discouraged, but permitted in cases of infidelity, insanity, etc.	
Sex	A woman who was caught in adultery was brought before Jesus and he said "He who is without sin cast the first stone"; then, he told the woman "to go and sin no more."	In the case of premarital sex or adultery, Muhammad recommended that four witnesses must testify in order for the fornicators to be stoned to death. This shows the high level of proof needed before this punishment may be applied.
Attitude Towards Gender	• Believed men and women had equal value/worth in the eyes of God; however, men and women had different roles and responsibilities in society (a womans primary responsibility was that of being a good homemaker, wife, and mother). • Raised the status of women in the patriarchal and male chauvinist societies of their times. However, Islam gave more rights to women than classical and medieval Christianity (especially in terms of inheritance, property ownership, and marriage).	
Attitude Towards Violence	• Was a pacifist believing in absolute non-violence, and encouraged his followers not to retaliate when attacked. • Was not involved in any military campaign.	• Concerned about threats posed and wars waged against the *ummah* (community of believers), and he prepared his followers to protect and defend themselves. • Was involved in several defensive military campaigns. • Justified the use of force when all peaceful means fail to protect the weak from the tyranny of armed oppressors.
Attitude Towards Economics	Frowned upon rapacious and exploitative individuals, and emphasized equality and socioeconomic justice.	Supported free enterprise (capitalism with a conscience), but also emphasized equality, socioeconomic justice, and a welfare state to take care of the poor and needy.
Select Quotes	• "So in everything, do to others what you would have them do to you" (Matthew 7: 12). • "Love your neighbor as yourself" (Matthew 12: 31). • "Love your enemies, bless them that curse you, do good to them that hate you, and pray for them which despitefully use you, and persecute you." (Luke 6: 28). • "Resist not evil, but whosoever shall smite thee on the right cheek, turn to him the other also". • "Blessed are the peacemakers, for they will be called sons of God." (Matthew 5:9).	• "None of you truly believes until you wish for others what you wish for yourself." • "All people are equal, as equal as the teeth of a comb. There is no merit of an Arab over a non-Arab, or of a white over a black person, or of a male over a female. Only God-fearing people merit preference." • "He who wishes to enter paradise, must please his father and mother." • "The ink of the scholar is holier than the blood of the martyr." • "Seek knowledge though it be in China."
Impact and Legacy		
Religious Acceptance	His message was rejected by most during his ministry; however, he had 12 well-known disciples during his lifetime and many admirers who feared publicly following him because of persecution from Roman authorities and Jewish fundamentalists.	His message was initially rejected by most Makkans; however, most Arabs in the Arabian peninsula became his followers towards the end of his lifetime.

TABLE 5: Cont'd

	Jesus	Muhammad
Impact and Legacy, continued		
Acceptance by Jews	Neither was accepted by Jews as a Prophet, and most Jews rejected their message.	
Establishment of a State	Did not establish or govern a state.	Like Moses, established a theocracy; first in Yathrib (622–630 CE/1–8 AH), known as *Madinat un-Nabi* (city of the prophet); and then in Makkah (630–632 CE/9–10 AH).
Political Impact	• His message created uncertainty and fear in the religiopolitical establishment. • Both Jewish elders and Roman leaders wanted to silence his peaceful revolutionary rhetoric.	• Transformed Arabia from a multitude of idolatrous, nomadic, and separated tribes into one united nation. • Successful in both the religious and secular realms.
Growth and Spread of Religion After Death	• Phenomenal expansion across Europe within 200 years of Jesus Christs passing. • Today, Christianity is the largest religion with 2.2 billion adherents.	• Within a century of Muhammads death, the Islamic empire was the largest in world history. • Today, Islam is the second largest religion with 1.3 billion adherents.
Status in Abrahamic Faiths	• Christians believe he founded Christianity and he was the earthly manifestation of God, or the "Son of God," as part of the Father, Son and Holy Spirit. • Muslims and Jews do not believe that he was God incarnate or the Son of God. • Muslims believe he was one of Gods most prominent prophets, teaching monotheism; most Jews do not believe he was a prophet or messiah. • Christians and Muslims believe he will return on/before the Day of Judgment to vanquish the Antichrist and establish peace, justice, and prosperity (Revelation 20:5; Qur'an 19:33).	• Most non-Muslims believe he founded Islam; Muslims believe that God is the founder of Islam. Most believe that he profoundly contributed to Islam. • Muslims believe he was the last and one of the most influential of Gods prophets, but a mortal human, *albeit insani-kamil* (perfect human being). • Muhammad was such a good role model and his name was so meaningful and significant, that the Prophets name is the most common male name in the world. • Muslims believe that God revealed His final message to him, which is the completion and perfection of the single monotheistic message taught by all Gods prophets from Adam to Muhammad. • Christians and Jews do not believe he was Gods prophet.
		• Many Sunnis believe Jesus and Muhammad were infallible only in purely religious matters (revelations from God that were later embodied in the Gospels of Jesus and the Qur'an); Shi`as believe they were both infallible/sinless.
Written Legacy		
Vehicle of Religiopolitical Statements	Used parables to protest the actions of his persecutors and authorities as well as confound those who would not follow him.	Sent letters to several non-Muslim leaders making the case for Islam and urging them to convert to the new faith.
Authority of Scripture	• Most Christians believe that the New Testament contains what Jesus Christ and his disciples said. • His gospels/teachings were not written down during his lifetime, rather many years later. • Muslims do not believe that the New Testament contains Gods revealed message. However, Muslims do believe that Gods divine message to Jesus was contained in the *Injeel* (the Gospels of Jesus Christ), which was corrupted by periodic revisions undertaken by fallible human beings.	• Muslims believe that God revealed the *Qur'an* to Muhammad between 610–632 CE. • Muslims believe his companions wrote down all the verses revealed to him just after he received them. • These sacred verses were collated and compiled into one holy book called the *Qur'an* in 653 CE, which is still in its orginal form.
Versions of Scripture	There are several versions of the Bible based on different translations. No single original version is available. The most popular English language version is the King James Bible.	Although there are several translations of the *Qur'an*, there is only one version of the *Qur'an* in Arabic—the original language in which it was revealed to Muhammad. Additionally, all Muslims believe that the Qur'an has been preserved in its original content and style.

The word "Muslim," which literally means "one who submits," is an active participle of *aslama* (to submit). Thus, Muslims are "those who submit to the will of God" and believe that only by totally submitting to God's will and by obeying His commands, as embodied in the Qur'an, can one achieve true happiness in this world and in the hereafter. Muslims also believe that Islam is God's final message to humankind, a reconfirmation and perfection of the messages that God has revealed through earlier prophets.

The Qur'an also states that Muhammad was not divine: ".... Muhammad is only a messenger; [other] messengers have [already] passed away before him." (3:144). Therefore, in Islam, Prophet Muhammad, like all the Old Testament prophets—including Noah, Abraham, Solomon, David, Moses, John the Baptist, and Jesus)—was a human being, albeit *khatam al-nabieen* (the last of God's prophets) and *insan-i-kamil* (perfect human being), sent by God to guide humankind back to "the straight path."

In order to avoid people deifying him, Prophet Muhammad himself said, "I am no more than a human being; when I order you do anything pertaining to religion, obey and follow it, and when I order you to do anything about the affairs of the world, then I am nothing more than human" and "my sayings do not abrogate the word of God [Qur'an], but the word of God can abrogate my sayings." He also asked his followers to refer to him as "the messenger of God," or "God's servant," or "God's slave."

In short, Prophet Muhammad did not create or establish the religion of Islam, was not Islam's architect or founder, and did not create a cult of personality. In Islam, God is the creator and founder of Islam as he is of the universe and everything in it. Furthermore, Muslims do not, should not, and cannot worship Muhammad. If any Muslim made the blunder of worshipping Prophet Muhammad, he would be guilty of *shirk* (the sin of associating someone with God), apostasy, or blasphemy for violating Islam's central principle of *tawhid* (the absolute oneness, unity, and uniqueness of Allah/God).

2. Islam's God is different from the Judeo-Christian God.

Many Christians and Jews are under the impression that Muslims worship a different God by the name of "Allah." In fact, "Allah" is simply the Arabic term for literally, "The God." Muslims worship the same omnipotent, omnipresent, omniscient, absolutely just, infinitely wise, and most merciful God of Adam, Noah, Abraham, David, Moses, Jesus, and many other prophets who preached the message of monotheism. Muslims, like Jews and Christians, also believe the chief purpose of human beings is to obey God's will as expressed in the divinely revealed holy books.

The following Qur'anic verses should clarify the fact that Muslims believe in and submit to the same God as Jews and Christians, and that Islam is merely the reconfirmation, completion, and perfection of the same monotheistic message that God revealed to all the prophets that preceded Muhammad:

- "Say (O Muhammad): We believe in God, and in the revelation given to us, and to Abraham, Ishmael, Isaac, Jacob, and the Tribes, and that given to Moses and Jesus, and that given to all Prophets from their Lord: We make no difference between one and another of them; And to Him we surrender" (2:136; 3:83)

- "The same religion has He established for you as that which He enjoined on Noah, that which We have sent to you as inspiration through Abraham, Moses, and Jesus, namely, that you should remain steadfast in religion and make no divisions within it." (42:13)

- "And in their footsteps, We sent Jesus, the son of Mary, confirming the Torah that had come before him: We sent him the *Injeel* [The Gospels]: therein was guidance and light. And confirmation of the Torah that had come before him: a guidance and an admonition to those who fear God." (5:46)

- "He has revealed to you, O Muhammad, the scripture with truth, confirming that which was revealed before it even as He revealed the Torah and the Gospel before as His guide to mankind and has revealed the Criterion for judging between right and wrong." (3:3-4).

- "O you who believe! Believe in God and His Apostle and the scripture which He has sent to His Apostle and the scripture which he sent to those before (him). Any who deny God, His angels, His Books, His Apostles, and the Day of Judgment, hath gone far, far astray" (4:136). It is noteworthy, that Judaism and Christianity also believe in five similar foundational principles, namely, monotheism, belief in angels, belief in the Old Testament prophets, belief in God's holy books, and belief in a Day of Judgment.

Based on their revealed scriptures, Jews and Christians are mentioned in the Qur'an as *Ahl al-Kitab* (People of the Book), and Muslim leaders/regimes have been commanded to give them most of the same rights of citizenship granted to Muslims (except political governance and serving in the armed forces) in Islamic states. Indeed, non-Muslims held prominent positions in Islamic Andalusian Empire, the Arab Abbasid Empire, the Egyptian Fatimid Empire, and the Indian Mughal Empire. Since Jews, Christians, and Muslims are all "People of the Book," Muslim men are also permitted to marry Jewish and Christian women without having them convert to Islam.

It is also noteworthy that on account of the many remarkable similarities between the Old Testament (Hebrew and Christian Bibles) and the Qur'an, many non-Muslims think and have suggested that Muhammad plagiarized the Qur'an from the Old Testament. Muslims believe that remarkable similarities between the Jewish, Christian, and Islamic holy books are due to the fact that all divine revelations come from the same source, namely Almighty God, and Islam is merely the continuation and completion of God's universal monotheistic message to humankind.

In pointing out the fallacies of Islam's critics, Muslims state that if Prophet Muhammad, who could not read or write, plagiarized the Qur'an from the Christian Old Testament, could not the doubters of Muhammad's honesty and integrity be just as wrong in erroneously believing that Jesus Christ plagiarized the Christian Bible from the Torah (both of which are also remarkably similar in content)? Furthermore, how can Islam's critics accuse Muhammad of plagiarizing the Qur'an from the Old Testament while at the same time stating that "Islam's God is different from the Judeo-Christian God"?

After all, Muhammad was calling people to worship and obey the same God of the Jews and Christians. God in the Qur'an and Muhammad in his *Hadith* referred to Jews and Christians as "People of the Book."

It is true, however, that Muslims, like Jews, reject the Christian beliefs in the "Holy Trinity" and Jesus Christ being the Son of God. In fact, Muslims, like Jews and Christians, consider Prophet Abraham, who was a staunch monotheist, to be their patriarch. So, Muslims believe that Judaism, Christianity, and Islam are "Abrahamic faiths," and Muslims believe they are actually following the Judeo-Christian-Islamic tradition.

In short, it will be illuminating for people of all religions to read the box, "The Ninety-Nine Names of Allah," to understand the ninety-nine attributes of Allah in Islam. Hopefully, this glimpse into nature, meaning, and significance of God will help non-Muslims get a better appreciation of the God that Muslims worship and whose guidance they follow.

3. Most Muslims are Arabs.

The Western mass media has engendered a confusion of Arab with Muslim. Even such prominent non-Arab Persian Muslims, like Ayatollah Ruhollah Khomeini, were subjected to this misconception. In the bombing campaign in Afghanistan in October 2001, most Westerners were not aware that the Afghans are themselves not Arabs. The Arabs in Afghanistan are foreigners.

While not all Arabs are Muslims (at least four percent of Arabs worldwide are Christians and Jews), it is true that 96 percent of Arabs are Muslims. However, it is factually incorrect to believe that most Muslims are Arabs. In fact, there are over 1.3 billion Muslims in the world, comprising many nationalities, races, ethnic groups, linguistic groups, tribal groups, and cultures. In other words, Muslims constitute over one-fourth of the world's 6.2 billion people and 80 percent of all Muslims are non-Arabs. On the other hand, there are 300 million Arab Muslims in the world (i.e. just over 20 percent of the total Muslim population in the world, but less than 5 percent of the world's population). Most of these Arab Muslims live in the present-day Middle East. But several thousand Arab Muslims also live in the U.S., Canada, Europe (especially what was known as Western Europe), and Australia. For instance, Arab Muslims (mainly Algerians, Tunisians, and Moroccans) make up most of the 10 percent of Muslims living in France. In fact, although 20 countries in the Middle East are Arab countries, nearly half of the Middle East is demographically made up of non-Arabs: 70 million Turks, 70 million Persians/Iranians, over 25 million Kurds, and several million Berbers. In other words, non-Arab Muslims constitute at least half of the Middle East, which many unfamiliar with the region, erroneously believe comprises mainly Arabs.

The five largest Muslim countries in the world are non-Arab: Indonesia (comprising 220 million Muslims), Pakistan (comprising over 145 million Muslims), Bangladesh (comprising 140 million Muslims), and predominantly Hindu India (comprising 140 million Muslims). Over one-third of sub-Sahara Black Africa is made up of Muslims; there are over 25 million Chinese Muslims, over 20 million Muslims in Europe, and 7 million Muslims in the United States.

4. Jihad is a holy war against non-Muslims and Islam was spread by the sword.

Jihad, which is one of the most misunderstood words in Islam, comes from the Arabic root j, h, d, and terms such as "to struggle," "to strive," "effort," and "labor" can be derived from it. In Islam, the term *jihad* means to struggle in the practice of one's faith despite obstacles or the hedonistic tendencies that arise within oneself. The word *jihad* appears several times in the Qur'an, wherein it is used to describe the efforts of Muslims to remain faithful to Islam despite heavy pressure from others to force the new converts to renounce their faith: "Therefore listen not to the unbelievers, but strive against them with it [the Qur'an] with the utmost strenuousness" (25:52) or "We have enjoined on people kindness to parents. But if they strive to make you ascribe partners with Me then obey them not" (29:8).

The translation of an Islamic "*jihad*" as "holy war," as is often done by non-Muslim scholars, is incorrect. The translation of "war" in Arabic is *harb*, and the term *haraba* is defined as "sowing corruption and chaos on earth." The translation of "holy war" in Arabic is actually *harbun muqaddastu*, which is not in the Qur'an, Prophet Muhammad's *Hadith*, or the *shariah* (Islamic law).

Prophet Muhammad made it abundantly clear to his followers to fight only when they were attacked. So, *jihad* was always intended as a defensive rather than an offensive operation. Once when returning to Madina after a successful military campaign, Muhammad told his army: "You have left the lesser or the smaller *jihad*, now you are returning to the greater *jihad* with yourself." So, there are at least two types of *jihad* in Islam. The first type of *jihad* is *jihad al-nafs* (struggle to control one's emotions and impulses), which Prophet Muhammad referred to as *jihad–i-akbar* (the greatest "sacred struggle"). This is a peaceful, spiritual struggle to keep one's heart, tongue, and mind free from evil as well as to avoid arrogance, jealousy, avarice, and selfishness. *Jihad* can include providing missionary services in a tough place, going to a far off land to study, donating money when it is a hardship, and going to school or university to gain knowledge.

The second type of *jihad* is that of an armed struggle fought in self-defense. This is a military campaign waged against aggressors, invaders, imperialists, occupiers, and tyrants who are persecuting the *ummah*. It has also been referred to as *jihad-i-asghar* (the smaller/lesser "holy struggle"). Yes, it is true that the *mujahideen* (jihadists) who die in a justified *jihad* that has been sanctioned by the *fatwas* of erudite *ulama* (often *muftis* in Sunni Islam and ayatollahs in Shi'a Islam) are regarded as *shaheed* (martyrs) who are destined to go to Heaven. However, there is no mention in the Qur'an about martyrs being taken care of by 72 *hurries* (virgin maidens). Abu Ibn al-Hadeed, a Hanbali scholar stated that this was one *hadith* of Prophet Muhammad, and other Hanbali and Wahhabi/Salafi scholars endorsed it and disseminated it widely. However, this so-called *hadith* of Prophet Muhammad is not to be found in *Sahih Muslim* or *Sahih Bukhari*—two of the most renowned sources of *Hadith* in Sunni Islam or in the authoritative Shi'a texts on Prophet Muhammad's *Hadith*. In fact, the Sunni *muftis* at al-Azhar University (the oldest and most influential center of Islamic learning in Sunni Islam) and the Shi'a ayatollahs have discredited al-Hadeed's *hadith*.

It is true that misguided Muslim extremists constantly use the term *jihad* for their terrorist acts and/or campaigns in which they indiscriminately target and kill non-combatants and innocent civilians (as they did in the U.S. on September 11th, 2001, Madrid, the Netherlands, and London, and are doing in Iraq, Afghanistan, Pakistan, and Israel). It is also true that these Muslim extremists often incorporate the term *jihad* in the name of their organizations (like Islamic Jihad) to justify their violent deeds. But the fact that they think they are engaging in a defensive *jihad*, does not make it so.

The Crusaders believed they were engaging in a "Just War" to take back the Holy Land (Palestine) from the Muslims (1095–1291 CE), and so did Ferdinand and Isabella when they instituted the Spanish Inquisition (1492, the Conquistadors when they conquered Latin America, Christopher Columbus in his treatment of the Native Americans, the European imperialists and colonialists in the developing world, the American cowboys killing the Red Indians, the Serbians against the Croatians, Bosnian Muslims, and Kosovars in the 1990s. Dr. Baruch Goldstein killed and wounded many Palestinian Muslims while they were praying at the Abraham Mosque in Hebron in Spring 1994. Several Israeli leaders have killed many Palestinians claiming that they are fighting a holy war against terrorism. Devout Hindus and devout Sikhs butchered Muslims during the Partition of the Indian subcontinent. There have also been many communal riots in India since its independence in 1947. Since the early 1990s, Hindu fundamentalists have killed Muslims in Kashmir, Ayodhya, and Gujarat.

If good people were not prepared to engage in a *jihad*, injustice would triumph. The Qur'an specifically encourages Muslims to help those who have been expelled from their homes, are oppressed, tortured, and are too weak to defend themselves: "Why should you not fight in the cause of Allah and of those who, being weak, are ill-treated and oppressed? Men, women, and children whose cry is: 'Our Lord! Rescue us from this town, whose people are oppressors! Raise for us from You one who will protect, and raise for us from You one who will help!' " (4:75). Another Qur'anic verse gives permission to Muslims to defend themselves against aggressors: "To those against whom war is made, permission is given to fight back, because they are wronged. And truly, Allah is most powerful for their aid. They are those who have been expelled from their homes in defiance of right, for no cause except that they say 'Our Lord is Allah' " (22:39–40).

Islam is committed to ending persecution and oppression, so that freedom and justice prevail. At all times, a violent military battle is to be used as a last resort, under the most extraordinary circumstances, when all other attempts at just and peaceful solutions to the dispute fail. Muslims are commanded to avoid initiating hostilities, engaging in aggression, or violating the rights of others. Prisoners of war and even the corpses of enemies killed in battle are to be treated with respect.

The claim of many non-Muslims that Islam was spread by sword has been disproved by a lengthy list of eminent Western historians and scholars of Islam. It will be instructive to read Sir Thomas W. Arnold's *The Preaching of Islam*, Marshall G. Hodgson's *The Venture of Islam*, Albert Hourani's *A History of the Arab People*, Ira Lapidus' History of Islamic Societies, and L. S. Starorianos' *A Global History: the Human Heritage*, to mention a few. Some Orientalists, like Bernard Lewis, are of the view that while some Muslims did abuse the concept of *jihad* and engage in forced conversions, Christians have far exceeded Muslims in the area of forced conversions.

According to Islamic doctrine, if faith does not spontaneously spring from one's deep convictions, it is neither sincere, nor acceptable to God. Quite simply a person cannot be forced to accept Islam (or any other religion, for that matter): "Let there be no compulsion in religion" (Qur'an, 2:256). Therefore, if a misguided Muslim does engage in *jihad* to force non-Muslims to accept Islam, he is violating basic Islamic principles: "Say, The Truth is from your Lord; Let him who will, believe, and let him who will, reject it" (Qur'an, 18:29). The Qur'an also advises Muslims to respond to non-Muslims with the words: "You have your religion, and I have mine" (109:6). The Qur'an also advises Muslims to: "Invite all to the Way of your Lord with wisdom and beautiful preaching, and argue with them in ways that are best and most gracious. For your Lord knows best who have strayed from His path, and who receive guidance. And if you punish, let your punishment be proportional to the wrong that has been done to you. But if you show patience, that is indeed the best course for those who are patient. And do be patient, for patience is from Allah. Nor grieve over them, and do not distress yourself because of their plots. For Allah is with those who restrain themselves, and those who do good." (16:125–128).

Muslims believe that Christians, who are part of the largest religion in the world with 2.1 billion adherents, have used force to gain converts. After all, the Crusades, the Spanish Inquisition, the Conquistadors in South America, the enslavement of African blacks in the 18th and 19th centuries, and European colonialism in Latin America, Africa, and Asia were by no means peaceful.

In short, those Muslims who did engage in spreading Islam by force and called it a *jihad* violated the basic moral and ethical principles of Islam: a) The Ten Commandments; (b) the Golden Rule, (c) he who kills/murders one person, it is as though he has murdered all of humanity, (d) "there shall be no compulsion in religion."

5. Islam encourages terrorism and suicide bombings.

The Qur'an clearly, categorically, and specifically condemns and prohibits terrorism and suicide. The indiscriminate killing of innocent people, which is always the result of terrorism and suicide missions engaged in by misguided Muslim zealots, is considered a sin in Islam. Human life is sacrosanct in Islam and only God has the right to bestow it and take it away. In fact, Islam emphasizes peace, moderation, and tolerance and opposes all types of violent extremism, including hostage taking, hijacking, planting bombs in public places, and killing innocent non-combatants. Below are some Qur'anic verses that address this issue:

- "Whoever kills a person not in retaliation for murder or to spread corruption in the land, it would be as if he murdered the whole of humankind. And (likewise) if anyone saved a life, it would be as if he saved the whole of humankind" (5:32).
- "Let there be no hostility except to those who practice oppression" (2:193)

Sensational Events in the Media about Islam and Muslims

While the terrorist attacks on America of September 11, 2001 may have heightened mass media coverage of Islam, Muslims, and Muslim countries, the World of Islam has been at the forefront of international news coverage since 1967, as the following list of major events illustrates:

- June 5, 1967: The Six-Day Arab-Israeli War begins with preemptive Israeli air strikes on Egypt and Syria. Israel occupies the Egyptian Sinai Peninsula and Gaza Strip, Syria's Golan Heights, and Jordan's West Bank. It quadruples the area of Israel's military occupation to four times its former geographical size. Israel's quick and spectacular victory demoralizes the Arabs.

- August 21, 1969: Michael Rohan, an Australian Christian fundamentalist, attempts to burn down the Al-Aqsa Mosque (literally, the furthest mosque) on the sacred Temple Mount in the old city of Jerusalem. The al-Aqsa Mosque is the third holiest Islamic shrine, after the great mosques in Makkah and Madina. This act of arson triggers protests throughout the Muslim world.

- September 22, 1969: Muslim heads of state meet in Rabat, Morocco, in response to the Al-Aqsa Mosque arson attack and decide to establish the Organization of the Islamic Conference (OIC) to represent the Muslim world/Islamic bloc.

- October 1973: The Yom Kippur War/Ramadan War/Arab-Israeli War that Egypt's Muhammad Anwar al-Sadat and Syria's Hafiz al-Assad initiate to take back the Egyptian Sinai and the Syrian Golan Heights that Israel conquered in the June 1967 Arab-Israeli War. Sadat and Assad are accused of invading Israel on *Yom Kippur* (Day of Atonement), one of the holiest days in the Jewish calendar because it is the day when Jews atone for their sins. Ironically, Sadat and Assad also attacked Israel during Islam's holiest month of Ramadan—the month when Muslims fast from dawn to dusk without food or water to atone for their sins as well.

- October 1973: First the predominantly Arab Muslim Organization of Arab Petroleum Exporting Countries (OAPEC) imposes an oil embargo on the United States and the Netherlands. Then, the Organization of Petroleum Exporting Countries (OPEC) raises oil prices to unprecedented levels through 1983.

- April 1975: In Lebanon, Christian Phalangists attack the increasingly restive Palestinians, sparking a civil war between the ruling Christian minority and the relatively poor, powerless, but restive Muslim majority. The Lebanese civil war goes on for the next fifteen years dragging in the other minorities.

- January 1978–February 1979: Islamic Revolution in Iran—the pro-Western and pro-American Shah is toppled by the Iranian masses and an anti-Western/anti-American Shi'a clerical establishment comes to power.

- November 4, 1979–January 20, 1981: American Embassy takeover and hostage crisis in Tehran, Iran, which results in negative mass media coverage of Islam (especially Shi'a Islam), Iran's clerical establishment, and Shi'a Muslims.

- November 20, 1979: Saudi Arabia's Wahhabi extremists take-over the Grand Mosque in Makkah that houses the Ka'abah. It takes two weeks for the elite French anti-terrorist unit and Saudi forces to end the siege of the Grand Mosque, which results in 160 people dead (including 75 Wahhabi zealots, 60 Saudi troops, and 25 civilian hostages and bystanders) and 175 zealots in the hands of Saudi authorities.

- December 24–27, 1979: The Soviet invasion of Afghanistan to keep the neighboring pro-Soviet Afghan regime in power and to crush the insurrection. The Soviet occupation of Afghanistan is fiercely resisted by the Afghan *mujahideen* (freedom fighters) with assistance from the U.S. and much of the Muslim world. The Soviets complete the withdrawal of all their fighting forces from Afghanistan as promised on February 15, 1989.

- September 1980–August 1988: Iran-Iraq War started by Saddam Hussein threatened the oil provided by Gulf countries through the Persian Gulf as well as peace in the region and in the world. Over one million Iranians and Iraqis lost their lives, thousands were wounded on both sides, several cities in both countries were devastated, Iraq used chemical weapons against Iranian troops and also sent SCUD missiles into Iranian cities. What is more, no one comes to Iran's assistance, while much of the Arab and Western worlds side with Saddam's regime during the war.

- October 6, 1981: Assassination by Egyptian revolutionary Islamists of Egyptian President Muhammad Anwar al-Sadat, who was condemned as a traitor by much of the global *ummah* (community of believers) for his historic visit to the disputed city of Jerusalem, which Muslims consider was militarily usurped from them by Israel with Western complicity, as well as Sadat's abandonment of the Palestinian cause by engaging in a separate peace treaty with Israeli Prime Minister Menachem Begin with the signing the Camp David Peace Accords (September 17, 1979.)

- June 6, 1982: Israel invades Lebanon to uproot the Palestine Liberation Organization's infrastructure, undermine the Muslim militias, and strengthen the Christian-dominated regime. By September, Israel pulls back to the Israeli-Lebanese border and a narrow "security zone" within Lebanon, 20,000 Lebanese are dead, over 100,000 wounded, and many thousands left homeless. The U.S. government-sponsored Multinational Force (comprising U.S. Marines, as well as French and Italian troops) arrives in Beirut to oversee the departure of PLO militias from Lebanon and act as peacekeepers.

- September 15–18, 1982: Maronite Christian Phalangist militiamen massacre several hundred Palestinian men, women, and children in the Sabra and Shatila Palestinian Refugee Camps in West Beirut. Israel is blamed for the massacre because the Israeli army under the leadership of General Ariel Sharon permitted the Phalangist militiamen into the camps.

- October 23, 1983: A Lebanese Shi'a suicide truck-bomber destroys the U.S. Marine headquarters in Beirut killing 242 Marines. Another suicide truck-bomber blows up the French military headquarters in Beirut, killing 58 French soldiers. This happens in retaliation for American troops siding with Lebanon's Christian minority against the Shi'a majority.

- January 1983–May 2000: Shi'a Hezbollah (Party of God) fighters that Iran had sent to protect and defend the predominantly Shi'a population of southern Lebanon also engage in suicide bombings against Israeli troops who occupy an 18 square mile swath of land across from the Israeli border in southern Lebanon. This strategy of "suicide bombings" or Hezbollah's so-called "martyrdom operations," finally bears fruit when Israeli Prime Minister decides to bring all Israeli troops back to Israel from southern Lebanon in May 2000.

- December 1987–August 1993: The First Palestinian *intifadah* (uprising) when Palestinian youth rise up to free themselves from Israeli occupation. Israel adopts an "iron fist policy" against the Palestinians in which the Palestinian population suffers grievously without any outside assistance. However, the *intifadah* does result in secret talks between Yasser Arafat's senior PLO negotiators and Israeli Prime Minister Yitzhak Rabin's representatives in Oslo, Norway, for the first seven months of 1993. The Declaration of Principles (DOP) drafted in secret talks in Oslo is signed by high-level PLO and Israeli government representatives on August 20, 1993.

- February 14, 1989: Iran's supreme spiritual leader Ayatollah Ruhollah Khomeini issues a *fatwa* (religious edict) condemning to death Salman Rushdie, the Indian Muslim novelist, for writing *The Satanic Verses*—a novel that slanders Prophet Muhammad and his family.

- August 2, 1990: Iraqi President Saddam Hussein orders his troops to invade and occupy the neighboring Arab Muslim oil-rich Emirate of Kuwait, claiming that Kuwait, which had been established and given its independence by the British colonialists, was historically part of Iraq.

55

Sensational Events in the Media about Islam and Muslims, cont'd

- August 9, 1990–January 15, 1991: The United States responds to the Iraqi takeover of Kuwait with Operation Desert Shield. It sends over 500,000 members of its armed forces to the Persian Gulf region to liberate Kuwait if the Iraqi army refuses to withdraw.
- January 17–February 28, 1991: Operation Desert Storm, in which the U.S. and its allies launch a massive military offensive against Iraq to liberate Kuwait. Their success in pushing Iraqi forces out is hailed as a major victory.
- January 11, 1992: The Algerian generals abort the national elections, which the Islamic Salvation Front (FIS) was winning, and unleash a reign of terror that lasts to this day.
- December 1992–March 1994: The U.S. humanitarian intervention in Somalia to feed starving Somalis turns into a nation-building effort that fails.
- 1992–2002: Kashmiri Muslims intensify their struggle to gain independence from India, but are ruthlessly suppressed by Indian troops.
- February 26, 1993: Misguided Muslim extremists detonate a truck bomb in the parking garage of the World Trade Center in New York City.
- September 13, 1993: The Oslo Declaration of Principles is greatly furthered when President Bill Clinton invites Arafat and Rabin to sign the DOP and shake hands on the White House lawn. Israel formally recognizes the PLO and gives them limited autonomy in the Gaza strip and in predominantly Palestinian Muslim West Bank towns.
- Spring 1992–December 1995: Serbian "ethnic cleansing"/genocide of Bosnian Muslims in the Bosnia-Herzegovina region of Yugoslavia
- 1994–Present: Russian state terrorism against the Chechen separatists in the Russian province of Chechnya
- August 7, 1998: In nearly simultaneous attacks, Al-Qaeda terrorists blow-up the American embassies in Nairobi, Kenya and Dar Es Salaam, Tanzania
- March–June 1999: Serbian "ethnic cleansing"/genocide of Kosovars (Albanian Muslims) in Yugoslavia's Kosovo province. The North Atlantic Treaty Organization (NATO) uses air power against Serbia to end Serbian state terrorism in Kosovo.
- September 1996–November 2001: The Taliban's puritanical Islamic rule in Afghanistan. Osama bin Laden comes to Afghanistan after being expelled from Sudan and establishes Al-Qaeda training camps.
- October 2000–Present: The second Palestinian *intifadah* and an intensification of an ongoing cycle of violence in the Israeli-Palestinian dispute, with Palestinian suicide bombings and Israeli Prime Minister Ariel Sharon's decision to militarily occupy the West Bank and Gaza (2001–2005)
- October 12, 2000: A misguided Muslim suicide bomber uses a motor boat full of explosives to ram and make a huge hole in the USS Cole off Yemen, killing 17 American sailors.
- September 11, 2001: American passenger airliners hijacked by misguided Muslim extremists are flown into the World Trade Center in New York City and the Pentagon in Washington, D.C. One hijacked plane crashes in a field in Pennsylvania. Over 3,000 people are killed.
- Fall 2001: The overthrow of the Taliban regime and uprooting of Al-Qaeda from Afghanistan by American forces

- October 12, 2002: A discotheque is bombed in Bali, Indonesia, killing 202 people. The attack is blamed on *Jama'ah al-Islamiyya* that is said to have ties to al-Qaeda. The majority of casualties are Australian vacationers.
- March 2003: The U.S. launches Operation Iraqi Freedom to overthrow Saddam Hussein's Ba'athist regime and bring democracy to Iraq.
- March 2003-Present: An insurrection plagues Iraq as Iraqi nationalists and misguided Muslim extremists engage in suicide bombings, kidnappings and beheadings of hostages, targeted assassinations, and economic sabotage.
- 2003–2004: Tragic ethnic violence in the Darfur province of western Sudan where government-sponsored Arab militiamen known as the *Janjaweed* (evil horsemen) conduct a campaign of terror to drive Darfur's black African Muslim and animist population from their farms
- March 11, 2004: Bombs explode on four commuter trains in Madrid, Spain, killing 191 people and injuring scores of others. The terrorist attack is the work of misguided Muslim extremists. The conservative Popular Party of Prime Minister Jose Maria Aznar loses Spain's national elections three days later to Socialist Party leader Jose Luis Rodriquez Zapatero. Aznar had sent Spanish troops to Iraq, a factor in the terrorist attack, while Zapatero promised to bring the Spanish troops home.
- April 2004: Revelations of American military police torturing Iraqi detainees at Abu Ghraib prison in Baghdad as well as information about torture of Muslim detainees in prisons in Guantanamo Bay, Cuba, and Afghanistan
- September 1–3, 2004: The Beslan school siege or hostage crisis, which began when armed Chechens, Inguish, and other misguided Muslim militants took hundreds of school children and adults hostage in the Russian town of Beslan in North Ossetia
- November 2, 2004: The murder of Dutch film maker Theo Van Gogh—great grandnephew of the celebrated Dutch painter Vincent Van Gogh—in the Netherlands at the hands of a Moroccan-Dutch Muslim extremist. Van Gogh had made a provocative and controversial film about violence against Muslim women in Islamic culture that aired on Dutch television.
- May 2005: Revelations of American soldiers and military police desecrating the Qur'an while interrogating Muslim prisoners and detainees
- July 7, 2005: Explosions in four subway stations and a bus in London, Britain, kill 59 civilians and wound scores of other people.

As a result of these and many other sensational international events highlighted in the world news, Islam is one of the most maligned and misunderstood religions. It is, therefore, imperative for non-Muslim students, scholars, journalists, politicians, and diplomats to attain a deeper and more meaningful understanding of Islam. It is also important for non-Muslims to differentiate between (a) the acts of the radicalized and desperate individuals driven by revolutionary religiopolitical ideologies, such as "Wahhabism/Salafism," (b) the acts of those who struggle against what they perceive as a foreign occupation of their ancestral homeland (such as Palestine, Chechnya, and Kashmir), and (c) the vast majority of the world's 1.3 billion Muslims who have coexisted harmoniously with their non-Muslim neighbors the world over.

- "Let there be no compulsion in religion. Truth stands out clearly from falsehood; whoever rejects evil and believes in God has grasped the most trustworthy handhold that never breaks. And God is All-Hearing and All-Knowing." (2:256)
- "And fight in the way of Allah those who fight you. But do not transgress the limits. Truly Allah loves not the transgressors" (2:190)

- "Let not the enmity of any people make you swerve to wrong and depart from justice" (5:8).
- "Those who spend (freely), whether in prosperity or adversity, who restrain their anger and pardon (all) human beings; For God loves those who do good" (3:134).
- "Humankind! We created you from a single (pair) of a male and female, and made you into nations and tribes, that ye

may know each other (not that ye may despise each other). Verily the most honored in the sight of God is (the) most righteous of you. And God has full knowledge and is well acquainted (with all things)" (49:13).

- "God does not forbid you from showing kindness and dealing justly with those who have not fought you about religion and have not driven you out of your homes. God loves those who are just." (60:8)
- "You who believe! Enter into Islam wholeheartedly; And follow not the footsteps of the Evil one; For he is to you An avowed enemy" (11:208).
- "Of all the communities raised among men you are the best, enjoining the good, forbidding the wrong, and believing in God."
- "…Nor kill (or destroy) yourselves…. If any do that in rancour and injustice, soon shall we cast them into the fire" (4:29-30).
- "And make not your own hands contribute to (your) destruction; but do good; for God loveth those who do good." (2:195).

The Prophet Muhammad made the following statements, which can be construed as condemning terrorism and suicide:

- "God has no mercy on one who has no mercy for others."
- "None of you truly believes until you wish for others what you wish for yourself."
- "Powerful is not he who knocks the other down; indeed powerful is he who controls himself in a fit of anger."
- "Indeed, whoever [intentionally] kills himself, then certainly he will be punished in the fire of hell, wherein he shall dwell forever."
- "Whoever kills himself with a weapon will have that weapon in his hand, and will kill himself forever in the fire of Hell."

Before every battle, Prophet Muhammad gave standing orders to his soldiers not to kill non-combatants (innocent men, women, and children, old people, and the sick); not to kill animals, destroy trees, burn crops, pollute waters, nor destroy homes, and houses of worship. Prophet Muhammad repeated these orders to his soldiers when he set out from Madina to conquer Makkah in 630 CE.

Prophet Muhammad once listed murder as the second biggest sin (after *shirk* or associating someone with God) and said that "The first cases that God will adjudicate on the Day of Judgment are those of murder."

Muslim revolutionaries and extremists have taken Qur'anic verses out of context, just as the Islamophobes and enemies of Islam are doing. What is more, misguided Muslim extremists have tried to divide the world into two principal camps/blocs: those who oppose Big Power control of Muslim countries and the exploitation of the Muslim world's resources through despotic, corrupt, and incompetent Muslim puppet regimes or the support of the status quo whereby the *ummah* will continue to be exploited and grow poorer and weaker while the Big Powers get richer and stronger at the expense of the Muslim world. President George W. Bush has also divided the world into two opposing camps/blocs with his statement, "You are either with us, or you are with the terrorists." Most Muslims tend to disagree with both the misguided Muslim revolutionaries/extremists as well the Bush administration's heavy-handed, unilateralist, and pre-emptive militaristic approach to solving the scourge of "terrorism." In

fact, both the misguided Muslim extremists and the Bush administration are doing everything possible to make the clash between the Islamic and Western civilizations inevitable.

Many Westerners constantly say, if Islam and Muslims are against terrorism, why don't Muslims strongly condemn it. The fact is that many prominent Muslims and Islamic organizations have condemned terrorism and suicide bombings against civilians as sinful acts that distort "true" Islam (as the Qur'anic quotes and Prophet Muhammad's *Hadith* clearly show); result in the death of many innocent Muslims as well as innocent non-Muslims; present Islam as a fanatical and violent faith, with uncivilized adherents; and create an environment of anarchy in Muslim countries thereby inhibiting their prospects for progress and prosperity.

6. Islam is intolerant of other religions.

Islam emphasizes tolerance. Several Qur'anic verses illustrate this honorable tradition:

- "There is no compulsion in religion" (2:256). This Qura'nic verse clearly implies that force must not be used to convert people.
- "O mankind! We created you from a single soul, male and female, and made you into peoples and tribes, so that you may come to know one another. Truly, the most honored of you in God's sight is the greatest of you in piety. God is All-Knowing, All-Aware" (49:13).
- "Did not Allah check one set of people by means of another, there would surely have been pulled down monasteries, churches, synagogues, and mosques, in which the name of Allah is commemorated in abundant measure" (22:40). In this verse, the Qur'an commands Muslims to respect and protect all houses of worship.

When Prophet Muhammad began governing Madina, he ordered all Muslims to deal with Christians and Jews with respect, kindness, and equality. A significant part of his final message focused on Muslims giving non-Muslims the same rights, provided they were law-abiding citizens. In Islamic Spain and in the Abbasid Empire, Christians and Jews enjoyed equal opportunities as Muslims did in getting into schools, colleges, research institutes, and jobs. The same tolerance was shown to non-Muslims in the Ottoman and Mughal Empires. It is not surprising, therefore, that many non-Muslim scientists and scholars made significant contributions to Islamic civilizations.

In his Farewell *Hajj*, among other things Prophet Muhammad said "One who kills a man under covenant (i.e. *dhimmi* or non-Muslim citizens of the Muslim state) will never smell the fragrance of Paradise."

Islam not only forbade Muslims from attacking people of other faiths, but encouraged *Al-Hewar Al-Aqaeedi* (interfaith dialogue to foster mutual understanding).

Islam is the only non-Christian faith that reveres *Issa* (Arabic name of Jesus Christ) as one of God's greatest messengers to humankind, believes he brought the *Injeel* (Gospels of Jesus Christ), and awaits his second coming. Of all the prophets, Jesus is probably the most written about in the Qur'an. In fact, there are about ninety Qur'anic verses spread across fifteen Qur'anic *surahs* (chapters) that favorably mention Jesus. Three

Qur'anic surahs: *Aal-e-Imran, Al-Maida,* and *Mariam,* have several Qur'anic verses devoted to Jesus and his noble mission. Various stories in the Qur'an discuss Jesus' miraculous birth, ministry, disciples, and the message he propagated to worship and obey the One True God (the Creator). During his prophetic mission, Jesus performed many miracles. The Qur'an informs us that Jesus said: "I have come to you with a sign from your Lord: I make for you out of clay, as it were, the figure of a bird, and breathe into it and it becomes a bird by God's leave. And I heal the blind, and the lepers, and I raise the dead by God's leave (3:49). In the Qur'an, Jesus is also believed to have said: "To attest the law which was before me. And to make lawful to you part of what was forbidden you; I have come to you with a sign from your Lord, so fear God and obey me (3:50)

Islam also regards Mary, mother of Jesus, as one of the most pure and exalted women of all creation. As the Qur'an says: "Behold! the angel said: "God has chosen you and purified you and has chosen you above the women of all nations. O Mary! God gives you the good news of a word from Him, whose name shall be Messiah, Jesus son of Mary, honored in this world and the hereafter, and one of those brought near to God" (3:42).

There are also several of Prophet Muhammad's *hadith* that portray Jesus' teaching and the ultimate purpose of his first and second coming. Islam regards its teachings to be a re-affirmation and culmination of the teachings of previous monotheistic religions like Judaism and Christianity. Hence, all Muslims believe in Moses and Jesus as Prophets of God. Prophet Muhammad was commanded to recite in the Qur'an: "Say, We believe in God, and that which was revealed unto us, and Isaac and Jacob, and the tribes; and that which was entrusted unto Moses and Jesus; and the Prophets from their Lord; We make no distinction between any of them, and unto Him we have submitted" (3:84).

In fact, if a Muslim does not revere Jesus and his teachings, he/she is considered a bad Muslim.

Jesus Christ's mother, Mary, is referred to as Maryam in the Qur'an. Muslims, like Christians, revere her as the purest woman in all creation. The Qur'an describes the Annunciation (Anchangel Gabriel's announcement of Jesus' incarnation to Mary) as follows: "Behold! God has chosen you, and purified you, and chosen you above the women of all nations. O Mary, God gives you good news of a word from Him whose name shall be the messiah, Jesus, son of Mary, honored in this world and the hereafter, and one of those brought near to God. He shall speak to the people from his cradle and in maturity, and shall be of the righteous." When Mary said "O my Lord! How shall I have a son when no man has touched me?" Gabriel said: "Even so; God creates what He will. When He decrees a thing, He says to it, "Be!" and it is" (Qur'an, 3:42–47). Many Muslims name their daughters Maryam after her. Also Prophet Muhammad once said that one of the greatest ladies in history is Jesus' mother: Mary.

When someone asked Prophet Muhammad, "what is religion?" He answered, "One's regard and conduct towards others."

7. The "Nation of Islam" and Islam are Synonymous.

It is true that the African American "Nation of Islam" that emerged in the United States in the 1930s has Islam in its name. But for the most part, the Nation of Islam (NOI) is very dif- ferent from mainstream Islam that Prophet Muhammad propagated in the Arabian Peninsula nearly fifteen-hundred years ago (610–632 CE).

The emergence of The Nation of Islam can be traced back to Wallace Fard Muhammad—an itinerant peddler selling trinkets, silks, and raincoats—in the predominantly African American ghettoes of Detroit, Michigan, in the early 1930s. He claimed to have been born in Makkah in the Arabian Peninsula and travelled widely in Africa. A year later, when Fard had several hundred followers, he established the first University of Islam (with a primary, middle, and high school) and Temple No. 1. Drawing on claims previously made by Noble Drew Ali (1886–1929)—founder of the Moorish Holy Temple of Science in Newark, New Jersey, in 1913—Fard told American blacks that they could trace their lineage back to the ancient and distinguished Muslim tribe of Shabazz in Africa; that racist whites were blue-eyed devils who would continue to deprive blacks the fruits of their labor and the benefits of American life; that blacks in the United States could free themselves from white racist domination, as well as earn God's favor only through self-knowledge, self-help, self-love, self-sufficiency, and solidarity in their own united Black Muslim Nation that was separate from the white race; that Allah had summoned him to redeem the original race of humankind: the black race; and that only through the Lost-Found Nation of Islam, with belief in a black God, could they expect to realize their just economic, political, and social rights.

By 1934, Fard had converted several hundred blacks to the Nation of Islam; developed a paramilitary organization, the Fruit of Islam, trained in the use of firearms to protect the Black Nations members and institutions; trained a spiritual minister and a cadre of administrators to run the organization; and anointed Elijah Poole (1897–1975)—a former member of the Moorish Temple of Science—as his successor. Then Fard disappeared without a trace, leaving Elijah Poole in charge of the organization.

Elijah Poole adopted the name Elijah Muhammad, moved to Chicago to establish Temple No. 2, and gave the impression that he was Gods prophet, while Fard, who had anointed him, was the divine savior of the black race, akin to the second coming of Jesus Christ, the long-awaited Messiah, and Mahdi. Elijah Muhammad claimed that God had originally created blacks to rule His kingdom, and that whites were the product of a eugenics experiment that had gone terribly wrong and created the devilish white race that sought to enslave blacks. On another occasion, Elijah Muhammad said that an evil scientist called Yaqub created whites in a fit of anger. According to him, the Nation of Islam's principal mission was to prepare blacks for the coming Battle of Armageddon, in which blacks would prevail over whites and regain their God-given right to control the world.

Besides Fard's divinity, his own prophethood, and the teachings of black supremacy and racial separation, Elijah Muhammad's pseudo-Islamic Nation of Islam was based on the following key ideas: the Qur'an and the scriptures of all the Old Testament prophets are equally valid (while Muslims believe the latter have been corrupted and only the Qur'an remains the authentic Word of God); on the Day of Judgment, only the souls of all human beings would be resurrected (while Muslims believe in the physical resurrection of all dead human beings, who

Table 6: Islam and Nation of Islam: A Comparative Overview

Key Subjects	Islam (Worldwide)	Nation of Islam (U.S.A.)
Mainstream Religion or Pseudo-Islamic Movement	• An established mainstream religion, very similar to Judaism and Christianity, that began in Palestine and the Arabian Peninsula. • Muslims believe that it can be traced all the way back to Adam (who was Islams first Prophet) • So comprehensive and holistic, that it is also referred to as a way of life	• A pseudo-Islamic movement inspired by charismatic black leaders—Wallace Fard 1930–1934), Elijah Muhammad (1934–1975), Wallace D. Muhammad (1975–1980), and Louis Farrakhan (1980–Present) in the United States. • Elijah Muhammad claimed that God created blacks to rule His kingdom, and whites were the result of a eugenics experiment that had gone terribly wrong, causing the creation of a devilish white race seeking to enslave blacks. On another occasion, Elijah Muhammad said that an evil scientist called Yaqub created whites in a fit of anger, and the Nation of Islams principal mission was to prepare blacks for the Battle of Armageddon in which blacks would regain their God-given right to control the world.
Concept of God	• Believe in Allah—the one and only unseen creator and sustainer of His creation—who is transcendent, omnipotent, omnipresent, omniscient, eternal, just, and merciful. • Believe God has never appeared in physical form on earth	• Believe God appeared in the person of a black man, Wallace D. Fard, in Detroit, Michigan, in July 1930. • Some believe Fard was the long awaited "messiah" of the Christians and the mahdi (savior) of the Muslims
Last Prophet	According to the Qur'an, Prophet Muhammad ibn Abdullah (570–632 CE) is Gods **last** prophet; Archangel Gabriel revealed Gods final message to the Prophet; and that this final message, embodied in the Qur'an, was the continuation of the same message that He sent earlier to Abraham, David, Moses, and Jesus.	Believe Elijah Muhammad and not Muhammad ibn Abdullah was Gods last messenger
Adherents	It is a global religion with 1.3 billion Muslims (one-fifth of the worlds population).	• It is an African American pseudo-Islamic movement that emerged in the United States in the early 1930s, • Almost all of its more than 250,000 followers are in the U.S.
Sacred Texts	• While believing in the original Old Testament, Muslims revere the Qur'an as Gods last and best preserved message to humankind. • Believe the Qur'an was revealed to Muhammad by Archangel Gabriel over a period of 22 years (610–632 CE), and was Muhammads greatest miracle. • Do not believe that the Psalms of David, the Hebrew Bible, Old Testament, and the Gospels of Jesus Christ are in their original form. Thus, do not believe that they contain the original Word of God.	• While believing in the scriptures of all Gods Prophets (including the Old Testament and the Qur'an), consider Elijah Muhammads religiopolitical ideology as Gods last message to humankind. • Believe that one day both the Bible and Qur'an will have to give way to the Nation of Islams "Holy Book."
Authentic *Hadith*	• Follow the compilation of Prophet Muhammads authentic sayings (hadith), which are the second most important textual source after the Qur'an. • Considered to be an indispensable guide for understanding Islam.	• Not essential to the core beliefs and practices of the faith, but selectively invoked from time to time.
Shariah Law (Islam Law)	• Devout Muslims should follow Gods laws embodied in the shariah in their daily lives. • Islamists would like to impose it in Islamic societies	Do not follow the Islamic shariah law.
Earning Gods Favor	Having faith (iman), performing the five obligatory duties (faraidh), following the advice in the Qur'an and Prophet Muhammads Sunnah, doing good works in society, and leading a righteous life.	Loving oneself, enlightening oneself, working diligently to improve ones status in life, promoting solidarity among blacks, and doing good works to improve the lot of underprivileged African Americans.
Race	The teachings of Islam hold that all human beings are equal before God and should be treated with equity and justice on earth. This anti-racist message is a factor in Islams universal appeal.	Religious ideology is based on the racial superiority of blacks; whites are considered "the blue-eyed devils" who have dominated and exploited the black race.
The Afterlife	• Believes that there is only one life in this finite world. • After death, individuals await Judgment Day, when they will be resurrected, judged, and sent to Paradise for doing good deeds or to Hell for doing evil deeds.	• Do not believe in a corporal resurrection, nor in Heaven and Hell.

Table 6: Cont'd

Key Subjects	Islam (Worldwide)	Nation of Islam (U.S.A.)
Ritual Prayer	Ritual prayers (*salah*) are required five times a day and include: standing, bowing, prostration with forehead touching the ground, and sitting on the floor (while reciting Qur'anic verses). After the ritual prayers are over, most Muslims say a spontaneous individual supplication (du`a) asking God for His forgiveness, and petitioning Him for assistance in their lives.	• No obligation to perform the five daily prayers. • When ritual prayers are performed, there is no bowing or prostration, only standing and sitting. • After the ritual prayers, supplication (du`a) is often said.
Fasting	Adults are required to fast (*sawm*) from dawn to dusk during the month of Ramadan (the ninth month of Islams lunar calendar).	• Fasting occurs in December (the twelfth month of the Gregorian solar calendar) only. • Fasting in the month of Ramadan is optional.
Almsgiving	An annual offering of 2.5 percent of ones total wealth is to be given to the poor and needy.	An annual donation for the poor called the "poor due" is expected. There is no fixed amount stipulated.
Pilgrimage	Pilgrimage to Makkah (*hajj*) is required for all believers once in a lifetime if finances and health permit.	The *hajj* is not required; Louis Farrakhan has made a pilgrimage to Makkah
Spiritual Leaders/Clerics (People of the Cloth)	*Mullahs, maulanas, moulvis, ulama* (Islamic scholars), *muftis* (authorities in Sunni Islam), and *ayatollahs* (authorities in Shi`ah Islam)	Ministers
Major Sects or Branches	Sunni and Shi`ah sects; several subsects within each. A few other sects (Ahmadis/Qadiyanis, Bahais, and Druze) have evolved into distinct faiths, but comprise a very small percentage of the total Muslim population.	Elijah Muhammads son Warith Deen Muhammad took two-thirds of the Nation of Islam with him into mainstream Sunni Islam, depleting the Nation of Islam membership.
Greetings among the Faithful	*Salaam Alaykum* (Peace be on/with you) and *Wa`Alaykum as-Salaam* (peace be on/with you too); call coreligionists "brother" and "sister."	
Religion and Politics	• Islamists believe religion and politics are inseparable and the government should be based on Islamic law (shariah), whereas Muslim secularists governing most Muslim countries believe that "church and state" should be separate.	Participation in American politics was discouraged until 1983, when Louis Farrakhan encouraged his followers to support Jesse Jackson's run for the presidency.
Proselytization	Both encourage the propagation of the faith and proselytization.	
Day of Worship	• For Muslims, every day is consecrated by offering the ritual prayers at dawn, noon, late afternoon, after dusk, and before midnight • Muslims are enjoined to offer congregational prayers in mosques/Islamic centers at noontime on Fridays.	Friday is a major congregational day of prayer, not for ritual prayers (*salah*) but to say a spontaneous individual prayer (*du`a*) and listen to a Minister.
Main Holy Days	• Festival of the Fast Breaking (*Eid al-Fitr*) at the end of the ninth Islamic calendar month of Ramadan • Festival of Sacrifice (*Eid al-Azha*) at the close of the ritual of *hajj* in the 12th Islamic calendar month of *Dhul Hijjah*, commemorating Abrahams willingness to sacrifice his son Ishmael.	• Celebrate Festival of the Fast Breaking around Christmas time every year. • Do not follow the Islamic lunar calendar, but the Western Gregorian calendar; so, they do not celebrate their holidays at the same time as mainstream Muslims.
"Unclean" Foods	• The Qur'an enjoined Muslims to eat kosher meat and avoid consuming pork. • Muslims have also been commanded not to imbibe any intoxicants (alcohol and drugs).	Nation of Islam followers are forbidden to eat pork, smoke cigarettes, or imbibe intoxicants (alcohol or drugs).

had turned to dust, from the time of Creation); adherents should pray to God every day (but not the five ritual Islamic prayers in Arabic that Muslims are expected to offer daily); adherents should fast during December, but fasting during the Islamic lunar month of Ramadan is optional; a poor due is required on income only and this goes to support only black members of the Nation of Islam (not the 2.5 percent of wealth that Muslims are obligated to contribute annually to needy Muslims irrespective of their color, ethnicity, or nationality anywhere in the world);

and there is no obligation to perform the *hajj* during the twelfth Islamic month of *Dhul-Hijjah*.

On Elijah Muhammad's death in 1975, his son, Wallace D. Muhammad, assumed the leadership of the Nation of Islam. He changed his name to Warith Deen Muhammad; called his father merely a teacher and not a divinely sent prophet; rejected the anti white racism of his father; encouraged non blacks to join the Nation of Islam; did away with the rigid dress code (including the long garments that covered women from head to toe); encouraged members to participate in American politics and permitted them to join the U.S. armed forces; renamed the organization the American Muslim Mission, then World Community of Islam, and finally Community of Al-Islam in the West; and in 1985 asked his followers to join mainstream Sunni Islam.

In 1980, Louis Farrakhan, born Louis Eugene Walcott in 1933—the charismatic minister and spellbinding orator of the Nation of Islam's New York temple—become the leader of a breakaway faction within the Nation of Islam that was committed to espousing much of Elijah Muhammad's religious ideology, while tempering the message of separatism. Interesting, Farrakhan too has gradually brought the Nation of Islam closer to mainstream Islam since the early 1990s.[4]

8) Islam is sexist

The stereotypical image of Muslim women wearing the *hijab* (veil) is all too prevalent in many non-Muslim minds (especially, images of Afghan and Pakistani women wearing the *burqa* (a tent like apparel that covers women from head to their toes with only a net in front of the face to see and breathe) or Iranian women wearing the *chador* (loose fitting black cloth that religious Iranian women wear to cover their head and body); forced to stay home all the time to take care of the children, cook, and clean the house; forbidden to shop without a male family member, work outside the home, and to drive a car; and subjugated and abused by insensitive Muslim men who often have four wives and large families. Although some Muslim countries may very well have laws relegating women to second class status (as Afghanistan did under the Taliban and Saudi Arabia does even today), this should not be seen as coming from Islam. Many of these countries are still developing societies where male chauvinism is part of the customs and traditions of these patriarchal cultures.

The following quotations from the Qur'an and Prophet Muhammad's *Hadith*—two of Islam's major textual sources—show that Islam actually raised the status of women. Unfortunately, patriarchal societies, male chauvinism, and cultural traditions in Muslim countries are holding women back (just as they are in non-Muslim societies like Japan, India, Latin America, and sub-Sahara Africa).

- In the Qur'anic account of Creation, woman was not created from the rib of man. Rather, the first person (indefinite gender) was created, and then that person's mate was created (4:1). Moreover, Eve was not considered the temptress and the cause of original sin; both Adam and Eve were equally responsible for the sin in the Garden of Eden (7:20–25; 20:21).

- The Qur'an prohibits the pagan Arab practice of female infanticide prevalent in pre-Islamic Arabia: "You shall not kill your children for fear of want; We will provide for them and for you. To kill them is a great sin" (17:31)

- In the Arabian peninsula of the sixth century CE, women who were lucky to survive to adulthood were treated like chattel, sold into marriage by their fathers, kidnapped, raped, and purchased both as concubines and as members of large harems. Some tribal chieftains had as many as fifty wives. Prophet Muhammad abhorred the practice of forced marriages made by a woman's guardian and instead converted marriage into a legal agreement or civil contract between two consenting individuals.

- Arabs in Muhammad's times had as many as ten or more wives, and considered them "property." Some tribal chieftains had up to fifty wives. Moreover, Arabs in those times fought many tribal wars, which resulted in numerous male fatalities. Consequently there was an overabundance of widows and orphans. Muhammad felt that through marriage the warring tribes could be brought closer, while providing care for widows and orphans. However, it was the Qur'an that ended the practice of concubines and harems, and limited the number of women any one man could marry to four, "provided they were treated equally" (4:3). The Qur'an later added that it was impossible for a man to do justice to more than one wife (4:129). It is also evident when one looks at the *ummah*, most Muslim men have only one wife. It is a very tiny percentage of wealthy and powerful Muslims who can afford more than one wife and think they can treat them equally, and thus have more than one wife. Of course, some Muslim men have also abused this privilege. I would venture to guess that no more than 0.1% of the 1.3 billion men may have more one wife.

- Islam gave women inheritance rights in the sixth century, long before the practice became common in the West. Although women were given half the amount assigned to corresponding males, this was still a big step forward in the Arabia of those days (4:11). This is in sharp contrast to many Western cultures, where until only a couple of centuries ago, daughters could not inherit anything if there were sons in the family. In fact, even in Great Britain, the so-called mother of democracies, women were granted the right to own property independent of their husbands only in 1870.

- The bridal gift was no longer payable to the guardian, but to the woman directly, to do with what she wanted. A woman was also given the right to own property, manage it herself, and bequeath it to whomsover she chose (4:11).

- A woman could earn her own living as an independent individual, without any obligation to contribute her income or wealth to her husband or her family (4:32).

- The Qur'an states: "O you who believe! You are forbidden to inherit women against their will. Nor should you treat them with harshness, that you may take away part of the dower you have given them, except where they have been guilty of open lewdness; On the contrary, live with them on a footing of kindness and equity. (4:19)

- The Qur'an emphasizes that all people, men and women, are equal, and "the noblest among you in the sight of God is the most Godfearing and the best in conduct" (46:13). It also states that a woman on the Day of Judgment will be absolutely equal to a man (4:124)

- The Qur'an also states: "They [women] are an apparel for you [men] and you are an apparel for them" (2:187). This Qur'anic verse is encouraging men and women to protect each other from dishonor and sin. It could also imply that a woman lends dignity and adds beauty to the existence of man, as man does to that of a woman. In other words, each sex complements the other, and neither is inferior in status and dignity.

- "Men and women who have surrendered, believing men and believing women, obedient men and obedient women, truthful men and truthful women, enduring men and enduring women, humble men and humble women, men and women who give charity, men who fast and women who fast, men and women who guard their private parts, men and women who remember God often—for them God has prepared forgiveness and a mighty wage" (33:35).

- "And We have enjoined on man to be good to his parents; In travail upon travail did his mother bear him....Show gratitude to Me and to thy parents: To Me is thy final Goal" (31:14) and "We have enjoined on man kindness to his parents; In pain did his mother bear him, and in pain did she given him birth (46:15).

- The tradition of veiling in Islam is associated with Islam because of a Qur'anic passage that states, "Say to the believing women that they should lower their gaze and guard their modesty. They should draw their veils over the bosoms and not display their beauty" (24:31) The Qur'an emphasizes modesty in dress for men as well, "Tell the believing men to lower their gaze and be modest" (24:30). So, the Qur'an recommends modesty in dress for both men and women, but does not mandate it or specify a particular type of covering. No wonder, millions of practicing Muslim women all over the world do not see the need to wear the *hijab*.

- During the *hajj* (pilgrimage) or *umrah* in Makkah, woman wear headscarves, but do not cover their face; walk shoulder to shoulder with their male family member(s); and pray side by side with their husband, brother(s), or son(s).

- Prophet Muhammad's progressive attitudes toward women can best be illustrated in his first marriage to Khadijah. She was a confident and mature widow, and an enterprising and self-actualized businesswoman who ran a successful trading company herself; earned her living outside the home in a patriarchal, male chauvinist, and sexist society; was the Prophet's employer under whom he actively and happily worked; and was fifteen years older than him (she was forty and he was twenty-five) when she proposed a love marriage in an era when arranged marriages were common. For nearly fifteen years thereafter, Muhammad and Khadijah were partners in their international trading company—the first recorded male-female partnership in the region. Prophet Muhammad never asked Khadijah to wear a veil or seclude herself at home, or even to stop interacting with men. She was the first person with whom he shared the news of Archangel Gabriel visiting him in the cave of Hira. Intimately knowing his impeccable character, she was the one who reassured him that God had anointed him as His Prophet, and she became his first convert. She also decided to contribute her entire fortune, time, and support to the spread of Islam in the teeth of fierce persecution by most of the residents of Makkah.

- Prophet Muhammad never stopped women from working outside the home during his time. Some were battlefield nurses, who were skilled in patching up wounds; others were well-versed in the use of herbal remedies; still others, ran their own businesses.

- Below are some of Prophet Muhammad's most noteworthy *Hadith* relating to the status of women in Islam. All of them can be found in two of the most highly reputable sources, namely, Sahih Muslim and Sahih Bukhari.

- Prophet Muhammad often stated that "all people are equal, as equal as the teeth of a comb. There is no merit of an Arab over a non-Arab, or of a white over a black person, or of a male over a female. Only God-fearing people merit preference."

- Three famous *Hadith* attributed to Prophet Muhammad are "Paradise lies at the feet of thy mother," "The most perfect believers are the best in conduct and best of you are those who are best to their wives," and "He who wishes to enter Paradise must please his father and mother."

- A woman can retain her name and does not have to adopt her husband's surname after she gets married. Prophet Muhammad's daughter Fatimah bint Muhammad remained Fatimah bint (daughter of) Muhammad even after she married Ali ibn Abu Talib.

- When several girls complained to Prophet Muhammad that the boys in their classes were surpassing them in learning the Qur'an and hadith, the Prophet assigned the girls special time for instruction so that they might catch up.

- It is nevertheless true that in Islam a woman is enjoined to dress modestly in public and give her full commitment to being a homemaker first and foremost. But what is often not mentioned is that Muslim men are expected to dress modestly too.

- Women in most Western countries—which have been developing democratic institutions over centuries instead of only a few decades, as in independent Muslim countries—did not gain the right to vote until the twentieth century. Great Britain enfranchised women in 1918, the United States in 1920, France in 1944, and Switzerland in 1971.

- While five Muslim women have governed Muslim countries the United States, the preeminent power in the Western world, has yet to have a female vice president or president.

- Benazir Bhutto was sworn in as Pakistan's prime minister in 1988. Although she lost power in 1990, she was popularly reelected by millions of Pakistanis in 1993.

- Bangladesh has had two female prime ministers since 1991: Khaleda Zia and Sheikh Hasina Wajed. Khalida Zia was Bangladesh's prime minister in 1991. Her party lost its majority in 1996. She was succeeded in power by Sheikh Hasina Wajed. In October 2001, when Hasina Wajed's party lost its majority, power reverted back to Khaleda Zia.

- Turkey elected Tansu Ciller as prime minister in 1993. Although she lost her position in 1996, she was appointed as foreign minister. Ciller was to serve as prime minister again in 1997, but her coalition government lost its majority later that year.

- Megawati Sukarnoputri served as the president of Indonesia (2001–2005)—the most populous Muslim country in the world, with over 200 million Muslims (and 20 million non-Muslims).

ISLAMOPHOBIA AND ANTI-WESTERNISM: TWO SIDES OF THE SAME COIN

For the first one-thousand years of Islamic history (610–1605 CE), Christian Europeans viewed Islam as a monolithic, powerful, and hostile adversary both militarily and intellectually.

Muslims not only enjoyed considerable military and political success against the Europeans, but also made remarkable contributions in the sciences and humanities (see Chapter 1). Additionally, Islam posed a serious religious challenge by winning millions of converts away from Christianity. Nothing before or since—with the exception of twentieth century Communism—has so alarmed the West as the Islamic challenge to Western supremacy. Unable to subdue Muslim armies on the field of battle, Christian Europeans vilified Muslims and denigrated Islam, describing it as a faith founded on deception and clumsy plagiarism of Jewish and Christian scriptures. Western propagandists depicted Muslims as gullible, emotional, and violent. Thus, post-9-11 Islamophobia (distrust and fear of Islam and Muslims) is merely the resurrection of those latent anti-Islamic misperceptions in the West.

Although Judaism, Christianity, and Islam shared a similar origin, different interpretations of God's message and an emphasis on these differences led to interreligious conflict. The Christian-Muslim conflict markedly increased when Muslims conquered Jerusalem (Palestine/Israel) in 638 CE, Andalusia (Spain) in 755 CE, and at different times conquered parts of southern Italy, central Europe and southern France. Christian-Muslim relations further deteriorated when Pope Urban II called on European Christians to rid the "wicked Heathens" (Muslims) from the Holy Land (1095 CE). While the Crusades waxed and waned for the next two-hundred years (1097–1291 CE), European Christians vilified and demonized Islam, Prophet Muhammad, and Muslims. This anti-Islamic propaganda profoundly influenced Western thinking about Islam and Muslims, and has carried over into future generations of Europeans.

Anti-Islamic/anti-Muslim sentiment was further compounded by the three-hundred year long *Reconquista* (1200–1492 CE) in which European Christians succeeded in gradually reconquering Andalusia from the Moors (Muslims). Muslim-Christian animus peaked during the Spanish Inquisition (1492 CE), instituted by King Ferdinand and Queen Isabella, when the majority of Muslims who refused to convert to Christianity faced imprisonment, torture, death, burning at the stake, or exile. Islamophobia generated by the Crusades and the Reconquista continued unabated due to the periodic military battles between the Ottoman Empire and European Christians for over five hundred years (1345-1918 CE).

Even during the European Renaissance (1350–1650 CE)—sparked in part by Muslims engaging in peaceful trade and commerce—and during the European Enlightenment (18th century), Islam continued to be maligned as a threat to Christendom and rationality. The Enlightenment scholars, while courageously debunking Christian Church propaganda, which had stigmatized Islam as a perverse hedonistic faith, were themselves particularly unenlightened about Islam, Muslims, and the Muslim world. In his Philosophical Dictionary, Voltaire, a prominent Enlightenment philosopher, referred to Prophet Muhammad as "a brazen impostor who deceived imbeciles."[5] Likewise, the paintings of Jean-Auguste-Dominique Ingres portrayed Ottoman Turks lolling around in their harems and thereby reinforced the stereotype of Muslims as permissive and promiscuous misogynists.

The rise of Europe intellectually, economically, politically, and militarily led to European imperialism and colonialism.

Consequently, Muslim-Christian relations plummeted when European Powers encroached on the fragmented and vulnerable Muslim societies in Africa, and then in Asia. The era of European colonialism peaked just after World War I, when Britain and France carved up the vanquished Ottoman Empire's Middle East possessions. During the European colonialist era, Islam was again reviled as a retrogressive religion. Devout Muslims were denigrated as backward. Muslims who fought to defend their land and their beliefs from the occupiers were called "terrorists," hunted down, imprisoned, tortured, and killed. Not understanding the Muslim mindset and their dedication to Islam, European colonialists glorified modernization and Westernization. Missionary/parochial schools as well as secular public schools were established to educate Muslims so that they could help the European colonialists govern their colonies. Ironically, it was the graduates of these Westernized schools that spearheaded the secular nationalist independence movements that swept the Muslim world in the aftermath of World War II.

When the Western Powers decolonized, they often left their colonies in the control of the brown-skinned, black-skinned, and yellow-skinned Muslim elite, who thought, dressed, spoke, and behaved the same as the departed Western colonizers. The legacy of European colonization was the split between the Westernized Muslim elite, who were determined to continue the modernization of their countries along Western lines, and the traditional religious masses who yearned for an Islamic state.

In the aftermath of World War II, the world also witnessed the decline of European Powers and the rise of two superpowers: the United States and the Soviet Union. During the Cold War (1947–1988), the U.S.-led bloc and the Soviet-led bloc kept their Muslim secularist allies in power in the developing Muslim countries with economic, military, and/or intelligence assistance. Although most of this aid was spent on industrialization, urbanization, and a security apparatus (armed forces, intelligence services, and police), some of the economic aid was used for prestige projects (such as colossal factories and huge government buildings). Some of this aid was also siphoned off into the Western bank accounts of influential political leaders, generals, bureaucrats, businessmen, and landlords who comprised the elite. It is not surprising, therefore, that the religiously-active Muslim masses (Islamists) came to see these Muslim secularist leaders as corrupt collaborators and pawns of the Western Powers or the Soviet Union. Whenever Islamists challenged the pro-Western elite, they were ruthlessly suppressed by the regimes' security forces, which had been trained and equipped by Western Powers. In reporting these clashes, the national and international media supported the pro-Western modernizers over the Islamists, labelling them as "Marxists," "Communists," "Muslim fanatics," or "terrorists."

ANTI-AMERICANISM IN THE MUSLIM WORLD: A CAUSAL ANALYSIS

In 1988, Alvin Z. Rubinstein and Donald E. Smith published an article, "Anti-Americanism in the Third World," wherein they defined anti-Americanism as "any hostile action or expression that becomes part and parcel of an undifferentiated attack on the foreign policy, society, culture, and values of the United

States."[6] Rubinstein and Smith claimed that anti-Americanism was growing exponentially in much of Asia, Africa, the Middle East, and Latin America, and causing major political and socio-economic problems for U.S. leaders in all facets of government, business, education, culture, and religion.[7] They also wrote that "the United States is still the lightening rod for much of the progress and chaos, hope and fear, prospects and resentments, inspiration and revulsion that permeates the thinking and policies of Third World elites."[8]

Rubinstein and Smith classify anti-Americanism into four types: issue-oriented, ideological, instrumental, and revolutionary. In this section, I will apply these four types of anti-Americanism to the Muslim world, by which I primarily mean the fifty-seven Organization of Islamic Conference (OIC) countries discussed in this book. However, before defining each of the four types of anti-Americanism and giving examples from the World of Islam for each of them, I would like to state that anti-Americanism began in the aftermath of World War II. From that time onwards, European Powers declined and surrendered their colonial possessions in Africa and Asia, while the United States emerged as a superpower (along with the Soviet Union), and dominated the world stage like a colossus. Since the U.S. became the economic, military, political, and sociocultural leader of the Western world, it inherited the anti-Western hostility dating back to the Crusades. Therefore, anti-Americanism is an expression of a broader anti-Westernism that has been around for over a thousand years.

Issue-Oriented Anti-Americanism

The first and most prevalent type of anti-Americanism in the Rubinstein and Smith typology is issue-oriented anti-Americanism. In this form of anti-Americanism, individuals and groups from developing countries opposed to U.S. policies and actions engage in verbal and/or violent military attacks directed against U.S. governmental institutions and personnel.[9] Some of the most prominent examples of issue-oriented anti-Americanism in the Muslim world have occurred in Iran, Lebanon, Libya, Sudan, Afghanistan, Somalia, and Iraq.

The biggest factor fueling issue-oriented anti-Americanism is the economic, military, and political support that the U.S. government has given to pro-American dictatorial, corrupt, and incompetent rulers/regimes all over the Muslim world since the late 1940s. Many of these regimes, have done a deplorable job of developing democratic institutions alleviating poverty, addressing the basic human needs of their populations, or bridging the growing gap between the rich minority and the poor majority. Thousands of opposition leaders and activists have lost their jobs, and have been imprisoned, tortured, and killed by these unpopular dictatorial regimes. The striking contrast between America's rhetoric of human rights, freedom, and democracy, and its unwillingness to recognize the brutality of these regimes is galling for both the victims of these pro-American regimes and informed observers all over the world.

In fact, the United States and other Western Powers have been ambivalent in persuading their allied Muslim autocrats such as the Shah of Iran (who left Iran in January 1979), Saudi King Fahd ibn Abdul Aziz ibn Saud (who died in August 2005) and now Saudi King Abdullah ibn Abdul Aziz ibn Saud, Indonesian President Suharto (ousted in 1998); Egyptian President Muhammad Hosni Mubarak, Pakistani President Pervaiz Musharraf, Morocco's King Hassan II (who died in 1999), Jordan's King Hussein (who died in 1999), Algeria's President Abdelaziz Bouteflika, Bahrain's King Hamad ibn Isa Al Khalifah, Qatar's King Sheikh Hamad bin Khalifa Al Thani, Qatar Uzbekistan's President Islam Karim, Kazakhistan's President Nursultan Abishuly Nazarbayev democratize because they fear the Islamists could come to power through democratic elections and adversely affect their national interests. The 1979 Islamic Revolution, which toppled the Shah of Iran's pro-American regime, brought to power Ayatollah Ruhollah Khomeini's anti-American and anti-Western Islamic theocracy. This is when the American foreign policy establishment in particular, and Western leaders in general, realized that it was better to live with "the devils they knew," than the revolutionary Islamists whom they perceived as "the bigger devils" they did not know and could not control.

The second major factor contributing to issue-oriented anti-Americanism is that the U.S. is perceived as a bully in the Muslim world. This widespread perception is based on America's "coercive diplomacy," which compels Muslim regimes to do its bidding or suffer harsh economic, diplomatic, and/or military consequences. For instance, the U.S. Central Intelligence Agency (CIA) covertly overthrew the democratically-elected nationalist regime of Prime Minister Muhammad Mossadegh when he nationalized the Anglo-Iranian Oil Company, and put the easily manipulated pro-American Shah Muhammad Reza Pahlavi II back on the Peacock Throne in 1953. What is more, the U.S.-government CIA-trained the Shah's secret police called SAVAK, which arrested, tortured, and killed thousands of Iranians from the late 1950s until the Shah's departure from Iran in January 1979.

Unlike America's covert operation in Iran, the U.S. government used disproportionate military force in Lebanon, Libya, Sudan, Afghanistan, Somalia, and above all, in Iraq. For instance, in 1958, the Eisenhower administration sent 10,000 American Marines to crush the Muslim insurrection against the Christian minority regime in Lebanon.

Again, in April 1986, the Reagan administration ordered the bombing of Tripoli and Benghazi in Libya to punish Muammar Gaddafi's regime for sending agents to bomb a West Berlin discotheque, which caused the death of a few American servicemen. Likewise, in 1998, the Clinton administration used American air power to destroy Sudan's Al-Shifa pharmaceutical plant, which was producing much needed medicines for nearly half the country of 36 million people. President Bill Clinton—who at the time was struggling to stave off his impeachment and removal from office due to his sexual affair with a White House intern named Monica Lewinski—claimed that Sudan was producing chemical weapons. And although Clinton's charge was later proved to be false, the U.S. government neither compensated the owner of the pharmaceutical plant, nor apologized for what was a cynical ploy to distract the mass media's attention from his sexual liaison and impeachment to weapons of mass destruction and international terrorism.

Muslims, who live by the Old Testament and Qur'anic concept of proportionate justice of "an eye for an eye," find the U.S. response to triggering events from the Muslim world are all too often totally disproportionate and deeply disturbing. For example, North Korea's announcement of its nuclear weapons program since 1993 has met with much U.S. rhetoric and negotiations, but no military response. Israel continually defies U.N. resolutions, and sometimes does not even do what the U.S. requests of it, but that has never stopped the U.S. from sending the Jewish state at least $3.2 billion in economic and military aid annually.

U.S. interventions in Iraq are classic examples of "overkill" in the Muslim world. When Iraq's President Saddam Hussein invaded and occupied Kuwait, President George H. W. Bush responded with Operation Desert Shield (August 9, 1990 to January 15th) and then Operation Desert Storm (January 16, 1991 to March 2, 1991). Muslims perceived Operation Desert Storm—that included the heaviest American aerial bombing since Vietnam of a poor, weak, and defenseless developing country since America's bombing of North Vietnam (1965–1975—as a disproportionately harsh military response to end Saddam Hussein's illegal occupation of Kuwait. The one-hundred day Operation Desert Storm ended with American bombers and helicopter gunships killing hundreds of Iraqis fleeing from Kuwait to Basra on the "highway of death," which a couple of American pilots jokingly referred to as a "turkey shoot." Over 100,000 Iraqi men, women, and children died in Operation Desert Storm. It is also noteworthy, that massive American air power and ground forces were used in Operation Iraqi Freedom in March 2003 because Saddam Hussein repeatedly refused to cooperate with U.N. inspectors who were searching for weapons of mass destruction. Many Iraqis have been arrested and detained, without due process of law. These detained Iraqis have also been denied their "prisoner of war" status as required by the Geneva Conventions and subjected to torture and cruel, inhuman, or degrading treatment. Terrible examples of torture and cruel and inhuman treatment occurred in Abu Ghraib prison in Baghdad as well as in Mosul, Camp Bucca, and Basra. The employment of American mercenaries and private contractors to carry out torture has served to significantly undermine accountability.

Besides Iraq, the U.S. experienced problems in war-torn and famine-ridden Somalia in the early 1990s. While President George H. W. Bush's "humanitarian intervention" to feed starving Somalis started with noble intentions, the U.S. armed forces got involved in the much larger, complex and difficult task of nation-building. When American commandos tried to apprehend General Muhammad Farrah Aideed, a popular and influential Somali clan leader, for opposing U.S. involvement in Somalia, they triggered the wrath of his big clan. Moreover, Al-Qaeda terrorists and sympathizers got involved in urban guerrilla warfare against the Americans, killing 18 U.S. Marines, and dragging the dead body of an American Marine through the streets of Mogadishu. This scene caused so much revulsion in the U.S. that the Clinton Administration decided to precipitously exit Somalia in 1994. This rushed exit emboldened Al-Qaeda to turn up the heat against pro-American Muslim regimes and Americans in other Muslim countries, with the ultimate goal of driving all Americans out of the Muslim world.

In late October and November 2001, the U.S. again used aerial bombardment against Afghanistan, one of the poorest and weakest Muslim countries in the world. Afghanistan was bombed for harboring the Al-Qaeda terrorist organization considered responsible for planning and executing the September 11, 2001 terrorist attack on America. After the Afghan Taliban regime was overthrown, America's special operation forces began uprooting Osama Bin Laden's infrastructure in Afghanistan. While the puritanical and autocratic Taliban regime was unpopular both in Afghanistan and abroad, Muslims the world over were astonished at the "overkill" used to overthrow the Taliban in retaliation for giving sanctuary to Osama Bin Laden's al-Qaeda. The Taliban was regarded as giving sanctuary to terrorists when Mullah Muhammad Omar, the Taliban leader, called Osama Bin Laden a guest and refused to hand him over to the Americans. President George W. Bush's request for the extradition of Osama bin Laden reminded Muslims of the U.S. government's refusal to hand over the Shah of Iran when the Iranian government asked for their former king to be tried for mass murder and the theft of billions of dollars from the Iranian treasury. Like Afghanistan's Taliban, the U.S. claimed the Shah was their guest and refused to hand him over.

The third major factor contributing to issue-oriented anti-Americanism is America's unwavering economic, military, and diplomatic support of Israel. The generous $3.2 billion economic and military support that the U.S. has given Israel for decades is a major irritant in the Muslim World. What is more, Muslims see Washington as having done nothing to stop the systematic usurpation of Palestinian lands and the loss of Palestinian lives and livelihoods. While calling them "obstacles to peace," Washington has done nothing to stop the building of Jewish settlements in the Israeli-occupied West Bank since the mid-1970s. Now there are as many as 300,000 Jewish settlers in the disputed West Bank. The Israeli annexation of Jerusalem infuriates the *ummah*, the community of Muslims all over the world who reverentially refer to this historic city as *Al-Quds* (The Holy) because of its many shrines associated with the Old Testament prophets, Jesus, and Muhammad.

Muslims the world over also resent the U.S. (and other Western Powers) for not making an issue over Israel's development of atomic weapons, while it has made a big international issue over the Pakistani, Iraqi, Libyan, and Iranian efforts in the development of their nuclear energy. The U.S. is also criticized in the Muslim world for vetoing over 50 United Nations Security Council Resolutions against Israel, while it has used the U.N. Security Council to isolate Iran after Iran took hostages in November 1979, Iraq after it invaded Kuwait in August 1990, Sudan after some of its diplomats were suspected of assisting some misguided Muslims who were implicated in planning terrorist attacks in New York.

The fourth major factor contributing to issue-oriented anti-Americanism is the U.S. government and American mass media making a big issue of Americans or Israelis being killed, while doing absolutely nothing to stop the killing of Muslims all over the world. For instance, the Palestinians have been suffering since 1948 when the Jewish state of Israel ceded much of their land. The cruel irony is that the Palestinians had absolutely nothing to do with the Jewish Holocaust. Nevertheless, most of their land has been systematically usurped in violation of international law and given to Jews coming from all over the world to settle in what they have claimed as Biblical Israel over one-thousand years ago and a land that God gave to Abraham. Not only does much of the

Muslim world see Zionists as usurpers of a land that does not belong to them, but as the victimizers of Palestinians. In fact, when the Palestinians began resisting their occupation, the Zionists labeled them as Palestinian terrorists. Jewish leaders and scholars as well as the American mass media has repeated the words "Palestinian terrorists" and "Palestinian terrorism" so often, that now the terms "Palestinian" and "terrorism" are synonymous in the Western mind.

In March 1991, just after the U.S.-led Gulf War, the U.S. did nothing when thousands of Shi'as were massacred by Saddam Hussein's Elite Republic Guard. In 1991, the U.S. did nothing to discourage or punish the Algerian Generals from aborting democratic national elections in Algeria and launching their reign of terror against the Islamists. That event, radicalized the Islamic Salvation Front (ISF) and spawned the feared Algerian Gama'a al-Islamiyyah (Islamic Group).

The U.S. has done nothing to help the Kashmiri Muslims in the Indian-occupied state of Kashmir in South Asia. India has never held the referendum in Kashmir that the United Nations resolution asked it to hold back in 1948. Instead, Kashmiri Muslims have been subjected to discrimination and persecution, which has gotten worse since 1992.

The U.S. is doing nothing to stop the Russians from committing genocide in Chechnya where over a hundred thousand Chechens have been killed, and many buildings leveled in the capital city of Grozny. In fact, in the aftermath of September 11, 2001, President George W. Bush pleased Russian President Putin by classifying Chechens separatists as "terrorists."

Likewise, just after September 11, 2001, the U.S. government sided with the totalitarian government of the People's Republic of China (PRC) in declaring the Uyghur Muslim separatists in PRC's Xinjiang Province as "terrorists." Both the Chechens and the Uyguars separatists were seen as "freedom fighters" in the pre-September 11, 2001 period. And in the post-September 11 era, global realpolitik deprived the Chechens and Uyghurs of their civil liberties and civil rights.

It is also ironic, that in the 1980s, the Ronald Reagan administration encouraged Muslims from all over the world to go and fight a jihad against the Soviet Communist occupiers of Afghanistan. Many Arabs and non-Arab Muslims accepted the call and went to northern Pakistan for training in guerrilla warfare. At the time, the Western world (and particularly the U.S. leaders and mass media) hailed these "Arab Afghans" and the Afghans fighting against Soviet occupation as the mujahideen (freedom fighters). Today, these very same people that Washington and the Pakistan armed forces trained are suspected of "terrorism" and being hunted down for interrogation and incarceration for an unspecified period of time.

In addition, the U.S. allowed the Serbian political and military leadership to get away with the "ethnic cleansing"/genocide of Bosnian Muslims in Bosnia Hezegovina for three years (1992–1995) before organizing a peace conference in Dayton, Ohio, which effectively rewarded President Slobodan Milosevik as a peacemaker and statesman, instead of revealing him as the mass murderer and war criminal that he was for contributing to the death of over 200,000 Bosnian Muslims, the rape of thousands of Bosnian Muslim women, and the displacement of hundreds of thousands of Bosnian Muslims. While Milosevik is in a comfortable prison in the International Court

of Justice at the Hague, the Bosnian Serb President Radovan Karadic and Ratko Mladic, the Bosnian Serb general who were guilty of horrible atrocities are still at large in Serbia or Bosnia-Hercegovina.

The fifth major factor in issue-oriented anti-Americanism is the U.S.A. Patriot Act of 2001 that has greatly heightened the surveillance of mosques, Islamic centers, and Muslims in the United States. The U.S. government has closed down several prominent Islamic charities for aiding and abetting terrorism by financing such organizations as Hamas, Islamic Jihad, Hezbollah, and/or even Al-Qaeda. Many Muslims have been incarcerated on suspicion that they violated the law without sufficient evidence of that fact. Since September 11, 2001, there have also been long delays that Muslim students have experienced in receiving their student visas to study at colleges/universities in the United States.

The sixth factor contributing to the rising tide of anti-Americanism are the degrading, disgusting, and shocking pictures of the torture of Muslim detainees and alleged "terrorists" in Abu Ghraib prison in Baghdad, Iraq, as well as in detention centers in Afghanistan and in Guantanamo Bay, Cuba. What is more, the mass media has reported stories of the CIA taking Muslim detainees and suspected terrorists to Muslim countries governed by pro-American regimes where the "terrorism suspects" have undergone torture. Many detainees have simply disappeared or died in captivity. Barely had the stories of torture subsided when there were reports of the alleged desecration of the Qur'an in Guantanamo Bay, Cuba, while interrogating Muslim prisoners and alleged terrorists is also contributing to deepening anti-Americanism.

The seventh factor contributing to anti-Americanism among the *ummah* is the anti-Islamic propaganda that Christian fundamentalist ministers and Christian fundamentalist organizations have launched against Islam in the post-September 11, 2001 era. While it is true that President George W. Bush as well as several U.S. government officials and American scholars and journalists have made favorable comments about Islam. However, it is bigoted anti-Islamic and anti-Muhammad comments, articles, and books that often get the sensationalist media attention. Below is a sampling of the derogatory remarks made by prominent religious and secular American leaders about Islam and its revered Prophet Muhammad, which have circulated widely in the Muslim world:

• The Reverend Franklin Graham—a Christian evangelist, founder and leader of the Samaritan Purse, a Christian missionary group, which provides aid to the poor and needy all over the world—referred to Islam in November 2001 as "a very evil and wicked religion… [that was] violent [and did not believe in]… the same god (as Christianity)." When NBC News reporter Jim Avila offered Franklin Graham the opportunity to clarify his comments Graham responded, "It wasn't Methodists flying into those buildings, and it wasn't Lutherans. It was an attack on this country by people of the Islamic faith." These remarks were noteworthy for two reasons: they followed the 9/11 attacks and the speaker is the son of famous evangelist, the Reverend Billy Graham, who has been a confidant to several U.S. Presidents.[10]

• Attorney General John Ashcroft said on Cal Thomas' radio program in November 2001 that "Islam is a religion in which

God requires you to send your son to die for Him. Christianity is a faith where God sent his Son [Jesus Christ] to die for you."[11]

- Again in November 2001, Representative C. Saxby Chambliss, the Republican Congressman from Georgia and Chairman of the House of Representatives' Congressional Subcommittee on Terrorism and Homeland Security and a Senate candidate, used Islamophobia when he remarked "Just turn [the sheriff] loose and have him arrest every Muslim that crosses the state line."[12]

- Reverend Jerry Vines—a pastor of the First Baptist Church of Jacksonville, Florida, and a former Southern Baptist Convention president—gave a speech in June 2002 at the Southern Baptist Convention, which included the following inflammatory statement "Islam was founded by Muhammad, a demon-possessed pedophile who had 12 wives and his last one was a 9-year old girl."[13]

- In September 2002, the Reverend Pat Robertson (Christian Coalition founder, owner and principal interviewer of the Christian 700 Club television program) proclaimed on the Fox Television News Channel's Hannity and Colmes program that "Muhammad was an absolute wild-eyed fanatic" and that to think Islam "is a peaceful religion is fraudulent."[14]

- The Reverend Jerry Falwell—a televangelist who founded the now-defunct Moral Majority political organization—labeled Prophet Muhammad a "terrorist" in his interview with Bob Simon in October 2002 on the Columbia Broadcasting Service's (CBS) 60 Minutes. Furthermore, he claimed to have studied both Muslim and non-Muslim literary works and concluded that Muhammad was "a violent man, a man of war."[15]

- Lieutenant General William "Jerry" Boykin (the Undersecretary of Defense for Intelligence, the Pentagon's pointman in charge of tracking down high profile targets in the antiterrorist campaign, and also a born-again Christian) has given talks in uniform to several evangelical churches around the U.S., proclaiming that the war on terrorism pits the Judeo-Christian tradition against "a guy named Satan." In October 2003, he also remarked that U.S. enemies "will only be defeated if we come against them in the name of Jesus." And speaking of a tribal Somali Muslim warlord named Farah Aidid in 1993, Boykin said, "My God was bigger than his [Allah]. I knew that my God was a real God, and his was an idol."[16]

- U.S. Representative Tom Tancredo (Republican from Colorado in the U.S. House of Representatives in Washington, D.C.) suggested that the United States could target Islamic "holy sites" if terrorists struck American cities with nuclear weapons.

IDEOLOGICAL ANTI-AMERICANISM

The second variant is ideological anti-Americanism, in which the United States is perceived as the greatest world threat because American society exemplifies and promotes a secular, permissive, and decadent culture that is at odds with the ideologies and cultures prevalent in much of the developing world.[17] Such ideological difference explains the hostility of communists, socialists, nationalists, Ba'athists, Nasserites, and funda-

mentalists of many religions (including Islamists) to the United States, which is viewed as undermining their culture and sociocultural institution and contributing to a selfish, materialistic, and unjust society.[18]

In the case of the World of Islam, ideological anti-Americanism results from Islamists accusing the U.S. of being the preeminent neo-imperialist power in the world that directly or indirectly controls the international economic system and through the manipulation of Muslim regimes, exploits the Muslim world's non-renewable resources, charges exorbitant interest rates on loans it gives, and contributes to a growing gap between the rich elite and the poor masses as well as between the West and the Muslim world.

Islamists also accuse the United States of "cultural imperialism." In this regard, American popular culture, and not the U.S. government, is the principal culprit and prime target of Islamist rage. Below are a few examples that will vividly illustrate America's "cultural imperialism" that is contributing to the "Islamic backlash."

Islamists blame European colonialism and American neoimperialism for promoting the Godless secularization of Muslim countries in the post-colonial period. This is because mainly pro-Western (especially pro-American) Muslim secularists assumed power in the post-independence period. These pro-American Muslim secularists promoted secularism, whereby they separated church/mosque and state, and rejected Islamic ideas as the basis of their political legitimacy. Through the mass media and public schools, these Muslim secularists also began transforming people's values from the strict adherence of Islamic beliefs and practices to an increasingly secular (nonreligious), liberal, pragmatic, and even Western orientation. They also tried to undermine and decrease the influence of religious leaders and groups in the Muslim societies. However, because most Muslim regimes have done a deplorable job in providing good education and health care to the masses, Islamist groups have been active in providing free food, free schooling (with a curriculum that is Islam-centric), and free health care for the poor.

Like American Christian fundamentalists/evangelicals, Islamists are alarmed at the decline of ethical, moral, and family values in American culture. Both Christian evangelicals and Islamists denounce the selfish individualism, excessive freedom, decadent hedonism, vulgar language, and sexual permissiveness that are present in American movies, television programs, music, computer games, books, and magazines. Islamists perceive American culture as being personified by the likes of Elvis Presley, Rock Hudson, Michael Jackson, Frank Sinatra, Elton John, Madonna, Jennifer Lopez, and Britney Spears. In fact, Islamists often point to Frank Sinatra's famous song "I did it my way" and Madonna's famous song "I am a material girl" as a couple of the insidious and pernicious ideas that are spreading in Muslim societies. Numerous Muslims are shocked to learn about the high level of premarital sex, extra-marital affairs, separations and divorce, rapes, homosexuality, lesbianism, same-sex marriages, alcohol and drug abuse, and violence (resulting in one of the highest incarceration rates in the world). All this information has created a strong backlash to Americanization (the spread of American socioeconomic culture) in Muslim societies.

While Islam condones capitalism—after all, Prophet Muhammad and several of his companions were businessmen—it is strongly opposed to avaricious, exploitative, and monopolistic capitalism. Islam is also against excessive materialism, like buying unnecessary consumer goods impulsively, or engaging in conspicuous consumption. Islamists believe that America's materialism is rapidly eroding Islam's ethical, moral, spiritual values. Traditionally, it was more important for Muslims to have good character than to have material wealth. Today, members of the Muslim elite are not only keeping up with the Jones', but constantly trying to outdo them

INSTRUMENTAL ANTI-AMERICANISM

The third variant is instrumental anti-Americanism. In this case, regimes in the developing world instigate and use hostility towards the United States to serve their own interests, namely increasing domestic support for the regime and providing a plausible scapegoat for its own failures, mismanagement, and corruption. The United States is a convenient target because it is the sole superpower, and is generally perceived to be intrusive and hypocritical; as a result this kind of anti-American "scapegoating" is easy and relatively cost-free.[19] "Instrumental anti-Americanism" is present in the following examples:

Gamal Abdel Nasser used anti-Americanism to mobilize Egyptians and the Arabs against the Western bloc led by the United States. He also used it to try and topple conservative and pro-American monarchies, receive Soviet economic and military aid, and become one of the leaders of the non-aligned movement (along with Chinese Premier Chou Enlai, Yugoslav President Josep Broz Tito, India's Prime Minister Jawaharlal Nehru, and Indonesian President Ahmad Soekarno).

Libya's Colonel Muammar Gaddafi used anti-Americanism to consolidate power after overthrowing the King Idris al-Sanusi's pro-American regime in 1969. For instance, the first thing Gaddafi did to show his nationalist credentials was to ask the British and the U.S. to close their military bases and leave the country. In 1988, his Libyan intelligence agents were involved in the explosion of a Pan-American civilian airliner over Lockerbie, Scotland.

Ayatollah Khomeini's regime in Iran frequently criticized the U.S. as the "Great Satan." By this Khomeini implied that the U.S. was an evil hegemonic power exploiting the resources of Muslim countries by controlling and manipulating pliant Muslim regimes to support its national interests. For Khomeini and other revolutionaries, the post-World War II era has been one of pax-Americana (an American global order) all over the world over American foreign policy as arrogant, hypocritical, biased towards Israel, and exploitative of Muslim countries.

Iraqi President Saddam Hussein's Ba'athist regime used anti-Americanism to blame all of Iraq's economic and social problems on the United States. He constantly railed against the comprehensive economic sanctions that the United States influenced the United Nations Security Council to impose on Iraq in August 1990. These sanctions remained in effect until 2003, with devastating consequences on the poorest and most vulnerable sections of the Iraqi population. Studies sponsored by the United Nations show that over one million Iraqis (mainly children) died due to inadequate food and medicines during those thirteen years until Operation Iraqi Freedom in March 2003.

To show that they are not puppets and stooges of the United States, even the leaders of pro-American regimes in the Muslim world condone varying degrees of anti-Americanism in their mass media and in the sermons delivered by mosque imams (preachers). In fact, some pro-American leaders even make critical statements from time to time about the U.S. government's economic and military support of Israel, the latter's horrible treatment of the Palestinians, and the decadent American culture. Saudi Arabia's King Faisal ibn Abdul Aziz ibn Saud (r. 1964–1975) went along with the decision in the Organization of Arab Petroleum Exporting Countries (OAPEC) to impose an oil embargo on the United States and the Netherlands for supporting Israel during the October 1973 Arab-Israeli War (the embargo was lifted within six months), and also went along with the increase in the price of petroleum charged by the Organization of Petroleum Exporting Countries (OPEC).

Saudi Arabia's regime tolerated much criticism of the U.S. in the kingdom's mass media when it was being criticized in the American mass media and by American scholars and politicians. However, Saudi Arabia's King Abdullah (Crown Pince under Fahd bin Abdul Aziz ibn Saud until Fahd died in August 2005, has called for moderation in the mass media, *madrassahs*, school curriculum, and in sermons given by clerics in mosques. Pakistan's President Pervez Musharraf is also attempting to revise the curriculum of madrassahs to please the George W. Bush administration.

In February 2003, the democratically-elected Turkish parliament voted against permitting the U.S.-led attack on Iraq from Turkish soil. This was particularly amazing considering Turkey is a North Atlantic Treaty Organization (NATO), a strong ally of the U.S. despite the fact that Prime Minister Recip Tayyeb Erdogan is a well known Islamist.

REVOLUTIONARY ANTI-AMERICANISM

The fourth and final variant is revolutionary anti-Americanism, which "is found among opposition groups seeking to overthrow regimes that are identified with the United States; attacking such regimes thus involves attacking the United States. After the overthrow of the pro-U.S. government, as in Iran and Nicaragua, revolutionary anti-Americanism becomes a mass phenomenon and a force justifying the rule of the new leadership. Accordingly, in Iran, for example, long after the fall of the shah, the Great Satan continues to be denounced as the deadliest enemy of the revolution. The new regime finds it useful to manipulate anti-American sentiment, as in the instrumental variant note earlier, but it is the revolutionary process that has pushed anti-Americanism to the center of both the regime's ideology an the mass consciousness."[20] Examples from the Muslim world include:

The first Palestinian *intifadah* (December 1987-August 1993) and the second Palestinian *intifadah* (October 2000-Present) in the Israeli-occupied West Bank and Gaza have obviously been anti-Israeli and anti-Zionist in character. However, the Palestinians suffering under Israeli occupation also blame the United States government for their plight because the United States supplies most of the weapons used by the Israelis against the Palestinians. Even the economic aid that the United States gives Israel has been used effectively control the Palestinians and to build Jewish settlements in the West Bank and Gaza.

We have been witnessing revolutionary anti-Americanism in the Iraqi insurgency that has been raging since Operation Iraqi Freedom began in March 2003. As of October 2005, 2,000 Americans and over twenty-five thousand Iraqis have died and thousands of Americans and Iraqis have been wounded. Virtually every day Iraqis working for the government as well as innocent bystanders are killed or wounded. America has already spent over $300 billion on the Iraqi military campaign and the war is far from over despite President Bush's overly optimistic declaration of "mission accomplished" back in March 2003.

Since the late 1970s, Saudi Arabia's version of Hanbali-Wahhabi Sunni Islam has been heavily promoted all over the world. The authentic version of Hanbali-Wahhabi Islam is puritanical, exclusivist, xenophobic, sexist, intolerant, anti-Western, and anti-American. The Saudi royal family, which is allied to the United States, promoted their version of Sunni Islam because it was flushed with petrodollars as a result of the oil price increases, and thus had the wherewithal to do so; wanted to appease the Hanbali-Wahhabi religious establishment in the kingdom, so that it would not turn the profoundly religious Saudi masses against the royal family; wanted to be seen by the Saudi religious establishment and their people as the standard-bearers of Islam who were promoting the Hanbali-Wahhabi version of Islam all over the world. Most offensive to the Saudi masses and many Muslims around the world was the stationing of over 500,000 American troops mainly in Saudi Arabia, referred to by many as "the land of Islam's two most holy cities." This did provoke several terrorist attacks in Saudi Arabia against the United States and the Saudi regime.

WHAT DO MUSLIMS WANT?

Now that we have examined what misguided Muslim extremists are doing and why in this post-September 11 world, let us get some idea of "what do Muslims want"?

- Muslims want Jews and Christians to stop focusing on differences between Judaism and Christianity on the one hand, and Islam on the other, while emphasizing the many commonalities between Islam, Judaism, and Christianity for a change.
- Muslims want Christians to know Islam is the only non-Christian faith that enjoins its adherents to believe Jesus was God's prophet and messenger; reveres Jesus Christ's mother, Mary, devoting one major chapter in the Qur'an to her; believes Mary miraculously gave birth to Jesus while she was still a virgin; and that Jesus Christ performed incredible miracles, ascended to heaven alive, and will return before the end of the world.
- Muslims want non-Muslims to stop stereotyping Muslims and vilifying Islam. Most Muslims believe Orientalists (non-Muslim Western scholars who have researched and written about the East and Islam) have undermined the Qur'an's integrity, Prophet Muhammad's personal character, and the authenticity of the last Prophet's *hadith* (sayings) and *sunnah* (sayings and deeds). Most Muslims also believe that Orientalists and post-9-11 Islamophobes have distorted the concept of *jihad* to mean only an aggressive and violent

"holy war"; over-emphasized Islam's conditional permission of polygamy; sensationalized the veiling, segregation, and the second-class status of women in the Muslim world; exaggerated the medievalism and barbarity of *shariah* (Islamic law) punishments; overstated the schisms, heresies, and fanaticism in the Muslim world; overplayed the anti-modern and anti-democratic nature of the Islamic state; denigrated the backwardness of Islamic culture; marginalized the achievements of Islamic civilization, choosing instead to dwell on its weaknesses and problems.

Muslims want the influential Western mass media to stop focusing on sensational aspects in the World of Islam. Muslims believe the mass media highlights only one strain of revolutionary Islamists—those engaging in terrorism and mistakenly calling it a *jihad*—while omitting the fact that an overwhelming majority of Muslims, and even Islamists (including the majority of revolutionary Islamists), are non-violent, law abiding citizens of their countries. By focusing on sensational extremism within Islam, the Western mass media perpetuates the myth of a monolithic, menacing, and inherently anti-modern and anti-Western Islamic world.

Muslims also believe the Western mass media's narrow and distorted coverage of Islam diverges markedly from the treatment of Christian and Jewish extremists. For example, when Muslim extremists commit terrorist acts, which are forbidden in Islam, they are referred to as "Islamic terrorists," the phenomenon is called "Islamic terrorism," and it adversely affects the attitudes of non-Muslims towards Islam and its 1.3 billion followers. However, when Christians or Jews perpetrate terrorist acts, they are rarely referred to as "Christian terrorists" and "Jewish terrorists," the phenomena is rarely called "Christian terrorism" or "Jewish terrorism," and the mass media never casts any doubt over the religions of Christianity or Judaism and their 2.2 billion and 18 million adherents respectively.

Most Muslims do not blame Christianity and/or Jesus Christ for the Crusades, the Spanish Inquisition, European Christian colonialism, the Jewish holocaust in Europe, the genocide of Native Americans in the Americas, slavery of the blacks, apartheid in South Africa, Serbian genocide (not merely "ethnic cleansing" as the Western mass media euphemistically called it) of Muslims in Bosnia-Herzegovina and in Kosovo, and the bombing of abortion clinics, and the killing of doctors and nurses performing abortions. In the same vein, most Muslims do not blame Judaism or the Jewish prophets for the Jewish State of Israel's overwhelming violence and "collective punishment" directed against Palestinians for decades. For instance, on February 25, 1994, a Jewish fundamentalist settler, Baruch Goldstein, killed Muslim worshippers while they were praying in the Abraham Mosque in Hebron, West Bank. However, most newspaper and magazine stories and television programs in the U.S. did not refer to Goldstein as a "Jewish terrorist" engaging in "Jewish terrorism," but a mentally distraught Israeli settler. Likewise, when Yigal Amir (a militant Jewish rabbinical student) assassinated Israeli Prime Minister Yitzhak Rabin on November 4, 1995, he was not referred to as a Jewish terrorist, but another mentally disturbed Israeli. In fact, the crimes of Christians and Jews are contextualized as exceptions of some lunatic fringe element, while the crimes committed by Muslims cast aspersions on all Muslims and the religion of Islam itself. Unless the Western mass media puts a human face on the suffering of Muslims, relations between the West and the Muslim world will continue to deteriorate.

- Muslims want Western journalists, politicians, preachers, and academics to stop connecting indiscriminate violence and terrorism committed by a few misguided Muslim extremists, who are erroneously referred to as "*gihadists*," with the teachings of Islam (see Myths and Misconception section on pp. 39). Muslims point to references in the Qur'an, which they believe is God's final message to humankind, to emphasize that Islam condemns terrorism, suicide, and evil deeds.
- Muslims want the West to stop labeling all Islamists as "Islamic fundamentalists" and Islamism as "Islamic fundamentalism." Muslims find the terms "Islamic fundamentalist" and "Islamic fundamentalism" offensive because the term "fundamentalism" has nothing to do with Islam. All devout Muslims adhere to the fundamentals of Islam. "Fundamentalism" was initially used for 19th century American Protestants who emphasized the literal interpretation and absolute inerrancy of the Bible. In the second half of the twentieth century, the Western mass media and scholars popularized the term "fundamentalism" to signify any religious group or individual who is conservative, radical, bigoted, or zealous. Because of these negative connotations, many Muslims object to the term's use in relation to Islam and Muslims.
- Muslims want the West to stop distorting the true meaning of *jihad* in Islam. In the post-9/11 world, Western politicians, academics, and the mass media have referred to the violence, terrorism, and "holy war" that Muslims engage in as a *jihad* and Muslim fanatics as *jihadists* or Muslim "holy warriors." In fact, the Arabic term for "holy war" is *harb un-muqaddastu*, which is not found in the Qur'an, *sunnah*, or *hadith*. In Arabic, *jihad* literally means "to strive" and "to struggle." In Islam, *jihad-i-akbar* (the greatest jihad) is the non-violent spiritual struggle to vanquish one's baser impulses and *jihad-i-asghar* (the lesser jihad) is to actively defend oneself against tyrants, aggressors, and colonizers. The Qur'an promises the mujahid (Muslim engaging in a *jihad*), who dies in the *jihad*, the honorific title of *shaheed* (martyr) and the reward of *al-Jannah* (Paradise). The overwhelming majority of Islamists engage in a non-violent *jihad* to promote truth and justice by writing, preaching, teaching, organizing, and peacefully demonstrating. An infinitesimally small number of revolutionary Islamists, however, have perpetrated terrorist acts against innocent civilians.
- Muslims want the West to distinguish between the progressive Islamic perspective on women and the unjust treatment of women in conservative, male chauvinist, and patriarchal Muslim societies. Too often, the veil worn by Muslim women is singled out as a symbol of Islamic oppression and discrimination against women. It is forgotten that the revered Christian, Saint Paul, encouraged women to cover their heads and, until the feminist revolution of the 1960s, few women would be seen in church without a scarf or a hat covering their hair. Nuns have been covered from head to toe, and although many nuns prefer to stay covered

in the traditional habit and robe, they enjoy great respect from society for being devoutly religious Catholics. Orthodox and even many conservative, Jewish, Hindu, and Sikh women are still expected to cover their heads loosely. Yet, among all these religious groups, only Muslim women seem to have been singled out as oppressed and suffering a second class status on account of their apparel.

- Muslims want the West to recognize Islamism as a legitimate political force. While separation of religion and politics is a political norm in Western societies, there is no separation between religion and politics in Islamic culture. Muslims, who have seen the failure of many secular "isms" to improve their lot, are eager to give the "Islamic Alternative" a chance for a change. For the Muslim masses, only Islam has been untainted by past failures and is associated with the glories of the past. Therefore, in the next decade or two, Islamists could very well come to power in the Muslim World, one country at a time. Accepting these new regimes and discounting their rhetoric as hostile or a threat to Western interests, is the surest way to avoid disastrous wars.
- Muslims want the West to recognize its past wrongs of imperialism and colonialism. During the colonial era, Western colonial powers exploited a large amount of the Muslim world's finite resources. Muslims were: enslaved to work in mines and in the fields to supply raw materials to the Western colonial masters; forced to purchase expensive technology and finished goods from their colonial masters; heavily taxed; and forced to take out loans at huge interest rates. Many Muslims believe pseudo-Westernized puppet regimes and elites in the Muslim world have allowed Western powers to exploit Muslim countries since the Western colonial powers left Muslim lands. Muslims want the West to provide restitution for colonialism and neocolonialism by: leading the fight on poverty, illiteracy, disease, and inequality in the Muslim world; lifting punitive economic sanctions it has imposed on several Muslim countries; significantly increasing economic assistance to the poorest Muslim countries; forgiving debts of the poorest Muslim countries; funding *grameen* banks—"poor people's banks" that give small amounts of loans to poor people keenly interested in starting a small private enterprise; and increasing the number of Peace Corps workers in the Muslim world.
- Muslims want the West to support an independent Palestinian state in the West Bank and Gaza, and give aid to that state. Muslims believe a terrible injustice was done to the Palestinians when half their land was given to the Jews in the newly created state of Israel in 1948. Palestinians had nothing to do with the suffering of the Jewish people in Europe, yet because of Western guilt over the German holocaust and influential pro-Israel lobbies, Palestinians were systematically deprived of their lands and birthright to accommodate Jews who flocked from all over the world. Muslims are angry at the West, especially the U.S., who gives Israel billions of dollars worth of weapons used to terrorize the Palestinian population in the occupied West Bank and Gaza. Muslims want U.S. policy makers to stop Prime Minister Ariel Sharon's brutal, collective punishment of Palestinians in the West Bank and Gaza, and they want the U.S., the European Union (EU), the United

Nations, and Russia to return the Palestinians' homeland back to them as well as provide the economic aid needed for development.

- Muslims want Americans to understand the deep-seated roots of Muslim rage and reasons for anti-Americanism in the Muslim world. The U.S. government's policies toward the Muslim world can never change if the perceptions of Americans are built on stereotypes. Since the U.S. has long-term interests in the Muslim world, it should forge long-term policies in the region and stay true to its democratic ideals. In fact, the U.S. can win the lasting friendship of the Muslim world by no longer supporting corrupt, despotic, and unpopular regimes that ruthlessly suppress their subjects and mismanage their economies. In fact, paranoid about Islamist regimes (like Iran in the Muslim world), the U.S. quells disquiet by supporting regimes targeted by popular revolution. Such a policy helps the pro-American regime stay in power, but ensures that any revolution that occurs will be decidedly anti-American.

- To reclaim their lands and religion, Islamists seek to drastically reduce U.S. global influence, force Israel to give up the West Bank, take over the governments of Muslim countries. Then, a United Muslim world led by devout, compassionate and just Muslim leaders will share the wealth more equitably with the needy ummah that is now concentrated in the hands of a few corrupt leaders and elites.

Muslims are painfully aware 9/11 may very have triggered a new East-West conflict. The East no longer symbolizes Communism and the Communist World, but revolutionary Islamism and the Muslim world. Muslims also know if efforts are not made by enlightened and moderate religious, political, media, and academic leaders on both sides of the great divide, this conflict could begin looking more and more like a Crusade. Unfortunately, Crusades are longer, bloodier, more costly, and debilitating than Cold Wars. In this particular Crusade, Muslims are the weaker side on virtually all fronts—economically, militarily, politically, and in their machinery of propaganda, and on the whole have more to lose than their Western counterparts.

Every effort should be made by both the Western powers and Muslim countries to end malicious propaganda, and attempt true understanding. In this regard, the governments, the mass media, and educational institutions have a vitally important role. For instance, many highly educated and qualified Muslims in Western countries could be hired by the foreign ministries and mass media outlets. Accepting the central place of the Islamic faith in the cultures of Muslim countries will avert misperceptions of a region strategically so important to the West. Regimes in Muslim countries should reciprocate by encouraging their mass media and educational institutions (including *madrassah* or Islamic schools) to adopt a more enlightened, tolerant, and open-minded approach towards the West. Both sides must try to "rehumanize" the other. Only by seriously engaging in a "dialogue of civilizations" will Samuel Huntington's "clash of civilizations" be averted in the twenty-first century.

Muslims feel a terrible sense of injustice, victimization, and humiliation. When they look nostalgically back to the past, Muslims see a golden age of Islamic civilization. Therefore, revolutionary Islamists are convinced that the *ummah* will progress and prosper, only when the corrupt, incompetent, and tyrannical Muslim Secularist regimes are overthrown by truly Islamic regimes and a united Islamic bloc is created.

REFERENCES

1. Some sections of Chapter 1 are revised versions of Chapters 1 and 2 in Mir Zohair Husain, *Global Islamic Politics*, 2nd edition, New York: Longman's Publishers, 2003.

2. Hereafter citations to the Qur'an will give the Qur'anic Surah (Chapter) number, followed by a colon, and then the number of the specific Qur'anic Ayah/Ayats (Verse/Verses). Thus this first Qur'anic citation is (112:1-4). Also refer to subsection on the Qur'an in this chapter: pp.6-7 (depending on pagination)

3. During the five ritual prayers Muslims say the *Sura-e-Fatihah* (The Opening), the first chapter in the *Qur'an*, seventeen times and this is how it goes: "In the name of Allah, the Most Beneficent, the Most Merciful; Praise be to Allah, the Lord of the worlds; the Most Beneficent, the Most Merciful; Master of the Day of Judgment; You alone we worship, You alone we ask for help; Guide us along the straight path: The path of those upon whom You have bestowed Your grace, not (the path) of those with whom You are angry, nor of those who go astray." This prayer could just as easily be said by Jews and Christians.

4. Kwame Anthony Appiah and Henry Louis Gates, Jr., eds., Africana: The Encyclopedia of the African and African American Experience (New York: Basic Civitas Books, 1999); Columbus Alley, The Black 100: A Ranking of the Most Influential African-Americans, Past and Present, 3rd ed. (Secausus, N.J.: Citadel Press, 1999); M. Amir Ali, A Comparison between Islam and Farrakhanism (under Pseudo-Islamic Cults at http://www.iiie.net.

5. Voltaire. *The Portable Voltaire*, edited by Ben Ray Redman (New York: Viking Press, 1961), p.187.

6. Alvin Z. Rubinstein and Donald E. Smith, "Anti-Americanism in the Third World," *The Annals of the American Academy of Political and Social Science* (Newbury Park: Sage, 1988), p. 35.

7. Ibid., p. 35.

8. Ibid., p. 38

9. Ibid., p. 38

10. http://www.islam-online.net/English/News/2001-11/21/article3.shtml; http://www.opinionjournal.com/extra/?id=95001576

11. http://www.counterpunch.org/leupp0724.html

12. Ibid.

13. Ibid; "Muslims angered by Baptist criticism," http://www.cnn.com/2002/ALLPOLITICS/06/13/cf.crossfire/ http://www.nljonline.com/fc/behind_scenes.html; Alan Cooperman, "Anti-Muslim Remarks Stir Tempest," washingtonpost.com, Thursday, June 20, 2002, p.A03; http://www....ontentId=A14499-2002Jun19&notFound=true/

14. Ibid, "Falwell remarks slam Islam: Televangelist calls the prophet Muhammad a 'terrorist.'" Mobile Press Register, October 4, 2002, pp.1A & 4 A.

15. Ibid, p.4A.

16. http://www.tompaine.com/feature2.cfm/ID/9249

17. Ibid, pp. 39-41.

18. Ibid, pp. 41-42.

19. Ibid., pp. 41-42

20. Source: Alvin Z. Rubinstein and Donald E. Smith, "Anti-Americanism in the Third World," in Thomas Perry Thornton, eds., Anti-Americanism: Origins and Context Vol. 497 of *The Annals of The American Academy of Political and Social Science*, May 1988, pp. 42-43.

Organization of the Islamic Conference (OIC)

Prior to 1969 Muslim countries were primarily concerned with their own national interests and lacked a central international organization. However, after the arson attack on the Al-Aqsa Mosque on August 21, 1969 in Jerusalem, Muslims saw the pressing need for cooperation among Muslim states in order to protect global Islamic interests. In order to create a united front, the leaders of Muslim countries met to discuss what needed to be done to further the cause of the *ummah* (community of believers/Muslims) including those Muslims living in non-Muslim countries. The result was the formation of the Organization of the Islamic Conference (OIC).

The OIC is based on a 1,400-year-old concept of the *ummah*. The OIC comprises 57 member-states plus three nonvoting observer states and at least 20 subsidiary bodies and affiliated specialized associations. Not all member-states have a majority Muslim population; in fact, while 50 are at least 45 percent Muslim, 7 have a very small percentage of Muslim inhabitants (Benin with 15%; Cameroon with 20%; Gabon with 1–3%; Guyana with 9–10%; Suriname with 20%; Togo with 10%, and Uganda with 16%).

According to its charter, the objectives of the OIC are as follows:

- To promote Islamic solidarity among member-states.
- To consolidate cooperation among member-states in economic, social, cultural, scientific, and other vital fields.
- To eliminate racial segregation and discrimination and to eradicate colonialism in all its forms.
- To take necessary measures to support international peace and security founded on justice.
- To aid the struggle of all Muslims with a view to safeguarding their dignity, independence, and national rights.

- To create a suitable atmosphere for the promotion of cooperation and understanding among member-states and other countries.

The OIC Charter also advocates total equality between member-states; the right to self-determination; noninterference in the domestic affairs of member-states; respect for the sovereignty, independence, and territorial integrity of member-states; settlement of conflicts by peaceful means (such as negotiation, mediation, reconciliation, or arbitration); and abstention from the threat or use of force against the territorial integrity, national unity, or the political independence of any member-state.

The OIC plays a vital role by organizing conferences to bring together Muslim leaders, government officials, and nongovernmental groups of the OIC member-states. These conferences foster a greater sense of solidarity in the fragmented Islamic bloc and institutionalize the global Islamic revival. Muslims the world over no doubt feel pleased and hopeful when leaders from Muslim countries meet to discuss their common problems, produce unanimous resolutions, and formulate solutions for the Muslim world in the true spirit of Islamic unity.

WEB SITES

http://www.infoplease.com/ce6/history/A0836844.html

http://www.oic-oci.org/

http://www.irna.com/oic/oicabout.htm

http://www.forisb.org/oic.html

http://www.infoplease.com/spot/oicstates1.html

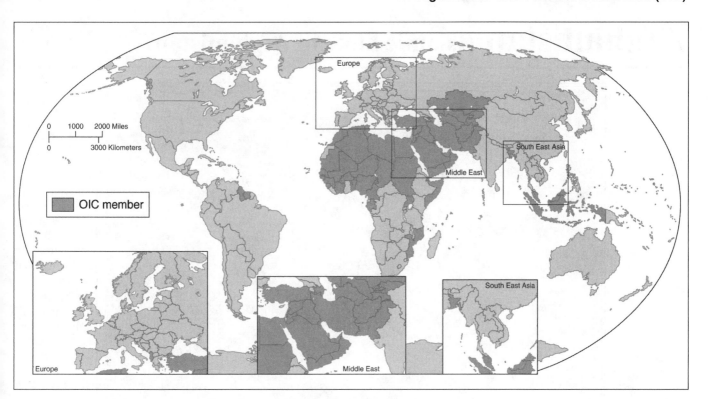

NAME	JOINING DATE	% MUSLIM
1 Islamic State of AFGHANISTAN	1969	99
2 Republic of ALBANIA	1992	70
3 Peoples Democratic Republic of ALGERIA	1969	99
4 Republic of AZERBAIJAN	1992	93
5 Kingdom of BAHRAIN	1972	85
6 Peoples Republic of BANGLADESH	1974	83
7 Republic of BENIN	1983	20
8 BRUNEI-DARUSSALAM	1984	67
9 BURKINA-FASO (then Upper Volta)	1974	50
10 Republic of CAMEROON	1974	20
11 Republic of CHAD	1969	51
12 Union of Comoros	1976	98
13 Republic of Cote dIvoire	2001	35–40
14 Republic of DJIBOUTI	1978	94
15 Arab Republic of EGYPT	1969	94
16 Republic of GABON	1974	1
17 Republic of The GAMBIA	1974	90
18 Republic of GUINEA	1969	85
19 Republic of GUINEA-BISSAU	1974	45
20 Republic of GUYANA	1998	10
21 Republic of INDONESIA	1969	88
22 Islamic Republic of IRAN	1969	98
23 Republic of IRAQ	1975	97
24 Hashemite Kingdom of JORDAN	1969	92
25 Republic of KAZAKHSTAN	1995	47
26 State of KUWAIT	1969	85
27 KYRGHYZ Republic	1992	75
28 Republic of LEBANON	1969	70
29 Socialist Peoples LIBYAN ARAB JAMAHIRIYA	1969	97
30 MALAYSIA	1969	53
31 Republic of MALDIVES	1976	100
32 Republic of MALI	1969	90
33 Islamic Republic of MAURITANIA	1969	100
34 Kingdom of MOROCCO	1969	99
35 Republic of MOZAMBIQUE	1994	20
36 Republic of NIGER	1969	80
37 Federal Republic of NIGERIA	1986	50
38 Sultanate of OMAN	1972	99
39 Islamic Republic of PAKISTAN	1969	97
40 State of PALESTINE	1969	98
41 State of QATAR	1972	95
42 Kingdom of SAUDI ARABIA	1969	96.6
43 Republic of SENEGAL	1969	94
44 Republic of SIERRA LEONE	1972	60
45 Republic of SOMALIA	1969	99.9
46 Republic of SUDAN	1969	70
47 Republic of SURINAME	1996	19.6
48 SYRIAN Arab Republic	1972	90
49 Republic of TAJIKISTAN	1992	90
50 Republic of TOGO	1997	20
51 Republic of TUNISIA	1969	98
52 Republic of TURKEY	1969	99
53 TURKMENISTAN	1992	89
54 Republic of UGANDA	1974	16
55 State of the UNITED ARAB EMIRATES	1972	96
56 Republic of UZBEKISTAN	1996	88
57 Republic of YEMEN	1969	100

Afghanistan (Islamic State of Afghanistan)

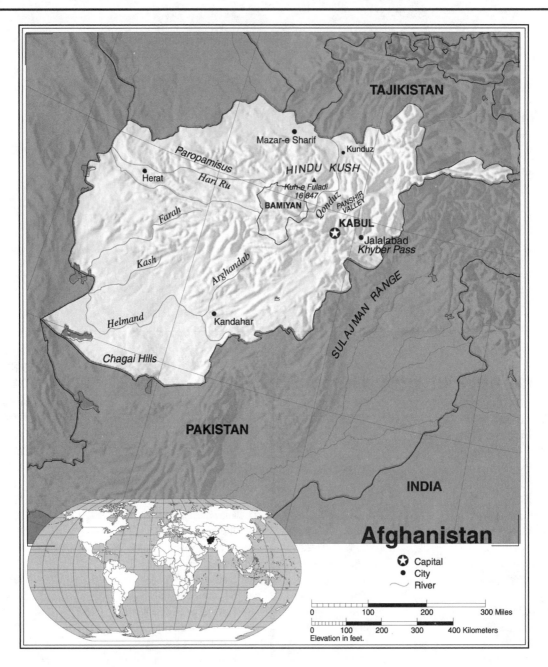

Afghanistan Statistics

GEOGRAPHY

Area in Square Miles (Kilometers): 249,935 (647,500) (about the size of Texas)

Capital (Population): Kabul (2,734,000)

Environmental Concerns: soil degradation; overgrazing; deforestation; desertification; limited freshwater resources; air and water pollution

Geographical Features: mostly rugged mountains; plains in the north and southwest; landlocked

Climate: arid to semiarid; cold winters and hot summers

PEOPLE

Population

Total: 28,513,677

Annual Growth Rate: 4.92% (rate does not take into consideration the recent war and its continuing impact)

Rural/Urban Population Ratio: 79/21

Major Languages: Pashtu; Dari; Turkic; 30 minor languages; much bilingualism

Ethnic Makeup: 42% Pushtun (Pushtun, or Pathan); 27% Tajik; 9% Hazara; 9% Uzbek; 4% Aimak; 3% Turkmen; 2% Baloch; 4% other

Religions: 80% Sunni Muslim; 19% Shi'a
   Muslim; 1% other

Health

Life Expectancy at Birth: 42.27 years
   (male); 42.66 years (female)
Infant Mortality: 165.96/1,000 live births
Physicians Available: 1/6,690 people
HIV/AIDS Rate in Adults: 0.01%

Education

Adult Literacy Rate: 36% (21% for females)
Compulsory (Ages): 7–14

COMMUNICATION

Telephones: 33,100 main lines
Daily Newspaper Circulation: 11 per
   1,000 people
Televisions: 10 per 1,000 people
Internet Users: 1,000

TRANSPORTATION

Highways in Miles (Kilometers): 13,049
   (21,000)

Railroads in Miles (Kilometers): 15.4
   (24.6)
Usable Airfields: 47
Motor Vehicles in Use: 67,000

GOVERNMENT

Type: trasitional Islamic State of
   Afghanistan
Independence Date: August 19, 1919
   (from United Kingdom control over
   Afghan foreign affairs)
Head of State/Government: chairman
   Hamid Karzai is currently head of state
   and head of government
Political Parties: in flux
Suffrage: 18 years of age; universal

MILITARY

Current Disputes: severe internal
   conflicts; border disputes with Pakistan

ECONOMY

Currency ($ U.S. Equivalent): 50 afghani
   = $1

Per Capita Income/GDP: $700 (2003 est.)
Labor Force by Occupation: 80%
   agriculture;10% industry; 10% services
Natural Resources: natural gas;
   petroleum; coal; copper; talc; barite;
   sulphur; lead; zinc; iron ore; salt;
   precious and semiprecious stones
Agriculture: opium; wheat; fruits; nuts;
   sheepskins; lambskins; wool; mutton
Industry: small-scale production of
   textiles, soap, furniture, shoes, fertilizer,
   and cement; handwoven carpets; natural
   gas; coal; copper
Exports: $98 million (not including illicit
   exports) (primary partners US, Pakistan,
   India, France)
Imports: $1.007 billion (primary partners
   Pakistan, South Korea, Japan, Germany)

SUGGESTED WEB SITES

http://www.afghan-web.com
http://www.cia.gov/cia/
   publications/factbook/geos/
   af.html

Afghanistan Country Report

Afghanistan is a rugged and mountainous country, nearly the size of Texas, divided through its center by a high mountain ridge. It is also divided by ethnic conflicts, competing political and religious ideologies, old superpower strategies, and war.

Only 12 percent of this land is arable; even more challenging to agricultural subsistence, the area receives an average rainfall of less than 12 inches a year. Severe drought conditions throughout the country since 1996 have drastically reduced even that rainfall for agricultural production and decimated the livestock of the Kuchi people, Afghanistan's nomadic herders. Toward the south, the land is normally inhospitable desert, racked by seasonal sandstorms that have been known to bury entire villages. The mountainous terrain in the north has mineral resources, primarily iron ore and natural gas, which are unexploited but hard to obtain.

The three-way slope of the landscape from the high ridge of the Hindu Kush divides Afghanistan into three distinct ethnic and linguistic regions. Northern Afghans are predominately Uzbeks and Turkmen, who share a strong sense of identity as well as the Turkic language with the peoples who live across their northern border in Turkmenistan and Uzbekistan—former republics of the Soviet Union.

The Tajik and Hazara peoples, who are 25 and 19 percent of the population, live in the central section and on the western slopes of the Hindu Kush toward Iran. They belong to different Islamic traditions. The Tajik, of ancient Persian origin, are primarily Sunni Muslim. The Hazara are Shi'a Muslims who trace their descent from the invaders of Genghis Khan from Mongolia in the thirteenth century A.D. The Tajiks and the Hazara share a common language, Dari, which is a dialect of Farsi, the language of Iran (where Shi'a Muslims are predominant).

DEVELOPMENT

In the 1980s, the Soviet government made a concerted effort to establish an industrial base, particularly in mining and processing Afghanistan's natural resources. With the increasing intensity of the warfare between the Afghan rebels and the Soviet occupying forces, these efforts collapsed. It is estimated that agricultural production declined by more than half, complicated by severe drought.

The Pashtuns (also called Pathans or Pushtuns), are the largest ethnic group, 10 million strong, about 38 percent of the total population. They live on the southeastern slope of the country and are themselves divided into two tribal groups, the Durrani and the Ghilzai. The Durrani Pashtuns have been politically the most dominant during the past 300 years. All of the Pashtuns are, like the Tajik and northern Afghans, predominantly Sunni Muslims, but they speak a different language, Pashto. They share both this language and their ethnic identity with a much larger population of Pashtuns, some 16 million, who live across the southeastern boundary of Afghanistan and are the predominant population of the northwest provinces in Pakistan.

FREEDOM

Millions who fled into Pakistan and Iran are slowly making their way back to their devastated lands.

MODERN HISTORY

Following a brief incursion of British forces into Afghan territory in 1878, the British withdrew to leave these lands under the nominal authority of Abdur Rahman Khan, the Emir of Kabul. During his reign, from 1880 to 1901, he committed himself to "breaking down the feudal and tribal system and substituting one grand community under one law and one rule.

In 1953, Sadar (Prince) Mohammed Daoud Khan, then commander of the Afghan army, seized the authority of prime minister to the Emir of Kabul, Zahir Shah. He instituted many economic and social reforms, leading up to the adoption of a constitutional monarchy with a nationally elected legislative assembly in 1964. Daoud's reforming zeal allowed women to remove the *chadri* (the traditional heavy veil worn in public) and to participate for the first time in that election.

Elections were held again in 1969, but this time local clan leaders, both religiously and socially conservative, better understood the electoral process. They gained control of the Assembly in order to preserve their traditional authority, and effectively limited further reform.

HEALTH/WELFARE

The family and tribe have been the traditional sources of welfare in Afghanistan. Because of continuing warfare and limited access to safe water supplies, disease is prevalent. The overall life expectancy and the literacy rate are among the lowest in South Asia. The ban on women's activities by the Taliban severely limited health and social services in the country.

Impatient with this resistance, Sadar Daoud, with the help of the army, overthrew the government in 1973. He sent Zahir Shah into exile and set himself up as military dictator. He strengthened the army and the bureaucracy to secure his rule. With Soviet aid, he strove to build an industrial sector to replace traditional agriculture and handicrafts as the primary source of the country's wealth. In 1977, he promulgated a new Constitution that outlawed all political parties other than his own, including the largely urban and intellectual Communist party. A new assembly then elected Daoud president of the Republic of Afghanistan.

The Soviet Occupation

Resistance to Daoud's nationalist reform program came from both sides of the political spectrum. From the more conservative elements in the countryside, a zealous group of militant clan leaders, armed and trained by Pakistan, arose to harass his government. Strengthened by a rising Islamic-fundamentalist zeal, they were called the *mujahideen*, "fighters for the faith." But Daoud was more concerned about the growing influence, encouraged by the Soviets, of the leftist, modernizing groups in the city of Kabul. He began to

purge suspected Communist Party members from the military and the bureaucracy. Within a year, army officers threatened by this purge staged a coup and assassinated him. Nur Mohammed Taraki, leader of the Peoples Democratic (Communist) party, then took over the reins of government.

Infighting amongst the Communist Party leadership led to President Taraki's assassination in 1979. He was followed by a former associate and arch-rival, Hafizullah Amin.

Mujahideen resistance intensified to a point where President Amin sought Soviet aid to protect his government in Kabul. The Soviet government, fearing that continuing civil strife in Afghanistan would diminish their influence and investment there and threaten the security of the adjoining Soviet states to the north, sent troops in December 1979. They came, however, not to protect, but to depose Amin and his radical faction of the Communist Party. The Soviet military installed Babrak Karmal to undertake a more moderate approach to socialist reform.

Forces of resistance in the countryside intensified in their opposition to foreign intervention in addition to the earlier reforms seeking centralization, industrialization, and modernization. And more than a third of the population of the country fled to neighboring peoples with whom they felt a strong sense of kinship. Supplied by Pakistani, Iranian, Arabic, and U.S. military and logistical support, many of them became powerful, holy adversaries (*mujahideen*).

This incursion of Soviet military forces in 1979 also intensified the Cold War confrontation between the United States and the Soviet Union, and transformed Afghanistan into a proxy international battlefield. During the years of occupation to 1989, the Soviets increased their military strength to 120,000 troops. Twelve thousand of 22,000 villages and more than 2,000 schools were destroyed, and 1 million Afghans and 13,000 Soviet soldiers were killed.

ACHIEVEMENTS

Given the warfare and devastation to their country that the Afghan people have been through during the past 2 ½ decades, their greatest achievement may simply be their survival.

The Soviet Withdrawal

In 1988 the leaders of seven *mujahideen* groups joined in Pakistan to form an interim government in exile. Faced with this resistance, the Soviet Union became unwilling to sustain the losses of an intensifying military stalemate and withdrew its forces by February, 1989.

In March 1992, Afghanistan president, Najibullah, was overthrown by his own army, and *mujahideen* forces, under the command of Ahmad Shah Masood, a Tajik from Panshir, overtook the city of Kabul. Their victory was followed by a *loya jirga*, "national council," to elect an interim president and draw up a new constitution for nationwide elections to be held in 1994. But the rivalry among the *mujahideen* leaders, particularly between Burhanuddin Rabbani, a Tajik elected as interim president, and Gulbuddin Hekmatyar, a Ghilzai Pashtun, led to intense fighting in Kabul and a further collapse of civil order throughout the country. The periodic assaults and bombings among rival *mujahideen* parties seeking control of the city reduced much of it to rubble.

In response to the militancy and corruption of the *mujahideen*, a group of Pashtun religious students called the Taliban ("seekers of religious knowledge"), from the southern city of Kandahar, rose up in indignation. Their reforming fervor spread rapidly among a people weary of uncontrolled violence, fear, and destruction. The Taliban became a formidable force, supplied by arms and logistics from Pakistan, manpower from local clan militias, war orphans from Islamic parochial schools called *madrassas*, religious volunteers (*jihadis*) from many countries, and financial support and training from al-Qaeda. By the fall of 1996, in control of the southern two-thirds of the country, they drove the *mujahideen* out of Kabul. They then established a reign of reactionary religious terror in a city that had aspired for so long to become modern. Their reforming zeal countenanced many human rights abuses. Most severely oppressed were the women, particularly widows, who were deprived of jobs, humanitarian aid, and education.

By the end of 2001, there were still 2.2 million refugees in Pakistan, 2.4 million in Iran, and around 1 million in refugee camps in Afghanistan itself.

RESTORATION

Following the terrorist attacks in the U.S. on September 11, 2001, an international coalition led by the United States joined forces with the Northern Alliance to oust the Taliban from Kabul. Pakistan's withdrawal of its support for the Taliban and the dismantling of al-Qaeda training camps created an opportunity for a new beginning toward political stability and reconstruction in the country.

An impressive list of regional leaders emerged to share in this effort. All had a part in the violent infighting following the Soviet withdrawal, based on their identification with the many diverse ethnic and tribal groups in the country. The most powerful of them retained their own private militias, and many were sustained by foreign aid and a flourishing trade in heroin production.

The United Nations initiated the rebuilding of Afghanistan by gathering representative leadership from across the country in Bonn, Germany, in December 2001. They were to design an interim administration of institutions to restore services, a supreme court, and a constitutional commission. The intent of this Bonn agreement was to establish a government with authority separate from the indigenous leaders' power. Despite the good intentions, according to Barnett Rubin, "the result was an Afghan government created at Bonn that rested on a power base of warlords."

Then in June 2002, a *loya jirga*, a council of 1,500 selected leaders, convened in Kabul on terms set under United Nations auspices in Bonn. This council created a transitional government and elected Hamid Karzai as interim president, a Pashtun with strong American support. Because he did not have an indigenous political base, he seemed most suited to hold the office above the taint and fray of traditional local clan power struggles and to attract international contributions for rehabilitation.

Steps toward a permanent government began with a national election for president in October 2004. Hamid Karzai won 55.4 percent of the vote, a victory for the UN agenda to promote an independent national government.

Encouraged by these initial steps to undertake the massive tasks of relief for a destitute people and reconstruction of a shattered infrastructure, the country has a new sense of freedom and hope. But the challenges are immense: 20 years of political decay and destruction, meager resources stretched by the return of millions of refugees to their ravaged homes among the land mines and the rubble, and remnants of the Taliban and other marauding forces attacking expensive rebuilding and relief projects.

Albania (Republic of Albania)

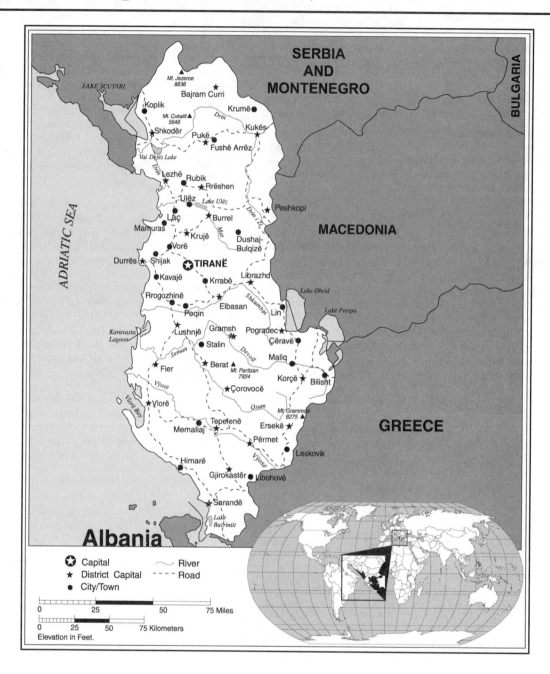

Albania Statistics

GEOGRAPHY

Area in Square Miles (Kilometers): 11,097
(28,489) (about the size of Maryland)
Capital (Population): Tirana (384,000)
Environmental Concerns: deforestation;
soil erosion; water pollution
Geographical Features: mostly mountains
and hills; small plains along the coast
Climate: mild temperate

PEOPLE

Population

Total: 3,544,808

Annual Growth Rate: 0.51%

Rural/Urban Population Ratio: 62/38

Major Languages: Albanian (Tosk is the
official dialect); Greek

Ethnic Makeup: 95% Albanian (Geg and
Tosk); 5% Greek, Vlach, Romani, and
Bulgarian

Religions: 70% Muslim; 20% Albanian
Orthodox; 10% Roman Catholic

Health

Life Expectancy at Birth: 74 years (male);
80 years (female)

78

Infant Mortality Rate (Ratio): 40/1,000
Physicians Available (Ratio): 1/585

Education

Adult Literacy Rate: 93%
Compulsory (Ages): 6–14; free

COMMUNICATION

Telephones: 255,000 main lines
Daily Newspaper Circulation: 54 per
1,000 people
Televisions: 1 per 11 people
Internet Users: 30,000

TRANSPORTATION

Highways in Miles (Kilometers): 11,160
(18,000)
Railroads in Miles (Kilometers): 277 (447)
Usable Airfields: 11

GOVERNMENT

Type: emerging democracy

Independence Date: November 28, 1912
(from Ottoman Empire)
Head of State/Government: President of
the Republic Alfred Moisiu; Prime
Minister Fatos Nano
Political Parties: Albanian Socialist Party;
Democratic Party; Social Democratic
Union Party; Social Democratic Party;
Unity for Human Rights Party; others
Suffrage: universal and compulsory at 18

MILITARY

Military Expenditures (% of GDP): 1.5%
Current Disputes: ethnic Albanians
experience discrimination in Kosovo, the
former Yugoslav Republic of Macedonia

ECONOMY

Currency ($ U.S. Equivalent): 141.80 leks
= $1
Per Capita Income/GDP: $3,000/$10.5
billion

GDP Growth Rate: 7.5%
Inflation Rate: 2.4%
Unemployment Rate: 16% officially, but
likely much higher
Labor Force: 1,692,000
Natural Resources: petroleum; natural gas;
coal; chromium; copper; timber; nickel
Agriculture: wide range of temperate-zone
crops; livestock
Industry: food processing; textiles and
clothing; lumber; oil; cement; chemicals;
mining; metals; hydropower
Exports: $425 million (primary partners
Italy, Greece, Germany)
Imports: $1.76 billion (primary partners
Italy, Greece, Turkey, Germany)

SUGGESTED WEBSITES

http://lcweb2.loc.gov/frd/cs/
altoc.htm
http://www.albania.co.uk

Albania Country Report

Since its independence from the Turkish Ottoman Empire in 1912, Albania has been threatened by foreign enemies seeking to partition and annex it. Albania is vulnerable because of its small size; its lack of natural resources for an effective military defense; and the sharp differences between the country's largest social groups, the Gegs and the Tosks. Moreover, its location astride the Strait of Otranto, which links the Adriatic Sea to the Mediterranean, has made Albania a tempting target of its powerful neighbors, Italy and the former Yugoslavia. In the 1920s and 1930s, Benito Mussolini's Italy had designs on Albania; Italy expanded its political influence in Tirana, the Albanian capital, until it finally invaded and occupied the country in 1939. And when Albania regained its independence after Italy left World War II in 1943, a new threat came from the Yugoslav Communists, who helped the newly formed Albanian Communist Party to take over the country at the end of the war.

The Albanian Communist Party, founded in 1941, had an obsession with security that bordered on paranoia. This obsession explains the speed with which the Communists adopted the Soviet style of political dictatorship, which would assure the unity and defense of Albania. By 1953 the Albanian Communists had transformed their country into a Marxist-Leninist police state.

COMMUNIST RULE WEAKENS

In the late 1980s, the country's small intelligentsia began to criticize the government's harsh political repression, lamenting its frequent violations of human rights. The intelligentsia advocated genuine political change.

Parliamentary elections, held on March 31, 1991, were the first contested elections that Albania had had since 1923. The Communists won due to benefiting from the enormous resources at their disposal. The elections did, however, tend to confirm what was already evident: a steady and seemingly irreversible movement away from communism.

ECONOMIC PROBLEMS

As the Communist government moved toward pluralism, it had to cope with a severely debilitated economy. Throughout the period of Communist rule following World War II, most Albanians lived with ox- and donkey-drawn carts, grimy steam-powered factories, and threshers dating back to the 1950s. Towns and villages had few shops, and workers either walked to their jobs or traveled on rickety buses. Conditions like these persist today. Recognizing the extreme backwardness of their economy, some Albanian reformers were ready to accept the "shock therapy" version of economic reform, namely a rapid curtailment of state control over the country's economic life that would lead to a free market, increased productivity, and a rise in

living standards, which were and remain among the lowest in Europe, east as well as west. In the summer of 1991, the Albanian government began an immediate and extensive reduction of government expenditures for administration, the military, and price subsidies and an acceleration of privatization. And in September 1991, it began a reform of the banking and currency systems.

THE COLLAPSE OF COMMUNIST RULE

In March 1992 Albanians elected a new parliament, and the Democratic Party won an overwhelming majority of the popular vote, with its leader, Dr. Sali Berisha, elected president.

Economic Difficulties

Perhaps the biggest political liability of Berisha's leadership by the mid-1990s was continuing economic hardship. Albania lagged far behind most other countries in the region in developing a free-market economy. In 1993, some 40 percent of the Albanian workforce were unemployed—a figure that did not include the 10 percent of the population who had fled abroad to find work. Electric power, heat, and water in Tirana were interrupted for long periods of time. Hospitals had virtually no resources. Schools had no textbooks, since millions of the heavily ideological books of the past had been scrapped. With the large agricultural collectives, which had produced enough to maintain a low but adequate nutritional level under the Communists, now split up into privately owned but inefficient small units (an average 3.5 acres), farm productivity declined to one-tenth of that in the European Union, forcing Albania to import expensive foreign grain.

Unable to pull itself up by its own bootstraps, Albania had to rely on foreign aid, which financed 50 to 60 percent of the national budget for most of the 1990s.

The End of the Berisha Era

In 1996 financial scandals traumatized Albania. These scandals involved so-called pyramid investment schemes, which destroyed the life savings of a large number of Albanian citizens and led eventually to a political crisis ending with the return of the former Communists to power and the resignation of President Berisha. This crisis divided, demoralized, and debilitated Albanian society and severely compromised its progress toward political and economic democracy.

The 1997 Parliamentary Elections

Parliamentary elections held in June 1997 resulted in a victory for the Socialists, who won an absolute majority. Socialist leader Fatos Nano subsequently asked Berisha to honor his pledge to resign the presidency if

his party were defeated. However, unable to keep his fragile coalition cabinet unified— his parliamentary majority was fragmented and conflict-ridden—Nano finally resigned on September 28, 1998.

UNSTABLE LEADERSHIP, 1998–2000

On October 4, 1998, President Mejdani nominated the Socialist politician Pandeli Majko as prime minister. He was only 31 years old, the youngest prime minister in Europe. He had a lot of support within the Socialist Party because of his youth; he represented a new, post-Communist generation of Social-Democratic-type reformist politicians who had taken control of the former Communist party.

Impact of the Crisis in Kosovo, 1999–2000

Throughout 1999 Albanian society had to cope with a horrendous refugee problem, caused by the conflict in Kosovo and made worse by a NATO bombing campaign over Kosovo territory in the spring. Kosovar Albanians fled into Albania also because of the murderous behavior of Serb military, paramilitary, and police personnel who wantonly and indiscriminately evicted Kosovar Albanians from their homes, killing many of them. The country was hard put to feed and house the refugees, but it nevertheless absorbed about 440,000 of them, more than any other country. About 70 percent of the refugees found a place to sleep and survive in Albanian homes. The West provided much food and tents, pledging long-term aid to help Albanian economic recovery and the modernization of its army, which was suffering the same degree of impoverishment that had afflicted the rest of society.

Kosovo and Albanian Relations With the West

Partly as a result of the crisis in Kosovo, the West began to show a new and substantial interest in Albania's political and economic future, convinced that it had an important role to play in maintaining regional peace and security. In April 1999, at the NATO 50th anniversary meeting in

Washington, Alliance members pledged to protect Baltic members of the Partnership for Peace and held out the long-term prospect of full membership in NATO. Albania was specifically mentioned as being eligible for consideration for future NATO membership, although no negotiations were envisaged in the near future, since in almost every respect Albania was clearly not ready to join.

The European Union showed an equivalent concern for Albania in the wake of the Kosovo crisis. The new policy was announced at an EU conference in Bonn in May 1999. The European Commission offered both Albania and Macedonia "stabilization and association agreements" but no commitment about future membership.

Kosovo and the Albanian Economy

There was a remarkable increase in Albanian economic development through the summer of 1999. As soon as foreigners and troops began to flood in, facilities for them were quickly provided, generating new employment in the construction and service industries, especially in Tirana. Humanitarian agencies and the armed forces employed local labor for work on refugee facilities and on road building, paying far higher wages than the domestic norm. The infusion of foreign money to help Albania offset the costs of caring for the refugees did wonders for the national economy, stimulating productivity and raising living standards slightly, hikes in the budget deficit and a decline in revenue notwithstanding. Also, privatization continued in Albania, a sign of the country's slow but steady movement toward some version of the free-market economy.

Meta Succeeds Majko as Prime Minister in 1999

On October 25, 1999, one year after having taken office, Prime Minister Majko resigned. Majko's successor as prime minister was Deputy Prime Minister Ilir Meta, a compromise between conservative ex-Communists like Nano and a new reformist-oriented group of Socialists. Meta was pro-West and eager to strengthen Albania's relations with the European Union.

However, following the aftermath of the June 2001 parliamentary elections—and partly as a result of it—the two most influential Socialist politicians in the country, Prime Minister Meta and Socialist chairman Nano, began a feud over the party's choice of candidate to run for president in the election scheduled for mid-2002. Eventually Nano scored an advantage. Meta resigned as prime minister in early 2002, in favor of Majko, at the time defense minister. Majko had been on better terms with Nano. Majko lasted as prime minister until summer 2002, when he stepped aside and Nano succeeded him.

Nano Tries to Lead, 2002–2004

Under Nano Albanian politics again was stymied, with Parliament unable to address issues of economic reform and also because of worsening factionalism inside the Socialist party between Nano and Meta, who resigned his post as foreign minister in July 2003. Meta bolted the Socialist Party to form a new political organization loyal to him and opposed to Nano's perceived ambition to become president. Nano continued to prevail because a majority of the rump Socialist Party supported him, reelecting him party leader at a party congress held at the end of December 2003. In the early months of 2004, Albanian politics was as unstable and unpredictable as it has been for most of the post-Communist era, with Meta and his ex-Socialist followers alienated and Berisha and the Democrats looking for ways to oust Nano from power in parliamentary elections scheduled for mid-2005.

RECENT FOREIGN POLICY

Despite internal political quarrels, Albania's foreign policy has been consistent in its focus on good relations with the West. Today Albanian political leaders of all ideological persuasions agree on the necessity of friendship and cooperation with both NATO, the European Union, and the United States as one of the most impoverished states in Europe, Albania needs Western help with its movement toward a free market. And from a purely strategic point of view, Albania needs Western support of its security, which can never be taken for granted in the conflict-ridden Balkan region.

Albania, Yugoslavia, and Kosovo After Milosevic

In the past few years, Prime Minister Nano has proceeded very carefully with regard to the volatile issue of independence for Kosovo, telling Kosovo President Ibrahim Rugova in the spring of 2004 that the political future of the region is "a complex question." Nano is between a rock and a hard place on Kosovo. He is under continuing pressure from Rugova to help the cause of independence for Kosovo. At the same time he is not so sure an independent Kosovo is in Albania's best interest, especially given the opposition to it in Belgrade, with which he wants Albania to remain on good terms. That said, there is no doubt of Nano's sympathy for the principle of Kosovo's separation from Serbia, and he discussed this issue with top Kosovo leaders in the spring of 2004.

Support of Western Policy After Kosovo

Albania and the European Union

Nano was and remains committed to Albanian membership in the European Union. The EU has been responsive but very cautious given the depressed level of economic output of Albania and the country's chronic political instability, pervasive corruption, and frequent divergence from Western democratic norms, especially with regard to elections where there has been rampant fraud and dishonesty. EU officials in recent years have warned the Albanian government about these flaws in its efforts to develop a Western-style parliamentary democracy and move the country toward some version of the free-market economy. Nano has promised the EU policies to accommodate its criticisms, but little has changed in Albanian development in the early years of the new century.

The EU has gone out of its way to encourage and assist Albania to resolve the political and economic problems that make imminent membership unlikely. On January 31, 2003, then-EU president Romano Prodi launched efforts to conclude with Tirana a Stabilization and Association Process, a framework in which Albania would receive assistance, technical advice, trade preferences, and cooperation in fields such as justice and home affairs and would engage in a political dialogue leading to the conclusion of a Stabilization and Association Agreement, which would bring the country into a closer association with the EU. The end of this process will be when Albania is integrated with the EU.

Cooperation With the United States

The Nano government has gone out of its way to cultivate the United States in recent

years. In fact Nano sees no contradiction supporting U.S. policy when it is at odds with the European Union, which he wants Albania to join. Both are potential friends of Albania in a position to help the country, especially in the economic sphere. In March 2003 Nano's government offered 70 noncombat troops for deployment in Iraq. Despite possible criticism from the EU, Nano said his government would not shirk from the operation to disarm Iraq "and rid its suffering people of unbearable tyranny." Also in May, Nano brought Albania into a United States-sponsored partnership of Adriatic countries that included Macedonia and Croatia as a first step along a road that could lead to the membership of these countries in NATO.

Algeria (Peoples' Democratic Republic of Algeria)

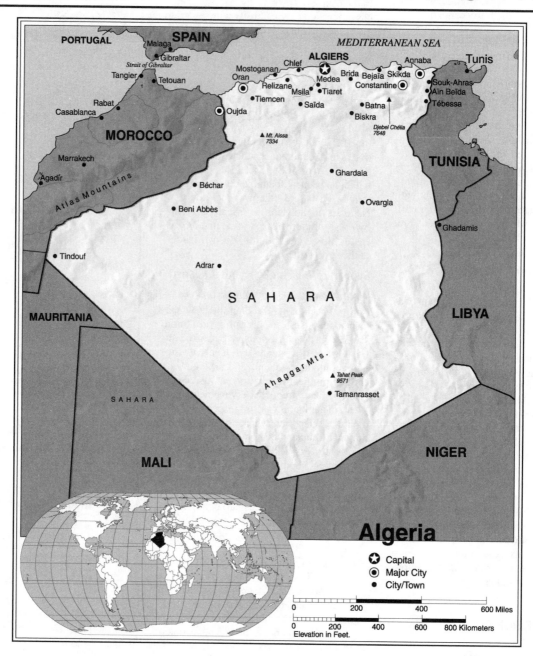

Algeria Statistics

GEOGRAPHY

Area in Square Miles (Kilometers): 919,352 (2,381,740) (about 3 1/2 times the size of Texas)

Capital (Population): Algiers (3,705,000)

Environmental Concerns: soil erosion; desertification; water pollution; inadequate potable water

Geographical Features: mostly high plateau and desert; some mountains; narrow, discontinuous coastal plain

Climate: arid to semiarid; mild winters and hot summers on coastal plain; less rain and cold winters on high plateau; considerable temperature variation in desert

PEOPLE

Population

Total: 32,277,942

Annual Growth Rate: 1.68%

Rural/Urban Population Ratio: 44/56

Major Languages: Arabic; Berber dialects; Ahaggar (Tuareg); French

Ethnic Makeup: 99% Arab-Berber; less than 1% European

Religions: 99% Sunni Muslim (Islam is the state religion); 1% Shia Muslim, Christian, and Jewish

Health

Life Expectancy at Birth: 68.97 years (male); 71.67 years (female)

Infant Mortality Rate (Ratio): 39/1,000 live births

Physicians Available (Ratio): 1/1,066 people

Education

Adult Literacy Rate: 61.6%

Compulsory (Ages): 6–15

COMMUNICATION

Telephones: 2,300,000 (1998); 500,000 new lines being connected in 2003, plus 33,500 cellular phones

Daily Newspaper Circulation: 52 per 1,000 people

Televisions: 71 per 1,000 people

Internet Users: 2 (2000)

TRANSPORTATION

Highways in Miles (Kilometers): 63,605 (102,424)

Railroads in Miles (Kilometers): 2,963 (4,772)

Usable Airfields: 136

Motor Vehicles in Use: 920,000

GOVERNMENT

Type: republic

Independence Date: July 5, 1962 (from France)

Head of State/Government: President Abdelaziz Bouteflika; Prime Minister Ali Benfis

Political Parties: National Liberation Front (FLN), majority party; National Democratic Rally (RND), National Reform Movement, chief minority parties; others include Movement for a Peaceful society; Islamic Salvation Front (FIS) outlawed since April 1992

Suffrage: universal at 18

MILITARY

Military Expenditures (% of GDP): 4.1%

Current Disputes: disputed southeastern border with Libya; Algeria supports Polisario Front which seeks to establish an independent Western Sahara, currently occupied by Morocco

ECONOMY

Currency ($ U.S. Equivalent): 78 Algerian dinars = $1

Per Capita Income/GDP: $5,600/$177 billion

GDP Growth Rate: 3.8%

Inflation Rate: 3%

Unemployment Rate: 34%

Labor Force: 9,400,000

Natural Resources: petroleum; natural gas; iron ore; phosphates; uranium; lead; zinc

Agriculture: wheat; barley; oats; grapes; olives; citrus fruits; sheep; cattle

Industry: petroleum; natural gas; light industries; mining; electrical; petrochemicals; food processing

Exports: $19.6 billion (primary partners Italy, United States, France)

Imports: $10.6 billion (primary partners France, United States, Italy)

Algeria Country Report

The modern state of Algeria occupies the central part of North Africa, a geographically distinctive and separate region of Africa that includes Morocco, Tunisia, and Libya.

The official name of the state is the Democratic and Popular Republic of Algeria. It is the second-largest nation in Africa (after Sudan). The overall population density is low, but the population is concentrated in the northern third of the country.

GEOGRAPHY

Algeria's geography is a formidable obstacle to broad economic and social development. About 80 percent of the land is uncultivable desert, and only 12 percent is arable without irrigation. Moreover, a large-scale exodus of rural families into the cities, with consequent neglect of agriculture, has resulted in a vast increase in urban slums.

Algeria is unique among newly independent Middle Eastern countries in that it gained its independence through a civil war. For more than 130 years (1830–1962), it was occupied by France and became a French department (similar to a U.S. state). The modern Algerian nation is the product of the interaction of native Muslim Algerians with the European settlers, who also considered Algeria home.

The original inhabitants of the entire North African region were Berbers. Berbers make up about 30 percent of the total population.

The Arabs, who brought Islam to North Africa in the seventh century A.D., converted the Algerian Berbers after a fierce resistance. The Arabs brought their language as a unifying feature, and religion linked the Algerians with the larger Islamic world. Today, most follow Sunni Islam, but a significant minority, about 100,000, are Shi'a Muslims. They refer to themselves as *Ibadis*, from their observance of an ancient Shia rite, and live in five "holy cities" clustered in a remote Saharan valley where centuries ago they took refuge from Sunni rulers of northern Algeria. One of many pressures on the government today is that of an organized Kabyle movement, which seeks greater autonomy for the region and an emphasis on Berber language in schools, along with the revitalization of Kabyle culture.

The French Conquest

In 1830, a French army landed on the coast west of the city, marched overland, and entered it with almost no resistance. The French, who had been looking for an excuse to expand their interests in North Africa, now were not sure what to do with Algiers. In the 1830s, they rallied behind their first national leader, Emir Abd al-Qadir.

Abd al-Qadir was the son of a prominent religious leader and, more important, was a descendant of the Prophet Muhammad. Abd al-Qadir had unusual qualities of leadership, military skill, and physical courage. From 1830 to 1847, he carried on guerrilla warfare against a French army of more than 100,000 men with such success that at one point the French signed a formal treaty recognizing him as head of an Algerian nation in the interior.

In order to defeat Abd al-Qadir, the French commander used "total war" tactics, burning villages, destroying crops, killing livestock, and levying fines on peoples who continued to support the emir. In 1847, Abd al-Qadir surrendered to French authorities. He was imprisoned for several years, then he spent the rest of his life in exile.

Abd al-Qadir is venerated as the first Algerian nationalist, able by his leadership and Islamic prestige to unite warring groups in a struggle for independence from foreign control.

THE AGONY OF INDEPENDENCE

On July 5, 1962, with the signing of a treaty with France, Algeria became an independent nation for the first time in its history.

The first leader to emerge from intraparty struggle to lead the nation was Ahmed Ben Bella, who laid the groundwork for an Algerian political system centered on the National Liberation Front (FLN) as a single legal political party, and in September 1963, he was elected president. In June 1965 he was overthrown in a military coup headed by the defense minister, Colonel Houari Boumedienne.

FREEDOM

Algeria's constitution, issued in 1976 and amended three times, defines the country as a multiparty republic. However, it specified that no political association may be formed that is based on religious, linguistic, race, gender, or regional differences. The gradual restoration of parliamentary democracy was expedited with the 2002 election for a National Popular Assembly and election by regional and municipal assemblies of two-thirds of the 144 members of the upper house (Council of Nations). And in what was described by outside observers as the cleanest, most open, and free election in the history in the Arab world, Bouteflika was reelected president in April 2004, by an 83 percent majority, defeating five rivals, including the prime minister and an avowed Islamist candidate. For the first time since their suppression of the 1992 elections, military leaders declared their strict neutrality, in effect leaving politics to the politicians and reflecting the will of the people.

Boumedienne declared that the coup was a "corrective revolution, intended to reestablish authentic socialism and put an end to internal divisions and personal rule."[8] A National Charter (Constitution) was approved by voters in 1976. The Charter defined Algeria as a socialist state, with Islam as the state religion, basic citizens' rights guaranteed, and leadership by the FLN as the only legal political party.

THE ECONOMY

Today the hydrocarbons sector provides the bulk of government revenues and 90 percent of exports. Algeria provides 29 percent of the liquefied natural gas (LNG) imported by European countries, much of it through undersea pipelines to Italy and Spain.

After a number of years of negative economic growth, the government initiated an austerity program in 1992. Imports of luxury products were prohibited and several new taxes introduced. The program was approved by the International Monetary Fund (IMF), Algeria's main source of external financing.

HEALTH/WELFARE

The 1984 Family Law improved women's rights in marriage, education, and work opportunities. But professional women and, more recently, rural women and their chidren have become special targets of Islamic violence. Some 400 professional women were murdered in 1995, and more than 400 were killed in a one-day rampage in January 1998.

The agricultural sector employs 47 percent of the labor force and accounts for 12 percent of gross domestic product. But inasmuch as Algeria must import 70 percent of its food, better agricultural production is essential to overall economic development.

The key features of current President Abdelaziz Bouteflika's economic reform program, one designed to attract foreign investment, include banking reforms, reduction of the huge government bureaucracy, favorable terms for foreign companies, and privatization of state-owned enterprises.

ACHIEVEMENTS

A new pipeline from the vast Hassi Berkine oil field, the African continent's largest, went into production in 1998, with exports of 300,000 barrels per day. Increased foreign investment due to expansion of the hydrocarbons sector, privatization of state-owned enterprises, and favorable terms for foreign companies increased GDP growth to 5% in 2001.

THE FUNDAMENTALIST CHALLENGE

Despite the growing appeal of Islamic fundamentalism in numerous Arab countries in recent years, Algeria until very recently seemed an unlikely site for the rise of a strong fundamentalist movement. But the failure of successive Algerian governments to resolve severe economic problems, plus the lack of representative political institutions nurtured within the ruling FLN, brought about the rise of fundamentalism as a political party. Fundamentalists organized the Islamic Salvation Front (FIS), which soon claimed 3 million adherents among the then 25 million Algerians.

Timeline: PAST

1518–1520
Establishment of the Regency of Algiers

1827–1830
The French conquest, triggered by the "fly-whisk incident"

1847
The defeat of Abd al-Qadir by French forces

1871
Algeria becomes an overseas department of France

1936
The Blum-Viollette Plan, for Muslim rights, is annulled by opposition

1943
Ferhat Abbas issues the Manifesto of the Algerian People

1954–1962
Civil war, ending with Algerian independence

1965
Ben Bella is overthrown by Boumedienne

1976
The National Charter commits Algeria to revolutionary socialist deveopment

1978
President Boumedienne dies

1980s
Land reform is resumed with the breakup of 200 large farms into smaller units; Arabization campaign

1990s
President Bendjedid steps down; the Islamic Salvation Front becomes a force and eventually is banned; the economy undergoes an austerity program; civil war

PRESENT

2000s
Efforts to restore the mutliparty system
Continued civil conflict

The first local elections in the country's history were held in 1997. Elections for a 389-seat National Popular Assembly took place in May 2002, with candidates elected by popular vote. The FLN won the majority of seats, 199. Although the FIS continued to be excluded from political participation, its leaders were released from house arrest in July 2003. They are still prohibited from political activity. Bouteflika's first term has been marked by improved security. The death toll from violence averages 100 monthly, compared with 1,200 per month in the mid-1990s.

NOTES

1. Raphael Danziger, *Abd al-Qadir and the Algerians* (New York: Holmes and Meier, 1977), notes that Turkish intrigue kept the

tribes in a state of near-constant tribal warfare, thereby preventing them from forming dangerous coalitions, p. 24.

2. The usual explanation for the quick collapse of the regency after 300 years is that its forces were prepared for naval warfare but not for attack by land. *Ibid.*, pp. 36–38.

3. Quoted in Harold D. Nelson, *Algeria, A Country Study* (Washington, D.C.: American University, Foreign Area Studies, 1979), p. 31.

4. Marnia Lazreg, *The Emergence of Classes in Algeria* (Boulder, CO: Westview Press, 1976), p. 53.

5. For Algerian Muslims to become French citizens meant giving up their religion, for all practical purposes, since Islam recognizes only Islamic law and to be a French citizen means accepting French laws. Fewer than 3,000 Algerians became French citizens during the period of French rule. Nelson, *op. cit.*, pp. 34–35.

6. John E. Talbott, *The War Without a Name: France in Algeria, 1954–1962* (New York: Alfred A. Knopf, 1980).

7. Georges Suffert, in *Esprit*, 25 (1957), p. 819.

8. Nelson, *op. cit.*, p. 68.

Azerbaijan

Map No. 3761 Rev. 5   UNITED NATIONS
June 2004

Department of Peacekeeping Operations
Cartographic Section

Azerbaijan Statistics

GEOGRAPHY

Area in Square Miles (Kilometers):
33,428 (86,600) (about the size of Maine)
Capital (Population): Baku (1,848,000)

PEOPLE

Population

Total: 7,772,000
Annual Growth Rate: 0.32%
Major Languages: Azeri; Russian;
  Armenian
Ethnic Makeup: 90% Azerbaijani (Azeri);
  3% Daghestani; 7% Russian, Armenian,
  and others

Religions: 93% Muslim; 7% Russian
  Orthodox, Armenian Orthodox, and others

Health

Life Expectancy at Birth: 59 years (male);
  68 years (female)
Infant Mortality Rate (Ratio): 82.5/1,000

Education

Adult Literacy Rate: 97%

GOVERNMENT

Type: republic
Head of State/Government: President Heydar
  Aliyev; Prime Minister Artur Rasizade

Political Parties: New Azerbaijan Party;
  Musavat Party; National Independence
  Party; Social Democratic Party;
  Azerbaijan Popular Front; Communist
  Party; others

ECONOMY

Currency ($ U.S. Equivalent): 3,865
  manats = $1
Per Capita Income/GDP: $3,000/$23.5
  billion
Inflation Rate: 1.8%
Exports: $1.9 billion
Imports: $1.4 billion

Azerbaijan Country Report

During the 1990s Russian leaders, especially conservatives seeking to strengthen Russia's links with other ex-Soviet republics and concerned about a strengthening of Azerbaijani links to the Islamic world, supported President Heydar Aliyev. The Kremlin offered to help the Azerbaijani in their war with the Karabakh Armenians. By November 1993 the Kremlin had military advisers in Azerbaijan to reorganize and strengthen the demoralized army. But Aliyev was very uncomfortable over what he and other Azerbaijani nationalists considered an ill-concealed Russian effort to restore Moscow's influence over the Caspian region.

New Problems With Azerbaijan, 1998–2004

By the late 1990s, Aliyev was ready to pursue an independent course in his foreign policy. In response to offers from the Kremlin of military advisers and troops, he said he did not need them "to help him maintain law and order." In addition, he was ready to deny Russia a major role in the production and marketing of Caspian oil. He could afford to pursue this independent path because Azerbaijan was politically stable. Moreover, other countries, notably Turkey and Iran, offered to support Aliyev's efforts to maintain independence

of the Kremlin. They did not want Russia exerting an undue influence over the marketing of Caspian oil, nor did they want to see Azerbaijan permanently lose the Nagorno-Karabakh territory.

In the spring of 2004, the new Azeri government, led by Aliev's son Ilam, announced its intention of regaining control of Nagorno-Karabakh by force if necessary, adding that the Azeri army was being geared up to go on the offensive. The stated objective was to restore Azerbaijan's territorial integrity by force given the failure over the years to reach a settlement with Armenia acceptable to both sides.

Russia and Caspian Oil

Azerbaijan is of significant interest to the rest of the world in part by its access to Caspian oil. The Caspian Sea is reputed to have oil reserves equivalent to about 200 billion barrels, plus comparable reserves of natural gas. By 2010 the Caspian could provide as much oil as the North Sea does today, making it one of the world's main production centers.

By 1999, the competition between Russia and outside nations—in particular the United States and, to a lesser degree, Turkey, Georgia, Iran, and Pakistan—focused

on the construction of pipelines to transport the oil to foreign markets, especially in the West. Russia wanted to use existing pipelines built in the Soviet era to send Caspian oil to Baltic and Central/Eastern European markets. The United States, Azerbaijan, Georgia, Turkey, and Iran have opposed a Russian route, which would naturally increase Russian leverage in the Caucasus. The U.S. government has favored a route through Georgia to Turkey, which would benefit those two countries economically and strategically.

At the end of 1999, the leaders of Georgia, Azerbaijan, Turkey, and Kazakhstan agreed to support the construction of a $2.4 billion pipeline to carry Caspian oil to Western markets on a route that did not pass through either Russia or Iran. The groundwork for this agreement had been laid in April 1998, when Aliyev, Georgia's Eduard Shevardnadze, and Turkish president Suleyman Demirel agreed to the Baku-Tbilisi-Ceyhan route to transport Caspian natural gas. In making this agreement, Aliyev dismissed Russian annoyance over the prospect of being excluded from making such plans.

Bahrain (State of Bahrain)

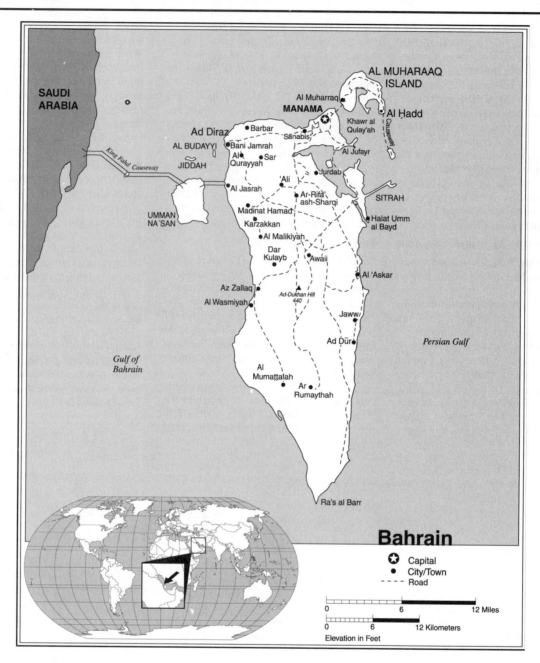

Map legend:
Bahrain
⭐ Capital
● City/Town
--- Road

Places shown on map: SAUDI ARABIA, AL MUHARAAQ ISLAND, Al Muharraq, MANAMA, Al Hadd, Ad Diraz, Barbar, Sanabis, Khawr al Qulay'ah, AL BUDAYYI, Bani Jamrah, Al Qurayyah, Sar, Al Jufayr, JIDDAH, 'Ali, Jurdab, Al Jasrah, Ar-Rifa ash-Sharqi, SITRAH, Madinat Hamad, UMMAN NA'SAN, Karzakkan, Halat Umm al Bayd, Al Malikiyah, Dar Kulayb, Awali, Al 'Askar, Az Zallaq, Ad-Dukhan Hill 440, Al Wasmiyah, Jaww, Ad Dur, Persian Gulf, Gulf of Bahrain, Al Mumattalah, Ar Rumaythah, Ra's al Barr, King Fahd Causeway

Scale: 0 — 6 — 12 Miles; 0 — 6 — 12 Kilometers; Elevation in Feet

Bahrain Statistics

GEOGRAPHY

Area in Square Miles (Kilometers): 266 (688) (about 3 1/2 times the size of Washington, D.C.)

Capital (Population): Manama (166,200)

Environmental Concerns: desertification; coastal degradation resulting from oil spills and discharges from ships and industry; no natural freshwater

Geographical Features: mostly low desert plain, rising gently to low central escarpment

Climate: hot and humid summers; temperate winters

PEOPLE

Population

Total: 688,345

Annual Growth Rate: 1.51%

Rural/Urban Population Ratio: 9/91

Major Languages: Arabic; English

Ethnic Makeup: 63% Bahraini; 19% Asian; 10% other Arab; 8% Iranian

Religions: 70% Shia Muslim; 15% Sunni Muslim; 15% Bahai, Christian, and others

Health

Life Expectancy at Birth: 71 years (male);
76 years (female)
Infant Mortality Rate (Ratio): 17.2/1,000
live births
Physicians Available (Ratio): 1/1,115
people

Education

Adult Literacy Rate: 89.1%
Compulsory (Ages): 6–17; free

COMMUNICATION

Telephones: 185,800 main lines
Daily Newspaper Circulation: 128 per
1,000 people
Televisions: 442 per 1,000 people
Internet Users: 195,700 (2003)

TRANSPORTATION

Highways in Miles (Kilometers): 1,927
(3,459)
Railroads in Miles (Kilometers): none

Usable Airfields: 4
Motor Vehicles in Use: 172,000

GOVERNMENT

Type: constitutional monarchy as of 2001
Independence Date: August 15, 1971
(from the United Kingdom)
Head of State/Government: King Hamad
bin Isa al-Khalifa; Prime Minister
Shaykh Salman bin Hamad al-Khalifa
Political Parties: none, but direct elections
held in October 2002 for 40-member
Chamber of Deputies (Parliament)
Suffrage: 18 years of age; universal

MILITARY

Military Expenditures (% of GDP): 6.3%
Current Disputes: none; dispute with
Qatar resolved in 2001

ECONOMY

Currency ($ U.S. Equivalent): 0.376 dinar
= $1 (fixed rate)

Per Capita Income/GDP: $19,200/$13.01
billion
GDP Growth Rate: 5%
Inflation Rate: 2%
Unemployment Rate: 15%
Labor Force: 370,000
Natural Resources: oil; associated and
nonassociated natural gas; fish
Agriculture: fruits; vegetables; poultry;
dairy products; shrimp; fish
Industry: petroleum processing and
refining; aluminum smelting; offshore
banking; ship repairing; tourism
Exports: $8.2 billion (primary partners
India, United States, Saudi Arabia)
Imports: $5.8 billion (primary partners
France, United States, United Kingdom)

SUGGESTED WEB SITES

```
http://lcweb2.loc.gov/frd/cs/
  bhtoc.html
http://www.usembassy.com.bh
```

Bahrain Country Report

Bahrain is the smallest Arab state. It is also the only Arab island state, consisting of an archipelago of 33 islands, just five of them inhabited. The largest island, also named Bahrain (from the Arabic *bahrayn*, or "two seas"), has an area of 216 square miles.

Although it is separated from the Arabian mainland, Bahrain is not far away; it is just 15 miles from Qatar and the same distance from Saudi Arabia. Oil was discovered there in 1932. Its head start in the exportation of oil enabled the government to build up an industrial base over a long period and to develop a large, indigenous, skilled labor force. As a result, today about two-thirds of the population are native-born Bahrainis.

DEVELOPMENT

Bahrain's economy continues to develop and diversify. GDP growth held steady at 4.5–5% annually from 1998 to 2003. The country has the highest concentration of Islamic banking institutions in the region and leads the Arab Middle East in direct foreign investment.

HISTORY

In 1782 clan leader, Shaykh Ahmad al-Khalifa established control over Bahrain and founded the dynasty that rules the state

today. (The al-Khalifas belong to the same clan as the al-Sabahs, the rulers of Kuwait, and are distantly related to the Saudi Arabian royal family.)

INDEPENDENCE

Bahrain became fully independent in 1971.

The gradual development of democracy in Bahrain reached a peak after independence. Shaykh Khalifa (now called emir) approved a new constitution and a law establishing an elected National Assembly of 30 members. The Assembly met for the first time in 1973, but it was dissolved by the emir only two years later.

FREEDOM

Reinstatement of the 1973 Constitution and the Election of a new Chamber of Deputies in 2002 underlined the ruler's commitment to parliamentary democracy. The National Action Charter gives women the right to vote and run for public office; although none were elected to the Chamber, seven were subsequently appointed to the Cabinet of Ministers.

What Had Happened?

Bahrain is an example of a problem common in the Middle East: the conflict between traditional authority and popular

democracy. Governmental authority in Bahrain is defined as hereditary in the al-Khalifa family, according to the 1973 Constitution. The succession passes from the ruling emir to his eldest son. Since Bahrain has no tradition of representative government or political parties, the National Assembly was set up to broaden the political process without going through the lengthy period of conditioning necessary to establish a multiparty system. Members were expected to debate laws prepared by the Council of Ministers and to assist with budget preparation. But as things turned out, Assembly members spent their time arguing with one another or criticizing the ruler instead of dealing with issues. When the emir dissolved the Assembly, he said that it was preventing the government from doing what it was supposed to do.

Since that time, government in Bahrain has reverted to its traditional patriarchal authority structure. However, Shi'a demands for reinstatement of the Assembly, a multiparty system with national elections, and greater representation for Shi'as in government have been met in part through changes in the governing structure. In 1993, the emir appointed a 30-member *Shura* (Council), composed of business and industry leaders along with members of the ruling family.

King Hamad, who changed his title as part of the country's move toward constitutional monarchy, has taken several long steps in that direction in recent years. In 2000 the Shura was enlarged to 40 members, including women and representatives of the large Shi'a community.

THREATS TO NATIONAL SECURITY

The 1979 Revolution in Iran caused much concern in Bahrain. However, after seeing the results of the Iranian Revolution, few Bahraini Shi'a Muslims wanted the Iranian form of fundamentalist Islamic government.

AN OIL-LESS ECONOMY?

Bahrain was an early entrant in the oil business and may be the first Gulf state to face an oil-less future. Current production from its own oil fields is 42,000 barrels per day. The Bahrain Petroleum Company (Bapco) controls all aspects of production, refining, and export. However, Bapco must import 70,000 b/d from Saudi Arabia to keep its refinery operating efficiently.

HEALTH/WELFARE

In January 2002 the American Mission Hospital, the first in Bahrain, marked its 100th anniversary. It was built in 1902 with a $6,000 gift from the Mason family, medical missionaries in Arabia. A 1993 labor law allows unions to organize and requires 60% local labor in new industries, both Bahraini and foreign-owned.

In the past, Bahrain's economic development was characterized by conservative management. This policy changed radically with the current ruler rise to power. A January 2001 decree allows foreign companies to buy and own property, particularly for non-oil investment projects. (Oil currently accounts for 80 percent of exports and 60 percent of revenues.)

The slow decline in oil production in recent years has been balanced by expansion of the liquefied natural gas (LNG) sector. Current production is 170 million cubic feet per day. But with 9 billion cubic feet of

ACHIEVEMENTS

In 2002 a female lawyer, Dr. Mariam bint Hassan Al-Khalifa, was appointed president of Bahrain University, the first to hold such a position in the Arab world. And in 2003 Bahrain's economy was named as the freest in the Arab Middle East by the Heritage Foundation.

proven reserves, production of LNG will long outlast oil production.

Aluminium Bahrain (ALBA), which accounts for 60 percent of Bahrain's non-oil exports, expanded its production in 2001 to become the world's largest aluminium smelter, with an annual output of 750,000 tons. Some 450,000 of this is exported. A seawater-desalination plant was completed in 1999. It uses waste heat from the smelter to provide potable water for local needs.

INTERNATIONAL FINANCE

"Offshore Banking Units" (OBUs) are set up to attract deposits from governments or large financial organizations such as the World Bank as well as to make loans for development projects. OBUs are "offshore" in the sense that a Bahraini cannot open a checking account or borrow money. However, OBUs bring funds into Bahrain without interfering with local growth or undercutting local banks.

In 2001 BNP Paribas, the sixth largest bank in the world, relocated its Middle East operations office to Bahrain, as did Turkey's Islamic Bank, an emerging giant in the Islamic banking system.

THE FUTURE

For a brief time after independence, the state experimented with representative government. But the hurly-burly of politics, with its factional rivalries, trade-offs, and compromises found in many Western democratic systems, did not suit the Bahraini temperament or experience. Democracy takes time to mature.

The emir demonstrated his commitment to gradual democratization in 2000, issuing an edict, confirmed in a national referendum, that defines Bahrain as a constitutional monarchy ruled by a king. He scheduled elections for municipal councils for May 2002 and parliamentary elections for October, which were held on schedule.

NOTES

1. UN Security Council *Resolution 287*, 1970. Quoted from Emile Nakhleh, Bahrain (Lexington, KY: Lexington Books, 1976), p. 9.

2. Fuad I. Khuri, *Tribe and State in Bahrain* (Chicago: University of Chicago Press, 1981), p. 219.

3. *Gulf Daily News* (May 15, 1982).

4. Nakhleh, *op. cit.*, p. 11.

Timeline: PAST

1602–1782
Periodic occupation of Bahrain by Iran after the Portuguese ouster

1783
The al-Khalifa family seizes power over other families and groups

1880
Bahrain becomes a British protectorate

1971
Independence

1973–1975
The new Constitution establishes a Constituent Assembly, but the ruler dissolves it shortly thereafter

1990s
Bahrain takes aggressive steps to revive and diversify its economy

PRESENT

2000s
Territorial disputes with Qatar resolved; important changes in representation and participation in government

Bangladesh (People's Republic of Bangladesh)

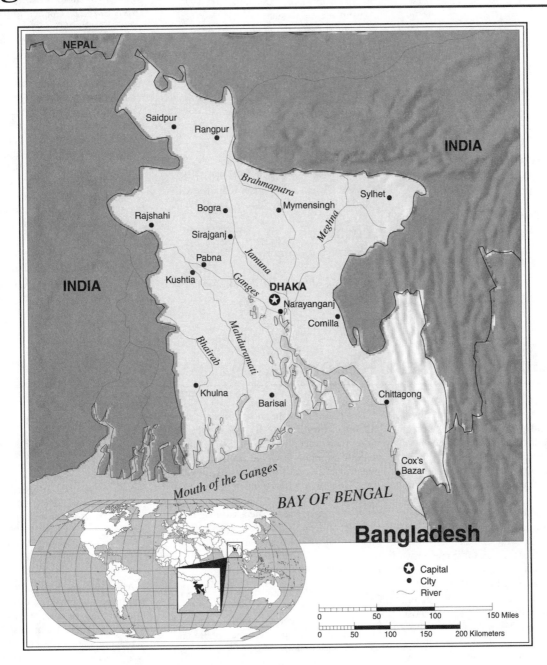

Bangladesh Statistics

GEOGRAPHY

Area in Square Miles (Kilometers): 55,584 (144,000) (slightly smaller than Iowa)

Capital (Population): Dhaka (8,545,000)

Environmental Concerns: water-borne disease and pollution; soil degradation; deforestation; severe overpopulation

Geographical Features: mostly flat alluvial plain; hilly in the southeast

Climate: tropical; monsoon; cool, mild winter; hot, humid summer

PEOPLE

Population

Total: 141,340,476

Annual Growth Rate: 2.08%

Rural/Urban Population Ratio: 81/19

Major Languages: Bangla (Bengali); English

Ethnic Makeup: 98% Bengali; 2% non-Bengali Muslims and various tribes

Religions: 83% Muslim; 16% Hindu; 1% other

Health

Life Expectancy at Birth: 61.8 years (male); 61.61 years (female)

91

Infant Mortality: 64.32/1,000 live births
Physicians Available: 1/4,759 people
HIV/AIDS Rate in Adults: less than 0.1%

Education

Adult Literacy Rate: 43.1%
Compulsory (Ages): 6–11; free

COMMUNICATION

Telephones: 740,000 main lines
Daily Newspaper Circulation: 0.4 per 1,000 people
Internet Users: 243,000 (2003)

TRANSPORTATION

Highways in Miles (Kilometers): 128,926 (207,486)
Railroads in Miles (Kilometers): 1,681 (2,706)
Usable Airfields: 16
Motor Vehicles in Use: 227,000

GOVERNMENT

Type: parliament democracy
Independence Date: December 16, 1971 (from West Pakistan)
Head of State/Government: President Iajuddin Ahmed; Prime Minister Zhaleda Zia
Political Parties: Bangladesh Nationalist Party; Awami League; Jatiya Party; Jamaat-e-Islami; Bangladesh Communist Party
Suffrage: universal at 18

MILITARY

Military Expenditures (% of GDP): 1.2%
Current Disputes: boundary disputes with India, sometimes violent

ECONOMY

Currency ($ U.S. equivalent): 58.15 takas = $1
GDP-Per Capita: purchasing power parity -$1,900
GDP Growth Rate: 5.3%
Inflation Rate: 5.6%
Unemployment Rate: 40%
Labor Force by Occupation: 63% agriculture; 26% services; 11% industry
Population Below Poverty Line: 35.6%
Natural Resources: natural gas; arable land; timber
Agriculture: rice; jute; tea; wheat; sugarcane; potatoes; tobacco; pulses; oilseeds; spices; fruit; beef; milk; poultry
Industry: jute; garments; textiles; food processing; newsprint; cement; light engineering; fertilizer; sugar
Exports: $6.713 billion (primary partners United States, Germany, United Kingdom, France)
Imports: $9.459 billion (primary partners India, China, Singapore, Japan, Hong Kong)

SUGGESTED WEB SITES

http://www.virtualbangladesh.com
http://southasia.net/Bangladesh

Bangladesh Country Report

Bangladesh, the youngest nation of South Asia, won its independence from Pakistan in 1971. It is a delta country fed by three major rivers, the Brahmaputra, the Ganges, and the Maghma. They draw upon and expand into 700 rivers that flow in intricate and shifting channels into the Sundarbans, "tide country," leading into the Bay of Bengal.

In the monsoon season, flooding waters frequently overflow the embankments surrounding settlements along these many rivers. Natural disasters remain a constant threat to all aspects of life in Bangladesh.

Although it is one of the smaller countries of the subcontinent, it is also the most densely populated. More than 141 million people—half the population of the United States—live in an area smaller than the state of Wisconsin, at an average rural density of more than 2,000 per square mile. Only 19 percent live in cities. The land is crowded, and unemployment is over 35 percent. Yet the population continues to grow, though at a decreasing rate (currently about 1.54 percent per year).

Bangladesh remains one of the poorest countries in the world; 61 percent of the urban population is below the poverty line, according to a recent Asian Development Bank survey, and over half of the total population lives on less than $1 a day. The nation's languages are obscure in origin; some have never been studied.

Bangladesh has the most cohesive population in South Asia. Except for the remote tribal peoples, almost all citizens share a common Bengali ethnic and language identity, and most are Sunni Muslims. However, with so much upon which to build a democratic nation—language, religion, culture, and a successful fight for its independence—the country still struggles to achieve political stability.

COLONIAL HISTORY

The origin of Bangladesh as an independent nation began in 1905, when Lord Curzon, the British viceroy in India, attempted to divide the Colonial Province of Bengal into a predominantly Muslim East Bengal (which then included Assam) and a Hindu West Bengal. In the 1947 partition of the subcontinent, when India and Pakistan received their independence from the British Raj, a truncated yet predominantly Muslim province of East Bengal became the eastern wing of Pakistan.

INDEPENDENCE

In December 1971 India attacked Pakistan in support of the Bengali resistance and freed the people of East Bengal from Pakistan military rule. Mujibur Rahman then became prime minister of the new nation of Bangladesh.

DEVELOPMENT

Bangladesh is an agricultural country with a very small industrial sector, few natural resources, and 35% unemployment plus substantial underemployment. Bangladesh's per capita income has grown an average of only 0.4% per year since 1960. The country continues to rely heavily on relief aid from the international community.

Although he was a popular leader, Mujib did not prove an effective administrator in the face of severe overpopulation, poverty, famine, and natural disasters. His increasingly authoritarian rule as an executive president led to a military coup in 1975, in which he and most of his family were killed.

In the political turmoil that followed, General Ziaur Rahman, army chief of staff, took over as martial-law administrator. To lead the country back to democracy, General Zia created his own political party, the Bangladesh Nationalist Party (BNP), and encouraged others to participate in national elections to elect 300 members to the national legislature. To assure administrative control of the government, Zia retained the independent executive presidency established by Mujibur Rahman. In 1981 dissident military officers assassinated General

Zia. A national referendum in September 1991 reduced the power of the president of Bangladesh by placing executive power in the hands of the prime minister of the national legislature.

FREEDOM

Bangladesh has reverted to martial law in order to maintain social order several times since its independence in 1971. With reports of an estimated 3 million children in the workforce, their abuse is also a source of concern. In 1994 novelist Taslima Nasreen was prosecuted on charges of blasphemy, raising an international outcry.

The new legislature still enacted an important initiative for women in government. This law reserves for women 3 of the 10 directly elected seats in the 4,298 local councils that form the lowest tier of government in Bangladesh. Elections for these councils started in December 1997, and more than 45,000 women were elected to council seats. This local initiative was an important step toward increasing the place of women in a country where traditional religious teachings and social custom have advocated their repression.

Sheikh Hasina's Awami League government was able to complete a full five-year term in control of the national legislature. But her liberalizing initiatives to establish modern secular rule in Bangladesh and build its relationship with India came to a sudden and surprising end in the elections of October 2001. Begum Zia's BNP campaigned on a pro-Islamic and isolationist platform, in alliance with three other conservative parties in order not to split their votes. Their alliance came to power in a landslide victory. There were many indigenous causes for the rout of the Awami League. But the terrorist attacks in the United States the month before may have stirred Islamic fundamentalist fervor in Bangladesh, as they did in many places in the Islamic world.

HEALTH/WELFARE

In spite of many obstacles, overall life expectancy has increased from 27 to 61 years over the past 2 decades. Forty-five% of the population has access to health care, and the number of hospital beds per population has doubled. Literacy has also increased, from 20% to 56%. The country has made significant strides in reducing the rate of population growth, from 3.3% to 1.59% per year.

CHALLENGES

Because of its large and growing population, its limited resources, unemployment, corruption, and a succession of natural disasters, Bangladesh has struggled since its independence to achieve prosperity for its people.

ACHIEVEMENTS

Surviving extensive flooding in 1975 and a horrific cyclone in 1991, the resilient people of Bangladesh continue to develop their wealth of human resources, mostly through volunteer and nongovernment agencies such as the Grameen Bank. In 1991 a national referendum to restrain the military and restrict the power of the executive branch of government made a strong commitment to parliamentary democracy.

Natural gas is the country's greatest potential resource, with reserves sufficient to provide for its energy needs. But without other natural resources to broaden its industrial base and create new employment, and with a decline in the world market for their jute and textiles, the country's largest exports, a sustained GDP growth of 5.3 percent is difficult to maintain. Lack of adequate education and other human development initiatives also contribute to high unemployment and slow economic growth.

Bangladesh has also been fortunate in the support it has received from many gov-

ernments and independent agencies. It received an estimated $1.575 billion in foreign aid in 2000. And it received a $2 million grant of credit from the World Bank in immediate response to the devastation of the floods in 2004. Because of corruption, a lack of significant planning in government, and a large drop in foreign aid from industrial countries, most aid is now going more directly to nongovernmental organizations (NGOs).

Timeline: PAST

A.D. 1757–1947
British control over Bengal

1947–1971
East Pakistan

1971
The birth of Bangladesh

1972–1975
Mujibur Rahman's presidential rule

1974
Severe flooding causes 400,000 deaths

1975–1989
Martial law

1990s
In 1991 a cyclone causes 130,000 deaths; flooding in 1998 kills 800 and leaves 30 million homeless; Bangladesh returns to parliamentary government

PRESENT

2000s
Women seek more reserved seats in the national Legislature

Bangladeshis continue to seek grassroot solutions to their country's severe economic and social problems

2004
Almost 2/3 of country flooded by monsoon, causing $7 billion in damage

Benin (Republic of Benin)

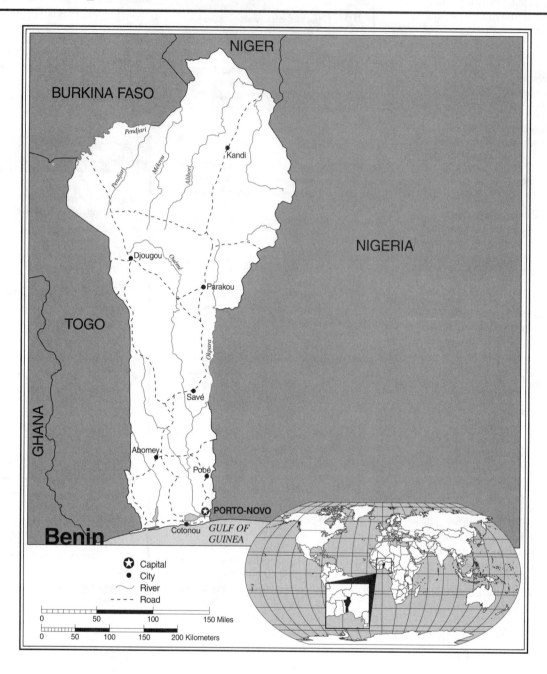

Benin Statistics

GEOGRAPHY

Area in Square Miles (Kilometers): 43,483 (112,620) (about the size of Pennsylvania)

Capital (Population): official: Porto-Novo (225,000); de facto: Cotonou (750,000)

Environmental Concerns: drought; insufficient potable water; poaching; deforestation; desertification

Geographical Features: mostly flat to undulating plain; some hills and low mountains

Climate: tropical to semiarid

PEOPLE

Population

Total: 7,250,033

Annual Growth Rate: 2.91%

Rural/Urban Population Ratio: 58/42

Major Languages: French; Fon; Yoruba; others
Ethnic Makeup: 99% African (most important groupings Fon, Adja, Yoruba, and Bariba); 1% European
Religions: 70% indigenous beliefs; 15% Muslim; 15% Christian

Health

Life Expectancy at Birth: 49 years (male); 51 years (female)
Infant Mortality: 88.5/1,000 live births
Physicians Available: 1/14,216 people
HIV/AIDS Rate in Adults: 4.1%

Education

Adult Literacy Rate: 37%
Compulsory (Ages): 6–12; free

COMMUNICATION

Telephones: 66,500 main lines
Daily Newspaper Circulation: 2 per 1,000 people
Televisions: 4 per 1,000 people
Internet Users: 70,000 (2003)

TRANSPORTATION

Highways in Miles (Kilometers): 4,208 (6,787)
Railroads in Miles (Kilometers): 360 (578)
Usable Airports: 5
Motor Vehicles in Use: 55,000

GOVERNMENT

Type: republic
Independence Date: August 1, 1960 (from France)
Head of State/Government: President Mathieu Kérékou is both head of state and head of government
Political Parties: Alliance for Democracy and Progress; Front for Renewal and Development; African Movement for Democracy and Progress; many others
Suffrage: universal at 18

MILITARY

Military Expenditures (% of GDP): 1.2%
Current Disputes: territorial disputes with Niger and Nigeria

ECONOMY

Currency ($ U.S. Equivalent): 581 CFA francs = $1
Per Capita Income/GDP: $1,100/$7.7 billion
GDP Growth Rate: 5.4%
Inflation Rate: 1.5%
Population Below Poverty Line: 37%
Natural Resources: small offshore oil deposits; limestone; marble; timber
Agriculture: palm products; cotton; corn; rice; yams; cassava; beans; sorghum; livestock
Industry: textiles; construction materials; food production; chemical production
Exports: $35.3 million (primary partners Brazil, France, Indonesia)
Imports: $437 million (primary partners France, China, United States)

SUGGESTED WEB SITES

http://www.benindaily.com
http://www.cia.gov/cia/
  publications/factbook/geos/
  bn.html

Benin Country Report

Over the past decade, Benin has emerged as one of one of Africa's most stable and democratic states. This has coincided with improved economic growth, though the country remains among the world's poorest in terms of both per capita income and human development.

DEVELOPMENT

Palm-oil plantations were established in Benin by Africans in the mid-nineteenth century. They have continued to be African-owned and capitalist-oriented. Today there are some 30 million trees in Benin, and palm-oil products are a major export used for cooking, lighting, soap, margarine, and lubricants.

Since gaining its independence from France in 1960, Benin has experienced a series of shifts in political and economic policy that have so far failed to lift most Beninois out of chronic poverty. In this respect, the country's ongoing struggle for development can be seen as a microcosm of the challenges facing much of the African continent. Politically, Benin has been in the forefront of those nations on the continent making the transition away from an authoritarian centralized state toward greater democracy and market reforms.

This process has not as yet been accompanied by a decisive shift toward a new generation of leadership.

Kérékou's leadership did not result in any significant moves away from his predecessor's economic reforms, which had resulted in a modest rise in GDP, increased investment, reduced inflation, and an easing of the country's debt burden. He is under pressure, however, to raise the living standards of Benin's impoverished masses.

FREEDOM

Since 1990 political restrictions have been lifted and prisoners of conscience freed. More recently, however, a number of citizens have been arrested for supposedly inciting people against the government and encouraging them not to pay taxes.

THE OLD ORDER FALLS A COUNTRY OF MIGRANTS

Benin is one of the least-developed countries in the world. Having for decades experienced only limited economic growth, in recent years the nation's real GDP has actually declined. No wonder the migration of Beninois in search of job opportunities to neighboring states has become a way of life.

HEALTH/WELFARE

One-third of the national budget of Benin goes to education, and the percentage of students receiving primary education has risen to 50% of the school-age population. College graduates serve as temporary teachers through the National Service System, but more teachers and higher salaries are needed.

THE ECONOMY

Nigeria's urban areas have been major markets for food exports. This has encouraged Beninois farmers to switch from cash crops (such as cotton, palm oil, cocoa beans, and coffee) to food crops (such as yams and cassava), which are smuggled across the border to Nigeria. The emergence of this parallel export economy has been encouraged by the former regime's practice of paying its farmers among the lowest official produce prices in the region. Given that agriculture, in terms of both employment and income generation, forms the largest sector of the Beninois economy, the rise in smuggling activities has inevitably contributed to a growth of graft and corruption.

Benin's small industrial sector is primarily geared toward processing primary products, such as palm oil and cotton, for export. It has thus been adversely affected by the shift away from producing these cash crops for the local market. Small-scale manufacturing has centered around the production of basic consumer goods and construction materials. The biggest enterprises are state-owned cement plants. One source of hope is that with privatization and new exploration, the country's small oil industry will undergo expansion.

ACHIEVEMENTS

 Fon appliquéd cloths have been described as "one of the gayest and liveliest of the contemporary African art forms." Formerly these cloths were used by Dahomeyan kings. Now they are sold to tourists, but they still portray the motifs and symbols of past rulers and the society they ruled.

Transport and trade are other important activities. Many Beninois find legal as well as illegal employment carrying goods. Due to the relative absence of rain forest (an impediment to travel), Benin's territory has historically served as a trade corridor between the coastal and inland savanna regions of West Africa. Today the nation's roads are comparatively well developed,

Timeline: PAST

1625
The kingdom of Dahomey is established

1892
The French conquer Dahomey and declare it a French protectorate

1960
Dahomey becomes independent

1972
Mathieu Kérékou comes to power in the sixth attempted military coup since independence

1975
The name of Dahomey is changed to Benin

1990s
Kérékou announces the abandonment of Marxism-Leninism as Benin's guiding ideology; multiparty elections are held; Kérékou loses power to Nicephore Soglo; Kérékou is reelected 5 years later

PRESENT

2000s
Benin marks its 40th year of independence; poverty remains an overwhelming problem

and the railroad carries goods from the port at Cotonou to northern areas of the country. The government has also tried, with little success, to attract tourists in recent years, through such gambits as selling itself as the "home of voodoo."

POLITICS AND RELIGION

Kérékou's narrow victory margin in 1996 amid charges and countercharges of electoral fraud underscored the continuing north-south division of Beninois politics and society. Although he is now a self-proclaimed Christian, Kérékou's political base remains the mainly Muslim north, while Soglo enjoyed majority support in the more Christianized south.

Religious allegiance in Benin is complicated, however, by the prominence of the indigenous belief system known as voodoo. Having originated in Benin, belief in voodoo spirits has taken root in the Americas, especially Haiti, as well as elsewhere in West Africa.

Brunei (State of Brunei Darussalam)

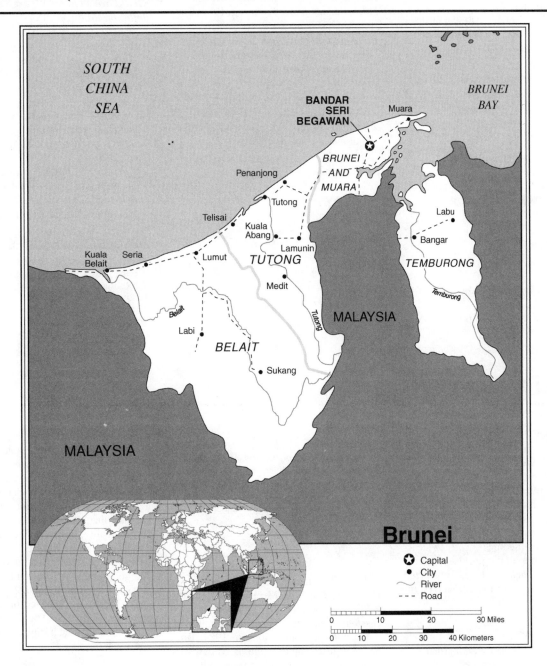

Brunei Statistics

GEOGRAPHY

Area in Square Miles (Kilometers): 2,228 (5,770) (about the size of Delaware)

Capital (Population): Bandar Seri Begawan (46,000)

Environmental Concerns: water pollution; seasonal smoke/haze resulting from forest fires in Indonesia

Geographical Features: flat coastal plain rises to mountains in east; hilly lowlands in west

Climate: tropical; hot, humid, rainy

PEOPLE

Population

Total: 365,251

Annual Growth Rate: 1.95%

Rural/Urban Population (Ratio): 28/72

Major Languages: Malay; English; Chinese; Iban; native dialects

Ethnic Makeup: 67% Malay; 15% Chinese; 18% others

Religions: 67% Muslim; 13% Buddhist; 10% Christian; 10% indigenous beliefs and others

Health

Life Expectancy at Birth: 72 years (male);
77 years (female)
Infant Mortality: 13.05/1,000 live births
Physicians Available: 1/1,398 people
HIV/AIDS Rate in Adults: 0.2%

Education

Adult Literacy Rate: 88%
Compulsory (Ages): 5–17; free

COMMUNICATION

Telephones: 79,000 main lines
Daily Newspaper Circulation: 70 per
1,000 people
Televisions: 308 per 1,000 people
Internet Users: 28,000 (2001)

TRANSPORTATION

Highways in Miles (Kilometers): 1521
(2,525)
Railroads in Miles (Kilometers): 8 (13)
Usable Airfields: 2
Motor Vehicles in Use: 165,000

GOVERNMENT

Type: constitutional sultanate (monarchy)
Independence Date: January 1, 1984 (from
the United Kingdom)
Head of State/Government: Sultan and
Prime Minister Sir Hassanal Bolkiah is
both head of state and head of
government
Political Parties: Brunei Solidarity
National Party (the only legal party);
Brunei People's Party (banned); Brunei
National Democratic Party
(deregistered)
Suffrage: none

MILITARY

Military Expenditures (% of GDP): 5.9%
Current Disputes: dispute over the Spratly
Islands

ECONOMY

Currency ($ U.S. Equivalent): 1.73 Brunei
dollars = $1

Per Capita Income/GDP: $18,600/$6.5
billion
GDP Growth Rate: 3%
Inflation Rate: 1%
Unemployment Rate: 10%
Labor Force by Occupation: 48%
government; 42% industry and services;
10% agriculture
Natural Resources: petroleum; natural
gas; timber
Agriculture: rice; cassava (tapioca);
bananas; water buffalo
Industry: petroleum; natural gas;
contruction
Exports: $3.43 billion (primary partners
Japan, South Korea, Thailand, Australia)
Imports: $1.4 billion (primary partners
Singapore, United Kingdom, Malaysia)

SUGGESTED WEB SITES

http://www.odci.gov/cia/
publications/factbook/geos/
bx.html
http://www.brunet.bn
http://www.brunei.gov.bn/
index.htm

Brunei Country Report

Home to only 351,000 people and a size about that of Delaware, Brunei boasts one of the highest living standards in the world. Moreover, the sultan of Brunei, with assets of $37 billion, is considered the richest person in the world. The secret? Oil. Today petroleum and natural gas almost entirely support the sultanate's economy. The government's annual income is nearly twice its expenditures, despite the provision of free education and medical care, subsidized food and housing, and the absence of income taxes.

DEVELOPMENT

Brunei's economy is a mixture of the modern and the ancient: foreign and domestic entrepreneurship, government regulation and welfare statism, and village tradition. Chronic labor shortages are managed by the importation of thousands of foreign workers.

Muslim sultans ruled over the entire island of Borneo and other nearby islands during the sixteenth century. Tropical rain forests and swamps occupy much of the country—conditions that are maintained by heavy monsoon rains for about five months each year. Oil and natural-gas deposits are found both on- and offshore.

FREEDOM

Although Islam is the official state religion, the government practices religious tolerance. The Constitution provides the sultan with supreme executive authority, which he has used to suppress opposition groups and political parties.

In 1967, Sultan (and Prime Minister) Sir Hassanal Bolkiah Mu'izzaddin Waddaulah, who became the 29th ruler in succession, oversaw Brunei's gaining of independence from Britain in 1984. Brunei's largest ethnic group is Malay, accounting for 64 percent of the population. Indians and Chinese constitute sizable minorities, as do indigenous peoples such as Ibans and Dyaks.

HEALTH/WELFARE

The country's massive oil and natural-gas revenues support wide-ranging benefits to the population, such as subsidized food, fuel, and housing, and free medical care and education. This distribution of wealth is reflected in Brunei's generally favorable quality-of-life indicators.

Brunei is an Islamic nation with Hindu roots. Islam is the official state religion, and in recent years, the sultan has proposed bringing national laws more closely in line with Islamic ideology. Modern Brunei is officially a constitutional monarchy, headed by the sultan, a chief minister, and a Council; in reality, however, the sultan and his family control all aspects of state decision making. The extent of the sultan's control of the government is revealed by his multiple titles: in addition to sultan, he is Brunei's prime minister, minister of defense, and minister of finance. The Constitution provides the sultan with supreme executive authority in the state.

ACHIEVEMENTS

An important project has been the construction of a modern university accommodating 1,500 to 2,000 students. Since independence, the government has tried to strengthen and improve the economic, social, and cultural life of its people.

In recent years, Brunei has been plagued by a chronic labor shortage. The government and Brunei Shell (a consortium owned jointly by the Brunei government and Shell Oil) are the largest employers in the country. They provide generous fringe benefits and high pay. Non-oil private-sector companies with fewer resources find it difficult to recruit within the country and have, therefore, employed many foreign workers. Indeed, one-third of all workers today in Brunei are foreigners. This situation is of considerable concern to the government, which is worried that social tensions between foreigners and residents may flare up at any time.

Timeline: PAST

A.D. 1521
Brunei is first visited by Europeans

1700
Brunei is known as haven for pirates

1800s
Briton James Brooke is given Sarawak as reward for help in a civil war

1847
The island of Labuan is ceded to Britain

1849
Britain attacks and ends pirate activities in Brunei

1888
The remainder of Brunei becomes a British protectorate

1963
Brunei rejects confederation with Malaysia

1984
Brunei gains its independence

1990s
Foreign workers are "imported" to ease the labor shortage; Brunei joins the International Monetary Fund

PRESENT

2000s
The sultan's brother agrees to return billions of dollars in stolen state assets Brunei declares itself a nuclear-free zone

The sultan signs a new constitution allowing for direct elections of 15 members of a redesigned Legislative Council; the Crown Prince weds a half-Swiss commoner in a lavish ceremony

Burkina Faso

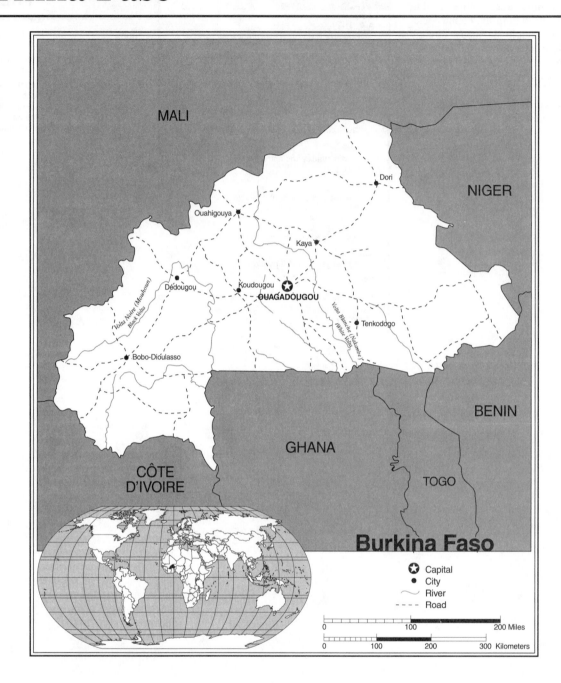

Burkina Faso Statistics

GEOGRAPHY

Area in Square Miles (Kilometers): 106,000 (274,500) (about the size of Colorado)

Capital (Population): Ouagadougou (862,000)

Environmental Concerns: drought; desertification; overgrazing; soil erosion; deforestation

Geographical Features: mostly flat to dissected, undulating plains; hills in west and southeast; landlocked

Climate: tropical; semiarid

PEOPLE

Population

Total: 13,574,820

Annual Growth Rate: 2.64%

Rural/Urban Population Ratio: 82/18

Major Languages: French; Mossi; Senufo; Fula; Bobo; Mande; Gurunsi; Lobi

Ethnic Makeup: about 40% Mossi; Gurunsi; Senufo; Lobi; Bobo; Mande; Fulani

Religions: 50% Muslim; 40% indigenous beliefs; 10% Christian

Health

Life Expectancy at Birth: 45 years (male); 47 years (female)
Infant Mortality: 105.3/1,000 live births
Physicians Available: 1/27,158 people
HIV/AIDS Rate in Adults: 6.44%

Education

Adult Literacy Rate: 36%
Compulsory (Ages): 7–14; free

COMMUNICATION

Telephones: 65,400 main lines
Televisions: 4.4 per 1,000 people
Internet Users: 48,000 (2003)

TRANSPORTATION

Highways in Miles (Kilometers): 7,504 (12,506)
Railroads in Miles (Kilometers): 385 (622)
Usable Airfields: 33
Motor Vehicles in Use: 55,000

GOVERNMENT

Type: parliamentary
Independence Date: August 5, 1960 (from France)
Head of State/Government: President Blaise Compaoré; Prime Minister Ernest Paramanga Yonli
Political Parties: Congress for Democracy and Progress; African Democratic Rally—Alliance for Democracy and Federation; others
Suffrage: universal

MILITARY

Military Expenditures (% of GDP): 1.4%
Current Disputes: two villages are in a dispute with Benin

ECONOMY

Currency ($ U.S. Equivalent): 581 CFA francs = $1
Per Capita Income/GDP: $1,100/$14.5 billion
GDP Growth Rate: 5.2%
Inflation Rate: 1.9%
Labor Force by Occupation: 90% agriculture
Population Below Poverty Line: 45%
Natural Resources: manganese; limestone; marble; gold; antimony; copper; bauxite; nickel; lead; phosphates; zinc; silver
Agriculture: peanuts; shea nuts; cotton; sesame; millet; sorghum; corn; rice; livestock
Industry: cotton lint; beverages; agricultural processing; soap; cigarettes; textiles; gold
Exports: $265 million (primary partners Venezuela, Benelux, Italy)
Imports: $580 million (primary partners Côte d'Ivoire, Venezuela, France)

SUGGESTED WEB SITES

http://burkinaembassy-usa.org
http://www.sas.upenn.edu/
  African_Studies/Country_Specific/
  Burkina.html

Burkina Faso Country Report

Notwithstanding some notable achievements, especially in the utilization of the Volta River and in the promotion of indigenous culture, Burkina Faso (formerly called Upper Volta) remains an impoverished country searching for a governing consensus. Recently its government has faced both domestic and external criticism over the state of the economy, human rights, and allegations that it has been involved in the smuggling of arms for diamonds ("blood diamonds") to the now-defeated rebel movements in Sierra Leone and Angola. Since falling gold prices forced the closure of its biggest gold mine, Burkina Faso has had little in the way of legitimate exports, leaving the landlocked, semiarid country with few economic prospects, and causing many of its citizens to seek opportunities elsewhere.

The restoration of multiparty democracy in 1991 under the firm guidance of former military leader Blaise Compaoré seemed to usher in an era of greater political stability. Along with his party, the Popular Democratic Organization–Worker's Movement (ODP–MT), he won elections against fragmented opposition in 1991 and 1995, as well as 1998.

Before adopting the mantle of democracy, Compaoré rose to power through a series of coups, the last of which resulted in the overthrow and assassination of the charismatic and controversial Thomas Sankara. A man of immense populist ap-

peal for many Burkinabé, Sankara remains as a martyr to their unfulfilled hopes.

DEBILITATING DROUGHTS

At the time of its independence from France, in 1960, the landlocked country then named the Republic of Upper Volta inherited little in the way of colonial infrastructure. Since independence, progress has been hampered by prolonged periods of severe drought. Much of the country has been forced at times to depend on international food aid. To counteract some of the negative effects of this circumstance, efforts have been made to integrate relief donations into local development schemes.

DEVELOPMENT

Despite political turbulence, Burkina Faso's economy has recorded positive, albeit modest, annual growth rates for more than a decade. Most of the growth has been in agriculture. New hydroelectric projects have significantly reduced the country's dependence on imported energy.

Particularly hard-hit has been pastoral production, long a mainstay of the local economy, especially in the north. It is estimated that a recent drought destroyed about 90 percent of the livestock in Burkina Faso. To counteract the effects of

drought while promoting greater development, the Burkinabé government has developed two major hydroelectric and agricultural projects over the past decade. The Bagre and Kompienga Dams, located east of Ouagadougou, have significantly reduced the country's dependence on imported energy, while also supplying water for largescale irrigation projects. This has already greatly reduced the need for imported food. Most Burkinabé continue to survive as agriculturalists and herders, but many people are dependent on wage labor. In the urban centers, there exists a significant working-class population that supports the nation's politically powerful trade-union movement.

FREEDOM

There has been a surprisingly strong tradition of pluralism in Burkina Faso despite the circumscribed nature of human rights under successive military regimes. Freedoms of speech and association are still curtailed, and political detentions are common. The Burkinabé Movement for Human Rights has challenged the government.

Another population category—whose numbers exceed those of the local wage-labor force—are individuals who seek employment outside of the country. At least 1 million

Burkinabé work as migrant laborers in other parts of West Africa. Returning workers have infused the rural areas with consumer goods and a working-class consciousness.

HEALTH/WELFARE

The inadequacy of the country's public health measures is reflected in the low Burkinabé life expectancy. Mass immunization campaigns have been successfully carried out, but in an era of structural economic adjustment, the prospects for a dramatic improvement in health appear bleak.

UNIONS FORCE CHANGE

As is the case in much of Africa, it is the salaried urban population (at least, next to the army) who have exercised the greatest influence over successive Burkinabé regimes. Yet despite this support base, the government has moved to restructure the until recently all-encompassing public sector of the economy by reducing its wage bill. This effort has impressed international creditors.

Beyond its core of support, the ODP–MT government has generally been met with sentiments ranging from hostility to indifference. The government has generally sought to cultivate good relations with France (the former colonial power) and other members of the Organization for Economic Cooperation and Development,

ACHIEVEMENTS

In 1997, a record total of 19 feature films competed for the Etalon du Yennenga award, the highest distinction of the biannual Pan-African Film Festival, hosted in Ouagadougou. Over the past three decades, this festival has contributed significantly to the development of the film industry in Africa. Burkina Faso has nationalized its movie houses, and the government has encouraged the showing of films by African filmmakers.

as well as the major international financial institutions. But Compaoré has alienated himself from some of his West African neighbors, as well as the Euro–North American diplomatic consensus, through his close ties to Libya and past military support for Charles Taylor's National Patriotic Front in Liberia. Along with Taylor, Compaoré has more recently been accused of, but denies, providing support for the Revolutionary United Front rebels in Sierra Leone.

Since October 2002 the Ivory Coast has continually accused Burkina Faso of sheltering dissident Ivorian soldiers, many of whom are descendents of individuals who first arrived from Burkina Faso. In turn Burkina Faso raised concerns about attacks on Burkinabés in the Ivory Coast after the September 2002 Ivorian military uprising.

Timeline: PAST

1313
The first Mossi kingdom is founded

1896
The French overcome Mossi resistance and claim Upper Volta

1932
Upper Volta is divided among adjoining French colonies

1947
Upper Volta is reconstituted as a colony

1960
Independence under President Maurice Yameogo

1980s
Captain Thomas Sankara seizes power and changes the country's name to Burkina (Mossi for "land of honest men") Faso (Dioula for "democratic republic"); Sankara is assassinated in a coup; Blaise Compaoré succeeds as head of state

1990s
Compaoré introduces multipartyism, but his critics are skeptical

PRESENT

2000s
The country marks 4 decades of independence; Burkina Faso is believed to be involved in the "blood diamonds" trade

Cameroon (Republic of Cameroon)

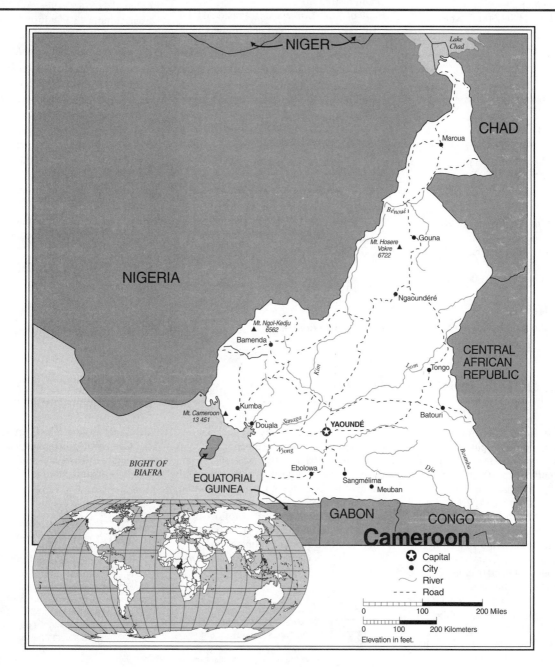

Cameroon Statistics

GEOGRAPHY

Area in Square Miles (Kilometers): 183,568 (475,400) (about the size of California)

Capital (Population): Yaoundé (1,119,000)

Environmental Concerns: deforestation; overgrazing; desertification; poaching; overfishing; water-borne disease

Geographical Features: diverse, with coastal plain in southwest, dissected plain in center, mountains in west, and plains in north

Climate: from tropical to semiarid

PEOPLE

Population

Total: 16,185,000

Annual Growth Rate: 1.97%

Rural/Urban Population Ratio: 54/46

Major Languages: English; French; Fulde; Ewondo; Duala; Bamelke; Bassa; Bali; others

Ethnic Makeup: 31% Cameroonian Highlander; 19% Equatorial Bantu; 11% Kirdi; 10% Fulani; 29% others

Religions: 40% indigenous beliefs; 40% Christian; 20% Muslim

Health

Life Expectancy at Birth: 54 years (male); 55 years (female)
Infant Mortality: 68.8/1,000 live births
Physicians Available: 1/11,848 people
HIV/AIDS Rate in Adults: 7.73%

Education

Adult Literacy Rate: 79%
Compulsory (Ages): 6–12; free

COMMUNICATION

Telephones: 95,000 main lines
Televisions: 72 per 1,000 people
Internet Users: 60,000 (2002)

TRANSPORTATION

Highways in Miles (Kilometers): 20,580 (34,300)
Railroads in Miles (Kilometers): 693 (1,111)
Usable Airfields: 49
Motor Vehicles in Use: 153,000

GOVERNMENT

Type: unitary republic

Independence Date: January 1, 1960 (from UN trusteeship under French administration)
Head of State/Government: President Paul Biya; Prime Minister Peter Mafany Musonge
Political Parties: Democratic Rally of the Cameroon People; National Union for Democracy and Progress; Social Democratic Front; Cameroonian Democratic Union; Union of Cameroonian Populations; others
Suffrage: universal at 20

MILITARY

Military Expenditures (% of GDP): 1.4%
Current Disputes: various border conflicts, especially with Nigeria

ECONOMY

Currency ($ U.S. equivalent): 529.43 CFA francs = $1
Per Capita Income/GDP: $1,700/$26.4 billion
GDP Growth Rate: 4.2%

Inflation Rate: 2%
Unemployment Rate: 30%
Labor Force by Occupation: 70% agriculture; 13% industry and commerce; 17% other
Population Below Poverty Line: 48%
Natural Resources: petroleum; timber; bauxite; iron ore; hydropower
Agriculture: coffee; cocoa; cotton; rubber; bananas; oilseed; grain; roots; livestock; timber
Industry: petroleum production and refining; food processing; light consumer goods; textiles; lumber
Exports: $2.1 billion (primary partners Italy, France, Netherlands)
Imports: $1.5 billion (primary partners France, Germany, United States, Japan)

SUGGESTED WEB SITES

http://www.sas.upenn.edu/
  African_Studies/
  Country_Specific/Cameroon.html
http://www.cameroon.net

Cameroon Country Report

Over the past decade, Cameroon has had a long-simmering border dispute with neighboring Nigeria over the Bakassi Peninsula. The latter conflict was referred by both countries to the International Court of Justice for resolution. But when the Court ruled in Cameroon's favor in October 2002, the government of Nigeria reneged on its previous agreement to accept the verdict. In August 2003, after talks in Cameroon, Nigeria said that it would not hand over the Bakassi Peninsula for at least three years. Yet in December 2003, Nigeria did in fact hand over 32 villages to Cameroon as part of the 2002 International Court of Justice's ruling. In January 2004, Nigeria agreed to have joint border patrols with Cameroon.

DEVELOPMENT

The Cameroon Development Corporation coordinates more than half of the agricultural exports and, after the government, employs the most people. Cocoa and coffee comprise more than 50% of Cameroon's exports. Lower prices for these commodities in recent years have reduced the country's income.

Although it claims to operate a multiparty democracy, freedom of expression is severely limited in Cameroon. Politically,

Cameroonians are deeply divided. During the October 2004 general elections, incumbent president Paul Biye was once again reelected by a large majority, even with many of the opposition parties boycotting. The poll, which was boycotted by the largest opposition parties, was a follow-up to the controversial elections of March 1992, which ended a quarter-century of one-party rule by Biya's Cameroon People's Democratic Party (CPDM).

HEALTH/WELFARE

The overall literacy rate in Cameroon, about 63%, is among the highest in Africa. There exists, however, great disparity in regional figures as well as between males and females. In addition to public schools, the government devotes a large proportion of its budget to subsidizing private schools.

In geographical terms, Cameroon's land is divided between the tropical forests in the south, the drier savanna of the north-central region, and the mountainous country along its western border, which forms a natural division between West and Central Africa.

In terms of religion, the country has many Christians, Muslims, and followers of indigenous belief systems. More than a dozen major languages, with numerous di-

alects, are spoken. The languages of southern Cameroon are linguistically classified as Bantu. English and French are Cameroon's official mediums.

ACHIEVEMENTS

The strong showing by Cameroon's national soccer team, the Indomitable Lions, in the 1990 and 1994 World Cup competitions is a source of pride for sports fans throughout Africa. Their success, along with the record numbers of medals won by African athletes in the 1988 and 1992 Olympics, is symbolic of the continent's coming of age in international sports competitions.

An upsurge of prodemocracy agitation began in 1990. In March, the Social Democratic Front (SDF) was formed in Bamenda, the main town of the Anglophonic west, over government objections. In May as many as 40,000 people from the vicinity of Bamenda, out of a total population of about 100,000, attended an SDF rally. Government troops opened fire on school children returning from the demonstration. This action led to a wave of unrest, which spread to the capital city of Yaoundé. The SDF called for a transition government, a new constitution, and multiparty elections.

One unrealized hope has been that democratic reform would help move Cameroon away from its consistent Transparency International rating as one of the world's most corrupt countries. Endemic corruption has become associated with environmental degradation. In recent years conservationists have been especially concerned about the construction of an oil pipeline, funded by the World Bank, without an environmental-impact study, and the allocation of about 80 percent of the country's forest for logging.

Timeline: PAST

1884
The establishment of the German Kamerun Protectorate

1916
The partition of Cameroon; separate British and French mandates are established under the League of Nations

1955
The UPC (formed in 1948) is outlawed for launching revolts in the cities

1960
The Independent Cameroon Republic is established, with Ahmadou Ahidjo as the first president

1961
The Cameroon Federal Republic reunites French Cameroon with British Cameroon after a UN-supervised referendum

1972
The new Constitution creates a unitary state

1980s
Ahidjo resigns and is replaced by Paul Biya; Lake Nyos releases lethal volcanic gases, killing an estimated 2,000 people

1990s
Nationwide agitation for a restoration of multiparty democracy; Biya retains the presidency in disputed elections

PRESENT

2000s
New clashes over the Bakassi Peninsula

Chad (Republic of Chad)

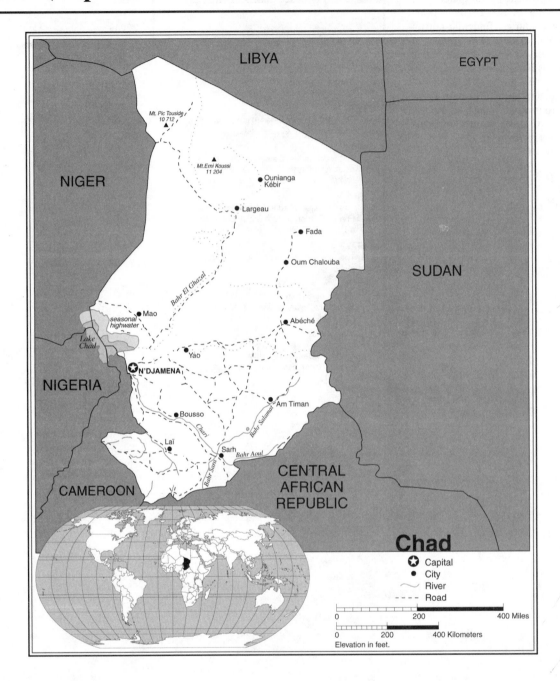

Chad Statistics

GEOGRAPHY

Area in Square Miles (Kilometers): 496,000 (1,284,634) (about 3 times the size of California)

Capital (Population): N'Djamena (826,000)

Environmental Concerns: soil and water pollution; desertification; insufficient potable water; waste disposal

Geographical Features: broad, arid plains in the center; desert in the north; mountains in the northwest; lowlands in the south; landlocked

Climate: tropical in the south; desert in the north

PEOPLE

Population

Total: 9,538,544
Annual Growth Rate: 3.27%

Rural/Urban Population Ratio: 77/23
Major Languages: French; Arabic; Sara; Sango; others
Ethnic Makeup: 200 distinct groups
Religions: 51% Muslim; 35% Christian; 7% animist; 7% others

Health

Life Expectancy at Birth: 49 years (male); 53 years (female)
Infant Mortality: 93.4/1,000 live births
Physicians Available: 1/27,765 people
HIV/AIDS Rate in Adults: 5%–7%

Education

Adult Literacy Rate: 40%
Compulsory (Ages): 6–14

COMMUNICATION

Telephones: 10,300 main lines
Televisions: 8 per 1,000 people
Internet Users: 15,000 (2002)

TRANSPORTATION

Highways in Miles (Kilometers): 19,620 (32,700)

Railroads in Miles (Kilometers): none
Usable Airfields: 49
Motor Vehicles in Use: 24,000

GOVERNMENT

Type: republic
Independence Date: August 11, 1960 (from France)
Head of State/Government: President Idriss Déby; Prime Minister Moussa Faki Mahamat
Political Parties: Patriotic Salvation Movement; National Union for Development and Renewal; many others
Suffrage: universal at 18

MILITARY

Military Expenditures (% of GDP): 2.1%
Current Disputes: civil war; border conflicts over Lake Chad area

ECONOMY

Currency ($ U.S. equivalent): 581 CFA francs = $1

Per Capita Income/GDP: $1,030/$8.9 billion
GDP Growth Rate: 8%
Inflation Rate: 3%
Labor Force by Occupation: 80%+ agriculture
Population Below Poverty Line: 80%
Natural Resources: petroleum; uranium; natron; kaolin; fish (Lake Chad)
Agriculture: subsistence crops; cotton; peanuts; fish; livestock
Industry: livestock products; breweries; natron; soap; textiles; cigarettes; construction materials
Exports 172 million (primary partners Portugal, Germany, Thailand)
Imports: $223 million (primary partners France, Nigeria, Cameroon)

SUGGESTED WEB SITES

http://www.chadembassy.org/site/index.cfm
http://www.sas.upenn.edu/African_Studies/Country_Specific/Chad.html

Chad Country Report

After decades of civil war between northern- and southern-based armed movements, in 1997 Chad completed its transition to civilian rule, under the firm guidance of its president, Idriss Déby. A former northern warlord who seized power in 1990, in 1996 Déby achieved a second-round victory in the country's first genuinely contested presidential elections since its independence in 1960.

DEVELOPMENT

Chad has potential petroleum and mineral wealth that would greatly help the economy if stable central government can be created. Deposits of chromium, tungsten, titanium, gold, uranium, and tin as well as oil are known to exist. Roads are in poor condition and are dangerous.

In June 2001 Chad's highest court confirmed Déby's reelection, after a controversial poll in which the results of about one-quarter of the polling stations were cancelled due to alleged irregularities. While Déby's success—through both the ballot and bullet—in defeating, marginalizing, and/or reconciling rival factions has restored a semblance of statehood to Chad

over the past five years, he continues to preside over a bankrupt government whose control over much of the countryside is tenuous.

FREEDOM

Despite some modest improvement, Chad's human-rights record remains poor. Its security forces are linked to torture, extra-judicial killings, beatings, disappearances, and rape. A recent Amnesty International report on Chad was entitled "Hope Betrayed." Antigovernment rebel forces are also accused of atrocities. The judiciary is not independent.

CIVIL WAR

Chad's conflicts are partially rooted in the country's ethnic and religious divisions. It has been common for outsiders to portray the struggle as being between Arab-oriented Muslim northerners and black Christian southerners, but Chad's regional and ethnic allegiances are much more complex. Geographically, the country is better divided into three zones: the northern Sahara, a middle Sahel region, and the southern savanna. Within each of these ecological areas live

peoples who speak different languages and engage in a variety of economic activities. Wider ethno-regional and religious loyalties have emerged as a result of the Civil War, but such aggregates have tended to be fragile and their allegiances shifting.

HEALTH/WELFARE

In 1992 there were reports of catastrophic famine in the countryside. Limited human services were provided by external aid agencies. Medicines are in short supply or completely unavailable.

A BETTER FUTURE?

The good news from Sudan during the period of 2002 to 2004 was that in October 2003 Chad became an oil exporter with the opening of a pipeline connecting its oil fields with Cameroon. Its funding comes from the World Bank, which has stipulated that at least 80 percent of these oil revenues must be allocated to social and infrastructure programs as to ensure that the masses share in the benefits of the country's new resources.

The long, drawn-out conflict in Chad has led to immense suffering. Up to a half

ACHIEVEMENTS

In precolonial times, the town of Kanem was a leading regional center of commerce and culture. Since independence in 1960, perhaps Chad's major achievement has been the resiliency of its people under the harshest of circumstances. The holding of truly contested elections is also a significant accomplishment.

a million people—the equivalent of 10 percent of the total population—have been killed in the fighting.

Timeline: PAST

1960
Independence is achieved under President François Tombalbaye

1965–1966
Revolt breaks out among peasant groups; FROLINAT is formed

1978
Establishment of a Transitional Government of National Unity (GUNT) with Hissène Habré and Goukkouni Oueddie

1980s
Habré seizes power and reunites the country in a U.S.–supported war against Libya

1990s
Habré is overthrown by Idriss Déby; Déby promises to create a multiparty democracy, but conditions remain anarchic

PRESENT

2000s
Chad's northern provinces bordering Libya remain heavily land mined; persistent armed insurgency in the north Dèby is confirmed as reelected, after a controversial poll

Even if peace could be restored, the overall prospects for national development are bleak. The country has potential mineral wealth, but its geographic isolation and current world prices are disincentives to investors. Local food self-sufficiency should be obtainable despite the possibility of recurrent drought, but geography limits the potential of export crops. Chad thus appears to be an extreme case of the more general African need for a radical transformation of prevailing regional and global economic interrelationships.

Comoros (Union of Comoros)

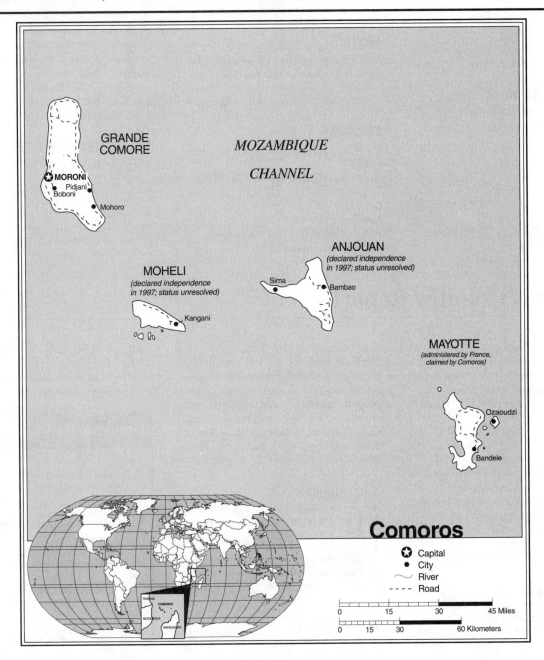

Comoros Statistics

GEOGRAPHY

Area in Square Miles (Kilometers): 838 (2,171) (about 12 times the size of Washington, D.C.)

Capital (Population): Moroni (49,000)

Environmental Concerns: soil degradation and erosion; deforestation

Geographical Features: volcanic islands; interiors vary from steep mountains to low hills

Climate: tropical marine

PEOPLE

Population

Total: 631,901

Annual Growth Rate: 2.99%

Rural/Urban Population Ratio: 69/31

Major Languages: Arabic; French; Comoran

Ethnic Makeup: Antalote; Cafre; Makoa; Oimatsaha; Sakalava

Religions: 98% Sunni Muslim; 2% Roman Catholic

Health

Life Expectancy at Birth: 58 years (male); 62 years (female)

Infant Mortality: 81.7/1,000 live births

Physicians Available: 1/6,600 people

HIV/AIDS Rate in Adults: 0.12%

Education

Adult Literacy Rate: 57.3%
Compulsory (Ages): 7–16

COMMUNICATION

Telephones: 13,200 main lines
Internet Users: 5,000 (2003)

TRANSPORTATION

Highways in Miles (Kilometers): 522 (870)
Railroads in Miles (Kilometers): none
Usable Airfields: 4

GOVERNMENT

Type: republic
Independence Date: July 6, 1975 (from France)
Head of State/Government: President Azali Assoumani

Political Parties: Rassemblement National pour le Development; Front National pour la Justice
Suffrage: universal at 18

MILITARY

Military Expenditures (% of GDP): 3%
Current Disputes: Comoros claims the French-administered island of Mayotte; Moheli and Anjouan seek independence

ECONOMY

Currency ($ U.S. Equivalent): 435 francs = $1
Per Capita Income/GDP: $700/$441 million
GDP Growth Rate: 2%
Inflation Rate: 3.5%
Unemployment Rate: 20%; extreme underemployment

Labor Force by Occupation: 80% agriculture
Population Below Poverty Line: 60%
Natural Resources: negligible
Agriculture: perfume essences; copra; coconuts; cloves; vanilla; bananas; cassava
Industry: tourism; perfume distillation
Exports: $35.3 million (primary partners France, United States, Singapore)
Imports: $44.9 million (primary partners France, South Africa, Kenya)

SUGGESTED WEB SITES

http://www.arabji.com/Comoros/index.htm
http://www.sas.upenn.edu/African_Studies/Country_Specific/Comoros.html
http://www.cia.gov/cia/publications/factbook/geos/cn.html

Comoros Country Report

A small archipelago consisting of three main islands—Grande Comore, Moheli, and Anjouan (a fourth island, Mayotte, has voluntarily remained under French rule)—in recent years Comoros has struggled to maintain its fragile unity. In 1997 separatists seized control of Anjouan and Moheli, subsequently declaring independence. But after years of failed mediation efforts by other African states, in December 2001 voters throughout Comoros were able to overwhelmingly agree on a new constitution designed to reunite their country as a loose federation. This followed the seizure of power by a "military committee" on Anjouan that was committed to reunification.

DEVELOPMENT

One of the major projects undertaken since independence has been the ongoing expansion of the port at Mutsamundu, to allow large ships to visit the islands. Vessels of up to 25,000 tons can now dock at the harbor. In recent years, there has been a significant expansion of tourism to Comoros.

FREEDOM

Freedom was abridged after independence under both Ahmed Abdullah and Ali Soilih. The government elected in 1990 ended human-rights abuses.

The years since independence from France, in 1975, have not been kind to Comoros, which has been consistently listed by the United Nations as one of the world's least-developed countries. Lack of economic development has been compounded at times by natural disasters, eccentric and authoritarian leadership, political violence, and external interventions. The 1990 restoration of multiparty democracy, along with subsequent elections in 1992–1993, has so far failed to provide a basis for national consensus.

HEALTH/WELFARE

Health statistics improved during the 1980s, but a recent World Health Organization survey estimated that 10% of Comoran children ages 3 to 6 years are seriously malnourished and another 37% are moderately malnourished.

ACHIEVEMENTS

Comoros has long been the world's leading exporter of ylangylang, an essence used to make perfume. It is also the second-leading producer of vanilla and a major grower of cloves. Together, these cash crops account for more than 95% of export earnings. Unfortunately, the international prices of these crops have been low for the past 2 decades.

Meanwhile, the entire archipelago remains impoverished. While many Comorans remain underemployed as subsistence farmers, more than half of the country's food is imported. The Comoros archipelago was populated by a number of Indian Ocean peoples, who—by the time of the arrival of Europeans during the early 1500s—had combined to form the predominantly Muslim, Swahili-speaking society found on the islands today.

Timeline: PAST

1500s
Various groups settle in the islands, which become part of a Swahili trading network

1886
A French protectorate over the remaining Comoros islands is proclaimed

1914–1946
The islands are ruled as part of the French colony of Madagascar

1975
Independence is followed by a mercenary coup, which installs Ali Soilih

1978
Ali Soilih is overthrown by mercenaries; Ahmed Abdullah is restored

1980s
Abdullah proclaims a one-party state; real power remains in the hands of mercenary leader Bob Denard

1990s
The assassination of Abdullah leads to the removal of Denard and to multiparty elections

PRESENT

2000s
The country is renamed "Union of Comoros"; despite the name change, Comoros's political unity has not been achieved

Côte d'Ivoire (Republic of Côte d'Ivoire)

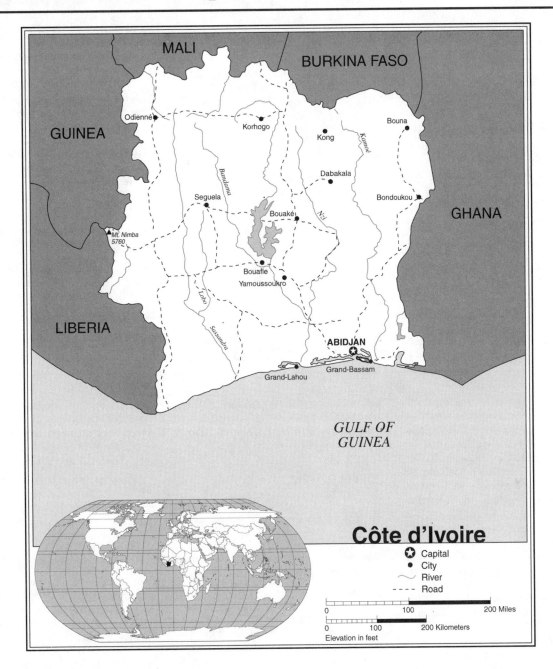

Côte d'Ivoire Statistics

GEOGRAPHY

Area in Square Miles (Kilometers): 124,503 (323,750) (about the size of New Mexico)

Capital (Population): Abidjan (administrative) (3,956,000); Yamoussoukro (political) (120,000)

Environmental Concerns: water pollution; deforestation

Geographical Features: mostly flat to undulating plains; mountains in the northwest

Climate: tropical to semiarid

PEOPLE

Population

17,327,724

Annual Growth Rate: 2.11%

Rural/Urban Population Ratio: 54/46

Major Languages: French; Dioula; many indigenous dialects

Ethnic Makeup: 42% Akan; 18% Voltaics or Gur; 11% Krous; 16% Northern Mandes; 10% Southern Mandes; 3% others

Religions: 60% Muslim; 22% Christian; 18% indigenous

Health

Life Expectancy at Birth: 43 years (male);
46 years (female)
Infant Mortality: 92.2/1,000 live births
Physicians Available: 1/11,745 people
HIV/AIDS Rate in Adults: 10.76%

Education

Adult Literacy Rate: 50.9%
Compulsory (Ages): 7–13; free

COMMUNICATION

Telephones: 328,000 main lines
Televisions: 57 per 1,000 people
Internet Users: 90,000 (2002)

TRANSPORTATION

Highways in Miles (Kilometers): 30,240
(50,400)
Railroads in Miles (Kilometers): 408 (660)
Usable Airfields: 36
Motor Vehicles in Use: 255,000

GOVERNMENT

Type: republic
Independence Date: August 7, 1960 (from
France)
Head of State/Government: President
Laurent Gbagbo; Prime Minister Seydou
Diarra
Political Parties: Democratic Party of
Côte d'Ivoire; Ivoirian Popular Front;
Rally of the Republicans; Ivoirian
Workers' Party; others
Suffrage: universal at 18

MILITARY

Military Expenditures (% of GDP): 1.3%
Current Disputes: civil war

ECONOMY

Currency ($ U.S. Equivalent): 581 CFA
francs = $1
Per Capita Income/GDP: $1,400/$24 billion
GDP Growth Rate: -1.9%

Inflation Rate: 3.4%
Unemployment Rate: 13%
Natural Resources: petroleum; diamonds;
manganese; iron ore; cobalt; bauxite;
copper; hydropower
Agriculture: coffee; cocoa beans; bananas;
palm kernels; corn; rice; manioc; sweet
potatoes; sugar; cotton; rubber; timber
Industry: foodstuffs; beverages; oil
refining; wood products; textiles;
automobile assembly; fertilizer;
construction materials; electricity
Exports: $3.6 billion (primary partners
France, the Netherlands, United States)
Imports: $2.4 billion (primary partners
France, Nigeria, China)

SUGGESTED WEB SITES

http://www.sas.upenn.edu/
African_Studies/
Country_Specific/Cote.html
http://www.cia.gov/cia/
publications/factbook/geos/
iv.html

Côte d'Ivoire Country Report

Once considered an island of political stability and a model of economic growth in West Africa, since the death in 1993 of its first president, Félix Houphouët-Boigny, Côte d'Ivoire (previously known by its English name, Ivory Coast) has been shaken by a series of military crises as well as sustained economic decline. In September 2002 a military mutiny sparked fighting that has left the country divided along regional and sectarian lines. The predominantly Muslim northern half of the country has come under the control of rebel soldiers, while the mainly Christian southern half has remained under the rule of the embattled government of Laurent Ghagbo. Although a partial truce between the two sides, upheld by French troops, was negotiated in October, intensive mediation efforts by neighboring states failed to reconcile the two sides. By the end of 2002, the opportunity for a quick end to the crisis appeared to be fading. In fact the October ceasefire collapsed in November 2002 as armed groups clashed with government forces in a battle for the key cocoa-industry town of Daloa. Moving desperately toward reconciliation in January 2003, President Gbagbo accepted a peace deal at talks in Paris, which proposed a power-sharing government. By March 2003 political parties and the rebels agreed on a new government to include nine members from rebel ranks. "Consensus" Prime Minister Seydou Diarra was tasked

with forming a cabinet. In May 2003 the armed forces signed a "full" cease-fire with rebel groups in May 2003 to end almost eight months of rebellion.

DEVELOPMENT

It has been said that Côte d'Ivoire is "power hungry." The Soubre Dam, being developed on the Sassandra River, is the sixth and largest hydroelectric project in Côte d'Ivoire. It will serve the eastern area of the country. Another dam is planned for the Cavalla River, between Côte d'Ivoire and Liberia.

Attempting to halt the violence, the UN deployed a contingent of peacekeepers into the country in May 2004. After a six-month period of initial success in curtailing the violence, the civil war was reignited in November 2004 when the Ivoirian Air Force attacked the rebels. The UN imposed an arms embargo against all the combatants in the Ivory Coast in November 2004.

POLITICAL POLARIZATION

Religious and ethnic divisions among Ivoirians in recent years have been aggravated by growing xenophobia against immigrants, who make up at least one-third of the country's total population. Under Houphouët-Boigny, people from other Af-

rican states were allowed to settle and even vote in Côte d'Ivoire. But his paternalistic autocracy, exercised through the Democratic Party of Côte d'Ivoire (PDCI), had begun to break down before his death.

Political life entered a new phase in 1990. Months of mounting prodemocracy protests and labor unrest had led to the legalization of opposition parties, previously banned under the country's single-party government.

Houphouët-Boigny was succeeded by Konan Bédié, a Christian southerner who came out ahead in a power struggle with Allassane Ouatarra, a northern technocrat who had occupied the post of prime minister. Once in power, Bédié stirred up ethnic discord and xenophobia against Muslim northerners.

Bédié's increasingly unpopular rule came to an abrupt end on December 24, 1999, when General Robert Guei assumed power following the country's first coup d'état.

FREEDOM

Former president Konan Bédié showed little tolerance for dissent, within either the PDCI or society as a whole. Journalists by the score were jailed for such "offenses" as writing "insulting" articles. Six Ivoirian gendarmes were charged in connection with a mass grave discovered near Abidjan in 2000.

ECONOMIC DOWNTURN

The primary explanation for the downturn of Côte d'Ivoire's once-vibrant economy is the decline in revenue from cocoa and coffee, which have long been the country's principal export earners. This has led to mounting state debt, which in turn has pressured the government to adopt unpopular austerity measures.

During its first two decades of independence, Côte d'Ivoire enjoyed one of the highest economic growth rates in the world. The nation had become the world's leading producer of cocoa and third-largest coffee producer.

HEALTH/WELFARE

 Côte d'Ivoire has one of the lowest soldier-to-teacher ratios in Africa. Education absorbs about 40% of the national budget. The National Commission to Combat AIDS has reported significant success in its campaign to promote condom use, by targeting especially vulnerable groups.

About two-thirds of the workforce are employed in agriculture, with coffee alone being the principal source of income for some 2.5 million people. In addition to coffee, Ivoirian planters grow cocoa, bananas, pineapples, sugar, cotton, palm oil, and other cash crops for export. While some of these farmers are quite wealthy, most have only modest incomes. In recent years, the circumstance of Ivoirian coffee and cocoa planters has become much more precarious, due to fluctuations in commodities prices.

DEBT AND DISCONTENT

Other factors may determine how much an Ivoirian benefits from the country's development. Professionals in the cities make better salaries than do laborers on farms or in small industries. Yet persistent inflation and recession have made daily life difficult for the middle class as well as poorer peasants and workers.

ACHIEVEMENTS

 Ivoirian textiles are varied and prized. Block printing and dyeing produce brilliant designs; woven cloths made strip by strip and sewn together include the white Korhogo tapestries, covered with Ivoirian figures, birds, and symbols drawn in black. The Ivoirian singer Alpha Blondy has become an international superstar as the leading exponent of West African reggae.

Serious brush fires, mismanagement, and the clearing of forests for cash-crop plantations have put the nation's once-sizable timber industry in jeopardy. Out of a former total of 12 million hectares of forest, 10 1/2 million have been lost. Plans for expansion of offshore oil production have not been implemented due to an inability to raise investment capital.

Difficulty in raising capital for oil development is a reflection of the debt crisis that has plagued the country since the collapse of its cocoa and coffee earnings. With the country now on the brink of full-scale civil war, for most Ivoirians the harsh economic conditions are likely to continue.

Timeline: PAST

1700s
Agni and Baoulé peoples migrate to the Ivory Coast from the East

1893
The Ivory Coast officially becomes a French colony

1898
Samori Touré, a Malinke Muslim leader and an empire builder, is defeated by the French

1915
The final French pacification of the country takes place

1960
Côte d'Ivoire becomes independent under Félix Houphouët-Boigny's leadership

1980s
The PDCI approves a plan to move the capital from Abidjan to Houphouët-Boigny's home village of Yamoussoukro

1990s
Prodemocracy demonstrations lead to multiparty elections; Houphouët-Boigny dies

PRESENT

2000s
Côte d'Ivoire adjusts after the startling coup in late 1999; Laurent Gbagbo becomes president; a mass grave of 57 bullet-ridden bodies is discovered near Abidjan

Djibouti (Republic of Djibouti)

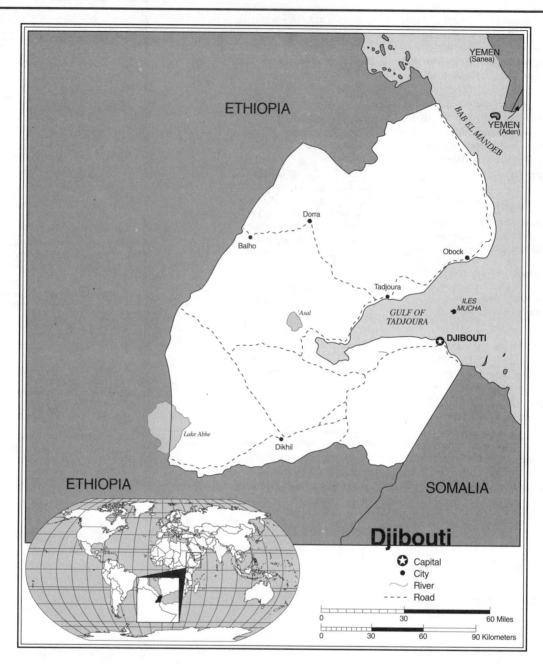

Djibouti Statistics

GEOGRAPHY

Area in Square Miles (Kilometers): 8,492 (22,000) (about the size of Massachusetts)

Capital (Population): Djibouti (542,000)

Environmental Concerns: Insufficient potable water; desertification

Geographical Features: coastal plain and plateau, separated by central mountains

Climate: desert

PEOPLE

Population

Total: 466,900

Annual Growth Rate: 2.1%

Rural/Urban Population Ratio: 17/83

Major Languages: French; Arabic; Somali; Afar

Ethnic Makeup: 60% Issa/Somali; 35% Afar; 5% French, Arab, Ethiopian, Italian

Religions: 94% Muslim; 6% Christian

Health

Life Expectancy at Birth: 50 years (male); 53 years (female)

Infant Mortality: 99.7/1,000 live births

Physicians Available: 1/3,790 people

HIV/AIDS Rate in Adults: 11.75%

Education
Adult Literacy Rate: 46.2%

COMMUNICATION
Telephones: 10,000 main lines
Televisions: 43 per 1,000 people
Internet Users: 6,500 (2003)

TRANSPORTATION
Highways in Miles (Kilometers): 1,801
   (2,906)
Railroads in Miles (Kilometers): 60 (97)
Usable Airfields: 12
Motor Vehicles in Use: 16,000

GOVERNMENT
Type: republic
Independence Date: June 27, 1977 (from
   France)

Head of State/Government: President
   Ismail Omar Guellah; Prime Minister
   Dileita Mohamed Dileita
Political Parties: People's Progress
   Assembly; Democratic Renewal Party;
   Democratic National Party; others
Suffrage: universal for adults

MILITARY
Military Expenditures (% of GDP): 4.4%
Current Disputes: ethnic conflict; border
   clashes with Eritrea

ECONOMY
Currency ($ U.S. Equivalent): 177 francs
   = $1
Per Capita Income/GDP: $1,400/$586
   million
GDP Growth Rate: 3.5%

Inflation Rate: 2%
Unemployment Rate: 50%
Population Below Poverty Line: 50%
Natural Resources: geothermal areas
Agriculture: livestock; fruits; vegetables
Industry: port and maritime support;
   construction
Exports: $260 million (primary partners
   Somalia, Yemen, Ethiopia)
Imports: $440 million (primary partners
   France, Ethiopia, Italy)

SUGGESTED WEB SITES
http://www.sas.upenn.edu/
   African_Studies/Country_Specific/
   Djibouti.html
http://www.republiquedjibouti.com
http://www.cia.gov/cia/
   publications/factbook/geos/
   dj.html

Djibouti Country Report

After a decade of civil unrest, Djibouti has settled down under the leadership of its second president, Ismail Omar Guellah. In April 1999, Guellah succeeded the aging Hassan Gouled Aptidon, who stepped down due to ill health. The new president has since consolidated his authority by building on the process of national reconciliation that had begun under his predecessor.

DEVELOPMENT

Recent discoveries of natural gas reserves in Djibouti could result in a surplus for export. A number of small-scale irrigation schemes have been established. There is also a growing, though still quite small, fishing industry.

Since achieving its independence from France, Djibouti has also had to strike a cautious balance between the competing interests of its larger neighbors, Ethiopia and Somalia. In the past, Somalia has claimed ownership of the territory, based on the numerical preponderance of Djibouti's Somali population, variously estimated at 50 to 70 percent. However, local Somalis as well as Afars also have strong ties to communities in Ethiopia. Furthermore, Djibouti's location at the crossroads of Africa and Eurasia has made it a focus of continuing strategic concern to nonregional powers, particularly France, which maintains a large military presence in the country.

In January 2002 German warships and 1,000 sailors arrived in Djibouti to patrol shipping lanes in the Red Sea area, in support of U.S. actions in Afghanistan. Although Djibouti says it won't be used as a base for attacks against another country in the region, some 900 U.S. troops also set up camp in support of the U.S.-led war on terror. The effort by Djibouti's government to fight the war on terror had one major political consequence as the government, in September 2002, passed a law allowing three other parties to compete in elections, thus opening the way for full multiparty politics.

FREEDOM

The government continues to harass and detain its critics. Prison conditions are harsh, with the sexual assault of female prisoners being commonplace.

In January 2003 the Union for Presidential Majority Coalition candidate, Ismael Omar Gelleh, won Djibouti's first free multiparty elections since independence in 1977. In September 2003 one of President Gelleh's first actions after assuming office was to begin a drive to detain and expel illegal immigrants, thought to make up 15 percent of the population.

On June 27, 1977, the Republic of Djibouti became independent. Internally, political power was divided by means of

Timeline: PAST

1862
France buys the port of Obock

1888
France acquires the port of Djibouti

1917
The Addis Ababa-Djibouti Railroad is completed

1958
Djibouti votes to remain part of Overseas France

1977
Independence; the Ogaden War

1980s
The underground Union of Movements for Democracy is formed as an interethnic, antigovernment coalition

1990s
Civil war rends the country; Ismail Omar Guellah is elected to replace President Hassan Gouled Aptidon

PRESENT

2000s
Ethnic conflict continues

ethnically balanced cabinets. War broke out between Ethiopia and Somalia a few months after Djibouti's independence. Djibouti remained neutral, but ethnic tensions mounted with the arrival of Somali refugees.

HEALTH/WELFARE

Progress has been made in reducing infant mortality, but health services are strained in this very poor country.
However, on the positive side, school enrollment has expanded by nearly one-third since 1987.

Refugees have poured into Djibouti for years now, fleeing conflict and famine in Ethiopia, Somalia, and Sudan. The influx has swelled the country's population by about one-third and has deepened Djibouti's dependence on external food aid. Massive unemployment among Djibouti's largely urban population remains a critical problem.

ACHIEVEMENTS

Besides feeding its own refugees, the government of Djibouti has played a major role in assisting international efforts to relieve the effects of recurrent famines in Ethiopia, Somalia, and Sudan.

Egypt (Arab Republic of Egypt)

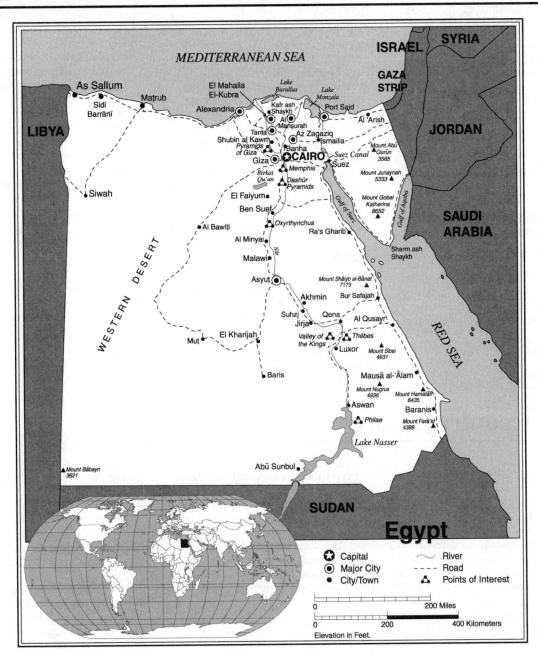

Egypt Statistics

GEOGRAPHY

Area in Square Miles (Kilometers): 386,258
  (1,001,258) (about 3 times the size of
  New Mexico)
Capital (Population): Cairo (6,800,000)
Environmental Concerns: loss of
  agricultural land; increasing soil
  salinization; desertification; oil pollution
  threatening coral reefs and marine
  habitats; other water pollution; rapid
  population growth
Geographical Features: a vast desert
  plateau interrupted by the Nile Valley
  and Delta
Climate: desert; dry, hot summers;
  moderate winters

PEOPLE

Population

Total: 70,712,345
Annual Growth Rate: 1.66%
Rural/Urban Population Ratio: 55/45
Major Languages: Arabic; English

Ethnic Makeup: 99% Eastern Hamitic
(Egyptian, Bedouin, Arab, Nubian); 1%
others
Religions: 94% Muslim (mostly Sunni);
6% Coptic Christian and others

Health

Life Expectancy at Birth: 62 years (male);
66 years (female)
Infant Mortality Rate (Ratio): 58.6/1,000
live births
Physicians Available (Ratio): 1/472 people

Education

Adult Literacy Rate: 51.4%
Compulsory (Ages): for 5 years, 6–13

COMMUNICATION

Telephones: 3,972,000 main lines
Daily Newspaper Circulation: 43 per
1,000 people
Televisions: 110 per 1,000 people
Internet Users: 600,000

TRANSPORTATION

Highways in Miles (Kilometers): 39,744
(64,000) R
Railroads in Miles (Kilometers): 2,973
(4,955)

Usable Airfields: 92
Motor Vehicles in Use: 1,703,000

GOVERNMENT

Type: republic
Independence Date: July 23, 1952, for the
republic; February 28, 1922, marking the
end of British rule
Head of State/Government: President
Mohammed Hosni Mubarak; Prime
Minister Atef Obeid
Political Parties: National Democratic
Party (NDP), majority party; others are
New Wafd; Tagammu (National
Progressive Unionist Group); Nasserist
Arab Democratic Party; Socialist Liberal
Party. NDP holds 88 percent majority in
Peoples Assembly
Suffrage: universal and compulsory at 18

MILITARY

Military Expenditures (% of GDP): 4.1%
Current Disputes: territorial dispute with
Sudan over the Hala'ib Triangle

ECONOMY

Currency ($ U.S. Equivalent): 5.99
Egyptian pounds = $1

Per Capita Income/GDP: $3,700/$258
billion
GDP Growth Rate: 2.5%
Inflation Rate: 2.3%
Unemployment Rate: 12%
Labor Force: 20,600,000
Natural Resources: petroleum; natural gas;
iron ore; phosphates; manganese; limestone;
gypsum; talc; asbestos; lead; zinc
Agriculture: cotton; sugarcane; rice; corn;
wheat; beans; fruits; vegetables;
livestock; fish
Industry: textiles; food processing;
tourism; chemicals; petroleum;
construction; cement; metals
Exports: $7.3 billion (primary partners
European Union, Middle East, Afro-
Asian countries)
Imports: $16.4 billion (primary partners
European Union, United States, Afro-
Asian countries)

SUGGESTED WEB SITE

http://www.cia.gov/cia/
publications/factbook/geog/
eg.html
http://www.yahoo.com/Regional/
countries/Egypt/Government
http://www.sis.gov
http://worldrover.com/Egypt.html

Egypt Country Report

The Arab Republic of Egypt is located at
the extreme northeastern corner of Africa,
with part of its territory—the Sinai Peninsula—serving as a land bridge to Southwest
Asia. The country's total land area is approximately 386,000 square miles. However, 96 percent of this is uninhabitable
desert. Except for a few scattered oases, the
only settled and cultivable area is a narrow
strip along the Nile River. The vast majority
of Egypt's population is concentrated in this
strip, resulting in high population density.
Migration from rural areas to cities has intensified urban density; Cairo's population
is currently 6.8 million, with an estimated
1.7 million more in the metropolitan area.

DEVELOPMENT

Egypt's GDP growth rate, which
held steady at 4–5% in the 90s,
has been hard-hit by the 9/11
terrorist attacks in the U.S. and
the U.S. invasion of Iraq in March 2003. The
tourism industry, which provides normally
12% of revenues, has been especially
affected. In March the government banned
imports of all but essential goods for 3 months
to conserve dwindling foreign exchange.

Egypt today identifies itself as an Arab nation and is a founding member of the League
of Arab States (which has its headquarters in
Cairo). Also, its development under British
tutelage gave the country a headstart over
other Arab countries or societies. Despite its
people's overall low level of adult literacy,
Egypt has more highly skilled professionals
than do other Arab countries.

HISTORY

Since the time of the pharaohs, Egypt has
been invaded many times, and it was under
foreign control for most of its history.
When Nasser, the first president of the new
Egyptian republic, came to power in 1954,
he said that he was the first native Egyptian
to rule the country in nearly 3,000 years.

The city of Alexandria, founded by Alexander the Great, became a center of Greek
and Roman learning and culture. Later, it
became a center of Christianity. The Egyptian Coptic Church was one of the earliest
organized churches. The Copts, direct descendants of the early Egyptians, are the
principal minority group in Egypt today.
(The name Copt comes from *aigyptos*,
Greek for "Egyptian.") The Copts wel-

comed the Arab invaders, who brought Islam to Egypt, preferring them to their
oppressive Byzantine Christian rulers. Muslim rulers over the centuries usually protected the Copts as "Peoples of the Book,"
leaving authority over them to their religious leaders, in return for allegiance and
payment of a small tax. But in recent years,
the rise of Islamic fundamentalism has
made life more difficult for Egypt's Christians. As a minority group, they are caught
between the fundamentalists and government forces seeking to destroy them.

Egypt also had, until very recently, a
small but long-established Jewish community that held a similar position under various Muslim rulers. Most of the Jews
emigrated to Israel after 1948.

THE INFLUENCE OF ISLAM

Islam was the major formative influence in
the development of modern Egyptian society. Islamic armies from Arabia invaded
Egypt in the seventh century A.D. Large
numbers of nomadic Arabs followed, set-
tling the Nile Valley until, over time, they
became the majority in the population.
Egypt was under the rule of the caliphs

John Feeney/Saudi Aramco World/PADIA
(1815_045)

The Muhammad Ali Mosque dominates the Citadel in cairo, Egypt, and honors the legacy of Muhammad Ali who overthrew the Fatimid dynasty and took over Cairo in 1805. Appointed Viceroy of Egypt by the Ottoman Sultan, Muhammad Ali proved to be a successful military commander and competent administrator who modernized Egypt's educational system, armed forces, and economy for his forty-four year reign.

("successors" of the Prophet Muhammad) until the tenth century, when a Shi'a group broke away and formed a separate government. The leaders of this group also called themselves caliphs. To show their independence, they founded a new capital in the desert south of Alexandria. The name they chose for their new capital was prophetic: *al-Qahira*—"City of War"—the modern city of Cairo.

EGYPT ENTERS THE MODERN WORLD

In the sixteenth century, Egypt became a province of the Ottoman Empire.

In 1805 the Ottoman sultan appointed Muhammad Ali, an Albanian officer, governor of Egypt. Muhammad Ali set up an organized, efficient tax-collection system. He took personal charge of all Egypt's exports. Cotton, a new crop, became the major Egyptian export and became known the world over for its high quality. Dams and irrigation canals were dug to improve cultivation and expand arable land.

EGYPTIAN NATIONALISM

In order to avoid conflict with the Ottomans, the British established a protectorate over Egypt that lasted from 1882 to 1956. An Egyptian nationalist movement gradually developed in the early 1900s, inspired by the teachings of religious leaders and Western-educated officials in the khedives' government. They advocated a revival of Islam and its strengthening to enable Egypt and other Islamic lands to resist European control. At the end of World War I, Egyptian nationalist leaders organized the *Wafd* (Arabic for "delegation").

THE EGYPTIAN REVOLUTION

During World War II, the British, fearing a German takeover of Egypt, reinstated the protectorate. Egypt became the main British military base in the Middle East. This action galvanized the officers into forming a revolutionary movement.

When Jewish leaders in Palestine organized Israel in May 1948, Egypt, along with other nearby Arab countries, sent troops to destroy the new state. Nasser and several of his fellow officers were sent to the front. The Egyptian Army was defeated; Nasser himself was trapped with his unit, was wounded, and was rescued only by an armistice. Even more shocking to the young officers was the evident corruption and weakness of their own government. The weapons that they received were inferior and often defective, battle orders were inaccurate, and their superiors proved to be incompetent in strategy and tactics.

Nasser and his fellow officers attributed their defeat not to their own weaknesses but to their government's failures. When they returned to Egypt, they were determined to overthrow the monarchy. They formed a secret organization, the Free Officers. It was not the only organization dedicated to the overthrow of the monarchy, but it was the best disciplined and had the general support of the army.

On July 23, 1952, the Free Officers launched their revolution. It came six months after "Black Saturday," the burning of Cairo by mobs protesting the continued presence of British troops in Egypt. The Free Officers persuaded King Farouk to abdicate, and they declared Egypt a re-

AP Photo (AP004)

Colonel Gamal Abdel Nasser (1918–1970) was the founder and leader of the Free Officers Movement that ousted King Farouk in 1952. By 1954, Nasser bacame the president of Egypt. His Egyptian nationalism, Arab socialism, pan-Arabism, opposition to Western neoclonialism, and non-alignment became the core of "Nasserism." He became popular in the Arab world when he prevailed over Britain, France, and Israel in the 1956 Suez Crisis, but suffered a humiliating defeat during Israel's preemptive war in June 1967.

public. A nine-member Revolutionary Command Council (RCC) was established to govern the country.

(WIKI001)

Syyid Qutb (1906–1966), the ideologue of the Egyptian Muslim Brotherhood, believed that Islam calls for political activism and provides answers to all political and swocioeconomic problems. Egyptian President Gamal Abdel Nasser's regime imprisoned him in 1954, and after releasing him in the early 1960s, had him rearrested and executed in 1966. His writings are still a major source of inspiration to most revolutionary Sunni Islamist organizations like *al-Jjihad, Hamas,* the *Ikhwan, Gama'a al-Islamiyyah,* and *al-Qaeda.*

EGYPT UNDER NASSER

By 1954 Nasser had emerged as Egypt's leader. When the monarchy was formally abolished in 1954, he became president, prime minister, and head of the RCC. Nasser came to power determined to restore dignity and status to Egypt, to eliminate foreign control, and to make his country the leader of a united Arab world.

The lowest point in Nasser's career came in June 1967. Israel invaded Egypt and defeated his Soviet-trained army, along with those of Jordan and Syria, and occupied the Sinai Peninsula in a lightning six-day war. The Israelis were restrained from marching on Cairo only by a United Nations ceasefire. Nasser took personal responsibility for the defeat, calling it *al-Nakba* ("The Catastrophe"). He announced his resignation, but the Egyptian people refused to accept it. The public outcry was so great that he agreed to continue in office. One observer wrote, "The irony was that Nasser had led the country to defeat, but Egypt without Nasser was unthinkable."[4] Nasser had little success in his efforts to unify the Arab world. Arab leaders respected Nasser but were unwilling to play second fiddle to him in an organized Arab state.

United Nations Photo (129736)

Muhammad Anwar al-Sadat (1918–1981) became president of Egypt onNasser's death in 1970. He secretly planned the invasion of Israel in October 1973 to recover Arab lands lost in the June 1967. He reduced Egypt's reliance on the Soviet Union and expanded his country's relationship with the West (especially, the United States). He also discontinued Nasser's policies of socialism and introduced capitalism in Egypt. In 1979, he signed the Camp David Accords and committed his country to peace with Israel, while Israel promised to return the Sinai Peninsula to Egypt. In 1981, while reviewing a military parade in Cairo, Sadat was assassinated by revolutionary Islamists for signing the camp David Accords and for becoming the new pharaoh.

ANWAR AL-SADAT

Nasser was succeeded by his vice president, Anwar al-Sadat, in accordance with constitutional procedure.

In October 1973, Egyptian forces crossed the Suez Canal in a surprise attack and broke through Israeli defense lines in occupied Sinai. The attack was coordinated with Syrian forces invading Israel from the east, through the Golan Heights. The Israelis were driven back with heavy casualties on both fronts, and although they eventually regrouped and won back most of the lost ground, Sadat felt he had won a moral and psychological victory. After the war, Egyptians believed that they had held their own with the Israelis and had demonstrated Arab ability to handle the sophisticated weaponry of modern warfare.

Anwar al-Sadat's most spectacular action took place in 1977. It seemed to him that the Arab-Israeli conflict was at a stalemate. Neither side would budge from its position, and the Egyptian people were angry at having so little to show for the 1973 success.

Sadat's successes in foreign policy, culminating in the 1979 peace treaty with Israel, gave him great prestige internationally.

On October 6, 1981, President Sadat was killed. The assassins, most of them young military men, were immediately arrested. They belonged to *Al Takfir Wal Hijra* ("Repentance and Flight from Sin"), a secret group that advocated the reestablishment of a pure Islamic society in Egypt—by violence, if necessary. Their leader declared that the killing of Sadat was an essential first step in this process.

They accused Sadat of favoring Western capitalism through his Infitah ("open door") policy, of making peace with the "enemy of Islam" (Israel), and of not being a good Muslim. At their trial, Sadat's assassins said that they had acted to rid Egypt of an unjust ruler, a proper action under the laws of Islam.

MUBARAK IN POWER

Vice President Hosni Mubarak, former Air Force commander and designer of Egypt's 1973 success against Israel, succeeded Sadat without incident.

Mubarak began rebuilding bridges with other Arab states that had been damaged after the peace treaty with Israel. Egypt was readmitted to membership in the Islamic Conference, the Islamic Development Bank, the Arab League, and other Arab regional organizations.

But relations worsened after the election in 1996 of Benjamin Netanyahu as head of a new Israeli government. Egypt had strongly supported the Oslo accords for a Palestinian state, and it had set up a free zone for transit of Palestinian products in 1995. The Egyptian view that Netanyahu was not adhering to the accords led to a "war of words" between the two countries. The Israeli-Palestinian conflict has generated a great increase in anti-Israeli sentiments among the Egyptians.

Internal Politics

The first free multiparty national elections held since the 1952 Revolution took place in 1984—although they were not entirely free, because a law requiring political parties to win at least 8 percent of the popular vote limited party participation.

Mubarak was elected to a fourth six-year term in September 1999, making him Egypt's longest-serving head of state in the country's independent history. His victory margin was 94 percent, two points less than in 1993, when as per usual he was the only candidate.

AT WAR WITH FUNDAMENTALISM

Egypt's seemingly intractable social problems—high unemployment, an inadequate

Photograph courtesy of Luke Juran (LJ001)

A *suq* (marketplace) in Egypt. Such marketplaces or *bazaars* are major focal poionts of trading, commerce, and social gatherings in all Middle Eastern countries. Close to most suqs are mosques, frequented by both sellers and buyers alike.

HEALTH/WELFARE

Egypt's women won a significant victory in 1999 when the Court of Cassation upheld a government law banning female circumcision, a time-honored practice in many African societies, including Egypt. Women also won the right to file for divorce under the new 2001 Family Law, and in 2003 the first female judge was appointed in the court system.

job market flooded annually by new additions to the labor force, chronic budgetary deficits, and a bloated and inefficient bureaucracy, to name a few—have played into the hands of Islamic fundamentalists, those who would build a new Egyptian state based on the laws of Islam. Although they form part of a larger fundamentalist movement in the Islamic world, one that would replace existing secular regimes with regimes that adhere completely to spiritual law and custom (*Shari'a*), Egypt's fundamentalists do not harbor expansionist goals. Their goal is to replace the Mubarak regime with a more purely "Islamic" one, faithful to the laws and principles of the religion and dominated by religious leaders.

Egypt's fundamentalists are broadly grouped under the organizational name al-Gamaa al-Islamiya, with the more militant ones forming subgroups such as the Vanguard of Islam and Islamic Jihad, itself an outgrowth of al-Takfir wal-Hijra, which had been responsible for the assassination of Anwar al-Sadat. Ironically, Sadat had formed Al-Gamaa to counter leftist political groups. However, it differs from its parent organization, the Muslim Brotherhood, in advocating the overthrow of the government by violence in order to establish a regime ruled under Islamic law.

FREEDOM

The Islamic fundamentalist challenge to Egypt's secular government has caused the erosion of many rights and freedoms enshrined in the country's constitution. A state of emergency first issued in 1981 is still in effect; it was renewed in 2001 for a 3-year period. In June 2003 the Peoples' Assembly approved establishment of a National Council for Human Rights that would monitor violations or misuse of government authority.

Islamic Jihad's chief aim is the overthrow of the Mubarak government and its replacement by an Islamic one. Its hostility to the United States stems from American support for that government and for the U.S. alliance with Israel against the Palestinians.

One important reason for the rise in fundamentalist violence stems from the government's ineptness in meeting social crises. After the disastrous earthquake in Egypt of October 1992, Islamic fundamentalist groups were first to provide aid to the victims, distributing $1,000 to each family made homeless, while the cumbersome, multilayered government bureaucracy took weeks to respond to the crisis.

The Mubarak government's response to rising violence has been one of extreme re-

ACHIEVEMENTS

Alexandria, founded in 332 B.C. by Alexander the Great, was one of the world's great cities in antiquity, with its Library, its Pharos (Lighthouse), its palaces, and other monuments. Most of them were destroyed by fire or sank into the sea long ago, as the city fell into neglect. Then, in 1995, underwater archaelogists discovered the ruins of the Pharos; its location had not been known previously. Other discoveries followed—the palace of Cleopatra, the remains of Napoleon's fleet (sunk by the British in the Battle of the Nile), Roman and Greek trading vessels filled with amphorae, etc. The restoration of the Library was completed in 2000, with half of its 11 floors under the Mediterranean; visitors in the main reading room are surrounded by water cascading down its windows. After centuries of decay, Alexandria is again a magnet for tourists.

pression. An unfortunate result of government repression of the militants is that Egypt, traditionally an open, tolerant, and largely nonviolent society, has taken on many of the features of a totalitarian state. Human rights are routinely suspended, the prime offenders being officers of the dreaded State Security Investigation (SSI). Indefinite detention without charges is a common practice, and torture is used extensively to extract "confessions" from suspects or their relatives.

Due to the extremism of methods employed by both sides, the conflict between the regime and the fundamentalists has begun to polarize Egyptian society.

Despite its huge majority in the Assembly and its ruthless pursuit of Islamic militants, the Mubarak regime thus far has failed to deal effectively with the political, economic, and social inequities and lack of freedoms that continue to hamper Egypt's development. Observers have commented on Mubarak's mindset about Islamic groups, arguing that he makes no distinction between militants and moderates. As a result, Islamists now control the trade and student unions, schools, even the judiciary, forcing the general public to choose between them and a repressive regime.

A STRUGGLING ECONOMY

Egypt's economy rests upon a narrow and unstable base, due to rapid demographic growth and limited arable land and because political factors have adversely influenced national development. The country has a relatively high level of education and, as a result, is a net exporter of skilled labor to other Arab countries. But the overproduction of university graduates has produced a bloated and inefficient bureaucracy, as the government is required to provide a position for every graduate who cannot find other employment.

Agriculture is the most important sector of the economy, accounting for about one-third of national income. The major crops are long-staple cotton and sugarcane.

Egypt was self-sufficient in foodstuffs as recently as the 1970s but now must import 60 percent of its food. Such factors as rapid population growth, rural-to-urban migration with consequent loss of agricultural labor, and Sadat's open-door policy for imports combined to produce this negative food balance. Subsidies for basic commodities, which cost the government nearly $2 billion a year, are an important cause of inflation, since they keep the budget continuously in deficit. The government kept prices in check. However, inflation, which had dropped to 8 percent in 1995 due to International Monetary Fund stabilization policies required for loans, rose to 37 percent in 1999 as the new free-market policy produced a tidal wave of imports. As a result, the foreign trade deficit increased drastically.

Egypt has important oil and natural-gas deposits, and new discoveries continue to strengthen this sector of the economy. Oil reserves increased to 3.3 billion barrels in 2001, due to new fields being brought on stream in the Western Desert. Proven natural-gas reserves are 51 trillion cubic feet, sufficient to meet domestic needs for 30 years at current rates of consumption.

Egypt also derives revenues from Suez Canal tolls and user fees, from tourism, and

Timeline: PAST

2500–671 B.C.
Period of the pharaohs

671–30 B.C.
The Persian conquest, followed by Macedonians and rule by Ptolemies

30 B.C.
Egypt becomes a Roman province

A.D. 641
Invading Arabs bring Islam

969
The founding of Cairo

1517–1800
Egypt becomes an Ottoman province

1798–1831
Napoleon's invasion, followed by the rise to power of Muhammad Ali

1869
The Suez Canal opens to traffic

1882
The United Kingdom establishes a protectorate

1952
The Free Officers overthrow the monarchy and establish Egypt as a republic

1956
Nationalization of the Suez Canal

1958–1961
Union with Syria into the United Arab Republic

1967
The Six-Day War with Israel ends in Israel's occupation of the Gaza Strip and the Sinai Peninsula

1970
Gamal Abdel Nasser dies; Anwar al-Sadat succeeds as head of Egypt

1979
A peace treaty is signed at Camp David between Egypt and Israel

1980s
Sadat is assassinated; he is succeeded by Hosni Mubarak; a crackdown on Islamic fundamentalists

1990s
The government employs totalitarian tactics in its battle with fundamentalists

PRESENT

2000s
Deep social and economic problems persist

from remittances from Egyptian workers abroad, mostly working in Saudi Arabia and other oil-producing Gulf states. Egypt's approach to terrorism has also had an economic impact on the country.

By 2000 the government's harsh repression had seriously weakened the fundamentalist movement, albeit at a heavy cost.

Some 1,200 police officers and militants had been killed during the 1990s, and 16,000 persons remained jailed without charges on suspicion of membership in Islamic Jihad or other organizations. However, public disaffection continues to grow and to involve inceasing numbers of non-fundamentalists.

Egypt's own difficulties with fundamentalists caused some reluctance on its part when support for the U.S.-led international coalition against terrorism formed after the September 11, 2001, bombings of the World Trade Center in New York City and the Pentagon near Washington, D.C. The reluctance stemmed in part from public anger over continued American support for Israel against the Palestinians and the suffering of Iraq's fellow Arabs under the 11-year sanctions imposed on that country.

In March 2004 the government reached agreement with Israel to set up a number of Qualifying Industrial Zones (Q.I.Z.) in an effort to boost its flagging economy. Egyptian manufacturers, notably of textiles, will be able to export goods duty-free to the United States provided that 35 percent of goods exported were locally produced and a percentage was reserved for Israeli products. Egypt's total exports to the United States of $3.3 billion included $336 million in textiles and clothing. The Q.I.Z.s will add significantly to this total.

NOTES

1. Leila Ahmed, in *A Border Passage* (New York: Farrar, Strauss & Giroux, 1999), deals at length with Egyptian vs. Arab identity from the perspective of growing up in British-controlled Egypt.
2. An English observer said, "In arms and firing they are nearly as perfect as European troops." Afaf L. Marsot, *Egypt in the Reign of Muhammad Ali* (Cambridge, England: Cambridge University Press, 1984), p. 132.
3. Quoted in P. J. Vatikiotis, *Nasser and His Generation* (New York: St. Martin's Press, 1978), p. 35.
4. Gamal Abdel Nasser, *The Philosophy of the Revolution* (Cairo: Ministry of National Guidance, 1954), p. 52.
5. Derek Hopwood, *Egypt: Politics and Society 1945–1981* (London: George Allen and Unwin, 1982), p. 77.
6. Quoted in Vatikiotis, *op. cit.*, p. 245.
7. Hopwood, *op. cit.*, p. 106.
8. David Hirst and Irene Beeson, *Sadat* (London: Faber and Faber, 1981), p. 255.
9. "Banners slung across the broad thoroughfares of central Cairo acclaimed The Hero of the Crossing (of the October 1973 War)." *Ibid.*, pp. 17–18.
10. Said Ashmawy, quoted in "In God He Trusts," *Jerusalem Post Magazine* (July 7, 1995).
11. Reported in *The New York Times*, July 2003.

Gabon (Gabonese Republic)

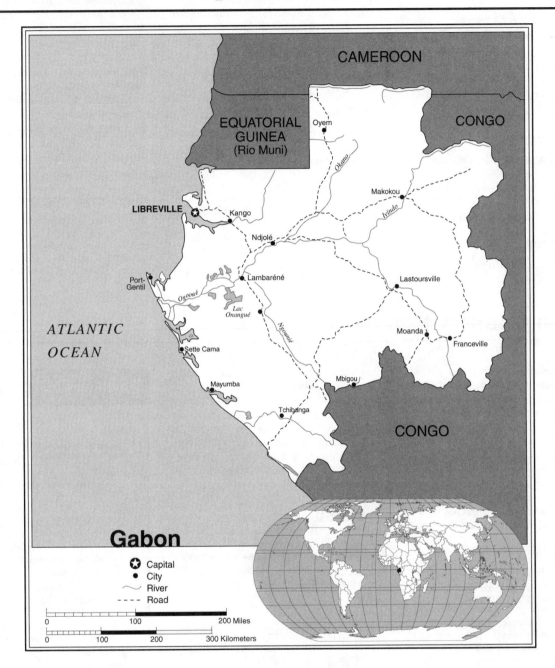

Gabon Statistics

GEOGRAPHY

Area in Square Miles (Kilometers): 102,317 (264,180) (about the size of Colorado)
Capital (Population): Libreville (573,000)
Environmental Concerns: deforestation; poaching
Geographical Features: narrow coastal plain; hilly interior; savanna in the east and south
Climate: tropical

PEOPLE

Population

Total: 1,355,246

Annual Growth Rate: 2.5%

Rural/Urban Population Ratio: 19/81

Major Languages: French; Fang; Myene; Eshira; Bopounou; Bateke; Bandjabi

Ethnic Makeup: about 95% African, including Eshira, Fang, Bapounou, and Bateke; 5% European

Religions: 55%–75% Christian; less than 1% Muslim; remainder indigenous beliefs

Health

Life Expectancy at Birth: 48 years (male); 50 years (female)

Infant Mortality: 93.5/1,000 live births

Physicians Available: 1/2,337 people
HIV/AIDS Rate in Adults: 8.1%

Education
Adult Literacy Rate: 63.2%
Compulsory (Ages): 6–16

COMMUNICATION
Telephones: 39,000 main lines
Televisions: 35 per 1,000 people
Internet Users: 35,000 (2002)

TRANSPORTATION
Highways in Miles (Kilometers): 4,650
  (7,500)
Railroads in Miles (Kilometers): 402 (649)
Usable Airfields: 59
Motor Vehicles in Use: 33,000

GOVERNMENT
Type: republic; multiparty presidential
  regime

Independence Date: August 17, 1960
  (from France)
Head of State/Government: President El
  Hadj Omar Bongo; Prime Minister Jean-
  Francois Ntoutoume-Emane
Political Parties: Gabonese Democratic
  Party; Gabonese Party for Progress;
  National Woodcutters Rally; others
Suffrage: universal at 21

MILITARY
Military Expenditures (% of GDP): 2%
Current Disputes: maritime boundary
  dispute with Equatorial Guinea

ECONOMY
Currency ($ U.S. equivalent): 529.43 CFA
  francs = $1
Per Capita Income/GDP: $5,500/$6.7
  billion
GDP Growth Rate: 2.5%
Inflation Rate: 1.5%

Unemployment Rate: 21%
Labor Force by Occupation: 60%
  agriculture; 25% services and
  government; 15% industry and commerce
Natural Resources: petroleum; iron ore;
  manganese; uranium; gold; timber;
  hydropower
Agriculture: cocoa; coffee; palm oil
Industry: petroleum; lumber; mining;
  chemicals; ship repair; food processing;
  cement; textiles
Exports: 2.5 billion (primary partners
  United States, France, China)
Imports: $921 million (primary partners
  France, Côte d'Ivoire, United States)

SUGGESTED WEB SITES
http://www.gabonnews.com
http://www.sas.upenn.edu/African
  Studies/Country_Specific/
  Gabon.html
http://www.presidence-gabon.com/
  index-a.html

Gabon Country Report

Since independence, Gabon has achieved one of the highest per capita gross domestic products in Africa, due to exploitation of the country's natural riches, especially its oil. But there is a wide gap between such statistical wealth and the real poverty that still shapes the lives of most Gabonese. Disparities in income have helped fuel crime. In a controversial response, in July 2002 the government razed four village suburbs of the capital city Libreville, saying that the areas had become havens for foreign criminal gangs.

DEVELOPMENT

The Trans-Gabonais Railway is one of the largest construction projects in Africa. Work began in 1974 and, after some delays, most of the line is now complete. The railway has opened up much of Gabon's interior to commercial development. The Chinese have become very important foreign investors in Gabon in recent years. In April 2004 the French oil firm Total signed a contract to export Gabonese oil to China. In September 2004 yet another agreement was signed with a Chinese company, this time to exploit iron ore. Both contracts represent a major boost for the Gabonese economy as they will generate thousands of jobs.

Guided by only two presidents since independence from France in 1960, Gabon has proven to be one of the most stable nations in Africa. With more than 40 tribal groups in the nation, the country has managed to avoid the ethnic violence that has

frequently wreaked havoc on many of the other African states. At the top of the local governing elite is President Omar Bongo, whose main palace, built a decade ago at a reported cost of $300 million, symbolizes his penchant for grandeur. First elected in 1967, Bongo is now able to remain in office indefinitely due to a constitutional change in July 2003.

FREEDOM

Since 1967 Bongo has maintained power through a combination of repression and the deft use of patronage. The current transition to a multiparty process, however, has led to an improvement in human rights.

HEALTH/WELFARE

The government claims to have instituted universal, compulsory education for Gabonese up to age 16. Independent observers doubt the government's claim but concur that major progress has been made in education. Health services have also expanded greatly.

ACHIEVEMENTS

Gabon will soon have a second private television station, funded by a French cable station. Profits will be used to fund films that will be shown on other African stations. Gabon's first private station is funded by Swiss and Gabonese capital.

Timeline: PAST

1849
Libreville is founded by the French as a settlement for freed slaves

1910
Gabon becomes a colony within French Equatorial Africa

1940
The Free French in Brazzaville seize Gabon from the pro-Vichy government

1960
Independence is gained; Leon M'ba becomes president

1967
Omar Bongo becomes Gabon's second president after M'ba's death

1968
The Gabonese Democratic Party (PDG) becomes the only party of the state

1990s
Bongo agrees to multiparty elections but seeks to put limits on the opposition; riots in Port-Gentil

PRESENT

2000s
The PDG retains power

The Gambia (Republic of The Gambia)

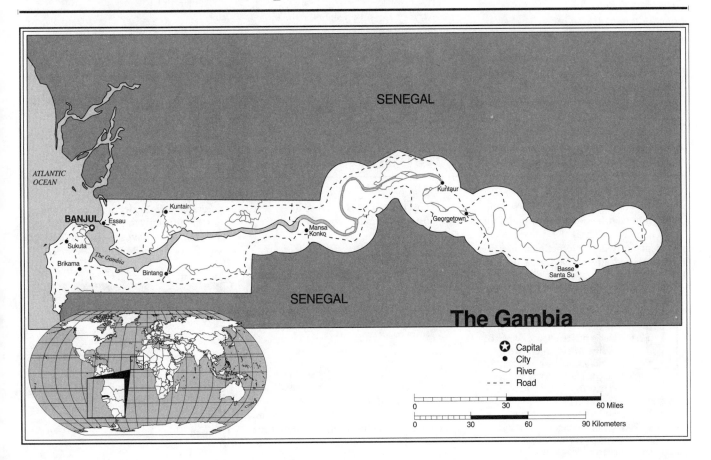

The Gambia Statistics

GEOGRAPHY

Area in Square Miles (Kilometers): (4,361) (11,295) (about twice the size of Delaware)
Capital (Population): Banjul (418,000)
Environmental Concerns: deforestation; desertification; water-borne diseases
Geographical Features: floodplain of The Gambia River flanked by some low hills
Climate: tropical; hot rainy season, cooler dry season

PEOPLE

Population

Total: 1,546,848
Annual Growth Rate: 2.98%
Rural/Urban Population Ratio: 68/32
Major Languages: English; Mandinka; Wolof; Fula; Sarakola; Diula; others
Ethnic Makeup: 42% Mandinka; 18% Fula; 16% Wolof; 24% others (99% African; 1% non-Gambian)
Religions: 90% Muslim; 9% Christian; 1% indigenous beliefs

Health

Life Expectancy at Birth: 52 years (male); 56 years (female)
Infant Mortality: 76.3/1,000 live births
Physicians Available: 1/14,536 people
HIV/AIDS Rate in Adults: 1.95%

Education

Adult Literacy Rate: 47.5%
Compulsory (Ages): 7–13; free

COMMUNICATION

Telephones: 38,000 main lines
Internet Users: 25,000 (2002)

TRANSPORTATION

Highways in Miles (Kilometers): 1,584 (2,640)
Railroads in Miles (Kilometers): none
Usable Airfield: 1
Motor Vehicles in Use: 9,000

GOVERNMENT

Type: republic
Independence Date: February 18, 1965 (from the United Kingdom)
Head of State/Government: President Yahya Jammeh is both head of state and head of government
Political Parties: Alliance for Patriotic Reorientation and Construction; National Reconciliation Party; People's Democratic Organization for Independence and Socialism; others
Suffrage: universal at 18

MILITARY

Military Expenditures (% of GDP): 0.3%
Current Disputes: internal conflicts; boundary dispute with Senegal

ECONOMY

Currency ($ U.S. Equivalent): 19.91 dalasis = $1

Per Capita Income/GDP: $1,770/$2.5 billion

GDP Growth Rate: 3%

Inflation Rate: 14%

Labor Force by Occupation: 75% agriculture; 19% industry and services; 6% government

Natural Resources: fish

Agriculture: peanuts; millet; sorghum; rice; corn, cassava; livestock; fish and forest resources

Industry: processing peanuts, fish, and hides; tourism; beverages; agricultural machinery assembly; wood- and metalworking; clothing

Exports: $139 million (primary partners Benelux, Japan, United Kingdom)

Imports: $200 million (primary partners China, Hong Kong, United Kingdom, the Netherlands)

SUGGESTED WEB SITES

http://www.gambianet.com
http://www.cia.gov/cia/
  publications/factbook/geos/
  ga.html

The Gambia Country Report

Since his seizure of power in a 1994 coup, Yahya Jammeh has dominated politics in The Gambia. In 2001 he was reelected president in what international election monitors generally viewed as a free and fair poll.

DEVELOPMENT

Since independence, The Gambia has developed a tourist industry. Whereas in 1966 only 300 individuals were recorded as having visited the country, the figure for 1988–1989 was over 112,000. Tourism is now the second-biggest sector of the economy. Still, tourism has declined since 2000. With the February 2004 announcement of the discovery of large oil reserves, there is expected to be a major upturn in economic activity.

In April 2000 Gambians were shocked when student protests in the capital city, Banjul, resulted in the killing of 14 people and the wounding of many more by government security forces. Many interpreted the violence as an ominous official response to the reemergence of independent voices within the media and civil society, which have been pushing for greater openness and accountability in government.

FREEDOM

Despite the imposition of martial law in the aftermath of the 1981 coup attempt, The Gambia has had a strong record of respect for individual liberty and human rights. Under its current regime, The Gambia has forfeited its model record of respect for freedoms of speech and association.

Jammeh came to power in July 1994, after The Gambia's armed forces overthrew the government of Sir Dawda Jawara, bringing to an abrupt end what had been postcolonial West Africa's only example of uninterrupted multiparty democracy. Meanwhile, The Gambia's already weak

economy has suffered from reduced revenues from tourism and foreign donors.

HEALTH/WELFARE

Forty percent of Gambian children remain outside the primary-school setup. Economic Recovery Program austerity has made it harder for the government to achieve its goal of education for all.

The Gambia is Africa's smallest non-insular nation. Except for a small seacoast, it is entirely surrounded by its much larger neighbor, Senegal. Gambians have much in common with Senegalese. The Gambia's three major ethnolinguistic groups—the Mandinka, Wolof, and Fula (or Peul)—are found on both sides of the border. The Wolof language serves as a *lingua franca* in both the Gambian capital of Banjul and the urban areas of Senegal. Islam is the major religion of both countries, while each also has a substantial Christian minority. The economies of the two countries are also similar, with each being heavily reliant on the cultivation of ground nuts as a cash crop.

ACHIEVEMENTS

Gambian *griots*—hereditary bards and musicians such as Banna and Dembo Kanute—have maintained a traditional art. Formerly, griots were attached to ruling families; now, they perform over Radio Gambia and are popular throughout West Africa.

In the aftermath of the 1981 coup attempt, The Gambia was modestly successful in rebuilding its politics. Whereas the 1982 elections were arguably compromised by the detention of the main opposition leader, Sherif Mustapha Dibba, on charges (later dismissed) of complicity in a revolt, the 1987 and 1992 polls restored most people's confidence in Gambian de-

mocracy. In both elections, opposition parties significantly increased their share of the vote, while Jawara's People's Progressive Party retained majority support.

Timeline: PAST

1618
The British build Fort James at the current site of Banjul, on the Gambia River

1807
The Gambia is ruled by the United Kingdom through Sierra Leone

1965
Independence

1970
President Dawda Jawara comes to power

1980s
An attempted coup against Jawara; the rise and fall of the Senegambia Confederation

1990s
Jawara is overthrown by a military coup; Yahya Jammeh becomes head of state

PRESENT

2000s
Government security forces kill 14 people during student protests; Jammeh is reelected president, but the opposition gains in parliamentary elections; discovery of large oil reserves

The Gambia has always been a poor country. During the 1980s conditions worsened as a result of bad harvests and falling prices for groundnuts, which usually account for half of the nation's export earnings. The tourist industry was also disrupted by the 1981 coup attempt. Faced with mounting debt, the government submitted to International Monetary Fund pressure by cutting back its civil service and drastically devaluing the local currency. The latter step initially led to high inflation, but prices have become more stable in recent years, and the economy as a whole has begun to enjoy a gross domestic product growth rate of up to 5 percent per year. As elsewhere, the negative impact of Structural Adjustment has proved especially burdensome to urban dwellers.

Guinea (Republic of Guinea)

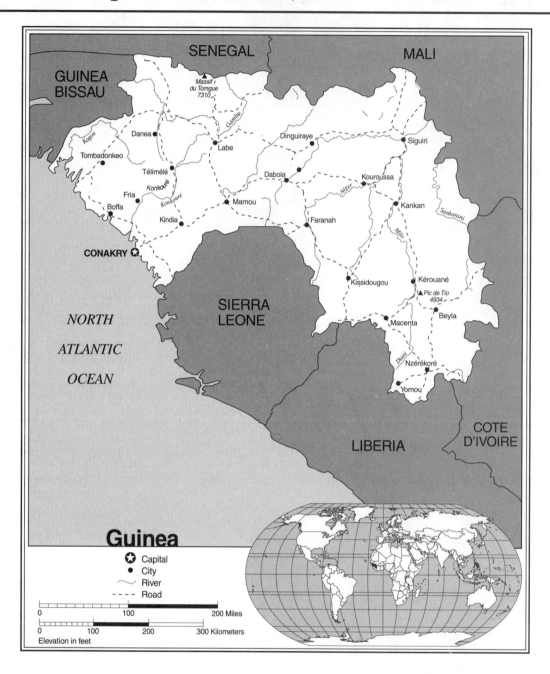

Guinea

- ⭐ Capital
- ● City
- 〰 River
- --- Road

0   100   200 Miles
0   100   200   300 Kilometers
Elevation in feet

Guinea Statistics

GEOGRAPHY

Area in Square Miles (Kilometers): 95,000 (246,048) (about the size of Oregon)

Capital (Population): Conakry (1,272,000)

Environmental Concerns: deforestation; insufficient potable water; desertification; soil erosion and contamination; over fishing; overpopulation

Geographical Features: mostly flat coastal plain; hilly to mountainous interior

Climate: tropical

PEOPLE

Population

Total: 9,246,462

Annual Growth Rate: 2.37%

Rural/Urban Population Ratio: 68/32

Major Languages: French; many tribal languages

Ethnic Makeup: 40% Peuhl; 30% Malinke; 20% Soussou; 10% other African groups

Religions: 85% Muslim; 8% Christian; 7% indigenous beliefs

Health

Life Expectancy at Birth: 43 years (male); 48 years (female)

Infant Mortality: 127/1,000 live births
Physicians Available: 1/9,732 people
HIV/AIDS Rate in Adults: 1.54%

Education

Adult Literacy Rate: 36%
Compulsory (Ages): 7–13; free

COMMUNICATION

Telephones: 37,000 main lines
Televisions: 10 per 1,000 people
Internet Users: 40,000 (2003)

TRANSPORTATION

Highways in Miles (Kilometers): 18,060
(30,100)
Railroads in Miles (Kilometers): 651 (1,086)
Usable Airfields: 15
Motor Vehicles in Use: 33,000

GOVERNMENT

Type: republic

Independence Date: October 2, 1958
(from France)
Head of State/Government: President
(General) Lansana Conté; Prime
Minister Francois Lonseny Fall
Political Parties: Party for Unity and
Progress; Union for the New Republic;
Rally for the Guinean People; many
others
Suffrage: universal at 18

MILITARY

Military Expenditures (% of GDP): 3.3%
Current Disputes: refugee crisis as a result
of unrest in Sierra Leone and Liberia

ECONOMY

Currency ($ U.S. Equivalent): 1,975
Guinean francs = $1
Per Capita Income/GDP: $2,100/$19
billion
GDP Growth Rate: 3.3%

Inflation Rate: 14.8%
Labor Force by Occupation: 80%
agriculture; 20% industry and services
Population Below Poverty Line: 40%
Natural Resources: bauxite; iron ore;
diamonds; gold; uranium; hydropower; fish
Agriculture: rice; cassava; millet; sweet
potatoes; coffee; bananas; palm
products; pineapples; livestock
Industry: bauxite; gold; diamonds;
alumina refining; light manufacturing
and agricultural processing
Exports: $695 million (primary partners
Belgium, United States, Ireland)
Imports: $555 million (primary partners
France, United States, Belgium)

SUGGESTED WEB SITES

http://www.sas.upenn.edu/African
Studies/Country_Specific/
Guinea.html
htt://www.cia.gov/cia/
publications/factbook/geos/
gv.html

Guinea Country Report

In recent years, Guinea has managed to maintain internal peace in the face of armed conflict along its borders. But renewed fighting in neighboring Sierra Leone, Liberia, and Côte d'Ivoire has revived fears that the country is being dragged into a wider regional conflict.

Since the end of 2000, incursions by rebels along Guinea's border regions with Liberia and Sierra Leone have claimed more than 1,000 lives and caused massive population displacement. The United Nations high commissioner for refugees, Ruud Lubbers, warned that the country's refugee crisis, mostly the result of the conflicts in Sierra Leone and Liberia, was in danger of getting out of control. The country shelters more than half a million (estimates vary widely) cross-border refugees.

DEVELOPMENT

A measure of economic growth in Guinea was reflected in the rising traffic in Conakry harbor, whose volume rose 415% over a 4-year period. Plans are being made to improve the port's infrastructure, but regional conflicts threaten further development.

At home, the harassment of journalists and opposition leaders has underscored the government's continued insecurity despite

the 1992 transition to multiparty politics. In a constitutional referendum that took place in November 2001, voters endorsed President Lansana Conté's proposal to extend the presidential term from five to seven years. But the opposition boycotted the poll, accusing Conté of trying to stay in office for life. Conté has proven adept at surviving challenges to his authority. In April 1992 he announced that a new constitution guaranteeing freedom of association would take immediate effect. Within a month, more than 30 political parties had formed. This initiative was a political second chance for a nation whose potential had been mismanaged for decades, under the dictatorial rule of its first president, Sekou Touré.

FREEDOM

Human rights continue to be restricted in Guinea, with the government's security forces being linked to disappearances, abuse of prisoners and detainees, torture by military personnel, and inhumane prison conditions.

Following Guinea's independence from France in 1958, the ability of Touré's Democratic Party of Guinea (PDG) to step into the administrative vacuum was the basis for Guinea's quick transformation into the

African continent's first one-party socialist state, a process that was encouraged by the Soviet bloc. Touré's rule was characterized by economic mismanagement and the widespread abuse of human rights. It is estimated that 2 million people—at the time about one out of every four Guineans—fled the country during his rule. At least 2,900 individuals disappeared under detention by the government.

HEALTH/WELFARE

The life expectancy of Guineans is among the lowest in the world, reflecting the stagnation of the nation's health service during the Sekou Touré years.

By the late 1970s, Touré, pressured by rising discontent and his own apparent realization of his country's poor economic performance, began to modify both his domestic and foreign policies. This shift led to better relations with Western countries but little improvement in the lives of his people.

On April 3, 1984, a week after Touré's death, the army stepped in, claiming that it wished to end all vestiges of the late president's dictatorial regime. A new government was formed, under the leadership of then-colonel Conté, and a 10-point program for national recovery was set forth, including the restoration of human rights and the renovation of the economy.

ACHIEVEMENTS

More than 80% of the programming broadcast by Guinea's television service is locally produced. This output has included more than 3,000 movies. A network of rural radio stations is currently being installed.

Faced with an empty treasury, the new government committed itself to a severe Structural Adjustment Program (SAP). This has led to a dismantling of many of the socialist structures that had been established by the previous government. While international financiers have generally praised it, the government has had to weather periodic unrest and coup attempts. In spite of these challenges, however, it has remained committed to SAP.

Timeline: PAST

1700s
A major Islamic kingdom is established in the Futa Djalon

1898
Samori Touré is defeated by the French

1958
Led by Sekou Touré, Guineans reject continued membership in the French Community; an independent republic is formed

1978
French president Giscard d'Estaing visits Guinea: the beginning of a reconciliation between France and Guinea

1980s
Sekou Touré's death is followed by a military coup; the introduction of SAP leads to urban unrest

1990s
President Lansana Conté begins to establish a multiparty democracy; multiparty elections are held for the presidency; Conté claims victory

PRESENT

2000s
Guinea stays the course of Structural Adjustment despite severe hardships; fears intensify regarding a regional conflict; Guinea, Sierra Leone, and Liberia agree on measures to secure mutual borders and to tackle insurgency; Prime Minister Lounseny resigns from office

Guinea is blessed with mineral resources, which could lead to a more prosperous future. The country is rich in bauxite and has substantial reserves of iron and diamonds. New mining agreements, leading to a flow of foreign investment, have already led to a modest boom in bauxite and diamond exports. Small-scale gold mining is also being developed. These initiatives, however, are being threatened by the conflicts in neighboring states.

Guinea's greatest economic failing has been the poor performance of its agricultural sector. Unlike many of its neighbors, the country enjoys a favorable climate and soils. But, although some 80 percent of Guineans are engaged in subsistence farming, only 3 percent of the land is cultivated, and foodstuffs remain a major import. In 1987, the government initiated an ambitious plan of road rehabilitation, which, along with better produce prices, has encouraged farmers to produce more for the domestic market.

Guinea-Bissau (Republic of Guinea-Bissau)

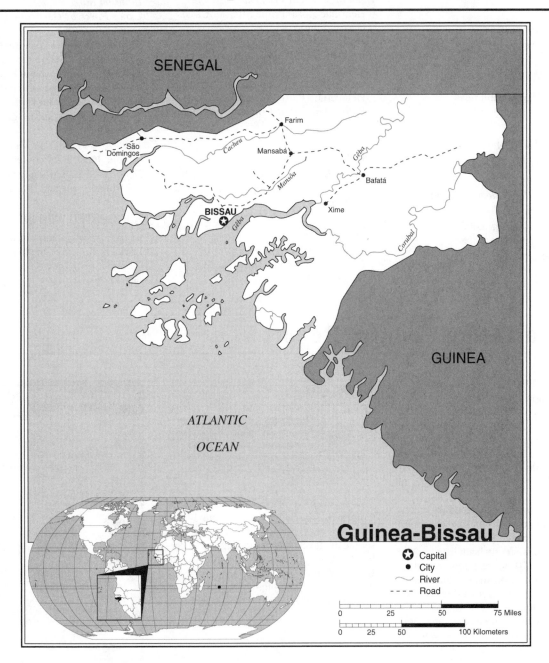

Guinea-Bissau Statistics

GEOGRAPHY

Area in Square Miles (Kilometers): 13,948 (36,125) (about 3 times the size of Connecticut)

Capital (Population): Bissau (292,000)

Environmental Concerns: soil erosion; deforestation; overgrazing; overfishing

Geographical Features: mostly low coastal plain, rising to savanna in the east

Climate: tropical

PEOPLE

Population

Total: 1,388,363

Annual Growth Rate: 1.99%

Rural/Urban Population Ratio: 77/23

Major Languages: Portuguese; Kriolo; various African languages

Ethnic Makeup: 30% Balanta; 20% Fula; 14% Manjaca; 13% Mandinka; 23% others (99% African; 1% others)

Religions: 50% indigenous beliefs; 45% Muslim; 5% Christian

Health

Life Expectancy at Birth: 47 years (male); 52 years (female)

Infant Mortality: 118/1,000 live births

Physicians Available: 1/9,477 people
HIV/AIDS Rate in Adults: 2.5%

Education

Adult Literacy Rate: 54%
Compulsory (Ages): 7–13

COMMUNICATION

Telephones: 10,600 main lines
Internet Users: 19,000 (2003)

TRANSPORTATION

Highways in Miles (Kilometers): 2,610 (4,350)
Railroads in Miles (Kilometers): none
Usable Airfields: 28
Motor Vehicles in Use: 6,000

GOVERNMENT

Type: republic

Independence Date: September 10, 1974 (from Portugal)
Head of State/Government: President Henrique Rosa; Prime Minister Carlos Gomes Junior
Political Parties: African Party for the Independence of Guinea-Bissau and Cape Verde; Front for the Liberation and Independence of Guinea; United Social Democratic Party; Social Renovation Party; Democratic Convergence; others
Suffrage: universal at 18

MILITARY

Military Expenditures (% of GDP): 2.8%
Current Disputes: trouble along the border with Senegal

ECONOMY

Currency ($ U.S. Equivalent): 581 Communaute Financiere Africaine francs (XOF) = $1

Per Capita Income/GDP: $900/$1.2 billion
GDP Growth Rate: -7%
Inflation Rate: 4%
Labor Force by Occupation: 82% agriculture
Natural Resources: fish; timber; phosphates; bauxite; petroleum
Agriculture: corn; beans; cassava; cashew nuts; cotton; fish and forest products; peanuts; rice; palm kernels
Industry: agricultural-products processing; beverages
Exports: $80 million (primary partners India, Italy, South Korea)
Imports: $55.2 million (primary partners Portugal, Senegal, Thailand)

SUGGESTED WEB SITES

```
http://www.guineabissau.com
http://www.sas.upenn.edu/African
   Studies/Country_Specific/
   G_Bissau.html
```

Guinea-Bissau Country Report

In February 2000 Kumba Yala of the Social Renovation Party (PRS) took 72 percent of the vote in the second round of presidential elections. Yala's reign came to an end when he was ousted from the presidency in a bloodless military coup in September 2003. Carlos Gomes Júnior was elected as the new Prime Minister in March 2004.

The Yala government faced the unenviable challenge of promoting economic development. Since independence the country has consistently been listed as one of the world's 10 poorest countries. Unfortunately, the period since Yala's installation has been marred by continued political instability. Prior to the 2003 coup, there had been three other attempted coups, hundreds of lives lost in war and political violence, and the pulling out of the ruling coalition by one of the major partners due to lack of consultation. An International Monetary Fund team praised improvements in financial controls, but this came after the country had lost tens of millions of dollars in revenue from corrupt practices of government officials. Meanwhile, the head of the Supreme Court and three judges were dismissed by Yala for allegedly overturning the president's decision to expel leaders of a Muslim sect from the country.

To many outsiders, the nation has been better known for its prolonged liberation war, from 1962 to 1974, against Portuguese colonial rule.

DEVELOPMENT

With help from the UN Development Program, Guinea-Bissau has improved the tourism infrastructure of the 40-island Bijagos Archipelago in the hopes of bringing in much-needed revenues.

The origins of Portuguese rule in Guinea-Bissau go back to the late 1400s. The area was raided for centuries as a source of slaves, who were shipped to Portugal and its colonies of Cape Verde and Brazil. With the nineteenth-century abolition of slave trading, the Portuguese began to impose forced labor within Guinea-Bissau itself.

FREEDOM

The police have engaged in arbitrary arrests and torture. The fighting between government and rebel troops resulted in some 13,000 civilian casualties during the 1990s.

In 1956 six *assimilados*—educated Africans who were officially judged to have assimilated Portuguese culture—led by Amilcar Cabral, founded the African Party for the Independence of Guinea-Bissau and Cape Verde (PAIGC) as a vehicle for the liberation of Cape Verde as well as Guinea-Bissau. Widespread participation throughout Guinea-Bissau in the 1973

Timeline: PAST

1446
Portuguese ships arrive; claimed as Portuguese Guinea; slave trading develops

1915
Portugal gains effective control over most of the region

1956
The African Party for the Independence of Guinea-Bissau and Cape Verde is formed

1963–1973
Liberation struggle in Guinea-Bissau under the PAIGC and Amilcar Cabral

1973
Amilcar Cabral is assassinated; the PAIGC declares Guinea-Bissau independent

1974
Revolution in Portugal leads to recognition of Guinea-Bissau's independence

1980
João Vieira comes to power through a military coup, ousting Luis Cabral

1990s
The country moves toward multipartyism; "Government of National Unity"

PRESENT

2000s
Kumba Yala of the Social Renovation (or Renewal) Party is elected president

election of a National Assembly encouraged a number of countries to formally recognize the PAIGC declaration of state sovereignty.

HEALTH/WELFARE

Guinea-Bissau's health statistics remain appalling: an overall 48-year life expectancy, 12% infant mortality, and more than 90% of the population infected with malaria.

INDEPENDENCE

Since 1974 the leaders of Guinea-Bissau have tried to confront the problems of independence while maintaining the ideal-ism of their liberation struggle. The nation's weak economy has limited their success. Guinea-Bissau has little in the way of mining or manufacturing, although explorations have revealed potentially exploitable reserves of oil, bauxite, and phosphates. More than 80 percent of the people are engaged in agriculture, but urban populations depend on imported foodstuffs. This situation has been generally attributed to the poor infrastructure and a lack of incentives for farmers to grow surpluses. Efforts to improve the rural economy during the early years of independence were hindered by severe drought. Only 8 percent of the small country's land is cultivated.

ACHIEVEMENTS

With Portuguese assistance, a new fiber-optic digital telephone system is being established in Guinea-Bissau.

Under financial pressure, the government adopted a Structural Adjustment Program (SAP) in 1987. The peso was devalued, civil servants were dismissed, and various subsidies were reduced. The painful effects of these SAP reforms on urban workers were cushioned somewhat by external aid.

Guyana (Cooperative Republic of Guyana)

Guyana Statistics

GEOGRAPHY

Area in Square Miles (Kilometers): 82,990
(215,000) (about the size of Idaho)

Capital (Population): Georgetown (248,500)

Environmental Concerns: water pollution;
deforestation

Geographical Features: mostly rolling
highlands; low coastal plain; savanna in
the south

Climate: tropical

PEOPLE*

*Note: Estimates explicitly take into account the
effects of excess mortality due to AIDS.

Population

Total: 705,813

Annual Growth Rate: 0.61%

Rural/Urban Population Ratio: 74/36

Major Languages: English; indigenous
dialects; Creole; Hindi; Urdu

Ethnic Makeup: 51% East Indian, 30% black; 14% mixed; 4% Amerindian; 2% white and Chinese
Religions: 50% Christian; 33% Hindu; 9% Muslim; 8% others

Health

Life Expectancy at Birth: 60 years (male); 64 (female)
Infant Mortality Rate (Ratio): 37.22/1,000
Physicians Available (Ratio): 1/3,000

Education

Adult Literacy Rate: 98%
Compulsory (Ages): 6–14; free

COMMUNICATION

Telephones: 80,400 main lines
Daily Newspaper Circulation: 97 per 1,000 people
Televisions: 1 per 26 people
Internet Users: 125,000

TRANSPORTATION

Highways in Miles (Kilometers): 4,949 (7,970)

Railroads in Miles (Kilometers): (187)
Usable Airfields: 1
Motor Vehicles in Use: 33,000

GOVERNMENT

Type: republic
Independence Date: May 26, 1966 (from the United Kingdom)
Head of State/Government: President Bharrat Jagdeo; Prime Minister Samuel Hinds
Political Parties: People's National Congress; Alliance for Guyana People's Progressive Party; United Force; Democratic Labour Movement; People's Democratic Movement; National Democratic Front; others
Suffrage: universal at 18

MILITARY

Military Expenditures (% of GDP): 0.8%
Current Disputes: territorial disputes with Venezuela and Suriname

ECONOMY

Currency ($ U.S. Equivalent): 190.672002) Guyanese dollars = $1
Per Capita Income/GDP: $4,000/$2.8 billion
GDP Growth Rate: 0.3%
Inflation Rate: 4.7%
Unemployment Rate: 9.1%
Natural Resources: bauxite; gold; diamonds; hardwood timber; shrimp; fish
Agriculture: sugar; rice; wheat; vegetable oils; livestock; potential for fishing and forestry
Industry: bauxite; sugar; rice milling; timber; fishing; textiles; gold mining
Exports: $5.12 million (primary partners United States, Canada, United Kingdom)
Imports: $612 million (primary partners United States, Trinidad and Tobago, Netherland Antilles)

SUGGESTED WEB SITE

http://www.cia.gov/cia/
publications/factbook/geos/
gy.html

Guyana Country Report

The first European settlers were the Dutch, who settled in Guyana late in the sixteenth century. Dutch control ended in 1796, when the British gained control of the area. In 1831 the former Dutch colonies were consolidated as the Crown Colony of British Guiana.

DEVELOPMENT

Moderate economic growth was achieved in 2001–2003 by the expansion of the agricultural and mining sectors, a favorable climate for business, a more realistic exchange rate, and modest inflation.

Guyana is a society deeply divided along racial and ethnic lines. East Indians make up the majority of the population. They predominate in rural areas, constituting the bulk of the labor force on the sugar plantations, and they comprise nearly all of the rice-growing peasantry. They also dominate local businesses and are prominent in the professions. Blacks are concentrated in urban areas, where they are employed in clerical and secretarial positions in the public bureaucracy, in teaching, and in semiprofessional jobs. A black elite dominates the state bureaucratic structure..

Before Guyana's independence in 1966, plantation owners, large merchants, and

FREEDOM

One of the priorities of the Jagan governments was the elimination of all forms of ethnic and racial discrimination, a difficult task in a country where political parties are organized along racial lines. It was hoped that Guyana's indigenous peoples would be offered accelerated development programs to enhance their health and welfare.

British colonial administrators consciously favored some ethnic groups over others, providing them with a variety of economic and political advantages. The regime of President Forbes Burnham revived old patterns of discrimination for political gain

HEALTH/WELFARE

The government has initiated policies designed to lower the cost of living for Guyanese. Prices for essentials have been cut. Money has been allocated for school lunch programs and for a "food-for-work" plan. Pensions have been raised for the first time in years. The minimum wage, however, will not sustain an average family.

Burnham, after ousting the old elite when he nationalized the sugar plantations and the bauxite mines, built a new regime

that simultaneously catered to lower-class blacks and discriminated against East Indians. In an attempt to address the blacks' basic human needs, the Burnham government greatly expanded the number of blacks holding positions in public administration.

Timeline: PAST

1616
The first permanent Dutch settlements on Essequibo River

1815
The Netherlands cedes the territory to Britain

1966
Independence

1985
President Forbes Burnham dies

1990s
The government promises to end racial and ethnic discrimination

PRESENT

2000s
Territorial disputes with Suriname and Venezuela persist; politics remains bitterly divided along ethnic lines

In the mid-1970s, a faltering economy and political mismanagement generated an increasing opposition to Burnham that cut across ethnic lines. The government increased the size of the military, packed Parliament through rigged elections, and amended the Constitution so that the president held virtually imperial power. There has been some improvement since Burnham's death in 1985.

In politics, the election of Indo-Guyanese leader Cheddi Jagan to the presidency reflected deep-seated disfavor with the behavior and economic policies of the previous government of Desmond Hoyte. During his campaign, Jagan stated that

ACHIEVEMENTS

The American Historical Association selected Walter Rodney for the 1982 Beveridge Award for his study of the Guyanese working people. The award is for the best book in English on the history of the United States, Canada, or Latin America. Rodney, the leader of the Working People's Alliance, was assassinated in 1980.

government should not be involved in sectors of the economy where private or cooperative ownership would be more efficient. Jagan's policies stimulated rapid socioeco-

nomic progress as Guyana embarked on the road to economic recovery.

Following Jagan's death, new elections were held in December 1997, and Janet Jagan, the ex-president's 77-year-old widow, was named president. In August 1999 she stepped down due to health reasons and named Finance Minister Bharrat Jagdeo to succeed her.

Jagdeo's presidency has only exacerbated ethnic tensions. The Afro-Guyanese, who represent less than half of Guyana's population, have responded to their lack of power by confronting the government on its policies, sometimes violently.

Indonesia (Republic of Indonesia)

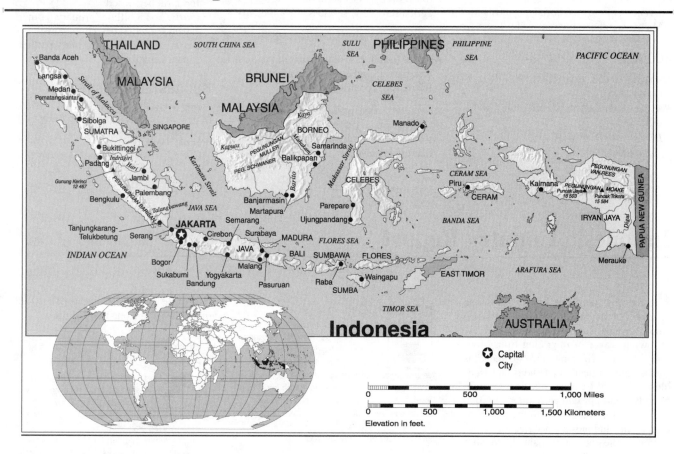

Indonesia Statistics

GEOGRAPHY

Area in Square Miles (Kilometers): 740,903 (1,919,440) (nearly 3 times the size of Texas)

Capital (Population): Jakarta (11,429,000)

Environmental Concerns: air and water pollution; sewage; deforestation; smoke and haze from forest fires

Geographical Features the world's largest archipelago; coastal lowlands; larger islands have interior mountains

Climate: tropical; cooler in highlands

PEOPLE

Population

Total: 238,452,952

Annual Growth Rate: 1.49%

Rural/Urban Population Ratio: 60/40

Major Languages: Bahasa Indonesian; English; Dutch; Javanese; many others

Ethnic Makeup: 45% Javanese; 14% Sundanese; 7.5% Madurese; 7.5% coastal Malay; 26% others

Religions: 88% Muslim; 8% Christian; 4% Hindu, Buddhist, and others

Health

Life Expectancy at Birth: 66 years (male); 71 years (female)

Infant Mortality: 39.4/1,000 live births

Physicians Available: 1/6,570 people

HIV/AIDS in Adults: 0.05%

Education

Adult Literacy Rate: 87%

Compulsory (Ages): 7–16

COMMUNICATION

Telephones: 7.75 million main lines

Daily Newspaper Circulation: 20 per 1,000 people

Televisions: 145 per 1,000 people

Internet Users: 4,400,000 (2002)

TRANSPORTATION

Highways in Miles (Kilometers): (1999) 212,474 (342,700)

Railroads in Miles (Kilometers): 3,875 (6,450)

Usable Airfields: 490

Motor Vehicles in Use: 4,800,000

GOVERNMENT

Type: republic

Independence Date: December 27, 1949 (legally; from the Netherlands)

Head of State/Government: President Susilo Bambang Yudhoyono is both head of state and head of government

Political Parties: Golkar; Indonesia Democracy Party-Struggle; Development Unity Party; Crescent Moon and Star Party; National Awakening Party; others

Suffrage: universal at 17; married persons regardless of age

MILITARY

Military Expenditures (% of GDP): 1.3%

Current Disputes: territorial disputes with Malaysia, others; internal strife

ECONOMY

Currency ($ U.S. Equivalent): 8,577 rupiahs = $1

Per Capita Income/GDP: $3,200/$758 billion

GDP Growth Rate: 4.1%

Inflation Rate: 11.5%

Unemployment Rate: 8.7%%

Labor Force by Occupation: 45% agriculture; 39% services; 16% industry

Population Below Poverty Line: 27%

Natural Resources: petroleum; tin; natural gas; nickel; timber; bauxite; copper; fertile soils; coal; gold; silver

Agriculture: rice; cassava; peanuts; rubber; cocoa; coffee; copra; other tropical; livestock products; poultry; beef; pork; eggs

Industry: petroleum; natural gas; textiles; mining; cement; chemical fertilizers; food; rubber; wood

Exports: $63.8 billion (primary partners Japan, United States, Singapore)

Imports: $40.2 billion (primary partners Japan, United States, Singapore)

SUGGESTED WEB SITES

```
http://www.cia.gov/cia/
  publications/factbook/geos/
  id.html
http://www.bps.go.id
·http://www.britannica.com/search
```

Indonesia Country Report

Present-day Indonesia is a kaleidoscope of some 300 languages and more than 100 ethnic groups. In the thirteenth century, following waves of migration from Mongolia, China, Thailand and Vietnam, as well as the influence of Hindus and Buddhists that had transpired during different periods over approximately the past 6,000 years, Muslim traders began the Islamization of the Indonesian people; today, 87 percent of the population claim the Muslim faith—meaning that there are more Muslims in Indonesia than in any other country of the world, including the states of the Middle East.

Consider what all the following past influences in Indonesia mean for the culture of modern Indonesia. Some of the most powerful ideologies ever espoused by hu-

DEVELOPMENT

Indonesia continues to be hamstrung by its heavy reliance on foreign loans, a burden inherited from the Sukarno years. Current Indonesian leaders speak of "stabilization" and "economic dynamism," but there are always obstacles—government corruption, and such natural disasters as the devastating tsunami of 2004—that hamper smooth economic improvement.

mankind—supernaturalism, Islam, Hinduism, Buddhism, Christianity, mercantilism, colonialism, and nationalism—have had an impact on Indonesia. Communal feasts in Hindu Bali, circumcision ceremonies in Muslim Java, and Christian baptisms among the Bataks of Sumatra all represent

borrowed cultural traditions. Thus, out of many has come one rich culture.

FREEDOM

Demands for Western-style human rights are frequently heard, but until recently, only the army has had the power to impose order on the numerous and often antagonistic political groups. However, some progress is evident: in 2004 Indonesians directly elected their president for the first time in decades.

Indonesia has more Muslims than any other country in the world, and the hundreds of Islamic socioreligious, political, and paramilitary organizations intend to

photo courtesy of tasikmalaya.go.id (TASIK001)

This mosque in Tasikmalaya on the island of Java in Indonesia was built in the last one hundred years. It has a dome, which is found in the Middle East (along with European colonial influences), instead of earlier Southeast Asian mosques with their layered roofs.

The *Istiqlal* (Freedom) Mosque in Indonesia's capital of Jakarta. Indonesia, with over 200 million Muslims, is the largest Muslim country in the world.

keep it that way. Some 9,000 people in the eastern provincial capital of Ambon in the Maluku islands, many of them Christians desiring independence from Indonesia, were killed in Muslim-Christian sectarian violence in 2001, and gangs from both religions fought street battles there again in 2004, leaving more than two dozen dead and scores wounded. In addition to exploding bombs and hacking people to death with swords, the gangs set fire to churches and destroyed a United Nations office. Clearly, Indonesians have a long way to go in developing mutual respect and tolerance for the diversity of cultures in their midst.

A LARGE LAND, LARGE DEBTS

Unfortunately, Indonesia's economy is not as rich as its culture. Three-quarters of the population live in rural areas; more than half of the people engage in fishing and small-plot rice and vegetable farming. The average income per person is only US$3,200 a year, based on gross domestic product. A 1993 law increased the minimum wage in Jakarta to $2.00 *per day*.

Also worrisome is the level of government debt. Indonesia is blessed with large oil reserves (Pertamina is the state-owned oil company) and minerals and timber of every sort (also state-owned), but to extract these natural resources has required massive infusions of capital, most of it borrowed. In fact, Indonesia has borrowed more money than any other country in Asia. The country must allocate 40 percent of its national budget just to pay the interest on loans. Low oil prices in the 1980s made it difficult for the country to

keep up with its debt burden. Extreme political unrest and an economy that contracted nearly 14 percent in 1998 have seriously exacerbated Indonesia's economic headaches in recent years.

HEALTH/WELFARE

Indonesia has one of the highest birth rates in the Pacific Rim. Many children will grow up in poverty, never learning even to read or write their national language, Bahasa Indonesian.

Indonesia's financial troubles seem puzzling, because in land, natural resources, and population, the country appears quite well-off. Indonesia is the second-largest country in Asia (after China). But transportation and communication are problematic and costly in archipelagic states.

Illiteracy and demographic circumstances also constrain the economy. Indonesia's population of 238.5 million is one of the largest in the world, but 12 percent of adults (17 percent of females) cannot read or write. Only about 600 people per 100,000 attend college, as compared to 3,580 in nearby Philippines. Moreover, since almost 70 percent of the population reside on or near the island of Java, on which the capital city, Jakarta, is located, educational and development efforts have concentrated there, at the expense of the communities on outlying islands. Over the past 20 years, poverty has been reduced from 60 percent (the current poverty rate is about 27 percent), but Indonesia was seriously damaged by the Asian financial crisis and by a series of natural disasters in 2004,

including the mammoth tsunami that devastated Aceh province, and experts expect that the economy will not return to normal in the near future.

ACHIEVEMENTS

Balinese dancers' glittering gold costumes and unique choreography epitomize the "Asian-ness" of Indonesia as well as the Hindu roots of some of its communities.

With 2.3 million new Indonesians entering the labor force every year, and with half the population under age 20, serious efforts must be made to increase employment opportunities.

MODERN POLITICS

Establishing the current political and geographic boundaries of the Republic of Indonesia has been a bloody and protracted task. So fractured is the culture that many people doubt whether there really is a single country that one can call Indonesia. During the first 15 years of independence (1950–1965), there were revolts by Muslims and pro-Dutch groups, indecisive elections, several military coups, battles against U.S.-supported rebels, and serious territorial disputes with Malaysia and the Netherlands. In 1966, nationalistic President Sukarno, who had been a founder of Indonesian independence, lost power to Army General Suharto.

In 1975, ignoring the disapproval of the United Nations, President Suharto invaded and annexed East Timor, a Portuguese colony.

With the economy in serious trouble in 1998, and with the Indonesian people tired of government corruption and angry at the control of Suharto and his six children over much of the economy, rioting broke out all over the country, ending in Suharto's resignation. In the first democratic elections in years, a respected Muslim cleric, Abdurrahman Wahid, was elected president, with Megawati Sukarnoputri (daughter of Indonesia's founding father, Sukarno) as vice president.

In the 2004 elections, in which 24 parties vied for 14,000 seats at all levels of government and fielded 450,000 candidates, Susilo Bambang Yudhoyono won the presidency in a a landslide victory. However, Yudhoyono had barely taken office when the country was hit by a devastating natural disaster, the December 2004 tsunami. Caused by a mammoth earthquake in the Indian Ocean, a massive wave over five stories tall and traveling at speeds of 500 mph smashed into northern Sumatra. Over 100,000 Indonesians were confirmed dead, and many thousands more were unaccounted for. Yudhoyono's approach to this tragedy will likely determine his ability to solve some of Indonesia's many other pressing problems.

Timeline: PAST

750,000 B.C.
Java Man lived here

A.D. 600
Buddhism gains the upper hand

1200
Muslim traders bring Islam to Indonesia

1509
The Portuguese begin to trade and settle in Indonesia

1596
Dutch traders begin to influence Indonesian life

1942
The Japanese defeat the Dutch

1949–1950
Indonesian independence from the Netherlands; President Sukarno retreats from democracy and the West

1966
General Suharto takes control of the government from Sukarno and establishes his New Order, pro-Western government

1975
Indonesia annexes East Timor

1990s
Suharto steps down after 32 years in power; East Timor votes for independence; violence erupts in Borneo

PRESENT

2000s
The economy remains stalled; East Timor obtains independence; Aceh Province signs a peace agreement ending a 130-year armed rebellion; a peace agreement in separatist Aceh Province mutes, but does not eliminate, some of the violence there; moderate Susilo Bambang Yudhoyono, age 55, wins a landslide election to become the first Indonesian president directly elected by the voters since the end of the Suharto dictatorship; a series of natural disasters, including a volcanic eruption in northeastern Indonesia, rain-triggered landslides in Sumatra, powerful earthquakes in Papua, and a mammoth tsunami in Aceh, kill tens of thousands and add further woes to the struggling economy

Iran (Islamic Republic of Iran)

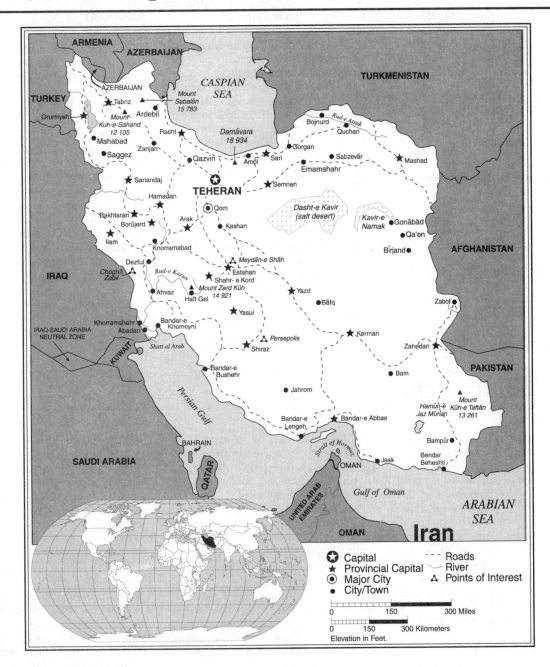

Legend:
- ✪ Capital
- ★ Provincial Capital
- ⊙ Major City
- • City/Town
- --- Roads
- River
- ⚐ Points of Interest

0 — 150 — 300 Miles
0 — 150 — 300 Kilometers
Elevation in Feet.

Iran Statistics

GEOGRAPHY

Area in Square Miles (Kilometers): 636,294 (1,648,000) (about the size of Alaska)
Capital (Population): Teheran (6,836,000)
Environmental Concerns: air and water pollution; deforestation; overgrazing; desertification; oil pollution; insufficient potable water
Geographical Features: a rugged, mountainous rim; a high central basin with deserts and mountains; discontinuous plains along both coasts
Climate: mostly arid or semiarid; subtropical along Caspian Sea coast

PEOPLE

Population

Total: 68,917,860
Annual Growth Rate: 0.86%
Rural/Urban Population Ratio: 40/60
Major Languages: Farsi (Persian); Azeri Turkish; Kurdish
Ethnic Makeup: 51% Persian; 24% Azeri; 8% Gilaki and Mazandarani; 7% Kurd; 10% others
Religions: 89% Shi'a Muslim; 9% Sunni Muslim; 2% Zoroastrian, Jewish, Christian, or Bahai

141

Health

Life Expectancy at Birth: 68 years (male); 71 years (female)
Infant Mortality Rate (Ratio): 41 per 1,000 live births
Physicians Available (Ratio): 1 per 1,600 people

Education

Adult Literacy Rate: 79.4%
Compulsory (Ages): 6–10; free

COMMUNICATION

Telephones: 14,571,100 main lines
Daily Newspaper Circulation: 20 per 1,000 people
Televisions: 117 per 1,000
Internet Service Providers: 8 (2000)

TRANSPORTATION

Highways in Miles (Kilometers): 86,924 (167,157)
Railroads in Miles (Kilometers): 3,472 (7,203)
Usable Airfields: 305
Motor Vehicles in Use: 2,189,000

GOVERNMENT

Type: theocratic republic
Independence Date: April 1, 1979 (Islamic Republic of Iran proclaimed)
Head of State/Government: Supreme Guide Ayatollah Ali Hoseini-Khamenei; President Mahmoud Ahmadinejad
Political Parties: none legally recognized; various political "organizations" present candidates for Majlis elections, the most recent one being in 2000; these include Assembly of the Followers of the Imam's Line, Freethinkers' Front, Moderation and Development Group, Servants of Construction, Society of Self-Sacrificing Devotees
Suffrage: universal at 15

MILITARY

Military Expenditures (% of GDP): 3.3%
Current Disputes: maritime boundary with Iraq in Shatt al-Arab not formally demarcated, and prisoner exchange not complete. Iran's occupation of Greater and Lesser Tunbs Islands disputed by United Arab Emirates (U.A.E.); Iran disagrees with Azerbaijan, Russia, Kazakhstan, and Turkmenistan over sharing of Caspian Sea waters.

ECONOMY

Currency ($ U.S. Equivalent): 8,614 rials = $1 (changed from multi-exchange to fixed single rate in 2004)
Per Capita Income/GDP: $7,700/$516.7 billion
GDP Growth Rate: 6.3%
Inflation Rate: 15.5%
Unemployment Rate: 11.2%
Labor Force: 23,000,000
Natural Resources: petroleum; natural gas; coal; chromium; copper; iron ore; lead; manganese; zinc; sulfur
Agriculture: grains; sugar beets; fruits; nuts; cotton; dairy products; wool; caviar
Industry: petroleum; petrochemicals; textiles; cement and other construction materials; food processing; metal fabrication; armaments
Exports: $38.7 billion (primary partners Japan, Italy, United Arab Emirates)
Imports: $31.3 billion (primary partners Germany, China, Italy, Japan, South Korea)

Iran Country Report

Iran is in many respects a subcontinent, ranging in elevation from Mount Demavend (18,386 feet) to the Caspian Sea, which is below sea level. Most of Iran consists of a high plateau ringed by mountains. Much of the plateau is covered with uninhabitable salt flats and deserts—the Dasht-i-Kavir and Dasht-i-Lut, the latter being one of the most desolate and inhospitable regions in the world. The climate is equally forbidding. The so-called Wind of 120 Days blows throughout the summer in eastern Iran, bringing dust and extremely high temperatures.

Most of the country receives little or no rainfall.

Water is so important to the Iranian economy that all water resources were nationalized in 1967. Lack of rainfall caused the development of a sophisticated system of underground conduits, qanats, to carry water across the plateau from a water source, usually at the base of a mountain. Many qanats were built thousands of years ago and are still in operation. They make existence possible for much of Iran's rural population.

ETHNIC AND RELIGIOUS DIVERSITY

Due to Iran's geographic diversity, the population is divided into a large number of separate and often conflicting ethnic groups. Ethnic Iranians constitute the majority. The Iranians (or *Persians*, from Parsa, the province where they first settled) are an Indo-European people whose original home was probably in Central Asia. They moved into Iran around 1100 B.C. and gradually dominated the entire region, establishing the world's first empire (in the sense of rule over various unrelated peoples in a large territory).

The largest ethnic minority group is the Azeri (or Azerbaijani) Turks. The Azeris live in northwestern Iran. Turkish dynasties originating in Azerbaijan controlled Iran for several centuries and were responsible for much of premodern Islamic Iran's political power and cultural achievements.

The Kurds are another large ethnic minority. Iran's Kurd population is concentrated in the Zagros Mountains along the Turkish and Iraqi borders. The Kurds are Sunni Muslims, as distinct from the Shi'a majority. Kurds are strongly independent mountain people who lack a politically recognized homeland and who have been unable to unite to form one.

The Arabs are another important minority group (Iran and Turkey are the two Islamic countries in this region of the world with a non-Arab majority). The Arabs live in Khuzestan Province, along the Iraqi border. The Baluchi, also Sunni Muslims, are located in southeast Iran and are related to Baluchi groups in Afghanistan and Pakistan. They are seminomadic and have traditionally opposed any form of central-government control. Non-Islamic minorities include Jews, Zoroastrians, and Armenians and other Christians. Altogether they make up 1 percent of the population.

The Bahais, a splinter movement from Islam founded by an Iranian mystic called the *Bab* ("Door," i.e., to wisdom) and organized by a teacher named Baha'Ullah in the nineteenth century, are the largest non-Muslim minority group. Although Baha'Ullah taught the principles of universal love, peace, harmony, and brotherhood, his proclamations of equality of the sexes, ethnic unity, the oneness of all religions, and a universal rather than a Muslim God aroused the hostility of Shi'a religious leaders.

Despite Iran's official hostility toward Israel, its own Jewish population is recognized as a minority under the 1979 Constitution and has lived there for centuries.

CULTURAL CONFORMITY

Despite the separatist tendencies in Iranian society caused by the existence of these

Photo courtesy of Holger Spamann (HS001)

Iran's holy city of Qom, with Fatimah al-Masuma's mausoleum. Qom, with its many Islamic seminaries, has been a major center for the training of Shi'a *ulama* (islamic scholars) and one of the places of Shi'a pilgrimage since the ninth century. In 817 CE, Fatimah *al-Masuma* (literally, "the sinless one"), the sister of the eighth Shi'a Imam Muhammad Reza, died in Qom. Her mausoleum, with its huge golden dome, dominates the Qom skyline.

various ethnic groups and religious divisions, there is considerable cultural conformity. Most Iranians, regardless of background, display distinctly Iranian values, customs, and traditions. Unifying features include the Farsi language, Islam as the overall religion, the appeal (since the sixteenth century) of Shi'a Islam as an Iranian nationalistic force, and a sense of nationhood derived from Iran's long history and cultural continuity.

Iranians at all levels have a strongly developed sense of class structure. It is a three-tier structure, consisting of upper, middle, and lower classes. Under the republic, these norms have been increasingly Islamized as religious leaders have asserted the primacy of Shi'a Islam in all aspects of Iranian life.

HISTORY

Arab armies defeated Sassanid's monarchy in Iran and brought Islam to the land. The establishment of Islam brought significant changes into Iranian life. The Arabs gradually established control over all the former Sassanid territories, converting the inhabitants to Islam as they went. But the well-established Iranian cultural and social system provided refinements for Islam that were lacking in its early existence as a purely Arab religion. The Iranian converts to Islam converted the religion from a particularistic Arab faith to a universal faith.

Islamic culture, in the broad sense—embracing literature, art, architecture, music, certain sciences, and medicine—owes a great deal to the contributions of Iranian Muslims such as the poets Hafiz and Sa'di, the poet and astronomer Omar Khayyam, and many others.

DEVELOPMENT

The Iranian economy grew by 4.8 percent in real terms in 2001–2002 compared with 5.7% in 2000–2001. However, GDP per capita was 30 percent lower in those years than in the 1970s under the Shah's regime. These days civil servants and even military officers must hold two or more jobs to keep up with the 17 percent inflation. The regime's "buy-back" system, whereby foreign companies develop oil-related projects and are reimbursed in dollars, has helped foreign exchange. But a lack of qualified Iranians has increased their costs by having to employ foreign expatriates to run the projects.

Shi'a Muslims, currently the vast majority of the Iranian population and represented in nearly all ethnic groups, were in the minority in Iran during the formative centuries of Islam. Only one of the Twelve Shi'a Imams—the eighth, Reza—actually lived in Iran. (His tomb at Meshed is now the holiest shrine in Iran.) *Taqiya* ("dissimulation" or "concealment")—the Shi'a practice of hiding one's beliefs to escape.

Sunni persecution—added to the difficulties of the Shi'a in forming an organized community.

In the sixteenth century, the Safavids, who claimed to be descendants of the Prophet Muhammad, established control over Iran with the help of Turkish tribes. The first Safavid ruler, Shah Ismail, proclaimed Shiism as the official religion of his state and invited all Shi'as to move to Iran, where they would be protected. Shi'a domination of the country dates from this period. Shi'a Muslims converged on Iran from other parts of the Islamic world and became a majority in the population. In

more recent years, the Khomeini government issued a call to Iranians to carry on war against the Sunni rulers of Iraq, indicating that Shi'a willingness to struggle and, if necessary, incur martyrdom, was still very much alive in Iran.

King of Kings

Nasr al-Din Shah, Iran's ruler for most of the nineteenth century, was responsible for a large number of concessions to European bankers, promoters, and private companies. His purpose was to demonstrate to European powers that Iran was becoming a modern state and to find new revenues without having to levy new taxes, which would have aroused more dangerous opposition. The various concessions helped to modernize Iran, but they bankrupted the treasury in the process. The shah realized that the establishment of a trained professional army would not only defend Iran's territory but would also demonstrate to the European powers that the country was indeed "modern." A new group of Iranian intellectuals and Iran's mullahs both felt that the shah was giving away Iran's assets and resources to foreigners. By the end of the nineteenth century, the people were roused to action, the mullahs had turned against the ruler, and the intellectuals were demanding a constitution that would limit his powers.

The mosque is the bastion of religious opinion; its preachers can, and do, mobilize the faithful to action through thundering denunciations of rulers and government officials. Mosque and bazaar came together in 1905 to bring about the first Iranian Revolution, a forerunner, at least in pattern, of the 1979 revolt. A mullah was arrested and killed for criticizing the ruler in a Friday sermon. Further protests were met with mass

Reza Khan or Raza Shah Pahlavi I (1877–1944) led a military coup and became prime minister of Persia in 1921. In 1925, Reza Khan made himself the new Shah and established the Pahlavi dynasty. For the next sixteen years, he promoted rapid modernization, Westernization, and centralization. His close ties with Germany during World War II, resulted in Britain and the Soviet Union forcing him to abdicate the throne in favor of his son, Muhammad Reza.

arrests and then gunfire; "a river of blood now divided the court from the country."[6]

In 1906 nearly all of the religious leaders left Teheran for the sanctuary of Qum, Iran's principal theological-studies center. The bazaar closed down again, a general strike paralyzed the country, and thousands of Iranians took refuge in the British Embassy in Teheran. With the city paralyzed, the shah gave in. He granted a constitution that provided for an elected Majlis, the first limitation on royal power in Iran in its history. In 1925, Reza Khan, a villager from an obscure family who had risen through the ranks on sheer ability, was crowned as shah, with an amendment to the Constitution that defined the monarchy as belonging to Reza Shah and his male descendants in succession

Reza Shah was one of the most powerful and effective monarchs in Iran's long history. He brought all ethnic groups under the control of the central government and established a well-equipped standing army to enforce his decrees. He did not tamper with the Constitution; instead, he approved all candidates for the Majlis and outlawed political parties, so that the political system was entirely responsible to him alone.

Reza Shah's New Order

Reza Shah wanted to build a "new order" for Iranian society, and he wanted to build it in a

hurry. He was a great admirer of Mustafa Kemal Ataturk, founder of the Turkish Republic. Like Ataturk, Reza Shah believed that the religious leaders were an obstacle to modernization, due to their control over the masses. He set out to break their power through a series of reforms. Lands held in religious trust were leased to the state, depriving the religious leaders of income. A new secular code of laws took away their control, since the secular code would replace Islamic law. Other decrees prohibited the wearing of veils by women and the fez, the traditional brimless Muslim hat, by men. When religious leaders objected, Reza Shah had them jailed; on one occasion, he went into a mosque, dragged the local mullah out in the street, and horsewhipped him for criticizing the ruler during a Friday sermon. Only one religious leader, a young scholar named Ruhollah al-Musavi al-Khomeini, consistently dared to criticize the shah, and he was dismissed as being an impractical teacher.

Iran declared its neutrality during the early years of World War II. But Reza Shah was sympathetic to Germany; he had many memories of British interference in Iran. He allowed German technicians and advisers to remain in the country, and he refused to allow war supplies to be shipped across Iran to the Soviet Union. In 1941 British and Soviet armies simultaneously occupied Iran. Reza Shah abdicated in favor of his son, Crown Prince Mohammed, and was taken into exile on a British warship. He never saw his country again.

The shah announced a 400 percent increase in the price of Iranian oil in 1973 and declared that the country would soon become a "Great Civilization." Money poured into Iran, billions of dollars more each year. The army was modernized with the most sophisticated U.S. equipment available. A new class of people, the "petro-bourgeoisie," became rich at the expense of other classes. Instead of the concessions given to foreign business firms by penniless Qajar shahs, the twentieth-century shah became the dispenser of opportunities to businesspeople and bankers to develop Iran's great civilization with Iranian money—an army of specialists imported from abroad.

In 1976, the shah seemed at the pinnacle of his power. His major adversary, Khomeini, had been expelled from Iraq and was now far away in Paris. U.S. President Jimmy Carter visited Iran in 1977 and declared, "Under your leadership (the country) is an island of stability in one of the more troubled areas of the world." Yet just a month later, 30,000 demonstrators marched on the city of Qum, protesting an unsigned newspaper article (reputed to have been written by the shah) that had at-

Crown Prince Muhammad Reza (1919–1980) became Shah of Iran in 1941. He continued his father's polices of modernizing and Westernizing Iran. By the late 1970s, the despotic and corrupt Shah became unpopular among most segments of the Iranian population. The highly organized and influential Shi'a clerical establishment assumed leadership of the 1979 revolution in Iran, forcing the Shah into exile. He died a year later in Cairo.

tacked Khomeini as being anti-Iranian. The police fired on the demonstration, and a massacre followed.

Gradually, a cycle of violence developed. It reflected the distinctive rhythm of Shi'a Islam, wherein a death in a family is followed by 40 days of mourning, and every death represents a martyr for the faith. Massacre followed massacre in city after city. In spite of the shah's efforts to modernize his country, it seemed to more and more Iranians that he was trying to undermine the basic values of their society by striking at the religious leaders. Increasingly, marchers in the streets were heard to shout, "Death to the shah!"

Even though the shah held absolute power, he seemed less and less able or willing to use his power to crush the opposition. It was as if he were paralyzed.

THE ISLAMIC REPUBLIC

The shah and his family left Iran for good in January 1979. Ayatollah Ruhollah Khomeini, who had been exiled by the shah, returned practically on his heels, welcomed by millions who had fought and bled for his return. The shah's Great Civilization lay in ruins. Like a transplant, it had been an attempt to impose a foreign model of life on the Iranian community, a surgical attachment that had been rejected.

In April 1979 Khomeini announced the establishment of the Islamic Republic of Iran. He called it the first true republic in Islam since the original community of believers was formed by Muhammad. Khomeini said that religious leaders would assume active leadership, serve in the Majlis, even fight Iran's battles as "warrior mullahs." A "Council of Guardians" was set up to interpret laws and ensure that they were in conformity with the sacred law of Islam. Although its rulers failed to conquer Greece and thereby extend their empire into Europe, such achievements as their imperial system of government, the Persian language (Farsi), the monumental architecture of their capital at Persepolis, and their distinct cultural/historical heritage provide modern Iranians with pride in their ancient past and a national identity, unbroken to the present day.

FREEDOM

Iran's constitution calls its political system a "religious democracy," leaving the term ambiguous. However, the struggle between advocates of openness and justice and those who would preserve rigid orthodoxy under the clerical regime has underscored freedom's limits. In recent years there has been some relaxation of social restrictions, particularly the dress code and public contacts between men and women, especially teenagers.

Khomeini, as the first Supreme Guide, embodied the values and objectives of the republic. Because he saw himself in that role, he consistently sought to remain above factional politics yet be accessible to all groups and render impartial decisions. But the demands of the war with Iraq, the country's international isolation, conflicts between radical Islamic fundamentalists and advocates of secularization, and other divisions forced the aging Ayatollah into a day-to-day policy-making role. It was a role that he was not well prepared for, given his limited experience beyond the confines of Islamic scholarship.

The Islamic Republic staggered from crisis to crisis in its initial years. Abol Hassan Bani-Sadr, a French-educated intellectual who had been Khomeini's right-hand man in Paris, was elected president in 1980 by 75 percent of the popular vote. But it was one of the few postrevolutionary actions that united a majority of Iranians. Although the United States, as the shah's supporter and rescuer in his hour of exile, was proclaimed the "Great Satan" and thus helped to maintain Iran's revolutionary fervor, the prolonged crisis over the holding of American Embassy hostages by guards who would take orders from no one but Khomeini embarrassed Iran and damaged its credibility more than any gains made from tweaking the nose of a superpower.

HEALTH/WELFARE

Drugs and heroin cross-border smuggling from Afghanistan have become a major problem in Iran, costing the country some $800 million a year. Over 3,000 border guards have been killed by smugglers since 1999, and an average of a dozen police die monthly in urban shootouts with dope dealers. It was estimated that Iran had 1.3 million addicts in 2000, and that number is rising. In 2003 it was estimated that there were 200,000 street children in Teheran alone, many of them addicts and abandoned by their families.

Historically, revolutions often seem to end by devouring those who carry them out. A great variety of Iranian social groups had united to overthrow the shah. They had different views of the future; an "Islamic republic" meant different things to different groups. The Revolution first devoured all those associated with the shah, in a reign of terror intended to compensate for 15 years of repression. Islamic tribunals executed thousands of people—political leaders, intellectuals, and military commanders.

The major opposition to Khomeini and his fellow religious leaders came from the radical group Mujahideen-i-Khalq. The group favored an Islamic socialist republic and was opposed to too much influence on government by religious leaders. However, the Majlis was dominated by the religious leaders, many of whom had no experience in government and knew little of politics beyond the village level. As the conflict between these groups sharpened, bombings and assassinations occurred almost daily.

The instability and apparently endless violence during 1980–1981 suggested to the outside world that the Khomeini government was on the point of collapse. Iraqi president Saddam Hussain thought so, and in September 1980, he ordered his army to invade Iran—a decision that proved to be a costly mistake. President Bani-Sadr was dismissed by Khomeini after an open split developed between him and religious leaders over the conduct of the war; he escaped to France subsequently and has remained out of politics.

INTERNAL POLITICS

What may be described as the "surreal world" of Iranian politics is largely the result of institutions grafted onto the structure of the pre-revolutionary government by clerical leaders. The clerical regime preserved that structure, which consisted of the Majlis, cabinet of ministers, civil service and the armed forces. SAVAK was replaced by a similar and equally repressive security and intelligence called SAVAM. Then a parallel structure of government was formed under the authority and leadership of the Supreme Legal Guide, responsible only to him as the final repository of Islamic law.

This structure consists of a 12-member Council of Constitutional Guardians (CCG), an 88-member Assembly of Experts elected for 8-year terms, and a 31-member appointed Expediency Council. These three bodies function within the system as a sort of checks and balances on each other. Thus the Assembly of Experts, based in Qum and popularly elected, chooses the Supreme Legal Guide when there is a vacancy. All Assembly members must be clerics and after being elected must be "approved" by the CCG before taking their seats. The die is further loaded by the fact that half of the members of the CCG must also be clerical leaders.

The Expediency Council was set up to resolve disputes over legislation between the Majlis and the CCG and to verify whether laws passed by the Majlis are compatible or not with Islamic law. The Supreme Legal Guide also controls the judiciary, the Radio-TV Ministry, the chiefs of the armed forces, the Revolutionary Guard and SAVAM, and the police.

An important change between the monarchy and the republic concerns the matter of appropriate dress. Decrees issued by Khomeini required women to wear the enveloping chador and *hijab* (headscarf) in public. Painted nails or too much hair showing would often lead to arrests or fines, sometimes jail. The decrees were enforced by Revolutionary Guards and *komitehs* ("morals squads") patrolling city streets and urban neighborhoods. Also, the robe and turban worn by Ayatollah Khomeini and his fellow clerics were decreed as correct fashion, preferred over the "Mr. Engineer" business suit and tie of the shah's time. The necktie in particular was considered a symbol of Western decadence and derided as a "donkey's tail" by the country's new leaders.

IRAN AFTER KHOMEINI

In June 1989 Ayatollah Ruhollah Khomeini died of a heart attack in a Teheran hospital. He was 86 years old and had struggled all his life against the authoritarianism of two shahs.

The Imam left behind a society entirely reshaped by his uncompromising Islamic ideals and principles. Every aspect of social life in republican Iran is governed by these principles, from prohibition of the production and use of alcohol and drugs to a strict dress code for women outside the home, compulsory school prayers, emphasis on theological studies in education, and required fasting during Ramadan. One positive result of this Islamization program has been a renewed awareness among Iranians of their cultural identity and pride in their heritage.

FOREIGN POLICY

Although Iranians continue to view the American people favorably, the clerical regime and its hard-line supporters insist that the U.S. government is the cause of their failure to establish a sound economy, and an obstacle to improved relations with the outside world.

Hence, with U.S companies excluded from the Iranian market, Russia has become the country's main source of weaponry as well as technical aid for its nuclear power program. Russian experts began building the first nuclear power plant, at Bushire, in 1995. Fully operational in 2004, it generates 1,000 megawatts (MW), enough to provide electric power for 20 percent of the population. The discovery of important uranium reserves near Yazd ensures that Iran will no longer need to rely on Russia for its nuclear fuel.

There remains a considerable reservoir of goodwill among ordinary Iranians toward the United States. After the southeastern city of Bam, with its ancient citadel, was leveled by a massive earthquake with some 45,000 casualties, the United States sent a medical disaster team along with volunteers from many humanitarian agencies. The door between the two countries opened a crack wider when Iran agreed to participate in an international donors' conference devoted to Iraq's reconstruction, agreeing to provide potable water and electricity.

Iran's foreign policy in recent years has been essentially regional. In 2001 it signed an agreement with Saudi Arabia for joint efforts to combat terrorism and drug trafficking. Iran's relations with the newly independent Iran has objected strenuously to the U.S.–sponsored plan for a pipeline to carry Azerbaijani oil from Baku to the Turkish port of Ceyhan (Adana) on the Mediterranean, thus bypassing Iranian territory.

An important element in Iran's willingness to cooperate with the United States against the Afghanistan-based al-Qaeda network and its leader, Osama bin Laden, stemmed from drug smuggling. The Taliban regime, which controlled 90 percent of

that country until its overthrow in late 2001, had encouraged drug cultivation as a means of income and turned a blind eye to smuggling, much of it through Iran. Since 1996 some 3,000 Iranian border guards have been killed by smugglers, and easy access to drugs has resulted in a large number of Iranian addicts.

ACHIEVEMENTS

Although the Ayatollah Khomeini was not always supportive of women's rights, the relaxation of dress and other social restriction in 2002–2003 have helped women participate more fully in public and national life than their sisters in other Islamic countries. Iranian women drive their own cars and work outside the home. There are women representatives in the Majlis, and a former American hostage-taker, Masoumah Ebtekar, is one of four vice presidents. A bill passed by the Majlis in 2003 gives women the right to file for divorce, although it will not become law until approved by the CCG.

But any further thawing of U.S.-Iranian relations was quickly refrozen when President George W. Bush included Iran in his "axis of evil" speech, covering countries supposedly sponsoring terrorism. The charge was made more explicit in August 2003 with revelations that the country was "well advanced" toward a nuclear weapons capability. Iranian officials insist that extraction of newly discovered uranium resources near the town of Natanz, along with the heavy water plant at Arak, both serve its intention to develop peaceful uses for nuclear energy. Indeed, the International Atomic Energy Agency (IAEA's) 2003 inspection revealed no evidence of nuclear arms development but announced Iran had provided some faulty information and did possess the reactor parts necessary to enrich uranium.

ELECTION SURPRISES

In May 1997 Iranian voters went to the polls to elect a new president. Four candidates had been cleared and approved by the CCG: a prominent judge; a former intelligence-agency director; Majlis Speaker Ali Akbar Nalegh-Nouri; and Mohammed Khatami, the former minister of culture and Islamic guidance, a more or less last-minute candidate, since he had been out of office for five years and was not well known to the public. With 25 million out of Iran's 33 million potential voters casting their ballots, Khatami emerged as the winner in a startling upset, with 69 percent of the votes as compared to 25 percent for Nalegh-Nouri. Support for the new president came mainly from women, but he was also

backed by the large number of Iranians under age 25, who grew up under the republic but are deeply dissatisfied with economic hardships and Islamic restrictions on their personal freedom.

The contest between "hard-liners" holding fast to the Islamic structure as laid out by Khomeini and implemented by his successor has intensified in recent years.

In the ninth presidential election held in July 2005, a 49-year-old revolutionary Islamist in the person of Mahmoud Ahmadinejad vanquished the well known former revolutionary Islamist (and now the much more moderate and progressive Islamist) in the person of Ali Akbar Hashemi Rafsanjani, who has served as the Speaker of the National Assembly for two terms, the President of Iran for two-four year terms, and on the influential Council of Guardians. After the success of the Islamic Revolution in 1979, Ahmadinejad served as the top commander of the *Pasdaran* (Islamic Revolutionary Guards), in the Shi'a establishment's Office for Strengthening Unity (OSU), in the right-wing Association of Engineers, in the Central Council of the Society of the Devotees of the Islamic Revolution, and as the Mayor of Tehran (2003–2005). Just before he assumed power on August 1, 2005, he himself mentioned that he will stress "justice" rather than "freedom" in governing Iran for the next four years.

THE ECONOMY

Iran's bright economic prospects during the 1970s were largely dampened by the 1979 Revolution. Petroleum output was sharply reduced, and the war with Iraq crippled industry as well as oil exports. Ayatollah Khomeini warned Iranians to prepare for a decade of grim austerity before economic recovery would be sufficient to meet domestic needs.

Iran's remarkable turnaround since the end of the war with Iraq, despite the U.S.–imposed trade restrictions, suggests that the late Ayatollah Khomeini was a better theologian than economist. The country's foreign debts were paid off by 1990. Since then, however, loans for new development projects and purchase of equipment, including a nuclear reactor for peaceful uses set up by Russian technicians in 1998, along with reduced oil revenues, have generated foreign debts of $30 billion. Additionally, formerly self-sufficient in food, Iran is now the world's biggest wheat importer.

Petroleum is Iran's major resource and the key to economic development. Oil was discovered there in 1908, making the Iranian oil industry the oldest in the Middle

Timeline: PAST

551–331 B.C.
The Persian Empire under Cyrus the Great and his successors includes most of ancient Near East and Egypt

A.D. 226–641
The Sassanid Empire establishes Zoroastrianism as the state religion

637–641
Islamic conquest at the Battles of Qadisiya and Nihavard

1520–1730
The Safavid shahs develop national unity based on Shi'a Islam as the state religion

1905–1907
The constitutional movement limits the power of the shah by the Constitution and Legislature

1925
The accession of Reza Shah, establishing the Pahlavi Dynasty

1941
The abdication of Reza Shah under Anglo-Soviet pressure; he is succeeded by Crown Prince Mohammed Reza Pahlavi

1951–1953
The oil industry is nationalized under the leadership of Prime Minister Mossadegh

1962
The shah introduces the White Revolution

1979–1980
Revolution overthrows the shah; Iran becomes an Islamic republic headed by the Ayatollah Khomeini

1980s
The Iran-Iraq war; Khomeini dies

1990s
Iran's economy begins to recover; foreign relations improve; debate over how Islamic the Islamic Republic should be

PRESENT

2000s
President Mohammed Khatami wins reelection handily; U.S. president George W. Bush calls Iran part of "evil axis" of terror, reigniting tensions with Iran

---

East. In 1973 the industry was nationalized for a second time and was operated by the state-run National Iranian Oil Company.

After the Revolution, political difficulties affected oil production, as the United States and its allies boycotted Iran due to the hostage crisis.

The instability of world oil prices, along with domestic energy subsidies (gasoline prices in Iran are about 10 percent lower than world prices) has led the country to boost natural gas production from huge reserves. However, difficulties of access to foreign markets and the hard bargaining involved for foreign companies have kept production low.

In addition to its oil and gas reserves, Iran has important bauxite deposits, and in 1994 it reported the discovery of 400 million tons of phosphate rock to add to its mineral resources. It is now the world's sixth-largest exporter of sulfur. However, oil and gas remain the mainstays of the economy. Oil reserves are 88 billion barrels; with new gas discoveries each year, the country sits astride 70 percent of the world's known oil reserves.

Iran's great natural resources, large population, and strong sense of its international importance have fueled its drive to become a major industrial power. The country is self-sufficient in cement, steel, petrochemicals, and hydrocarbons (as well as sugar—Iranians are heavy users). Production of electricity meets domestic needs.

A new foreign investment law was passed by the Majlis in 2002 and approved by the CCG, but heavy taxes, extensive bargaining over agreements and the high costs of doing business continue to deter foreign companies from investing in Iran's potentially huge market.

A REVOLUTION FROM WITHIN?

Two decades after the Revolution that brought the first Islamic republic into existence, a debate is still under way to determine how "Islamic" Iranian society should be. The debate is between two vocal groups in Iranian society. Two decades after the Revolution that brought the first Islamic republic into existence, a debate is still under way to determine how "Islamic" Iranian society should be. The debate is between two vocal groups in Iranian society. One group has been referred to in the mass media as "hardliners," while the other group has been referred to as "reformers." The former, generally speaking, are those who would preserve at all costs the theocratic rule and Islamic values bequeathed to the republic by its founders in 1979. The latter have always envisioned a more pluralist and tolerant society, with a vibrant "civil society," and a state that enjoys good relations with the whole world (including the West). The newly-elected Iranian president, Ahmadinejad, is considered a hardliner, while the former president whom he replaced, Muhammad Khatami (1997–2005), was regarded as a reformer. In fact, in the last election, even Ali Akbar Hashemi Rafsanjani—Speaker of the Iranian *Majlis* (National Assembly/Parliament) during the 1980s, president for two-terms (1989–1997), and member of the influential Council of Guardians and who ran as a progressive Islamist—lost to the revolutionary Islamist Ahmadinejad. This new development does not bode well for Iran in the near future as Western Powers try to further isolate the Islamic Republic for proceeding with its nuclear program.

NOTES

1. A 1991 memo from Ayatollah Khamenei ordered that Bahais should be prevented from attaining "positions of influence" and denied employment and access to education. The memo is in sharp contrast to UN General Assembly *Resolution 52/142*, which calls on Iran to "emancipate" its Bahai population.

2. Golamreza Fazel, "Persians," in Richard V. Weekes, ed., *Muslim Peoples: A World Ethnographic Survey*, 2nd ed. (Westport, CT: Greenwood Press, 1984), p. 610. "Face-saving is in fact one of the components of *Ta'aruf*, along with assertive masculinity *(gheyrat)*."

3. John Malcolm, *History of Persia* (London: John Murray, 1829), vol. II, p. 303.

4. Behzad Yaghmaian, *Social Change in Iran* (Albany, NY: State University of New York Press, 2001), p. 127.

5. Roy Mottahedeh, *The Mantle of the Prophet* (New York: Simon & Schuster, 1985), p. 52.

6. *Ibid.*, p. 34.

7. Until recently, the CIA had always been credited with engineering Mossadegh's overthrow and had made no effort to deny this charge. Publication recently of the agency's secret history of "Operation Ajax" clearly emphasized its limited role and lack of effectiveness. The unpublished memoirs of Ardeshir Zahedi, the general's son ("Five Decisive Days, August 14–18, 1953") indicate that U.S. involvement was incidental to a genuine popular uprising.

8. Imam Khomeini, *Islam and Revolution*, transl. by Hamid Algar, tr. (Berkeley, CA: Mizan Press, 1981), p. 175.

9. Mohammed Reza Pahlavi, Shah of Iran, *Answer to History* (New York: Stein and Day, 1980), pp. 152–153.

10. Sepehr Zabih, *Iran's Revolutionary Upheaval: An Interpretive Essay* (San Francisco, CA: Alchemy Books, 1979), pp. 46–49.

11. Elizabeth Rabin, "The Cult of Rajavi," *New York Times* magazine, July 13, 2003, pp. 26–31.

12. "Wearing red headbands and inspired by professional chanters before battle, their heads were filled with thoughts of death and martyrdom and going to Paradise." V. S. Naipaul, "After the Revolution," *The New Yorker* (May 26, 1997), p. 46.

13. "A Survey of Iran," *The Economist*, January 18, 2003.

14. Thomas Friedman, "Dinner with the Sayyids," *New York Times* Op-Ed, August 10, 2003.

15. David Menashri, *Post-Revolutionary Politics in Iran* (London: Frank Cass, 2001), p. 322.

Iraq (Republic of Iraq)

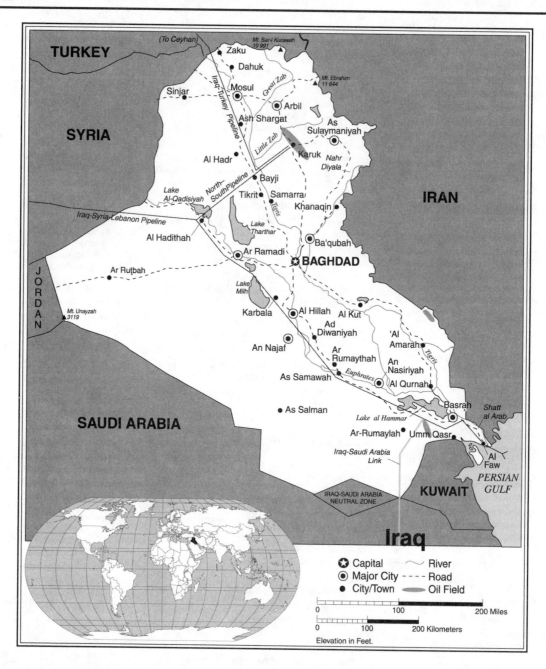

✪ Capital	∿ River
◉ Major City	- - - Road
● City/Town	▨ Oil Field

Iraq

Elevation in Feet.

Iraq Statistics

GEOGRAPHY

Area in Square Miles (Kilometers): 168,710 (437,072) (about twice the size of Idaho)

Capital (Population): Baghdad (3,842,000)

Environmental Concerns: draining of marshes near An Nasiriyah has affected wetlands and destroyed ecosystems with heavy impact on wildlife; inadequacy of potable water; air and water pollution in cities; soil degradation due to excess salinity and erosion; desertification

Geographical Features: broad plains shading to desert in central and south; mountains in north and northwest; hilly north of Baghdad. The area near the confluence of the Tigris and Euphrates river, some 3,000 square miles, was largely drained in the 1990s for a vast land reclamation project but has been partially restored since the U.S. invasion and occupation.

Climate: dry and extremely hot, with very short winters, except in northern mountains, which have cold winters with much snow and temperate summers

PEOPLE

Population

Total: 26,074,906 (2005 estimate)
Annual Growth Rate: 2.7%
Rural/Urban Population Ratio: 25/75
Major Languages: Arabic; Kurdish
Ethnic Makeup: 75% Arab; 20% Kurdish; 5% Turkoman, and others
Religions: 60–65% Shi'a Muslim; 32–37% Sunni Muslim; 3% others (Christian, Yazidi, Sabaean)

Health

Life Expectancy at Birth: 67 years (male); 69 years (female)
Infant Mortality Rate: 50/1,000 live births
Physicians Available (Ratio): 1/2,181 people

Education

Adult Literacy Rate: 40.4% (males 55.9%, females 24%) (Note: Iraq had a much higher rate prior to Saddam's wars. War disruption and UN sanctions have lowered the literacy rate significantly. In the 1970s Iraq had the highest level in the Arab world.)
Compulsory (Ages): 6–12; free

COMMUNICATION

Telephones: 675,000 (A huge number of lines were destroyed or sabotaged during and after the 2003 U.S. invasion and occupation and have not yet been restored)
Daily Newspaper Circulation: n/a (same reason)
Televisions: n/a (same reason)
Internet Users: 25,000 (2002)

TRANSPORTATION

Highways in Miles (Kilometers): 29,435 (45,550)
Railroads in Miles (Kilometers): 1,262 (2,200)
Usable Airfields: 111
Motor Vehicles in Use: 1,040,000

GOVERNMENT

Type: In transition since the U.S. occupation in March 2003. Following the appointment by U.S. administrators of a 25-member Governing Council, its members endorsed in March 2004 an interim constitution as the basis for a federal-style republic.
Independence Date: October 3, 1932, from Britain; July 14, 1958, as republic after the overthrow of the monarchy
Head of State/Government: Prime Minister Ibrahim al-Jafari (since April 2005)
Political Parties: formerly the Iraqi Ba'th was the sole legal party. The Iraq Communist Party, which was recognized as a legal party during the mandate and under the monarchy, was suppressed by the Ba'th when it seized power in 1968 and was banned permanently in 1978. Thereafter it went underground. Its present secretary-general serves on the Governing Council set up after the overthrow of Saddam Hussein.
Suffrage: universal at 18; however the only elections allowed after Saddam Hussein became president were those for him in that office, with no term limits

MILITARY

Military Expenditures (% of GDP): n/a ($1.3 billion)
Current Disputes: prisoner exchanges, navigation rights and other issues from the 1980–1988 war with Iran not yet formally settled although diplomatic relations were restored in 1990; dispute with Turkey over sharing of Tigris and Euphrates waters; guerrilla warfare against U.S. forces since the occupation

ECONOMY

Currency ($U.S. Equivalent): during the UN sanctions period the Iraqi dinar dropped in value to 1,890 = $1; under U.S. occupation new 25,000 and 10,000 notes lacking Saddam's portrait have been placed in circulation with approximately the same value
Per Capita Income/GDP: $2,100/$54.4 billion
GDP Growth Rate: 52.3%
Inflation Rate: 25.4%
Labor Force: 6,700,000
Natural Resources: petroleum; natural gas; phosphates; sulfur; lead; gypsum; iron ore
Agriculture: wheat; barley; rice; vegetables; dates; cotton; sheep; cattle
Industry: petroleum; chemicals; textiles; construction materials; food processing
Exports: $10.1 billion, exclusively crude oil (primary partners United States, France, Russia)
Imports: $9.9 billion (primary partners France, Australia, Italy)

Iraq Country Report

In ancient times, Iraq's central portion was called *Mesopotamia*, a word meaning "land between the rivers." Those rivers are the Tigris and the Euphrates, which originate in the highlands of Turkey and flow southward for more than a thousand miles to join in an estuary called the Shatt al-Arab, which carries their joint flow into the Persian (or, to Iraqis, the Arab) Gulf.

The fertility of the land between the rivers encouraged human settlement and agriculture from an early date.

Present-day Iraq (*Iraq* is an Arabic word meaning "cliff" or, less glamorously, "mud bank") occupies a much larger territory than the original Mesopotamia.

HISTORY

The "land between the rivers" has had many occupiers in its long history as a settled area, and it has seen many kingdoms and empires rise and fall. Over the centuries many peoples—Sumerians, Babylonians, Assyrians, Persians, Arabs and others—added layer upon layer to the mix of Mesopotamian civilization. The world's first cities probably began there, as did agriculture, the growing of food crops, made possible by an ingenious irrigation system developed by Sumerian "engineers" to bring Tigris-Euphrates water from those rivers to their fields. Since theirs was essentially an agricultural society, the Sumerians developed a system of recording land

ownership and grain sales on clay tablets, in what is generally considered the world's first written alphabet. Their transactions were recorded in cube-shaped letters called cuneiform, rather than the picture-words (hieroglyphs) used in ancient Egypt, which were much more cumbersome.

Successor Mesopotamian peoples also contributed much to our modern world. The Babylonian king Hammurabi developed the first code of laws; there are 282 of them in all, inscribed on *steles* (pillars) placed at strategic points in his kingdom to warn people what they should or should not do, and the consequences thereof. A later Babylonian king, Nebuchadnezzar, built the world's first capital city, at Babylon. Its Hanging Gardens, a series of over-

Michael Spencer/Saudi Aramco World/PADIA (SA1301007)

Abbisid Caliph Abul Fadl al-Mutawwakil's Great Mosque in Samarra, Iraq. Completed in 852 CE, it was the largest mosque in the Muslim world for centuries. Its 150 foot high spiral minaret was inspired by ancient Mesopotamian ziggurats.

hanging terraces planted with flowers and trees and watered by hidden waterwheels, was considered one of the Seven Wonders of the ancient world.

Other contributions have come down to us from this ancient land. The first political system, based on sovereign city-states, began there. One would think that the modern Iraqis would take great pride in their storied heritage.

The most important influence in Iraqi social and cultural life today comes from the conquest of the region by Islamic Arabs. In A.D. 637 an Arab army defeated the Persians, who were then rulers of Iraq, near the village of Qadisiya, not far from modern Baghdad, a victory of great symbolic importance for Iraqis today. Arab peoples settled the region and intermarried with the local population, producing the contemporary Iraqi-Arab population.

Aside from Saddam's mythmaking, the most important influence on Iraq's people has been that of Islam, brought to their ancestors by Arabs from Arabia in the seventh century A.D. In 637 an invading Arab army defeated the Persians, who ruled Mesopotamia at that time, in the battle of Qadisiyya, near modern Baghdad.

During the early years of Islam, Iraq played an important role in Islamic politics. It was a center of Shi'a opposition to the Sunni Muslim caliphs on the west to the plains of India some 2,000 miles east. An eighth century caliph, Al-Mansur, built a new capital for the Islamic world to signify his authority, some 60 miles west of the ruins of Babylon. He named his new capital Baghdad. The tombs of Ali, Muhammad's son-in-law and the fourth and last leader of a united caliphate, and his son Husayn, martyred in a power struggle with his Damascus-based rival Yazid, are both in Iraq (at Najaf and Karbala, respectively).

In the period of the Abbasid caliphs (A.D. 750–1258), Iraq was the center of a vast Islamic empire stretching from Morocco on the west to the plains of India. Caliph al-Mansur laid out a new capital for the world of Islam, some 60 miles from the ruins of Babylon. He named his new capital Baghdad, possibly derived from a Persian word for "garden," and, according to legend, laid bricks for its foundations with his own hand. Baghdad was a round city, built in concentric circles, each one walled, with the caliph's green-domed palace and mosque at the center. It was the world's first planned city, in the sense of having been laid out in a definite urban configuration and design. Under the caliphs, Baghdad became a center of science, medicine, philosophy, law, and the arts, at a time when London and Paris were mud-and-wattle villages. The city became wealthy from the goods brought by ships from Africa, Asia, and the Far East, since it was easily reachable by shallow-draught boats from the Gulf and the Indian Ocean moving up the Tigris to its harbor.

Baghdad was destroyed by an invasion of Central Asian Mongols in A.D. 1258. In addition to ravaging cities, they ruined the complex irrigation system that made agriculture possible and productive. Modern Iraq has yet to reach the level of agricultural productivity of Abbasid times, even with the use of sophisticated technology.

After the fall of Baghdad, Iraq came under the rule of various local princes and dynasties. In the sixteenth century, it was included in the expanding territory of the Safavid Empire of Iran. The Safavid shah championed the cause of Shi'a Islam; as a result, the Ottoman sultan, who was Sunni, sent forces to recover the area from his hated Shi'a foe. Possession of Iraq went back and forth between the two powers, but the Ottomans eventually established control until the twentieth century.

The British Mandate

World War I found England and France at war with Germany and the Ottoman Empire. British forces occupied Iraq, which they rechristened Mesopotamia, early in the war. British leaders had worked with Arab leaders in the Ottoman Empire to launch a revolt against the sultan; in return, they promised to help the Arabs form an independent Arab state once the Ottomans

had been defeated. A number of prominent Iraqi officers who were serving in the Ottoman Army then joined the British and helped them in the Iraqi campaign.

The British promise, however, was not kept. The British had made other commitments, notably to their French allies, to divide the Arab provinces of the Ottoman Empire into British and French "zones of influence." An independent Arab state in those provinces was not in the cards.

The most that the British (and the French) would do was to organize protectorates, called mandates, over the Arab provinces, promising to help the population become self-governing within a specified period of time. The arrangement was approved by the new League of Nations in 1920. Iraq then became a British mandate, with Faisal ibn Hussein as its king, but with British advisers appointed to manage its affairs.

The British kept their promise with the mandate. They worked out a constitution for Iraq in 1925 that established a constitutional monarchy with an elected legislature and a system of checks and balances. In 1932 the mandate formally ended, and Iraq became an independent kingdom under Faisal. The British kept the use of certain air bases, and their large capital investment in the oil industry was protected through a 25-year treaty. Otherwise, the new Iraqi nation was on its own.

The Iraqi Monarchy: 1932–1958

The new kingdom cast adrift on perilous international waters was far from being a unified nation. It was more of a patchwork of warring and competing groups. The Muslim population was divided into Sunni and Shi'a, as it is today, with the Sunnis forming a minority but controlling the government and business and dominating urban life. The Shi'as, although a majority, were mostly rural peasants and farmers, many of them migrants to the cities, where they formed a large underclass.

The country also had large Christian and Jewish communities, the latter tracing its origins back several thousand years to the exile of Jews from Palestine to Babylonia after the conquest of Jerusalem by Nebuchadnezzar. The Assyrians for a time formed the largest Christian group.

These social and religious divisions in the population plus great economic disparities made the new state almost impossible to govern or develop politically.[2] King Faisal I was the single stabilizing influence in Iraqi politics, so his untimely death in 1933 was critical. As a result, there was little political stability or progress toward national unity.

THE REVOLUTION OF 1958

To their credit, the king's ministers kept the country's three broad social divisions—the Kurdish north, the Sunni Arab center, and the Shi'a Arab south—in relative balance and harmony. Oil revenues were channeled into large-scale development projects. The formation of a modern school system with a Western-model curriculum, along with adult literacy programs, establishment of a national army, and opportunities for its officers to attend British military academies such as Sandhurst, gave Iraq a head start toward self-government, well ahead of other Arab states. Education was promoted strongly, which may explain why Iraq has a much higher literacy rate than most other Middle Eastern countries. The press was free, and, though it had a small and ingrown political elite, there was much participation in legislative elections. Despite its legitimate Arab credentials as one of the successor states fashioned by the British after World War I, however, a new generation of pan-Arab nationalist Iraqis viewed the royal regime as a continuation of foreign rule, first Turkish and then British.

Resentment crystallized in the Iraqi Army. On July 14, 1958, a group of young officers overthrew the monarchy in a swift, predawn coup. The king, regent, and royal family were killed. Iraq's new leaders proclaimed a republic that would be reformed, free, and democratic, united with the rest of the Arab world and opposed to all foreign ideologies, "Communist, American, British or Fascist."

Iraq has been a republic since the 1958 Revolution, and July 14 remains a national holiday. But the republic has passed through many different stages, with periodic coups, changes in leadership, and political shifts, most of them violent. Continuing sectarian and ethnic hatreds, maneuvering of political factions, ideological differences, and lack of opportunities for legitimate opposition to express itself without violence have created a constant sense of insecurity among Iraqi leaders.

The republic's first two leaders were overthrown after a few years. Several more violent shifts in the Iraqi government took place before the Ba'th Party seized control in 1968. Since that time, the party has dealt ruthlessly with internal opposition. A 1978 decree outlawed all political activity outside the Ba'th for members of the armed forces. Many Shi'a clergy were executed in 1978–1979 for leading antigovernment demonstrations after the Iranian Revolution; and following Saddam Hussein's rise to the presidency, he purged a number of members of the Revolutionary Command

Council (RCC), on charges that they were part of a plot to overthrow the regime.

THE BA'TH PARTY IN POWER

The Ba'th Party in Iraq began as a branch of the Syrian Ba'th founded in the 1940s by two Syrian intellectuals: Michel Aflaq, a Christian teacher, and Salah al-Din Bitar, a Sunni Muslim. Like its Syrian parent, the Iraqi Ba'th was dedicated to the goals of Arab unity, freedom, and socialism. However, infighting among Syrian Ba'th leaders in the 1960s led to the expulsion of Aflaq and Bitar. Aflaq went to Iraq, where he was accepted as the party's true leader. Eventually, he moved to Paris, where he died in 1989. His body was brought back to Iraq for burial, giving the Iraqi Ba'th a strong claim to legitimacy in its struggle with the Syrian Ba'th for hegemony in the movement for Arab unity.

The basis of government under the Ba'th is the 1970 Provisional Constitution, issued unilaterally by the Revolutionary Command Council (RCC), the party's chief decision-making body. It defines Iraq as a sovereign peoples' democratic republic. The Constitution provides for an "elected" National Assembly with responsibility for ratification of laws and RCC decisions.

SADDAM HUSSEIN

In the late 1970s and early 1980s, one of Iraq's leaders, Saddam Hussein, emerged from the pack to become an absolute ruler. Saddam Hussein's early history did not suggest such an achievement. He was born in 1937 in the small town of Tikrit, on the Tigris halfway between Baghdad and Mosul. Tikrit's chief claim to fame, until the twentieth century, was that it was the birthplace of Saladin, hero of the Islamic world in the Middle Ages against the Crusaders.

As a teenager Saddam left home for Baghdad, lived with an uncle, and joined the Ba'th Party. Eventually he worked his way up to vice-chairman, and then chairman, of the Revolutionary Command Council, the party's ruling body. As chairman, he automatically became president of Iraq under the 1970 Constitution. As there are no constitutional provisions limiting the terms of office for the position, the National Assembly named him president-for-life in 1990.[5]

As one might expect from a leader whose political experience was limited to intraparty intrigue and antigovernment plots, Saddam Hussein came to office with none of the attributes needed for leader and statesman. He had never served in the army, traveled only as far as Egypt, and had little knowledge of foreign affairs or non-Arab peoples. His first effort was to instill in the Iraqi people a "climate of fear," which would enable him to govern unopposed.

The Iran-Iraq War of the 1980s was a severe test for the Ba'th and its leader. A series of Iraqi defeats with heavy casualties in the mid-1980s suggested that the Iranian demand for Saddam Hussein's ouster as a precondition for peace might ignite a popular uprising against him. But Iranian advances into Iraqi territory, and in particular the capture of the Fao Peninsula and the Majnoon oil fields, united the Iraqis behind Saddam. For one of the few times in its history, the nation coalesced around a leader and a cause.

RECENT DEVELOPMENTS

As a survivor of many party conflicts, one would expect Saddam Hussein to make bold moves and take great risks when his survival seemed to be at stake. Such moves also characterized his foreign policy. To further his goal of establishing Iraq as a major regional power and threatening its enemies, notably Israel, he undertook a large-scale project of building an arsenal of weapons of mass destruction (WMD), mainly nuclear, chemical, and biological. The first one made by Iraq would be dropped unannounced on Israel. Such a bomb was tested in 1987, but the project was halted in 1990 by the invasion of Kuwait. By that time, it had employed 12,000 engineers and scientists and cost more than $10 billion.[7]

DEVELOPMENT

The Security Council formally ended sanctions on Iraq in May 2003. Aside from their devastating impact on the population, the 13-year sanctions had severely limited oil production and led to the deterioration of oil refinery installations, industries, and service systems. Oil production was 3.5 million barrels per day (b/d) prior to 1991 but dropped to 2.6 million b/d during the sanctions period and stopped entirely during the U.S. invasion. Since the occupation began, sabotage has further delayed economic recovery. (Turkey, the major export outlet, has been shut down several times since it reopened). In September 2003 the new Iraq Governing Council announced that the economy would be "privatized" with state-owned companies, which had dominated the Ba'thist socialist economy under Saddam Hussein, made available to foreign investors. The one exception would be the oil industry, which would be kept under government control.

THE KURDS

The Kurds, the largest non-Arab minority in Iraq today, form a relatively compact society in the northern mountains. Formerly the Ottoman province (*vilayet*) of Mosul, the territory was occupied by British troops after World War I and included in the mandate over Iraq by the League of Nations, despite angry protests by the Turks demanding its inclusion in the new Republic of Turkey. The Kurds living there agitated for self-rule periodically during the monarchy; for a few months after World War II, they formed their own republic in Kurdish areas straddling the Iraq-Iran and Iraq-Turkey borders.

In the 1960s, the Kurds rebelled against the Iraqi government, which had refused to meet their three demands (self-government in Kurdistan, use of Kurdish in schools, and a greater share in oil revenues). The government sent an army to the mountains but was unable to defeat the Kurds, masters of guerrilla warfare.

However, with the end of the Iraq-Iran war in 1988, the Iraqi Army turned on the Kurds in a savage and deliberate campaign of genocide. Operation *Anfal* ("spoils," in Arabic) involved the launching of chemical attacks on such villages as Halabja and the forced deportation of Kurdish villagers from their mountains to detention centers in the flatlands. Under Anfal, 4,000 Kurdish villages were destroyed, and 5,000 Kurds—mostly old men, women, and children—were killed in a cyanide gas attack on the border town of Halabya. In total 182,000 Kurds were slaughtered during the anti-Kurdish campaign.[8]

FREEDOM

Although violence has continued and even accelerated since the occupation, with not only U.S. soldiers but ordinary Iraqis in the newly-formed police force, Shi'as and even Sunnis accused of collaborating with Coalition forces as targets, progress toward building a new Iraqi nation under representative government continues, albeit at a slow pace. In September 2003 the U.S. administrator formed a 25-member Governing Council with representatives from women, Kurds, Sunni and Shi'a communities, Turkoman tribes, and Assyrian Christians. In March 2004 the Council reached agreement on an interim constitution as the basis for electing a National Assembly in 2005. The Constitution includes a 13-article Bill of Rights.

THE OPPOSITION

Saddam Hussein's ruthless repression of opposition, made possible by his control of security services, the brutality of his sons, and his legion of spies and informers, made sure that no organized group of opponents would emerge to challenge his rule.

OTHER COMMUNITIES

The Shi'a community, which forms approximately two-thirds of the total population of Iraq, has been ruled by the Sunni minority since independence. Shi'as have been consistently underrepresented in successive Ba'thist governments and are the most economically deprived component of the population. However, they remained loyal to the regime (or at least quiescent) during the war with Iran. In a belated attempt to undo decades of deprivation and assure their continued loyalty, the government invested large sums in the rehabilitation of Shi'a areas in southern Iraq after the war ended. Roads were built, and sacred Shi'a shrines were repaired.

Long-held Shi'a grievances against Ba'thist rule erupted in a violent uprising after Iraq's defeat in the Gulf War. The uprising was crushed, however, as Iraqi troops remained loyal to Saddam Hussein. Some 600 troops were killed in an Alamo-type siege of the sacred shrines, which were badly damaged.

THE ECONOMY

Iraq's economy since independence has been based on oil production and exports. The country also has large natural-gas reserves as well as phosphate rock, sulfur, lead, gypsum, and iron ore. Ancient Mesopotamia was probably the first area in the world to develop agriculture, using the fertile soil nourished by the Tigris and Euphrates Rivers. Until recently, Iraq was the world's largest exporter of dates. However, by 1999 the UN embargo and the longest drought in a century had brought food production to a near standstill. An estimated 70 percent of wheat and barley crops, mainstays of agriculture, were lost, and government officials described the situation as a "food catastrophe" comparable to the collapse of the health care system. The Ba'th economic policies emphasized state control of the economy while the party was in power, under the Ba'thist rubric of guided socialism. In 1987 the regime began a major economic restructuring program. More than 600 state organizations were abolished, and young technocrats replaced many senior ministers. In 1988 the government began selling off state-run industries, reserving only heavy industry and hydrocarbons for state operation.

The oil industry was developed by the British during the mandate but was nationalized in the early 1970s. Nationalization and price increases after 1973 helped to accelerate economic growth. The bulk of Iraqi oil shipments exported via pipelines across Iraq has proven oil reserves of some 100 billion barrels, the fifth largest in the world, and new discoveries continue to augment the total.

In 1988 Iraq's GDP of $50 billion was the highest in the Arab world, after Saudi Arabia's. With a well-developed infrastructure and a highly trained workforce, Iraq appeared ready to move upward into the ranks of the developed nations.

THE UN EMBARGO

Iraq's invasion and occupation of Kuwait and the resulting Gulf War drew a red line through any optimistic prospects. Bombing raids destroyed much of Iraq's infrastructure, knocking out electricity grids, bridges, and sewage and water-purification systems and refurbishing of industries, oil refineries and installations. Although much of this infrastructure has been repaired, the oil industry and water and sanitation systems in particular have been operating at only about 40 percent of capacity.

The UN embargo (or sanctions) imposed on Iraq after the 1991 Gulf War to force compliance with resolutions ordering the country to dismantle its weapons program has not only brought development to a halt but has also caused untold suffering for the Iraqi population. The resolutions in question were *Resolution 687*, which required the destruction of all missile, chemical, and nuclear facilities; *Resolution 713*, which established a permanent UN monitoring system for all missile test sites and nuclear installations; and *Resolution 986*, which allowed Iraq to sell 700,000 barrels of oil per day for six months, in return for its compliance with the first two resolutions. Of the $1.6 billion raised through oil sales, $300 million would be paid into a UN reparations fund for Kuwait. Another $300 million would be put aside to finance the UN monitoring system as well as provide aid for the Kurdish population. The remainder would revert to Iraq to be used for purchases of food and medical supplies.

Saddam Hussein initially refused to be bound by *Resolution 986*, calling it an infringement of Iraq's national sovereignty. But in 1996 he agreed to its terms. By then the Iraqi people were nearly destitute, suffering from extreme shortages of food and medicines. The United Nations estimated that 750,000 Iraqi children were "severely malnourished." Half a million had died, and the monthly death toll from malnutrition-related illnesses was averaging 5,750, the majority of them children under age five, due to lack of basic medicines and hospital equipment.[12] In 1998 the Security Council increased approved Iraqi oil revenues to $5.26 billion every six months. Higher world oil prices and exemptions to make up for earlier shortfalls in its export quota due to equipment breakdowns brought total revenues to $7 billion in 1999. In all, Iraq has received $40 billion from oil sales since 1996; however it disbursed $365 million in payment of claims in September 2001. The largest single payment, $176.3 million, went to Botas Petroleum Pipeline Corporation to cover losses caused by the shutdown in the pipeline from Iraq to the Turkish port of Iskenderun. Since the establishment of the UN Compensation Commission, which is responsible for reparations to companies and individuals for losses sustained during the occupation of Kuwait, the commission has paid $35.4 billion to claimants.

Despite disagreement within the Security Council over the scope, effectiveness and moral legitimacy of the sanctions, they were kept in force in six-month increments until the U.S. invasion and overthrow of the Iraqi regime, the last renewal being in December 2002. However, concern in many countries about their devastating effect on the population and the economy led the Arab states and others who had been Iraq's trading partners to bypass or simply ignore them. By 2001 20 countries had resumed regular air service to Baghdad International Airport, much of it in humanitarian supplies. They included Turkey, Egypt, and Syria, all former members of the Desert Storm coalition. A free-trade agreement with Syria in January 2001 would triple the annual trade volume of the two countries, to $1 billion, and additional contracts with Jordan, Lebanon, and the U.A.E. would generate $4.7 billion in Iraqi exports.

Other loopholes in the sanctions enabled Iraq to bypass the "oil-for-food" program with direct oil shipments to Jordan, shipments to Syria to supplement the latter's lagging oil production, and a huge amount of oil smuggling by truck across the Iraqi Kurdish border into Turkey, eventually to reach both Turkish and overseas markets. The profits from these "extracurricular" sales efforts seldom reached the Iraqi people; the bulk went to the leadership and the small Sunni elite that had survived Saddam's purges.

GLORIOUS LEADER, VANQUISHED SURVIVOR

Under Saddam Iraq had become a huge prison; its people in a very real sense had bartered their freedom for his protection. After the UN-imposed sanctions, their jailers became even more isolated. The impact of sanctions in fact fell heaviest on the middle class. Prior to the 1990s, this sector of society had profited from oil-based development to become the best-educated and most productive in all the Arab states. But Saddam Hussein's excesses and particularly his ill-advised foreign policy ventures effectively ruined this class.

In addition to his numerous palaces, gigantic statues and posters of him in cities, on highway billboards, and before banks and other public buildings served as constant reminders of the Glorious Leader. In Baghdad victory arches and a statue of him were erected on the first anniversary of the U.S. air strikes. Saddam called it a "great victory," similar to the "defence" of the homeland after the 1991 Gulf War.

ACHIEVEMENTS

Despite the overall violence and resulting instability, there has been progress in many areas of national life. Iraqi-American political educator Ban Saraf has formed 85 neighborhood councils in Baghdad and other cities as the "core of democracy" in the country. The newly reopened, refurbished schools benefit from a student-centered interactive curriculum introduced by a U.S. firm, along with the elimination of Ba'thist propaganda from textbooks. In August Iraqi artist Essam Pasha al-Azzawy completed a giant mural depicting Iraq's incredible history as a work "meant to light the way toward a brighter future."

Saddam's skill in evading the direct impact of sanctions on his lifestyle and playing off more powerful countries against each other for Iraq's benefit was more than equaled by his internal actions. Those who survived arrest, torture, and incarceration in his infamous prisons, many of them skilled professionals, usually fled into exile. The assassination of Grand Ayatollah Sadiq al-Badr, spiritual head of the Shi'a community in Iraq, was a grim warning

that anyone who spoke out against the Iraqi leader or questioned his decisions would suffer the same fate.[13]

As a result the only organized opposition to the regime operated outside the country. It was the Iraqi National Congress, headed by Ahmad Chalabi. The other organized opposition group outside the country, the Supreme Council for Islamic Revolution in Iraq (SCIRI), was formed in 1982 in Iran. It was essentially an umbrella group for various Saddam opponents, most of them Shi'a. SCIRI's original goal was to establish an Islamic regime in Iraq similar to Khomeini's in Iran. Its military wing, the Badr Brigade, fought with Iranian forces against Iraq in the later stages of that war.

The Brigade entered Iraq after Saddam's fall and has cooperated with U.S. forces, even to the extent of laying down its weapons on request. SCIRI's spiritual leader, the Ayatollah Baqr al-Hakim, served as liaison between the two forces before his untimely assassination, and his brother Abdelaziz, also a Shi'a cleric, was appointed as a member of the Governing Council when it was formed in August 2003.

THE U.S. INVASION AND ITS IMPACT

The impact of the March 2003 invasion and overthrow of Saddam Hussein by U.S. and British forces on the Iraqi people as they struggle to put years of authoritarian rule behind them and construct a viable system of government—one based on law and human rights and buttressed by constitutional protections—has been and promises to continue to be one of the most difficult in the long history of this land.

From its beginnings as an artificial nation-state patched together by outsiders, Iraq has always lacked the essential ingredients for successful nationhood. It was traditionally fragmented into many different groups with different and often opposed identities. Iraqi society was, and to a great extent still is, tribal, ethnic, religious, linguistic, urban, and rural but not "national." Saddam Hussein was able to override these differences by sheer force or personality and absolute power. Amid a host of negative contributions, the "Butcher of Baghdad" must be credited for forcing these disparate elements into an Iraqi unitary state.

What lies ahead for this battered nation? In retrospect it is clear that the fall of Saddam Hussein could not be accomplished in any other way than by external invasion. But as should have been expected, the abrupt removal of an absolute ruler and the collapse of his regime left a huge political vacuum in Iraq.

What seems to have escaped awareness by U.S. policymakers was the deplorable condition of the Iraqi economy. This fact alone militated against any possibility of an ongoing weapons program there. The years of UN sanctions and U.S. bombings had destroyed most of its infrastructure. Roads, electricity, the water system, and health care had dropped to a primitive level, comparable with that of Bangladesh. The sudden collapse of the regime also set off an orgy of looting, revenge killings, and destruction of the remaining essential services and facilities. A tragic loss was the looting of the National Museum in Baghdad with its priceless collection of artifacts. (Fortunately many were returned, and thousands of others had been hidden by museum curators, but thousands more are still unaccounted for.)

Saddam himself was captured in December 2003 after being discovered bearded, disheveled, and anything but "glorious," trapped in an underground hideout in Adwar, near Tikrit. Since then the former Iraqi leader has been kept under guard, incommunicado, with access limited to CIA and other U.S. intelligence investigators. Under international pressure the United States now considers him a prisoner of war, under the terms of the Geneva Convention.

The "war that ended" with a premature presidential announcement unfortunately continues and has changed significantly in scope. Although U.S. casualties continued to mount, the brunt of the violence is directed at ordinary Iraqis, the police, security services, schoolchildren, women, and all who seem in any way connected with or supported by the U.S. forces. It is a vicious cycle—the more American troops attempt to curb the violence, the more they alienate the Iraqi people. As an Iraqi policeman told a reporter, "they (the soldiers) treat us like Palestinians. They treat us like dirt. Our chief of police is in jail right now."[13]

Meanwhile Iraq's children are trickling back to their reopened schools, business improves, the sanctions are lifted, and a sense of normalcy is slowly returning. Iraqis have elected officials for a transitional government, headed by newly elected Prime Minister Dr Ibrahim al-Ashaiqir al-Jaafari. The Iraqi Transitional Government has a tall task ahead of it in the latter part of 2005, as all parties try to hammer out a new national constitution.

NOTES

1. K. S. Husry, "The Assyrian Affair of 1933," *International Journal of Middle East Studies* (1974), p. 166. The Assyrians are also called Chaldeans.

2. Muhammad A. Tarbush, *The Role of the Military in Politics: A Case Study of Iraq to 1941* (London: Kegan Paul, 1982), p. 50.

3. Richard F. Nyrop, *Iraq: A Country Study.* Washington D.C.: American University, Foreign Area Studies (1979), p. 38. Faisal I had noted sadly just before his death: "There is no Iraqi people but unimaginable masses of human beings, devoid of any patriotic feeling, connected by no common tie, perpetually ready to rise against any government." Quoted in Hanna Batatu, *The Old Social Classes and the Revolutionary Movements in Iraq* (Princeton, NJ: Princeton University Press, 1978), pp. 25–26.

4. Joe Stork, "State Power and Economic Structure …" in Tim Niblock, *Iraq: The Contemporary State* (London: Croom Helm, 1982), p. 44.

5. Milton Viorst, "Letter From Baghdad," *The New Yorker* (June 24, 1991), p. 61.

6. Ofra Bengio, *Saddam's Word: Political Discourse in Iraq* (London: Oxford University Press, 1988), p. 24.

7. Khidr Hamza, with Jeff Stein, *Saddam's Bombmaker* (New York: Scribner's, 2001). Hamza was head of the team that designed the bomb.

8. "Anafal" is the Arabic name of the eighth sura (chapter) of the Koran and appeared as a revelation to Muhammad after the battle of Badr, the first victory of the Muslims over their Meccan enemies. It was viewed by them (and by Saddam) as proof that God and right were on their side. See Human Rights Watch, *Iraq's Crime of Genocide: The Anfal Campaign Against the Kurds* (New Haven, CT: Yale University Press, 1995), p. 4. The campaign would have never come to light but it was fully documented when 18 tons of Iraqi government documents were captured by Kurdish *pesh mergas* during the uprising that followed the Gulf War.

9. Henri J. Barkey, "Kurdish Geopolitics," *Current History* (January 1997), p. 2.

10. The INA was "managed" from Jordan by a special CIA team. After the coup had been thwarted—the regime had advance warning through penetration of the CIS's satellite-technology communications system—the team received a message: "We have arrested all your people. You might as well pack up and go home." The CIA team did just that. Andrew Cockburn and Peter Cockburn, *Out of the Ashes: The Resurrection of Saddam Hussein* (New York: HarperCollins, 1999), p. 229.

11. In June 2003 heavy spring rains and snow melt in the Turkish highlands, where the rivers begin, led occupation forces to join with the remaining marsh Arabs (the Ma'adan) to open floodgates and levees to allow water to flow back into the marshes. An international scientific team has been formed to resurrect the marshes, and it may be that in this case nature can heal herself with human help!

12. A judge who served on the Iraq Court of Appeals and had dared to rule one of Saddam's edicts unconstitutional was thrown in jail at the notorious Abu Ghraib prison outside Baghdad. A visitor who knew him visited the prison after the occupation and noted, in addition to chambers for torture and cells where prisoners were packed like vermin, there was a long bar with a deep pit with room for several nooses to be used at the same time.

13. Christian Parenti, "Two Sides: Scenes from a Nasty Brutish War," *The Nation*, Feb. 25, 2004, p. 14.

Timeline: PAST

1520–1920
Border province of the Ottoman Empire

1920–1932
British mandate

1932
Independent kingdom under Faisal I

1958
The monarchy is overthrown by military officers

1968
The Ba'th Party seizes power

1975
The Algiers Agreement between the shah of Iran and Hussein ends Kurdish insurrection

1980s
Iran-Iraq War; diplomatic relations are restored with the United States after a 17-year break

1990s
Iraq invades and occupies Kuwait, leading to the brief but intense Gulf War; Saddam Hussein retains power

PRESENT

2000s
Despite continuing UN sanctions, Saddam remains firmly in control; Iraq continues transition to a new government, while insurgency continues

Jordan (Hashimite Kingdom of Jordan)

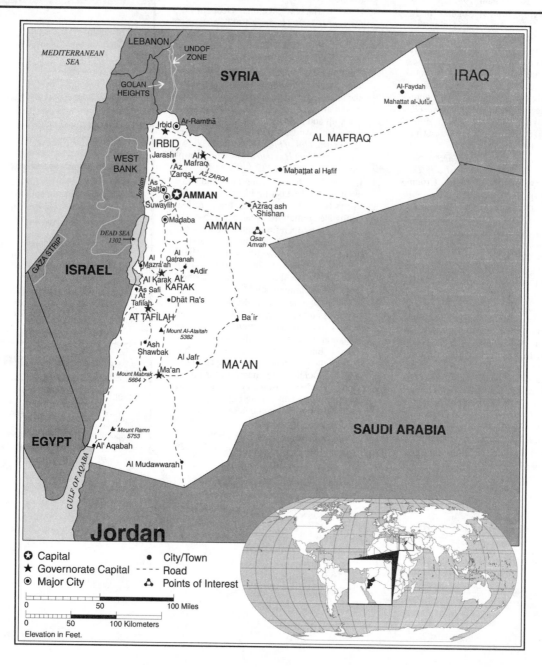

Map Legend

- ✪ Capital
- ★ Governorate Capital
- ◉ Major City
- ● City/Town
- --- Road
- △ Points of Interest

0 ___ 50 ___ 100 Miles
0 ___ 50 ___ 100 Kilometers
Elevation in Feet.

Jordan Statistics

GEOGRAPHY

Area in Square Miles (Kilometers): 35,000 (92,300) about the size of Indiana

Capital (Population): Amman (483,000)

Environmental Concerns: limited natural freshwater reserves; deforestation; overgrazing; soil erosion; desertification

Geographical Features: mostly desert plateau in the east; a highland area in the west; the Great Rift Valley separates the east and west banks of the Jordan River

Climate: mostly arid desert; a rainy season in the west

PEOPLE

Population

Total: 5,759,732

Annual Growth Rate: 2.56%

Rural/Urban Population Ratio: 28/72

Major Languages: Arabic; English widely understood

Ethnic Makeup: 98% Arab; 1% Circassian; 1% Armenian

Religions: 92% Sunni Muslim; 6% Christian; 2% Others

156

Health

Life Expectancy at Birth: 75 years (male); 80 years (female)
Infant Mortality Rate: 17.3/1,000 live births
Physicians Available (Ratio): 1/616 people

Education

Adult Literacy Rate: 91.3%
Compulsory (Ages): 6–16; free

COMMUNICATION

Telehones: 622,600 main lines
Daily Newspaper Circulation: 62 per 1,000 people
Televisions: 176 per 1,000
Internet Users: 457,000 (2003)

TRANSPORTATION

Highways in Miles (Kilometers): 4,968 (7,301)
Railroads in Miles (Kilometers): 420 (505)
Usable Airfields: 17
Motor Vehicles in Use: 265,000

GOVERNMENT

Type: constitutional monarchy
Independence Date: May 25, 1946 (from League of Nations mandate)
Head of State/Government: King Abdullah II; Prime Minister Adnan Badran
Political Parties: Al-Umma (Nation) Party; Jordanian Democratic Popular Unity Party; Islamic Action Front; National Constitutional Party; many others
Suffrage: universal at 18

MILITARY

Military Expenditures (% of GDP): 14.6%
Current Disputes: none

ECONOMY

Currency ($ U.S. Equivalent): 0.709 dinar = $1 (fixed rate)
Per Capita Income/GDP: $4,500/$25.5 billion
GDP Growth Rate: 5.1%
Inflation Rate: 3.2 %

Unemployment Rate: officially 15%; more likely 25%–30%
Labor Force: 1,410,000
Natural Resources: phosphates; potash; shale oil
Agriculture: wheat; barley; fruits; tomatoes; olives; livestock
Industry: phosphate mining; petroleum refining; cement; potash; light manufacturing
Exports: $3.2 billion (primary partners India, United States, Saudi Arabia)
Imports: $7.6 billion (primary partners Germany, United States, Italy; trade with Iraq, formerly Jordan's main trading partner, discontinued after U.S. invasion of that country in 2003)

SUGGESTED WEB SITES

http://lcweb2.loc.gov/frd/cs/jotoc.html
http://www.odci.gov/cia/publications/factbook/index.html

Jordan Country Report

The Hashimite Kingdom of Jordan (previously called Transjordan; usually abbreviated to Jordan) is one of the smaller Middle Eastern nations. The country formerly consisted of two regions: the East Bank (lying east of the Jordan River) and the West Bank of the Jordan. Israel occupied the West Bank in June 1967, although the region continued to be legally and administratively attached to Jordan and salaries of civil servants and others were paid by the Jordanian government. In 1988 King Hussein formally severed the relationship, leaving the West Bank under Israeli occupation de facto as well as de jure. Between 1948 and 1967, Jordanian-occupied territory also included the old city of Jerusalem (East Jerusalem), which was annexed during the 1948 Arab-Israeli War.

Modern Jordan is an "artificial" nation, the result of historical forces and events that shaped the Middle East in the twentieth century. It had no prior history as a nation and was known simply as the land east of the Jordan River, a region of diverse peoples, some nomadic, others sedentary farmers and herders. Jordan's current neighbors are Iraq, Syria, Saudi Arabia, and Israel. Their joint borders were all established by the British after World War I, when Britain and France divided the territories of the defeated Ottoman Empire between them.

Jordan's borders with Iraq, Syria, and Saudi Arabia do not follow natural geographical features. They were established mainly to keep nomadic peoples from raiding; over time, these borders have been accepted by the countries concerned. The boundary with Israel, which formerly divided the city of Jerusalem between Jordanian and Israeli control, became an artificial barrier after the 1967 Six-Day War and Israel's occupation of Jerusalem and the West Bank (of the Jordan River). The Jordan-Israel Peace Treaty of 1994 has resulted in a redrafting of borders. Israel returned 340 square miles captured in 1967 in the Arava Valley and south of the Galilee to Jordanian control. However, Israeli kibbutzim (communal farm settlements) will be allowed to continue cultivating some 750 acres in the territory under a 25-year lease.

HISTORY

Britain received a mandate from the League of Nations to administer and prepare Transjordan for eventual self-government. This mandate also entailed appointing a native ruler. During World War I, the British had worked with Sharif Husayn to organize an Arab revolt against the Ottomans. Husayn was a prominent Arab leader in Mecca who held the honorary position of "Protector of

the Holy Shrines of Islam." Two of the sharif's sons, Faisal and Abdullah, had led the revolt, and the British felt that they owed them something. When Iraq was set up as a mandate, the British made Faisal its king. Abdullah was offered the Transjordan territory. Because the population was primarily pastoral, he chose the traditional title of emir, rather than king, considering it more appropriate.

EMIR ABDULLAH

Through his father, Abdullah traced his lineage back to the Hashim family of Mecca, the clan to which the Prophet Muhammad belonged. This ancestry gave him a great deal of prestige in the Arab world, particularly among the nomads of Transjordan, who had much respect for a person's genealogy. Abdullah used the connection assiduously to build a solid base of support among his kinspeople. When the country became fully independent in 1946, Abdullah named the new state the Hashimite Kingdom of Jordan.

During the period of the mandate (1921–1946), Abdullah was advised by resident British officials. The British helped him draft a constitution in 1928, and Transjordan became independent in everything except financial policy and foreign relations.

Abdullah did not trust political parties or institutions such as a parliament, but he agreed to issue the 1928 Constitution as a step toward eventual self-government. He also laid the basis for a regular army. A British Army officer, John Bagot Glubb, was appointed in 1930 to train the Transjordanian Frontier Force to curb Bedouin raiding across the country's borders. Under Glubb's command, this frontier force eventually became the Arab Legion; during Emir Abdullah's last years, it played a vital role not only in defending the kingdom against the forces of the new State of Israel but also in enlarging Jordanian territory by the capture of the West Bank and East Jerusalem.[2]

Following the State of Israel being proclaimed in 1948, armies of the neighboring Arab states, including Jordan, immediately invaded Palestine. But they were poorly armed and untrained. Only the Jordanian Arab Legion gave a good account of itself. The Legion's forces seized the West Bank, originally part of the territory allotted to a projected Palestinian Arab state by the United Nations. The Legion also occupied the Old City of Jerusalem (East Jerusalem). Subsequently, Abdullah annexed both territories, despite howls of protest from other Arab leaders, who accused him of landgrabbing from his "Palestine brothers" and harboring ambitions to rule the entire Arab world.

Jordan now became a vastly different state. Its population tripled with the addition of half a million West Bank Arabs and half a million Arab refugees from Israel. Abdullah still did not trust the democratic process, but he realized that he would have to take firm action to strengthen Jordan and to help the dispossessed Palestinians who now found themselves reluctantly included in his kingdom. He approved a new constitution, one that provided for a bicameral legislature (similar to the U.S. Congress), with an appointed senate and an elected house of representatives. He appointed prominent Palestinians to his cabinet. A number of Palestinians were appointed to the Senate; others were elected to the House of Representatives.

On July 20, 1951, King Abdullah was assassinated as he entered the Al Aqsa Mosque in East Jerusalem for Friday prayers. His grandson Hussein was at his side and narrowly escaped death. Abdullah's murderer, who was killed immediately by royal guards, was a Palestinian. Many Palestinians felt that Abdullah had betrayed them by annexing the West Bank and because he was thought to have carried on secret peace negotiations with the Israelis (recent evidence suggests that he did so).

United Nations Photo (UN001)

King Hussein bin Talal (1935–1999) was the autocratic ruler of the Hashemite Kingdom of Jordan for 47 years (r. 1952–1999). Two weeks before he finally succumbed to cancer, he removed his brother, King Hasan, who had been Crown Prince for several decades from the line of succession, and made his son, Abdullah, heir apparent.

KING HUSSEIN

Abdullah's son Crown Prince Talal succeeded to the throne. He suffered from mental illness (probably schizophrenia) and had spent most of his life in mental hospitals. When his condition worsened, advisers convinced him to abdicate in favor of his eldest son, Hussein.

At the time of his death from cancer in February 1999, Hussein had ruled Jordan for 46 years, since 1953—the longest reign to date of any Middle Eastern monarch and one of the longest in the world in the twentieth century. To a great extent he was Jordan, developing a small desert territory with no previous national identity into a modern state.

The June 1967 Six-Day War produced a crisis in Jordan. Israeli forces occupied 10 percent of Jordanian territory, including half of its best agricultural lands. The Jordanian Army suffered 6,000 casualties, most of them in a desperate struggle to hold the Old City of Jerusalem against Israeli attack. Nearly 300,000 more Palestinian refugees from the West Bank fled into Jordan. To complicate things further, guerrillas from the Palestine Liberation Organization (PLO), formerly based in the West Bank, made Jordan their new headquarters. The

PLO considered Jordan its base for the continued struggle against Israel. Its leaders talked openly of removing the monarchy and making Jordan an armed Palestinian state.

DEVELOPMENT

The Israel-Jordan peace treaty has enabled Jordan to save $893 million in debts to the United States and European countries. But continued budgetary deficits and the cutoff in trade with Iraq, the country's main trading partner, have hampered development. U.S. aid in setting up free trade zones in 2000–2001 have generated 13,000 new jobs, and in July 2003 a thermal gas facility linked to Egypt via pipeline went into operation. It will supply Jordan with 2.7 billion cubic centimeters (cm^3) of Egyptian natural gas.

By 1970 Hussein and the PLO were headed toward open confrontation. The guerrillas had the sympathy of the population, and successes in one or two minor clashes with Israeli troops had made them arrogant. They swaggered through the streets of Amman, directing traffic at intersections and stopping pedestrians to examine their identity papers. Army officers complained to King Hussein that the PLO was really running the country. The king became convinced that unless he moved against the guerrillas, his throne would be in danger. He declared martial law and ordered the army to move against them.

FREEDOM

The National Charter guarantees full civil and other rights to all Jordanians. In practice, however, press freedom, political activity, and other rights are often circumscribed. In December 2002 Queen Rania roused a storm of criticism (mostly male) by a decree giving Jordanian women the same rights as men in passing their nationality onto their children. Tribal Bedouin, traditionally the monarchy's strongest supporters, objected that the decree would give citizenship to stateless Palestinians born to Palestinian-Jordanian mothers, giving Jordan a Palestinian majority in the population.

The ensuing Civil War lasted until July 1971, but in the PLO annals, it is usually referred to as "Black September," because of its starting date and because it ended in disaster for the guerrillas. Their bases were dismantled, and most of the guerrillas were driven from Jordan. The majority went to Lebanon, where they reorganized. In time they became as powerful there as they had been in Jordan.

For the remainder of his reign, there were no serious internal threats to King Hussein's rule. Jordan shared in the general economic boom in the Arab world that developed as a result of the enormous price increases in oil after the 1973 Arab-Israeli War. As a consequence, Hussein was able to turn his attention to the development of a more democratic political system. Accordingly, Hussein set up a National Consultative Council in 1978, as what he called an interim step toward democracy. The Council had a majority of Palestinians (those living on the East Bank) as members.

Hussein's arbitrary separation of Jordan from the West Bank has had important implications for internal politics in the kingdom. It enabled the king to proceed with political reforms without the need to involve the Palestinian population there.

In 1990 the king and leaders of the major opposition organization, the Jordanian National Democratic Alliance (JANDA), signed a historic National Charter, which provides for a multiparty political system. Elections were set under the charter for an 80-member house of representatives. Nine seats would be reserved for Christians and three for Circassians, an ethnic Muslim minority originally from the Caucasus.

In 1992 Hussein abolished martial law, which had been in effect since 1970. Henceforth, security crimes such as espionage would be dealt with by state civilian-security courts. New laws also undergirded constitutional rights such as a free press, free speech, and the right of public assembly.

With political parties now legalized, 20 were licensed by the Interior Ministry to take part in Jordan's first national parliamentary election since 1956.

The results were an affirmation of Hussein's policy of gradual democratization. Pro-monarchy candidates won 54 of the 80 seats in the House of Representatives to 16 for the Islamic Action Front, the political arm of the Muslim Brotherhood. The remaining seats were spread among minor parties and independents The electorate also surprised by choosing the first woman member, Toujan Faisal.

FOREIGN POLICY

During the 40-year cycle of hostilities between Israel and its Arab neighbors, there were periodic secret negotiations involving Jordanian and Israeli negotiators, including at times King Hussein himself, as Jordan sought to mend fences with its next-door neighbor. But in 1991 and 1992, Jordan became actively involved in the "peace process" initiated by the United States to resolve the vital issue of Palestinian self-government.

Peace with Israel became a reality in October 1994, with Jordan the second Arab nation to sign a formal treaty with the Israeli state. Subsequently, the normalization of relations moved ahead with lightning speed. In July 1995 the Senate voted to annul the last anti-Israel laws still on the books. Embassies opened in Amman and Tel Aviv under duly accredited ambassadors.

The late King Hussein worked tirelessly to mediate the conflict. King Abdullah II has been less involved. Other than closing down the Amman office of Hamas—the militant Islamic anti-Israeli organization in the West Bank and Gaza Strip—Abdullah's government observes the letter but not the spirit of the peace treaty. Early in 2001 Abdullah and Egyptian President Hosni Mubarak submitted a joint proposal to end the violence and to reinstate the peace talks on the basis of equality. Israel would halt settlement building in the West Bank in return for an end to the Palestinian *intifada*; but thus far the proposal has achieved no results.

The positive relationship established with successive U.S. administrations by the late King Hussein has been seriously weakened by the renewed cycle of Israeli-Palestinian conflict. In October 2001 the U.S. Senate approved the free-trade agreement with Jordan negotiated by the Bill Clinton administration and supported by that of George W. Bush. As a result Jordan became the fourth country (after Canada, Mexico, and Israel) to enjoy a tariff-free

association with the United States. Early in 2002 the king strongly criticized Israel's blockade and confinement of Palestinian national leader Yasir Arafat in his West Bank headquarters.

In recent years Islamic extremism and anti-American feeling have increased significantly in Jordan. At the end of the century, Jordanian intelligence agents uncovered a plot to bomb Amman hotels filled with American and Israeli tourists who had come to celebrate the millennium, and another scheme that would blow up Christian holy sites in Jordan. The plotters included a number of Jordanians who had fought the Soviets in Afghanistan and returned home after the Soviet withdrawl from that country.

Timeline: PAST

1921
Establishment of the British mandate of Transjordan

1928
The first constitution is approved by the British-sponsored Legislative Council

1946
Treaty of London; the British give Jordan independence and Abdullah assumes the title of emir

1948
The Arab Legion occupies the Old City of Jerusalem and the West Bank during the first Arab-Israeli War

1967
Jordanian forces are defeated by Israel in the Six-Day War; Israelis occupy the West Bank and Old Jerusalem

1970–1971
"Black September"; war between army and PLO guerrillas ends with expulsion of the PLO from Jordan

1990s
Politically, economically, and socially, Jordan is one of the primary losers in the Gulf crisis; Jordan signs a peace treaty with Israel; King Hussein dies and is succeeded by his son Abdullah

PRESENT

2000s
The Aqaba Special Economic Zone opens; Jordan supports the antiterrorism coalition

THE ECONOMY

Jordan is rich in phosphates. Reserves are estimated at 2 billion tons, and new deposits are constantly being reported. Phosphate rock is one of the country's main exports, along with potash, which is mined on the Jordanian side of the Dead Sea.

The mainstay of the economy is agriculture. The most productive agricultural area is the Jordan Valley. A series of dams and canals from the Jordan and Yarmuk Rivers has increased arable land in the valley by 264,000 acres and made possible production of high-value vegetable crops for export to nearby countries.

During the years of Israeli occupation of the West Bank, Jordan was estimated to have been deprived of 80 percent of its citrus crops and 45 percent of its vegetable croplands. It also lost access to an area that had provided 30 percent of its export market, as Israeli goods replaced Jordanian ones and the shekel became the medium of exchange there. The peace treaty guaranteed Jordan 7.5 billion cubic feet of water annually from the Jordan and Yarmuk Rivers, but to date the country has received less than half the agreed-on amount.

Jordan's economy traditionally has depended on outside aid and remittances from its large expatriate skilled labor force to make ends meet. A consequence of the Gulf War was the mass departure from Kuwait of some 350,000 Jordanian and Palestinian workers. Despite the loss in remittances and the added burden on its economy, Jordan welcomed them. But their return to Jordan

complicated the nation's efforts to meet the requirements of a 1989 agreement with the International Monetary Fund for austerity measures as a prerequisite for further aid. The government reduced subsidies, but the resulting increase in bread prices led to riots throughout the country. The subsidies were restored; but they were again reduced in 1991, this time with basic commodities (including bread) sold at fixed low prices under a rationing system. Later price increases that were required to meet budgetary deficits in 1996 and 1998 met with little public protest, as the population settled down stoically to face a stagnating economy.

Economic progress remains a large concern. As the result of the high birth rate—75 percent of the population are under age 29, with those age 15 to 29 accounting for 34.4 percent—there are not enough jobs. Unemployment for this age group is about 30 percent. The UN-financed Jordan Human Development Report 2000 found that Jordan's youth "are not well-equipped to meet the challenges of a globalizing world."

In addition to the free-trade pact, the United States has helped Jordan to set up a number of free-trade zones. A $300 million supplemental aid package for Jordan was approved by the U.S. Congress in 1999, and the country currently ranks fourth in

the Middle East in U.S. aid appropriations (after Israel, Egypt, and Turkey).

NOTES

1. The Ottomans paid subsidies to nomadic tribes to guard the route of pilgrims headed south for Mecca. Peter Gubser, *Jordan: Crossroads of Middle Eastern Events* (Boulder, CO: Westview Press, 1983).
2. Years later, Glubb wrote, "In its twenty-eight years of life it had never been contemplated that the Arab Legion would fight an independent war." Quoted in Harold D. Nelson, ed., *Jordan, A Country Study* (Washington, D.C.: American University, Foreign Area Studies, 1979), p. 201.
3. King Abdullah of Jordan, *My Memoirs Completed*, Harold W. Glidden, trans. (London: Longman, 1951, 1978), preface, xxvi.
4. The text of the proposal is in Abdullah's *Memoirs, Ibid.*, pp. 89–90.
5. Naseer Aruri, *Jordan: A Study in Political Development (1925–1965)* (The Hague, Netherlands: Martinus Nijhoff, 1967), p. 159.
6. Quoted in *Middle East Economic Digest* (June 16, 1995).
7. Helen Schary Motro, "Israel the Invisible," *The Christian Science Monitor* (January 12, 2000).
8. Laith Shbeilat, quoted in William A. Orme, "Neighbors Rally to Jordan," *The New York Times* (February 18, 1999).
9. Jeffrey Goldberg, "Learning to Be a King," *The New Times Magazine* (February 8, 2000).
10. *Ibid.*

Kazakhstan

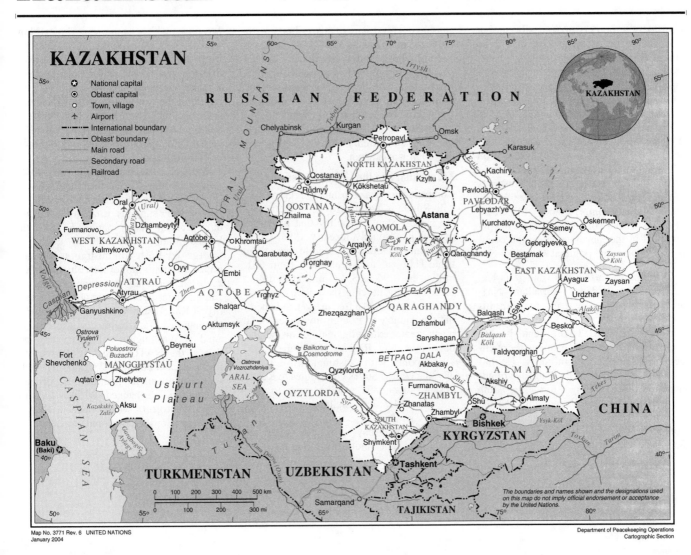

Kazakhstan Statistics

GEOGRAPHY

Area in Square Miles (Kilometers): 1,048,878
(2,717,300) (4 times the size of Texas)
Capital (Population): Almy (formerly
Alma-Ata) (271,000)

PEOPLE

Population

Total: 16,731,000
Annual Growth Rate: 0.03%
Major Languages: Kazalj; Russian
Ethnic Makeup: 42% Kazakh; 37%
Russian; 5% Ukrainian; 5% German; 2%
Uzbek; 2% Tatar; 7% others

Religions: 47% Muslim; 15% Russian
Orthodox; 2% Protestant;
36% others

Health

Life Expectancy at Birth: 58 years (male);
69 years (female)
Infant Mortality Rate (Ratio): 59.7/1,000

Education

Adult Literacy Rate: 98%

GOVERNMENT

Type: republic

Head of State/Government: President
Nursultan A. Nazarbayev; Prime
Minister Kazyrnzhomart Tokayev
Political Parties: People's Unity Party;
Communist Party; Republican People's
Party; others

ECONOMY

Currency ($ U.S. Equivalent): 141.78
tenges = $1
Per Capita Income/GDP: $5,000/$85.6
billion
Inflation Rate: 10.5%
Exports: $8.8 billion
Imports: $6.9 billion

Kazakhstan Country Report

Kazakhstan borders not only Russia but also China, the Caspian Sea, and three other Central Asian republics. Kazakhstan has nuclear installations and nuclear weapons that once belonged to the Soviet arsenal, which Russia wants under its control. Kazakhstan also has an abundance of gold, silver, chrome, zinc, iron ore, and oil, and it is an exporter of wheat and coal. This economic wealth has attracted the attention of the West, which wants to participate in its exploitation, especially the oil reserves of the Tengiz fields along the eastern Caspian. Russians comprise about 40 percent of Kazakhstan's population and are deeply involved in the management of the country's economy and political system.

Working to Russia's advantage is Kazakhstan's president, Nursultan Nazarbayev, who wisely tries to keep his country's fences mended with his great northern neighbor. To this end, he has gone out of his way to promote the well-being of the Russian minority. He has maintained Russian as the language of administration in Almy (formerly Alma Ata), and he ensured the equality of Russian with the Kazakh language in a new constitution. He also agreed to include Russia in Kazakhstan's major energy deal and has merged part of his military with the Russian Army.

Meanwhile, Putin continues former president Boris Yeltsin's policy of helping Kazakhstan defend its border against other Central Asian republics and the spread of Islamic fundamentalism from Iran and Afghanistan. Putin has offered to "beef up" the Russian military force already deployed in Kazakhstan.

Kazakhstan and the United States

Complicating Kazakhstan's relationship with Russia is Nazarbayev's cultivation of the United States, a policy that began to pay off handsomely in early 1994, when President Bill Clinton agreed to more than triple U.S. aid to Kazakhstan, from $91 million in 1994 to $311 million in 1995. Moreover, by moving the country slowly but steadily toward a free market and opening the country to foreign investment to a much greater extent than any of his neighbors, including Russia, Nazarbayev has scored points with Washington. Additionally, the United States contributes to Kazakhstan's economic stability and, to that extent, undercuts challenges to Nazarbayev's rule from extremists.

While Nazarbayev values American friendship, he cannot afford to antagonize Moscow, which alone can protect him from the spread of Islamic fundamentalism from Iran and Afghanistan. Moreover, Moscow has a pretext for intervening in Kazakh internal affairs—to protect the interests of the Russian minority in Kazakhstan. So far, Nazarbayev has skillfully balanced Kazakhstan's relations with Moscow and Washington, extracting the most he can from both.

More recently, in August 2003 Kazakhstan sent about 30 peacekeeping troops to Iraq to help with demining and the restoration of water supplies. Kazakhstan was the only Central Asian nation to give the United States some help in Iraq. The George W. Bush administration has continued Clinton's policy of cultivating Kazakhstan, assuring the country that the United States is concerned about the security of Kazakhstan's portion of the oil-rich Caspian Sea. Nazarbayev also was encouraged by Washington to become more active in the NATO-sponsored Partnership for Peace. On February 23, 2004, Kazakhstan announced its intention of formally joining the U.S.-backed, Western-built oil pipeline project, which needed Kazakh business in order to become profitable.

Kuwait (State of Kuwait)

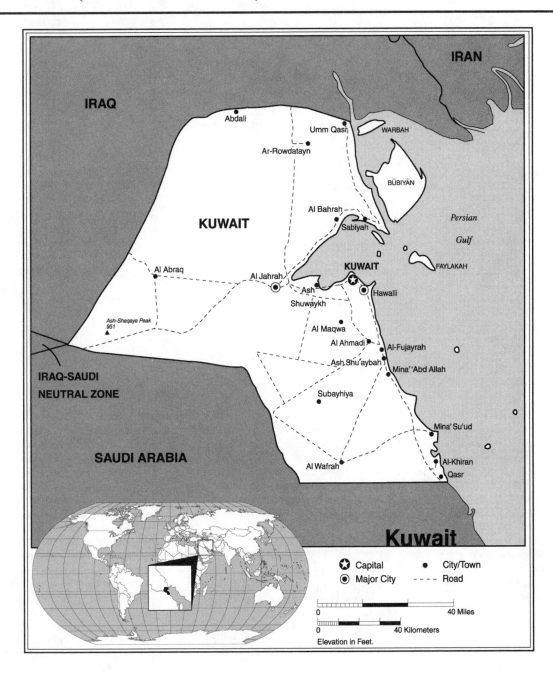

IRAN

IRAQ

Abdali

Umm Qasr

WARBAH

Ar-Rowdatayn

BŪBIYĀN

KUWAIT

Al Bahrah

Sabiyah

Persian

Gulf

Al Abraq

Al Jahrah

KUWAIT

FAYLAKAH

Ash Shuwaykh

Hawalli

Ash-Shaqaya Peak
951

Al Maqwa

Al Ahmadi

Al-Fujayrah

Ash Shu'aybah

Mina' 'Abd Allah

IRAQ-SAUDI
NEUTRAL ZONE

Subayhiya

Mina' Su'ud

SAUDI ARABIA

Al-Khiran

Qasr

Al Wafrah

Kuwait

⊗ Capital ● City/Town
◉ Major City --- Road

0   40 Miles
0   40 Kilometers
Elevation in Feet.

Kuwait Statistics

GEOGRAPHY

Area in Square Miles (Kilometers): 6,880
(17,818) (about the size of New Jersey)
Capital (Population): Kuwait (277,000)
Environmental Concerns: limited natural
freshwater reserves; air and water
pollution; desertification
Geographical Features: flat to slightly
undulating desert plain

Climate: intensely hot and dry summers;
short, cool winters

PEOPLE

Population

Total: 2,335,648 (includes 1,291,354
nonnationals)

Annual Growth Rate: 3.44% (reflects
increased immigration of expatriates,
mostly Arabs, after the 1991 Gulf War)

Rural/Urban Population Ratio: 3/97

Major Languages: Arabic; English

Ethnic Makeup: 45% Kuwaiti; 35% other
Arab; 9% South Asian; 4% Iranian; 7%
others

Religions: 85% Muslim (70% Suni, 30% Shi'a); 15% Christian, Hindu, Parsi, and others

Health

Life Expectancy at Birth: 76 years (male); 78 years (female)
Infant Mortality Rate: 9.95/1,000 live births
Physicians Available (Ratio): 1/533 people

Education

Adult Literacy Rate: 83.5%
Compulsory (Ages): 6–14; free

COMMUNICATION

Telephones: 486,900 main lines
Daily Newspaper Circulation: 401 per 1,000 people
Televisions: 390 per 1,000 people
Internet Service Providers: 2 (2000)

TRANSPORTATION

Highways in Miles (Kilometers): 2,763 (4,450)

Railroads in Miles (Kilometers): none
Usable Airfields: 7
Motor Vehicles in Use: 700,000

GOVERNMENT

Type: nominal constitutional monarchy
Independence Date: June 19, 1961 (from the United Kingdom)
Head of State/Government: Emir Jabir al-Ahmad al-Jabir al-Sabah; Prime Minister (Crown Prince) Saad al-Abdullah al-Salim al-Sabah
Political Parties: none legal
Suffrage: limited to male citizens over 21, including those naturalized; women and members of the armed services excluded

MILITARY

Military Expenditures (% of GDP): 5.3%
Current Disputes: Kuwait and Saudi Arabia continue negotiating a joint maritime boundary with Iran

ECONOMY

Currency ($ U.S. Equivalent): 0.294 dinars = $1 (fixed rate)
Per Capita Income/GDP: $21,300/$48 billion
GDP Growth Rate: 6.8%
Inflation Rate: 2.3%
Unemployment Rate: 2.2% (official rate)
Labor Force: 1,420,000
Natural Resources: petroleum; fish; shrimp; natural gas
Agriculture: fish
Industry: petroleum; petrochemicals; desalination; food processing; construction materials; salt; construction
Exports: $27.4 billion (primary partners Japan, United States, Singapore)
Imports: $11.1 billion (primary partners United States, Japan, United Kingdom)

SUGGESTED WEB SITES

http://lcweb2.loc.gov/frd/cs/kwtoc.html
http://kuwait-info.org

Kuwait Country Report

The State of Kuwait consists of a wedge-shaped, largely desert territory located near the head of the Persian Gulf and just southwest of the Shatt al-Arab. Kuwaiti territory includes the islands of Bubiyan and Failaka in the Gulf, both of them periodically claimed by Iraq. Kuwait also shares a Neutral Zone, consisting mainly of oil fields, which it administers jointly with Iraq and Saudi Arabia; oil production is supposedly divided equally among them. The Iraqi accusation that Kuwait was taking more than its share was one of the points of contention that led to Iraq's invasion of Kuwait in 1990.

HISTORY

Kuwait was inhabited entirely by nomadic peoples until the early 1700s. Then a number of clans of the large Anaiza tribal confederation settled along the Gulf in the current area of Kuwait. They built a fort for protection from raids—*Kuwait* means "little fort" in Arabic—and elected a chief to represent them in dealings with the Ottoman Empire, the major power in the Middle East at that time. The ruling family of modern Kuwait, the al-Sabahs, traces its power back to this period.

INDEPENDENCE

Kuwait continued its peaceful ways under the paternalistic rule of the al-Sabahs until

the 1950s. Then oil production increased rapidly. The small pearl-fishing port became a booming modern city. In 1961 Britain and Kuwait jointly terminated the 1899 agreement, where Kuwait had agreed to become a self-governing state under British protection, and Kuwait became fully independent under the al-Sabahs.

DEVELOPMENT

Declining oil revenues resulted in budgetary deficits, which reached $6 billion in 1998 and 1999. With the Assembly dissolved, the emir issued some 60 decrees, intended to begin to privatize the economy and reduce expenditures by 20%. In 2001 35% of ownership in the Kuwait Cement Company was turned over to private management.

A threat to the country's independence developed almost immediately, as Iraq refused to recognize Kuwait's new status and claimed the territory on the grounds that it had once been part of the Iraqi Ottoman province of Basra. Iraq was also interested in controlling Kuwaiti oil resources. The ruling shaykh, now called emir, asked Britain for help, and British troops rushed back to Kuwait. Eventually, the Arab League agreed that several of its members would send troops to defend Kuwait—and, incidentally, to en-

sure that the country would not revert to its previous protectorate status. The Arab contingents were withdrawn in 1963. A revolution had overthrown the Iraqi government earlier in the year, and the new government recognized Kuwait's independence. However, the Ba'thist Party's concentration of power in Saddam Hussein's hands in the 1970s led to periodic Iraqi pressure on Kuwait, culminating in the 1990 invasion and occupation. After the expulsion of Iraqi forces, Kuwait requested a realignment of its northern border, and in 1992 the United Nations Boundary Commission approved the request, moving the border approximately 1,880 feet northward. The change gave Kuwait full possession of the Rumaila oil fields and a portion of the Iraqi Umm Qasr naval base. Kuwait had argued that the existing border deprived it of its own resources and access to its territorial waters as specified in the 1963 agreement. Some 3,600 UN observers were assigned to patrol the new border; and Kuwaiti workers dug a 130-mile trench, paid for by private donations, as a further protection for the emirate.

REPRESENTATIVE GOVERNMENT

Kuwait differs from other patriarchally ruled Arabian Peninsula states in having a constitution that provides for an elected National Assembly. Its 50 members are elected for four-year terms.

Following years of friction between assembly members and Kuwait's rulers, a new Assembly was formed in 1981, with different members. The majority were traditional patriarchs loyal to the rulers, along with technical experts in various fields, such as industry, agriculture, and engineering. But the new Assembly fared little better than its predecessor in balancing freedom of expression with responsible leadership. The ruler suspended it, along with the Constitution, in 1986.

FREEDOM

Although women have not yet succeeded in gaining voting rights, the government submitted a decree for Assembly approval in May 2001 that would allow them to join the police force. It was subsequently approved.

Pressures to reinstate the Assembly have increased in recent years. Just prior to the Iraqi invasion, the ruler had convened a 75-member National Council "to appraise our parliamentary experiment." The process was halted during the Iraqi occupation; but, after the Iraqi withdrawal and the return to Kuwait of the ruling family, the emir pledged to hold elections for a new Assembly in October 1992.

The emir kept his pledge, and on October 5, 1992, the election took place as scheduled. However, the emir suspended the Assembly in May 1999, after opposition deputies had paralyzed government action by endless criticism of government ministers who were presenting their programs for legislative concurrence. However, he approved elections for a new Assembly to take place in July. During the suspension period he issued a decree giving women the right to vote and run for public office in 2003. When the new Assembly (all-male) took office, its members refused to approve the decree as required by Kuwaiti law. Since then Kuwaiti women have struggled, as yet without success, to gain the right to vote.

VULNERABILITY

Kuwait's location and its relatively open society make the country vulnerable to external subversion. In the early 1970s, the rulers were the target of criticism and threats from other Arab states because they did not publicly support the Palestinian cause. For years afterward, Kuwait provided large-scale financial aid not only to the Palestine Liberation Organization (PLO), but also to Arab states, such as Syria and Jordan, that were directly involved in the struggle with Israel because of their common borders.

A new vulnerability surfaced with the Iranian Revolution of 1979, which overthrew the shah. Kuwait has a large Shi'a Muslim population, while its rulers are Sunni. Kuwait's support for Iraq and the development of closer links with Saudi Arabia (and indirectly the United States) angered Iran's new fundamentalist rulers. Kuwaiti oil installations were bombed by Iranian jets in 1981, and in 1983 truck bombs severely damaged the U.S. and French embassies in Kuwait City. The underground organization Islamic Jihad, which claimed links to Iran, claimed responsibility for the attacks and threatened more if Kuwait did not stop its support of Iraq. Fear of Iran led Kuwait to join the newly formed Gulf Cooperation Council in 1981.

HEALTH/WELFARE

The 1.4 million foreign workers in Kuwait have had little protection under law until very recently. In November 2000 a large number of unemployed or underemployed Egyptians, the largest component of the expatriate labor force, rioted over bad working conditions and exploitation by sponsors who charge up to $3,000 for residency and work permits. The government agreed to review labor laws to limit payments to sponsors by mutual agreement.

The country also began making large purchases of weapons for defense, balancing U.S. with Soviet equipment. Its arms buildup made it the world's third-highest defense spender, at $3.1 billion, an average of $2,901 per capita.

THE IRAQI OCCUPATION AND AFTERMATH

The seven months of Iraqi occupation (August 1990–February 1991) had a devastating effect on Kuwait. Some 5,000 Kuwaitis were killed, and the entire population was held hostage to Iraqi demands. Oil production stopped entirely. Iraqi forces opened hundreds of oil storage tanks as a defense measure, pouring millions of gallons of oil into the sea, thus creating a serious environmental hazard. (As they retreated, the Iraqis also set 800 oil wells on fire, destroying production capabilities and posing enormous technical and environmental problems. These conflagrations were not extinguished for nearly a year.) In Kuwait City, basic water, electricity, and other services were cut off; public buildings were damaged; shops and homes were vandalized; and more than 3,000 gold bars, the backing for the Kuwaiti currency, were taken to Iraq.

ACHIEVEMENTS

Despite their exclusion from the franchise, Kuwaiti women have done well in other areas of national life. They may now serve in the police force. And in April 2000, the first all-female soccer tournament was held for teams from Kuwait University, institutes, and foreign schools, despite criticism from Islamic fundamentalists that such a public activity was "forbidden and a disobedience to God."

THE PEOPLE

Until the economic recession in the region, the country had a high rate of immigration. As a result, there are more non-Kuwaitis than Kuwaitis in the population, though dislocation resulting from the Iraqi occupation has changed the balance. Today, approximately 45 percent of the population are native Kuwaitis.

About one-third of the total population, both citizens and noncitizens, are Shi'a Muslims.

Timeline: PAST

1756
Establishment of the al-Sabah family as the rulers of Kuwait

1899
Agreement with Great Britain making Kuwait a protectorate

1961–1963
Independence, followed by Iraqi claim and British/Arab League intervention

1971
Elections for a new National Assembly

1976
The ruler suspends the Assembly on the grounds that it is a handicap to effective government

1980s
Bombings by Islamic Jihad; massive deportation of Iranians after public buildings and oil installations are sabotaged; the government places the tanker fleet under U.S. protection by reflagging ships and providing naval escorts in the Gulf

1990s
Iraqi forces occupy Kuwait: Kuwait is liberated in the Gulf War; tension between the government and the Assembly; tensions rise between Kuwaitis and foreign workers

PRESENT

2000s
Kuwait joins the international coalition against terrorism

THE ECONOMY

Kuwait's only abundant resource is petroleum. Less than 1 percent of the land can be cultivated, and there is almost no fresh water. Drinking water comes from seawater converted to fresh water by huge desalination plants.

Kuwait's oil reserves of 94 billion barrels are the world's third largest, comprising 10 percent of global reserves. According to a 1996 study by the International Monetary Fund, the oil industry—and, with it, the economy—has recovered "impressively" from the effects of the Iraqi occupation. Oil production in 1997 reached 2 million barrels per day. The 1995–2000 Five-Year Plan approved by the Assembly projects a balanced budget by the end of the plan, largely through privatization of state enterprises, increased oil and non-oil revenues, and expansion of petrochemical industries.

As a result, the Kuwaiti economy has rebounded to such an extent that, in 1996, Kuwait became the first Gulf state to receive an "A" rating from the International Banking Credit Association, an organization that evaluates countries on the basis of short- and long-term risks.

In addition to restoring its oil fields to full production, by 2001 nearly all the land mines left by the retreating Iraqis had been cleared from Kuwait's vast stretches of desert. An enormous oil slick from oil-well destruction that had threatened to pollute the water supply (which comes from desalinization) had also been cleared up.

NOTE

1. Cameron Barr, in *The Christian Science Monitor* (March 2001).

Kyrgyzstan (Kyrgyzstan Republic)

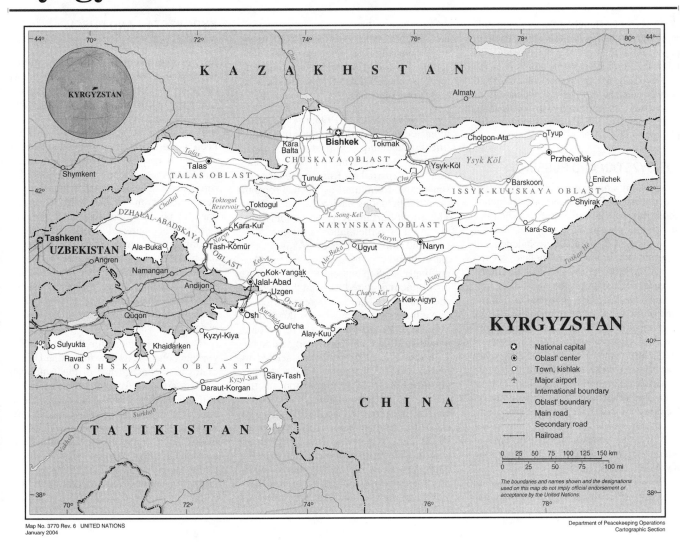

Map No. 3770 Rev. 6   UNITED NATIONS
January 2004

Department of Peacekeeping Operations
Cartographic Section

Kyrgyzstan Statistics

GEOGRAPHY

Area in Square Miles (Kilometers): 76,621 (198,500) (about the size of South Dakota)

Capital (Population): Bishkek (590,000)

PEOPLE

Population

Total: 4,753,000

Annual Growth Rate: 1.44%

Major Languages: Kirghiz; Russian; Uzbek

Ethnic Makeup: 52% Kirghiz; 18% Russian; 13% Uzbek; 3% Ukrainian; 14% others

Religions: 75% Muslim; 20% Russian Orthodox; 5% others

Health

Life Expectancy at Birth: 59 years (male); 68 years (female)

Infant Mortality Rate (Ratio): 76/1,000

Education

Adult Literacy Rate: 97%

GOVERNMENT

Type: republic

Head of State/Government: President Askar Akayev; Prime Minister Kurmanbek Bakiyev

Political Parties: Social Democratic Party; Kyrgyz Democratic Movement; National Unity; Communist Party; others

ECONOMY

Currency ($ U.S. Equivalent): 30.25 soms = $1

Per Capita Income/GDP: $2,700/$12.6 billion

Inflation Rate: 18.4%

Exports: $482 million

Imports: $579 million

167

Kyrgyzstan Country Report

The Kyrghyz Republic (more commonly referred to as Kyrgyzstan) is one of the least populated of the Central Asian republics. Its Islamic culture has become a prominent aspect of daily life, now that communist-inspired atheism no longer exists. It is relatively well endowed with mineral resources and has a fairly homogeneous population.

KYRGYZSTAN AND RUSSIA

Kyrgyzstan's biggest problems with Russia concern its Russian minority, which is about one-fifth of the population. Nationalist politicians in the Kyrgyz Parliament have insisted that the newly independent republic is a "national homeland" of the Kyrgyz people, whose interests should be considered ahead of the minorities, including the Russians. They insist that the land of the republic belongs to the Kyrgyz people—a principle that, if accepted into law, would deprive non-Kyrgyz people of ownership rights. President Akar Akayev has resisted these nationalistic pressures to harass and embarrass the Russian residents and other minorities in his country. He does not want to antagonize the Kremlin, and he certainly does not want to destabilize his multinational society, in which only half of the population is ethnic Kyrgyz.

However, Akayev was unsuccessful in preventing Parliament's growing discrimi-

nation against Russians and other minorities, which included a declaration of Kyrgyz as the state language, an increasing Islamicization of the society, and preferential treatment given to ethnic Kyrgyz workers in search of scarce jobs.

Between 1989 and 1993, tired of being relegated to second-class status by the political leadership of post–Soviet Kyrgyzstan, 15 percent of the Russian minority departed for Russia, even though some came from families that had roots in the republic dating back almost a century. This flight hurt the Kyrgyz economy, depriving it of skilled labor in the construction and other industries. Akayev was alarmed and tried to reverse the trend. Accordingly, in September 1994 the Kyrgyz government declared Russian the "second state language" for a 10-year period, a move that opened the way for the temporary use of Russian in all areas of national administration and provided Russians with the time many said they needed to master a difficult tongue. This and other gestures, such as revitalization of the economy, the introduction of a modern banking system, and a careful policy to assure the secular character of Kyrgyzstan in the face of pressure from a religious elite to give more official attention to Islamic practices, apparently have had a positive outcome. Emigration of non-Kyrgyz minorities has declined accordingly.

KYRGYZSTAN AND RUSSIA AFTER 2000

Akayev had become a close ally of the Kremlin in Central Asia, supporting most of Russia's influence-building initiatives in the region, including efforts to promote collective security through agreements on military cooperation. In return, Russia has been a consistent and dedicated supporter of Akayev despite his growing authoritarian tendencies, evident in the results of a referendum in early 2003 establishing a new constitution, which greatly strengthened the power of the president while preserving the outward appearance of a parliamentary democracy. The Kremlin has had no objection to Akayev's authoritarianism, especially if it is what Akayev needs to keep his regime secure against political opposition until the end of 2005, when his current term as president is supposed to be over.

The main problem for Russia in Kyrgyzstan concerns its new ties to the United States as a consequence of the American war on terrorism following the September 11th attacks. The Kremlin has responded to American influence with an enhanced military presence in Kyrgyzstan now that U.S. troops have come to the country. Kyrgyzstan has also cooperated with Washington by supplying it with intelligence about militant Islamic groups operating in the country.

Lebanon (Lebanese Republic)

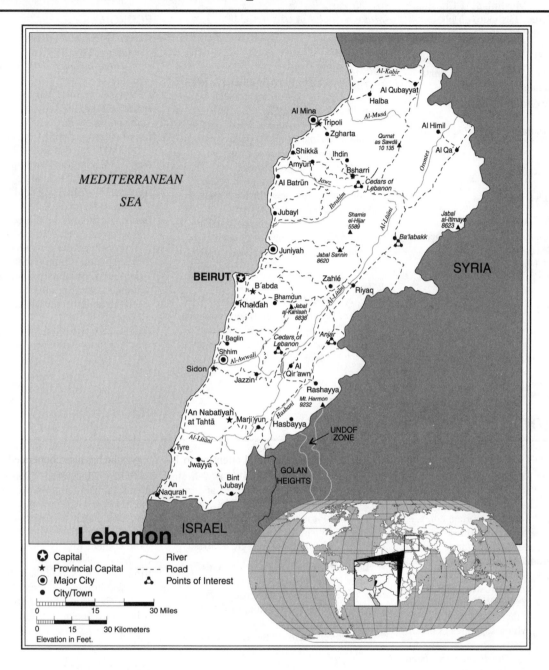

Map legend:
- ✪ Capital
- ★ Provincial Capital
- ◉ Major City
- • City/Town
- ∼ River
- - - - Road
- △ Points of Interest

0   15   30 Miles
0   15   30 Kilometers
Elevation in Feet.

Lebanon Statistics

GEOGRAPHY

Area in Square Miles (Kilometers): 4,015 (10,452) (smaller than Connecticut)

Capital (Population): Beirut (1,826,000)

Environmental Concerns: deforestation; soil erosion; air and water pollution

Geographical Features: a narrow coastal plain; the Biqa' Valley separates Lebanon and the Anti-Lebanon Mountains

Climate: Mediterranean (hot, humid summers; cool, damp winters); heavy winter snows in mountains

PEOPLE

Population

Total: 3,826,018
Annual Growth Rate: 1.26%
Rural/Urban Population Ratio: 12/88
Major Languages: Arabic; French; English

169

Ethnic Makeup: 95% Arab; 4% Armenian;
1% others
Religions: 59.7% Muslim; 39% Christian
(Maronite, Greek Orthodox, Melkite,
Armenian, and Protestant); 1.3% other

Health

Life Expectancy at Birth: 70 years (male);
75 years (female)
Infant Mortality Rate: 24.52/1,000 live
births
Physicians Available (Ratio): 1/529 people

Education

Adult Literacy Rate: 87.4%

COMMUNICATION

Telephones: 678,800 main lines
Daily Newspaper Circulation: 172 per
1,000 people
Televisions: 291 per 1,000 people
Users: 400,000 (2000)

TRANSPORTATION

Highways in Miles (Kilometers): 4,380
(7,300)

Railroads in Miles (Kilometers): 138
(401)
Usable Airfields: 8
Motor Vehicles in Use: 1,183,000

GOVERNMENT

Type: republic
Independence Date: November 22, 1943
(from League of Nations mandate under
French administration)
Head of State/Government: President Emile
Lahoud; Prime Minister Fuad Siniora
Political Parties: various parties are
identified with religious or
denominational groups; each group
nominates candidates for the National
Assembly (Parliament)
Suffrage: compulsory for males at 21;
authorized for women at 21 with
elementary-school education

MILITARY

Military Expenditures (% of GDP): 3.1%
Current Disputes: Syrian troops continue
de facto occupation in northeast and
central areas; Hezbollah dispute with

Israel over Shab'a Farms area in Israeli-
occupied Golan Heights

ECONOMY

Currency ($ U.S. Equivalent): 1,507
pounds = $1
Per Capita Income/GDP: $5,000/$18.8
billion
GDP Growth Rate: 4%
Inflation Rate: 2%
Unemployment Rate: 18%
Labor Force: 2,600,000 (plus an estimated
1,000,000 foreign workers)
Natural Resources: limestone; iron ore;
salt; water; arable land
Agriculture: fruits; vegetables; olives;
tobacco; hemp (hashish); sheep; goats
Industry: banking; food processing;
jewelry; cement; textiles; mineral and
chemical products; wood and furniture
products; oil refining; metal fabricating
Exports: $1.7 billion (primary partners
United Arab Emirates, Saudi Arabia,
Switzerland, United States, Turkey,
France)
Imports: $8.16 billion (primary partners
Italy, France, Germany)

Lebanon Country Report

The Lebanese Republic is located at the eastern end of the Mediterranean Sea. The coastal plain, which contains the capital, Beirut, and all the other important cities, is narrow, rising just a few miles east of Beirut to a rugged mountain range, Mount Lebanon. Beyond Mount Lebanon is the Biqa', a broad, fertile valley that is the country's main wheat-growing region. At the eastern edge of the Biqa', the land rises again abruptly to the snow-capped Anti-Lebanon Range, which separates Lebanon from Syria.

Lebanon's geography has always been important strategically. Many invaders passed through it over the centuries on their conquests—Egyptians, Assyrians, Persians, Crusaders, Arabs, and Turks. However, they were seldom able to gain control of Mount Lebanon. For this reason, the mountain served as a refuge for ethnic and religious minorities, and it became in time the nucleus of the modern Lebanese state.

HISTORY

In ancient times, Lebanon was known as Phoenicia. The Phoenicians were great traders who traveled throughout the Mediterranean and probably out into the Atlan-

tic Ocean as far north as Cornwall in England, in search of tin, copper, and iron ore, which were valued in the ancient world for their many uses. Phoenician merchants established trading posts, some of which eventually grew into great cities.

Lebanon began to develop a definite identity much later, in the seventh century A.D. when a Christian group, the Maronites, took refuge in Mount Lebanon after they were threatened with persecution by the government of the East Roman or Byzantine Empire because of theological disagreements over the nature of Christ. The Muslim Arabs brought Islam to coastal Lebanon at about the same time, but they were unable to dislodge or convert the Maronites. Mount Lebanon's sanctuary tradition attracted other minority groups, Muslim as well as Christian. Shi'a Muslim communities moved there in the ninth and tenth centuries to escape persecution from Sunni Muslims, the Islamic majority. In the eleventh century, the Druze, adherents of an offshoot of Islam who followed the teachings of an Egyptian mystic and also faced persecution from Sunni Muslims, established themselves in the southern part of Mount Lebanon.

Lebanon acquired a distinct political identity under certain powerful families in the sixteenth and seventeenth centuries. The Ottoman Turks conquered it along with the rest of the Middle East, but they were content to leave local governance in the hands of these families in return for tribute. The most prominent was the Ma'an family, who were Druze. Their greatest leader, Fakhr al-Din (1586–1635), established an independent principality that included all of present-day Lebanon, Israel, and part of Syria.

The French Mandate

After the defeat of Ottoman Turkey in World War I, Lebanon became a French mandate. The French had originally intended the country to be included in their mandate over Syria; but in 1920, due to pressure from Maronite leaders, they separated the two mandates. "New" Lebanon was much larger than the old Maronite-Druze territory up on Mount Lebanon. The new "Greater Lebanon" included the coast—in short, the area of the current Lebanese state.

France gave Lebanon its independence in 1943, but French troops stayed on until

1946, when they were withdrawn due to British and American pressure on France.

THE LEBANESE REPUBLIC

The major shortcoming of the mandate was the French failure to develop a broad-based political system with representatives from the major religious groups. The French very pointedly favored the Maronites. The Constitution, originally issued in 1926, established a republican system under an elected president and a legislature. Members would be elected on the basis of six Christians to five Muslims. The president would be elected for a six-year term and could not serve concurrently. (The one exception was Bishara al-Khuri [1943–1952], who served during and after the transition period to independence. The Constitution was amended to allow him to do so.) By private French-Maronite agreement, the custom was established whereby the Lebanese president would always be chosen from the Maronite community.

In the long term, perhaps more important to Lebanese politics than the Constitution is the National Pact, an oral agreement made in 1943 between Bishara al-Khuri, as head of the Maronite community, and Riad al-Sulh, his Sunni counterpart. The two leaders agreed that, first, Lebanese Christians would not enter into alliances with foreign (i.e., Christian) nations and Muslims would not attempt to merge Lebanon with the Muslim Arab world; and second, that the six-to-five formula for representation in the Assembly would apply to all public offices. The pact has never been put in writing, but in view of the delicate balance of sects in Lebanon, it has been considered by Lebanese leaders, particularly the Maronites, as the only alternative to anarchy.

DEVELOPMENT

The end of the civil war and Hariri's energetic reform program have brought significant improvements to the Lebanese infrastructure. The GDP growth rate reached a high of 8 percent in 1994, although dropping steadily thereafter to average 1 percent annually. An austerity program introduced in 2000 emphasized privatization of state-owned enterprises, reduction in the size of the bureaucracy, and tax reform.

The large extended family, although an obstacle to broad nation building, served as an essential support base for its members, providing services that would otherwise have to have been drawn from government sources. These services included education, employment, bank loans, investment capital, and old-age security. The free-wheeling Lebanese economy was another important factor in Lebanon's relative stability. Per capita annual income rose from $235 in 1950 to $1,070 in 1974, putting Lebanon on a level with some of the oil-producing Arab states, although the country does not have oil.

The private sector was largely responsible for national prosperity. A real-estate boom developed, and many fortunes were made in land speculation and construction. Tourism was another important source of revenues. Many banks and foreign business firms established their headquarters in Beirut because of its excellent communications with the outside world; its educated, multilingual labor force; and the absence of government restrictions.

THE 1975–1976 CIVIL WAR

The titles of books on Lebanon in recent years have often contained adjectives such as "fractured," "fragmented," and "precarious." These provide a generally accurate description of the country's situation as a result of the civil war of 1975–1976. The main destabilizing element, and the one that precipitated the conflict, was the presence and activities of Palestinians.

In some ways Palestinians have contributed significantly to Lebanese national life. The first group, who fled there after the 1948 Arab-Israeli War, consisted mostly of cultured, educated, highly urbanized people who gravitated to Beirut and were absorbed quickly into the population. Many of them became extremely successful in banking, commerce, journalism, or as faculty members at the American University of Beirut. A second Palestinian group arrived as destitute refugees after the 1967 Six-Day War. They have been housed ever since in refugee camps run by the United Nations Relief and Works Agency. The Lebanese government provides them with identity cards but no passports. For all practical purposes, they are stateless persons.

Neither group was a threat to Lebanese internal stability until 1970, although Lebanon backed the Palestine Liberation Organization (PLO) cause and did not interfere with guerrilla raids from its territory into Israel. After the PLO was expelled from Jordan, the organization made its headquarters in Beirut. This new militant Palestinian presence in Lebanon created a double set of problems for the Lebanese. Palestinian raids into Israel brought Israeli retaliation, which caused more Lebanese than Palestinian casualties. Yet the Lebanese government could not control the Palestinians. To many Lebanese, especially the Maronites, their government seemed to be a prisoner in its own land.

In April 1975 a bus carrying Palestinians returning from a political rally was ambushed near Beirut by the Kata'ib, members of the Maronite Phalange Party. The incident triggered the Lebanese Civil War of 1975–1976. The war officially ended with a peace agreement arranged by the Arab League. But the bus incident also brought to a head conflicts derived from the opposing goals of various Lebanese power groups. The Palestinians' goal was to use Lebanon as a springboard for the liberation of Palestine. The Maronites' goal was to drive the Palestinians out of Lebanon and preserve their privileged status. Sunni Muslim leaders sought to reshape the National Pact to allow for equal political participation with the Christians. Shi'a leaders were determined to get a better break for the Shi'a community, generally the poorest and least represented in the Lebanese government. The Druze, also interested in greater representation in the system and traditionally hostile to the Maronites, disliked and distrusted all of the other groups.

Eventually Lebanon's importance as a regional trade, banking, and transit center ensured that outside powers would intervene. Syrian troops were ordered by the Arab League to occupy the country. Their purpose was not only to end the conflict but also to block Palestinian aspirations to use Lebanon as a launching pad for the recovery of their lands in Israel.

THE ISRAELI INVASION

The immediate result of the civil war was to divide Lebanon into separate territories, each controlled by a different faction. The Lebanese government, for all practical purposes, could not control its own territory. Israeli forces, in an effort to protect northern Israeli settlements from constant shelling by the Palestinians, established control over southern Lebanon. The Lebanese-Israeli border, ironically, became a sort of "good fence" open to Lebanese civilians for medical treatment in Israeli hospitals.

In March 1978 PLO guerrillas landed on the Israeli coast near Haifa, hijacked a bus, and drove it toward Tel Aviv. The hijackers were overpowered in a shootout with Israeli troops, but 35 passengers were killed along with the guerrillas. Israeli forces invaded southern Lebanon in retaliation and occupied the region for two months, eventually withdrawing after the United Nations, in an effort to separate Palestinians from Israelis, set up a 6,000-member "Interim Force" in Lebanon UNIFIL in the south, made up of units from various countries. UNIFIL's mandate was renewed in January 2004 for an additional six months.

The Lebanese factions themselves continued to tear the nation apart. Political assassinations of rival leaders were frequent. Many Lebanese settlements became ghost towns; they were fought over so much that their residents abandoned them. Some 300,000 Lebanese from the Israeli-occupied south fled to northern cities as refugees.

FREEDOM

Under an unwritten agreement made by Christian and Muslim leaders at independence, Lebanon is a "confessional democracy," with political representation based on religious affiliation. By tradition, the president is a Maronite Christian, the prime minister a Sunni Muslim, and the speaker of the Chamber of Deputies a Shi'a Muslim. Other government posts are similarly apportioned among the various religious denominations. However, demographic changes resulting in a non-Christian majority have yet to be reflected in the political structure.

The Israeli invasion of Lebanon in June 1982 was intended as a final solution to the Palestinian problem. It didn't quite work out that way. The Israeli Army surrounded Beirut and succeeded with U.S. intervention in forcing the evacuation of PLO guerrillas from Lebanon. The burden of war, as always, fell heaviest on the civilian population. A Beirut newspaper estimated almost 50,000 civilian casualties in the first two months of the invasion.

Israeli control over Beirut enabled the Christians to take savage revenge against the remaining Palestinians. In September 1983 Christian Phalange militiamen entered the refugee camps of Sabra and Shatila in West Beirut and massacred hundreds of people, mostly women and children. The massacre led to an official Israeli inquiry and censure of Israeli government and military leaders for indirect responsibility. But the Christian-dominated Lebanese government's own inquiry failed to fix responsibility on the Phalange.

The Lebanese Civil War supposedly ended in 1976, but it was not until 1990 that the central government began to show results in disarming militias and establishing its authority over the fragmented nation. In June 1985, following their withdrawal, the Israelis left behind a country that had become almost ungovernable. The growing power of the Shi'a Muslims, particularly the Shi'a organization Amal, presented a new challenge to the Christian leadership, while the return of the Palestinians brought bloody battles between Shi'a and PLO guerrillas. As the battles raged,

cease-fire followed cease-fire, and conference followed conference, but without noticeable success.

The Israeli withdrawal left the Syrians as the major power brokers in Lebanon. In 1985 Syrian president Hafez al-Assad masterminded a comprehensive peace and reform agreement that would expand the National Pact to provide equal Christian-Muslim representation in the Chamber of Deputies.

SYRIA INTERVENES

The collapse of peace efforts led Syria to send 7,000 heavily armed commandos into west Beirut in 1987 to restore law and order. They did restore a semblance of order to that part of the capital and opened checkpoints into east Beirut. But the Syrians were unable, or perhaps unwilling, to challenge the powerful Hizbullah faction (reputed to have held most Western hostages), which controlled the rabbit warren of narrow streets and tenements in the city's southern suburbs.

Aside from Hizbullah, Syria's major problem in knitting Lebanon together under its tutelage was with the Maronite community.

HEALTH/WELFARE

The withdrawal of Israeli forces from southern Lebanon left Hizbullah as the sole on-site agency for reconstruction of that war-torn region. In late 2000 teams of fighters-turned-humanitarian-workers cleaned village streets, set up potable water dispensers, sent mosquito-spraying trucks into the villages, and established and equipped mobile health clinics. Schools were reopened, and the former Israeli hospital at Bint Jbail, the regional capital, is now managed completely by Hizbullah doctors and nurses.

BREAKDOWN OF A SOCIETY

Following the reestablishment of central-government authority, a new transitional Council of Ministers (cabinet) was appointed by the then president Elias Hrawi, a Christian politician from the Maronite stronghold of Zahle, in 1992. Its responsibilities were to stabilize the economy and prepare for elections for a new Chamber of Deputies. In preparation for the elections the Chamber was enlarged from 108 to 128 seats.

The first national elections since the start of the civil war were held in 1992. Due in part to a boycott by Christian parties, which had demanded Syrian withdrawal as their price for participation, Shi'a candidates won 30 seats. Shi'a Amal leader Nibih Berri was elected speaker; Rafiq Hariri, a Sunni Muslim and millionaire, was named prime minister.

In any case, the growing demographic imbalance of Muslims and Christians indicated that, in the not too distant future, Lebanon would no longer be "a Christian island in a Muslim sea." By 1997 Christians numbered at most 30 percent of the population (composed of 800,000 Maronites, 400,000 Greek Orthodox, 300,000 Greek Catholics or Melkites, and 75,000 Armenians). Half a million Christians had left the country during the civil war. A 1996 amendment to the election law allowed government officials to run for office. The amendment enabled General Emile Lahoud, the Lebanese Army chief of staff, to run for president at the end of President Hrawi's term. Lahoud was elected in October 1998 for a six-year term to succeed him. Subsequently, new elections for the presidency and the National Assembly were scheduled for November 2004.

During his tenure, Israel decided to withdraw its troops. On May 24, 2000, the last Israeli soldiers pulled out of the zone, ending a 22-year occupation. The Israeli withdrawal resulted in jubilant celebrations throughout Lebanon. The government declared May 24 a national holiday, National Resistance Day, as crowds danced in the streets.

LEBANON AND THE WORLD

Aside from its vulnerability to international and inter-Arab rivalries because of internal conflicts, Lebanon drew world attention in the 1980s for its involvement in hostage taking. Lebanese militias such as Hizbullah, a Shi'a group backed by Iran as a means of exporting the Islamic Revolution, and shadowy organizations like the Islamic Jihad, Revolutionary Justice, and Islamic Jihad for the Liberation of Palestine kidnapped foreigners in Beirut. The conditions set for their release were rarely specific, and the refusal of the United States and other Western governments to "deal with terrorists" left them languishing in unknown prisons for years, seemingly forgotten by the outside world.

The changing Middle East situation and Lebanon's slow return to normalcy in the 1990s began to move the hostage-release process forward.

Since then, Lebanese-American relations have remained stable. However, the September 11, 2001 terrorist bombings in the United States and President George W. Bush's effort to form an international anti-terrorism coalition that would include Muslim states placed the Lebanese government in an awkward position. The U.S. ambassador to Lebanon commented in October 2001 that the country continued to shelter "terrorist organizations," including Hizbullah, since it had been responsible for the 1983 destruction of the American Embassy in Beirut and a truck-bomb onslaught on a U.S. Marine barracks that killed 241 Americans. Despite Hizbullah's newfound respectability as a social-service organization and political party represented in the Chamber of Deputies, the government feared that its past actions might motivate the United States to seek retribution, and include Lebanon in its antiterrorism campaign.

THE ECONOMY

In the mid-1970s, the Lebanese economy began going steadily downhill. The civil war and resulting instability caused most banks and financial institutions to move out of Beirut to more secure locations, notably Jordan, Bahrain, and Kuwait. Aside from the cost in human lives, Israeli raids and the 1982 invasion severely damaged the economy. The cost of the invasion in terms of damages was estimated at $1.9 billion. Remittances from Lebanese emigrants abroad dropped significantly. The Lebanese currency, once valued at 4.74 pounds to $1, had dropped in value to 3,000 to $1 by 1992, although rebounding to the present 1,507 to $1 11 years later.

Yet by a strange irony of fate, some elements of the economy continued to display robust health. Most middle-class Lebanese had funds invested abroad, largely in U.S. dollar accounts, and thus were protected from economic disaster.

ACHIEVEMENTS

The culivation of cannabis (opium poppy) in the Biqa' region, formerly one of the world's major sources, has been drastically reduced due to U.S. and Iranian aid, development of alternate crops, and cattle raising. Currently only 2,500 hectares are under cannabis cultivation.

The long, drawn-out civil conflict badly affected Lebanese agriculture, the mainstay of the economy. Both the coastal strip and the Biqa' Valley are extremely fertile, and in normal times produce crop surpluses for export. Lebanese fruit, particularly apples (the most important cash crop) and grapes, is in great demand throughout the Arab world. But these crops are no longer exported in quantity. Israeli destruction of crops, the flight of most of the farm labor force, and the blockade by Israeli troops of truck traffic

from rural areas into Beirut had a devastating effect on production.

Lebanon produces no oil of its own, but before the Lebanese Civil War and the Israeli invasion, the country derived important revenues from transit fees for oil shipments through pipelines across its territory. The periodic closing of these pipelines and damage to the country's two refineries sharply reduced revenues. The well-developed manufacturing industry, particularly textiles, was equally hard hit.

Timeline: PAST

9th–11th centuries
Establishment of Mount Lebanon as a sanctuary for religious communities

1860–1864
The first civil war, between Maronites and Druze, ending in foreign military intervention

1920–1946
French mandate

1958
Internal crisis and the first U.S. military intervention

1975–1976
Civil war, ended (temporarily) by an Arab League-sponsored cease-fire and peacekeeping force of Syrian troops

1980s
Israeli occupation of Beirut; Syrian troops reoccupy Beirut; foreigners are seized in a new outbreak of hostage taking; the economy nears collapse

1990s
The withdrawal of Israeli forces from Lebanon; all foreign hostages are released; Lebanon begins rebuilding

PRESENT

2000s
Hizbullah's presence in Lebanon causes tension with the United States; Najib Mikati is appointed prime minister

Armed with $458 million in aid from the World Bank, the European Union, and the Paris-based Mediterranean Development Agency, Prime Minister Hariri launched a major economic reform drive in February 2001. He laid off 500 employees from the bloated public sector and privatized the state-owned electricity company as a start toward further privatization. The cabinet also agreed to shut down the state-owned

TeleLiban, saving $33 million a year. Elimination of the sugar subsidy will save another $40 million annually.

Hariri's reform program faced significant obstacles. Lebanon's current public debt is $28 billion, 165 percent of gross domestic product and the fourth-highest debt-to-GDP ratio in the world (after Nicaragua, Zambia, and Malawi). Another obstacle is the time-honored practice of *wasta* (bribes), needed for all public services. In 2001 Syria stopped supplying Lebanon with electricy, due to an unpaid $120 million bill. In February 2001 the government introduced a value added tax (VAT) of 10 percent on most goods; it should generate $500 million in income. Increased tourism and a rise in purchases of real estate by wealthy Gulf Arabs offered some hope that the economy would rebound.

NOTES

1. David C. Gordon, *The Republic of Lebanon: Nation in Jeopardy* (Boulder, CO: Westview Press, 1983), p. 4.
2. Samir Khlaf, *Lebanon's Predicament* (New York: Columbia University Press, 1987), p. 69.
3. Gordon, *op. cit.*, p. 19.
4. *Ibid.*, p. 25. See also Baaklini, *op. cit.*, pp. 200–202, for a description of the coexistence process as used by Sabri Hamadeh, for many years head of the assembly.
5. Whether the Lebanese Civil War ever really ended is open to question. A cartoon in a U.S. newspaper in August 1982 shows a hooded skeleton on a television screen captioned "Lebanon" saying, "And now we return to our regularly scheduled civil war." Gordon, *op. cit.*, p. 113.
6. Shi'a religious leader Imam Musa al-Sadr's political organization was named Harakat al-Mahrumin ("Movement of the Disinherited") when it was founded in 1969–1970. See Marius Deeb, *The Lebanese Civil War* (New York: Praeger, 1980), pp. 69–70.
7. Gordon, *op. cit.*, p. 110.
8. *Ibid.*, p. 125.
9. Charles Issawi, "Economic Development and Political Liberalism in Lebanon," in Leonard Binder, ed., *Politics in Lebanon* (New York: John Wiley, 1966), pp. 80–81.
10. The Taif Accord, signed under Arab League auspices in Taif, Saudi Arabia, changes the power-sharing arrangement in the Lebanese government from a 6:5 Christian-Muslim ratio to one of equal representation in the government. The powers of the president are also reduced.
11. *Middle East Economic Digest* (October 10, 1990).
12. Joel Greenberg, in *The New York Times* (May 24, 2000).

Libya (Socialist People's Libyan Arab Jamahiriyya)

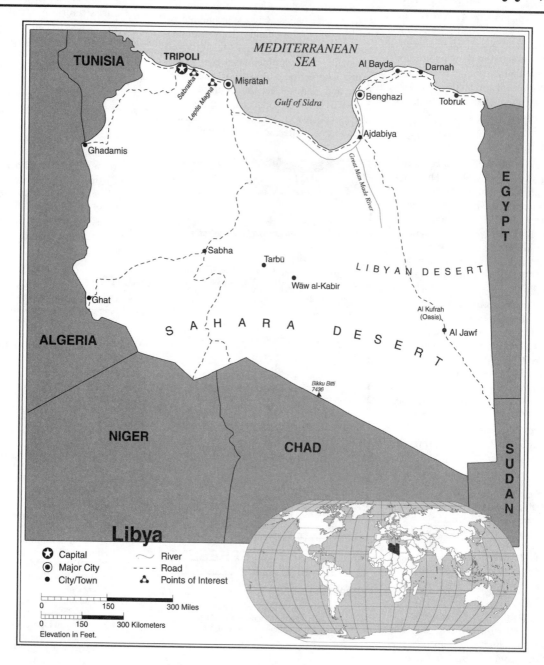

Libya Statistics

GEOGRAPHY

Area in Square Miles (Kilometers): 679,147 (1,759,450) (about the size of Alaska)

Capital (Population): Tripoli (1,681,000)

Environmental Concerns: desertification; very limited freshwater resources

Geographical Features: mostly barren, flat to undulating plains, plateaus, depressions

Climate: Mediterranean along the coast; dry, extreme desert in the interior

PEOPLE

Population

Total: 5,368,585 (includes 662,669 nonnationals of whom 500,000 are migrants from sub-Saharan Africa)

Annual Growth Rate: 2.4%

Rural/Urban Population Ratio: 14/86

Major Languages: Arabic; English; Italian

Ethnic Makeup: 97% Berber and Arab; 3% others

Religions: 97% Sunni Muslim; 3% others

Health

Life Expectancy at Birth: 74 years (male); 78 years (female)

Infant Mortality Rate: 27.9/1,000 live births
Physicians Available (Ratio): 1/948 people

Education

Adult Literacy Rate: 76.2%
Compulsory (Ages): 6–15

COMMUNICATION

Telephones: 380,000 main lines
Daily Newspaper Circulation: 15 per 1,000 people
Televisions: 105 per 1,000 people
Internet Users: 1 (2000)

TRANSPORTATION

Highways in Miles (Kilometers): 15,180 (24,484)
Railroads in Miles (Kilometers): none
Usable Airfields: 136
Motor Vehicles in Use: 904,000

GOVERNMENT

Type: officially a Jamahiriyya ("state belonging to the people") with government authority exercised by a General Peoples' Congress
Independence Date: December 24, 1951 (from Italy)
Head of State/Government: Revolutionary Leader Mahammad Au Minyar al-Qadhafi holds no official title but serves as de facto head of state; Mubarak al-Shamekh, secretary of the GPC, is the equivalent to prime minister
Political Parties: none
Suffrage: universal and compulsory at 18

MILITARY

Military Expenditures (% of GDP): 3.9%
Current Disputes: Libya claims about 19,400 square kilometers of land in northern Niger and part of southeastern algeria; both disputes currently dormant

ECONOMY

Currency ($ U.S. Equivalent): 2 dinars = $1; the official foreign trade rate was devalued in 2002 to 21.30 Libyan dinars = $1

Per Capita Income/GDP: $7,600/$40 billion
GDP Growth Rate: 3%
Inflation Rate: 18.5%
Unemployment Rate: 30%
Labor Force: 1,500,000
Natural Resources: petroleum; natural gas; gypsum
Agriculture: wheat; barley; olives; dates; citrus fruits; vegetables; peanuts; beef; eggs
Industry: petroleum; food processing; textiles; handicrafts; cement
Exports: $13.9 billion (primary partners Italy, Germany, Spain)
Imports: $7.6 billion (primary partners Italy, Germany, Tunisia)

SUGGESTED WEB SITES

http://lcweb2.loc.gov/frd/cs/lytoc.html
http://home.earthlink.net/~dribrahim/

Libya Country Report

The Socialist People's Libyan Arab Jamahiriya (Republic), commonly known as Libya, is the fourth largest of the Arab countries. Since it became a republic in 1969, it has played a role in regional and international affairs more appropriate to the size of its huge territory than to its small population.

Libya consists of three geographical regions: Tripolitania, Cyrenaica, and the Fezzan. Most of the population live in Tripolitania, the northwestern part of the country, where Tripoli, the capital and major port, is located. Cyrenaica, in the east along the Egyptian border, has a narrow coastline backed by a high plateau (2,400-feet elevation) called the Jabal al-Akhdar ("Green Mountain"). It contains Libya's other principal city, Benghazi. The two regions are separated by the Sirte, an extension of the Sahara Desert that reaches almost to the Mediterranean Sea. Most of Libya's oil fields are in the Sirte.

The Fezzan occupies the central part of the country. It is entirely desert, except for a string of widely scattered oases. Its borders are with Chad, Algeria, Niger, and Sudan.

HISTORY

Until modern times, Libya did not have a separate identity, either national or territo-rial. It always formed a part of some other territorial unit and in most cases was controlled by outsiders. However, control was usually limited to the coastal areas. The Berbers of the interior were little affected by the passing of conquerors and the rise and fall of civilizations.

Libya's culture and social structure have been influenced more by the Islamic Arabs than by any other invaders. The Arabs brought Islam to Libya in the early seventh century. Arab groups settled in the region and intermarried with the Berber population to such an extent that the Libyans became one of the most thoroughly Arabized peoples in the Islamic world.

DEVELOPMENT

Although continued U.S. sanctions prohibit American firms from operating in Libya, improved relations with other countries have begun to generate diversification of the Libyan economy. An agreement with Ireland to import 50,000 live Irish cattle was concluded in March 2001, and Italy's export credit agency wrote off $230 million in Libyan debts to encourage investment by Italian firms. New oil discoveries in the Murzuq field have aided economic recovery.

Coastal Libya, around Tripoli, was an outlying province of the Ottoman Empire for several centuries.

The Sanusiya Movement

At various stages in Islam's long history, new groups or movements have appeared committed to purifying or reforming Islamic society and taking it back to its original form of a simple community of believers led by just rulers. Several of these movements, such as the Wahhabis of Saudi Arabia, were important in the founding of modern Islamic states. The movement called the Sanusiya was formed in the nineteenth century. In later years, it became an important factor in the formation of modern Libya.

The founder, the Grand Sanusi, was a religious teacher from Algeria. He left Algeria after the French conquest and settled in northern Cyrenaica. The Grand Sanusi's teachings attracted many followers. He also attracted the attention of the Ottoman authorities, who distrusted his advocacy of a strong united Islamic world in which Ottomans and Arabs would be partners. In 1895, to escape from the Ottomans, the Grand Sanusi's son and successor moved Sanusiya headquarters to Kufra, a remote oasis in the Sahara.

The Sanusiya began as a peaceful movement interested only in bringing new converts to Islam and founding a network of *zawiyas* ("lodges") for contemplation and monastic life throughout the desert. But when European countries began to seize territories in North and West Africa, the Sanusi became warrior-monks and fought the invaders.

Italy Conquers Libya

The first attempt at Italian conquest of Libya took place in 1911. It would not be until 1932 (after nine years) for Italy to overcome all of Libya, despite Italy's vast superiority in troops and weapons. Sanusi guerrilla bands harried the Italians, cutting supply lines, ambushing patrols, and attacking convoys. Their leader, Shaykh Omar Mukhtar, became Libya's first national hero.

The Italians finally overcame the Sanusi by making Cyrenaica into a huge concentration camp, with a barbed-wire fence along the Egyptian border. Nomadic peoples were herded into these camps, guarded by soldiers to prevent them from aiding the Sanusi. Sanusi prisoners were pushed out of airplanes, wells were plugged to deny water to the people, and flocks were slaughtered. In 1931 Omar Mukhtar was captured, court-martialed, and hanged in public. The resistance ended with his death.

Independent Libya

Libya was a major battleground during World War II, as British, German, and Italian armies rolled back and forth across the desert. The British defeated the Germans and occupied northern Libya, while a French army occupied the Fezzan. The United States later built an important air base, Wheelus Field, near Tripoli. Thus the three major Allied powers all had an interest in Libya's future. But they could not agree on what to do with occupied Libya.

Italy wanted Libya back. Due to lack of agreement, the Libyan "problem" was referred to the United Nations General Assembly. Popular demonstrations of support for independence in Libya impressed a number of the newer UN members; in 1951 the General Assembly approved a resolution for an independent Libyan state, a kingdom under the Grand Sanusi, Idris.

THE KINGDOM OF LIBYA

Libya has been governed under two political systems since independence: a constitutional monarchy (1951–1969); and a Socialist republic (1969–), which has no constitution because all power "belongs" to the people. Monarchy and republic have had almost equal time in power. But Libya's sensational economic growth and aggressive foreign policy under the republic need to be understood in relation to the solid, if unspectacular, accomplishments of the regime that preceded it.

At independence, Libya was an artificial union of the three provinces. The Libyan people had little sense of national identity or unity. Loyalty was to one's family, clan, village, and, in a general sense, to the higher authority represented by a tribal confederation. The only other loyalty linking Libyans was the Islamic religion. The tides of war and conquest that had washed over them for centuries had had little effect on their strong, traditional attachment to Islam.

Political differences also divided the three provinces. Tripolitanians talked openly of abolishing the monarchy. Cyrenaica was the home and power base of King Idris; the king's principal supporters were the Sanusiya and certain important families. The king had his administrative capital at Baida, in the Jabal al-Akhdar.

The greatest problem facing Libya at independence was economics. Per capita income in 1951 was about $30 per year; in 1960 it was about $100 per year. Approximately 5 percent of the land was marginally usable for agriculture, and only 1 percent could be cultivated on a permanent basis. Most economists considered Libya to be a hopeless case, almost totally dependent on foreign aid for survival.

Despite its meager resources and lack of political experience, Libya was valuable to the United States and Britain in the 1950s and 1960s because of its strategic location. The United States negotiated a long-term lease on Wheelus Field in 1954, as a vital link in the chain of U.S. bases built around the southern perimeter of the Soviet Union due to the cold war. In return, U.S. aid of $42 million sweetened the pot, and Wheelus became the single largest employer of Libyan labor. The British had two air bases and maintained a garrison in Tobruk.

Political development in the kingdom was minimal. King Idris knew little about parliamentary democracy, and he distrusted political parties.

THE 1969 REVOLUTION

At dawn on September 1, 1969, a group of young, unknown army officers abruptly carried out a military coup in Libya. King Idris, who had gone to Turkey for medical treatment, was deposed, and a "Libyan Arab Republic" was proclaimed by the officers. These men, whose names were not known to the outside world until weeks after the coup, were led by Captain Muammar Muhammad al-Qadhafi.

Qadhafi's new regime made a sharp change in policy from that of its predecessor. Wheelus Field and the British air bases were evacuated and returned to Libyan control. Libya took an active part in Arab affairs and supported Arab unity, to the extent of working to undermine other Arab leaders whom Qadhafi considered undemocratic or unfriendly to his regime.

REGIONAL POLICY

To date, Qadhafi's efforts to unite Libya with other Arab states have not been successful. A 1984 agreement for a federal union with Morocco, which provided for separate sovereignty but a federated Assembly and unified foreign policies, was abrogated unilaterally by the late King Hassan II, after Qadhafi had charged him with "Arab treason" for meeting with Israeli leader Shimon Peres. Undeterred, Qadhafi tried again in 1987 with neighboring Algeria, receiving a medal from President Chadli Bendjedid but no other encouragement.

Although distrustful of the mercurial Libyan leader, other North African heads of state have continued to work with him on the basis that it is safer to have Qadhafi inside the circle than isolated outside. In 1989 Libya joined with other North African states in the Arab Maghrib Union (AMU), which was formed to coordinate their respective economies. However, the AMU has yet to become a viable organization due to political differences among its members.

SOCIAL REVOLUTION

Qadhafi's desert upbringing and Islamic education gave him a strong, puritanical moral code. In addition to closing foreign bases and expropriating properties of Italians and Jews, he moved forcefully against symbols of foreign influence. The Italian cathedral in Tripoli became a mosque, street signs were converted to Arabic, nightclubs were closed, and the production and sale of alcohol were prohibited.

But Qadhafi's revolution went far beyond changing names. In a three-volume work entitled *The Green Book*, he described his vision of the appropriate political system for Libya. Political parties would not be allowed, nor would constitutions, legislatures, even an organized court system. All of these institutions, according to Qadhafi, eventually become corrupt and unrepresentative. Instead, "people's committees" would run the government, business, industry, and even the universities. The country was renamed the Socialist People's Libyan Arab Jamahiriya, and titles of government officials were eliminated. Qadhafi became "Leader of the Revolution," and each government department was headed by the secretary of a particular people's committee.

Qadhafi then developed a so-called Third International Theory, based on the belief that neither capitalism nor communism could solve the world's problems. What was needed, he said, was a "middle way" that would harness the driving forces of human history—religion and nationalism—to interact with each other to revitalize humankind. Islam would be the source of that middle way because "it provides for the realization of justice and equity, it does not allow the rich to exploit the poor."

THE ECONOMY

Modern Libya's economy is based almost entirely on oil exports. Concessions were granted to various foreign companies to explore for oil in 1955, and the first oil strikes were made in 1957. Within a decade, Libya had become the world's fourth-largest exporter of crude oil. During the 1960s pipelines were built from the oil fields to new export terminals on the Mediterranean coast.

After the 1969 Revolution, Libya became a leader in the drive by oil-producing countries to gain control over their petroleum industries. The process began in 1971, when the new Libyan government took over the interests of British Petroleum in Libya. The Libyan method of nationalization was to proceed against individual companies rather than to take on the "oil giants" all at once. It took more than a decade before the last company, Exxon, capitulated.

FREEDOM

The General People's Congress (GPC) has the responsibility for passing laws and appointing a government. In 1994 the GPC approved legislation making Islamic law applicable in the country. They concerned retribution and blood money; rules governing wills, crimes of theft and violence, protection of society from things banned in the Koran, marriage, and divorce; and a ban on alcohol use.

Recent discoveries have increased Libya's oil reserves 30 percent, to 29.5 billion barrels, and recoverable natural-gas reserves to 1.6 billion cubic meters. With oil production reaching a record 1.4 million barrels per day, Libya has been able to build a strong petrochemical industry. The Marsa Brega petrochemical complex is one of the world's largest producers of urea, although a major contract with India was canceled in 1996 due to UN sanctions on trade with Libya.

Until recently, industrial-development successes based on oil revenues enabled Libyans to enjoy an ever-improving standard of living, and funding priorities were shifted from industry to agricultural development in the budget. But a combination of factors—mismanagement, lack of a cadre of skilled Libyan workers, absenteeism, low motivation of the workforce, and a significant drop in revenues (from $22 billion in 1980 to $7 billion in 1988)—cast doubts on the effectiveness of Qadhafi's *Green Book* socialistic economic policies.

In 1988 the leader began closing the book. In 1990 the General People's Congress (GPC), Libya's equivalent of a parliament, began a restructuring of government, adding new secretariats (ministries) to help expand economic development and diversity the economy.

HEALTH/WELFARE

In addition to 1 million sub-Saharan African workers, Libya has made use of skilled workers as well as unskilled ones from many other Arab countries. Palestinian workers were expelled after the 1993 Oslo Agreement with Israel, which Qadhafi opposed vehemently. A GPC regulation issued in 2001 fixed the total number of skilled foreign workers at 40,000.

In January 2000 Qadhafi abolished most of the secretariats and transferred their powers to "provincial cells" outside of Tripoli. Only five government functions—finance, defense, foreign affairs, information, and African unity—would remain under central-government control. For the first time he named a prime minister, Mubarak al-Shamekh, to head the stripped-down government. These changes came as the country needed to meet several challenges. For example, difficult climatic conditions and little arable land severely limit agricultural production; the country must import 75 percent of its food.

AN UNCERTAIN FUTURE

The revolutionary regime has been more successful than the monarchy was in making the wealth from oil revenues available to ordinary Libyans. Per capita income, which was $2,170 the year after the revolution, had risen to $10,900 by 1980.

This influx of wealth changed the lives of the people in a very short period of time. Extensive social-welfare programs, such as free medical care, free education, and low-cost housing, have greatly enhanced the lives of many Libyans. However, this wealth has yet to be spread evenly across society.

Qadhafi's principal support base rests on the armed forces and the "revolutionary committees," formed of youths whose responsibility is to guard against infractions of *The Green Book* rules.

ACHIEVEMENTS

The Great Man-Made River (GMR), called by Qadhafi the world's eighth wonder, went into its full operational phase in 2003, when subsurface water from deep in the Sahara Desert began flowing to Libya's cities through a network of 13-foot-diameter pipes from pumping stations. Excess water from the $27 billion project is to be stored in the Kufra basin, which has a capacity of 5,000 cubic meters. Pipeline blowouts continue to hamper completion. Once these problems are solved, water of 200 million cubic feet per day will flow. Without the support of the GMR, Libya would remain essentially uninhabitable.

Timeline: PAST

1835
Tripoli becomes an Ottoman province with the Sanusiya controlling the interior

1932
Libya becomes an Italian colony, Italy's "Fourth Shore"

1951
An independent kingdom is set up by the UN under King Idris

1969
The Revolution overthrows Idris; the Libyan Arab Republic is established

1973–1976
Qadhafi decrees a cultural and social revolution with government by people's committees

1980s
A campaign to eliminate Libyan opponents abroad; the United States imposes economic sanctions in response to suspected Libya-terrorist ties; U.S. planes attack targets in Tripoli and Benghazi; Libyan troops are driven from Chad, including the Aouzou Strip

1990s
Libya's relations with its neighbors improve; the UN votes to impose sanctions on Libya for terrorist acts; Qadhafi comes to an agreement with the UN regarding the trial of the PanAm/Lockerbie bombing suspects

PRESENT

2000s
Qadhafi makes changes to governmental structure

FOREIGN POLICY

Libya's relations with the United States have remained hostile since the 1969 Revolution, which not only overthrew King Idris but also resulted in the closing of the important Wheelus Field air base. Despite Qadhafi's efforts in more recent years to portray himself and Libya as respectable members of the world of nations, the country remains on the U.S. Department of State's list as one of the main sponsors of international terrorism.

However, Libya has made a series of efforts to repair the damage done to its image. In December 2003 Libya announced that it would abandon its programs to develop weapons of mass destruction, and in January of 2004 Libya agreed to compensate families of victims of the 1989 bombing of the French passenger aircraft over the Sahara desert. In August 2004 Libya agreed to pay 35 million to compensate victims of the bombing of a Berlin nightclub in 1986. In recognition of these efforts, and to the surprise of many observers, British Prime Minister Tony Blair visited Libya in March 2004 and met with Libyan leader Muammar Gaddafi. It was the first visit since 1943.

PROSPECTS

The tide of fundamentalism sweeping across the Islamic world and challenging secular regimes has largely spared Libya thus far, although there were occasional clashes between fundamentalists and police in the 1980s, and in 1992 some 500 fundamentalists were jailed briefly. However, the bloody civil uprisings against the regimes in neighboring Algeria and Egypt caused Qadhafi in 1994 to reemphasize Libya's Islamic nature. New laws passed by the General People's Congress would apply Islamic law (Shari'a) and punishments in such areas as marriage and divorce, wills and inheritance, crimes of theft and violence (where the Islamic punishment is cutting off a hand), and for apostasy. Libya's tribal-based society and Qadhafi's own interpretation of Islamic law to support women's rights and to deal with other social issues continue to serve as obstacles to Islamic fundamentalism.

While Libya currently has normal relations with Europe, the United States continues to insist that the country is a sponsor of global terrorism. In July 2001 the U.S. Senate approved a five-year extension of the Iran-Libya Sanctions Act (ILSA). The act bars U.S. companies from doing business in Libya, imposing fines for those investing more than $20 million in Libyan development projects. But in December 2003 Qadhafi again confounded his critics by agreeing to discontinue Libya's nuclear weapons development program and open its facilities to international inspection. The country also signed the Nuclear Non-Proliferation Treaty. In March 2004 the Libyan leader ordered 3,300 chemical bombs destroyed and agreed to halt further production.

Although he remains hostile to the United States and equally to Israel, Qadhafi has cultivated an image of respectability in recent years and has vigorously promoted African unity.

NOTES

1. "[I]rrigation, colonization and hard work have wrought marvels. Everywhere you see plantations forced out of the sandy, wretched soil." A. H. Broderick, *North Africa* (London: Oxford University Press, 1943), p. 27.

2. Religious leaders issued a *fatwa* ("binding legal decision") stating that a vote against independence would be a vote against religion. Omar el Fathaly, et al., *Political Development and Bureaucracy in Libya* (Lexington, KY: Lexington Books, 1977).

3. See *Middle East Journal*, vol. 24, no. 2 (Spring 1970), Documents Section.

4. John Wright, *Libya: A Modern History* (Baltimore, MD: Johns Hopkins University Press, 1982), pp. 124–126. Qadhafi's idol was former Egyptian president Nasser, a leader in the movement for unity and freedom among the Arabs. While he was at school in Sebha, in the Fezzan, he listened to Radio Cairo's Voice of the Arabs and was later expelled from school as a militant organizer of demonstrations.

5. *The London Times* (June 6, 1973).

6. Khidr Hamza, with Jeff Stein, *Saddam's Bombmaker* (New York: Scribner's, 2000), p. 289. The author was head of the Iraqi nuclear-weapons program before defecting to Libya and eventually the United States.

7. Donald G. McNeil Jr., in *The New York Times* (February 1, 2001).

Malaysia

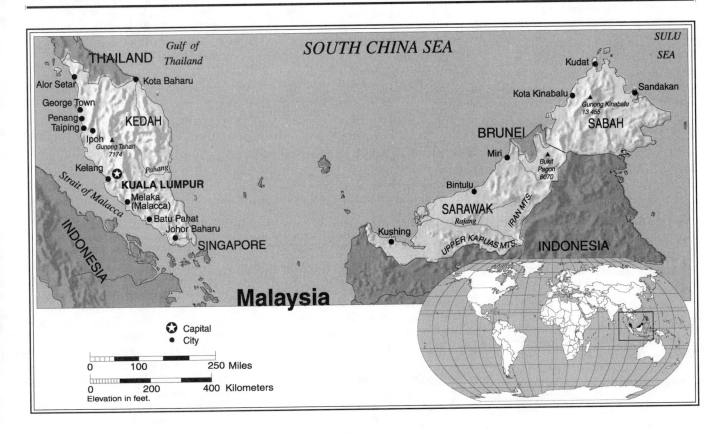

Malaysia Statistics

GEOGRAPHY

Area in Square Miles (Kilometers): 121,348
(329,750) (slightly larger than New
Mexico)

Capital (Population): Kuala Lumpur
(1,410,000)

Environmental Concerns: air and water
pollution; deforestation; smoke/haze
from Indonesian forest fires

Geographical Features: coastal plains
rising to hills and mountains

Climate: tropical; annual monsoons

PEOPLE

Population

Total: 23,522,482

Annual Growth Rate: 1.83%

Rural/Urban Population Ratio: 43/57

Major Languages: Peninsular Malaysia:
Bahasa Malaysia, English, Chinese
dialects, Tamil; Sabah: English, Malay,
numerous tribal dialects, Mandarin and
Hakka dialects; Sarawak: English,
Malay, Mandarin, numerous tribal
dialects, Arabic, others

Ethnic Makeup: 58% Malay and other
indigenous; 26% Chinese; 7% Indian;
9% others

Religions: Peninsular Malaysia: Malays
nearly all Muslim, Chinese mainly
Buddhist, Indians mainly Hindu; Sabah:
33% Muslim, 17% Christian, 45%
others; Sarawak: 35% traditional
indigenous, 24% Buddhist and
Confucian, 20% Muslim, 16% Christian,
5% others

Health

Life Expectancy at Birth: 69 years (male);
74 years (female)

Infant Mortality: 19.6/1,000 live births

Physicians Available: 1/2,153 people

HIV/AIDS in Adults: 0.42%

Education

Adult Literacy Rate: 88%

Compulsory (Ages): 6–16; free

COMMUNICATION

Telephones: 4,600,000 main lines

Daily Newspaper Circulation: 139 per
1,000 people

Televisions: 454 per 1,000 people

Internet Users: 5,700,000

TRANSPORTATION

Highways in Miles (Kilometers): 38,803
(64,672)

Railroads in Miles (Kilometers): 1,116
(1,800)

Usable Airfields: 116

Motor Vehicles in Use: 3,948,000

GOVERNMENT

Type: constitutional monarchy

Independence Date: August 31, 1957
(from the United Kingdom)

Head of State/Government: Paramount
Ruler Tuanku Syed Sirajuddin ibni
Almarhum Tuanku Syed Putra
Jamalullail; Prime Minister Abdullah bin
Ahmad Badawi

Political Parties: Peninsular Malaysia: National Front and others; Sabah: National Front and others; Sarawak: National Front and others

Suffrage: universal at 21

MILITARY

Military Expenditures (% of GDP): 2%

Current Disputes: complex dispute over the Spratly Islands; Sabah is claimed by the Philippines; other territorial disputes

ECONOMY

Currency ($ U.S. Equivalent): 3.80 ringgits = $1
Per Capita Income/GDP: $9,000/$207 billion
GDP Growth Rate: 5.2%
Inflation Rate: 1.5%
Unemployment Rate: 3.6%
Population Below Poverty Line: 8%
Natural Resources: tin; petroleum; timber; natural gas; bauxite; iron ore; copper; fish
Agriculture: rubber; palm oil; rice; coconut oil; pepper; timber

Industry: rubber and palm oil manufacturing and processing; light manufacturing; electronics; tin mining and smelting; logging and timber processing; petroleum; food processing

Exports: $98.4 billion (primary partners United States, Singapore, Japan)

Imports: $74.4 billion (primary partners Japan, United States, Singapore)

SUGGESTED WEB SITE

http://ianchai.50megs.com/
malaysia.html

Malaysia Country Report

About the size of Japan and famous for its production of natural rubber and tin, Malaysia sounds like a true political, economic, and social entity. Although it has all the trappings of a modern nation-state, Malaysia is one of the most fragmented nations on Earth.

Consider its land. West Malaysia, wherein reside 86 percent of the population, is located on the Malay Peninsula between Singapore and Thailand; but East Malaysia, with 60 percent of the land, is located on the island of North Borneo, some 400 miles of ocean away.

DEVELOPMENT

Efforts to move the economy away from farming and toward industrial production have been very successful. Manufacturing now accounts for 30% of GDP, and Malaysia is the third-largest producer of semiconductors in the world. With Thailand, Malaysia will build a $1.3 billion, 530-mile natural-gas pipeline.

Similarly, Malaysia's people are divided along racial, religious, and linguistic lines. Fifty-eight percent are Malays and other indigenous peoples, many of whom adhere to the Islamic faith or animist beliefs; 26 percent are Chinese, most of whom are Buddhist, Confucian, or Taoist; 7 percent are Indians, and 9 percent are Pakistanis and others, some of whom follow the Hindu faith. Bahasa Malaysia is the official language, but English, Arabic, two forms of Chinese, Tamil, and other languages are also spoken. Thus, although the country is called Malaysia (a name adopted only 35 years ago), many people living in Kuala Lumpur, the capital, or in the many villages in the countryside have a stronger

identity with their ethnic group or village than with the country of Malaysia per se.

Malaysian culture is further fragmented because each ethnic group tends to replicate the architecture, social rituals, and norms of etiquette peculiar to itself.

FREEDOM

Malaysia is attempting to govern according to democratic principles. Ethnic rivalries, however, severely hamper the smooth conduct of government and limit such individual liberties as the right to form labor unions. Evidence of undemocratic tactics, such as the government's treatment and imprisonment of ex-Deputy Prime Minister Anwar Ibrahim, bring out large numbers of protestors.

Malaysia was able to gain its colonial independence when the Japanese defeated the British in Southeast Asia during World War II.

After the war, Malaysian demands for independence from European domination grew more persuasive.

The three main ethnic groups—Malayans, comprised of 41 different Malay groups and represented by the United Malay National Organization (UMNO); Chinese, represented by the Malayan Chinese Association, or MCA; and Indians, represented by the Malayan Indian Congress, or MIC—were able to cooperate long enough in 1953 to form a single political party under the leadership of Abdul Rahman. This party demanded and received complete independence for the Federation in 1957, although some areas, such as Brunei, refused to join. Upon independence, the Federation of Malaya (not yet called Malaysia), became a member of the British Common-

wealth of Nations and was admitted to the United Nations.

Political troubles stemming from the deep ethnic divisions in the country, however, remain a constant feature of Malaysian life. With 9 of the 13 states controlled by independent sultans, every election is a test of the ability of the National Front, a multiethnic coalition of 11 different parties. As in the 2004 elections, the National Front held almost 80 percent of the 219-seat federal parliament and scored victories in regional races as well. The strong showing was apparently in reaction to the efforts of Islamic fundamentalists to win control and transform Malaysia into an Islamic state. In addition, voters seemed pleased with the efforts of their secular prime minister, Abdullah Ahmad Badawi, whose low-key, rational approach to politics was a refreshing break from the combative nationalism of his predecessor, Mahathir Mohamad. Despite the current success of the National Front coalition, it will continue to be difficult for any government to maintain political stability.

ECONOMIC DEVELOPMENT

For years, Malaysia's "miracle" economy kept social and political instability in check. Although it had to endure normal fluctuations in market demand for its products, the economy grew at 5 to 8 percent per year from the 1970s to the late 1990s, making it one of the world's top 20 exporters/importers. The manufacturing sector developed to such an extent that it accounted for 70 percent of exports. Then in 1998 a financial crisis hit. Malaysia was forced to devalue its currency, the ringgit, making it more difficult for consumers to buy foreign products, and dramatically slowing the economy.

Malaysia

HEALTH/WELFARE

City dwellers have ready access to educational, medical, and social opportunities, but the quality of life declines dramatically in the countryside. Malaysia has one of the highest illiteracy rates in the Pacific Rim. It spends only a small percentage of its GDP on education.

Malaysia continues to be rich in raw materials; therefore, it is not likely that the crisis of the late 1990s will permanently cripple its economy. Moreover, the Malaysian government has a good record of active planning and support of business ventures—directly modeled after Japan's export-oriented strategy. Malaysia launched a "New Economic Policy" (NEP) in the 1970s that welcomed foreign direct investment and sought to diversify the economic base. Japan, Taiwan, and the United States invested heavily in Malaysia. So successful was this strategy that economic-growth targets set for the mid-1990s were actually achieved several years early. In 1991 the government replaced NEP with a new plan, "Vision 2020." Its goal was to bring Malaysia into full "developed nation" status by the year 2020. Sectors targeted for growth included the aerospace industry, biotechnology, microelectronics, and information and energy technology. The government expanded universities and encouraged the creation of some 170 industrial and research parks, including "Free Zones," where export-oriented businesses were allowed duty-free imports of raw materials. Some of Malaysia's most ambitious projects, including a $6 billion hydroelectric dam (strongly opposed by environmentalists), have been shelved, at least until the full effects of the Asian financial crisis are overcome. That may not be long, for while the economy nose-dived, the growth rate has picked up and occasionally even exceeded the average world growth rate of 4 percent.

Despite Malaysia's substantial economic successes, serious social problems remain. They stem not from insufficient revenues but from inequitable distribution of wealth. The Malay portion of the population in particular continues to feel economically deprived as compared to the more affluent Chinese and Indian segments. Furthermore, most Malays are farmers, and rural areas have not benefited from Malaysia's economic boom as much as urban areas have.

ACHIEVEMENTS

Malaysia has made impressive economic advancements, and its New Economic Policy (NEP) has resulted in some redistribution of wealth to the poorer classes. Malaysia has been able to recover from the Asian financial crisis of the late 1990s and now expects solid GDP growth. The country has also made impressive social and political gains.

Nonetheless, social goals have been attained to a greater extent than most observers have thought possible. Educational opportunities for the poor have been increased, farmland development has proceeded on schedule, and the poverty rate has dropped below 10 percent.

THE LEADERSHIP

In a polity so fractured as Malaysia's, one would expect rapid turnover among political elites, but for over a decade, Malaysia was run, sometimes ruthlessly, by Malay Prime Minister Mahathir Mohamad of the United Malay Naitonal Organization. Most Malaysians were relieved that his aggressive nationalistic rhetoric was usually followed by more moderate behavior vis-à-vis other countries. The Chinese Democratic Action Party (DAP) was sometimes able to reduce his political strength in Parliament, but his successful economic strategies muted most critics.

However, in late 2003 Mahathir resigned due to scandals. Another Malay, Abdullah Ahmad Badawi, whose resistance to the creation of an Islamic state won him respect from the majority of the people, including many moderate Muslims, replaced him.

Timeline: PAST

A.D. 1403
The city of Malacca is established; it becomes a center of trade and Islamic conversion

1511
The Portuguese capture Malacca

1641
The Dutch capture Malacca

1824
The British obtain Malacca from the Dutch

1941
Japan captures the Malay Peninsula

1948
The British establish the Federation of Malaya; a communist guerrilla war begins, lasting for a decade

1957
The Federation of Malaya achieves independence under Prime Minister Tengku Abdul Rahman

1963
The Federation of Malaysia, including Singapore but not Brunei, is formed

1965
Singapore leaves the Federation of Malaysia

1980s
Malaysia attempts to build an industrial base

1990s
The NEP is replaced with Vision 2020; economic crisis

PRESENT

2000s
The economy rebounds; the environment suffers; former deputy prime minister Anwar Ibrahim is arrested and convicted under questionable circumstances; the World Court awards two tiny Celebes Sea islands to Malaysia in a dispute with Indonesia; Abdullah Ahmad Badawi replaces Mahathir Mohamad as prime minister; ex-deputy prime minister Anwar Ibrahim's conviction is overturned; he vows to push for democratic reforms

Maldives (Republic of Maldives)

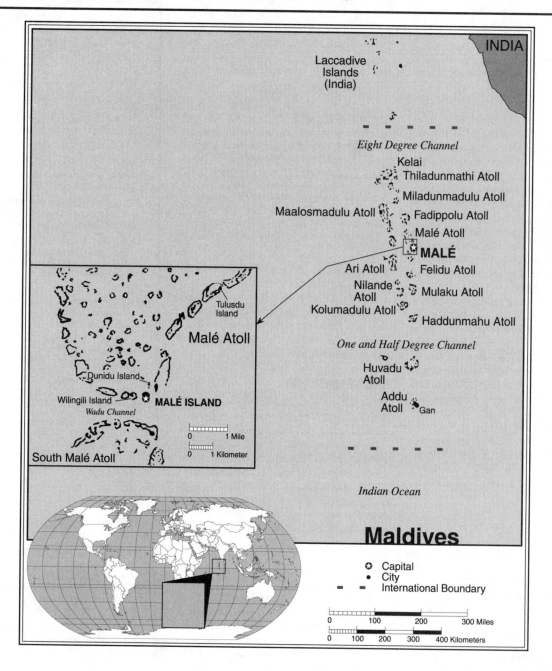

Maldives Statistics

GEOGRAPHY

Area in Square Miles (Kilometers): 186 (300) (about 1 1/2 times the size of Washington, D.C.)

Capital (Population): Malé (84,000)

Environmental Concerns: depletion of freshwater aquifers; global warming and sea-level rise; coral-reef bleaching

Geographical Features: flat, with white sandy beaches

Climate: tropical; hot; humid; monsoon

PEOPLE

Population

Total: 339,330
Annual Growth Rate: 2.86%
Rural/Urban Population Ratio: 73/27

Major Languages: Maldivian Dhivehi; English is spoken by most government officials

Ethnic Makeup: South Indians; Sinhalese; Arab

Religion: 100% Sunni Muslim

Health

Life Expectancy at Birth: 62.41 years (male); 65.01 years (female)

Infant Mortality: 58.32/1,000 live births
Physicians Available: 1/2,587 people
HIV/AIDS Rate in Adults: 0.1%

Education
Adult Literacy Rate: 97.2%

COMMUNICATION
Telephones: 28,700 main lines
Daily Newspaper Circulation: 32 per 1,000 people
Televisions: 19 per 1,000 people
Internet Users: 15,000 (2001)

TRANSPORTATION
Highways in Miles (Kilometers): 6 (9.6) in city of Malé
Railroads in Miles (Kilometers): none
Usable Airfields: 5

GOVERNMENT
Type: republic

Independence Date: July 26, 1965 (from the United Kingdom)
Head of State/Government: President Maumoon Abdul Gayoom is both head of state and head of government
Political Parties: although political parties are not banned, none exist
Suffrage: universal at 21

MILITARY
Military Expenditures (% of GDP): 8.6%
Current Disputes: none

ECONOMY
Currency ($ U.S. Equivalent): 12.8 rufiyaas = $1
GDP-Per Capita: purchasing power parity—$3,900
GDP Growth Rate: 2.3% (2001)
Inflation Rate: 1%
Unemployment Rate: negligible

Labor Force by Occupation: 60% services; 22% agriculture; 18% industry
Natural Resource: fish
Agriculture: fish; corn; coconuts; sweet potatoes
Industry: tourism; fish processing; shipping; boat building; coconut processing; garments; woven mats; rope; handicrafts; coral and sand mining
Exports: $90 million (primary partners United States, Thailand, Japan, Indonesia, United Kingdom, Sri Lanka)
Imports: $392 million (primary partners Singapore, India, Sri Lanka)

SUGGESTED WEB SITES
http://www.maldive.com/hist/
   mhisto.html
http://www.cia.gov/cia/
   publications/factbook/geos/
   mv.html
http://www.undp.org/missions/
   maldives
http://southasia.net/Maldives/

Maldives Country Report

Maldives is a string of 1,190 tiny tropical islands grouped into 26 atolls in the Indian Ocean about 400 miles southwest of India. The island chain stretches 510 miles north to south across the equator. The largest of the islands is less than five square miles in area, and the highest elevation is only 80 feet above sea level. Most of the islands are much smaller, rising barely six feet above sea level. They were easily submerged under the tsunami waves in 2004, and more frequently by storm swells. Because of a shortage of freshwater and arable land on most of the islands, only 200 of them are inhabited. About one-fifth of the total population of 339,330 live in the capital city on the island of Malé, which is just seven-tenths of a square mile.

DEVELOPMENT

A major economic activity of this nation of islands is fishing, which provides about 20% of its gross domestic product. Tourism has gained tremendously in importance and is attracting foreign investment. Maldives' gross domestic product per capita, though still low, has increased dramatically since 1960.

The earliest inhabitants of Maldives came from south India and Sri Lanka. The prevailing language of the islands is evidence of early Buddhist settlement. Because the Maldive islands lie across the maritime trade route between Africa and

East Asia, Arab traders often stopped there. The arrival of an Islamic Sufi saint in 1153 A.D. led to the conversion of the people to Islam. Today, citizenship is restricted to Sunni Muslims, and the country's legal system is based on Shari'a, the Islamic law.

FREEDOM

Maldives became a democratic republic in 1968. It adopted a popularly elected unicameral legislature and made provisions for an independently elected president, but it prohibited the formation of political parties. Rights of citizenship in Maldives, an Islamic nation, are restricted to Sunni Muslims.

THE RISE OF DEMOCRACY

Strongly united under the authority of a sultan (an Islamic monarch), the Maldivians remained fiercely independent through the centuries. Maldives became a protectorate under the British crown in 1887. Even then, the Maldivian leaders did not permit British interference in local governance. In 1953, the sultan, Muhammad Amin Didi, declared Maldives a democratic republic, with himself as president. But the power of governance remained with an appointed "Regency Committee."

Economic Development

President Gayoom's government benefited the people of Maldives in many ways. Enlightened economic policies encouraged

Timeline: PAST

300 B.C.
The earliest evidence of Indian Buddhist civilization

A.D. 1153
Conversion to Islam in Maldives

1153–1968
Maldives is an Islamic sultanate; Bodu Muhammed Takurufanu repulses brief Portuguese intrusion to the islands in 1573

1887–1968
Maldives is a British protectorate

1968
Maldives becomes an independent democratic republic without political parties

1988
An attempted coup is put down by the Indian Army

1990s
The government seeks to improve social services, incurring substantial debt in the process; Maldives agitates for global environmental responsibility

PRESENT

2000s
At the Coral Reef Symposium in October 2000, Maldives' marine environment is cited as heavily damaged by global warming

2004
Public protest for greater democracy leads to declaration of a state of emergency; tsunami kills 82, causes extensive damage to tourist and fishing industries

significant growth in the fishing and tourism industries. Almost half of the country's workforce is employed in fishing, mostly using traditional craft called *dhonis*.

HEALTH/WELFARE

Health and educational services are hard to provide to a population widely dispersed among the habitable islands of the country. Still, the government has developed an emergency rescue service that is able to reach 97% of the population. The average overall life expectancy is 63 years.

These industries, even with a reviving coconut crop and a modest shipping fleet, do not balance the import needs of the country, especially for food. The country receives more than 20 percent of its revenue as foreign aid, and it continues to accumulate debt. Like most regions of the world dependent upon tourism, Maldives' fortunes are based upon the prosperity of wealthier nations. With continuing foreign support, the country has sustained an impressive economic growth rate, around 7 percent since 1995, leading to the highest per capita income in South Asia.

ACHIEVEMENTS

Maldives has resisted superpower attempts to place a naval base on its territory. To preserve its fragile environment and its peace-loving character, the country has become a strong advocate to make the Indian Ocean an arms-free, and particularly a nuclear-free, zone.

The Maldivian government has also extended education and health services throughout the inhabited islands in the archipelago. Adult literacy has increased from 82 percent to 93 percent, a result of the outreach to the outer islands.

Maldives has no institutions of higher learning, and medical facilities are limited. There are only four hospitals in the country, plus an emergency medical rescue service among the outlying islands. The government, however, continues to work to improve water supplies and to eliminate water-borne diseases through water purification, desalinization, and other public-health measures.

Public Protest

Even with all of this beneficial support and growth, the people seek for greater democracy. The government responded initially by acts of suppression.

In November 1998 the Majlis amended the Constitution to guarantee citizens' civil rights, along with decentralizing government administration among the many islands of the country. In 2003 it established a human rights commission to look into reports of prison abuses.

Mali (Republic of Mali)

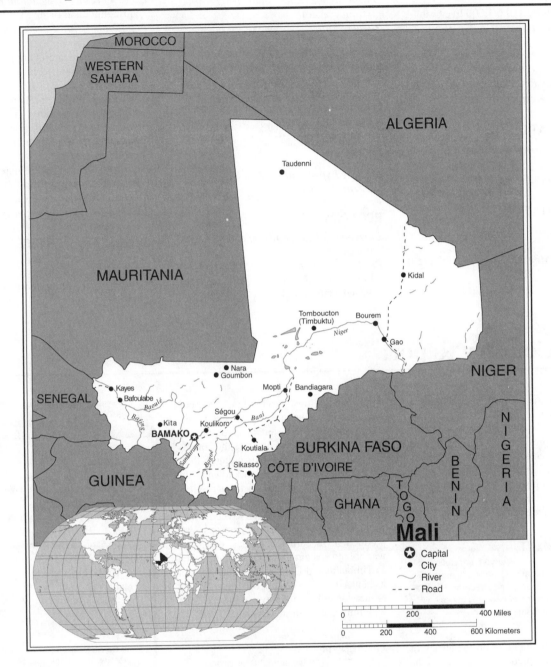

MOROCCO
WESTERN SAHARA
ALGERIA
Taudenni
MAURITANIA
Kidal
Tomboucton (Timbuktu)
Bourem
Niger
Gao
Nara
Goumbon
Mopti
Bandiagara
Kayes
Bafoulabe
Baoulé
Ségou
Bani
Kita
Koulikoro
BAMAKO
Koutiala
NIGER
Sikasso
BURKINA FASO
CÔTE D'IVOIRE
GUINEA
SENEGAL
GHANA
TOGO
BENIN
NIGERIA

Mali

⊛ Capital
● City
~ River
--- Road

0   200   400 Miles
0   200   400   600 Kilometers

Mali Statistics

GEOGRAPHY

Area in Square Miles (Kilometers): 478,819 (1,240,142) (about twice the size of Texas)

Capital (Population): Bamako (1,161,000)

Environmental Concerns: soil erosion; deforestation; desertification; insufficient potable water; poaching

Geographical Features: mostly flat to rolling northern plains covered by sand; savanna in the south; rugged hills in the northeast

Climate: subtropical to arid

PEOPLE

Population

Total: 11,956,788

Annual Growth Rate: 2.78%

Rural/Urban Population Ratio: 71/29

Major Languages: French; Bambara; numerous African languages

Ethnic Makeup: 50% Mande; 17% Peul; 12% Voltaic; 6% Songhai; 10% Tuareg and Maur (Moor); 5% others

Religions: 90% Muslim; 9% indigenous beliefs; 1% Christian

Health

Life Expectancy at Birth: 46 years (male);
48 years (female)
Infant Mortality: 119.6/1,000 live births
Physicians Available: 1/18,376 people
HIV/AIDS Rate in Adults: 1.7%

Education

Adult Literacy Rate: 38%
Compulsory (Ages): 7–16; free

COMMUNICATION

Telephones: 56,600 main lines
Televisions: 12 per 1,000 people
Internet Users: 25,000 (2002)

TRANSPORTATION

Highways in Miles (Kilometers): 9,362
(15,100)
Railroads in Miles (Kilometers): 452 (729)
Usable Airfields: 27
Motor Vehicles in Use: 41,000

GOVERNMENT

Type: republic
Independence Date: September 22, 1960
(from France)
Head of State/Government: President
Amadou Toumani Touré; Prime Minister
Ousmane Issoufi Maiga
Political Parties: Alliance for Democracy;
National Congress for Democratic
Initiative; Sudanese Union/African
Democratic Rally; others
Suffrage: universal at 18

MILITARY

Military Expenditures (% of GDP): 2%
Current Disputes: none

ECONOMY

Currency ($ U.S. Equivalent): 581 CFA
francs = $1
Per Capita Income/GDP: $900/$10.3
billion
GDP Growth Rate: 0.5%

Inflation Rate: 4.5%
Unemployment Rate: 14.6% in urban areas
Labor Force by Occupation: 80%
agriculture and fishing
Population Below Poverty Line: 64%
Natural Resources: hydropower; bauxite;
iron ore; manganese; tin; phosphates;
kaolin; salt; limestone; gold; uranium;
copper
Agriculture: millet; sorghum; corn; rice;
sugar; cotton; peanuts; livestock
Industry: food processing; construction;
phosphate and gold mining; consumer-
goods production
Exports: $575 million (primary partners
Brazil, South Korea, Italy)
Imports: $600 million (primary partners
Côte d'Ivoire, France, Senegal)

SUGGESTED WEB SITES

http://www.maliembassy-usa.org
http://www.cia.gov/cia/
publications/factbook/geos/
ml.html

Mali Country Report

Amadou Toumani Touré, the army general credited with rescuing Mali from military dictatorship and handing it back to its people, won the presidential elections of May 2002. He entered office on a program of anticorruption, peace, and development aimed at alleviation of poverty. This program resonated strongly with the population because corruption was viewed as rampant.

DEVELOPMENT

In 1989 the government received international funding to overhaul its energy infrastructure. The opening of new gold mines has provided the economy with a boost.

Touré will be building on the legacy of his immediate predecessor, Dr. Alpha Konare, who stepped down from power after two terms in office that moved Mali away from its authoritarian past. The current democratic order was inaugurated a year after a coup led by Touré ended the dictatorial regime of Moussa Traoré Konare, who ruled as an activist scholar. But his efforts to rebuild Mali were hampered by a weak economy, aggravated by the 1994 collapse in value of the CFA franc.

ENVIRONMENTAL CHALLENGES

Mali is one of the poorest countries in the world. About 80 percent of the people are employed in (mostly subsistence) agriculture and fishing, but the government usually has to rely on international aid to make up for local food deficits. Most of the country lies within either the expanding Sahara Desert or the semiarid region known as the Sahel, which has become drier as a result of recurrent drought. Much of the best land lies along the Senegal and Niger Rivers, which support most of the nation's agropastoral production. In earlier centuries, the Niger was able to sustain great trading cities such as Timbuktu and Djenne, but today most of its banks do not even support crops. Efforts to increase cultivation have so far been met with limited overall success.

FREEDOM

The human-rights situation in Mali has improved in recent years, though international attention was drawn to the suppression of opposition demonstrations in the run-up to the 1997 elections.

Mali's frequent inability to feed itself has been largely blamed on locust infestation, drought, and desertification. The inefficient state-run marketing and distribution systems, however, have also had a negative impact. Low official produce prices have encouraged farmers either to engage in subsistence agriculture or to sell their crops on the black

Timeline: PAST

1250–1400s
The Mali Empire extends over much of the upper regions of West Africa

late 1400s–late 1500s
The Songhai Empire controls the region

1890
The French establish control over Mali

1960
The Mali Confederation

1968
Moussa Traoré and the Military Committee for National Liberation grab power

1979
Traoré's Democratic Union of the Malian People is the single ruling party

1979–1980
School strikes and demonstrations; teachers and students are detained

1990s
The country's first multiparty elections are held; economic problems stir civic unrest

PRESENT

2000s
The Touré government explores ways to strengthen the economy; Ousmane Issoufi Maiga appointed prime minister

Courtesy of the Aga Khan Trust for Culture (ANIAA2744)
The Sankore Mosque in Timbuktu, Mali, was first built in the 14th to 15th centuries. At that time, this mosque was a major center of Islamic learning south of Africa's Sahara desert.

market. Thus, while some regions of the country remain dependent on international food donations, crops continue to be smuggled across Mali's borders. Recent policy commitments to liberalize agricultural trading, as part of an International Monetary Fund-approved Structural Adjustment Program (SAP), have yet to take hold.

HEALTH/WELFARE

About a third of Mali's budget is devoted to education. A special literacy program in Mali teaches rural people how to read and write, by using booklets that concern fertilizers, measles, and measuring fields.

In contrast to agriculture, Mali's mining sector has experienced promising growth. The nation exports modest amounts of gold, phosphates, marble, and uranium. Potentially exploitable deposits of bauxite, manganese, iron, tin, and diamonds exist. The Manantali Dam in southwestern Mali opened in December 2001. It is expected to provide electricity and jobs for thousands of Malians.

For decades, Mali was officially committed to state socialism. Its first president, Keita, established a command economy and one-party state during the 1960s. His attempt to go it alone outside the CFA Franc Zone proved to be a major failure. Under Traoré, socialist structures were modified but not abandoned. Agreements

ACHIEVEMENTS

For centuries, the ancient Malian city of Timbuktu was a leading center of Islamic learning and culture. Chronicles published by its scholars of the Middle Ages still enrich local culture.

with the IMF ended some government monopolies, and the country adopted the CFA franc as its currency. But the lack of a significant class of private entrepreneurs and the role of otherwise unprofitable public enterprises in providing employment discouraged radical privatization.

Courtesy of the Aga Khan Trust for Culture (ANIAA24369)
The Great Mosque in Djenne, Mali, was constructed with traditional clay and exhibits West African rather than international architectural mosque design. Djenne, which was two-hundred miles south of the major Islamic center of Timbuktu, became a commercial center to which goods were brought for import and export as well as for collection and distribution.

Mauritania (Islamic Republic of Mauritania)

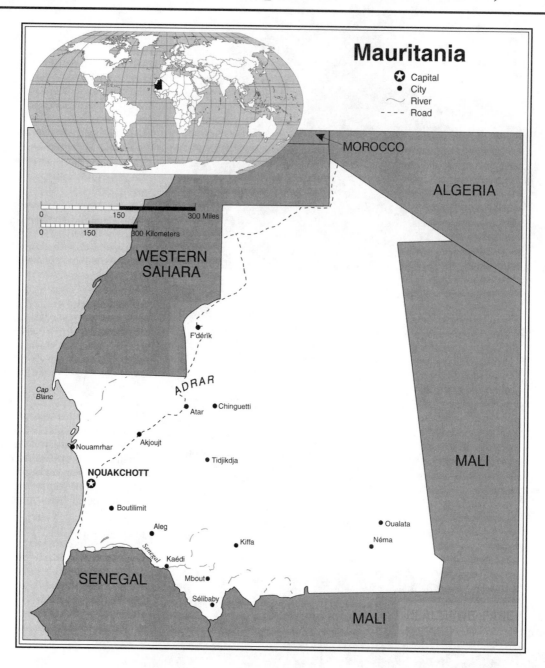

Mauritania
- ✪ Capital
- ● City
- ～ River
- --- Road

MOROCCO

ALGERIA

WESTERN SAHARA

F'dérîk

ADRAR

Cap Blanc

Atar ● Chinguetti

Nouamrhar Akjoujt

MALI

● Tidjikdja

NOUAKCHOTT

● Boutilimit

● Oualata

Aleg ● Kiffa ● Néma

Kaédi

SENEGAL Mbout

Sélibaby

MALI

Mauritania Statistics

GEOGRAPHY

Area in Square Miles (Kilometers): 398,000 (1,030,700) (about 3 times the size of New Mexico)

Capital (Population): Nouakchott (626,000)

Environmental Concerns: overgrazing; deforestation; soil erosion; desertification; very limited natural freshwater resources; overfishing

Geographical Features: mostly barren, flat plains of the Sahara; some central hills

Climate: desert

PEOPLE

Population

Total: 2,998,563

Annual Growth Rate: 2.92%

Rural/Urban Population Ratio: 44/56

Major Languages: Hasanixa; Soninke; Arabic; Pular; Wolof

Ethnic Makeup: 40% mixed Maur/black; perhaps 30% Maur; 30% black

Religion: 100% Muslim

Health

Life Expectancy at Birth: 49 years (male); 54 years (female)

Infant Mortality: 75.2/1,000 live births

Physicians Available: 1/11,085 people
HIV/AIDS Rate in Adults: 1.8%

Education

Adult Literacy Rate: 37.7%
Compulsory (Ages): 6–12

COMMUNICATION

Telephones: 31,500 main lines
Internet Users: 10,000 (2002)

TRANSPORTATION

Highways in Miles (Kilometers): 4,560
  (7,600)
Railroads in Miles (Kilometers): 422 (704)
Usable Airfields: 26
Motor Vehicles in Use: 26,500

GOVERNMENT

Type: republic

Independence Date: November 28, 1960
  (from France)
Head of State/Government: President
  Maaouya Ould Sid Ahmed Taya; Prime
  Minister Sghair Ould M'Bareck
Political Parties: Democratic and Social
  Republican Party; Union for Democracy
  and Progress; Popular Social and
  Democratic Union; others
Suffrage: universal at 18

MILITARY

Military Expenditures (% of GDP): 3.7%
Current Disputes: ethnic tensions

ECONOMY

Currency ($ U.S. equivalent): 276
  ouguiyas = $1
Per Capita Income/GDP: $1,800/$5 billion
GDP Growth Rate: %

Inflation Rate: 7%
Unemployment Rate: 21%
Labor Force by Occupation: 50%
  agriculture; 40% services; 10% industry
Population Below Poverty Line: 50%
Natural Resources: iron ore; gypsum; fish;
  copper; phosphates
Agriculture: millet; sorghum; dates; root
  crops; cattle and sheep; fish products
Industry: iron-ore and gypsum mining;
  fish processing
Exports: $359 million (primary partners
  France, Japan, Italy)
Imports: $335 million (primary partners
  France, United States, Spain)

SUGGESTED WEB SITE

http://www.cia.gov/cia/
  publications/factbook/geos/
  mr.html

Mauritania Country Report

Since the adoption of its current constitution in 1991, Mauritania has legally been a multiparty democracy. But in practice, power remains in the hands of President Ould Taya's Republican Social Democratic Party (PRDS). Multiparty politics has thus so far failed to assure either social harmony or a respect for human rights. Neither has it resolved the country's severe social and economic problems.

Amidst allegations of fraud, President Taya won the elections of November 2003 with more than 67 percent of the votes during the first round. There were attempted coups during June 2003 and August and September 2004. However, on August 3, 2005, Taya was finally removed from office by a military coup. Long-time police chief Colonel Ely Ould Mohamed Vall was named president. The military has promised to have free elections within two years. Regardless of who is in office many challenges will await.

DEVELOPMENT

Mauritania's coastal waters are among the richest in the world. During the 1980s the local fishing industry grew at an average annual rate of more than 10%. Many now believe that the annual catch has reached the upper levels of its sustainable potential.

For decades, Mauritania has grown progressively drier. Today, about 75 percent of the country is covered by sand. Less than 1 percent of the land is suitable for cultivation, 10 percent for grazing. To make matters worse, the surviving arable and pastoral areas have been plagued by grasshoppers and locusts.

FREEDOM

The Mauritanian government is especially sensitive to continuing allegations of the existence of chattel slavery in the country. While slavery is outlawed, there is credible evidence of its continued existence. In 1998 five members of a local advocacy group SOS-Esclaves (Slaves) were sentenced to 13 months' imprisonment for "activities within a non-authorized organization."

In the face of natural disaster, people have moved. Since the mid-1960s, the percentage of urban dwellers has swelled, from less than 10 percent to 53 percent, while the nomadic population during the same period has dropped, from more than 80 percent to perhaps 20 percent. In Nouakchott, the capital city, vast shanty-towns now house nearly a quarter of the population. As the capital has grown, from a few thousand to 626,000 in a single generation, its poverty—and that of the nation as a whole—has become more obvious. People seek new ways to make a living away from the land, but there are few jobs. The best hope for lifting up the economy may lie in offshore oil exploration. A prospecting report in 2002 has attracted the interest of major international oil companies.

Mauritania's heretofore faltering economy has coincided with an increase

Timeline: PAST

1035–1055
  The Almoravids spread Islam in the Western Sahara areas through conquest

1920
  The Mauritanian area becomes a French colony

1960
  Mauritania becomes independent under President Moktar Ould Daddah

1978
  A military coup brings Khouma Ould Haidalla and the Military Committee for National Recovery to power

1979
  The Algiers Agreement: Mauritania makes peace with Polisario and abandons claims to Western Sahara

1980
  Slavery is formally abolished

1990s
  Multiparty elections are boycotted by the opposition; tensions continue between Mauritania and Senegal

PRESENT

2000s
  Desertification takes its toll on the environment and the economy; it is estimated that 90,000 Mauritanians still live in servitude, despite the legal abolishment of slavery; Senegal and Mauritania seek better relations; President Taya re-elected to office; military coup removes Taya from office

in racial and ethnic tensions. Since independence, the government has been dominated by the Maurs (or Moors), who speak Hasaniya Arabic.

HEALTH/WELFARE

There have been some modest improvements in the areas of health and education since the country's independence, but conditions remain poor. Mauritania has received low marks regarding its commitment to human development.

The other half of Mauritania's population is composed of the "blacks," who mostly speak Pulaar, Soninke, or Wolof. Like the Maurs, all these groups are Muslim. Thus Mauritania's rulers have stressed Islam as a source of national unity. The country proclaimed itself an Islamic republic at independence, and since 1980 the Shari'a—the Islamic penal code—has been the law of the land.

Muslim brotherhood has not been able to overcome the divisions between the northern Maurs and southern blacks. One major source of friction has been official Arabization efforts, which are opposed by most southerners. In recent years, the country's desertification has created new sources of tension. As their pastures turned to sand, many of the Maurish nomads who did not find refuge in the urban areas moved southward. There, with state support, they began in the 1980s to deprive southerners of their land.

In recent years, the regime in Nouakchott has sent out conflicting sig-

ACHIEVEMENTS

There is a current project to restore ancient Mauritanian cities, such as Chinguette, which are located on traditional routes from North Africa to Sudan. These centers of trade and Islamic learning were points of origin for the pilgrimage to Mecca and were well known in the Middle East.

nals. Although the government has legalized some opposition parties, it has also continued to pursue its Arabization program and has clamped down on genuine dissent. Maur militias have been armed, and the army has been expanded with assistance from Arab countries.

Morocco (Kingdom of Morocco)

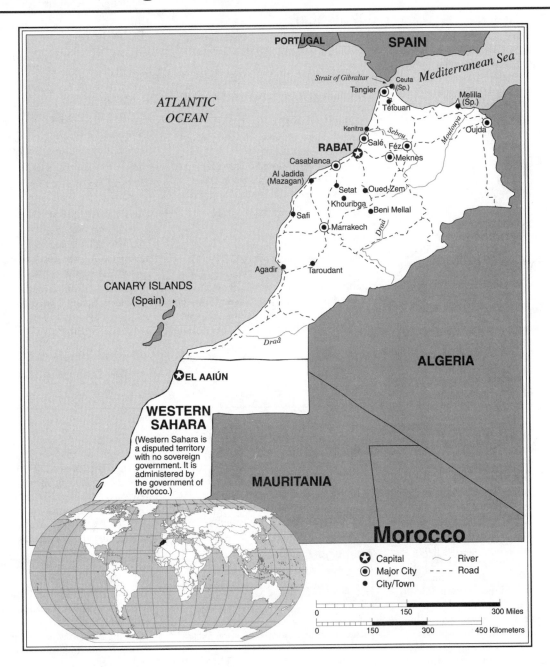

Morocco Statistics

GEOGRAPHY

Area in Square Miles (Kilometers): 274,400 (710,850) including the Western Sahara (102,675 [266,000]) about the size of California

Capital (Population): Rabat (1,293,000)

Environmental Concerns: Land degradation; desertification; soil erosion; overgrazing; contamination of water supplies; oil pollution of coastal waters

Geographical Features: the northern coast and interior are mountainous, with large areas of bordering plateaux, intermontane valleys, and rich coastal plains; south, southeast and entire Western Sahara is desert

Climate: varies from Mediterranean to desert

PEOPLE

Population

Total: 31,167,783
Annual Growth Rate: 1.68%
Rural/Urban Population Ratio: 47/53
Major Languages: Arabic; Tama-zight; various Berber dialects; French
Ethnic Makeup: 64% Arab; 35% Berber; 1% non-Morroccan and Jewish

Religions: 99% Sunni Muslim; 1%
  Christian and Jewish

Health

Life Expectancy at Birth: 67 years (male);
  72 years (female)
Infant Mortality Rate: 47/1,000 live births
Physicians Available (Ratio): 1/2,923
  people

Education

Adult Literacy Rate: 43.7%
Compulsory (Ages): 7–13

COMMUNICATION

Telephones: 1,515,000 main lines
Daily Newspaper Circulation: 13 per
  1,000 people
Televisions: 93 per 1,000 people
Internet Service Providers: 8 (2000)

TRANSPORTATION

Highways in Miles (Kilometers): 37,649
  (60,626)
Railroads in Miles (Kilometers): 1,184
  (1,907)

Usable Airfields: 69
Motor Vehicles in Use: 1,278,000

GOVERNMENT

Type: constitutional monarchy
Independence Date: March 2, 1956 (from
  France)
Head of State/Government: King
  Muhammad VI; Prime Minister Driss
  Jettou
Political Parties: National Rally of
  Independents; Popular Movement;
  National Democratic Party;
  Constitutional Union; Socialist Union of
  Popular Forces; Istiqlal; Kutla Bloc;
  Party of Progress and Socialism; others
Suffrage: universal at 21

MILITARY

Military Expenditures (% of GDP): 4%
Current Disputes: final resolution on the
  status of Western Sahara remains to be
  worked out; from time to time Morocco
  demands the retrocession of Ceuta and
  Melilla, cities located physically within

its territory but considered extensions of
mainland Spain (plazas de soberaniá by
the Spanish government)

ECONOMY

Currency ($ U.S. Equivalent): 9.37
  dirhams = $1
Per Capita Income/GDP: $3,500/$105
  billion
GDP Growth Rate: 8%
Inflation Rate: 2%
Unemployment Rate: 23%
Labor Force: 11,000,000
Natural Resources: phosphates, iron ore;
  manganese; lead; zinc; fish; salt
Agriculture: barley; wheat; citrus fruits;
  wine; vegetables; olives; livestock
Industry: phosphate mining and
  processing; food processing; leather
  goods; textiles; construction; tourism
Exports: $7.6 billion (primary partners
  France, Spain, United Kingdom)
Imports: $12.2 billion (primary partners
  France, Spain, Italy)

Morocco Country Report

The Kingdom of Morocco is the western-most country in North Africa. Morocco's population is the second largest (after Egypt) of the Arab states. The country's territory includes the Western Sahara (a claim made under dispute), formerly two Spanish colonies, Rio de Oro and Saguia al-Hamra. Morocco annexed part in 1976 and the balance in 1978, after Mauritania's withdrawal from its share, as decided in an agreement with Spain. Since then, Morocco has incorporated the Western Sahara into the kingdom as its newest province.

Two other territories physically within Morocco remain outside Moroccan control. They are the cities of Ceuta and Melilla, both located on rocky peninsulas that jut out into the Mediterranean Sea. They have been held by Spain since the fifteenth century. Spain's support for Morocco's admission to the European Union (EU) as an associate member has eased tensions between them over the enclaves.

Moroccan geography explains the country's dual population structure. About 35 percent of the population are Berbers, descendants of the original North Africans. The Berbers were, until recently, grouped into tribes, often taking the name of a common ancestor, such as the Ait ("Sons of") 'Atta of southern Morocco. Invading Arabs converted them to Islam in the eighth cen-

tury but made few other changes in Berber life. Unlike the Berbers, the majority of the Arabs who settled in Morocco were, and are, town-dwellers. The Berbers, more than the Arabs, derived unity and support from their extended families rather than from state control, whether real or putative.

DEVELOPMENT

Morocco has important reserves of phosphate rock, particularly in the Western Sahara. It also has exportable supplies of certain rare metal, such as antimony. Unfortunately it lacks oil resources. An oil strike in the Sahara in 2000 proved abortive. Abundant rainfall has improved agricultural production; GDP growth presently averages 5% annually.

HISTORY

Morocco has a rich cultural history, with many of its ancient monuments more or less intact. It has been governed by some form of monarchy for over a thousand years, although royal authority was frequently limited or contested by rivals. The current ruling dynasty, the Alawis, assumed power in the 1600s. One reason for their long rule is the fact that they descend from the Prophet Muhammad. Thus, Mo-

roccans have had a real sense of Islamic traditions and history through their rulers.

The first identifiable Moroccan "state" was established by a descendant of Muhammad named Idris, in the late eighth century. Idris had taken refuge in the far west of the Islamic world to escape civil war in the east. Because of his piety, learning, and descent from Muhammad, he was accepted by a number of Berber groups as their spiritual and political leader. His son and successor, Idris II, founded the first Moroccan capital, Fez. Father and son established the principle whereby descent from the Prophet was an important qualification for political power as well as social status in Morocco.

Also, in the eleventh and twelfth centuries, two Berber confederations developed that brought imperial grandeur to Morocco. These were the Almoravids and the Almohads. Under their rule, North Africa developed a political structure separate from that of the eastern Islamic world, one strongly influenced by Berber values.

The Almoravids began as camel-riding nomads from the Western Sahara who were inspired by a religious teacher to carry out a reform movement to revive the true faith of Islam. (The word *Almoravid* comes from the Arabic *al-Murabitun*, "men of the ribat," rather like the crusading

© CORBIS/Royalty-Free (DILDAF0013)

King Hassan II Mosque in Casablanca, Morocco, is named in honor of the country's former king, who ruled Morocco for thirty-eight years (1961–1999). This mosque in Morocco's most populous city is not only the largest in the country, but one of the largest in the world. The building also houses a *madrassah*, a library, and an exhibition hall.

religious orders of Christianity in the Middle Ages.) Fired by religious zeal, the Almoravids conquered all of Morocco and parts of western Algeria.

A second "imperial" dynasty, the Almohads, succeeded the Almoravids but improved on their performance. They were the first, and probably the last, to unite all of North Africa and Islamic Spain under one government. Almohad monuments, such as the Qutubiya tower, the best-known landmark of Marrakesh, and the Tower of Hassan in Rabat, still stand as reminders of their power and the high level of the Almohads' architectural achievements.

MULAY ISMAIL

The Alawis came to power and established their rule partly by force but also as a result of their descent from the Prophet Muham-mad. This link enabled them to win the support of both Arab and Berber populations. The real founder of the dynasty was Mulay Ismail, one of the longest-reigning and most powerful monarchs in Morocco's history.

Mulay Ismail unified the Moroccan nation. The great majority of the Berber groups accepted him as their sovereign. The sultan built watchtowers and posted permanent garrisons in Berber territories to make sure they continued to do so. He brought public security to Morocco also; it was said that in his time, a Jew or an unveiled woman could travel safely anywhere in the land, which was not the case in most parts of North Africa, the Middle East, and Europe.

In 1904 France, Britain, Spain, and Germany signed secret agreements partitioning the country. The French would be

FREEDOM

The "freest and fairest" elections in Moroccan history established a new 325-seat Chamber of Representatives equally balanced among the leading political parties. Some 35 women candidates were elected. King Muhammad VI's "National Action Plan" raises the legal marriageable age for women to 18 and gives other rights to them. In 2003 the king proposed revisions to the 1957 Mudawanna (Family Law), which were approved by the Chamber. Women now have the right to file for divorce, share equally in family property, and travel without prior consent from male family members.

given the largest part of the country, while Spain would receive the northern third as a protectorate plus some territory in the Western Sahara. In return, the French and

Spanish agreed to respect Britain's claim to Egypt and Germany's claim to East African territory.

The French protectorate over Morocco covered barely 45 years (1912–1956). But in that brief period, the French introduced significant changes into Moroccan life. For the first time, southern Morocco was brought entirely under central government control, although the "pacification" of the Berbers was not complete until 1934.

MOROCCO'S INDEPENDENCE STRUGGLE

The movement for independence in Morocco developed slowly. The only symbol of national unity was the sultan, Muhammad ibn Yusuf. But he seemed ineffectual to most young Moroccans, particularly those educated in French schools, who began to question the right of France to rule a people against their will.

The hopes of these young Moroccans got a boost during World War II. The Western Allies, Great Britain and the United States, had gone on record in favor of the right of subject peoples to self-determination after the war. When U.S. President Franklin D. Roosevelt and British Prime Minister Winston Churchill came to Casablanca for an important wartime conference, the sultan was convinced to meet them privately and get a commitment for Morocco's independence. The leaders promised their support.

In 1953 the French sent the sultan into exile, and named an elderly uncle as his replacement.

The sultan's departure had the opposite effect from what was intended. In exile, he became a symbol for Moroccan resistance to the protectorate. Violence broke out, French settlers were murdered, and a Moroccan Army of Liberation began battling French troops in rural regions. Although the French could probably have contained the rebellion in Morocco, they were under great pressure in neighboring Algeria and Tunisia, where resistance movements were also under way. In 1955 the French abruptly capitulated. Sultan Muhammad ibn Yusuf returned to his palace in Rabat in triumph.

INDEPENDENCE

Morocco became independent on March 2, 1956. It began its existence as a sovereign state with a number of assets—a popular ruler, an established government, and a well-developed system of roads, schools, hospitals, and industries inherited from the protectorate. Against these assets were the liabilities of age-old Arab-Berber and inter-Berber conflicts, little experience with political parties or democratic institutions, and an economy dominated by Europeans.

The sultan's goal was to establish a constitutional monarchy. His first action was to give himself a new title, King Muhammad V, symbolizing the end of the old autocratic rule of his predecessors.

Muhammad V did not live long enough to reach his goal. He died unexpectedly in 1961 and was succeeded by his eldest son, Crown Prince Hassan. Hassan II ruled until his death in 1999. While he fulfilled his father's promise immediately with a constitution, in most other ways Hassan II set his own stamp on Morocco.

The Constitution provided for an elected legislature and a multiparty political system. In addition to the Istiqlal, a number of other parties were organized, including one representing the monarchy. However, elections failed to produce a clear majority for any party, not even the king's.

In fact, following several attempts on his own life, Hassan II saw to a new constitution being issued in 1972 defining Morocco "as a democratic and social constitutional monarchy in which Islam is the established religion." However, the king retained the constitutional powers that, along with those derived from his spiritual role as "Commander of the Faithful" and lineal descendant of Muhammad, undergirded his authority.

HEALTH/WELFARE

In October 2000 the International Labor Organization (ILO) ranked Morocco as the third-highest country in the world, after China and India, in the exploitation of child labor. Moroccan children as young as five, all girls, are employed in the carpet industry, working up to 10 hours per day weaving the carpets that are at present Morocco's major source of foreign currency. In recent years, more and more Moroccan minors have been leaving their families and migrating illegally to Europe through the Spanish port city of Ceuta. Some 3,500 did so in 2002.

INTERNAL POLITICS

More recently, a referendum in 1996 approved several amendments to the constitution. One in particular replaced the unicameral legislature by a bicameral one. The Chamber of Representatives (lower house) is to be elected directly, for five-year terms. The Chamber of Counselors (upper house) is to be two-thirds elected and one-third appointed. In September 2002 elections were held for the 325-seat lower house. Some 26 parties, a dozen of them brand new, presented candidates.

The election results underlined the current broad spectrum of Moroccan politics. The Socialist Union of Popular Forces (USFP), headed by then prime minister

Youssoufi, won 50 seats, the venerable Istiqlal Party 48, the National Rally of Independents 41, and the National Popular Movement 27. The Party of Justice and Development, which had replaced the banned Islamist Justice and Development, won 42 seats; its predecessor had held only 18 in the outgoing Chamber. Also noteworthy was the election of 35 women; a quota of 30 had been reserved for them.

FOREIGN RELATIONS

During his long reign, King Hassan II served effectively in mediating the long-running Arab-Israeli conflict. He took an active part in the negotiations for the 1979 Egyptian-Israeli peace treaty and for the treaty between Israel and Jordan in 1994. For these services he came to be viewed by the United States and by European powers as an impartial mediator. However, his absolute rule and suppression of human rights at home caused difficulties with Europe. The European Union (EU) suspended $145 million in aid in 1992; it was restored only after Hassan had released long-time political prisoners and pardoned 150 alleged Islamic militants. In 1995 Morocco became the second African country, after Tunisia, to be granted associate status in the EU. In February 2003 a Casablanca court sentenced three Saudi members of al-Qaeda to 10 years in prison after they were accused of plotting to attack U.S. and British warships in the Straits of Gibraltar. In May 2003, 41 people were killed and many more injured in a series of suicide bomb attacks in the business capital of Casablanca. As a reward for their staunch support of U.S. policy and for their assistance, a free-trade agreement with the United States came into effect in July 2004. The deal followed Washington's designation of Morocco as a major non-NATO ally.

Thus far, Morocco's only venture in "imperial politics" has been in the Western Sahara. This California-size desert territory, formerly a Spanish protectorate and then a colony after 1912, was never a part of the modern Moroccan state. Its only connection is historical—it was the headquarters and starting point for the Almoravid dynasty, camel-riding nomads who ruled western North Africa and southern Spain in the eleventh century. But the presence of so much empty land, along with millions of tons of phosphate rock and potential oil fields, encouraged the king to "play international politics" in order to secure the territory. The 1975 Green March has been followed up by large-scale settlement of Moroccans there in the past two decades. Like the American West in the nineteenth century, it was Morocco's "last frontier." Moroccans were encouraged to move there, with government pledges of free land, tools, seeds, and equipment for farmers, as well as housing.

Since the 1976 partition, ownership of the Western Sahara has been challenged by the Polisario, an independence movement backed by Algeria. Acting under the aegis of its responsibility for decolonization and self-government of colonized peoples, the United Nations established a peacekeeping force for the Western Sahara (MINURSO) in 1991. A UN resolution thereafter called for a referendum that would give the population a choice between independence and full integration with Morocco. Voter registration would precede the referendum, in order to determine eligibility of voters.

A decade later, the referendum seems less and less likely to be held. King Hassan II unilaterally named the territory Morocco's newest province, and by 2001 Moroccan settlers formed a majority in the population of 244,593.

THE ECONOMY

Morocco has many of certain resources but too little of other, critical ones. It has two-thirds of the world's known reserves of phosphate rock and is the top exporter of phosphates. The major thrust in industrial development is in phosphate-related industries. Access to deposits was one reason for Morocco's annexation of the Western Sahara, although to date there has been little extraction there due to the political conflict. The downturn in demand and falling prices in the global phosphates market brought on a debt crisis in the late 1980s. Increased phosphate demand globally and improved crop production following the end of several drought years have strengthened the economy. Privatization of the government-owned tobacco monopoly, the first industry to be so affected, generated a budgetary surplus in 2002.

ACHIEVEMENTS

A Moroccan runner, Abdelkader Mouaziz, won the 31st New York City Marathon, two and one-half minutes ahead of his nearest rival. Another Moroccan, Youssef el Aynaoui, had become one of the world's premier tennis players and competed well in major tournaments before his retirement.

The country also has important but undeveloped iron-ore deposits and a small but significant production of rare metals such as mercury, antimony, nickel, and lead. In the past, a major obstacle to development was the lack of oil resources.

United Nations Photo (UN160937))

King Hassan II (1929–1999), also known as Hassan bin Mauhammad, ruled Morocco for 38 years (r. 1961–1999). He was opposed by Socialists, right-wing republicans (who want Morocco to be a republic), Islamists, and the Polisario Liberation Front in the Western Sahara. However, he was able to neutralize or crush the opposition through his astute politics, populist policies, and a pervasive security apparatus.

Although recurring droughts have hampered improvement of the agricultural sector, it still accounts for 20 percent of gross domestic product and employs 50 percent of the labor force. Production varies widely from year to year, due to fluctuating rainfall.

The fisheries sector is equally important to the economy, with 2,175 miles of coastline and half a million square miles of territorial waters to draw from. Fisheries account for 16 percent of exports; annual production is approximately 1 million tons. The agreement with the European Union for associate status has been very beneficial to the industry. Morocco received $500 million in 1999–2001 from European countries in return for fishing rights for their vessels in Moroccan territorial waters.

But the economic outlook and social prospects remain bleak for most people. Although the birth rate has been sharply reduced, job prospects are limited for the large number of young Moroccans entering the labor force each year. The "suicide bombers" who attacked a Jewish community center, a hotel, foreign consulates and other structures in Casablanca in May 2003, killing some 41 persons, were said to belong to the radical Islamist organization al-Sirat al-Mustakim (Righteous Path), believed to be linked with al-Qaeda. However, the fact that they came mostly from the impoverished Thomasville slum area of the city suggests that they acted not out of

a desire to overthrow the monarchy but out of frustration with the problems that face Morocco's youth today, namely unemployment, poverty, and lack of opportunities in the workplace.

PROSPECTS

King Hassan II died in July 1999. The king's eldest son, Crown Prince Muhammad, succeeded him without incident as Muhammad VI. Morocco's new ruler began his reign with public commitments to reform human-rights protections and an effort to atone for some aspects of Hassan's autocratic rule. The king's declared commitment to human rights and political reform have been undercut to a large extent by the repressive structure inherited from his father. This structure, comprising the security services, army leaders, and a coterie of senior ministers, is a major obstacle to civil change.

Timeline: PAST

788–790
The foundations of Moroccan nation are established by Idris I and II, with the capital at Fez

1062–1147
The Almoravid and Almohad dynasties, Morocco's "imperial period"

1672
The current ruling dynasty, the Alawi, establishes its authority under Mulay Ismail

1912
Morocco is occupied and placed under French and Spanish protectorates

1956
Independence under King Muhammad V

1961
The accession of King Hassan II

1975
The Green March into the Western Sahara dramatizes Morocco's claim to the area

1980s
Bread riots; agreement with Libya for a federal union; the king unilaterally abrogates the 1984 treaty of union with Libya

1990s
Elections establish parliamentary government; King Hassan dies and is succeeded by King Muhammad VI

PRESENT

2000s
King Muhammad VI works to improve human rights; the economic picture brightens

Muhammad VI also publicly admitted the existence of the Tazmamat "death camp" and other camps in the Sahara, where rebel army officers and political prisoners were held, often for years and without trial or access to their families. The new king also committed $3.8 million in compensation to the families of those who had been imprisoned.

The rise of Islamic fundamentalism as a political force is an obstacle to Muhammad VI's vision of Morocco. Hassan II kept fundamentalists on a tight rein. He suppressed the main Islamist movement, Adil wa Ihsan ("Justice and Charity"), and sent its leader to a mental institution. Hassan also used his religious credentials to pose as a fundamentalist leader of his people. Muhammad VI seems more willing to integrate the fundamentalists into the political structure. Recently he issued a "National Action Plan" guaranteeing rights for women, approving a free press, and promising other civil rights long absent from Moroccan society.

NOTES

1. Sue Miller, "Migration Station," *Christian Science Monitor,* June 26, 2003.
2. See David M. Hart, *Dadda 'Atta and His Forty Grandsons* (Cambridge, England: Menas Press, 1981), pp. 8–11. Dadda 'Atta was a historical figure, a minor saint or marabout.
3. See Malika Oufkir, with Michele Fitoussi, *Stolen Lives: Twenty Years in a Desert Jail* (New York: Hyperion Books, 1999). Another prisoner, Ahmed Marzouki, recently published his memoir of life there. Entitled *Cell 10,* it has sold widely in Morocco.

Mozambique (Republic of Mozambique)

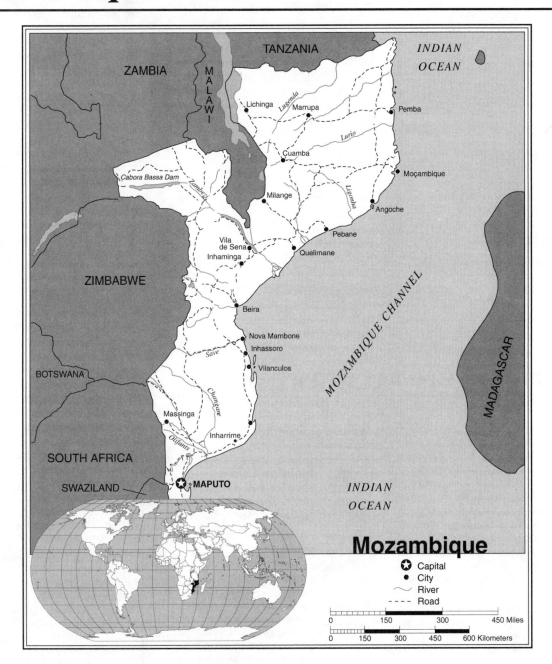

Mozambique Statistics

GEOGRAPHY

Area in Square Miles (Kilometers): 309,494
(801,590) (about twice the size of
California)

Capital (Population): Maputo (1,134,000)

Environmental Concerns: civil war and
drought have had adverse consequences
on the environment; water pollution;
desertification

Geographical Features: mostly coastal
lowlands; uplands in center; high
plateaus in northwest; mountains in west

Climate: tropical to subtropical

PEOPLE

Population

Total: 18,811,731

Annual Growth Rate: 1.22%

Rural/Urban Population Ratio: 61/39

Major Languages: Portuguese; indigenous
dialects

Ethnic Makeup: nearly 100% indigenous
groups

Religions: 50% indigenous beliefs; 30%
Christian; 20% Muslim

Health

Life Expectancy at Birth: 38 years (male);
37 years (female)
Infant Mortality: 138.5/1,000 live births
Physicians Available: 1/131,991 people
HIV/AIDS Rate in Adults: 12.6%–16.4%

Education

Adult Literacy Rate: 47.8%
Compulsory (Ages): 7–14

COMMUNICATION

Telephones: 83,700 main lines
Daily Newspaper Circulation: 8 per 1,000
people
Televisions: 3.5 per 1,000 people
Internet Users: 50,000 (2002)

TRANSPORTATION

Highways in Miles (Kilometers): 17,886
(29,810)
Railroads in Miles (Kilometers): 1,879
(3,131)
Usable Airfields: 166
Motor Vehicles in Use: 89,000

GOVERNMENT

Type: republic
Independence Date: June 25, 1975 (from
Portugal)
Head of State/Government: President
Joaquim Alberto Chissano; Prime
Minister Luisa Diogo
Political Parties: Front for the Liberation
of Mozambique (Frelimo); Mozambique
National Resistance—Electoral Union
(Renamo)
Suffrage: universal at 18

MILITARY

Military Expenditures (% of GDP): 1%
Current Disputes: none; cease-fire since
1992

ECONOMY

Currency ($ U.S. Equivalent): 23,467
meticais = $1
Per Capita Income/GDP: $1,200/$21.23
billion
GDP Growth Rate: 7%
Inflation Rate: 14%

Unemployment Rate: 21%
Labor Force by Occupation: 81%
agriculture; 13% services; 6% industry
Population Below Poverty Line: 70%
Natural Resources: coal; titanium; natural
gas; hydropower
Agriculture: cotton; cassava; cashews;
sugarcane; tea; corn; rice; fruits;
livestock
Industry: processed foods; textiles;
beverages; chemicals; tobacco; cement;
glass; asbestos; petroleum products
Exports: $795 million (primary partners
South Africa, Zimbabwe, Spain)
Imports: $1.14 billion (primary partners
South Africa, Portugal, United States)

SUGGESTED WEB SITES

```
http://
  www.mozambique.mz.eindex.htm
http://poptel.org.uk/mozambique-news
http://
  www.africaindex.africainfo.no/
  africaindex1/countries/
  mozambique.html
http://www.cia.gov/cia/
  publications/factbook/geos/
  mz.html
```

Mozambique Country Report

Mozambique has made steady economic and political progress over the past decade in the face of grinding poverty, natural disasters, and the immense burden of overcoming the legacy of a bitter civil war. Although many in the region note that the country has served as a kind of magnet for foreign investment, problems with human-rights issues remain with accusations of torture and harassment of any political opponent of the government. In June 2002 the ruling Mozambique Liberation Front (Frelimo) party chose Armando Guebuza, an independence-struggle veteran, as its presidential candidate for the December 2004 presidential elections, after its long-serving incumbent, Joaquim Chissano, declined to run again.

In February 2000 the eyes of the world focused on devastating floods in Mozambique. In some places the country's two main rivers, the Limpopo and Save, expanded miles beyond their normal banks, engulfing hundreds of villages and destroying property and infrastructure. Many Mozambicans were left homeless. The disaster was a serious setback for the nation, which had been making steady economic progress after three decades of civil war. Even before the floods, Mozambique (which remains one of the world's poorest countries) faced immense economic, political, and social challenges.

DEVELOPMENT

To maintain minimum services and to recover from wartime and flood destruction, Mozambique relies on the commitment of its citizens and international assistance. Western churches have sent relief supplies, food aid, and vehicles.

FREEDOM

While the status of political and civil liberties has improved, the government's overall human-rights record continues to be marred by security-force abuses (including extra-judicial killings, excessive use of force, torture, and arbitrary detention) and an ineffective and only nominally independent judicial system.

Frelimo originally came to power as a result of a liberation war. Between 1964 and 1974, it struggled against Portuguese colonial rule. At a cost of some 30,000 lives, Mozambique gained its independence in 1975 under Frelimo's leadership. Although the new nation was one of the least-developed countries in the world, many were optimistic that the lessons learned in the struggle could be applied to the task of building a dynamic new society based on Marxist-Leninist principles.

Timeline: PAST

1497
Portuguese explorers land in Mozambique

1820s
The Northern Nguni of Shosagaane invade southern Mozambique, establishing the Gaza kingdom

1962
The Frelimo liberation movement is officially launched

1975
The liberation struggle is successful

1980s
Increased Renamo attacks on civilian and military targets; President Samora Machel is killed in a mysterious airplane crash; Joaquim Chissano becomes president

1990s
Renamo agrees to end fighting, participate in multiparty elections

PRESENT

2000s
Floods lead to enormous losses in life, property, and infrastructure; Chissano decides not to run again; elections are scheduled for 2004

Unfortunately, hopes for any sort of postindependence progress were quickly dashed by Renamo, which was originally established as a counterrevolutionary fifth column by Rhodesia's (Zimbabwe) Central Intelligence Organization. More than 1 million people died due to the rebellion, a large proportion murdered in cold blood by Renamo forces. It is further estimated that, out of a total population of 17 million, some 5 million people were internally displaced, and about 2 million others fled to neighboring states. No African nation paid a higher price in its resistance to white supremacy.

HEALTH/WELFARE

Civil strife, widespread Renamo attacks on health units, and food shortages drastically curtailed healthcare goals and led to Mozambique's astronomical infant mortality rate.

Although some parts of Mozambique were occupied by the Portuguese for more than 400 years, most of the country came under colonial control only in the early twentieth century. For decades, the colonial state and many local enterprises also relied on forced labor. Even by the dismal standards of European colonialism in Africa, there continued to be a notable lack of concern for human development. At independence, 93 percent of the African population in Mozambique were illiterate.

ACHIEVEMENTS

Between 1975 and 1980, the illiteracy rate in Mozambique declined from 93% to 72% while classroom attendance more than doubled. Progress slowed during the 1980s due to civil war. Today, the overall literacy rate stands at about 40%.

However, the economy was already bankrupt due to the Portuguese policy of running Mozambique on a nonconvertible local currency. The rapid transition to independence compounded this problem by encouraging the sudden exodus of almost all the Portuguese settlers.

Perhaps even more costly to Mozambique in the long term was the polarization between Frelimo and African supporters of the former regime, who included about 100,000 who had been active in its security forces. While Frelimo did not subject the "compromised ones" to bloody reprisals, their rights were circumscribed, and many were sent, along with prostitutes and other "antisocial" elements, to "reeducation camps."

A TROUBLED INDEPENDENCE

Frelimo assumed power without the benefit or burden of a strong sense of administrative continuity. But Frelimo was initially able to fill the vacuum and launch aggressive development efforts. Health care and education were expanded, worker committees successfully ran many of the enterprises abandoned by the settlers, and communal villages coordinated rural development. However, efforts to promote agricultural collectivization as the foundation of a command economy generally led to peasant resistance and economic failure.

In its 1989 Congress, Frelimo formally abandoned its commitment to the primacy of Marxist-Leninist ideology and opened the door to further political and economic reforms. Multipartyism was formally embraced in 1991.

Niger (Republic of Niger)

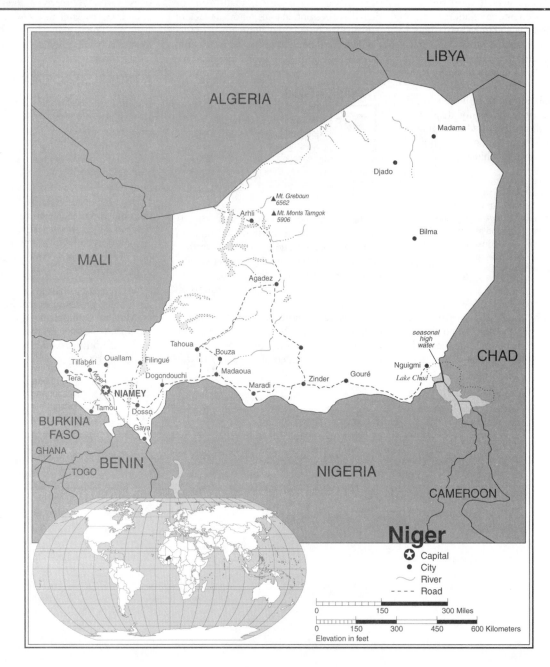

Niger Statistics

GEOGRAPHY

Area in Square Miles (Kilometers): 489,191 (1,267,000) (about twice the size of Texas)

Capital (Population): Niamey (821,000)

Environmental Concerns: overgrazing; deforestation; soil erosion; desertification; poaching and habitat destruction

Geographical Features: mainly desert plains and sand dunes; flat to rolling plains in the south; hills in the north; landlocked

Climate: desert; tropical in the extreme south

PEOPLE

Population

Total: 11,360,538
Annual Growth Rate: 2.67%
Rural/Urban Population Ratio: 80/20
Major Languages: French; Hausa; Djerma

Ethnic Makeup: 56% Hausa; 22% Djerma; 8% Fula; 8% Tuareg; 6% others
Religions: 80% Muslim; 20% indigenous beliefs and Christian

Health

Life Expectancy at Birth: 42 years (male); 42 years (female)
Infant Mortality: 122/1,000 live births
Physicians Available: 1/35,141 people
HIV/AIDS Rate in Adults: 4%

Education

Adult Literacy Rate: 15.3%
Compulsory (Ages): 7–15, free

COMMUNICATION

Telephones: 22,400 main lines
Televisions: 2.8 per 1,000 people
Internet Users: 15,000 (2002)

TRANSPORTATION

Highways in Miles (Kilometers): 6,262 (10,100)
Railroads in Miles (Kilometers): none
Usable Airfields: 27
Motor Vehicles in Use: 51,500

GOVERNMENT

Type: republic
Independence Date: August 3, 1960 (from France)
Head of State/Government: President Mamadou Tandja is both head of state and head of government
Political Parties: National Movement for a Developing Society—Nassara; Democratic and Social Convention—Rahama; Nigerien Party for Democracy and Socialism—Tarayya; Nigerien Alliance for Democracy and Social Progress—Zaman-lahia; others
Suffrage: universal at 18

MILITARY

Military Expenditures (% of GDP): 1.3%
Current Disputes: territorial dispute with Libya; boundary disputes over Lake Chad

ECONOMY

Currency ($ U.S. Equivalent): 581 CFA francs = $1

Per Capita Income/GDP: $820/$9 billion
GDP Growth Rate: 3.8%
Inflation Rate: 3%
Labor Force by Occupation: 90% agriculture; 6% industry and commerce; 4% government
Population Below Poverty Line: 63%
Natural Resources: uranium; coal; iron ore; tin; phosphates; gold; petroleum
Agriculture: millet; sorghum; peanuts; cotton; cowpeas; cassava; livestock
Industry: cement; brick; textiles; chemicals; agricultural products; food processing; uranium mining
Exports: $246 million (primary partners France, Nigeria, Spain)
Imports: $331 million (primary partners France, Côte d'Ivoire, United States)

SUGGESTED WEB SITES

```
http://www.friendsofniger.org
http://www.cia.gov/cia/
  publications/factbook/geos/
  ng.html
```

Niger Country Report

Niger is ranked by the United Nations as the world's second-poorest country, after war-ravaged Sierra Leone. This circumstance can in part be blamed on poor governance. For most of the past four decades, since it gained independence from France in 1960, Niger has been governed by a succession of military regimes that have left it bankrupt. This has led to chronic instability, as the government has regularly failed to pay its salaries, resulting in strikes by civil servants and mutinies by soldiers.

In November 1999 the current president, Mamadou Tandja, was elected under a new constitution. But ultimate power remains in the hands of the military, which, in January 1996 overthrew Niger's last elected government.

DROUGHT AND DESERTIFICATION

Most Nigeriens subsist through small-scale crop production and herding. Yet farming is especially difficult in Niger. Less than 10 percent of the nation's vast territory is suitable for cultivation even during the best of times. Most of the cultivable land lies along the banks of the Niger River. Unfortunately, much of the past four decades has

been the worst of times. During this period, Nigeriens have been constantly challenged by recurrent drought and an ongoing process of desertification.

In particular, many attribute environmental degradation to the introduction of inappropriate forms of cultivation, overgrazing, deforestation, and new patterns of human settlement.

DEVELOPMENT

Nigerien village cooperatives, especially marketing cooperatives, predate independence and have grown in size and importance in recent years. They have successfully competed with well-to-do private traders for control of the grain market. In September 2004 the Nigerien government granted gold mining permits to a number of European nations in an effort to increase gold mining and production.

Ironically, much of the debate on people's negative impact on the environment has been focused on some of the agricultural-development schemes that once were perceived as the region's salvation. These were designed to increase per-acre yields,

typically through the intensive planting of new seeds and reliance on imported fertilizers and pesticides. Such projects often led to higher initial local outputs that proved unsustainable, largely due to expensive overhead. In addition, many experts promoting the new agricultural techniques failed to appreciate the value of traditional technologies and forms of social organization in limiting desertification while allowing people to cope with drought. It is now appreciated that patterns of cultivation long championed by Nigerien farmers allowed for soil conservation and reduced the risks associated with pests and poor climate.

FREEDOM

Nigeriens have been effectively disenfranchised by the 1996 coup and subsequent fraudulent presidential election. Security forces are known to beat and intimidate opposition political figures. The private media are a target of repression, with a number of journalists having been detained. Opposition meetings and demonstrations are often banned.

Photo courtesy of r. Bartlett Moon at americandiplomacy.org (Moon001)

This mosque at Agagdes in Niger shows the synthesis of *Maghreb's* (Northwest Africa) Arab architectural style adapted to local architectural traditions in sub-Sahara Africa.

The government's recent emphasis has been on helping Niger's farmers to help themselves through the extension of credit, better guaranteed minimum prices, and improved communications. Vigorous efforts have been made in certain regions to halt the spread of desert sands by supporting village tree-planting campaigns. Given the local inevitability of drought, the government has also increased its commitment to the stockpiling of food in granaries.

HEALTH/WELFARE

A national conference on educational reform stimulated a program to use Nigerien languages in primary education and integrated the adult literacy program into the rural development efforts. The National Training Center for Literacy Agents is crucial to literacy efforts.

ACHIEVEMENTS

Niger has consistently demonstrated a strong commitment to the preservation and development of its national cultures through its media and educational institutions, the National Museum, and events such as the annual youth festival at Agades.

The Nigerien government's emphasis on agriculture has, in part, been motivated by the realization that the nation could not rely on its immense uranium deposits for future development. The opening of uranium mines in the 1970s resulted in the country becoming the world's fifth-largest producer. By the end of that decade, uranium exports accounted for some 90 percent of Niger's foreign-exchange earnings. Depressed international demand throughout the 1980s, however, resulted in substantially reduced prices and output. Although uranium still accounts for 75 percent of foreign-exchange earnings, its revenue contribution in recent years is only about a third of what it was prior to the slump.

Timeline: PAST

1200s–1400s
The Mali Empire includes territories and peoples of current Niger areas

1400s
Hausa states develop in the south of present-day Niger

1800s
The area is influenced by the Fulani Empire, centered at Sokoto, now in Nigeria

1906
France consolidates rule over Niger

1960
Niger becomes independent

1974
A military coup brings Colonel Seyni Kountché and a Supreme Military Council to power

1987
President Kountché dies and is replaced by Ali Saibou

1990s
The Nigerien National Conference adopts multipartyism; President Ibrahim Bare Mainassara is assassinated

PRESENT

2000s
President Mamadou Tandja holds power under the new constitution; the military retains significant influence

Nigeria (Federal Republic of Nigeria)

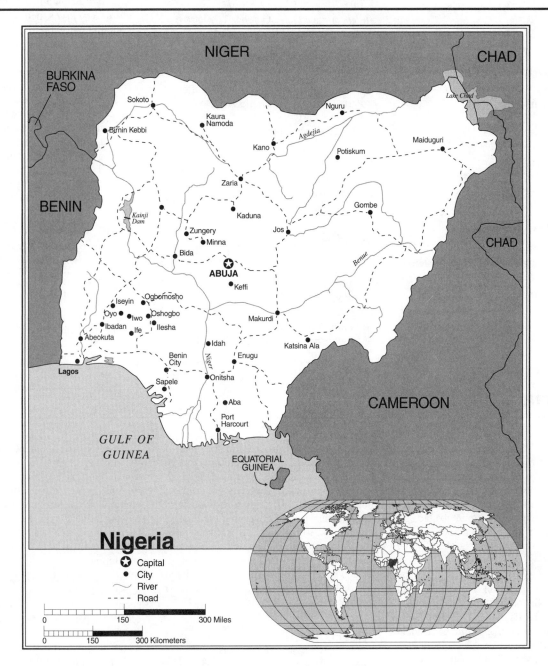

Nigeria Statistics

GEOGRAPHY

Area in Square Miles (Kilometers): 356,669 (923,768) (twice the size of California)

Capital (Population): Abuja (420,000)

Environmental Concerns: soil degradation; deforestation; desertification; drought

Geographical Features: southern lowlands merge into central hills and plateaus; mountains in southeast; plains in north

Climate: varies from equatorial to arid

PEOPLE

Population

Total: 137,253,133

Annual Growth Rate: 2.54%

Rural/Urban Population Ratio: 57/43

Major Languages: English; Hausa; Yoruba; Ibo; Fulani

Ethnic Makeup: about 21% Hausa; 21% Yoruba; 18% Ibo; 9% Fulani; 31% others

Religions: 50% Muslim; 40% Christian; 10% indigenous beliefs

Health

Life Expectancy at Birth: 51 years (male); 51 years (female)

Infant Mortality: 72.5/1,000 live births
Physicians Available: 1/4,496 people
HIV/AIDS Rate in Adults: 5.06%

Education

Adult Literacy Rate: 57%
Compulsory (Ages): 6–15; free

COMMUNICATION

Telephones: 853,100 main lines
Daily Newspaper Circulation: 18 per 1,000 people
Televisions: 38 per 1,000 people
Internet Users: 750,000 (2003)

TRANSPORTATION

Highways in Miles (Kilometers): 120,524 (194,394); but much of the road system is barely usable
Railroads in Miles (Kilometers): 2,226 (3,567)
Usable Airfields: 70 Motor Vehicles in Use: 954,000

GOVERNMENT

Type: republic in transition from military rule
Independence Date: October 1, 1960 (from the United Kingdom)
Head of State/Government: President Olusegun Obasanjo is both head of state and head of government
Political Parties: People's Democratic Party; Alliance for Democracy; All People's Party
Suffrage: universal at 18

MILITARY

Military Expenditures (% of GDP): 1%
Current Disputes: civil strife; various border disputes

ECONOMY

Currency ($ U.S. Equivalent): 128.3 nairas = $1
Per Capita Income/GDP: $900/$114 billion
GDP Growth Rate: 7.1%
Inflation Rate: 13.8%
Unemployment Rate: 28% (1992 est.)

Labor Force by Occupation: 70% agriculture; 20% services; 10% industry
Population Below Poverty Line: 45%
Natural Resources: petroleum; tin; columbite; iron ore; coal; limestone; lead; zinc; natural gas; hydropower
Agriculture: cocoa; peanuts; rubber; yams; cassava; sorghum; palm oil; millet; corn; rice; livestock; timber; fish
Industry: mining; petroleum; food processing; textiles; cement; building materials; chemicals; agriculture products; printing; steel
Exports: $20.3 billion (primary partners United States, Spain, India)
Imports: $13.7 billion (primary partners United Kingdom, United States, France)

SUGGESTED WEB SITES

```
http://www.nigeria.com
http://www.nigeriatoday.com
http://www.nigeriadaily.com
http://www.nigeriaworld.com
http://www.africanews.org/west/
  nigeria/
http://www.cia.gov/cia/
  publications/factbook/geos/
  ni.html
```

Nigeria Country Report

Nigeria's military has been active in the settlement of regional disputes in Liberia, Côte d'Ivoire, and Sierra Leone. But the country's regional diplomatic standing was compromised in October 2002, when it reneged on a previous agreement to abide by the judgment of the International Court of Justice in a long-running border dispute with Cameroon.

The first legislative elections since the end of military rule in 1999 were held throughout Nigeria in April 2003. Polling was marked by delays and allegations of fraud arising from the opposition. President Obasanjo's People's Democratic Party won a parliamentary majority, with President Obasanjo elected for a second term in office with more than 60 percent of the votes cast. Although a number of opposition parties rejected the result, and the EU observers say the polling was marred by "serious irregularities," Obasanjo was sworn into office as president, marking the first civilian transfer of power in Nigeria's history.

With a vast population of nearly 130 million, Nigeria's human resources are yet to be fully tapped in the interest of the country. Poverty and inequality between the rich and the poor remain extreme. Nigeria's industrious people hope that the restoration of democracy will allow them

to make renewed progress in the face of these challenges. In February 1999 Obasanjo was elected Nigeria's first civilian president in 15 years. His government has since struggled to push forward with the immense task of governing the diverse communities that make up Africa's most populous country. But ethnic/religious tension and corruption have continued to plague Nigeria. Transparency International has ranked the country as the second most corrupt in the world.

DEVELOPMENT

Nigeria hopes to mobilize its substantial human and natural resources to encourage labor-intensive production and self-sufficient agriculture. Recent bans on food imports will increase local production, and restrictions on imported raw materials should encourage research and local input for industry.

Since early 2000 attempts to introduce Shari'a (Islamic law) in northern areas of the country have touched off severe violence between Muslim and Christian communities, as well as international condemnation for stoning sentences against single mothers convicted of adultery.

Since Nigeria's independence in 1960, its citizens have been through an emotional, political, and material roller coaster ride. It has been a period marred by inter-ethnic violence, economic downturns, and mostly military rule. But there have also been impressive levels of economic growth, cultural achievement, and human development.

Nigeria's hard-working population is responsible for one of Africa's largest economies. But per capita income is still only $840 per year, which is about average for the globe's most impoverished continent but down from Nigeria's estimated 1980 per capita income of $1,500.

A decade ago, it was common to equate Nigeria's wealth with its status as Africa's leading oil producer, but oil earnings have since plummeted. Although hydrocarbons still account for about 90 percent of the country's export earnings and 75 percent of its government revenue, the sector's current contribution to total gross domestic product is a more modest 20 percent.

NIGERIA'S ROOTS

The British, who conquered Nigeria in the late nineteenth and early twentieth centuries, administered the country through a

Ikem Okoye, 1987, Courtesy of the Aga Khan Visual Archive, M.I.T. (ANIAF0064)

This mosque is in the northern Nigerian town of Kano, which flourished during the rule of Muhammad Rumfa (1463–1499 CE) and was a major Hausa city-state and commercial center on the trans-Saharan caravan routes. After the Fulani conquest of Hausaland in the early 19th century, Kano became the capital of an emirate within the Islamic Sokoto Caliphate. Kano today is a major industrial, commmerical, and educational center in Nigeria's predominantly Muslim northern region.

policy of divide-and-rule. In the predominantly Muslim, Hausa-speaking north, they co-opted the old ruling class while virtually excluding Christian missionaries. But in the south, the missionaries, along with their schools, were encouraged, and Christianity and formal education spread rapidly. Many Yoruba farmers of the southwest profited through their cultivation of cocoa. Although most remained as farmers, many of the Igbo of the southeast became prominent in nonagricultural pursuits, such as state employees, artisans, wage workers, and traders. As a result, the Igbo tended to migrate in relatively large numbers to other parts of the colony.

FREEDOM

Under Abacha, Nigeria had one of the world's worst human-rights records. In 1998, the Nigerian Advocacy Group for Human Rights joined other international groups in issuing a statement insisting that nothing essentially changed after Abubakar succeeded Abacha. With the transition to civilian rule under former political detainee Obasanjo, the situation should improve.

OIL BOOM—AND BUST

Nigeria, as a leading member of the Organization of Petroleum Exporting Countries (OPEC), experienced a period of rapid social and economic change during the 1970s. The recovery of oil production and the subsequent hike in its prices led to a massive increase in government revenue. This allowed for the expansion of certain types of social services. Universal primary education was introduced, and the number of universities increased from 5 (in 1970) to 21 (in 1983).

Timeline: PAST

1100–1400
Ancient life flourishes

1851
The first British protectorate is established at Lagos

1960
Nigeria becomes independent as a unified federal state

1966–1970
Military seizure of power; proclamation of Biafra; civil war

1979
Elections restore civilian government

1980s
Muhammed Buhari's military coup ends the Second Republic; later, Buhari is toppled by Ibrahim Babanguida; lean times

1990s
Babanguida resigns; Sani Abacha takes the reins; civil unrest and violence intensify; military strongman Abdulsalam Abubakar takes power; elections bring civilian Olusegun Obasanjo to power

PRESENT

2000s
Ethnic and religious conflict intensifies; hopes for democratic pluralism in Nigeria revive; first civilian transfer of power in Nigeria's history

Agriculture, burdened by inflationary costs and low prices, entered a period of crisis, leaving the rapidly growing cities dependent on foreign food. Nonpetroleum exports, once the mainstay of the economy, either virtually disappeared or declined drastically.

HEALTH/WELFARE

Nigeria's infant mortality rate is now believed to have dropped to about 72 per 1,000 live births. (Some estimate it to be as high as 150 per 1,000.) While social services grew rapidly during the 1970s, Nigeria's strained economy since then has led to cutbacks in health and education.

The oil industry, although responsible for the vast majority of Nigeria's foreign exchange earning, has caused a number of problems throughout the country. In July 2003 a nationwide strike took place for nine days in a successful attempt to get government to reduce the price of fuel. During September 2004 deadly battles between gangs in the oil city of Port Harcourt prompted a strong crackdown by troops. The human-rights group Amnesty International cited the death toll at 500, after the government authorities claimed that only 20 people died. A very successful four-day general strike over fuel prices took place in October 2004, stoking fears about the country's oil exports and driving up the price of oil worldwide.

ACHIEVEMENTS

When many of their leading writers, artists, and intellectuals were exiled, and the once-lively press was suppressed, Nigerians found some solace in the success of their world-class soccer team and other athletes. In September, Nigeria's first satellite, NigeriaSat-1, was launched by Russian rocket.

The golden years of the 1970s were also banner years for inappropriate expenditures, corruption, and waste. For a while, given the scale of incoming revenues, it looked as if these were manageable problems. But GDP fell drastically in the 1980s with the collapse of oil prices. As the economy worsened, populist resentment grew.

In 1980 an Islamic movement condemning corruption, wealth, and private property defied authorities in the northern metropolis of Kano. The army was called in, killing nearly 4,000.

Oman (Sultanate of Oman)

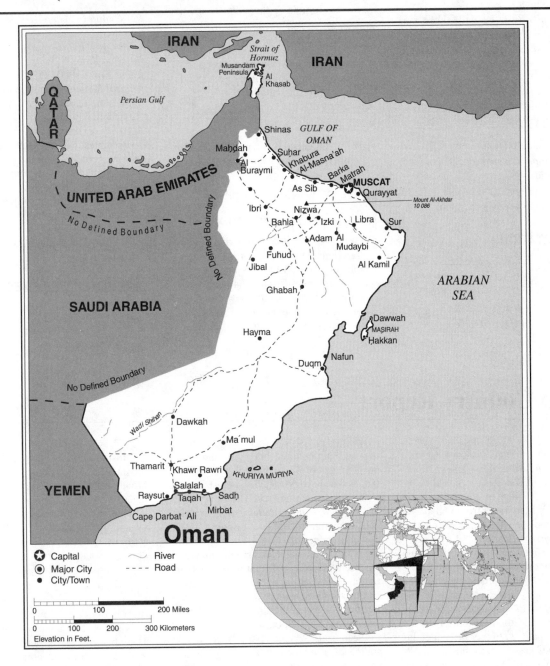

Oman Statistics

GEOGRAPHY

Area in Square Miles (Kilometers): 82,009 (212,460) (about the size of Kansas)

Capital (Population): Muscat (400,000)

Environmental Concerns: rising soil salinity; beach pollution from oil spills; very limited freshwater

Geographical Features: central desert plain; rugged mountains in the north and south

Climate: coast, hot and humid; interior, hot and dry

PEOPLE

Population

Total: 3,001,583 (includes 577,293 nonnationals)

Annual Growth Rate: 3.32%

Rural/Urban Population Ratio: 22/78

Major Languages: Arabic; English; various South Asian languages

Ethnic Makeup: almost entirely Arab; small Baluchi, South Asian, and African groups

Religions: 75% Ibadi Muslim; remainder Sunni Muslim, Shi'a Muslim, some Hindu

Health

Life Expectancy at Birth: 70 years (male); 75 years (female)

Infant Mortality Rate: 19.5/1,000 live births

Physicians Available (Ratio): 1/852 people

Education

Adult Literacy Rate: nearly 75.8%

COMMUNICATION

Telephones: 233,900 main lines

Daily Newspaper Circulation: 31 per 1,000 people

Televisions: 711 per 1,000 people

Internet Service Provider: 1 (2000)

TRANSPORTATION

Highways in Miles (Kilometers): 20,369 (34,965)

Railroads in Miles (Kilometers): none

Usable Airfields: 136

Motor Vehicles in Use: 347,000

GOVERNMENT

Type: monarchy; the monarch's absolute power is limited by the 1996 Basic Law

Independence Date: 1650 (expulsion of the Portuguese)

Head of State/Government: Sultan and Prime Minister Qabus ibn Said Al Said is both head of state and head of government

Political Parties: none

Suffrage: universal for over 21 except for members of military and security forces.

MILITARY

Military Expenditures (% of GDP): 11.4%

Current Disputes: boundary with United Arab Emirates(U.A.E.) agreed to bilaterally in 2003. Other boundaries, with U.A.E. Emirates Ras al-Khaymah and Sharjah, which separate the Musandam Peninsula from Oman proper, are administrative and not treaty-defined

ECONOMY

Currency ($ U.S. Equivalent): 0.3845 rials = $1

Per Capita Income/GDP: $13,100/$38.09 billion

GDP Growth Rate: 1.2%

Inflation Rate: 0.2%

Labor Force: 920,000

Natural Resources: petroleum; copper; asbestos; marble; limestone; chromium; gypsum; natural gas

Agriculture: dates; limes; bananas; alfalfa; vegetables; camels; cattle; fish

Industry: crude-oil production and refining; natural-gas production; construction; cement; copper

Exports: $13.4 billion (primary partners Japan, China, Thailand)

Imports: $6.37 billion (primary partners United Arab Emirates, Japan, United Kingdom)

SUGGESTED WEB SITES

http://lcweb2.loc.gov/frd/cs/ omtoc.htm

http://www.oman.org/

Oman Country Report

The Sultanate of Oman was, at least until about 1970, one of the least-known countries in the world. Yet it is a very old country with a long history of contact with the outside world. Merchants from Oman had a near monopoly on the trade in frankincense and myrrh.

In the twentieth century, Oman became important to the outside world for two primary reasons: it began producing oil in the 1960s and it has a strategic location on the Strait of Hormuz, the passageway for supertankers carrying Middle Eastern oil to the industrialized nations. Eighty percent of Japan's oil needs passes through Hormuz, as does sixty percent of Western Europe's.

GEOGRAPHY

Oman is the third-largest country in the Arabian Peninsula after Yemen and Saudi Arabia. However, the population is small, and large areas of land are uninhabited or sparsely populated. The geographical diversity—rugged mountains, vast gravelly plains, and deserts—limits large-scale settlement. The bulk of the population is centered in the Batinah coastal plain, which stretches from the United Arab Emirates border south to the capital, Muscat. Formerly this area was devoted to fish-

ing and agriculture; but with the rapid development of Oman under the current sultan, it has become heavily industrialized, with extensive commerce. The ancient system of *falaj*—underground irrigation channels that run for miles, bringing water downhill by gravity flow—has made farming possible, although the agricultural sector has been adversely affected in recent years by prolonged drought. Oman's southern Dhofar Province is more fertile and productive than the rest of the country, due to monsoon rains. In addition to citrus and other tropical fruits, Oman is the major world source of frankincense and gum from a small tree that grows wild and has been prized since ancient times.

DEVELOPMENT

Vision Oman 2020, the sultan's blueprint for long-term growth, sets among its objectives increasing economic diversity to reduce dependence on oil, developing a competitive private sector producing manufactured goods for export, and Omanization of the labor force. With one-half million youths entering the job market by 2005, reducing dependence on foreign workers is critical.

Most of Oman's oil wells are located in the interior of the country. The interior is a broad, hilly plain dotted with oasis villages, each one a fortress with thick walls to keep out desert raiders. The stony plain eventually becomes the Rub al-Khali ("Empty Quarter"), the great uninhabited desert of southeastern Arabia.

HISTORY

As was the case elsewhere in Arabia, the early social structure of Oman consisted of a number of tribal groups. Many of them were and still are nomadic (Bedouin), while others became settled farmers and herders centuries ago.

In the seventh century A.D., the Omanis were converted to Islam. They developed their own form of Islam, however, called Ibadism, meaning "Community of the Just," a branch of Shi'a Islam. The Ibadi peoples elect their own leader, called an Imam. The Ibadi Imams do not have to be descendants of the prophet Muhammad, as do the Imams in the main body of Shi'a Muslims. The Ibadi community believes that anyone, regardless of background, can be elected Imam, as long as the individual is pious, just, and capable. If no one is available who meets those requirements, the office may remain vacant.

Ibadi Imams ruled interior Oman with the support of family shaykhs until the eighteenth century. Well before then, however, coastal Oman was being opened up to foreign powers. The Portuguese captured Muscat in the 1500s for use as a stopping place for their ships on the trade route to India. The Portuguese were finally driven out in 1650. Since that time, Oman has not been ruled directly by any foreign power.

FREEDOM

Although Qabus is, both in theory and practice, an absolute ruler and governs by royal decree, in 1996 he issued a Basic Law that provides for an appointed Council of State (including a few women members) and a Majlis al-Shura, also appointed, which may draft legislation on social issues for his approval. If approved, the draft then becomes law. Unlike in other Gulf states, most Omani women are educated, and many play an active part in national life.

Oman's ruler for nearly four decades in the twentieth century was Sultan Said ibn Taimur (1932–1970). The most interesting aspect of his reign was the way in which he stopped the clock of modernization. Oil was discovered in 1964 in inland Oman; within a few years, wealth from oil royalties began pouring in. But the sultan was afraid that the new wealth would corrupt his people. He would not allow the building of schools, houses, roads, or hospitals for his people. Before 1970 there were only 16 schools in all of Oman. The sole hospital was the American mission in Muscat, established in the 1800s by Baptist missionaries. All 10 of Oman's qualified doctors worked abroad, because the sultan did not trust modern medicine. The few roads were rough caravan tracks; many areas of the country, such as the Musandam Peninsula, were inaccessible.

On the darker side, slavery was still a common practice. Women were almost never seen in public and had to be veiled from head to foot if they so much as walked to a neighbor's house to visit. And on the slightest pretext, prisoners could be locked up in the old Portuguese fort at Muscat and left to rot.

As the 1960s came to an end, there was more and more unrest in Oman. The opposition centered around Qabus ibn Said, the sultan's son. Qabus had been educated in England. When he came home, his father shut him up in a house in Salalah, a town far from Muscat, and refused to give him any responsibilities. He was afraid of his son's "Western ideas."

On July 23, 1970, supporters of Crown Prince Qabus overthrew the sultan, and Qabus succeeded him. Sultan Qabus ibn Said brought Oman into the twentieth century in a hurry. The old policy of isolation was reversed.

OMANI SOCIETY

Oman today is a land in flux, its society poised between the traditional past and a future governed increasingly by technology. An Omani business executive or industrial chief may wear a Western suit and tie to an appointment, but more than likely he will arrive for his meeting in a *dishdasha* (the traditional full-length robe worn by Gulf Arabs), with either a turban or an embroidered skullcap to complete the outfit. A ceremonial dagger called *kanjar* will certainly hang from his belt or sash. He will have a cellular phone pressed to his right ear and a digital watch on his wrist, courtesy of Oman's extensive trade with Japan. Older Omani women are also traditional in costume, covered head to toe with the enveloping *chador* and their faces (except for the eyes) hidden behind the black *batula*, the eagle-like mask common in the region. But increasingly their daughters and younger sisters opt for Western clothing, with only head scarves to distinguish them as Muslims.

HEALTH/WELFARE

Mobile health units that travel to remote areas have helped bring about a steep decline in infant mortality rates, from 34.3 per 1,000 in 1995 to 19.5 per 1,000 in 2003. Effective family-planning programs using mobile health units that cover the rural countryside have helped lower the high birth rate from 3.41 percent in 1998 to 2.5 percent in 2003. Oman's health care system was declared to be eighth best in the world by the World Health Organization (WHO) in 2000.

In social, economic, and even political areas of Omani life, Qabus has brought about changes that have proceeded at a dizzying pace during his three-decade rule. Education, health care, and roads were his three top priorities when he took office. By the 2001–2002 school year, 542,063 students were enrolled in the country's 1,000 state schools. The enrollment is 48.7 percent female. Sultan Qabus University, which opened in 1986 with a student body of 3,000, now has 6,000 students. These efforts, along with numerous adult-education programs, have increased Oman's literacy rate to 80 percent.

The sultan has also begun the process of replacing authoritarian rule by representative government. In 1996, his silver-anniversary year, he issued a Basic Law setting up a Majlis al-Shura (Council of State). Its 82 members are appointed by the ruler to represent Oman's provinces (*wilayats*) and cities. The Majlis has neither veto nor legislative powers, but it acts as an advisory body in the drafting of laws and the national budget. In 1998 an amendment to the Basic Law established local and municipal councils in order to exercise internal authority in these areas.

ACHIEVEMENTS

A new Iranian-built power plant began operations in 1999 in Oman, meeting domestic needs for electricity. Oman is also self-sufficient in cement and textiles, most of the latter made in factories located in the Rusayl free-trade zone near Muscat. The zone now has more than 60 industries and produces $60 million in finished goods, generating $24 million in exports.

Timeline: PAST

1587–1588
The Portuguese seize Muscat and build massive fortresses to guard the harbor

1749
The Al Bu Said Dynasty is established; extends Omani territory

late 1800s
The British establish a de facto protectorate; the slave trade is supposedly ended

1951
Independence

1970
Sultan Said ibn Taimur is deposed by his son, Prince Qabus

1975
With British and Iranian help, Sultan Qabus ends the Dhofar rebellion

1980s
Oman joins the Gulf Cooperation Council; Sultan Qabus sets up a Consultative Assembly as the first step toward democratization

1990s
The sultan focuses on expanding Oman's industrial base

PRESENT

2000s
Democratization continues with the extension of suffrage; WHO rates Oman's healthcare system 8th best in the world; Oman supports the coalition against terrorism

THE ECONOMY

Oman began producing and exporting oil in limited quantities in 1967. The industry was greatly expanded after the accession of Sultan Qabus. It is managed by a national corporation, Petroleum Development Oman (PDO). Oil production in the 1990s reached 900,000 barrels per day (b/d) but was reduced to 860,000 b/d in 2000–2001, in accordance with OPEC production cuts. Oman's oil reserves are 5.7 billion barrels. Natural-gas reserves are 29.3 trillion cubic feet. The new liquefied natural gas (LNG) plant at Qalhat produced 6.6 million tons of LNG in 2001.

Barely 2 percent of Oman's land is arable. Rainfall averages two to four inches annually except in monsoon-drenched Dhofar, and recent drought has largely dried up the long-established *falaj* system.

The interior oases and Dhofar provide for intensive cultivation of dates. They also grow coconuts and various other fruits. Agriculture provides 35 percent of non-oil exports and employs 12 percent of the labor force.

The fishing industry employs 10 percent of the working population, but obsolete equipment and lack of canning and freezing plants have severely limited the catch in the past. Another problem is the unwillingness of Omani fishermen to move into commercial production; most of them catch just enough fish for their own use.

FOREIGN RELATIONS

Oman joined with other Arab countries in opening links with Israel after its Oslo agreements with the Palestine Liberation Organization (PLO) for Palestinian autonomy and the 1994 Jordan-Israel peace treaty.

As a member of the Gulf Cooperation Council, Oman has become active in regional affairs, a role emphasized by its strategic location. Its long history of dealings with the United States—a relationship dating back to Andrew Jackson's presidency—has made Oman a natural partner in U.S. efforts to promote stability in the Gulf region.

After the September 11, 2001, terrorist attacks on the World Trade Center and the Pentagon, Sultan Qabus took the lead among the Gulf states in supporting the U.S.-led international coalition against terrorism.

Pakistan (Islamic Republic of Pakistan)

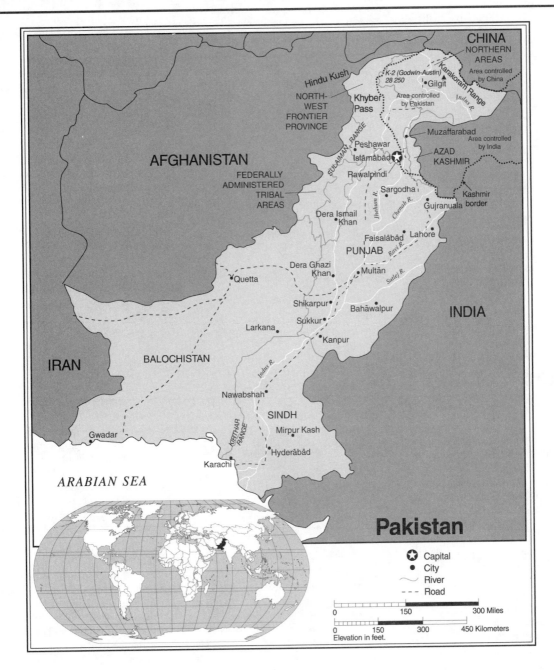

Pakistan Statistics

GEOGRAPHY

Area in Square Miles (Kilometers): 310,320 (803,940) (about twice the size of California)

Capital (Population): Islamabad (636,000)

Environmental Concerns: water pollution; deforestation; soil erosion; desertification; limited freshwater supplies

Geographical Features: flat plain in the east; mountains in the north and northwest; Balochistan plateau in the west

Climate: mostly hot, dry desert; temperate in the northwest; arctic in the north

PEOPLE

Population

Total: 159,196,336

Annual Growth Rate: 1.98%

Rural/Urban Population Ratio: 65/35

Major Languages: Punjabi; Sindhi; Siraiki; Pashtu; Urdu; Balochi; Hindko; English; others

Ethnic Makeup: 63% Punjabi; 12% Sindhi; 10% Pushtun (Pathan); Baloch, Muhajir

Religions: 97% Muslim; 3% other

Health

Life Expectancy at Birth: 61.69 years (male); 63.58 years (female)
Infant Mortality: 74.43/1,000 live births
Physicians Available: 1/1,863 people
HIV/AIDS Rate in Adults: 0.1%

Education

Adult Literacy Rate: 45.7%

COMMUNICATION

Telephones: 3,982,800 main lines
Daily Newspaper Circulation: 22 per 1,000 people
Televisions: 16 per 1,000 people
Internet Users: 1.5 million (2002)

TRANSPORTATION

Highways in Miles (Kilometers): 158,083 (254,410)
Railroads in Miles (Kilometers): 4,898 (8,163)
Usable Airfields: 129
Motor Vehicles in Use: 1,100,000

GOVERNMENT

Type: federal republic
Independence Date: August 14, 1947 (from the United Kingdom)
Head of State/Government: President, Chief Executive (General) Pervez Musharraf; Prime Minister Shaukat Aziz
Political Parties: many government and opposition parties
Suffrage: universal at 18; joint electorates and reserved parliamentary seats for women and non-Muslims

MILITARY

Military Expenditures (% of GDP): 3.9%
Current Disputes: border problems with Afghanistan; disputes over Kashmir and water-sharing problems with India; narcotics trade

ECONOMY

Currency ($ U.S. Equivalent): 57.75 rupees = $1

GDP-Per Capita: $2,100
GDP Growth Rate: 5.5%
Inflation Rate: 2.9%
Unemployment Rate: 7.7%
Labor Force by Occupation: 44% agriculture; 39% services; 17% industry
Population Below Poverty Line: 35%
Natural Resources: land; natural gas; petroleum; coal; iron ore; copper; salt; limestone
Agriculture: cotton; grains; sugarcane; fruits; vegetables; milk; mutton; eggs; livestock
Industry: textiles; food processing; construction materials; consumer goods
Exports: $11.7 billion (primary partners United States, United Kingdom, United Arab Emirates)
Imports: $12.51 billion (primary partners United Arab Emirates, Saudi Arabia, China)

SUGGESTED WEB SITE

http://www.clas.ufl.edu/users/gthursby/pak/

Pakistan Country Report

Pakistan, the second largest nation in South Asia, is about one-fourth the size of India. It lies in the Indus River Valley, between the mountainous border with Afghanistan—through which comes the famous Khyber Pass—to the northwest, the Great Indian Desert, and the Rann of Kutch, to the southeast. Long a land of transition between the rugged steppes of Inner Asia and the plains of India, it is today a new nation caught between the heritage of a glorious imperial past and the poetic image of an ideal theocratic future. Its goal to become an exemplary modern religious state, a truly Islamic republic, is affirmed by the name, Pakistan, given by the Muslim poet Muhammed Iqbal in 1930. It means "Land of the Pure."

The heritage of the people of Pakistan goes back to the earliest-known urban culture in South Asia. Excavations of the ancient cities of Harappa and Mohenjodaro, discovered in 1922, reveal an impressive civilization that dates from 3000 to 1500 B.C. The civilizations in the Mesopotamian valley to the west are distinctive for its knowledge of hydrology and its use of irrigation waters of the Indus River.

Islam has a long heritage in Pakistan. Invading princes from the west and wandering Sufi mystics, by their spiritual discipline and religious teaching, drew large numbers of indigenous peoples to

www.twf.org/bio/SAKhan.html (COL001)

Sayyid Ahmad Khan (1817–1898) is recognized as the torchbearer of progressive Islam. In his six-volume commentary on the Qur'an, he argued that Islam was a dynamic and flexible faith fully compatible with science, technology, justice, freedom, and other enlightened and humane Western concepts. He is credited with establishing a publishing house to translate English literature into Urdu and visaversa to further British-Muslim understanding as well as founding the Anglo-Muhammadan Oriental College in Lucknow (renamed Alligarh University) to educate Muslims. Many of Alligarh University's graduates were in the vanguard of the Pakistan Movement.

submission to the will of Allah (God) as early as the eighth century. This vibrant faith, now so firmly woven into the fabric of people's lives, led to the creation of Pakistan as an Islamic Republic in 1947. Today 97 percent of the 159 million people in the country are Muslim. Of these, 71 percent belong to the Sunni tradition.

The invasion of Moghul princes, who marched their conquering forces across the northern plains of South Asia to the Bay of Bengal in the sixteenth century, marked the period of greatest glory in the heritage of the Pakistani people. The Moghuls were militant Turks refined by the elegance of Persia and energized by their Islamic faith. Akbar (1556–1605), the greatest of these emperors, is remembered for the opulence and splendor of his court, for the far-reaching administrative control of his empire, and for his elaborate building projects that still stand as massive tribute to his commanding wealth and intellect. The Taj Mahal, built by his grandson, Shah Jahan, is the crowning architectural achievement of this magnificent imperial past.

In the middle of the nineteenth century, the Moghul Dynasty fell to British colonial rule. With the departure of the British Raj in 1947, Pakistan became an independent nation, created, especially by the 7.2 mil-

Nik Wheeler/Saudi Aramco World/PADIA (SA0422005)

Badshahi Masjid (Emperor's Mosque) in Lahore, Pakistan, was completed in 1674 CE by Mughal Emperor Muhammad Aurangzeb (1658–1707 CE). It was the last great Moghul architectural monument in the Indian subcontinent and arguably the largest mosque in the world until the Grand Mosque surpassed it in the late 1960s.

lion people who migrated from central India at the time of independence, to preserve the culture of a staunch Islamic and glorious Moghul imperial past. This heritage has been both an asset and an obstacle to its evolution as a modern nation state.

DEVELOPMENT

Pakistan's per capita income has grown substantially since 1960. Industry, primarily cotton textiles and food processing, has grown at an impressive rate since 1980. This sector now produces more of the GDP than the agricultural sector, although agriculture still employs nearly half of the labor force. However, there are vast inequities in income distribution among the people of Pakistan.

INDEPENDENCE MOVEMENT

The Muslim League was formed in 1906 to represent the interests of the Islamic minority in British India in the movement for freedom from colonial domination. Its leaders became convinced through the years of struggle with the British Raj that their people would be oppressed and even destroyed in an independent India dominated by Hindus. In 1940 the League voted to demand a separate state for the Muslim population of South Asia. Muhammad Ali Jinnah, through his persistence as leader of the League, realized this objective when the British Raj, departing in 1947, set the mechanism to establish two nations instead of one. Those districts that were under British control (about three-fifths of the subcontinent), where Muslims were predominant, would

become Pakistan; the districts where Hindus were in the majority would become India. The remaining areas—princely states not under direct British administrative control—would accede to either country by their own determination.

This scheme to partition a separate Islamic state out of British India created a smaller, more populous East Pakistan, and a larger, dominant West Pakistan—separated by nearly 1,000 miles of India.

This partition scheme had disastrous consequences. The Muslims in British India who most feared Hindu oppression were not those who had the security of living in Muslim majority districts, but those who lived in the Hindu-majority districts in north central India. They felt endangered in their own lands. Similarly, Hindu minorities in districts where the Muslims were in a majority also feared for their lives. This mutual fear caused the migration of 14 million people, Hindus and Muslims moving in opposite directions.

CHALLENGES TO POLITICAL STABILITY

The homelessness and bloodshed caused by the partition of British India in 1947 taxed to the limit the meager resources of the new nation of Pakistan. Because its lands were on the outer fringes of the British Raj, the country lacked adequate administrative services to pull itself together. The country's struggles to become a modern democratic republic have been difficult. And they continue to this day.

Muhammad Ali Jinnah, the leader of the movement to establish an independent Is-

AP/World Wide Photos (AP003)

Muhammad Ali Jinnah (1875–1948) was the architect and founding father of Pakistan. Although Anglicized and secular in his worldview, he infused the Pakistan Movement with vigor when he became its leader in the 1934, brought about an unprecedented Islamic resurgence in India during the 1940s, and carved out the new Muslim homeland of Pakistan in 1947 despite opposition from the All-India Congress Party, the British colonialists, and Islamic fundamentalist *Jamaat-e-Islami*. Pakistanis reverentially call him the *Quaid-i-Azam* (Great Leader).

lamic state, took upon himself the chief executive duties of governor general in the interim government. Unfortunately, he became ill and died 13 months later. The

S.M. Amin/Saudi Aramco World/PADIA (SA2046083)

The King Faisal Mosque in Islamabad, Pakistan, is named in honor of Saudi Arabia's King Faisal ibn Abdul Aziz ibn Abdul Rahman al-Saud (r. 1964–1975), who promised to finance the mosque when on an official visit to Pakistan's capital. The prayer hall can accommodate over 10,000 worshippers. Affiliated with this mosque is the Institute for Islamic Research, and since 1982, some sections of the International Islamic University.

Muslim League, which had been imported from British India, lost control of a unifying national agenda to the indigenous sources of provincial power: wealthy landowners and tribal leaders in five distinct provinces, each divided from the others by ethos and language.

Because the regional identities of these provinces have been the primary basis for the political parties that have brought the people into civic life, the differences between these regions have been accentuated rather than mitigated on the national level. In the case of the Bengali people in the province of East Pakistan, their political solidarity as a region led to their split from Pakistan to form an independent nation, Bangladesh, in 1971.

Each of the four remaining provinces in West Pakistan is defined not only by a distinct geography and ethnic group but also by a distinct language that takes regional precedence over Urdu as the declared national language of Pakistan. Urdu is spoken by only about 8 percent of the population, mostly the families of *mohajirs*, immigrants from India, who brought the language with them in 1947, and who live today primarily in the major cities of the country.

Because the vast majority of the people of Pakistan are Sunni Muslim, difference in religious identity is a significant factor mostly for Hindu and Christian communities as small minorities, and for members of the Ahmadiya Sect of Islam, whose faith is considered heretical by the orthodox. But a serious rift exists between fundamentalists and moderates within the Sunni fold over what kind of Islamic nation Pakistan is to be. More traditional Islamists have long felt their commitment to an exclusive, coercive theocracy challenged by the quest for modern, Westernized democracy. With the intrusion of Western values manifest in the fall of the Taliban in Afghanistan, their cause took on a new urgency. A coalition of fundamentalist parties, called the Muttahida Majlis-eamal (MMA), representing the provinces closest to Afghanistan in the National Assembly, has become a force in promoting their Islamist agenda both in those provinces and in the nation as a whole.

Amid all of these challenges to the formation of a single body politic, the military has been the strongest force for political unity, holding the country together under the fear of a life-threatening attack by India. Ironically, because of its dominant role in national government to maintain unity and stability, the military has also impeded the growth of democracy in Pakistan.

A constitution to establish a national parliamentary government was finally adopted in 1956, affirming the common sovereign identity of the two wings of Pakistan as an Islamic Republic. Yet this and each of the successive attempts to establish democratic rule—in 1971 and in 1988—occurred under the watchful eye of the military, and ended in a takeover: by General Ayub Khan in 1958, by General Yahya Khan in 1969, by General Zia-ul-Haq in 1977, and by General Pervez Musharraf in 1999. In all, the country has been under martial law for more than half of its years as an independent nation.

DEMOCRACY: 1971–1977

The separation of Bangladesh as an independent nation left the Pakistan People's Party with a majority in the National Assembly, and Zulfikar Ali Bhutto, a Western-educated diplomat from a large landholding family in the province of Sindh in West Pakistan and founder of the Pakistan People's Party, became the president of Pakistan. He set out immediately to bring what was left of the country together as a socialist state by nationalizing banking and such major industries as steel, chemicals, and cement. Bhutto thereby expanded an already cumbersome civil-service bureaucracy. His policy created employment opportunities in the central government but discouraged investment and led to a decline in industrial production.

Bhutto was more successful in restoring parliamentary government. He created a new Constitution—the third in 26 years—that was adopted in 1973. It established a National Assembly of 207 members, all of them elected directly for five-year terms. Under its provisions, Bhutto became prime minister, the chief executive of the government, elected by majority of the National Assembly.

However, in the 1977 national elections, nine parties united to form the Pakistan National Alliance (PNA). Bhutto's

FREEDOM

Pakistan has experienced long years of martial law since independence in 1947. The first popular elections were not held until 1970, and not again until 1988. With the increasing political power of religious conservatives, women are held to their traditional, subservient role in Islamic society. Human-rights abuses are charged against the government, particularly against Hindus in the province of Sindh.

Pakistan People's Party won the election. But the PNA, which won only 36 of 207 seats in the National Assembly, charged that the elections had been fixed and took to the streets in protest. Bhutto called in the army to restore order and sought to negotiate with the PNA to hold new elections. Before any agreement could be reached, Mohammad Zia-ul-Haq, chief of staff of the army, seized control of the government. He promised to hold elections within 90 days, but canceled them two weeks before they were to be held. Zia also brought forth charges against Bhutto of complicity in a political murder, which led to Bhutto's trial and execution on April 4, 1979.

MARTIAL LAW: 1977–1988

In the fall of 1979, Zia banned all political parties and imposed censorship on the press. The following year he removed the actions of his government and the decisions of the military courts from judicial review. Many of these measures were cloaked in a policy of "Islamization," through which his military regime sought to improve the religious quality of the people's public life by an appeal to traditional laws and teachings of Sunni Islam.

Zia's consolidation of power in Pakistan coincided with the collapse of the Shah of Iran, the rise of Saudi Arabia as a power in the Middle East, and the Soviet invasion of Afghanistan. The response of the United States to these developments gave Pakistan a strategic role in protecting western sources of oil and containing Soviet expansion. These vital interests placed a higher priority on the stability of the Zia government than on progress toward real democracy in Pakistan. U.S. support for his repressive military rule not only set back the quest for democracy but also ultimately weakened the authority of the Zia government itself.

DEMOCRACY: 1988–1999

A spirit of democracy did survive, if only partially, in a hasty referendum called in 1985 by General Zia to affirm his policy of Islamization by electing him an executive president for a five-year term. The Constitution of 1973 also survived, though altered by General Zia in the Eighth Amendment, to give the president (normally a formal position in parliamentary government) executive power to dismiss the prime minister. He thus set the stage for legislative elections in November of 1988. These elections did take place, in spite of his death in a plane crash in August. A ruling of the Supreme Court removed the ban on political parties, and Bhutto's Pakistan People's Party, led by his daughter, Benazir Bhutto, won 93 seats in the 217-member National Assembly. Although not commanding a majority of the legislature, she was invited to become prime minister. Then just 35 years old, she was the youngest person and the first woman to lead an Islamic nation.

In 1989, Benazir Bhutto tried to restore the full authority of the prime minister's office by having the Eighth Amendment of the Constitution repealed. She failed to get the necessary two-thirds vote of the legislature. In the summer of 1990, her opposition in the National Assembly tried to defeat her but did not have enough votes. So President Ghulam Ishaq Khan asserted his authority under the Eighth Amendment to dismiss her government. Thus began a cycle of brief tenures of prime ministers ended by presidential decree.

In the elections that followed the 1990 dismissal of the Bhutto government, Mian Nawaz Sharif, chief minister of Punjab and head of the Islami Jamhorri Ittehad (IJI), or Islamic Democratic Alliance, brought his conservative party together with the communist-leaning Awami National party, dominant in the North-West Frontier Province, and the fundamentalist Jamiat-Ulema-i-Islam party. Their coalition won 105 seats in the 217-member National Assembly by winning 36.86 percent of the popular vote. Sharif, a member of a successful industrial family who migrated from Amritsar in East Punjab to Pakistan in 1947, became prime minister.

Even without their support, Nawaz Sharif still called upon Islam as a unifying force in holding the country together and in harmony with its neighboring countries to the west. Sharif's government enacted blasphemy laws and pushed to amend the Constitution to make the Koran "the supreme law of land." These acts were understood as efforts not only to divert attention from increasing economic instability and other political issues but also to contain the potentially volatile force of religious fundamentalism as a threat to stability in the country.

In the fall 1993 elections, Benazir Bhutto and her Pakistan People's Party were returned to power by a slim margin.

In her second term as prime minister, Benazir Bhutto pursued a disastrous series of policies that destabilized the nation's economy, compromised foreign investment, and drove the inflation rate to 20 percent. In response, she imposed a sales tax that proved very unpopular. An image of rampant corruption in government, together with an attempt to appoint sympathetic judges to the high courts, also eroded her popular support. She was once again dismissed on charges of corruption and nepotism under the Eighth Amendment by President Leghari. New elections were called for February 3, 1997. To avoid any legal action against her, Benazir Bhutto fled the country.

HEALTH/WELFARE

Emphasis on the military budget has slighted government attention to education and social services. Because of increasing agricultural production through the Green Revolution, life expectancy has doubled since 1960. The literacy rate among women is half that of the adult male population.

Even though voter turnout was low, Mian Nawaz Sharif and his Pakistan Muslim League Party won a two-thirds majority in the National Assembly. Then, in response to Prime Minister Sharif's repudiation of the military attack into the Kargil District of Kashmir in the summer of 1999, the army chief of staff, General Pervez Musharraf, staged a coup in October.

He then brought charges against Sharif for treason and attempted murder. The courts found Sharif guilty, and sentenced him to life in prison, which General Musharraf commuted to a life in exile.

MARTIAL RULE SINCE 1999

General Musharraf's coup overthrew the parliamentary government that had been elected in 1997. In June 2001 he took over the title of president from Rafiq Tarar, who was elected to a five-year term in that office in 1998. General Musharraf came under considerable international pressure to return Pakistan to a democratic form of government. In response, he portrayed himself as an interim administrator, committed to rooting out corruption and restoring confidence in Pakistan's economy in anticipation of early elections to restore democratic government. But then came the war on terror following the terrorist attacks on the United States on September 11, 2001, and Pakistan suddenly had a vital role in its pursuit that required a firm, decisive, and stable government. General Musharraf took over.

ACHIEVEMENTS

Pakistan has experienced political instability, warfare with India, the loss of East Pakistan, and the incursion of 3 million refugees from Afghanistan. Yet there has still been substantial industrial growth, and the Constitution, adopted in 1973, is working. The country continues to seek a government that is adequate to the needs of its peoples in the modern world and that is consistent with its Islamic faith and tradition.

The primary objective of the war on terror was to remove Osama bin Laden and al-Qaeda bases from Afghanistan. Pakistan, as the friendliest of Afghanistan's neighbors to the United States, became a necessary ally to provide bases and logistical support for American forces conducting military operations in Afghanistan. Equally important, President Musharraf courageously rejected the policy that had created and was continuing to sustain the Taliban regime there. By withdrawing support for the Taliban, he stirred strong opposition among a growing Islamic fundamentalist movement in his own country. He sought both stronger political support for his own rule and greater strategic depth against India by allying himself with the United States.

Still aware of the call to return to democracy, President Musharraf set elections for a national legislature for the fall of 2002. In anticipation of these elections, he called for and won a national referendum on April 30 to extend his presidency for another five years, regardless of the outcome of the legislative elections.

The election results in October did not yield the popular support that Musharraf had sought. A pro-Taliban, anti–United States coalition of Islamic fundamentalist parties, called the Muttahida Majlis-e-amal (MMA), won sufficient support in Baluchistan and the North-West Frontier Province, closest to Afghanistan, to gain 60 of 342 seats in the National Assembly. Benazir Bhutto's PPP won 81 seats. Musharraf's own PAL(Q) won a plurality of 118 seats, but not a majority.

INTERNAL CHALLENGES

Many international forces and events have encumbered Pakistan's quest to become a democratic Islamic republic. But most of its challenges have their origin within the country itself. Areas of concern include a disproportionately high defense budget ($194 billion, or 21.5 percent of the 2004 federal budget), a high rate of population growth (1.98 percent), corruption in gov-

ernment, the loss of human rights through the imposition of religious blasphemy laws, and, most significantly, the lack of human resources development.

More recently, the United Nations Human Development Programme (UNDP) has ranked Pakistan 144th out of 175 countries, the lowest in South Asia, on its Human Development Index. This ranking points to a significant neglect in education (2.7 percent of total federal expenditure) and health (1.09 percent), especially among the poor.

The limited—and elitist—opportunity for education in Pakistan is also a significant indicator of the need for human resources development. The level of literacy in the country is now at 45.8 percent—small improvement over the level, accord-

ing to UNICEF, when Pakistan received its independence in 1947.

Women are excluded even more from education. Their level of literacy is half that of the men (30.6 percent to 59.8 percent). This lack of education reflects the traditional expectation of subservience and seclusion in Islamic society.

Pakistan remains apprehensive about its survival as a unified, sovereign state. It is threatened by divisive political, social, and religious forces both without and within, and by substantive economic and human development challenges. Affirming its integrity as an Islamic republic, its greatest challenge is to become a fully developed modern nation while remaining faithful to the teachings of Islam.

Palestine (State of Palestine)

Palestine Country Report

The lands known as Palestine are of great religious significance for Judaism, Christianity, and Islam. Many different people have come to live on it throughout the years with each of the three religions being emphasized in the region at different periods. This is the reason that today both Jews (the Israelis) and Muslims (the Palestinians) both hold that the lands are theirs by birthright. For Muslims, Palestine is home of the Dome of the Rock (built where the Temple of Solomon once stood). This is where Muslims believe was a halting place for Muhammad on his way to heaven. Nearby is also the Aqsa mosque. They were built in 691 CE and 750 CE, respectively, during the time when the Persians controlled Palestine. Moreover, many of the Muslim Arabs felt the state of Palestine was part of a promise made by the British for Arab support during World War I, especially since a majority of the population in the region was indeed Muslim Arabs. Hence it is that Palestinians believe they have been given the short end of the stick for well over the past 80 years, while their homes were arbitrarily taken away and

Masjid al-Aqsa (the farthest mosque), which is situated in Jerusalem's hallowed precinct, Mount Moriah, known to Muslims as *Haram al-Sharif* or The Noble Sanctuary, and to Jews and Christians as the Temple Mount. This mosque is sacred because Muhammad was miraculously transported here from Makkah on his mystical night journey before ascending to heaven from the Foundation Rock for his meeting with God.

have been repressed by the Israelis who now hold sovereignty over much of the lands that comprise Palestine. Currently, most Palestinians have been left to reside in the West Bank and the Gaza Strip. While the West Bank is located to the east of Israel and west of Jordan, the Gaza Strip is found between Israel and Egypt along the Mediterranean Coast. These two territories are expected to become the basis of a future new state of Palestine.

THE BRITISH MANDATE

The peace settlement arranged after World War I by the new League of Nations gave Palestine to Britain as a mandate. As a result, the name *Palestine* came into common usage for the territory. It is probably derived from Philistine, from the original tribal inhabitants (who are also called Canaanites), but this covenanted land had been ruled by many other peoples and their rulers for centuries, due to its location as a strategic corridor between Asia and Africa. After it became part of the Ottoman Empire, along with Lebanon, it was divided into *vilayets* (provinces), those of Beirut and Acre, respectively; Jerusalem was administered separately as a *sanjak* (subprovince).

The majority of the population were small farmers living in compact villages and rarely traveling elsewhere. Most were Muslims, but there was a substantial minority of Christians. Leadership, such as it was, was held by a small urban elite, the principal families being the Husseinis and Nashashibis of Jerusalem.

DEVELOPMENT

By international standards, Israel is a "developed" country with a per capita income, GDP, and other economic levels comparable to those of Europe. However, the Palestinian *intifada,* which has cost the country $8 billion since it began in 2000, and other factors such as huge government debts over spending on welfare programs and bureaucratic inefficiency have brought on a severe recession. Some 17 percent of Israeli companies were at high risk of bankruptcy as of mid-2003, the ones most affected being in the food industry. The Treasury Ministry predicts a budgetary shortfall of NIS 32 billion for the year, 6 percent of GDP.

After World War I and the peace settlement, the Zionists (Zionism is a movement with the goal of established Palestine as a Jewish homeland) assumed that the Balfour Declaration (a promise by the British to aid in establishing a Jewish home in Palestine) authorized them to begin building a national home for dispersed Jews in Palestine. Great Britain's obligation under the mandate was to prepare Palestine's inhabitants for eventual self-government. However, British officials assigned to Palestine tended to favor Jewish interests over those of the native population. This was due in part to their Judeo-Christian heritage but also to the active support of Jews in Britain during the war. Britain's "view with favor" toward Zionism weighed heavily in the application of mandate requirements to Palestine. Jews were allowed to emigrate, buy land, develop agriculture, and establish banks, schools, and small industries.

Compounding the difficulties of adjustment of two different peoples to the same land was the fact that most Zionist leaders had never been to Palestine. They envisaged it as an empty land waiting for development by industrious Jews. David Ben-Gurion, for example, once claimed that one could walk for days there without meeting a soul; Palestine, he told his compatriots, was a land without a people for a people without a land. Palestine was indeed underpopulated, but it did have a substantial population, many of its members living in villages settled by their ancestors centuries earlier.

Palestinian Arabs were opposed to the mandate, to the Balfour Declaration, and to Jewish immigration. They turned to violence on several occasions, against the British and the growing Jewish population.

In 1936 Arab leaders called a general strike to protest Jewish immigration, which led to a full-scale Arab rebellion. The British tried to steer a middle ground between the two communities. But they were unwilling (or unable) either to accept Arab demands for restrictions on Jewish immigration and land purchases or Zionist demands for a Jewish majority in Palestine.

British policy reports and White Papers during the mandate wavered back and forth. In 1937, the Peel Commission, set up after the Arab revolt, recommended a halt to further Jewish immigration, and subsequently the 1939 White Paper stated that the mandate should be replaced by a self-governing Arab state with rights assured for the Jewish minority.

One important difference between the Palestinian Arab and Jewish communities was in their organization. The Jews were organized under the Jewish Agency, which operated as a "state within a state" in Palestine. Jews in Europe and the United States also contributed substantially to the agency's finances and made arrangements for immigration. The Palestinian Arabs, in contrast, were led by heads of urban families who often quarreled with one another. The Palestinian Arab cause also did not have outside Arab support; leaders of neighboring Arab states were weak and were still under British or French control.

Adolf Hitler's policy of genocide (total extermination) of Jews in Europe, developed during World War II, gave a special urgency to Jewish settlement in Palestine. American Zionist leaders condemned the 1939 British White Paper and called for unrestricted Jewish immigration into Palestine and the establishment of an independent, democratic Jewish state. After World War II, the British, still committed to the White Paper, blocked Palestine harbors and turned back the crowded, leaking ships carrying desperate Jewish refugees from Europe. World opinion turned against the British.

Supplies of smuggled weapons enabled Haganah, the Jewish militia, to fend off attacks by Palestinian Arabs, while Jewish terrorist groups such as the Stern Gang and Irgun Zvai Leumi carried out acts of murder and sabotage against British troops and installations.

PARTITION AND INDEPENDENCE

In 1947 the British decided that the Palestine mandate was unworkable. They asked the United Nations to come up with a solution to the problem of "one land, two peoples." A UN Special Commission on Palestine (UNSCOP) recommended partition of Palestine into two states—one Arab, one Jewish—with an economic union between them. A minority of UNSCOP members recommended a federated Arab-Jewish state, with an elected legislature and minority rights for Jews. The majority report was approved by the UN General Assembly on November 29, 1947, by a 33–13 vote, after intensive lobbying by the Zionists.

The partition would establish a Jewish state, with 56 percent of the land, and a Palestinian Arab state, with 44 percent. The population at that time was 60 percent Arab and 40 percent Jewish. Due to its special associations for Jews, Muslims, and Christians, Jerusalem would become an international city administered by the United Nations.

FREEDOM

Israel is a multiparty democracy with a parliament (Knesset) and representative political and judicial institutions. Its Basic Laws guarantee free speech, among other human rights. However the full range of human rights has never been extended to Israeli Arabs. They are discriminated against in access to higher education, adequate schools, jobs, and other "guaranteed" rights. The Israeli-Arab political position has improved in recent years with the formation of "Arab" political parties and election of Arab members to the Knesset. However, in January 2003 two Arab members were stripped of their parliamentary immunity on the grounds that they had questioned the "Jewish character" of the state, arguing that it should be a "state for all citizens."[21]

The Jewish delegation accepted the partition plan approved by the UN General Assembly. But Palestinian Arab leaders, backed strongly by the newly independent Arab states, rejected the plan outright. On May 14, 1948, in keeping with Britain's commitment to end its mandate, the last British soldiers left Palestine. On May 15 the United States and the Soviet Union recognized the new state, even as the armies of five Arab states converged on it to "push the Jews into the sea."

INDEPENDENT ISRAEL

Long before the establishment of Israel, the nation's first prime minister, David Ben-Gurion, had come to Palestine as a youth.

After a clash between Arab nomads and Jews from the kibbutz where he lived had injured several people, Ben-Gurion wrote prophetically, "It was then I realized... that sooner or later Jews and Arabs would fight over this land, a tragedy since intelligence and good will could have avoided all bloodshed."[8] In the five decades of independence, Ben-Gurion's prophecy has been borne out in five Arab-Israeli wars. In between those wars, conflict between Israel and the Palestinians has gone on more or less constantly, like a running sore.

Some 700,000 to 800,000 Palestinians fled Israel during the War for Independence. After the 1967 Six-Day War, an additional 380,000 Palestinians became refugees in Jordan. Israeli occupation of the West Bank brought a million Palestinians under military control.

The unifying factor among all Palestinians is the same as that which had united the dispersed Jews for 20 centuries: the recovery of the sacred homeland. Abu Iyad, a top PLO leader, once said, "... our dream....[is] the reunification of Palestine in a secular and democratic state shared by Jews, Christians and Muslims rooted in this common land.... There is no doubting the irrepressible will of the Palestinian people to pursue their struggle... and one day, we will have a country."[9] Indeed, in 1964, the PLO was created to stand up against Israel to take their homeland back. Their leader, Yasir Arafat, would bring their cause to the floor of the United Nations 10 years later, with Palestinians becoming the first government without a state to do so.

The land vacated by the Palestinians has been transformed in the decades of Israeli development. Those Israelis actually born in Palestine—now in their third generation—call themselves Sabras, after the prickly pear cactus of the Negev. The work of Sabras and of a generation of immigrants has created a highly urbanized society, sophisticated industries, and a productive agriculture.

HEALTH/WELFARE

The 2002–2003 recession has punched large holes in the safety net provided for Israelis by the government and its adjunct organization, Histadrut. The increases in both unemployment and families below the poverty line suggest that the country can no longer function as a welfare state. One result of the recession is that more Russian Jews are emigrating to Germany than to Israel due to the more stable German economy.

JEWISH EXTREMISTS, ARAB EXTREMISTS

The deep divisions in Israeli society regarding future relations with the Palestinian population in the occupied territories (for many Israelis, these lands are Judea and Samaria,

Qubbat as-Sakhra (Dome of the Rock) on Mount Moriah in the Old City of Jerusalem houses the rock of Foundation from where Muslims believe Prophet Muhammad ascended to Heaven for a meeting with God. The same rock is the site where Jews and Christians believe Abraham came to sacrifice his son Isaac. Completed by Umayyad Caliph Abdul Malik ibn Marwan in 691 CE, this shrine is one of the oldest and most important architectural monuments of Islamic civilization and the third holiest site in Islamdom after the Ka'abah in Makkah and Prophet Muhammad's Mosque in Madina.

part of the ancestral Jewish homeland) were underscored by the uncovering in the 1980s of a Jewish underground organization that had attacked Palestinian leaders in violent attempts to keep the territories forever Jewish. The group had plotted secretly to blow up the sacred Islamic shrines atop the Dome of the Rock. A number of the plotters were given life sentences by a military court. But such was the outcry of support from right-wing groups in the population that their sentences were later commuted by then-president Chaim Herzog.

A more virulent form of anti-Arab, anti-Palestinian violence emerged in 1984 with the founding of Kach, a political party that advocated expulsion of all Arabs from Israel. Its founder, Brooklyn, New York-born Rabbi Meir Kahane, was elected to the Knesset in 1984, giving him parliamentary immunity, and he began organizing anti-Arab demonstrations. The Knesset subsequently passed a law prohibiting any political party advocating racism in any form from participation in national elections. On that basis, the Israeli Supreme Court barred Kach and its founder from participating in the 1988 elections. Kahane was murdered by an Egyptian-American while in New York for a speaking engagement.

His son Binyamin formed a successor party, *Kahane Chai* ("Kahane Lives"), based in the West Bank Jewish settlement of Tapuah. Both Kach and Kahane Chai were labeled terrorist groups by the U.S. Department of State. They were also outlawed in Israel after a member, Baruch Goldstein, murdered 29 Muslims in a mosque in Hebron. In September 2000

Binyamin Kahane and his wife were killed in an ambush while driving their children to school, in another blow to the struggling Palestinian-Israeli peace negotiations.

Arab extremism, or, more accurately, Palestinian extremism, evolved in the 1990s largely as a result of Palestinian anger and disillusionment over the peace agreements with Israel, which were seen as accommodation on the part of Palestinian leaders, notably Yassir Arafat, to Israel rather than negotiations to establish a Palestinian state. The main Palestinian extremist group is *Hamas* (the Arabic acronym for the Islamic Resistance Movement, or IRM). Hamas developed originally as a Palestinian chapter of the Muslim Brotherhood, which has chapters in various Islamic Arab countries where it seeks to replace their secular regimes by a government ruled under Islamic law. However, Hamas broke with its parent organization over the use of violence, due largely to the lack of success of the intifada in achieving Palestinian self-rule.

A number of violent attacks on Israelis, including the murder of a border policeman in 1992, led Israel to deport 415 Hamas activists to southern Lebanon. However, the Lebanese government refused to admit them. Lebanon and other Arab countries filed a complaint with the UN Security Council. The Council passed *Resolution 799*, calling for the return of the deportees.

Although Israel seldom responds to UN resolutions, in this case the 1993 Oslo Agreement provided additional motivation, and eventually the deportees were allowed to return to their homes.

THE INTIFADA

The Palestinian intifada (literally, "shaking off") in the West Bank and Gaza Strip, which began in December 1987, came as a rude shock to Israel. Coming as it did barely two and a half years after the trauma of the Lebanon War, the uprising found the Israeli public as well as its citizen army unprepared. The military recall of middle-aged reservists and dispatch of new draftees to face stone-throwing Palestinian children created severe moral and psychological problems for many soldiers.

Military authorities devised a number of methods to deal with the uprising. They included deportation of suspected terrorists, demolition of houses, wholesale arrests, and detention of Palestinians without charges for indefinite periods. However, growing international criticism of the policy of "breaking the bones" of demonstrators (particularly children) developed by then-defense minister Yitzhak Rabin brought a change in tactics, with the use of rubber or plastic dum-dum bullets, whose effect is less lethal except at close range.

The government also tried to break the Palestinian resistance through arbitrary higher taxes, arguing that this was necessary to compensate for revenues lost due to refusal of Palestinians to pay taxes, a slowdown in business, and lowered exports to the territories. A value added tax (VAT) imposed on olive presses just prior to the processing of the West Bank's major crop was a particular hardship. Along with the brutality of its troops, the tax-collection methods drove Palestinians and Israelis further apart, making the prospect of any amicable relationship questionable.

The opening of emigration to Israel for Soviet Jews added an economic dimension to the intifada. Increased expropriation of land on the West Bank for new immigrant families, along with the expansion of Jewish settlements there, added to Palestinian resentment. Many Palestinians felt that because the new immigrants were unable to find professional employment, they were taking menial jobs ordinarily reserved for Palestinian workers in Israel.

In October 1990 the most serious incident since the start of the intifada occurred in Jerusalem. Palestinians stoned a Jewish group, the Temple Mount Faithful, who had come to lay a symbolic cornerstone for a new Jewish Temple near the Dome of the Rock. Israeli security forces then opened fire, killing some 20 Palestinians and injuring more than 100. The UN Security Council approved a resolution condemning Israel for excessive response (one of many that the Israeli state has ignored over the years).

The success of the intifada lay in demonstrating for Israelis the limits to the use of force against a population under occupation. It also served as a pointed reminder to Israelis that "incorporating the occupied territories would commit Israel to the perpetual use of its military to control and repress, not 'Arab refugees' but the whole Palestinian population living in these lands."[19]

THE PEACE AGREEMENT

Prior to September 1993, there were few indications that a momentous breakthrough in Palestinian-Israeli relations was about to take place. The new Israeli Labor Party government had cracked down on the Palestinians in the occupied territories harder than had its predecessor in six years of the intifada. In addition to mass arrests and deportations of persons allegedly associated with Hamas, the government sealed off the territories, not only from Israel itself but also from one another. With 120,000 Palestinians barred from their jobs in Israel, poverty, hunger, and unemployment became visible facts of life in the West Bank and the Gaza Strip.

However, what 11 rounds of peace talks, five wars, and 40 years of friction had failed to achieve was accomplished swiftly that September, with the signing of a peace and mutual-recognition accord (referred to as the Oslo Agreement) between Israel and Palestinians. The accord was worked out in secret by Israeli and PLO negotiators in Norway and under Norwegian Foreign Ministry sponsorship. It provided for mutual recognition, transfer of authority over the Gaza Strip and the West Bank city of Jericho (but not the entire West Bank) to an elected Palestinian council that would supervise the establishment of Palestinian rule, withdrawal of Israeli forces and their replacement by a Palestinian police force, and a Palestinian state to be formed after a transitional period. So it was that the Palestinian Authority took control of the these territories with Arafat as its elected leader.

Opposition to the accord from within both societies was to be expected, given the intractable nature of Palestinian-Israeli differences—two peoples claiming the same land. Implementation of the Oslo agreements has been hampered from the start by groups opposed to any form of Palestinian-Israeli accommodation. On the Israeli side, some settler groups formed vigilante posses for defense, even setting up a "tent city" in Jerusalem to protest any giveaway of sacred Jewish land. Palestinian gunmen and suicide bombers responded with attacks on Jews, sometimes in alleyways or on lonely stretches of road outside the cities, but also in public places.

Labor's return to power in 1992 suggested that, despite this virulent opposition, the peace process would go forward under its own momentum. The new government, headed by Yitzak Rabin as prime minister, began to implement the disengagement of Israeli forces and the transfer of power over the territories to Yassir Arafat's Palestine National Authority (PNA). The Gaza Strip, Jericho, and several West Bank towns were turned over to PNA control. Israel's seeming commitment to the peace process at that time helped to improve relations with its Arab neighbors. An Arab boycott of Israeli goods and companies was lifted. In 1994 the country signed a formal peace treaty with Jordan and opened trade offices in several Gulf states.

RABIN'S DEATH AND ITS CONSEQUENCES

The second stage in transfer of authority over the West Bank had barely begun when Rabin was assassinated by an Orthodox Jew while speaking at a Peace Now rally in Jerusalem on November 4, 1995.

Then, in the 1996 elections, Likud party leader Benjamin Netanyahu became Israel's new prime minister. His victory, by a scant 16,000 votes, foreshadowed what would prove to be a near-total deadlock in the peace process. The deadlock was also marked by a deep and angry division within the Israeli society.

In addition to not honoring the Oslo agreements, Netanyahu encouraged in-

creased Jewish settlements in the West Bank and Gaza. He used his office to cultivate various groups and parties at the expense of other groups, changing sides when it suited him. However, Netanyahu would fail to win reelection, which presented a new crossroads for Israeli-Palestinian relations.

Ariel Sharon's well-publicized visit on September 28, 2000, to the Dome of the Rock (referred to as Haram al-Sharif by Muslims) not only set off a new Palestinian intifada (it is often referred to as the al-Aqsa intifada); it also had a direct impact on a muddled Israeli political system. Additionally, Sharon won the new elections.

The new prime minister took office amid foreboding on the part of many Israelis, as well as by the country's Arab neighbors and the world at large. At the time, Sharon's record included masterminding the 1982 invasion of Lebanon and ultimate responsibility for the slaughter of Palestinians by Israel's Christian allies in Lebanese refugee camps.

Sharon's first year in office coincided with the renewal of the Palestinian intifada, which has brought Israel and the Palestinians into a head-on conflict verging on total war. The accelerated cycle of violence has been marked by new tactics on both sides—relentless suicide bombings by Palestinians, mostly against Israeli civilians; and use of massive retaliation by Israeli tanks, missiles, and helicopter gunships.

By 2004 the conflict had taken on many aspects of a civil war. In four years, nearly 4,000 people had become casualties of the second intifada (of which approximately 3,000 were Palestinians). On the Israeli side there is increasing divergence between the population at large, 39 percent of whom favor accommodation with the Palestinians, and the Sharon government. On the official side, several former heads of Shin Bet, the Israeli security service, publicly denounced the government's repressive measures, and the military Chief of Staff,

United Nations Photo (UN162036)

Yasser Arafat (1929–2004) was the chairman and commander-in-chief of the Palestine Liberation Organization (PLO) since he was elected by that multi-faction guerrilla organization in 1968. In 1994, he was the co-winner of the Nobel Peace Prize for his agreement to work toward peaceful coexistence with Israel. Two years later, he was elected president of the Palestinian National Authority (PNA) in the Israel-occupied West Bank and Gaza. Although he died in Novemeber 2004 without achieving his goal of Palestinian independence, he earned a place in history as the father of Palestinian nationalism.

General Ayalon, warned that the measures would only "generate hatred that will explode in our face." Several officials spoke openly of a unilateral withdrawal from the occupied territories.

A similar extremism marked the relationship between Sharon and the late Yassir Arafat. In December 2001 Sharon declared Arafat "irrelevant" to the peace process. Israeli security forces blockaded his Ramallah headquarters, confining him to house arrest.

Relations improved temporarily with the election of Prime Minister Mahmoud Abbas to expedite the Palestinian side of the "road map to peace." However Arafat retained final decision-making powers in the Palestinian hierarchy and remained a symbol of hope for generations of Palestinians in their struggle to establish a state of their own. After all, it was Arafat who had finally succeeded in bringing the world's attention to the plight of his people. The blockade was lifted in May 2002 under heavy U.S. pressure.

Timeline: PAST

691
Dome of the Rock is complete

750
The Adsa mosque is built

1897
The Zionist movement is organized by Theodor Herzel

1917
The Balfour Declaration

1922–1948
British mandate over Palestine

1947–1948
A UN partition plan is accepted by the Jewish community; following British withdrawal, the State of Israel is proclaimed

1964
The Palestinian Liberation Organization is created

1967
The Six-Day War; Israeli occupation of East Jerusalem, the Gaza Strip, and the Sinai Peninsula

1987
The first Palestinian intifada begins

1990s
Israeli-Palestinian efforts toward peace; violence escalates on both sides in response

PRESENT

2000s
Ariel Sharon visits the Dome of the Rock; the second (al-Aqsa) intifada begins; the Palestinian-Israeli conflict reaches new extremes of violence; "road map" to peace is unveiled; Arafat dies; Abbas becomes Palestinian Authority's new president

RECENT DEVELOPMENTS

The "road map" for peace that was constructed by the United States, United Nations, European Union and Russia has gotten off to a slow start. Both sides initially did little to move towards the outlined goals to bring about an end to the continued violence. Many held that Arafat refused to do little to slow down Palestinian militant attacks on Israel. Moreover, Sharon continued building his "security fence" to divide Israel and Palestine despite the condemnation of the UN (although he did change its route as to not take away lands from the Palestinians). However, since the ascension of Abbas to president following the death of Arafat on November 10, 2004, greater efforts seem to be being made. Both sides pledged a ceasefire on February 8, 2005, but the violence has continued. Also, in August of 2005 Israel began removing some (but not all) settlements from the West Bank and Gaza Strip.

NOTES

1. Ashkenazi, derived from Ashkenaz (Genesis 10:3), is the name given to Jews who lived in Europe, particularly Germany, and followed particular traditions of Judaism handed down from biblical days. Sephardim (from Sepharah, Obadiah 1:20) refers to Jews originally from Spain who were expelled and emigrated to the Middle East-North Africa. R. J. Zwi Werblowsky and Geoffrey Wigoder, eds., *The Encyclopedia of the Jewish Religion* (New York: Holt, Rinehart & Winston, 1965).

2. Dan V. Segre, *A Crisis of Identity: Israel and Zionism* (Oxford, England: Oxford University Press, 1980), p. 25.

3. Ben Lynfield, in *The Christian Science Monitor*, August 8, 2003.

4. Herod's palaces, adorned with copious mosaics and furnished with mineral baths and saunas, have been excavated and reveal not only his opulent lifestyles but also his very real contributions to the architecture of his time, including renovation of the Temple. Other links with Jesus' time are less definite. An ossuary (burial box) discovered in 2002 and thought to contain the bones of his elder brother James has been proven to be a forgery.

5. Yaron Ezrahi, *Rubber Bullets: Power and Conscience in Modern Israel* (New York: Farrar, Straus & Giroux, 1997), p. 269.

6. Abraham Shulman, *Coming Home to Zion* (Garden City, NY: Doubleday, 1979), p. 14.

7. The text is in "Documents on Palestine," *The Middle East and North Africa* (London: Europa Publications, 1984), p. 58.

8. David Ben-Gurion, *Memoirs* (Cleveland: World Publishing, 1970), p. 58.

9. Abu Iyad with Eric Rouleau, *My Home, My Land: A Narrative of the Palestinian Struggle*, Linda Butler Koseoglu, tr. (New York: New York Times Books, 1981), pp. 225–226.

10. Ezrahi, *op. cit.*, pp. 274–275.

11. Milton Viorst, What Shall I Do With These People?; Jews and the Fractious Politics of Judaism (New York: Free Press, 2 2002), p. 215.

Qatar (State of Qatar)

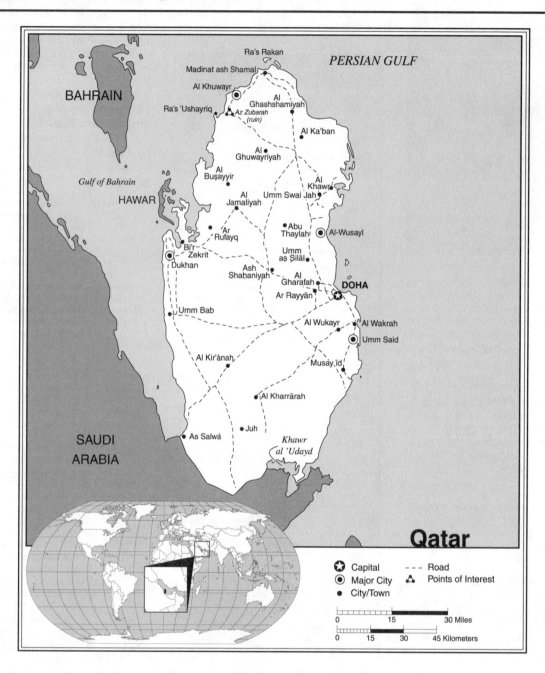

Qatar

- ⭐ Capital
- ◉ Major City
- ● City/Town
- - - - Road
- △ Points of Interest

| 0 | 15 | 30 Miles |

| 0 | 15 | 30 | 45 Kilometers |

Qatar Statistics

GEOGRAPHY

Area in Square Miles (Kilometers): 4,400 (11,400) (about the size of Connecticut)

Capital (Population): Doha (340,000)

Environmental Concerns: limited natural freshwater supplies; increasing dependence on large-scale desalination facilities

Geographical Features: mostly flat and barren desert covered with loose sand and gravel

Climate: desert; hot and dry; humid and sultry summers

PEOPLE

Population

Total: 853,051
Annual Growth Rate: 2.61%
Rural/Urban Population Ratio: 8/92
Major Languages: Arabic; English widely used

Ethnic Makeup: 40% Arab; 18% Pakistani;
18% Indian; 10% Iranian; 14% others
Religions: 95% Muslim; 5% others

Health

Life Expectancy at Birth: 71 years (male);
76 years (female)
Infant Mortality Rate: 18.6/1,000 live
births
Physicians Available (Ratio): 1/793 people

Education

Adult Literacy Rate: 79.4%

COMMUNICATION

Telephones: 184,500 main lines
Daily Newspaper Circulation: 143 per
1,000 people
Televisions: 451 per 1,000 people
Internet Service Provider: 1 (2000)

TRANSPORTATION

Highways in Miles (Kilometers): 764 (1,230)
Railroads in Miles (Kilometers): none

Usable Airfields: 4
Motor Vehicles in Use: 183,000

GOVERNMENT

Type: traditional monarchy
Independence Date: September 3, 1971
(from the United Kingdom)
Head of State/Government: Emir Hamad
bin Khalifa al-Thani; Prime Minister
Abdallah bin Khalifa al-Thani
Political Parties: none
Suffrage: 18 years of age; universal

MILITARY

Military Expenditures (% of GDP): 10%
Current Disputes: none; territorial dispute
with Bahrain settled in 2001 by the
International Court of Justice

ECONOMY

Currency ($ U.S. Equivalent): 3.64 rials =
$1 (fixed rate)

Per Capita Income/GDP: $23,200/$19.49
billion
GDP Growth Rate: 8.7%
Inflation Rate: 3%
Labor Force: 140,000
Unemployment Rate: 2.7%
Natural Resources: petroleum; natural
gas; fish
Agriculture: fruits; vegetables; poultry;
dairy products; beef; fish
Industry: crude-oil production and
refining; fertilizers; petrochemicals; steel
reinforcing bars; cement
Exports: $15 billion (primary partners
Japan, Singapore, South Korea)
Imports: $6.15 billion (primary partners
France, United Kingdom, Japan,
Germany)

SUGGESTED WEB SITES

http://lcweb2.loc.gov/frd/cs/
qatoc.html
http://www.qatar-info.com/

Qatar Country Report

Qatar is a shaykhdom on the eastern
(Gulf) coast of Arabia. It is the second
smallest Middle Eastern state, after Bahrain; but due to its oil wealth, it has an extremely high per capita annual income.
Before 1949, when its oil exports began,
there were about 20,000 Qataris, all descendants of peoples who had migrated to
the coast centuries ago in search of a dependable water supply. Since then, rapid
economic growth has attracted workers
and residents from other Arab countries
and distant Muslim states such as Pakistan.
As a result, Qatar has a high number of immigrants and expatriates, which makes for
some tension.

HISTORY

Although the peninsula has been inhabited
since 4000 B.C., little is known of its history before the nineteenth century. At one
time, it was ruled by the al-Khalifa family,
the current rulers of Bahrain. It became
part of the Ottoman Empire formally in
1872, but the Turkish garrison was evacuated during World War I. The Ottomans
earlier had recognized Shaykh Qassim al-
Thani, head of the important al-Thani family, as emir of Qatar, and the British followed suit when they established a
protectorate after the war.

The British treaty with the al-Thanis
was similar to ones made with other

shaykhs in Arabia and the Persian Gulf in
order to keep other European powers out of
the area and to protect their trade and communications links with India. In 1916 the
British recognized Shaykh Abdullah al-
Thani, grandfather of the current ruler, as
ruler of Qatar and promised to protect the
territory from outside attack either by the
Ottomans or overland by hostile Arabian
groups. In return, Shaykhal-Thani agreed
not to enter into any relationship with any
other foreign government and to accept
British political advisers.

Qatar remained a tranquil British protectorate until the 1950s, when oil exports
began. Since then, the country has developed rapidly, though not to the extent of
producing the dizzying change visible in
other oil-producing Arab states.

INDEPENDENCE

Qatar became independent in 1971. The
ruler, Shaykh Ahmad al-Thani, took the title of emir. Disagreements within the ruling family led the emir's cousin, Shaykh
Khalifa, to seize power in 1972. Khalifa
made himself prime minister as well as
ruler and initiated a major program of social and economic development, which his
cousin had opposed.

Shaykh Khalifa limited the privileges of
the ruling family. There were more than
2,000 al-Thanis, and most of them had

been paid several thousand dollars a month
whether or not they worked. Khalifa reduced their allowances and appointed
some nonmembers of the royal family to
the Council of Ministers, the state's chief
executive body. In 1992, he set up a Consultative Council of 30 members to advise
the cabinet on proposed legislation and
budgetary matters. Subsequently, the cabinet itself was enlarged, with new ministries
of Islamic affairs, finance, economy, and
industry and trade. While the majority of
cabinet and Consultative Council members
belonged to the royal family, the appointment of a number of nonfamily members to
both these organizations heralded the
"quiet revolution" toward power sharing to
which Shaykh Khalifa was committed.

DEVELOPMENT

Qatar's huge gas reserves are
among the largest in the world,
but are concentrated in a single
field. They form the basis for
ongoing economic development. New
petrochemical and related fertilizer industries
are beginning to diversify sources of revenue.

FOREIGN RELATIONS

Because of its small size, great wealth, and
proximity to regional conflicts, Qatar is
vulnerable to outside intervention. The

government fears especially that the example of the Iranian Shi'a Revolution may bring unrest to its own Shi'a Muslim population. After the discovery of a Shi'a plot to overthrow the government of neighboring Bahrain in 1981, Qatari authorities deported several hundred Shi'a Qataris of Iranian origin. But thus far the government has avoided singling out the Shi'a community for heavy-handed repression, preferring to concentrate its efforts on economic and social progress.

THE ECONOMY

The Qatari economy is currently based on oil, but in the very near future, oil will be replaced by natural gas as its major mineral resource. Until recently, the Qatari oil industry was considered to be in a state of terminal decline, with dwindling reserves and low production. New discoveries and production-sharing agreements have revived the industry. Proven oil reserves are sufficient for 23 years at current rates of production.

Depletion of water supplies due to heavy demand and dependence on outdated desalination plants for its fresh water have prompted the country to undertake some innovative food-production projects. One such project, begun in 1988, uses solar energy and seawater to cultivate food crops in sand. As a result of such projects, Qatar produces sufficient food both to meet domestic needs and to export vegetables to neighboring states.

SOCIETAL CHANGES

Qatar was originally settled by nomadic peoples, and their influence is still strong. Traditional Bedouin values, such as honesty, hospitality, pride, and courage, have carried over into modern times.

FREEDOM

Since he deposed his father, the ruling emir has abolished press censorship, established Al-Jazeerah as a service of uncensored news to the Arab world, and appointed younger members of the ruling family to replace his father's advisers and ministers.

Most Qataris belong to the strict puritanical Wahhabi sect of Islam, which is also dominant in Saudi Arabia. They are similar to Saudis in their conservative outlook, and Qatar generally defers to its larger neighbor in foreign policy. There are, however, significant social differences between Qataris and Saudis. Western movies may be shown in Qatar, for example, but not in Saudi Arabia. Furthermore, Qatar does not have religious police or "morals squads" to enforce Islamic conventions, and foreigners may purchase alcoholic beverages legally.

Qatar also differs from its Arab peninsular neighbors and the Arab world generally in permitting free discussion in the media of issues generally suppressed by Arab rulers. Following his accession to the throne, the new emir abolished press censorship and eliminated the Information Ministry from his cabinet. In 1997 his government licensed a new satellite TV network station called Al-Jazeera ("Peninsula," in Arabic), supported by an annual subsidy to meet its operating costs. Despite its freewheeling broadcasting style and frequent criticism of Arab rulers, including its own, the ruling emir does not attempt to censor the station or close it down.

HEALTH/WELFARE

Qatar's first private hospital opened in 1996 and is now fully staffed by Qatari doctors and nurses, who have replaced expatriate medical personnel. Among the Arab states, Qatar has an unusually high ratio of physicians to population.

The most significant societal change in Qatar involves the position of women. In 1998 the new emir granted women the right to vote and to run for and hold public office.

Roughly 30 percent of Qatari women are employed in the labor force, and many are not only educated but also well qualified professionally. Unlike their sisters in some other Gulf states, they drive cars, work in offices and juggle careers and family responsibilities.

INTERNAL POLITICS

Elections for a unicameral Central Municipal Council of 29 members for Doha were held first in 1999 and subsequently in 2003, two "firsts" for the emirate. Some 221 men and 3 women competed for the 29 seats. One of the women was elected, the first female to hold elective office not only in Qatar but in the entire Gulf region. As a first step toward constitutional government, the Council has consultative powers, although these are limited to improving municipal services.

The "quiet revolution" initiated by the new emir entered a new stage in March 1999, with elections for a Doha Central Municipal Council, the country's first

ACHIEVEMENTS

Qatar played host to the World Trade Conference annual meeting in November 2001. Despite threats of disruption by activists opposed to WTO policies, the meeting opened on schedule, albeit under tight security. It produced a compromise agreement among the 144 member states on global-market reforms that will expedite free trade while protecting the interests of the poorer nations.

public elections. The Council does not have executive powers, but it is intended as a transitional body between patriarchal rule and the establishment of an elected parliament. All Qataris over age 18 were allowed to vote, including women (who make up 44 percent of registered voters). Six women ran with 221 men for the Council's 29 seats.

NOTES

1. Qatar News Agency (November 23, 1981).
2. Douglas Jehl, *The New York Times International* (July 20, 1997).
3. Mary Anne Weaver, "Democracy by Decree," *The New Yorker* (November 20, 2000), p. 57.
4. Fouad Ajami, "What the Muslim World Is Watching," *The New York Times Magazine* (November 18, 2001).
5. Weaver, op cit.

Timeline: PAST

1916
Britain recognizes Shaykh Abdullah al-Thani as emir

1949
The start of oil production in Qatar

1971
An abortive federation with Bahrain and the Trucial States (U. A. E.), followed by independence

1972
The ruler is deposed by Shaykh Khalifa

1990s
Qatar condemns the Iraqi invasion of Kuwait and expels resident Palestinians; Crown Prince Hamad al-Thani deposes his father and takes over as emir

PRESENT

2000s
The World Court decides a territorial dispute in favor of Bahrain; Qatari-funded Al-Jazeerah news station achieves global prominence

Saudi Arabia (Kingdom of Saudi Arabia)

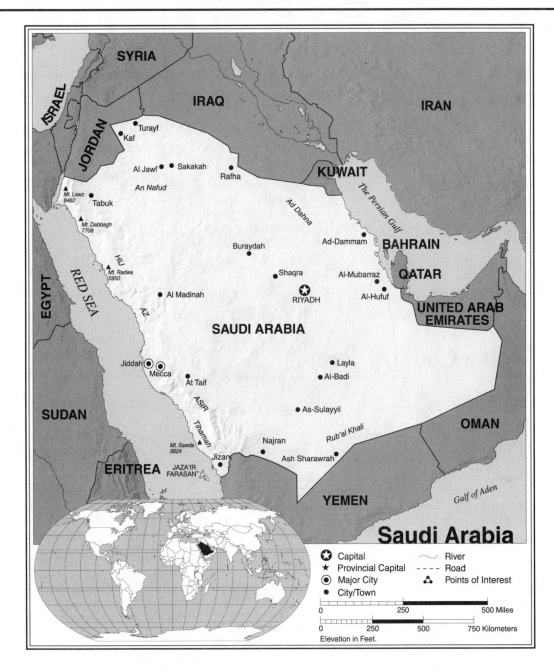

Saudi Arabia Statistics

GEOGRAPHY

Area in Square Miles (Kilometers): 756,785 (1,960,582) (about 1/5 the size of the United States)

Capital (Population): Riyadh (2,625,000)

Environmental Concerns: desertification; depletion of underground water resources; coastal pollution from oil spills

Geographical Features: mostly uninhabited sandy desert

Climate: harsh, dry desert, with great extremes of temperature

PEOPLE

Population

Total: 26,417,599 (includes 5,576,076 nonnationals)

Annual Growth Rate: 2.3%

Rural/Urban Population Ratio: 16/84

Major Languages: Arabic; English widely used

Ethnic Makeup: 90% Arab; 10% Afro-Asian

Religion: 100% Muslim

Health

Life Expectancy at Birth: 73 years (male); 77 years (female)

Infant Mortality Rate: 13.24/1,000 live
  births
Physicians Available (Ratio): 1/590 people

Education
Adult Literacy Rate: 78.8%

COMMUNICATION
Telephones: 3,502,600, plus 7 million
  mobile cellular phones
Daily Newspaper Circulation: 54 per
  1,000 people
Televisions: 257 per 1,000 people
Internet Service Providers: 42 (2001)

TRANSPORTATION
Highways in Miles (Kilometers): 87,914
  (152,044)
Railroads in Miles (Kilometers): 863 (1,392)
Usable Airfields: 201
Motor Vehicles in Use: 2,800,000

GOVERNMENT
Type: hereditary monarchy

Independence Date: September 23, 1932
  (unification)
Head of State/Government: King and
  Prime Minister Abdallah bin Abd al-
  Aziz Al Saud
Political Parties: none; prohibited
Suffrage: adult male citizen age 21 or older

MILITARY
Military Expenditures (% of GDP): 10%
Current Disputes: border with Yemen
  fixed by treaty but not demarcated due to
  frequent use by nomadic tribes.
  Boundary with U.A.E. not formally
  demarcated but recognized de facto;
  Yemen protests Saudi erection of a
  concrete-filled pipe as a security barrier
  in 2004 to stem illegal cross-border
  activities in sections of the boundary

ECONOMY
Currency ($ U.S. Equivalent): 3.745 riyals
  = $1

Per Capita Income/GDP: $12,000/$310.2
  billion
GDP Growth Rate: 5%
Inflation Rate: 0.8%
Labor Force: 6,620,000
Unemployment Rate: 25% (unofficial)
Natural Resources: petroleum; natural
  gas; iron ore; gold; copper
Agriculture: wheat; barley; tomatoes;
  melons; dates; citrus fruits; mutton;
  chickens; eggs; milk
Industry: crude-oil production; petroleum
  refining; basic petrochemicals; cement;
  construction; fertilizer; plastics
Exports: $113 billion (primary partners
  Japan, United States, South Korea)
Imports: $36.2 billion (primary partners
  United States, Japan, Germany)

SUGGESTED WEB SITES
http://lcweb2.loc.gov/frd/cs/
  satoc.html
http://www.saudinf.com/main/
  start.htm

Saudi Arabia Country Report

The Kingdom of Saudi Arabia is the geographical giant of the Arabian Peninsula. It is also a giant in the world economy because of its oil. To many people, the name Saudi Arabia is a synonym for oil wealth. Indeed, its huge oil reserves, large financial surpluses from oil production, and ability to use oil as a political weapon (as in the 1973 embargo) enable the country to play an important part in international as well as regional affairs.

Saudi Arabia's population is small in relation to the country's size and is heavily urbanized. Urban growth has been very rapid, considering that only 1 percent of the land can be used for agriculture and all employment opportunities are in the cities or in the oil-producing regions. The kingdom has relied strongly on expatriate workers, skilled as well as unskilled, in its development. The economic dislocation of the Gulf War, along with the support given Iraq by Palestinians and the government of Yemen, led to the expulsion of nearly 1 million foreign workers, most of them Palestinians and Yemenis. But due to the unwillingness of most Saudis to take on low-paying work that seems to be below them professionally, the government has had to continue its dependence on expatriates. Some 67 percent of government jobs and 95 percent of those in private industry are still held by foreigners.

The country contains three main geographical regions: the Hejaz, along the Red Sea; the Nejd, a vast interior plateau that comprises the bulk of Saudi territory; and the Eastern Province. The kingdom's largest oases, al-Hasa and Safwa, are located in this third region, along with the major oil fields and industrial centers. The Empty Quarter (al-Rub' al-Khali), an uninhabited desert where rain may not fall for a decade or more, occupies the entire southeastern quadrant of the country.

THE WAHHABI MOVEMENT

In the eighteenth century, most of the area included in present-day Saudi Arabia was the home of nomads, as it had been for centuries. These peoples had no central government and owed allegiance to no one except their chiefs. They spent much of their time raiding one another's territories in the struggle for survival. Inland Arabia was a great blank area on the map—a vast, empty desert.

The only part of modern Saudi Arabia under any government control in the eighteenth century was the Hejaz, which includes the Islamic holy cities of Makkah and Madina. It was a province of the Ottoman Empire, the major power in the Middle East at that time.

Saudi Arabia became a nation, in the modern sense of the word, in 1932. But the origins of the Saudi nation go back to the eighteenth century. One of the tribes that roamed the desert beyond Ottoman control was the tribe of Saud. Its leader, Muhammad ibn Saud, wanted to gain an advantage over his rivals in the constant search for water and good grazing land for animals. He approached a famous religious scholar named Abd al-Wahhab, who lived in an oasis near the current Saudi capital, Riyadh. Abd al-Wahhab promised Allah's blessing to ibn Saud in his contests with his rivals. In return, the Saudi leader agreed to protect al-Wahhab from threats to his life by opponents of the strict doctrines he taught and preached, and he swore an oath of obedience to these doctrines. The partnership between these two men gave rise to a crusading religious movement called Wahhabism.

Wahhabism is basically a strict and puritanical form of Sunni Islam. The Wahhabi code of law, behavior, and conduct is modeled on that of the original Islamic community established in Makkah and Madina by the Prophet Muhammad. Although there has been some relaxation of the code due to the country's modernization, it remains the law of Saudi Arabia today. Interpretation of Islamic law is the responsibility of the *ulama* (a body of religious scholars and jurists, in Sunni Islam). As a result, Saudi society is more conservative and puritanical than many other Islamic societies, including

S.M. Amin/Saudi Aramco World/PADIA (SA2100018)

Masjid-al-Nabawi (Prophet Muhamad's Mosque) in Madina, Saudi Arabia. This was the first mosque that Prophet Muhammad assisted in building when he first moved from Makkah to Madina, offered his prayers in, used as his headquarters to govern the first Islamic state in history, and was buried in.

those of its Persian Gulf neighbors. The Taliban, the Islamic fundamentalist movement that held power in Afghanistan from 1996 to 2001, is thus far the only movement in Islam to have embraced Wahhabism.

Wahhabi-based social and cultural restrictions and strict observance of Islamic law are still the norm in Saudi Arabia. The government maintains separate schools for boys and girls at the precollege level. Women are not allowed to drive cars, although this may change with the continued economic downturn, as more women are forced to enter the workforce. And Islamic law continues to be applied with severity. Alcohol consumption is prohibited, and its use may bring jail sentences or expulsion of foreigners. Public floggings, amputations, and even executions are mandatory for crimes ranging from harassment of women to robbery, homosexual behavior in public, adultery, or occasionally murder.

The *ulama* includes a number of Wahhab's descendants—he had a very large family—and the Saudi-Wahhabi partnership has enabled them to play an important role in decision making. The late grand mufti, Shaykh Abd al-Aziz Bin Baz (who was famous for declaring that Earth was not round but flat), played such a role in the crisis that followed the Iraqi invasion of Kuwait.

The September 11, 2001, terrorist attacks in the United States and the resulting war on terrorism proclaimed by President George W. Bush against Osama bin Laden and his al-Qaeda network placed the Saudi government in an awkward position. As a valued ally, it was expected to provide active support for the international antiterrorism coalition. But a large section of the Saudi

population is opposed to U.S. policy in the Middle East because of its support for Israel. A number of Wahhabi religious leaders ranged themselves in opposition to the monarchy due to its alliance with the "infidel West," some of them even urging its overthrow. In October 2001 a senior Wahhabi cleric, Shaykh Hamoud Ben Oqla, issued a *fatwa* (religious edict) to the effect that "it is a duty to wage jihad on anyone who supports the [American] attack on Afghanistan by hand, tongue or money; whoever helps the infidel against Muslims is to be considered an infidel." Although the Saudi government in October ended its recognition of the Taliban as the legitimate government of Afghanistan, the presence of 5,000 U.S. troops on "sacred Saudi Islamic soil" and bin Laden's popularity as a symbol of Muslim defiance against American "arrogance" in stationing them there forced the monarchy to walk a tightrope in balancing its international obligations with the views of its own people.

Fears that Saudi Arabia would be next on Saddam Hussain's invasion list after Kuwait led to the formation of the coalition of United Nations-sponsored forces that carried out Operation Desert Storm. This action involved stationing of American and other non-Muslim troops in the kingdom. The Saudi leadership was divided on the issue. But at this critical juncture, Bin Baz issued a fatwa. His edict said that in an extreme emergency, it was permissible for an Islamic state to seek help from non-Islamic ones. A later edict ruled that the campaign against Iraq was a jihad, further justifying the coalition and buildup of non-Muslim troops on Saudi soil.

In the late 1700s, the puritanical zeal of the Wahhabis led them to declare a "holy war" against the Ottoman Turks, who were then in control of Mecca and Medina, in order to restore these holy cities to the Arabs. In the 1800s, Wahhabis captured the cities. Soon the Wahhabis threatened to undermine Ottoman authority elsewhere. Wahhabi raiders seized Najaf and Karbala in Iraq, centers of Shi'a pilgrimage, and desecrated Shi'a shrines. In Mecca, they removed the headstones from the graves of members of the Prophet's family, because in their belief system, all Muslims are supposed to be buried unmarked.

The Ottoman sultan did not have sufficient forces at hand to deal with the Wahhabi threat, so he called upon his vassal, Muhammad Ali, the *khedive* (viceroy) of Egypt. Muhammad Ali organized an army equipped with European weapons and trained by European advisers. In a series of hard-fought campaigns, the Egyptian Army defeated the Wahhabis and drove them back into the desert.

Saudi Aramco World/PADIA (SA2119041)

King Abdul Aziz ibn Abdul Rahman al-Saud (1880–1953), also known as Ibn Saud, used his loyal Arabian tribesmen called the *Ikhwan* (the Brethren) and at least twenty marriages with the daughters of tribal chieftains in several regions of the Arabian Peninsula to establish the Kingdom of Saudi Arabia within its current international boundaries in 1932. By the time he died in 1953, he had produced 68 children (37 of whom were princes) and established a strong relationship between his kingdom and western powers (especially the United States) that endures to this day.

Inland Arabia reverted to its old patterns of conflict. The Saudis and other rival tribes were Wahhabi in belief and practice, but this religious bond was countered by age-old disputes over water rights, territory, and control over trade routes. In the 1890s, the Saudis' major rivals, the Rashidis, seized Riyadh. The Saudi chief escaped across the desert to Kuwait, a town on the Persian Gulf that was under British protection. He took along his young son, Abd al-Aziz ibn Saud.

IBN SAUD

Abd al-Aziz al-Rahman Al Sa'ud, usually referred to simply as Ibn Saud (son of Sa'ud), was the father of his country, in both a political and a literal sense.[1] He grew up in exile in Kuwait, where he brooded and schemed about how to regain the lands of the Saudis. When he reached age 21, in

Photo courtesy of the Royal Embassy of Saudi Arabia, Washignton, DC (RESA002)

King Faisal ibn Abdul Aziz ibn Abdul Rahman al-Saud (1904–1975) became the King of Saudi Arabia in 1964. He greatly accelerated the economic and social development of the kingdom. He was highly respected in Saudi Arabia and much of the Muslim world because of his piety, honesty, and competent governance of his kingdom.

1902, he decided on a bold stroke to reach his goal. On 5 Shawwal 1319 (January 1902), he led a force of 48 warriors across the desert from Kuwait to Riyadh. They scaled the city walls at night and seized the Rashidi governor's house, and then the fort in a daring dawn raid. The population seems to have accepted the change of masters without incident, while Bedouin tribes roaming in the vicinity came to town to pledge allegiance to Ibn Saud and applaud his exploit.

Over the next three decades, Ibn Saud steadily expanded his territory. He said that his goal was "to recover all the lands of our forefathers."[2] In World War I, he became an ally of the British, fighting the Ottoman Turks in Arabia. In return, the British provided arms for his followers and gave him a monthly allowance. The British continued to back Ibn Saud after the war, and in 1924 he entered Mecca in triumph. His major rival, Sharif Husayn, who had been appointed by the Ottoman government as the "Protector of the Holy Places," fled into exile. (Sharif Husayn was the great-grandfather of King Hussein I of Jordan.)

Ibn Saud's second goal, after recovering his ancestral lands, was to build a modern nation under a central government. The first step was to gain recognition of Saudi Arabia as an independent state. Britain recognized the country in 1927, and other countries soon followed suit. In 1932 the country took its current name of Saudi Arabia, a union of the three provinces of Hejaz, Nejd, and al-Hasa.

INDEPENDENCE

Ibn Saud's second step in his "grand design" for the new country was to establish order under a central government.

Ibn Saud also established the country's basic political system. The basis for the system was the Wahhabi interpretation of Islamic law. He saw no need for a written constitution, and as yet Saudi Arabia has none. Ibn Saud decreed that the country would be governed as an absolute monarchy, with rulers always chosen from the Saud family. Yet Ibn Saud was himself democratic, humble in manner, and spartan in his living habits. He remained all his life a man of the people and held every day a public assembly (*majlis*) in Riyadh at which any citizen had the right to ask favors or present petitions. (The custom of holding a daily majlis has been observed by Saudi rulers ever since.) More often than not, petitioners would address Ibn Saud not as Your Majesty but simply as Abd al-Aziz (his given name), a dramatic example of Saudi democracy in action.

Ibn Saud died in 1953. He had witnessed the beginning of rapid social and economic change in his country due to oil revenues. Yet his successors have presided over a transformation beyond the wildest imaginations of the warriors who had scaled the walls of Riyadh half a century earlier. Riyadh then had a population of 8,000. Today, it has 2.6 million inhabitants. It is one of the fastest-growing cities in the world.[4]

Ibn Saud was succeeded by his eldest surviving son, Crown Prince Saud.

DEVELOPMENT

The new Saudi 5-Year Plan sets a growth rate of 3.16% annually, with increased diversification of the economy to reduce dependence on oil. With revenues dropping to half of the 1980 totals, an abnormally high birth rate and high unemployment, there are simply not enough jobs being created for the 100,000 Saudis entering the workforce each year.

By 1958 the country was almost bankrupt due to the frivolous disbursement of money by Saud and his son. The royal family was understandably nervous about a possible coup supported by other Arab states, such as Egypt and Syria, which were openly critical of Saudi Arabia because of its lack of political institutions. The senior princes issued an ultimatum to Saud: First he would put Faisal (Ibn Saud's second son, who had more experience in foreign affairs and economic management) in charge of straightening out the kingdom's finances, and, when that had been done, he would abdicate.

When the financial overhaul was complete, with the kingdom again on a sound footing, Saud abdicated in favor of Faisal.

The transfer of authority from Saud to Faisal illustrates the collective principle of government of the Saudi family monarchy. The sovereign rules in theory; but in practice, the inner circle of Saudi senior princes, along with ulama leaders, make all decisions concerning succession, foreign policy, the economy, and other issues. The reasons for a decision must always be guessed at; the Saudis never explain them.

FAISAL AND HIS SUCCESSORS

In terms of state-building, the reign of King Faisal (1964–1975) is second in importance only to that of Ibn Saud. Encouraged by his wife, Queen Iffat, he introduced education for girls into the kingdom. Before Faisal, the kingdom had had no systematic development plans.

In foreign affairs, Faisal ended the Yemen Civil War on an honorable basis for both sides; took an active part in the Islamic world in keeping with his role as Protector of the Holy Places; and, in 1970, founded the Organization of the Islamic Conference, which has given the Islamic nations of the world a voice in international affairs. Faisal laid down the basic strategy that his successors have followed, namely, avoidance of direct conflict, mediation of disputes behind the scenes, and use of oil wealth as a political weapon when necessary. The king never understood the American commitment to Israel, any more than his father had. But Faisal's distrust of communism was equally strong. This distrust led him to continue the ambivalent yet close Saudi alliance with the United States that has continued up to the present.

King Faisal was assassinated in 1975 by a deranged nephew while he was holding the daily majlis.

THE ECONOMY

Oil was discovered in Saudi Arabia in 1938, but exports did not begin until after World War II. Reserves in 1997 were 261 billion barrels, 26 percent of the world's oil supply. The oil industry was controlled by Aramco (Arabian-American Oil Company), a consortium of four U.S. oil companies. In 1980 it came under Saudi government control, but Aramco continued to manage marketing and distribution services. The last American president of Aramco retired in 1989 and was succeeded by a Saudi. The company was renamed Saudi Aramco. But after a quarter-century of exclusion of foreign firms from the oil and gas industry, Saudi Arabia opened the gates in June 2001. A consortium of foreign oil companies was granted

Photo courtesy of the Royal Embassy of Saudi Arabia, Washignton, DC (RESA001)

King Abdullah ibn Abul Aziz ibn Abdul Rahman al-Saud (1923–) was formally enthroned as King of Saudi Arabia on August 3, 2005 after the death of King Fahd ibn Abdul Aziz ibn Abdul Rahman al-Saud. He served for nearly two decades as Crown Prince (1982–2005), and a decade (1995–2005) as the de facto ruler of Saudi Arabia under his incapacitated half brother, King Fahd. He is a devout Hanbali Muslim who enjoys the goodwill of Saudi Arabia's religious establishment.

exploration rights in a desert area the size of Ireland. As a spin-off from the concession, the consortium will develop the existing South Ghawar gas field, and related power, desalination, and petrochemical plants.

The pressures of unemployment (14 percent for male Saudis), a population growth rate of 3.2 percent annually, and a stagnating economy have motivated the government to seek foreign capital investment. The new investment law passed in 2000 permits 100 percent foreign ownership of projects. Import duties were reduced from 12 to 5 percent in 2001. As a result, foreign investment doubled to $9 billion. Some 60 percent of this amount comes from two projects: a Japanese-built desalination plant and a U.S. contract to build 3,000 schools with connections to the Internet.

King Faisal's reorganization of finances and development plans in the 1960s set the kingdom on an upward course of rapid development. The economy took off after 1973, when the Saudis, along with other Arab oil-producing states, reduced production and imposed an export embargo on Western countries as a gesture of support to Egypt in its war with Israel. After 1973 the price per barrel of Saudi oil continued to increase, to a peak of $34.00 per barrel in 1981. (Prior to the embargo, it was $3.00 per barrel; in 1979, it was $13.30 per bar-

rel.) The outbreak of the Iran-Iraq War in 1980 caused a huge drop in world production. The Saudis took up the slack.

The huge revenues from oil made possible economic development on a scale undreamed of by Ibn Saud and his Bedouin warriors. Riyadh experienced a building boom; Cadillacs bumped into camels on the streets, and the shops filled up with imported luxury goods. Every Saudi, it seemed, profited from the boom through free education and health care, low-interest housing loans, and guaranteed jobs.

The economic boom also lured many workers from poor countries, attracted by the high wages and benefits available in Saudi Arabia. Most came from such countries as Pakistan, Korea, and the Philippines, but the largest single contingent was from Yemen, next door.

Continued low world oil prices in the 1990s had a very bad effect on what was formerly a freewheeling economy. In 1998 the country's oil income dropped 40 percent, to $20 billion; after a two-year surplus, the budget showed a $13 billion deficit. Lowered oil prices accounted only in part for the deficit. Monthly stipends ranging from $4,000 to $130,000 given to the 20,000-plus descendants of Ibn Saud continued to drain the treasury, while free education, health care, and other benefits guaranteed for all Saudis under the Basic Law of Government generated some $170 billion in internal debts. The steady downturn in the economy, along with significant population increase (it doubled in the past two decades) and high unemployment have called these social benefits into question.

FREEDOM

Saudi Arabia's strict adherence to Islamic law not only imposes harsh punishments for many crimes, but also restricts human rights. The country ranks second in the world in executions per million population: 123 in 2000. Sharia law applies equally to Saudis and non-Saudis; in 2001, 4 Britons were flogged publicly for dealing in alcohol. A new Code of Criminal Procedure took effect in July 2001. But although Saudi judges (qadis) in theory are bound to respect judicial procedure and legal rights (e.g. of lawyers to defend their clients), they often revert to arbitrary decisions and base these purely on Islamic law.

The Saudi economy experienced a two-year surge in growth in 2003–2004, aided by the highest global oil price increases in two decades, with a $12 billion budget surplus after three years of defcits. The surplus is to be invested in infrastructure projects, particularly transportation and utilities. However, the country's heavy reliance on

oil production continues to affect the non-oil sector. It grew barely 3.4 percent in 2003 compared with 14 percent for the oil sector. Unemployment remains high, with an estimated 13 percent of the work force idled. And the Saudi-ization of business and industry, with consequent reduction of expatriate labor, has been adversely affected by the lower job skills and expectations on young Saudis entering the labor force.

Following the death of King Fahd in July 2005, Crown Prince Abdallah, his half-brother, who had been serving as the country's de facto head of state since 1995, ascended to the Saudi throne. To his credit, Abdallah has demonstrated leadership capabilities in the past. He initiated various reforms in 2000–2001 to keep the country solvent. The state telephone service and several other public enterprises were privatized. Visa document fees for foreign workers were doubled, and subsidies for gasoline and electricity were discontinued. For the first time in 18 years, national income equaled public debt.

A CHANGING KINGDOM, INCH BY INCH

The modern version of the Saudi-Wahhab partnership permits the ruler to appoint the Council of Senior Theologians, whose job it is to ensure Islamic cultural and social "rules" (such as women driving). In return, their presence and prescripts on Islamic behavior serve as an endorsement of the monarchy.

Pressure to broaden participation in political decision making outside of the royals has increased markedly in recent years. This is due not only to greater contact by educated Saudis with more democratic political systems, but also to the vastly increased use of satellite dishes and the Internet. While agreeing in principle to changes, the House of Saud, strongly supported by the religious leaders, has held fast to its patriarchal system.

Given these strictures, it was somewhat surprising in 1991 when the ulama submitted a list of 11 "demands" to King Fahd. The most important one was the formation of a *Majlis al-Shura* (Consultative Council), which would have the power to initiate legislation and advise the government on foreign policy. The king's response, developed in deliberate stages with extensive behind-the-scenes consultation, in typical Saudi style, was to issue in February 1992 an 83-article "Organic Law," comparable in a number of respects to a Western constitution. The law sets out the basic rules for Saudi government.

Further evidence of the kingdom's glacial progress toward reform was the announcement in late 2003 that the first-ever election for municipal councils would be held "within a year." The councils would supplement the Majlis al-Shura, first appointed in 1993, as a third voice of authority after the ruling family and the religious authorities. And in another nudge forward, the Majlis was empowered to introduce or amend laws without prior approval from the king.

Saudi Arabia is defined in the Organic Law as an Arab Islamic sovereign state (Article 5), with Islam the state religion (Article 1), and as a monarchy under the rule of Ibn Saud's descendants. Other articles establish an independent judiciary under Islamic law (*shari'a*) and define the powers and responsibilities of the ruler.

HEALTH/WELFARE

Although Saudi schools are administratively under the Ministry of Education, the curriculum is controlled by the religious authorities. After a disastrous fire at a girls' school in which a number of students died after religious police blocked their escape on grounds they were not fully covered, the government transferred responsibility for female education to the Ministry. Also a nonpartisan advisory group was formed in 2003 to revise the Saudi school curriculum to remove unfavorable references to other religions, and to strengthen instruction in higher education to prepare Saudi youth better to function in a world of globalization and high technology.

Aside from some internal pressures, mainly from intellectuals, the main reason for Fahd's decision to broaden the political process was the Gulf War, which exposed the Saudi system to international scrutiny and pointed up the risks of patriarchal government. A major difference between the Saudi Organic Law and Western-style constitutions is the absence of references to political, civil, and social rights.

Since the Gulf War, the country's purchases of large amounts of weaponry and the stationing of 5,000 American air and ground forces on Saudi soil have been strongly criticized by the Saudi public as well as by other Arab countries. Other Arab leaders have even accused Saudi Arabia (and Kuwait) of becoming U.S. satellites. In the past, the monarchy ignored such criticism; alignment with United States as its major ally and protector have been cornerstones of Saudi foreign policy since World War II. However, U.S. support for Israel and the presence of American forces on sacred Islamic soil have begun to fray the strands holding the alliance together. Further damage resulted from the revelation that the hijackers in the September 11, 2001, attack on U.S. targets were Saudis.

Despite the American presence and its own vigilance, the country continues to be threatened by Islamic fundamentalists. After the seizure of the Great Mosque in Mecca by Sunni fundamentalists in 1979, several hundred of them were deported to Afghanistan, where they joined the resistance to the Soviet occupation. After the Soviet withdrawal in 1989, many of these "Arab Afghans" returned to Saudi Arabia and other Middle Eastern Islamic countries. Some even migrated to Europe or Canada, ultimately entering the United States. Most of them were Saudi nationals; they included Osama bin Laden. Although bin Laden was deprived of his Saudi citizenship and deported (to Sudan) in 1994, the nucleus of his terrorist organization remained in Saudi Arabia and presents a serious underground threat to the monarchy. The threat became reality in May 2003 when suicide bombers attacked three residential compounds in Riyadh, killing 35 non-Saudis, including 9 Americans. The November bombing set off a vast manhunt for al-Qaeda members suspected as responsible for this and earlier attacks, some by suicide bombers. Bounties of $267,000 each were posted for 26 leading suspects. A series of raids during the year netted some 300 other suspects who were captured or killed by Saudi police.

ACHIEVEMENTS

In 2000, Saudi doctors performed the world's first uterus transplant, from a 46-year-old woman to a 26-year-old woman who had a hemorrhage after childbirth. The transplant was successful at first, but it had to be removed after 90 days due to blood clotting in the patient.

The government also cooperated with U.S. and other intelligence organizations in closing down international banks that had served as fronts for al-Qaeda funding. But due to the large number of mujahideen fighters who had returned from the wars in Afghanistan to infiltrate Saudi society, a full-scale crackdown remained difficult. Saudi officials estimated their number at between 10,000 and 60,000.

The presence of American, non-Muslim forces in the country is certainly conducive to terrorism, as is the appeal of Osama bin Laden and his organization for young Saudis. But Saudi vulnerability stems more from internal weaknesses than external threats, as was the case earlier when Iraqi forces seized Kuwait. Not only has the economy not kept pace with the demands of a growing population, but the heavy hand of Wahhabism also limits social changes.

FOREIGN POLICY

The Iraqi invasion and occupation of Kuwait caused a major shift in Saudi policy, away from mediation in regional conflicts and bankrolling of popular causes (such as the Palestinian) to one of direct confrontation. For the first time in its history, the Saudi nation felt directly threatened by the actions of an aggressive neighbor. Diplomatic relations were broken with Iraq and subsequently with Jordan and Yemen, due to their support of the Iraqi occupation. Yemeni workers were rounded up and expelled, and harsh restrictions were imposed on Yemeni business owners in the kingdom. Profiting by the example of Israel's "security fence" built to block Palestinian gunmen and suicide attacks, Saudi Arabia closed its border with Yemen in January 2004. The purpose was to block entry of al-Qaeda activists based in Yemen. Yemeni leaders protested the action as a violation of the Treaty of Taif. That treaty, approved in 2000, established a neutral zone between the two states, which allows nomadic tribes to move about freely. After Yemeni president Saleh visited Riyadh to discuss the

Timeline: PAST

1800
Wahhabis seize Mecca and Medina

1902
Ibn Saud captures Riyadh in a daring commando raid

1927
Ibn Saud is recognized by the British as the king of Saudi Arabia

1946
Oil exports get under way

1963
King Saud, the eldest son and successor of Ibn Saud, is deposed in favor of his brother Faisal

1975
Faisal is assassinated; succession passes by agreement to Khalid

1979
The Great Mosque in Mecca is seized by a fundamentalist Muslim group

1980s
King Khalid dies; succession passes to Crown Prince Fahd; Saudi jets shoot down an Iranian jet for violation of Saudi air space

1990s
Saudi Arabia hosts foreign troops and shares command in the Gulf War

PRESENT

2000s
The Saudi economy stabilizes; the Saudi-U.S. relationship is scrutinized in the wake of the September 11th terrorist attacks

matter, the Saudis agreed to dismantle the barrier in return for increased joint border patrols to deal with smuggling and terrorist infiltration. Establishment of the UN/U.S.-led coalition against Iraq led to the stationing of foreign non-Muslim troops on Saudi soil, also a historic first.

Relations with neighboring Gulf states have improved. Long-time border disputes with Qatar and Yemen have been resolved amicably, with demarcation through largely featureless desert territory. In the Yemeni case, the border was demarcated by a joint arbitration commission to extend from Jebel Thar to the Omani border, on the basis of the 1934 Treaty of Taif.

Now that "terrorism" has become a household word in the West, and one particularly associated with Islam, many scholars and analysts have traced it to Wahhabism, Saudi Arabia's version of the faith. The partnership between the House of Sa'ud and the Wahhabi religious establishment has been a source of strength to the Saudi state. But it has also resulted in a state which supports and encourages militant Islam worldwide, providing significant funding thereto. Internally Wahhabism has also applied its version of Islamic principles to its population, often at the expense of basic human rights. Thus punishment by flogging, prescribed in the Qur'an only for adultery or libel of female honor and limited in application, is carried out for a variety of misdemeanors by thousands of lashes.

NOTES

1. He had 24 sons by 16 different women during his lifetime (1880–1953). See William Quandt, *Saudi Arabia in the 1980's* (Washington, D.C.: Brookings Institution, 1981), Appendix E, for a genealogy.
2. George Rentz, "The Saudi Monarchy," in Willard A. Beling, ed., *King Faisal and the Modernization of Saudi Arabia* (Boulder, CO: Westview Press, 1980), pp. 26–27.
3. *Ibid.*, p. 29.
4. "Saudi Arabia's Centennial," *Aramco World*, Vol. 50, No. 1 (January–February 1999), pp. 21–22. The walls and gates were demolished in 1953 under the "relentless pressure" of modernization, but the Masmak and other structures dating from Ibn Saud's time have been preserved as museums to celebrate the nation's past.
5. The wall was torn down by his successor, King Faisal. Justin Coe, in *The Christian Science Monitor* (February 13, 1985).
6. Gordon Gaskill, "Saudi Arabia's Modern Monarch," *Reader's Digest* (January 1967), p. 118.
7. Ministry of Information, Kingdom of Saudi Arabia, *Faisal Speaks* (n.d.), p. 88.
8. Douglas Jehl, in *The New York Times* (March 20, 1999).
9. Susan Sachs, in *The New York Times* (December 4, 2000).
10. David Hirst, "Corruption, Hard Times Fuel Desert Discontent," *The Washington Times* (September 29, 1999), p. 150.
11. Quoted by Nicholas Blanford, "Reformist impulse in Saudi Arabia," *Christian Science Monitor,* June 5.
12. Stephen Schwartz, *The Two Faces of Islam the House of Sa'ud From Tradition to Terror* (New York: Doubleday, 2002) pp. 64–65. A man in Jiddah was given 4,750 lashes for adultery with his sister-in-law, although the Qur'anic limit is 100.

Senegal (Republic of Senegal)

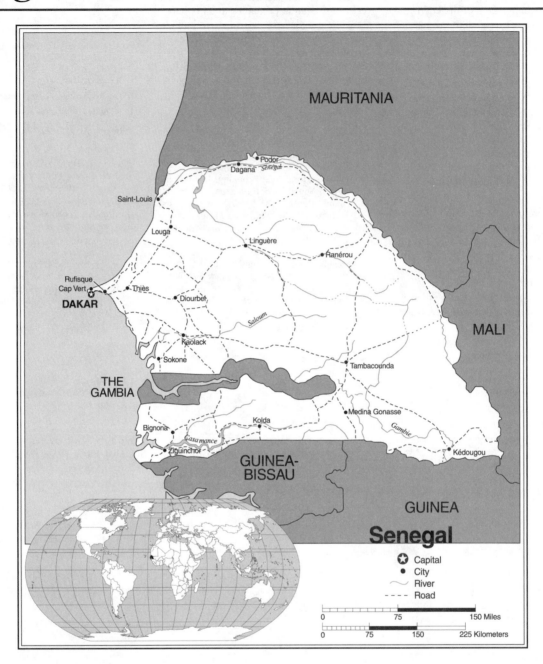

Senegal Statistics

GEOGRAPHY

Area in Square Miles (Kilometers): 76,000 (196,840) (about the size of South Dakota)

Capital (Population): Dakar (2,160,000)

Environmental Concerns: poaching; deforestation; overgrazing; soil erosion; desertification; overfishing

Geographical Features: low, rolling plains, foothills in the southeast; Gambia is almost an enclave of Senegal

Climate: tropical

PEOPLE

Population

Total: 10,852,147

Annual Growth Rate: 2.52%

Rural/Urban Population Ratio: 53/47

Major Languages: French; Wolof; Pulaar; Diola; Mandinka

Ethnic Makeup: 43% Wolof; 24% Pular; 15% Serer; 18% others

Religions: 94% Muslim; 5% Christian; 1% indigenous beliefs

Health

Life Expectancy at Birth: 61 years (male); 65 years (female)
Infant Mortality: 55.4/1,000 live births
Physicians Available: 1/14,825 people
HIV/AIDS Rate in Adults: 1.4%

Education

Adult Literacy Rate: 39%
Compulsory (Ages): 7–13

COMMUNICATION

Telephones: 235,000 main lines
Televisions: 6.9/1,000 people
Internet Users: 225,000 (2003)

TRANSPORTATION

Highways in Miles (Kilometers): 8,746 (14,576)
Railroads in Miles (Kilometers): 565 (905)
Usable Airfields: 20
Motor Vehicles in Use: 160,000

GOVERNMENT

Type: republic
Independence Date: April 4, 1960 (from France)
Head of State/Government: President Abdoulaye Wade; Prime Minister Macky Sall
Political Parties: Socialist Party; Senegalese Democratic Party; Democratic League-Labor Party Movement; Independence and Labor Party; others
Suffrage: universal at 18

MILITARY

Military Expenditures (% of GDP): 1.4%
Current Disputes: civil unrest; issue with The Gambia; tensions with Mauritania and Guinea-Bissau

ECONOMY

Currency ($ U.S. equivalent): 581 CFA francs = $1
Per Capita Income/GDP: $1,600/$17 billion
GDP Growth Rate: 5.7%
Inflation Rate: 0%
Unemployment Rate: 48%
Labor Force by Occupation: 70% agriculture
Population Below Poverty Line: 54%
Natural Resources: fish; phosphates; iron ore
Agriculture: peanuts; millet; sorghum; corn; rice; cotton; vegetables; livestock; fish
Industry: agricultural and fish processing; phosphate mining; fertilizer production; petroleum refining; construction materials
Exports: $1 billion (primary partners France, Italy, Spain)
Imports: $1.3 billion (primary partners France, Nigeria, Germany)

SUGGESTED WEB SITES

http://www.senegal-online.com/anglais/index.html
http://www.sas.upenn.edu/African_Studies/Country_Specific/Senegal.html

Senegal Country Report

In March 2000 Senegalese politics entered a new era with the electoral victory of veteran opposition politician Abdoulaye Wade over incumbent Abdou Diouf. Like his predecessors, Wade faces daunting challenges. Much of Senegal's youthful, relatively well-educated population remains unemployed. Widespread corruption and a long-running separatist rebellion in the southern region of Casamance will also test the new regime. However, Senegal under Wade has already adopted a new constitution in January 2001 that permits opposition parties and gives both genders equal property rights.

THE IMPACT OF ISLAM

The vast majority of Senegalese are Muslim. Islam was introduced into the region by the eleventh century A.D. and was spread through trade, evangelism, and the establishment of a series of theocratic Islamic states from the 1600s to the 1800s.

DEVELOPMENT

The recently built Diama and Manantali Dams will allow for the irrigation of many thousands of acres for domestic rice production. At the moment, large amounts of rice are imported to Senegal, mostly to feed the urban population.

Today, most Muslims are associated with one or another of the Islamic Brotherhoods. The leaders of these Brotherhoods, known as *marabouts*, often act as rural spokespeople as well as the spiritual directors of their followers. The Brotherhoods also play an important economic role. For example, the members of the Mouride Brotherhood, who number about 700,000, cooperate in the growing of the nation's cash crops.

FREEDOM

Senegal's generally favorable human-rights record is marred by persistent violence in its southern region of Casamance, where rebels are continuing to fight for independence. A 2-year cease-fire broke down in 1995 after an army offensive was launched against the rebel Movement of Democratic Forces of Casamance.

POLITICS

Under Diouf, Senegal strengthened its commitment to multipartyism. After succeeding Leopold Senghor, the nation's scholarly first president, Diouf liberalized the political process by allowing an increased number of opposition parties effectively to compete against his own ruling Socialist Party (PS). He also restructured his administration in ways that were credited with making it less corrupt and more efficient. Some say that these moves did not go far enough, but Diouf, who inclined toward reform, had to struggle against reactionary elements within his own party.

HEALTH/WELFARE

Like other Sahel countries, Senegal has a high infant mortality rate and a low life expectancy rate. Health facilities are considered to be below average, even for a country of Senegal's modest income, but recent child-immunization campaigns have been fairly successful.

THE ECONOMY

Many believe that the *Sopi* (Wolof for "change") riots of 1988 were primarily motivated by popular frustration with Senegal's weak economy, especially among its youth (about half of the Senegalese are under age 21), who face an uncertain future. Senegal's relatively large (47 percent) urban population has suffered from rising rates of unemployment and inflation, which have been aggravated by the country's attempt to implement an International

Monetary Fund-approved Structural Adjustment Program (SAP). In recent years, the economy has grown modestly but has so far failed to attract the investment needed to meet ambitious privatization goals. Among rural dwellers, drought and locusts have also made life difficult. Fluctuating world market prices and disease as well as drought have undermined groundnut exports.

ACHIEVEMENTS

Dakar, sometimes described as the "Paris of West Africa," has long been a major cultural center for the region. Senegalese writers, such as former president Leopold Senghor, were founders of the Francophonic African tradition of Negritude.

Timeline: PAST

1659
The French occupy present-day St. Louis and, later, Gorée Island

1700s
The Jolof kingdom controls much of the region

1848
All Africans in four towns of the coast vote for a representative to the French Parliament

1889
Interior areas are added to the French colonial territory

1960
Senegal becomes independent as part of the Mali Confederation; shortly afterward, it breaks from the Confederation

1980s
President Leopold Senghor retires and is replaced by Abdou Diouf; Senegalese political leaders unite in the face of threats from Mauritania

1990s
Serious rioting breaks out in Dakar protesting the devaluation of the CFA franc

PRESENT

2000s
Tensions remain with Guinea-Bissau and Mauritania; Abdoulaye Wade wins the presidency

Sierra Leone (Republic of Sierra Leone)

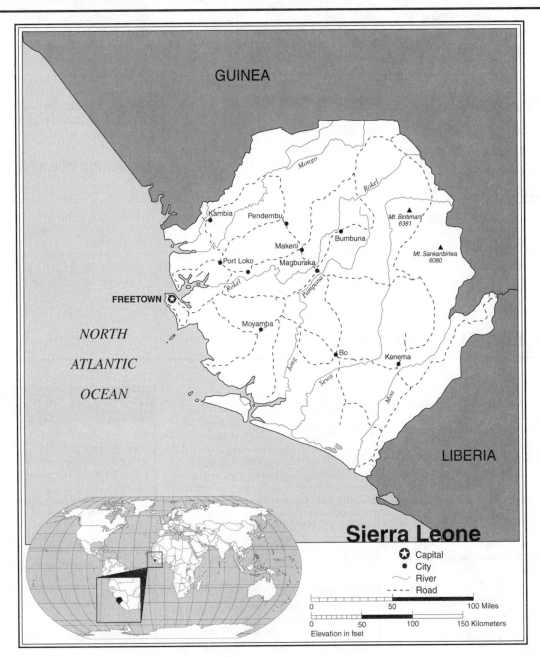

Sierra Leone Statistics

GEOGRAPHY

Area in Square Miles (Kilometers): 27,925 (72,325) (about the size of South Carolina)

Capital (Population): Freetown (837,000)

Environmental Concerns: soil exhaustion; deforestation; overfishing; population pressures

Geographical Features: a coastal belt of mangroves; wooded, hilly country; upland plateau; mountainous east

Climate: tropical; hot, humid

PEOPLE

Population

Total: 5,883,889

Annual Growth Rate: 2.27%

Rural/Urban Population Ratio: 64/36

Major Languages: English, Krio, Temne, Mende

Ethnic Makeup: 30% Temne; 30% Mende; 30% other African; 10% others

Religions: 60% Muslim; 30% indigenous beliefs; 10% Christian

Health

Life Expectancy at Birth: 43 years (male);
49 years (female)
Infant Mortality: 144.3/1,000 live births
Physicians Available: 1/10,832 people
HIV/AIDS Rate in Adults: 2.99%

Education

Adult Literacy Rate: 31.4%

COMMUNICATION

Telephones: 25,000 main lines
Internet Users: 20,000 (2001)

TRANSPORTATION

Highways in Miles (Kilometers): 7,020
(11,700)
Railroads in Miles (Kilometers): 52 (84)
Usable Airfields: 10
Motor Vehicles in Use: 44,000

GOVERNMENT

Type: constitutional democracy
Independence Date: April 27, 1961 (from
the United Kingdom)
Head of State/Government: President
Ahmad Tejan Kabbah is both head of
state and head of government
Political Parties: Sierra Leone People's
Party; National Unity Party; others
Suffrage: universal at 18

MILITARY

Military Expenditures (% of GDP): 1.5%
Current Disputes: hopes for a lasting
peace after a decade of civil war

ECONOMY

Currency ($ U.S. Equivalent): 2,347
leones = $1
Per Capita Income/GDP: $500/$2.7 billion
GDP Growth Rate: 6.5%
Inflation Rate: 10%

Population Below Poverty Line: 68%
Natural Resources: diamonds; titanium
ore; bauxite; gold; iron ore; chromite
Agriculture: coffee; cocoa; palm kernels;
rice; palm oil; peanuts; livestock; fish
Industry: mining; petroleum refining;
small-scale manufacturing
Exports: $65 million (primary partners
New Zealand, Belgium, United States)
Imports: $145 million (primary partners
Czech Republic, United Kingdom,
United States)

SUGGESTED WEB SITES

http://www.sierra-leone.org
http://www.sierraleonenews.com
http://www.fosalone.org
http://www.africanews.org/west/
sierraleone/
http://www.sas.upenn.edu/
African_Studies/
Country_Specific/S_Leone.html

Sierra Leone Country Report

In 2002 Sierra Leone emerged from a decade of civil war with the help of Britain (its former colonial power), a large United Nations peacekeeping mission, and other international elements. More than 17,000 UN troops disarmed tens of thousands of rebels and militia fighters. Currently the country is rebuilding its infrastructure and civil society. President Ahmed Tejan Kabbah won a landslide victory in May elections, in which his Sierra Leone People's Party also secured a majority in Parliament. In July 2002 a "Truth and Reconciliation Commission" was established to help the people of Sierra Leone overcome the trauma of the war, which was characterized by widespread atrocities.

DEVELOPMENT

The recently relaunched Bumbuna hydroelectric project should reduce Sierra Leone's dependence on foreign oil, which has accounted for nearly a third of its imports. In response to threats of boycotting, the country's Lungi International Airport was upgraded. Persistent inflation and unemployment have taken a severe toll on the country's people.

Although rich in its human as well as natural resources at independence, today Sierra Leone is ranked as one of the world's poorest countries. Revenues from diamonds (which formed the basis for

FREEDOM

The deposed AFRC/RUF regime unleashed a terror campaign, including extra-judicial killings, torture, mutilation, rape, beatings, arbitrary arrest, and the detention of unarmed civilians. Junta forces killed and/or amputated the arms of detainees. Prior to the coup, RUF was infamous for its murderous attacks on civilians during raids in which children were commonly abducted and forced to commit atrocities against their relatives as a form of psychological conditioning.

HEALTH/WELFARE

Life expectancy for both males and females in Sierra Leone is only in the 40s, while the infant mortality rate, 144.3 per 1,000 live births, remains appalling. In 1990, hundreds, possibly thousands, of Sierra Leone children were reported to have been exported to Lebanon on what amounted to slave contracts. The UNEP Human Development Index rates Sierra Leone last out of 174 countries.

prosperity during the 1950s) and gold have steadily fallen due to the depletion of old diggings and massive smuggling. The two-thirds of Sierra Leone's labor force employed in agriculture have suffered the most from the nation's faltering economy. Poor producer prices, coupled with an international slump in demand for cocoa and

Timeline: PAST

1400–1750
Early inhabitants arrive from Africa's interior

1787
Settlement by people from the New World and recaptured slave ships

1801
Sierra Leone is a Crown colony

1898
Mende peoples unsuccessfully resist the British in the Hut Tax War

1961
Independence

1978
The new constitution makes Sierra Leone a one-party state

1985
President Siaka Stevens steps down; Joseph Momoh, the sole candidate, is elected

1990s
Debt-servicing cost mounts; SAP; Liberian rebels destabilize Sierra Leone; Momoh is overthrown

PRESENT

2000s
Civil war ends; Ahmed Kabbah wins reelection

ACHIEVEMENTS

The Sande Society, a women's organization that trains young Mende women for adult responsibilities, has contributed positively to life in Sierra Leone. Beautifully carved wooden helmet masks are worn by women leaders in the society's rituals. Ninety-five percent of Mende women join the Society.

robusta coffee, have cut into rural incomes. Like its minerals, much of Sierra Leone's agricultural production has been smuggled out of the country. In 1989 the cost of servicing Sierra Leone's foreign debt was estimated to be 130 percent of the total value of its exports. This grim figure led to the introduction of an International Monetary Fund-supported Structural Adjustment Program (SAP), whose austerity measures made life even more difficult for urban dwellers.

Somalia

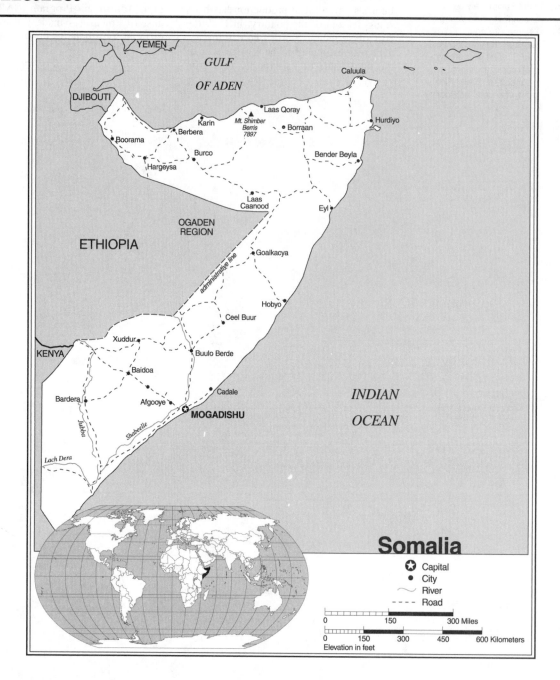

Somalia Statistics

GEOGRAPHY

Area in Square Miles (Kilometers): 246,331 (638,000) (about the size of Texas)

Capital (Population): Mogadishu (1,212,000)

Environmental Concerns: famine; contaminated water; deforestation; overgrazing; soil erosion; desertification

Geographical Features: principally desert; mostly flat to undulating plain, rising to hills in the north
Climate: arid to semiarid

PEOPLE

Population

Total: 8,304,601*
Annual Growth Rate: 3.46%

Rural/Urban Population Ratio: 73/27
Major Languages: Somali; Arabic; Italian; English
Ethnic Makeup: 85% Somali; Bantu; Arab
Religion: Sunni Muslim

*Note: Population statistics in Somalia are complicated by the large number of nomads and by refugee movements in response to famine and clan warfare.

240

Health

Life Expectancy at Birth: 45 years (male); 47 years (female)
Infant Mortality: 122/1,000 live births
Physicians Available: 1/19,071 people

Education

Adult Literacy Rate: 38%
Compulsory (Ages): 6–14; free

COMMUNICATION

Telephones: 100,000 main lines
Televisions: 18 per 1,000 people
Internet Users: 89,000 (2002)

TRANSPORTATION

Highways in Miles (Kilometers): 13,702 (22,100)
Railroads in Miles (Kilometers): none
Usable Airfields: 54
Motor Vehicles in Use: 20,000

GOVERNMENT

Type: "Transitional National Government"
Independence Date: July 1, 1960 (from a merger of British Somaliland and Italian Somaliland)
Head of State/Government: President Abdullahi Yusuf Ahmed; Prime Minister Ali Muhammad Ghedi
Political Parties: none
Suffrage: universal at 18

MILITARY

Military Expenditures (% of GDP): 0.9%
Current Disputes: civil war; border and territorial disputes with Ethiopia

ECONOMY

Currency ($ U.S. Equivalent): 11,000 shillings = $1
Per Capita Income/GDP: $550/$4.1 billion
Inflation Rate: NA

Labor Force by Occupation: 71% agriculture; 29% industry and services
Natural Resources: uranium; iron ore; tin; gypsum; bauxite; copper; salt
Agriculture: livestock; bananas; sugarcane; cotton; cereals; corn; sorghum; mangoes; fish
Industry: sugar refining; textiles; limited petroleum refining
Exports: $186 million (primary partners Saudi Arabia, United Arab Emirates, Yemen)
Imports: $314 million (primary partners Djibouti, Kenya, India)

SUGGESTED WEB SITES

http://www.unsomalia.org
http://www.somalianews.com
http://somalinet.com
http://somaliawatch.org
http://www.cia.gov/cia/
   publications/factbook/geos/
   so.html

Somalia Country Report

Wracked by violence, ruled by warlords, torn asunder not just by tribal but also petty clan disputes (some of which go back centuries), there seems to be nowhere to look for a spark of hope toward peace in Somalia. The list of transgressions committed by Somalia's leaders over the last 15 years is immense. The country has thrown out their traditional allies, waged war with their regional neighbors, killed numerous international volunteers (who were supplying the starving residents with food and medical supplies), and fought viciously with one another in an unprecedented anarchy.

In what looked like a chance for peace in Somalia, there was a breakthrough in January 2004 at peace talks held in Kenya when the warlords and a few politicians signed a deal to set up a new parliament. Within four months, however, renewed fighting broke out, killing 100 people as ethnic militias clashed in the southern town of Bula Hawo. The violence notwithstanding, a new transitional parliament was inaugurated in August 2004 at a ceremony in Kenya. In October the body elected Abdullahi Yusuf as president of Somalia. The election took place in Kenya because the Somali capital was regarded as being too dangerous.

President Yusuf pledged to do his best to promote reconciliation and to set about rebuilding the country. He called on the international community to provide aid and peacekeepers. President Yusuf's leadership style is said to be authoritarian. Clearly, in the eyes of the assembled representatives of Somalia, what the country needed in 2004 was another separatist dictator, who arose from the ranks of the warlords themselves, to resolve the pressing issues of the Somalian state.

DEVELOPMENT

 Most development projects have ended. Somalia's material infrastructure has largely been destroyed by war and neglect, though some local rebuilding efforts are under way, especially in the more peaceful central and northern parts of the country. In 1996, the European Union agreed to finance the reconstruction of the port of Berbera.

Somalia has in effect been without a central government since 1991, when after the overthrow of President Siad Barre, the country entered a period of chaos from which it has never recovered. The country has been dominated by "warlords" responsible for small fiefdoms supported by heavily armed militias under their control. The resulting intermilitia fighting, added to the inability to deal with famine and disease, has led to the deaths of up to 1 million people. There appears to be little hope for an early resolution to the continuing conflicts in Somalia. The international donor community has long vanished, fundamentally giving up efforts to work out a peaceful solution to the problems of the nation. To compound matters, the northern portion of the country has broken away from the south and is now called Somaliland.

For much of the outside world, Somalia has become a symbol of failure of both international peacekeeping operations and the postcolonial African state. For the Somalis themselves, Somalia is an ideal that has ceased to exist—but may yet be recreated. Literally hundreds of thousands of Somalis starved to death in 1991–1992 before a massive U.S.–led United Nations intervention—officially known as UNITAF but labeled "Operation Restore Hope" by the Americans—assured the delivery of relief supplies.

SOMALI SOCIETY

The roots of Somalia's suffering run deep. Somalis have lived with the threat of famine for centuries, as the climate is arid even in good years. Traditionally, most Somalis were nomadic pastoralists, but in recent years, this way of life has declined dramatically. Prior to the 1990s crisis, about half the population were still almost entirely reliant on livestock.

A quarter of the Somali population has long combined livestock-keeping with agriculture. Cultivation is possible in the area between the Juba and Shebelle Rivers and in portions of the north. Although up to 15 percent of the country is potentially arable, only about 1 percent of the land has been put to plow at any given time. Bananas, cotton, and frankincense have been major cash crops, while maize and sorghum are subsistence crops. Like Somali pastoralists, farmers walk a thin line between abundance and scarcity, for locusts as well as drought are common visitors.

The delicate nature of Somali agriculture helps to explain recent urbanization. One out of every four Somalis lives in the large towns and cities. The principal urban center is Mogadishu, which, despite being divided by war, still houses well over a million people. Unfortunately, as Somalis have migrated in from the countryside, they have found little employment. Even before the recent collapse, the country's manufacturing and service sectors were small.

FREEDOM

Plagued by persistent hunger and internal violence, and with the continuing threat of governance by the anarchic greed of the warlords, the living have no true freedom in Somalia.

Until recently, many outsiders assumed that Somalia possessed a greater degree of national coherence than most other African states. Somalis do share a common language and a sense of cultural identity. Islam is also a binding feature. However, competing clan and subclan allegiances have long played a divisive political role in the society. Membership in all the current armed factions is congruent with blood loyalties. Traditionally, the clans were governed by experienced, wise men. But the authority of these elders has now largely given way to the power of younger men with a surplus of guns and a surfeit of education and a lack of moral decency.

Somalia became independent on July 1, 1960, when the new national flag, a white, five-pointed star on a blue field, was raised in the former British and Italian territories. The star symbolized the five supposed branches of the Somali nation—that is, the now-united peoples of British and Italian Somalilands and the Somalis still living in French Somaliland (modern Djibouti), Ethiopia, and Kenya.

THE RISE AND FALL OF SIAD BARRE

Siad Barre came to power in 1969, through a coup promising radical change. As chairman of the military's Supreme Revolutionary Council, Barre combined Somali nationalism and Islam with a commitment to "scientific socialism." Some genuine efforts were made to restructure society through the development of new local councils and worker management committees. New civil and labor codes were written. The Somali Revolutionary Socialist Party was developed as the sole legal political party.

Initially, the new order seemed to be making progress. The Somali language was alphabetized in a modified form of Roman script, which allowed the government to launch mass-literacy campaigns. Various rural-development projects were also implemented. In particular, roads were built, which helped to break down isolation among regions.

HEALTH/WELFARE

Somalia's small health service has almost completely disappeared, leaving the country reliant on a handful of international health teams. By 1986 education's share of the national budget had fallen to 2%. Somalia had 525 troops per teacher, the highest such ratio in Africa.

The promise of Barre's early years in office gradually faded. Little was done to follow through the developments of the early 1970s, as Barre increasingly bypassed the participatory institutions that he had helped to create. His government became one of personal rule; he took on emergency powers, relieved members of the governing council of their duties, surrounded himself with members of his own Marehan branch of the Darod clan, and isolated himself from the public.

ACHIEVEMENTS

Somalia has been described as a "nation of poets." Many scholars attribute the strength of the Somali poetic tradition not only to the nomadic way of life, which encourages oral arts, but to the role of poetry as a local social and political medium.

In mid-1992, the International Red Cross estimated that, of southern Somalia's 4.5 million people, 1.5 million were in danger of starvation. Another 500,000 or so had fled the country. More than 300,000 children under age five were reported to have perished.

A small UN presence, known as UNISOM, was established in August 1992, but its attempts to police the delivery of relief supplies proved to be ineffectual.

Timeline: PAST

1886–1887
The British take control of northern regions of present-day Somalia

1889
Italy establishes a protectorate in the eastern areas of present-day Somalia

1960
Somalia is formed through a merger of former British and Italian colonies under UN Trusteeship

1969
Siad Barre comes to power through an army coup; the Supreme Revolutionary Council is established

1977–1978
The Ogaden war in Ethiopia results in Somalia's defeat

1980s
SNM rebels escalate their campaign in the north; government forces respond with genocidal attacks on the local Issaq population

1990s
The fall of Barre leaves Somalia without an effective central government; U.S.-led UN intervention feeds millions while attempting to restore order; In the face of mounting losses, foreign troops pull out of Somalia

PRESENT

2000s
Chaos still reigns in Somalia, causing untold suffering; Abdiqassim Salah Hassan is named interim president

2004
275-member Transitional Federal Government replaces the Transitional National Government

Sudan (Republic of the Sudan)

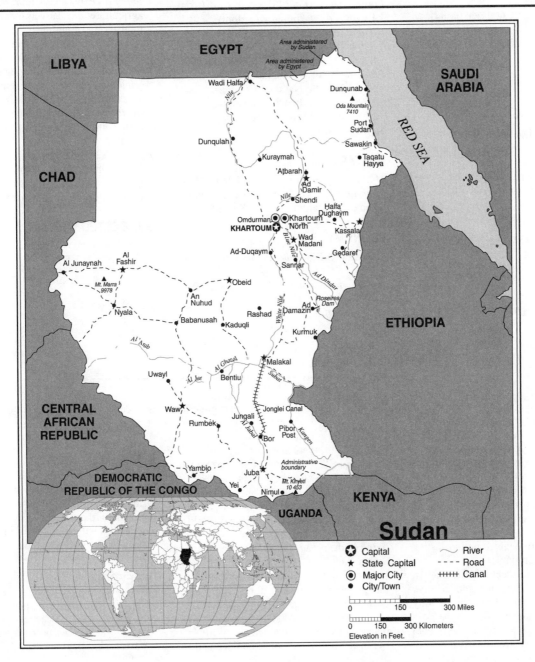

Sudan Statistics

GEOGRAPHY

Area in Square Miles (Kilometers): 967,247
(2,505,810) (about 1/4 the size of the
United States)

Capital (Population): Khartoum (2,853,000)

Environmental Concerns: insufficient
potable water; excessive hunting of
wildlife; soil erosion; desertification

Geographical Features: generally flat,
featureless plain; mountains in the east
and west

Climate: arid desert to tropical

PEOPLE

Population

Total: 39,148,162

Annual Growth Rate: 2.73%

Rural/Urban Population Ratio: 65/35

Major Languages: Arabic; Sudanic
languages; Nubian; English; others

Ethnic Makeup: 52% black; 39% Arab;
6% Beja; 3% others

Religions: 70% Sunni Muslim, especially
in north; 25% indigenous beliefs; 5%
Christian

Health

Life Expectancy at Birth: 56 years (male); 58 years (female)
Infant Mortality: 67/1,000 live births
Physicians Available: 1/11,300 people
HIV/AIDS Rate in Adults: 0.99%

Education

Adult Literacy Rate: 46%

COMMUNICATION

Telephones: 900,000 main lines
Daily Newspaper Circulation: 21 per 1,000 people
Televisions: 8.2 per 1,000 people
Internet Users: 300,000 (2003)

TRANSPORTATION

Highways in Miles (Kilometers): 7,198 (11,610)
Railroads in Miles (Kilometers): 3,425 (5,516)
Usable Airfields: 65
Motor Vehicles in Use: 75,000

GOVERNMENT

Type: transitional
Independence Date: January 1, 1956 (from Egypt and the United Kingdom)
Head of State/Government: President Umar Hasan Ahmad al-Bashir is both head of state and head of government
Political Parties: National Congress Party; Popular National Congress; Umma; Sudan People's Liberation Movement (Army); others
Suffrage: universal at 17

MILITARY

Military Expenditures (% of GDP): 2.5%
Current Disputes: civil war; border disputes and clashes with Egypt and Kenya

ECONOMY

Currency ($ U.S. Equivalent): 260 pounds = $1
Per Capita Income/GDP: $1,900/$70.95 billion
GDP Growth Rate: 5.9%

Inflation Rate: 8.8%
Unemployment Rate: 18.7%
Labor Force by Occupation: 80% agriculture; 13% government; 7% industry and commerce
Natural Resources: petroleum; iron ore; chromium ore; copper; zinc; tungsten; mica; silver; gold; hydropower
Agriculture: cotton; sesame; gum arabic; sorghum; millet; wheat; sheep; groundnuts
Industry: textiles; cement; cotton ginning; edible oils; soap; sugar; shoes; petroleum refining
Exports: $2.1 billion (primary partners Japan, China, Saudi Arabia)
Imports: $1.6 billion (primary partners China, Saudi Arabia, United Kingdom)

SUGGESTED WEB SITES

http://www.sudan.net
http://sudanhome.com
http://www.sudmer.com
http://www.sunanews.net
http://www.cia.gov/cia/
publications/factbook/geos/
su.html

Sudan Country Report

The name *Sudan* comes from the Arabic *bilad al-sudan*, or "land of the blacks." Today, Sudan is Africa's largest country. Apart from an 11-year period of peace, it has been torn since its indpendence in 1956 by civil war between the mainly Muslim north and the animist and Christian south. Sudan's tremendous size as well as its great ethnic and religious diversity have frustrated the efforts of successive postindependence governments to build a lasting sense of national unity.

The current president, Omar Bashir, was reelected in 2001 for another five years. The Machakos Protocol of July 2002, which was signed by both the government and the two largest southern rebel groups, calls for a six-year interval period, after which there will be a referendum held on self-determination for the south. However, the Muslim-led Sudanese government has continued to attack the southern rebels; through the age-old tactic of divide-and-conquer, it has been able to make periodic inroads into the rebels' African strongholds. Ethnic groups are pitted against one another. Meanwhile, there has been evidence of the widespread enslavement of blacks in the south. In December 2001, for example, more than 14,550 slaves, mainly blacks, were freed following campaigning by human-rights activists.

Listed by the U.S. government as a major supporter of terrorism, until 1997 Sudan's Islamic fundamentalist government provided refuge for Osama bin Laden. Since then, the government has been keen to overcome its image as a pariah state. The challenges facing Sudan have also been complicated by the discovery of major oil fields in the south. The government has sought to establish safe enclaves for the exploitation of the oil fields, at the cost of relocating people who were living in the area. The oil fields may make Sudan rich, but they remain a primary source of alienation, as funds generated by the government from oil revenues have been used to purchase weapons against the southern rebels. In 2004 an agreement was reached to split the oil revenues evenly between the north and south and seemed to give a new hope for peace, but fighting between the two continues.

DEVELOPMENT

Many ambitious development plans have been launched since independence, but progress has been limited by political instability. The periodic introduction and redefinition of "Islamic" financial procedures have complicated long-term planning.

The future looks like continued civil war until Sudan ceases to enslave its people, grants the southerners self-determination, and ceases trying to impose an Islamic state on its religiously mixed population.

HISTORY

The Nile river provides water to most of the 80 percent of Sudanese who survive by farming. From ancient times, the Upper Nile region of northern Sudan has been the site of a series of civilizations whose histories are closely intertwined with those of Egypt.

FREEDOM

The current regime rules through massive repression. In 1992 Africa Watch accused it of practicing genocide against the Nuba people. Elsewhere, tales of massacres, forced relocations, enslavement, torture, and starvation are commonplace. The insurgent groups have also been responsible for numerous atrocities.

The last ruler to unite the Nile Valley politically was the nineteenth-century Turko-Egyptian ruler Muhammad Ali. After absorbing northern Sudan, by then predominantly Arabized Muslim, into his Egyptian state, Ali gradually expanded his authority to the south and west over non-Arabic and, in many cases, non-Muslim groups. This process, which was largely motivated by a desire for slave labor, united for the first time the diverse regions

Mahammad Ahmad Abdullah al-Mahdi (1843–1885), a puritanical Sudanese Islamist, launched the *Mahdiyyah* movement in Sudan (1881). In January 1885, the Mahdi of Sudan routed the Ottoman Empire's Egyptian forces, defeated the British, and became the undisputed ruler of Sudan. However, within a few months, the Mahdi himself died and his successor, Abdullahi al-Ta'ashi, ruled Sudan until 1898, when Anglo-Egyptian armies reconquered the country.

that today make up Sudan. In the 1880s much of Sudan fell under the theocratic rule of the Mahdists, a local anti-Egyptian Islamic movement. The Mahdists were defeated by an Anglo-Egyptian force in 1898. Thereafter, the British dominated Sudan until its independence, in 1956.

Sudanese society has remained divided ever since. There has been strong pan-Arab sentiment in the north, but 60 percent of Sudanese, concentrated in the south and west, are non-Arab. About a third of Sudanese, especially in the south, are also non-Muslim. Despite this fact, many, but by no means all, Sudanese Muslims have favored the creation of an Islamic state. Ideological divisions among various socialist- and nonsocialist-oriented factions have also been important. Sudan has long had a strong Communist Party, drawing on the support of organized labor, and an influential middle class.

The division between northern and southern Sudan has been especially deep. A mutiny by southern soldiers prior to independence escalated into a 17-year rebellion by southerners against what they perceived to be the hegemony of Muslim Arabs. Some 500,000 southerners perished before the Anya Nya rebels and the government reached a compromise settlement, recognizing southern autonomy in 1972.

In northern Sudan, the first 14 years of independence saw the rule of seven different civilian coalitions and six years of military rule. Despite this chronic instability, a tradition of liberal tolerance among political factions was generally maintained. Government became increasingly authoritarian during the administration of Jaafar Nimeiri, who came to power in a 1969 military coup.

Nimeiri quickly moved to consolidate his power by eliminating challenges to his government from the Islamic right and the Communist left. His greatest success was ending the Anya Nya revolt, but his subsequent tampering with the provisions of the peace agreement led to renewed resistance. In 1983 Nimeiri decided to impose Islamic law throughout Sudanese society. This led to the growth of the Sudanese People's Liberation Army (SPLA), under the leadership of John Garang, which quickly seized control of much of the southern Sudanese countryside. Opposition to Nimeiri had also been growing in the north, as more people became alienated by the regime's increasingly heavy-handed ways and inability to manage the declining economy. Finally, in 1985, he was toppled in a coup.

HEALTH/WELFARE

Civil strife and declining government expenditures have resulted in rising rates of infant mortality. Warfare has also prevented famine relief from reaching needy populations, resulting in instances of mass starvation.

In March 1989 a new government, made up of the northern-based Umma and the Democratic Union (DUP), committed itself to accommodating the SPLA. However, a month later, on the day the cabinet was to ratify an agreement with the rebels, there was a coup by pro-National Islamic Front (NIF) officers.

Besides leading to a breakdown in all efforts to end the SPLA rebellion, the NIF/military regime has been responsible for establishing the most intolerant, repressive government in Sudan's modern history. Extra-judicial executions have become commonplace. Instances of pillaging and enslavement of non-Muslim communities by government-linked militias have increased. NIF-affiliated security groups have become a law unto themselves, striking out at their perceived enemies and intimidating Muslims and non-Muslims alike to conform to their fundamentalist norms. Islamic norms are also being invoked to justify a radical campaign to undermine the status of women.

ECONOMIC PROSPECTS

Although it has great potential, political conflict has left Sudan one of the poorest nations in the world. Persistent warfare and lack of financing are blocking needed infrastructural improvements. Sudan's unwillingness to pay its foreign debt has led to calls for its expulsion from the International Monetary Fund.

ACHIEVEMENTS

Although his music is banned in his own country, Mohammed Wardi is probably Sudan's most popular musician. Now living in exile, he has been imprisoned and tortured for his songs against injustice, which also appeal to a large international audience, especially in North Africa and the Middle East.

Nearly 7 million Sudanese (out of a total population then of 23 million) had been displaced by 1988—more than 4 million by warfare, with drought and desertification contributing to the remainder. Sudan has been a major recipient of international emergency food aid for years, but warfare, corruption, and genocidal indifference have often blocked help from reaching the needy. In 1994 the United Nations estimated that 700,000 southern Sudanese faced the prospect of starvation.

Timeline: PAST

1820
Egypt invades northern Sudan

1881
The Mahdist Revolt begins

1956
Independence

1969
Jaafar Nimeiri comes to power

1972
Hostilities end in southern Sudan

1980s
Islamic law replaces the former penal code; renewed civil war in the south; Nimeiri is overthrown in a popular coup; an elected government is installed

1990s
The hard-line Islamic fundamentalist regime becomes increasingly repressive

PRESENT

2000s
Famine threatens large segments of the population; Omar al-Bashir claims victory in boycotted elections

Suriname (Republic of Suriname)

Suriname Statistics

GEOGRAPHY

Area in Square Miles (Kilometers): 63,037 (163,265) (about the size of Georgia)

Capital (Population): Paramaribo (216,000)

Environmental Concerns: deforestation; water pollution; threatened wildlife populations

Geographical Features: mostly rolling hills; a narrow coastal plain with swamps; mostly tropical rain forest

Climate: tropical

PEOPLE

Population

Total: 436,935

Annual Growth Rate: 0.31%

Rural/Urban Population Ratio: 50/50

Major Languages: Dutch; Sranantonga; English; Hindustani

Ethnic Makeup: 37% Hindustani (locally called East Indian); 31% Creole; 15% Javanese; 10% Bush Negro; 3% Amerindian; 3% Chinese

Religions: 27% Hindu; 25% Protestant; 23% Roman Catholic; 20% Muslim; 5% others

Health

Life Expectancy at Birth: 66 years (male); 71 years (female)
Infant Mortality Rate (Ratio): 25/1,000
Physicians Available (Ratio): 1/1,348

Education

Adult Literacy Rate: 93%
Compulsory (Ages): 6–16; free

COMMUNICATION

Telephones: 78,700 main lines
Daily Newspaper Circulation: 107 per 1,000 people
Televisions: 146 per 1,000 people
Internet Users: 20,000 (2002)

TRANSPORTATION

Highways in Miles (Kilometers): 2,813 (4,530)
Railroads in Miles (Kilometers): 103 (166)

Usable Airfields: 46
Motor Vehicles in Use: 66,000

GOVERNMENT

Type: constitutional democracy
Independence Date: November 25, 1975 (from the Netherlands)
Head of State/Government: President Runaldo Ronald Venetiaan is both head of state and head of government
Political Parties: New Front; Progressive Reform Party; National Democratic Party; National Party; others
Suffrage: universal at 18

MILITARY

Military Expenditures (% of GDP): 0.7%
Current Disputes: territorial disputes with Guyana and French Guiana

ECONOMY

Currency ($ U.S. Equivalent): 2,346 guilders = $1

Per Capita Income/GDP: $3,500/$1.53 billion
GDP Growth Rate: 1.5%
Inflation Rate: 17%
Unemployment Rate: 17%
Labor Force: 100,000
Natural Resources: timber; hydropower; fish; kaolin; shrimp; bauxite; gold; nickel; copper; platinum; iron ore
Agriculture: paddy rice; bananas; palm kernels; coconuts; plantains; peanuts; livestock; forest products; shrimp
Industry: bauxite and gold mining; alumina and aluminum production; lumbering; food processing; fishing
Exports: $495 million (primary partners Norway, Netherlands, United States)
Imports: $604 million (primary partners United States, Netherlands, Trinidad and Tobago)

SUGGESTED WEB SITE

http://www.cia.gov/cia/
publications/factbook/index.html

Suriname Country Report

Settled by the British in 1651, Suriname, a small colony on the coast of Guiana, prospered with a plantation economy based on cocoa, sugar, coffee, and cotton. The colony came under Dutch control in 1667. When slavery was finally abolished, in 1863, plantation owners brought contract workers from China, India, and Java.

DEVELOPMENT

The bauxite industry, which had been in decline for 2 decades, now accounts for 15 percent of GDP and 70 percent of export earnings.

On the eve of independence of the Netherlands in 1975, Suriname was a complex, multiracial society. Although existing ethnic tensions were heightened as communal groups jockeyed for power in the new state, other factors cut across racial lines. Even though Creoles (native-born whites) were dominant in the bureaucracy as well as in the mining and industrial sectors, there was sufficient economic opportunity for all ethnic groups, so acute socioeconomic conflict was avoided.

THE POLITICAL FABRIC

Until 1980 Suriname enjoyed a parliamentary democracy. The various ethnic, politi-

cal, and economic groups that comprised Surinamese society were united and found their expression in government.

FREEDOM

The Venetiaan government successfully brought to an end the Maroon insurgency of 8 years' duration. Under the auspices of the Organization of American States, the rebels turned in their weapons, and an amnesty for both sides in the conflict was declared.

Through the interplay of the various groups, integration in the political process and accommodation of their needs were achieved. Despite the fact that most interests had access to the center of power, and despite the spirit of accommodation and cooperation, the military seized power early in 1980.

THE ROOTS OF MILITARY RULE

The coup originated vis-a-vis officers that resented what they perceived as discrimination by a wasteful and corrupt government. Their demands for reforms, including recognition of an officers' union, were ignored.

The coup, masterminded and led by Sergeant Desire Bouterse, had a vague, unde-

Timeline: PAST

1651
British colonization efforts

1667
The Dutch receive Suriname from the British in exchange for New Amsterdam

1975
Independence of the Netherlands

1980s
A military coup

1990s
A huge drug scandal implicates high-level government officials

PRESENT

2000s
The Netherlands extends loan aid

fined ideology. It claimed to be nationalist; and it revealed itself to be puritanical, in that it lashed out at corruption and demanded that citizens embrace civic duty and a work ethic. Ideological purity was maintained by government control or censorship of a once-free media. Wavering between left-wing radicalism and middle-of-the-road moderation, the rapid shifts in

Bouterse's ideological declarations suggest that this was a policy designed to keep the opposition off guard and to appease factions within the military.

HEALTH/WELFARE

Amerindians and Maroons (the descendants of escaped African slaves) who live in the interior have suffered from the lack of educational and social services, partly from their isolation and partly from insurgency. With peace, however, it is hoped that the health, education, and general welfare of these peoples will improve.

With regard to Suriname's economic policy, most politicians see integration into Latin American and Caribbean markets as critical. The Dutch, who suspended economic aid after the 1990 coup, restored their assistance with the election of President Ronald Venetiaan in 1991.

High on Venetiaan's agenda were economic reform necessary to ensure Dutch aid and establish the country's eligibility for international credit, and the need to re-establish ties with the interior to consolidate an Organization of American States.

A loan negotiated with the Dutch in 2001 will help Suriname to develop agri-

ACHIEVEMENTS

Suriname, unlike most other developing countries, has a small foreign debt and a relatively strong repayment capacity. This is substantially due to its export industry.

culture "bauxite" and the gold-mining industry. Unfortunately the development policy also threatens deforestation, because of timber exports, and the pollution of waterways as a result of careless mining practices.

Syria (Syrian Arab Republic)

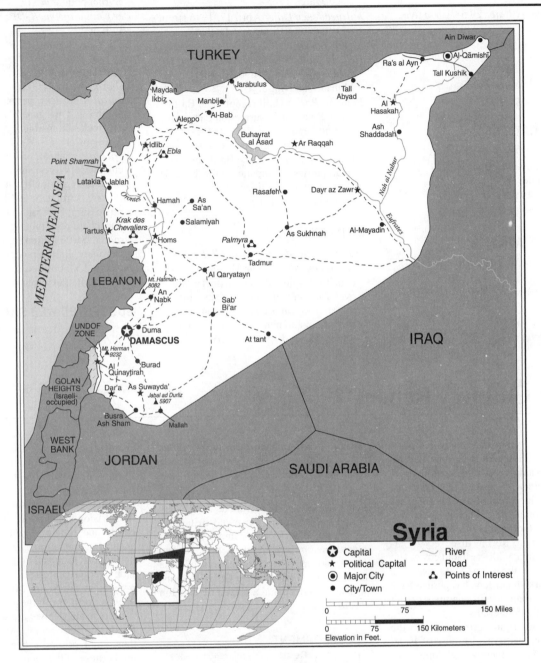

Syria Statistics

GEOGRAPHY

Area in Square Miles (Kilometers): 71,500 (185,170) (about the size of North Dakota)
Capital (Population): Damascus (1,549,000)
Environmental Concerns: deforestation; overgrazing; soil erosion; desertification; water pollution; insufficient potable water
Geographical Features: primarily semiarid and desert plateau; narrow coastal plain; mountains in the west

Climate: predominantly desert; considerable variation between the interior and coastal regions

PEOPLE

Population

Total: 18,448,752 (plus 20,000 living in the Israeli-occupied Golan Heights)
Annual Growth Rate: 2.34%

Rural/Urban Population Ratio: 47/53

Major Languages: Arabic, Kurdish, various minority languages, e.g. Aramaic, Hebrew

Ethnic Makeup: 90.3% Arab; 9.7% Kurd, Armenian, and others

Religions: 74% Sunni Muslim; 16% Alawite, Druze, and other Muslim sects; 10% Christian and Jewish

Health

Life Expectancy at Birth: 68 years (male); 71 years (female)
Infant Mortality Rate: 29.53/1,000 live births
Physicians Available (Ratio): 1/953 people

Education

Adult Literacy Rate: 76.9%
Compulsory (Ages): 6–12

COMMUNICATION

Telephones: 2,099,300 main lines
Daily Newspaper Circulation: 19 per 1,000 people
Televisions: 49 per 1,000 people
Internet Users: 220,000 (2000)

TRANSPORTATION

Highways in Miles (Kilometers): 25,741 (45,697)
Railroads in Miles (Kilometers): 1,650 (2,711)
Usable Airfields: 100
Motor Vehicles in Use: 353,000

GOVERNMENT

Type: republic under a military regime since March 1963
Independence Date: April 17, 1946 (from a League of Nations mandate under French administration)
Head of State/Government: President Bashar al-Assad; Prime Minister Muhammad Naji-al_Utri
Political Party: Until recently the Ba'th (Arab Socialist Resurrection Party) was the only legal party. The late President Hafez al-Assad formed a National Progressive Front of the Ba'th and six small parties in preparation for the 2003 parliamentary elections
Suffrage: universal at 18

MILITARY

Military Expenditures (% of GDP): 5.9%
Current Disputes: Golan Heights is Israeli-occupied; dispute with Turkey over Turkish water-development plans; Syrian troops in Lebanon; 2004 agreement and pending demarcation settles border dispute with Jordan

ECONOMY

Currency ($ U.S. Equivalent): 11.225 Syrian pounds = $1
Per Capita Income/GDP: $3,400/$60.4 billion
GDP Growth Rate: 2.3%
Inflation Rate: 2.1%
Unemployment Rate: 20%
Labor Force: 5,1200,000
Natural Resources: petroleum; phosphates; chrome and manganese ores; asphalt; iron ore; rock salt; marble; gypsum; hydropower
Agriculture: wheat; barley; cotton; lentils; chickpeas; olives; sugar beets; beef; mutton; eggs; poultry; milk
Industry: petroleum; textiles; food processing; beverages; tobacco; phosphate-rock mining
Exports: $6.08 billion (primary partners Germany, Italy, France)
Imports: $5.04 billion (primary partners France, Italy, Germany)

SUGGESTED WEB SITES

http://lcweb2.loc.gov/frd/cs/ sytoc.html

Syria Country Report

The modern Syrian state is a pale shadow of ancient Syria, which at various times in its history was a great kingdom, incorporating the lands of present-day Lebanon, Israel, Iraq, Jordan, and a part of Turkey within its boundaries. Ancient Syria was also a part of the great civilization centered in Mesopotamia. Recent discovery by archaeologists of a 6,000-year-old city at Hamonkar, in northeastern Syria near the Iraqi and Turkish borders, has pushed back the start of urban design centuries earlier than that of the Sumerians.

Syrian kings figure prominently in the Old Testament as rivals to those of Israel and Judah. One of these kings, Antiochus, divided the empire of Alexander the Great. Antiochus's kingdom dominated the Near East prior to the establishment of the Roman empire, with Syria as its center.

Syria also figured prominently in the expansion of Islam. After the death of the Prophet Muhammad, his successors, called *caliphs,* expanded Islamic rule over a territory greater than Rome. They moved their capital from Mecca to Damascus. The Umayyad Caliphate, so called because of its family origins in Muhammad's clan, spread the Arabic language and Islamic culture from North Africa to the western border of India. Due to its centrality, Arab geogra-

phers and cartographers termed Syria *Bilad ash-Sham,* literally "east," whence the sun rose over the lands of Islam.

Modern Syria is a nation of artificial boundaries. Its borders were determined by agreement between France and Britain after World War I. The country's current boundaries are with Turkey, Iraq, Jordan, Israel, and Lebanon. (The only one of these boundaries in dispute is the Golan Heights, which was seized and annexed by Israel in the 1970s.)

DEVELOPMENT

Despite some relaxation of state controls and reforms such as authorization for private banks, the economy has remained sluggish, with population increasing faster than the annual 2.5% GDP growth rate. Nightmarish bureaucratic rules particularly hamper foreign investment, which is urgently needed in the important oil industry.

Syria is artificial in another sense: Its political system was established by outside powers. Since becoming independent in 1946, the Syrians have struggled to find a political system that works for them. The large number of coups and frequent

changes in government are evidence of this struggle. The most stable government in Syria's independent history is the current one, which has been in power since 1970.

Syrian political instability stems from the division of the population into separate ethnic and religious groups. The Syrians are an amalgamation of many different ethnoreligious groups that have settled the region over the centuries. The majority of the population are Sunni Muslim Arabs. The Alawis form the largest minority group. Although the Alawis are nominally Shi'a Muslims, the Sunni Muslims distrust them—not primarily because of religion, but because of the secret nature of their rituals and because as a minority they are very clannish. The next-largest minority, the Druze, live in Israel and Lebanon as well as Syria. They are nominally Muslims, but their (secret) rituals include Christian liturgical elements such as the Eucharist, when they drink the blood and eat the body not of Christ but of Ali, Muhammad's closest relative and for Shi'as his legitimate successor as Caliph of Islam.

The largest non-Arab minority in Syria are Kurds, Sunni Muslims found in much larger numbers in Iraq, Turkey, and Iran. The country also has small but long-established Christian and Jewish communities. The Assad regime, probably due to its own minority status within the larger Syrian Muslim community, has allowed them full religious and social freedom. Five of the late president's advisers were Christians. This tolerant attitude may explain why relatively few Syrian Jews have emigrated to Israel over the years. The Christian population is equally well treated.

HISTORY

Syria's greatest period was probably that of the Umayyad caliphs (A.D. 661–750). These caliphs were rulers of a vast Islamic empire. The first Umayyad caliph, Mu'awiya, is considered one of the political geniuses of Islam.

During this period of Umayyad rule, Damascus became a great center of learning and culture. But later Umayyad caliphs were no more successful than their modern Syrian counterparts in developing effective government. They ruled by fear, repression, and heavy taxation. They also made new non-Arab converts to Islam pay a special tax from which Arab Muslims were exempted. They were finally overthrown by non-Arab Muslim invaders from Iraq. From that time until Syria became an independent republic, its destiny was determined by outsiders.

After the Ottoman Turks had established their empire and expanded their rule to the Arab lands of the Middle East, Syria became an Ottoman province governed by a pasha. The name "Syria" did not come into use until shortly before World War I and was adopted by France after the war when Syria became a League of Nations mandate under French sponsorship.

The French Mandate

In the years immediately preceding World War I, numbers of young Syrian Christians and some Muslims were exposed through mission schools to ideas of nationalism and human rights. A movement for Arab independence from Turkish rule gradually developed, centered in Damascus and Beirut. After the start of World War I, the British, with French backing, convinced Arab leaders to revolt against the Ottoman government. The Arab army recruited for the revolt was led by Emir Faisal, the second son of Sharif Husayn of Mecca, leader of the powerful Arab Hashimite family, and the Arab official appointed by the Ottomans as "Protector of the Holy Shrines of Islam." Faisal's forces, along with a British army, drove the Ottomans out of Syria. In 1918, the emir entered Damascus as a conquering hero, and in 1920 he was proclaimed king of Syria.

Faisal's kingdom did not last long. The British had promised the Arabs independence in a state of their own, in return for their revolt. However, they had also made secret agreements with France to divide the Arab regions of the defeated Ottoman Empire into French and British protectorates. The French would govern Syria and Lebanon; the British would administer Palestine and Iraq. The French now moved to collect their pound of flesh. They sent an ultimatum to Faisal to accept French rule. When he refused, a French army marched to Damascus, bombarded the city, and forced him into exile.

The Syrians reacted angrily to what they considered betrayal by their former allies. Resistance to French rule continued throughout the mandate period (1920–1946), and the legacy of bitterness over their betrayal affects Syrian attitudes toward outside powers, particularly Western powers, to this day.

The French did some positive things for Syria. They built schools, roads, and hospitals, developed a productive cotton industry, and established order and peaceful relations among the various communities. But the Syrians remained strongly attached to the goals of Arab unity and Arab independence, first in Syria, then in a future Arab nation.[4]

INDEPENDENT SYRIA

Syria became independent in 1946. The French had promised the Syrians independence during World War II but delayed their departure after the war, hoping to keep their privileged trade position and military bases. Eventually, pressure from the United States, the Soviet Union, and Britain forced the French to leave both Syria and Lebanon.

FREEDOM

The 1973 Constitution defines Syria as a socialist, populist democracy. The Hafez al-Assad regime limited press freedom along with human rights. President Bashar has restored some of these rights. Also, the new budget was presented to the People's Assembly for approval before being issued. But the country still has a long way to go to become truly free, populist, and democratic.

The new republic began under adverse circumstances. Syrian leaders had little experience in government; the French had not given them much responsibility and had encouraged personal rivalries in their divide-and-rule policy. The Druze and Alawi communities feared that they would be under the thumb of the Sunni majority. In addition, the establishment in 1948 of the State of Israel next door caused great insta-

bility in Syria. The failure of Syrian armies to defeat the Israelis was blamed on weak and incompetent leaders.

For two decades after independence, Syria had the reputation of being the most unstable country in the Middle East. There were four military coups between 1949 and 1954 and several more between 1961 and 1966. There was also a brief union with Egypt (1958–1961), which ended in an army revolt.

One reason for Syria's chronic instability was that political parties were simply groups formed around individuals. At independence, the country had many such parties. Other parties were formed on the basis of ideology, such as the Syrian Communist Party. In 1963, one party, the Ba'th, acquired control of all political activities. Since then, Syria has been a single-party state.

THE BA'TH

The Ba'th Party (the Arabic word *ba'th* means "resurrection") began in the 1940s as a political party dedicated to Arab unity. It was founded by two Damascus schoolteachers, both French-educated: Michel Aflaq, a Greek Orthodox Christian, and Salah Bitar, a Sunni Muslim. In 1953 the Ba'th merged with another political party, the Arab Socialist Party. Since then, the formal name of the Ba'th has been the Arab Socialist Resurrection Party.

The Ba'th was the first Syrian political party to establish a mass popular base and to draw members from all social classes. Its program called for freedom, Arab unity, and socialism. The movement for Arab unity led to the establishment of the branches of the party in other Arab countries, notably Iraq and Lebanon. The party appealed particularly to young officers in the armed forces; and it attracted strong support from the Alawi community, because it called for social justice and the equality of all Syrians.

The Ba'th was instrumental in 1958 in arranging a merger between Syria and Egypt as the United Arab Republic (U.A.R.). The Ba'thists had hoped to undercut their chief rival, the Syrian Communist Party, by the merger. But they soon decided that they had made a mistake. The Egyptians did not treat the Syrians as equals but as junior partners. Syrian officers seized control and expelled the Egyptian advisers. It was the end of the U.A.R.

For the next decade, power shifted back and forth among military and civilian factions of the Ba'th Party. The process had little effect on the average Syrian, who liked to talk about politics but was wary, with good reason, of any involvement. Gradually, the military faction got the upper hand, and in 1970, Lieutenant General Hafez al-Assad, the defense minister of one of the country's innumerable previous governments, seized power in a bloodless coup.[5]

THE HAFEZ AL-ASSAD REGIME

Syria can be called a presidential republic, in the sense that the head of state has extensive powers, which are confirmed in the constitution approved in 1973. He decides and executes policies, appoints all government officials, and commands the armed forces. He is also head of the Ba'th Party. Under the Constitution, he has unlimited emergency powers "in case of grave danger threatening national unity or the security… of the national territory" (Article 113), which only the president can determine.

Hafez al-Assad ruled Syria for nearly three decades, becoming in the process the longest-serving elected leader of any Arab state. He was first elected in 1971 (as the only candidate) and thereafter for five consecutive seven-year terms, the last in 1999. Over the years he broadened the political process to some extent, establishing a People's Assembly with several small socialist parties as a token opposition body in the Legislature. In 1990 elections were held for an enlarged, 250-member Assembly. Ba'th members won 134 seats to 32 for the opposition; the remainder were won by independents. Assad then approved the formation of a National Progressive Front, which included the independents. But mindful of Syria's long history of political instability in the years before he took office, he decreed that its only function would be approval of laws issued by the Ba'th Central Committee.

Syria's Role in Lebanon

Assad's position was strengthened domestically in the 1970s due to his success (or perceived success) in certain foreign-policy actions. The Syrian Army fought well against Israel in the October 1973 War, and Syria subsequently received both military and financial aid from the Soviet Union as well as its Arab brothers. The invitation by the Arab League for Syria to intervene in Lebanon, beginning with the 1975–1976 Lebanese Civil War, was widely popular among Syrians. They never fully accepted the French action of separating Lebanon from Syria during the mandate period, and they continue to maintain a proprietary attitude toward Lebanon. Assad's determination to avoid conflict with Israel led him in past years to keep a tight rein on Syrian-based Palestine Liberation Organization (PLO) operations.

When the Lebanese Civil War broke out, Assad pledged that he would control the Palestinians in Lebanon. He sent about 2,000 al-Saiqa guerrillas to Beirut in early 1976. The peacekeeping force approved by the Arab League for Lebanon included 30,000 regular Syrian troops.

The 30,000–35,000 Syrian troops in Lebanon have been reduced in stages since the end of the Lebanese civil war, the most recent withdrawal in July 2003. Aside from continued Lebanese resentment over their presence, the withdrawal seemed a positive gesture toward the United States, which has been critical of anti-Israeli groups operating out of Damascus and of Syrian support for the regime of Saddam Hussein of Iraq prior to the American invasion of that country.

HEALTH/WELFARE

Syria's high birth rate has generated a young population. With insufficient jobs available, the unemployment rate is around 30%. A mandatory family-planning program will eventually lower the birth rate, and a grant from the European Union is being used to expand the public sector and provide salary increases for those already employed there.

Internal Opposition

Opposition to the Hafez al-Assad regime was almost nonexistent in the 1990s. A major cause for resentment among rank-and-file Syrians, however, is the dominance of the Alawi minority over the government, armed forces, police, and intelligence services. The main opposition group was the Syrian branch of the Muslim Brotherhood (a Sunni organization spread throughout the Arab world). The Brotherhood opposed Assad because of his practice of advancing Alawi interests over those of the Sunni majority. Its main stronghold was the ancient city of Hama, famed for its Roman waterwheels. In 1982 Assad's regular army moved against Hama after an ambush of government officials there. The city was almost obliterated by tanks and artillery fire, with an estimated 120,000 casualties. Large areas were bulldozed as a warning to other potentially disloyal elements in the population.[6]

The "lessons of Hama" have not been forgotten. The calculated savagery of the attack was meant not only to inflict punishment but to provide a warning for future generations of Syrians. It did have a positive result. In ensuring the survival of his regime, Assad guaranteed political stability, along with prosperity for the largely Sunni merchant class. Thus other Arab states look toward the "Hama solution" with nostalgia.

Assad's control over the various levers of power, notably the intelligence services (*mukhabarat*), the security police, and the military, ensured his rule during his lifetime, despite his narrow support base as head of a minority group. After Hama, no organized opposition group remained to challenge his authority. As a result, he was able to give Syria the political stability that his predecessors had never provided.

Syrian popular support for the aging president grew in the 1990s, as he continued to resist accommodation with Israel, while other Arab states were establishing relations or even recognizing the State of Israel. This broader support enabled Assad to loosen the reins of government. At the start of his fourth term he included several Sunni ministers in his cabinet. Political prisoners were released, most of them Muslim Brotherhood members.

THE ECONOMY

At independence, Syria was primarily an agricultural country, although it had a large merchant class and a free-enterprise system with considerable small-scale industrial development. When it came to power, the Ba'th Party was committed to state control of the economy. Agriculture was collectivized, with land expropriated from large landowners and converted into state-managed farms. Most industries were nationalized in the 1960s. The free-enterprise system all but disappeared.

Cotton was Syria's principal export crop and money earner until the mid-1970s. But with the development of oil fields, petroleum became the main export. Syria produced enough oil for its own needs until 1980. However, the changing global oil market and the reluctance of foreign companies to invest in Syrian oil exploration under the unfavorable concession terms set by the government have hampered development. Oil production, formerly 580,000 barrels per day (b/d), fell to 340,000 b/d in the mid-1990s. It increased to 450,000 b/d in 2000 and 550,000 b/d in 2001, due largely to imports of Iraqi oil for further export through the Kirkuk-Banias pipeline. Syria's position is that the arrangement did not violate the United Nation's oil-for-food program any more than that of Iraqi exports of crude oil to Jordan.

Agriculture, which accounts for 30 percent of gross domestic product annually at present and employs 33 percent of the labor force, benefited in the early 1990s from expanded irrigation, which brought additional acreage under cultivation. Production of cotton, the major agricultural crop, reached a record 1.1 million tons in 2000, with 270,000 tons exported.

The end of Syria's special relationship with the Soviet Union due to the breakup of that country in 1991 encouraged a modest liberalization of the Ba'thist economic system. Syria's large number of educated and skilled managers, along with a dependable and productive labor force, has encouraged foreign investment.

Hafez al-Assad's death in June 2000 and the accession of his son Bashar to the presidency have been felt most strongly in the economic sector. In December 2000 the Ba'th Regional Command, the party's central committee, approved the establishment of private banks, ending 40 years of state monopoly over banking and foreign-exchange transactions.

FOREIGN RELATIONS

Syria's often prickly relations with its neighbors and its rigid opposition to Israel have made the country the "odd man out" in the region at various times. Following rough relations between Iraq and Syria due to the latter's support of Iran during the Iraq-Iran war, the UN sanctions on Iraq brought the two Arab neighbors closer together.

ACHIEVEMENTS

Ghada Shonaa brought honor and glory to Syria when she became the first Syrian to win an Olympic gold medal. She won the women's heptathlon at the 1996 Olympic Games in Atlanta, Georgia. And although the United States and Syria remain estranged politically, the Host House Trio, an American jazz group, joined with Syrian musicians in 1999 in a concert in Damascus.

Syria's role as an alleged major sponsor of international terrorism has adversely affected its relations with Western countries for years. Yet Syria did send troops to support the U.S.–led coalition in the Gulf War, despite its close economic relationship with Iraq. Following the September 11, 2001 attacks on the United States by al-Qaeda terrorists, Syria provided intelligence information on its network. However, the Assad regime's continued support and sponsorship of anti-Israeli organizations such as Hamas and Hezbollah have tarnished its image abroad, notably in the United States. After the U.S. invasion and occupation of Iraq, Bush administration policymakers charged that its open border with that country enabled weapons and terrorists to enter and thus delay the reconstruction of Iraq. In December 2003 Congress passed the Syria Accountability Act. It bans exports of dual-use items (those which have both civilian and military applications). In March 2004 Bush ordered the imposition of economic sanctions in implementation of the act.

Syria's inclusion in the Department of State list as a state supporter of terrorism had been based on the harboring of groups engaged in violence, usually against Israel but also against Yassir Arafat's Palestinian organization. The groups included Hamas, the Popular Front for the Liberation of Palestine (PFLP), and Islamic Jihad. However, the Assad government was careful not to allow them to launch anti-Israeli operations from Syrian territory. The September 11, 2001, terrorist attacks on the United States brought a change in the equation. President Bashar denounced the terrorist attacks and criticized Osama bin Laden and his al-Qaeda network for giving Islam a bad name. However, he declared that the Palestinian-Israeli conflict ultimately bore responsibility for the terrorism. In March 2002 Bashar announced strong support for the Saudi proposal for recognition of Israel by the Arab states in return for Israel's withdrawal to its pre-1967 borders.

PROSPECTS

Hafez al-Assad died on June 10, 2000, the last of a group of autocratic rulers who had dominated the Middle East for more than a generation. His younger son, Bashar, was elected to succeed him on June 25 by the People's Assembly, confirmed by 97.5 percent of voters in a nationwide referendum.

Syria's new leader was trained as an opthalmologist in Britain and had little experience in national politics before being summoned back to replace his elder brother Basil (killed in an auto accident in 1994) as the heir-apparent. His only public post was that of commander of the Republican Guard. After his election to the presidency (he was the only candidate, like his father), Bashar became head of the armed forces and of the Ba'th Regional Command.

While cynical observers joked that Syria had exchanged a dictator for an eye doctor, Bashar brought fresh air into a moribund political system and a stagnant economy. Bashar changed the composition of the Ba'th Regional Command, bringing in younger army commanders as well as some women. In other essentially cosmetic changes, private universities were established to supplement, and revitalize, the moribund state system, and in 2002 private banks were allowed to form. By mid-2003 six such banks were in operation.

NOTES

1. The statement is found in many chronicles of the Umayyads. See Richard Nyrop, ed., *Syria, A Country Study* (Washington, D.C.: American University, Foreign Area Studies, 1978), p. 13.

2. Philip Khoury, *Urban Notables and Arab Nationalism: The Politics of Damascus 1860–1920* (Cambridge, England: Cambridge University Press, 1983), pp. 8–9.

3. Umar F. Abd-Allah, *The Islamic Struggle in Syria* (Berkeley, CA: Mizan Press, 1983), p. 39.

4. "Syrians had long seen themselves as Arabs...who considered the Arab world as rightly a single entity." John F. Devlin, *Syria: Modern State in an Ancient Land* (Boulder, CO: Westview Press, 1983), p. 44.

5. He was barred from attending a cabinet meeting and then surrounded the meeting site with army units, dismissed the government, and formed his own. *Ibid.*, p. 56.

6. Thomas L. Friedman, in *From Beirut to Jerusalem*, coined the phrase "Hama rules" to describe Assad's domestic political methods. "Hama rules" means no rules at all.

7. Quoted in Scott Peterson, in *The Christian Science Monitor* (July 12, 2000).

8. Helena Cobban, in *The Christian Science Monitor* (December 19, 2002).

Timeline: PAST

661–750
The capital of Umayyads is removed to Damascus; Syria becomes the center of the Islamic world

1517–1917
Ottoman province

1920
An independent Arab Kingdom of Syria is proclaimed under Faisal; shot down by French

1920–1946
French mandate, followed by independence

1958–1961
Union with Egypt into the United Arab Republic

1976
Syrian troops are sent to Lebanon as a peacekeeping force

1980s
Syria's association with international terrorism leads some European countries to break relations and some to impose economic sanctions

1990s
Assad's efforts to gain the release of hostages in Lebanon leads the United States and other countries to resume aid and diplomatic relations

PRESENT

2000s
Hafez al-Assad dies; his son Bashar is elected to succeed him; Syria denounces the September 11, 2001, terrorist attacks

Tajikistan

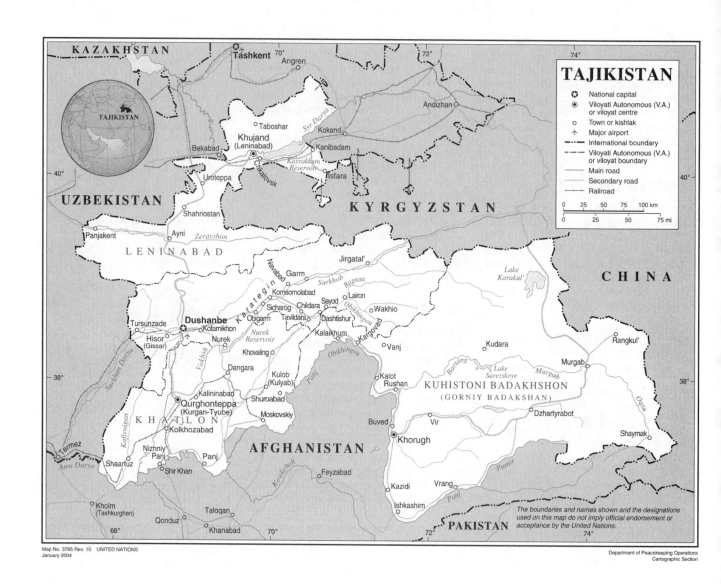

Tajikistan Statistics

GEOGRAPHY

Area in Square Miles (Kilometers): 55,237
  (143,100) (about the size of Wisconsin)
Capital (Population): Dushanbe (524,000)

PEOPLE

Population

Total: 6,579,000

Annual Growth Rate: 2.12%

Major Languages: Tajik; Russian

Ethnic Makeup: 65% Tajik; 25% Uzbek;
  3% Russian; 7% others

Religions: 80% Sunni Muslim; 5% Shi'a
  Muslim; 15% others

Health

Life Expectancy at Birth: 61 years (male);
  67 years (female)

Infant Mortality Rate (Ratio): 116/1,000

Education

Adult Literacy Rate: 98%

GOVERNMENT

Type: republic

Head of State/Government: President
Emomali Rahmanov; Prime Minister
Oqil Oqilov

Political Parties: People's Democratic
Party; Tajik Socialist Party; Communist
Party; Islamic Renaissance Party; others

ECONOMY

Currency ($ U.S. Equivalent): 998 Tajik
rubles = $1

Per Capita Income/GDP: $1,140/$7.3
billion

Inflation Rate: 33%

Exports: $761 million

Imports: $782 million

Tajikistan Country Report

Tajikistan is the most conflict-ridden of
the Central Asian republics. Neo-Commu-
nists and militant Islamic fundamentalists
began fighting each other following the
collapse of the Soviet state. Democratic elements and discontented poverty-stricken
minorities, such as the Garmis and Pamiri
Tajiks in the eastern part of the country,
who suffered under communist rule, have
tended to align with Islamists against the
Communists.

CIVIL WAR

From the beginning of the post-Soviet era,
the Tajik Communists have opposed a succession of democratic and religion-based
political groups, in particular the Islamic
Rebirth Party. The former head of the Tajik
Communist Party, Rakhman Nabiyev, presided over a conservative Parliament beginning in 1991. Democratic-, Islamic-,
and rural-based opposition groups relent-
lessly opposed Nabiyev. They condemned
the corruption and repression of the
Nabiyev order and spoke for the people living in eastern Tajikistan, who complained
about the poverty of their villages and the
evident discrimination against them by the
Nabiyev regime. They also spoke for
Tajiks living in the remote mountainous areas of the country, whose interests had
been all but forgotten by the urban Marxist
leaders in Dushanbe. Nabiyev drew most
of his support from the tribal groups living
in the western part of the country in the regions of Kurgan-Tyube, Kulyab, and
Khodzhent.

RUSSIAN INVOLVEMENT

Russia and other neighboring republics, in
particular Uzbekistan, worried that the
Tajik civil strife could spread quickly
throughout the region. At the end of 1992,
Russia contributed the major portion of a

commonwealth of Independent States
(C.I.S.)-sponsored peacekeeping force of
about 1,000 troops to try to maintain order in Dushanbe. Subsequently, Russia
decided to send a much larger Russian
contingent to prop up the Communist
government. By February 1993 there
were about 3,500 Russian troops in
Tajikistan and 20,000 Russian military
personnel. Russia pledged to rebuild the
Tajik Army and to provide help at the
frontier with Afghanistan.

Meanwhile, the Uzbek leadership, concerned about the safety of the large Uzbek
minority in Tajikistan (about 25 percent of
the total Tajik population), decided to back
the Communists as the only political force
capable of preventing the establishment of
an Iranian-style fundamentalist regime.

By the mid-1990s, Tajikistan had become virtually a satellite of Moscow. In a
monetary agreement with Russia, the Tajik
government, now under Emomali Rakhmanov, agreed to turn over control of currency and credit to the Russian Central Bank
and to use the Russian ruble as the country's
medium of exchange. By 1994 Russia was
paying nearly 70 percent of the Tajik state
budget and had 25,000 troops deployed in
the country to protect the government of
President Rakhmanov against its challeng-
ers, especially the fundamentalist insurgents
who continued to receive support from the
Afghanistan government, despite its own
troubles. In fact, by 1993 the Afghan fundamentalist government had recruited an estimated 65,000 Tajiks in guerrilla training
centers, for the purpose of returning them to
Tajikistan to fight with the Islamists against
the neo-communist Tajik governments supported by Russia. So it was that Russian
forces occasionally found themselves fighting Islamic insurgents.

To the dismay of the Kremlin, President
Rakhmanov's hardline government was

unable to fulfill its expectations. By early
1997 Rakhmanov's regime controlled only
a few slices of Tajik territory, about 20 percent of the country. It survived mainly because of Russian support and the backing
of some local warlords determined to prevent the establishment of an Islamic state
led by a fundamentalist—not by any means
a possibility. Today, it is not an exaggera-
tion to say that the term government is
meaningless in Tajikistan.

RECENT DEVELOPMENTS

Tajikistan has joined other Central Asian
republics in strengthening the role of an already powerful and autocratic presidency
in a referendum held in June 2003, which
returned President Rakhmanov for two
more seven-year terms following the expi-
ration of his present term in 2006. Tajik
voters approved the extension of his tenure
because they see Rakhmanov as founder
and saviour of today's independent and
sovereign Tajikistan, administered at least
in theory by, for, and in the interest of ethnic Tajiks, a pleasingly novel situation
given the long subjugation of Tajiks to
Russians in recent Tajik history.

Despite Rakhmanov's popularity the government did take some high-handed steps to
assure the outcome of the referendum—the
turnout was 96 percent of eligible voters,
and 93 percent of them approved the
change. The heavily state-controlled media
called on voters to go the polls and to vote
yes. Given a view that Tajik voters lack an
understanding of democratic politics and
are interested in primarily one issue, stability, the government's intervention was
overkill and clearly in violation of the spirit
if not the letter of Tajikistan's alleged democratic and parliamentary system of government.

Togo (Togolese Republic)

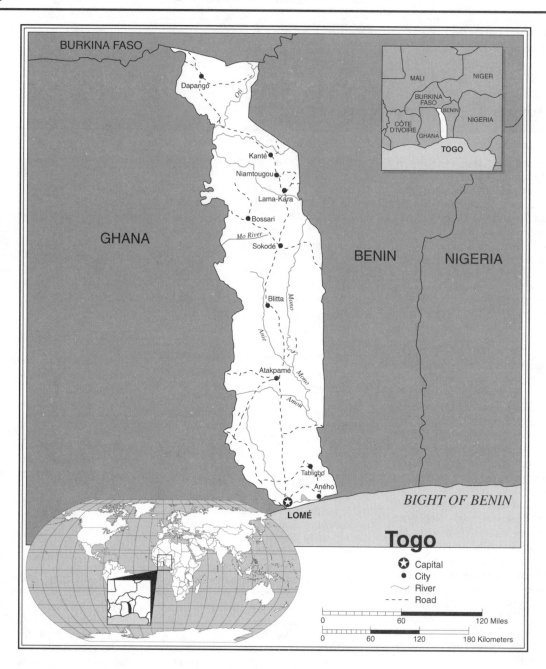

Togo Statistics

GEOGRAPHY

Area in Square Miles (Kilometers): 21,853 (56,600) (about the size of West Virginia)
Capital (Population): Lomé (732,000)
Environmental Concerns: drought; deforestation
Geographical Features: gently rolling savanna in north; central hills; southern plateau; low coastal plain with extensive lagoons and marshes
Climate: tropical to semiarid

PEOPLE

Population

Total: 5,556,812
Annual Growth Rate: 2.27%
Rural/Urban Population Ratio: 67/33
Major Languages: French; Ewe; Mina; Dagomba; Kabye; Dasomsa
Ethnic Makeup: 99% African—Ewe; Mina; Kabye; many others
Religions: 70% indigenous beliefs; 20% Christian; 10% Muslim

Health

Life Expectancy at Birth: 52 years (male);
56 years (female)
Infant Mortality: 69.3/1,000 live births
Physicians Available: 1/11,270 people
HIV/AIDS Rate in Adults: 5.98%

Education

Adult Literacy Rate: 51.7%
Compulsory (Ages): 6–12

COMMUNICATION

Telephones: 60,600 main lines
Televisions: 36 per 1,000 people
Internet Users: 210,000 (2003)

TRANSPORTATION

Highways in Miles (Kilometers): 4,512
(7,520)
Railroads in Miles (Kilometers): 352 (532)
Usable Airfields: 9
Motor Vehicles in Use: 109,000

GOVERNMENT

Type: republic under transition to
multiparty democratic rule
Independence Date: April 27, 1960 (from
French-administered UN trusteeship)
Head of State/Government: President
Gnassingbé Eyadéma; Prime Minister
Koffi Sama
Political Parties: Assembly of the
Togolese People; Coordination des
Forces Nouvelles; Action Committee for
Renewal; Patriotic Pan-African
Convergence; Union of Forces for
Change; others
Suffrage: universal for adults

MILITARY

Military Expenditures (% of GDP): 1.8%
Current Disputes: civil unrest; tensions
with Benin

ECONOMY

Currency ($ U.S. Equivalent): 581 CFA
francs = $1

Per Capita Income/GDP: $1,500/$7.6
billion
GDP Growth Rate: 3.3%
Inflation Rate: -1%
Labor Force by Occupation: 65%
agriculture; 30% servies; 5% industry
Population Below Poverty Level: 32%
Natural Resources: phosphates;
limestone; marble; arable land
Agriculture: coffee; cocoa; yams; cassava;
millet; sorghum; rice; livestock; fish
Industry: phosphates mining; textiles;
handicrafts; agricultural processing;
cement; beverages
Exports: $306 million (primary partners
Benin, Nigeria, Ghana)
Imports: $420 million (primary partners
Ghana, France, Côte d'Ivoire)

SUGGESTED WEB SITES

```
http://www.republicoftogo.com/
   english/index.htm
http://www.republicoftogo.com/
http://www.sas.upenn.edu/
   African_Studies/Country_Specific/
   Togo.html
```

Togo Country Report

In recent years Togo has become a prime example of the difficulty of achieving democratic reform in the face of determined resistance by a ruling clique that enjoys military backing and a strong ethnic support base. For the past four decades, the country has been politically dominated by supporters of its long-serving president, Gnassingbé Eyadéma.

Emerging from the ranks of the military, Eyadéma first seized power in 1967. This followed a period of instability in the wake of the assassination of the country's first president, Sylvanius Olympio, by the Togolese military. In 1969 Eyadéma institutionalized his increasingly dictatorial regime as a one-party state. All Togolese have been required to belong to the Rally of the Togolese People (RPT). But in 1991, faced with mass prodemocracy demonstrations in Lomé, the capital city, Eyadéma acquiesced to opposition calls for a "National Conference" that would end the RPT's monopoly of power. Since then, Eyadéma has survived Togo's turbulent return to multiparty politics with characteristic ruthlessness, skillfully taking advantage of the weakness of his divided opponents.

In December 2002 the Parliament altered the Constitution by removing a clause that would have barred President Eyadéma

from seeking a third presidential term. In June 2003 Eyadéma was reelected president of the country.

STRUCTURAL ADJUSTMENT

Togo's political crisis has taken place against a backdrop of economic restructuring. In 1979, Togo adopted an economic recovery strategy that many consider to have been a forerunner of other Structural Adjustment Programs (SAPs) introduced throughout most of the rest of Africa. Faced with mounting debts as a result of falling export revenue, the government began to loosen the state's grip over the local economy. Since 1982 a more rigorous International Monetary Fund/World Bank-supported program of privatization and other market-oriented reforms has been pursued.

The livelihoods of certain segments of the Togolese population have materially

improved during the past decade. Beneficiaries include some of the two-thirds of the workforce employed in agriculture. Encouraged by increased official purchase prices, cash-crop farmers have expanded their outputs of cotton and coffee. This is especially true in the case of cotton production, which tripled between 1983 and 1989. Nearly half the nation's small farmers now grow the crop.

Balanced against the growth of cotton has been a decline in cocoa, which emerged as the country's principal cash crop under colonialism. Despite better producer prices during the mid-1980s, output fell as a result of past decisions not to plant new trees. Given the continuing uncertainty of cocoa prices, this earlier shift may prove to have been opportune. The long-

HEALTH/WELFARE

The nation's health service has declined as a result of austerity measures. Juvenile mortality is 15%. Self-induced abortion now causes approximately 17% of the deaths among Togolese women of child-bearing age. School attendance has dropped in recent years.

term prospects of coffee are also in doubt, due to a growing global preference for the arabica beans of Latin America over the robusta beans that thrive throughout much of West Africa. As a result, the government had to reverse course in 1988, drastically reducing its prices for both coffee and cocoa, a move that it hopes will prove to be only temporary.

Eyadéma's regime has claimed great success in food production, but its critics have long countered official reports of food self-sufficiency by citing the importation of large quantities of rice, a decline in food production in the cotton-growing regions, and widespread childhood malnutrition. The country's food situation is complicated by an imbalance between the drought-prone northern areas and the more productive south. In 1992 famine threatened 250,000 Togolese, mostly northerners.

There have been improvements in transport and telecommunications. The national highway system, largely built by the European Development Fund, has allowed the port of Lomé to develop as a transshipment center for exports from neighboring states as well as Togo's interior. At the same time, there has been modest progress in cutting the budget deficit. But it is in precisely this area that the cost of Togo's SAP is most apparent. Public expenditures in health and education declined by about 50 percent between 1982 and 1985. Whereas school enrollment rose from 40 percent to more than 70 percent during the 1970s, it has slipped back below 60 percent in recent years.

ACHIEVEMENTS

The name of Togo's capital, Lomé, is well known in international circles for its association with the Lomé Convention, a periodically renegotiated accord through which products from various African, Caribbean, and Pacific countries are given favorable access to European markets.

The ultimate justification for Togo's SAP has been to attract overseas capital investment. In addition to sweeping privatization, a Free Trade Zone has been established. But overseas investment in Togo has always been modest. There have also been complaints that many foreign investors have simply bought former state industries on the cheap rather than starting up new enterprises. Furthermore, privatization and austerity measures are blamed for unemployment and wage cuts among urban workers. One-third of the state-divested enterprises have been liquidated.

Timeline: PAST

1884
Germany occupies Togo

1919
Togo is mandated to Britain and France by the League of Nations following Germany's defeat in World War I

1956–1957
UN plebiscites result in the independence of French Togo and incorporation of British Togo into Ghana

1960
Independence is achieved

1963
Murder of President Sylvanus Olympio; a new civilian government is organized after the coup

1967
The coup of Colonel Etienne Eyadéma, now President Gnassingbé Eyadéma

1969
The Coalition of the Togolese People becomes the only legal party in Togo

1990s
Prodemocracy demonstrations lead to interim government and the promise of multiparty elections; Eyadéma survives escalating violence and controversial elections

PRESENT

2000s
Eyadéma retains power; Eyadéma is named chairman of the OAU

Tunisia (Republic of Tunisia)

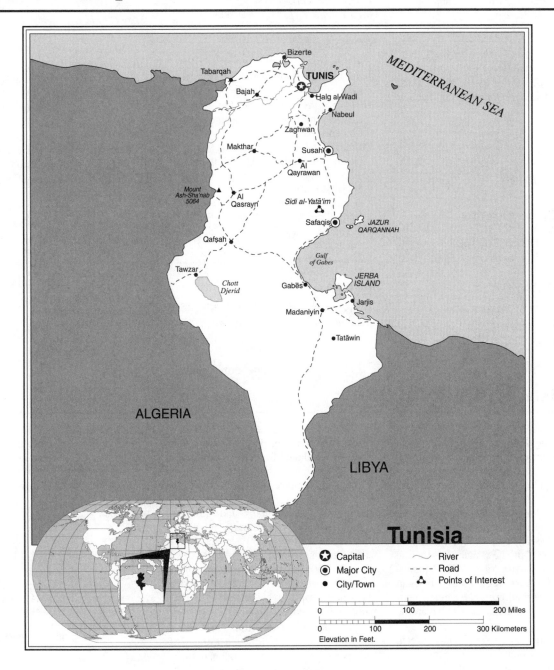

Tunisia Statistics

GEOGRAPHY

Area in Square Miles (Kilometers): 63,153 (163,610) (about the size of Georgia)

Capital (Population): Tunis (675,000)

Environmental Concerns: hazardous waste disposal; water pollution; limited freshwater resources; deforestation; overgrazing; soil erosion; desertification

Geographical Features: mountains in north; hot, dry central plain; semiarid south merges into Sahara

Climate: hot, dry summers; mild, rainy winters; desert in the south, temperate in the north

PEOPLE

Population

Total: 9,815,644

Annual Growth Rate: 1.12%

Rural/Urban Population Ratio: 37/63

Major Languages: Arabic; French

259

Ethnic Makeup: 98% Arab-Berber; 1%
 European; 1% others
Religions: 98% Muslim; 1% Christian;
 less than 1% Jewish

Health

Life Expectancy at Birth: 72.5 years
 (male); 74 years (female)
Infant Mortality Rate: 28/1,000 live births
Physicians Available (Ratio): 1/1,640 people

Education

Adult Literacy Rate: 70.8%
Compulsory (Ages): 6–16

COMMUNICATION

Telephones: 1,313,000 main lines
Daily Newspaper Circulation: 45 per
 1,000 people
Televisions: 156 per 1,000 people
Internet Service Provider: 1 (2000)

TRANSPORTATION

Highways in Miles (Kilometers): 14,345
 (23,100)

Railroads in Miles (Kilometers): 1,403
 (2,260)
Usable Airfields: 32
Motor Vehicles in Use: 531,000

GOVERNMENT

Type: republic
Independence Date: March 20, 1956 (from
 France)
Head of State/Government: President
 Zine El Abidine Ben Ali; Prime Minister
 Mohammed Ghannouchi
Political Parties: Constitutional
 Democratic Rally (RCD), ruling party;
 others are Al-Tajdid Movement, Liberal
 Socialist Party (PSL), Movement of
 Democratic Socialists (MDS), Popular
 Unity Party, Unionist Democratic Union
 (Al-Nahda "Resistance"), Islamic
 fundamentalist party (currently outlawed)
Suffrage: universal at 20

MILITARY

Military Expenditures (% of GDP): 1.5%
Current Disputes: none

ECONOMY

Currency ($ U.S. Equivalent): 1.26 dinars
 = $1
Per Capita Income/GDP: $6,500/$62.8
 billion
GDP Growth Rate: 4.8%
Inflation Rate: 3%
Unemployment Rate: 15.6%
Labor Force: 6,259,000
Natural Resources: petroleum;
 phosphates; iron ore; lead; zinc; salt
Agriculture: olives; dates; oranges;
 almonds; grain; sugar beets; grapes;
 poultry; beef; dairy products
Industry: petroleum; mining; tourism;
 textiles; footwear; food; beverages
Exports: $6.1 billion (primary partners
 Germany, France, Italy)
Imports: $8.4 billion (primary partners
 France, Germany, Italy)

SUGGESTED WEB SITES

http://www.cia.gov/cia/
 publications/factbook/index.html
http://www.tunisiaonline.com

Tunisia Country Report

Tunisia, the smallest of the four North African countries, is less than one-tenth the size of Libya, its neighbor to the east. However, its population is nearly twice the size of Libya's.

Tunisia's long coastline has exposed it over the centuries to a succession of invaders from the sea. The southern third of the country is part of the Sahara Desert; the central third consists of high, arid plains. Only the northern region has sufficient rainfall for agriculture. This region contains Tunisia's single permanent river, the Medjerda.

The country is predominantly urban. There is almost no nomadic population, and there are no high mountains to provide refuge for independent mountain peoples opposed to central government. The Tunis region and the Sahel, a coastal plain important in olive production, are the most densely populated areas. Tunis, the capital, is not only the dominant city but also the hub of government, economic, and political activity.

HISTORY

Tunisia has an ancient history that is urban rather than territorial. Phoenician merchants from what is today Lebanon founded a number of trading posts several

thousand years ago. The most important one was Carthage, founded in 814 B.C. It grew wealthy through trade and developed a maritime empire. Its great rival was Rome; after several wars, the Romans defeated the Carthaginians and destroyed Carthage. Later, the Romans rebuilt the city, and it became great once again as the capital of the Roman province of Africa. Rome's African province was one of the most prosperous in the empire. Modern Tunisia has yet to reach the level of prosperity it had under Roman rule.

The collapse of the Roman Empire in the fifth century A.D. affected Roman Africa as well. Cities were abandoned; the irrigation system that had made the farms prosperous fell into ruin.

Arab armies from the east brought Islam to North Africa in the late seventh century. After some resistance, the population accepted the new religion, and from that time on the area was ruled as the Arab-Islamic province of *Ifriqiya.* The Anglicized form of this Arabic word, "Africa," was eventually applied to the entire continent.

The Arab governors did not want to have anything to do with Carthage, since they associated it with Christian Roman rule. They built a new capital on the site of a village on the outskirts of Carthage, named Tunis. The

fact that Tunis has been the capital and major city in the country for 14 centuries has contributed to the sense of unity and nationhood among most Tunisians.[1]

DEVELOPMENT

Associate membership in the European Union has resulted in a number of advantages to Tunisia. One important one is favorable terms for its agricultural exports. Privatization of some 140 state-owned industries, a liberal investment code, and tax reform have made possible a GDP growth rate averaging 4.5 to 5 percent annually.

The original Tunisian population consisted of Berbers, a people of unknown origin. During the centuries of Islamic rule, many Arabs settled in the country. Other waves of immigration brought Muslims from Spain, Greeks, Italians, Maltese, and many other nationalities. Until recently, Tunisia also had a large community of Jews, most of whom emigrated to the State of Israel when it was founded in 1948. The blending of ethnic groups and nationalities over the years has created a relatively homogeneous and tolerant society, with few of the conflicts that marked other societies in the Islamic world.

From the late 1500s to the 1880s, Tunisia was a self-governing province of the Ottoman Empire.

In 1881 a French army invaded and occupied all of Tunisia, almost without firing a shot. The French said that they had intervened because the bey's government could not meet its debts to French bankers and capitalists, who had been lending money for years to keep the country afloat. There was concern also about the European population. Europeans from many countries had been pouring into Tunisia, ever since the bey had given foreigners the right to own land and set up businesses.

HABIB BOURGUIBA

Habib Ben Ali Bourguiba, born in 1903, once said he had "invented" Tunisia, not historically but in the sense of shaping its existence as a modern sovereign nation. The Neo-Destour Party, under Bourguiba's leadership, became the country's first mass political party. It drew its membership from shopkeepers, craftspeople, blue-collar workers, and peasants, along with French-educated lawyers and doctors. The party became the vanguard of the nation, mobilizing the population in a campaign of strikes, demonstrations, and violence in order to gain independence. It was a long struggle. Bourguiba spent many years in prison. But eventually the Neo-Destour tactics succeeded. On March 20, 1956, France ended its protectorate and Tunisia became an independent republic, led by Habib Bourguiba.

One of the problems facing Tunisia today is that its political organization has changed very little since independence. A constitution was approved in 1959 that established a "presidential republic"—that is, a republic in which the elected president has great power. Bourguiba was elected president in 1957.

Bourguiba was also the head of the Neo-Destour Party, the country's only legal political party. The Constitution provided for a National Assembly, which is responsible for enacting laws. But to be elected to the Assembly, a candidate had to be a member of the Neo-Destour Party. Bourguiba's philosophy and programs for national development in his country were often called Bourguibism. It was tailored to the particular historical experience of the Tunisian people. Since ancient Carthage, Tunisian life has been characterized by the presence of a strong central government able to impose order and bring relative stability to the people. The predominance of cities and villages over nomadism reinforced this sense of order. The experience of Carthage, and even more so that of Rome, set the pattern.

In 1961 Bourguiba introduced a new program for Tunisian development that he termed "Destourian Socialism." It combined Bourguibism with government planning for economic and social development. The name of the Neo-Destour Party was changed to the Destour Socialist Party (PSD) to indicate its new direction. Destourian Socialism worked for the general good, but it was not Marxist; Bourguiba stressed national unanimity rather than class struggle and opposed communism as the "ideology of a godless state." Bourguiba took the view that Destourian Socialism was directly related to Islam. He said once that the original members of the Islamic community (in Muhammad's time in Mecca) "were socialists … and worked for the common good."[2] For many years after independence, Tunisia appeared to be a model among new nations because of its stability, order, and economic progress. Particularly notable were Bourguiba's reforms in social and political life. Islamic law was replaced by a Western-style legal system, with various levels of courts. Women were encouraged to attend school and enter occupations previously closed to them, and they were given equal rights with men in matters of divorce and inheritance.

Bourguiba strongly criticized those aspects of Islam that seemed to him to be obstacles to national development. He was against women wearing the veil; polygyny; and ownership of lands by religious leaders, which kept land out of production. He even encouraged people not to fast during the holy month of Ramadan, because their hunger made them less effective in their work.

The new generation coming of age in Tunisia is deeply alienated from the old. Young Tunisians (half the population are under age 15) increasingly protest their inability to find jobs, their exclusion from the political decision-making process, the unfair distribution of wealth, and the lack of political organizations. It seems as if there are two Tunisias: the old Tunisia of genteel politicians and freedom fighters; and the new one of alienated youths, angry peasants, and frustrated intellectuals. Somehow the two have gotten out of touch with each other.

FREEDOM

The campaign against Islamic fundamentalists have significantly reduced the civil rights normally observed in Tunisia. Foreign travel is routinely restricted, passports randomly confiscated and journalists arrested for articles that are said to "defame" the state. Tunisia was expelled from the World Press Organization in 1999 for its restrictions on press freedom.

The division between these groups has been magnified by the growth of Islamic fundamentalism, which in Bourguiba's view, was equated with rejection of the secular, modern Islamic society that he created. The Islamic Tendency Movement (MTI) emerged in the 1980s as the major fundamentalist group.

THE END OF AN ERA

In 1984 riots over an increase in the price of bread signaled a turning point for the regime. For the first time in the republic's history, an organized Islamic opposition challenged Bourguiba, on the grounds that he had deformed Islam to create a secular society. The Tunisian Labor Confederation (UGTT) was disbanded, and the government launched a massive purge of fundamentalists.

A decision that would prove crucial to the needed change in leadership was made by Bourguiba in September 1987, when he named Ben Ali as prime minister. Six weeks later, Ben Ali carried out a bloodless coup, removing the aging president under the 1974 constitutional provision that allows the prime minister to take over in the event of a president's "manifest incapacity" to govern. A council of medical doctors affirmed that this was the case.

NEW DIRECTIONS

President Ben Ali (elected to a full five-year term in April 1989) initiated a series of bold reforms designed to wean the country away from the one-party system. Political prisoners were released under a general amnesty. Prodded by Ben Ali, the Destour-dominated National Assembly passed laws ensuring press freedom and the right of political parties to form as long as their platforms are not based exclusively on language, race, or religion. The Assembly also abolished the constitutional provision establishing the position of president-for-life, which had been created expressly for Bourguiba. Henceforth Tunisian presidents would be limited to three consecutive terms in office.

After the 1994 election the Chamber of Deputies was enlarged from the present 144 to 160 deputies. Twenty seats would be reserved for members from opposition parties. In the presidential election, Ben Ali was reelected for a third term and again in 1999 for a fourth term.

The Chamber was enlarged again in time for the 1999 elections, this time to 182 seats, to broaden representation for Tunisia's growing population. Opposition parties all together increased their representation from 19 seats to 34.

Timeline: PAST

264–146 B.C.
Wars between Rome and Carthage, ending in the destruction of Carthage and its rebuilding as a Roman city

800–900 A.D.
The establishment of Islam in Ifriqiya, with its new capital at Tunis

1200–1400
The Hafsid dynasty develops Tunisia as a highly centralized urban state

1500–1800
Ottoman Turks establish Tunis as a corsair state to control Mediterranean sea lanes

1881–1956
French protectorate

1956
Tunisia gains independence, led by Habib Bourguiba

1974
An abortive merger with Libya

1980s
Bourguiba is removed from office in a "palace coup;" he is succeeded by Ben Ali

1990s
Tunisia's economic picture brightens; Ben Ali seeks some social modernization; women's rights are expanded

PRESENT

2000s
Human-rights abuses continue

THE ECONOMY

The challenge to Ben Ali lies not only in broadening political participation but also in improving the economy. After a period of impressive expansion in the 1960s and 1970s, the growth rate began dropping steadily, largely due to decreased demand and lowered prices for the country's three main exports (phosphates, petroleum, and olive oil). Tunisia is the world's fourth-ranking producer of phosphates, and its most important industries are those related to production of superphosphates and fertilizers.

Problems have dogged the phosphate industry. The quality of the rock mined is poor in comparison with that of other phosphate producers, such as Morocco.

Tunisia's oil reserves are estimated at 1.65 billion barrels. New offshore discoveries and a 1996 agreement with Libya for 50/50 sharing of production from the dis-puted Gulf of Gabes oil field have improved oil output, currently about 4.3 million barrels annually.

Tunisia became an associate member of the European Union (EU) in 1998, the first Mediterranean country to do so. The terms of the EU agreement require the country to remove trade barriers over a 10-year period. In turn, Tunisian products such as citrus and olives receive highly favorable export terms in EU countries. The EU also provides technical support and training for the government's Mise A Nouveau (Upgrading and Improvement) program intended to enhance productivity in business and industry and compete internationally.

HEALTH/WELFARE

Tunisia has overhauled its school and university curricula to emphasize respect for other monotheistic religions. They require courses on the Universal Declaration of Human Rights, democracy, and the value of the individual. The new curricula are at variance with government repressive policies, but they do stress Islamic ideals of tolerance for the school-age population.

Tunisia's political stability—albeit one gained at the expense of human rights—and its economic reforms have made it a favored country for foreign aid over the years. During the period 1970–2000 it received more World Bank loans than any other Arab or African country. Its economic reform program, featuring privatization of 140 state-owned enterprises since 1987, liberalizing of prices, reduction of tariffs, and other reforms, is lauded as a model for development by international financial institutions.

The funding has been equitably distributed, so that 60 percent of the population are middle class, and 80 percent own their own homes.

THE FUTURE

Tunisia's "Islamic nature" was reaffirmed by such actions as the reopening of the venerable Zitouna University in Tunis, a center for Islamic scholarship, along with its counterpart in Kairouan. But like other Islamic countries, it has not been free from the scourge of militant Islamic fundamentalism. The fundamentalist movement Al-Nahda ("Renaissance"), advocates a Tunisian government based on Islamic law. Many of its members, including the leader, were subsequently arrested, and it was out-lawed as a political party. However, the success of Osama bin Laden's al-Qaeda movement is attracting young Muslims everywhere, and it has emboldened those members still at large.

ACHIEVEMENTS

With domestic electric demand rising at the rate of 77 percent annually, the country has moved rapidly to add new power plants. The new Rades plant, powered by a combination of diesel fuel and natural gas, went into operation in mid-2003; it increases national output from 2000 megawatts (mw) to 2,480. Some 94% of Tunisian homes now have electric power.

In subsequent years, Tunisia has become an increasingly closed society. The press is heavily censored. Telephones are routinely tapped. More than 1,000 Ennahda members have been arrested and jailed without trial. In December 2000 a dozen members of another Islamic fundamentalist group were given 17-year jail sentences for forming an illegal organization; their lawyers walked out of the trial to protest the court's bias and procedural abuses.

The regime's repression of Islamic groups, even moderate nonviolent ones, has changed its former image as a tolerant, progressive Islamic country. The Tunisian League for Human Rights, oldest in the Arab world, was closed in 1992. Arrest and harassment of intellectuals, journalists, and others for alleged criticism of the regime are routine. Foreign publications are banned, and opposition leaders are pilloried in the state-controlled press as fundamentalists.

NOTES

1. Harold D. Nelson, ed., *Tunisia: A Country Study* (Washington, D.C.: American University, Foreign Area Studies, 1979), p. 68.
2. *Ibid.*, p. 42.
3. *Ibid.*, p. 194. What Nelson means, in this case, by "authoritarianism" is that the French brought to Tunisia the elaborate bureaucracy of metropolitan France, with levels of administration from the center down to local towns and villages.
4. *Ibid.*, p. 196.
5. Jim Rupert, in *The Christian Science Monitor* (November 23, 1984).
6. Mamoun Fandy, in *The Christian Science Monitor* (October 25, 1999).
7. Georgie Ann Geyer, in *The Washington Post* (October 23, 1999).
8. Noted in *The Economist* (April 15, 2000).

Turkey (Republic of Turkey)

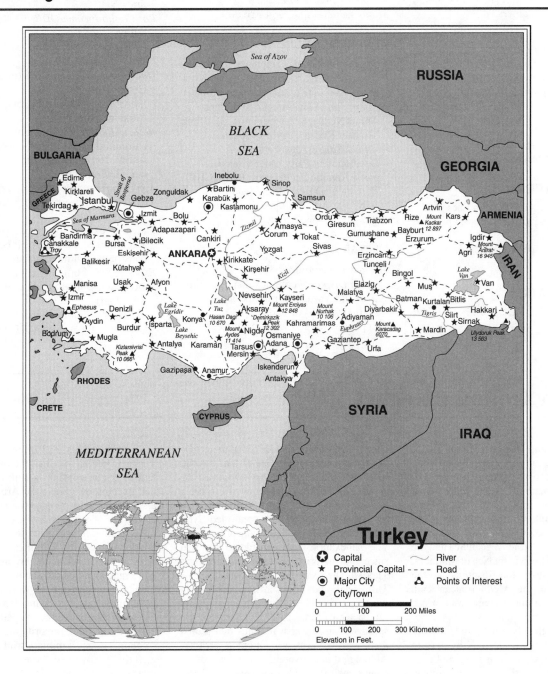

Map legend:
- ✪ Capital
- ★ Provincial Capital
- ◉ Major City
- ● City/Town
- 〜 River
- - - - Road
- △ Points of Interest

0   100   200 Miles
0 100 200 300 Kilometers
Elevation in Feet.

Turkey

Map labels: Sea of Azov, BLACK SEA, RUSSIA, BULGARIA, GEORGIA, ARMENIA, GREECE, IRAN, SYRIA, IRAQ, RHODES, CRETE, CYPRUS, MEDITERRANEAN SEA, Sea of Marmara, Strait of Bosporus.

Cities: Edirne, Kirklareli, Tekirdag, Istanbul, Gebze, Izmit, Bolu, Bandirma, Canakkale, Troy, Bursa, Bilecik, Adapazari, Cankiri, Balikesir, Eskisehir, ANKARA, Kutahya, Kirikkate, Manisa, Usak, Afyon, Kirsehir, Izmir, Ephesus, Denizli, Lake Egridir, Konya, Nevsehir, Aksaray, Kayseri, Aydin, Burdur, Isparta, Lake Beysehir, Nigde, Kahramarimas, Bodrum, Mugla, Antalya, Karaman, Tarsus, Mersin, Adana, Osmaniye, Gaziantep, Urfa, Gazipasa, Anamur, Iskenderun, Antakya, Inebolu, Bartin, Sinop, Zonguldak, Karabuk, Kastamonu, Samsun, Ordu, Giresun, Trabzon, Rize, Artvin, Kars, Amasya, Tokat, Gumushane, Bayburt, Erzurum, Igdir, Corum, Sivas, Yozgat, Erzincan, Tunceli, Agri, Bingol, Elazig, Mus, Van, Malatya, Batman, Kurtalan, Bitlis, Diyarbakir, Siirt, Hakkari, Adiyaman, Mardin, Sirnak.

Lakes/features: Lake Tuz, Lake Van, Kizil, Tigris, Euphrates, Izmit.

Mountains: Mount Kackar 12 897, Mount Ararat 16 945, Mount Erciyas 12 848, Mount Nurhak 10 106, Demirkazik Peak 12 302, Hasan Dagi 10 670, Mount Aydes 11 414, Mount Karacadag 6070, Kizlarsivrisi Peak 10 066, Ulydoruk Peak 13 563.

Turkey Statistics

GEOGRAPHY

Area in Square Miles (Kilometers): 301,303 (780,580) (about the size of Texas)

Capital (Population): Ankara (2,940,000)

Environmental Concerns: water and air pollution; deforestation; threat of oil spills from Bosporus ship traffic

Geographical Features: mostly mountains; a narrow coastal plain; a high central plateau (Anatolia)

Climate: temperate; hot, dry summers and mild wet winters along coasts; much drier and more extreme in temperatures in interior plateau and mountains

PEOPLE

Population

Total: 69,660,559

Annual Growth Rate: 1.09%

Rural/Urban Population Ratio: 29/71

Major Languages: Turkish; Kurdish; Arabic

Ethnic Makeup: 80% Turk; 17% Kurd; 3% others

Religions: 99% Muslim (about 79% Sunni, 20% Shi'a); 1% others

Health

Life Expectancy at Birth: 69 years (male); 74 years (female)

Infant Mortality Rate: 41/1,000 live births

Physicians Available (Ratio): 1/1,200 people

Education

Adult Literacy Rate: 86.5%

Compulsory (Ages): 6–16

COMMUNICATION

Telephones: 18,916,700 main lines

Daily Newspaper Circulation: 44 per 1,000 people

Televisions: 171 per 1,000 people

Internet Users: 5.5 million (2003)

TRANSPORTATION

Highways in Miles (Kilometers): 237,747 (354,421)

Railroads in Miles (Kilometers): 5,336 (8,697)

Usable Airfields: 119

Motor Vehicles in Use: 4,320,000

GOVERNMENT

Type: republican parliamentary democracy

Independence Date: October 29, 1923 (successor state to the Ottoman Empire)

Head of State/Government: President Ahmet Necdet Sezer (ceremonial); Prime Minister Recep Tayyip Erdogan

Political Parties: Justice and Development Party (AKP); majority party; Republican Peoples' Party (CHP), True Path (DYP); Motherland Party (ANAP), principal opposition parties

Suffrage: universal at 18

MILITARY

Military Expenditures (% of GDP): 5.3%

Current Disputes: complex disputes with Greece; Cyprus question; periodic friction with Syria and Iraq over Euphrates River's water resources

ECONOMY

Currency ($ U.S. Equivalent): 1,425,600 lira = $1

Per Capita Income/GDP: $7,400/$508.7 billion

GDP Growth Rate: 8.2%

Inflation Rate: 9.3%

Unemployment Rate: 9.3% (plus 4.0% Underemployment)

Labor Force: ,25,300,000, plus 1,200,000 Turks working abroad

Natural Resources: antimony; coal; chromium ore; mercury; copper; boray; sulfur; iron ore; meerschaum; arable land; hydropower

Agriculture: tobacco; cotton; grains; olives; sugar beets; pulse; citrus; livestock

Industry: textiles; food processing; automobiles; mining; steel; petroleum; construction; lumber; paper

Exports: $69.4 billion (primary partners Germany, United States, Italy, United Kingdom)

Imports: $94.5 billion (primary partners Germany, Italy, Russia, United States)

Turkey Country Report

Except for a small area in extreme Southeastern Europe called Thrace, the Republic of Turkey comprises the large peninsula of Asia Minor (Anatolia), which forms a land bridge between Europe and Asia. Asiatic Turkey is separated from European Turkey by the Bosporus, a narrow strait connecting the Black Sea with the Aegean Sea and the Mediterranean Sea via the Sea of Marmara. Throughout history, the Bosporus and the Dardanelles, at the Mediterranean end, have been important strategic waterways, fought over by many nations.

Except for the Syrian border, Asiatic Turkey's borders are defined by natural limits, with seas on three sides and rugged mountains on the fourth. European Turkey's frontiers with Greece and Bulgaria are artificial; they fluctuated considerably in the nineteenth and twentieth centuries before the Republic of Turkey was established.

Modern Turkey occupies a much smaller area than did its predecessor, the Ottoman Empire. The Ottoman Turks were the dominant power in the Middle East for more than five centuries. After the defeat of the empire in World War I, Turkey's new leader, Mustafa Kemal Ataturk, turned away from the imperial past, limiting the new republic to territory with a predominantly Turkish population. Since then, Turkey has not attempted to annex land beyond its natural Anatolian borders—with two exceptions. One was the Hatay, formerly a province of Syria that was ceded to Turkey by the French (who then controlled Syria under mandate from the League of Nations). The annexation was considered justified since the majority of the population was Turkish. The second exception was Cyprus. This island republic has a Greek majority in the population, but a significant minority (20 percent) are Turkish Cypriots, descended from Turkish families that settled there when Cyprus was Ottoman territory. Although it is a sovereign state, fears of violence against the Cypriot Turks led Turkish forces to occupy the northern third of the island in 1974. They have been there since then, with no agreement as yet on reunification of Cyprus.

Asia Minor has an ancient history of settlement. Most of the peninsula is a plateau ringed by mountains. The mountains are close to the coast; over the centuries, due to volcanic action, the coastline became cracked, with deep indentations and islands just offshore. The inland plateau has an area of arid steppe with dried-up salt lakes at the center, but most of it is rolling land, well suited to agriculture.

In terms of national unity, the modern Turkish state has not had the thorny problem of ethnic conflicts—with two important exceptions. One is the Armenians, an ancient Christian people who ruled over a large part of what is now eastern Turkey many centuries ago. With the outbreak of World War I, the Ottoman government aligned itself with Germany against Britain, France, and its old enemy Russia. Following a declaration of war, the Czarist government invited Armenians living in Ottoman territory to revolt against the Sultan's rule. A small minority did so, and the "Young Turks," a military triumvirate that effectively governed the empire used the pretext of an "armed Armenian revolutionary uprising" to eliminate its entire Armenian population. In what is usually, and effectively, described as the first twentieth century genocide, approximately 800,000 Armenians were uprooted from their towns and villages and deported to Syria and other nearby Ottoman territories. The deportations were carried out under harrowing conditions, and few survived.

The other exception to Turkish homogeneity is the Kurds, who make up 17 percent of the population officially but may be closer to 20 percent. There are also Kurdish populations in Iraq, Syria, and Iran, but Tur-

© Getty Images/John A. Rizzo (DIL89124)

The *Hagai Sophia* (Divine Wisdom) in Istanbul, Turkey, was first built as a church by Roman Emperor Constantine two years after his conversion to Christianity in 322 CE. In 537 CE, Roman Emperor Justinian I, commissioned the present basilica, which was dedicated in Constantinople (named after Emperor Constantine), an d used for magnificent religious ceremonies. In 1453 CE, the Ottoman Turks conquered Constantinople and converted the church into a mosque (with minarrets). Since 1935, it has been a museum.

key's Kurds form the largest component of this "people without a nation," one of the last ethnic peoples in the world who do not have their own indigenous government. Their clannish social structure and fierce spirit of independence have led to periodic Kurdish uprisings against the governments that rule them. In Turkey the Ataturk regime crushed Kurdish rebellions in the 1920s, and from then on, Kurds were officially referred to as "Mountain Turks." Until the 1980s Turkey's Kurds were considered an unimportant, albeit economically deprived, population group. Large numbers of them have moved to Istanbul, Ankara, and other cities and have been assimilated into the surrounding Turkish culture. Those who remain are grouped in compact villages and are mostly farmers or herders.

An estimated 20 percent of Turkey's population are *Alevis*, a blanket term for various Muslim communities whose Islamic rituals and beliefs differ from those of the Sunni majority. Some are Shi'as; others are ethnic and religious compatriots of the Alawis, who currently rule Syria and live close by in the Hatay and other areas

near the Syrian border. Other Alevis form compact communities in such small Anatolian towns as Sivas, Corum, and Kahramanras, and Istanbul has a substantial Alevi population. Alevi rituals differ from those of both Sunnis and Shi'as in that they incorporate music and dancing into their services. They have no religious leaders, but each Alevi community has a *dede* ("old man") who directs community affairs.

HISTORY: A PARADE OF PEOPLES

The earliest political unit to develop in the peninsula was the Empire of the Hittites (1600–1200 B.C.), inventors of the two-wheeled chariot and one of the great powers of the ancient Near East.

Following the collapse of the Roman Empire in the fifth century A.D., Asia Minor became the largest part of the East Roman or Byzantine Empire, named for its capital, Byzantium. The city was later renamed Constantinople, in honor of the Roman emperor Constantine, after he had become Christian. For a thousand years, this empire was a center and fortress of

DEVELOPMENT

The loans pledged by the IMF and World Bank to resolve Turkey's economic crisis require the country to maintain a 4% budget surplus, excluding interest on foreign debts. Inflation and the loss of purchasing power have made that objective almost impossible to reach. A new tracking system that requires an official personal identification number (PIN) for transactions over $3,000 or to hold a bank or stock account should reduce cheating and create a financial database. It will also provide for more equitable tax collection.

Christianity against hostile neighbors and later against the forces of Islam.

The Ottoman Centuries[4]

Various nomadic peoples from Central Asia began migrating into Islamic lands from the ninth century onward. Among them were the ancestors of the Turks of today. They settled mostly along the borders between Christian and Islamic powers in Asia Minor and northwest Iran. Although

Mustafa Kemal Ataturk (1881–1938) rose through the ranks of the Ottoman army to become its commander-in-chief and then-the first president of modern Turkey (1923–1938). His fifteen-year presidency was marked by rapid modernization and the secularization of the educational, legal, economic, and political systems. His pro-Western legacy resulted in Turkey being aligned with the West in the North Atlantic Treaty Organization (NATO). In 1934, he assumed the title of Atatürk, which means "father of the Turks."

divided into families and clans and often in conflict, the Turks had a rare sense of unity as a nation. They were also early converts to Islam. Its simple faith and requirements appealed to them more than did Christian ritual, and they readily joined in Islam's battles as *Ghazis*, "warriors for the faith." Asia Minor, having been wrested from the Greeks by the Turks, also gave the Turks a strong sense of identification with that particular place. To them it was Anadolu (Anatolia), "land of the setting sun," a "sacred homeland" giving the Turks a strong sense of national identity and unity.

The Ottomans were one of many Turkish clans in Anatolia.

Although the Ottomans started out with a small territory, they were fortunate in that Osman and his successors were extremely able rulers. Osman's son, Orkhan, captured the important Greek city of Bursa, across the Sea of Marmara from Constantinople (modern-day Istanbul). It became the first Ottoman capital. Later Ottoman rulers took the title of sultan to signify their temporal authority over expanding territories. A series of capable sultans led the Ottoman armies deep into Europe. Constantinople was surrounded, and on May 29, A.D. 1453,

Mehmed II, the seventh sultan, captured the great city amid portents of disaster for Christian Europe.[6] On two occasions his armies besieged Vienna, and during the rule of Sultan Sulayman I, a contemporary of Queen Elizabeth I of England, the Ottoman Empire was the largest and most powerful in the world.

One reason for the success of Ottoman armies was the Janissaries, an elite corps recruited mostly from Christian villages and converted to Islam by force. Janissary units were assigned to captured cities as garrisons.

Another factor that made the Ottoman system work was the religious organization of non-Muslim minority groups as self-governing units termed *millets*, a Turkish word meaning "nations." Each millet was headed by its own religious leader, who was responsible to the sultan for the leadership and good behavior of his people. The three principal millets in Turkey were the Armenians, Greek Orthodox Christians, and Jews. Although Christians and Jews were not considered equal to freeborn Muslims, they were under the sultan's protection. Armenian, Greek, and Jewish merchants rendered valuable services to the empire due to their linguistic skills and trade experience, particularly after the wars with Europe were replaced by peaceful commerce.

The Ottoman Reforms

In the eighteenth and nineteenth centuries, the Ottoman Empire gradually weakened, while European Christian powers grew stronger. European countries improved their military equipment and tactics and began to defeat the Ottomans regularly. The sultans were forced to sign treaties and lost territories, causing great humiliation, since they had never treated Christian rulers as equals before. To make matters worse, the European powers helped the Greeks and other Balkan peoples to win their independence from the Ottomans.

One or two sultans in the nineteenth century tried to make reforms in the Ottoman system. Sultan Mahmud II issued an imperial decree called *Tanzimat* (literally, "reordering"). It gave equal rights under the law to all subjects, Muslims and non-Muslims alike, in matters such as taxation, education, and property ownership.

World War I: Exit Empire, Enter Republic

During World War I, the Ottoman Empire was allied with Germany against Britain, France, and Russia. Ottoman armies fought bravely against heavy odds but were eventually defeated. A peace treaty signed in 1920 divided up the empire into British and French protectorates, except for a small

part of Anatolia that was left to the sultan. At this point in the Turkish nation's fortunes, however, a new leader appeared. He would take it in a very different direction.

This new leader, Mustafa Kemal, had risen through the ranks of the Ottoman Army to become one of its few successful commanders. Mustafa Kemal took advantage of Turkish anger over the occupation of Anatolia by foreign armies, particularly the Greeks, to launch a movement for independence. It would be a movement not only to recover the sacred Anatolian homeland but also for independence from the sultan.

The Turkish independence movement began in the interior, far from Constantinople. Mustafa Kemal and his associates chose Ankara, a village on a plateau, as their new capital. They issued a so-called National Pact stating that the "New Turkey" would be an independent republic. Its territory would be limited to areas where Turks were the majority of the population. The nationalists resolutely turned their backs on Turkey's imperial past. The Turkish War of Independence lasted until 1922. It was fought mainly against the Greeks. The Greeks were defeated in a series of fierce battles; and eventually France and Britain signed a treaty recognizing Turkey as a sovereign state headed by Mustafa Kemal.

FREEDOM

Turkey's drive to join the European Union has generated a number of constitutional reforms. In October 2001 the GNA eliminated the death penalty except in cases of terrorism. A court order is now required for searches of private property; public protests and demonstrations opposing government policy may be held; thus the opposition to the use of Turkish bases by American troops against Iraq roused a storm of public protest, even to the use of posters reading "Vahsete Ortak Olma" ("Don't Cooperate for Savagery!") In an updating of the 1926 civil code, women are now given full equality with men in matters of divorce and the workplace, and they share ownership of property acquired during the marriage.

THE TURKISH REPUBLIC

The Turkish republic has passed through several stages of political development since it was founded. The first stage, dominated by Mustafa Kemal, established its basic form. "Turkey for the Turks" meant that the republic would be predominantly Turkish in population; this was accomplished by rough surgery, with the expulsion of the Armenians and most of the Greeks. Peace with Turkey's neighbors and the abandonment of imperialism enabled Mustafa Kemal to concentrate on internal changes. By design, these changes would be far-reaching, in order to break what he viewed as the dead hand of Islam on Turkish life. Turkey would become a secular democratic state on the European model. A constitution was approved in 1924, the sultanate and the caliphate were both abolished, and the last Ottoman sultan went into exile. Religious courts were also abolished, and new European law codes were introduced to replace Islamic law. An elected Grand National Assembly was given the responsibility for legislation, with executive power held by the president of the republic.

The most striking changes were made in social life, most bearing the personal stamp of Mustafa Kemal. The traditional Turkish clothing and polygyny were outlawed. Women were encouraged to work, were allowed to vote (in 1930), and were given equal rights with men in divorce and inheritance. Turks were now required to have surnames; Mustafa Kemal took the name *Ataturk*, meaning "Father of the Turks."

Mustafa Kemal Ataturk died on November 10, 1938.

Ismet Inonu, Ataturk's right-hand man, succeeded Ataturk and served as president until 1950. Ataturk had distrusted political parties; the only political party he allowed was the Republican People's Party (RPP). It was not dedicated to its own survival or to repression, as are political parties in many single-party states. The RPP based its program on six principles, the most important, in terms of politics, being *devrimcilik* ("revolutionism" or "reformism"). It meant that the party was committed to work for a multiparty system and free elections.

HEALTH/WELFARE

Improved prison conditions is an important prerequisite for Turkey's membership in the European Union. A hunger strike by inmates protesting these conditions in 2001 led to 31 deaths. An amendment to the penal code allows for reduced sentences for "honor killings," those carried out by husbands or other relatives on women who have "shamed" their families by adultery or other forms of misbehavior.

Agitation for political reforms began during World War II. Later, when Turkey applied for admission to the United Nations, a number of National Assembly deputies pointed out that the UN Charter specified certain rights that the government was not providing. Reacting to popular demands and pressure from Turkey's allies, Inonu announced that political parties could be established. The first new party in the republic's history was the Democratic

Party, organized in 1946. In 1950 the party won 408 seats in the National Assembly, to 69 for the Republican People's Party. The Democrats had campaigned vigorously in rural areas, winning massive support from farmers and peasants. Having presided over the transition from a one-party system with a bad conscience to a two-party one, President Inonu stepped down to become head of the opposition.

MILITARY INTERVENTIONS

Modern Turkey has struggled for decades to develop a workable multiparty political system. An interesting point about this struggle is that the armed forces have seized power three times, and three times they have returned the nation to civilian rule. This fact makes Turkey very different from other Middle Eastern nations, whose army leaders, once they have seized power, have been unwilling to give it up.

Ataturk deliberately kept the Turkish armed forces out of domestic politics. He believed that the military had only two responsibilities: to defend the nation in case of invasion and to serve as "the guardian of the reforming ideals of his regime."[10] Since Ataturk's death, military leaders have seized power only when they have been convinced that the civilian government had betrayed the ideals of the founder of the republic.

RETURN TO CIVILIAN RULE

Following the third coup in 1980, the military regime approved a new constitution in 1982. It provided for a multiparty political system, although pre-1980 political parties were specifically excluded. (Several were later reinstated, notably the RPP). Three new parties were allowed to present candidates for a new Grand National Assembly (GNA), and elections were scheduled for 1983. However, the party least favored by the generals, the Motherland Party (ANAP), ran an American-style political campaign, using the media to present its candidates to the country. It won handily.

However, there was a shift in the October 1991 elections for a new National Assembly, when candidates of the True Path Party won 180 seats to 113 for the Motherland Party, taking 27 percent of the popular vote, as compared to 24 percent for the majority party. The Social Democratic Populist Party (SHP) garnered 20 percent of the vote, followed by the Islamic Welfare Party (Refah), whose growing strength was reflected in its 16 percent support from voters. Lacking a majority in the Assembly, the True Path (DYP) formed a coalition government with the SHP in November 1991. Party leader Suleyman Demirel be-

came prime minister. In 1993, the DYP, founded by former prime minister and current president Suleyman Demirel of the former Justice Party, elected Tansu Ciller, a U.S.-trained economist and university professor, as Turkey's first woman prime minister, one of two in the Muslim world (the other was Benazir Bhutto of Pakistan).

Ciller's first two years in office were marked by economic difficulties; growing tendencies toward Islamic fundamentalism, spearheaded by Refah, and intensified violence by Kurdish separatists of the Workers' Party of Kurdistan (PKK), in the southeastern region. Nevertheless, her government, a coalition of the DYP and the RPP, representing the center left and the center right, seemed to be governing effectively in at least some respects. By early 1995 the army had regained control of much of the southeast from PKK forces, and in March, agreement was reached for a customs union with the European Union. Municipal elections in June also favored the ruling coalition. It won 61.7 percent of Council seats against 17.4 percent for Refah candidates and 13.4 percent for those of ANAP.

Thus the collapse of the coalition government in September came as a surprise to most observers. RPP head Deniz Baykal had set certain terms for continuation of his party's alliance with DYP. These included repeal of a strict antiterrorism law, which had drawn international condemnation for its lack of rights for detained dissidents; tighter controls over Islamic fundamentalists; and pay raises of 70 percent for public workers to offset inflation. When these terms were rejected, he withdrew his party from the coalition.

Elections in December 1995 brought another shock, with Refah winning 158 seats to 135 for True Path and 132 for ANAP. For the first time in modern Turkish history, an Islamic-oriented party had won more seats in the Grand National Assembly than its rivals. Refah leader Necmettin Erbakan was named Turkey's first "Islamist" prime minister, taking office in April 1996. However, his party lacked a clear majority in the Assembly. As a result, coalition government became necessary. Erbakan's cabinet included ministers from the three major parties, and Ciller became foreign minister.

The septuagenarian Erbakan initially brought a breath of fresh air into the country's stale political system. With his round face and Italian designer ties, he seemed more like a Turkish uncle than an Islamic fundamentalist. And during his year in office, his government reaffirmed traditional secularism, state socialism, and other elements of the legacy of Ataturk. The government also stressed NATO membership in its foreign policy and continued the drive for an economic and customs union with the European Community (EC), begun by its predecessors.

With Refah's victory at the polls, Turkey's military leaders believed that the party was determined to dismantle the secular state founded by Ataturk and replace it with an Islamized one. In 1997 they demanded Erbakan's resignation. Inasmuch as they have final authority over political life under the 1980 Constitution, Erbakan had no choice. After his resignation, the state prosecutor filed suit to outlaw Refah on the grounds that its programs were intended to impose Islamic law on Turkish society. The court agreed, and Erbakan was barred from politics for five years.

President Demirel then named ANAP leader Mesut Yilmaz to head a caretaker government. But he also resigned following a no-confidence resolution in the Grand National Assembly (GNA).

In the April 1999 GNA elections, however, a relatively new party, Democratic Left, surprised observers by winning a clear majority of seats. A strong pro-nationalistic party, Nationalist Action (MHP), ran second, with 18 percent of the popular vote, winning 130 seats. The Virtue Party, reformed from the ruins of Refah, finished with 102 seats and 15 percent of the popular vote.

Virtue then set out to distance itself from Islamic fundamentalism. Its members opposed the ban on wearing headscarves in university classes and government offices. Its governing board even approved the celebration of St. Valentine's Day as an appropriate secular holiday.

Unfortunately, the "new image" of Virtue did not convince the country's military and civilian leaders, who are adamant in their defense of Ataturk's legacy. In July 2000 an appeals court upheld the one-year jail sentence imposed on Erbakan, and the following year the Constitutional Court, the country's highest court, banned Virtue as a political party. The action came over the objections of many political leaders, including Ecevit. Despite the ban Virtue deputies in the GNA would be allowed to keep their seats, as independents.

In August 2001 yet another Islamic-related political party was formed, the 281st since the 1876 Constitution allowed them to form. The new party, Justice and Development (AKP), included many former Virtue leaders, including the charismatic ex-mayor of Istanbul, Recep Tayyip Erdogan. He had been banned from politics for five years in 1998 for criticizing the country's nonadherence to traditional Is-

lam, but he was released under the 2000 amnesty law for political prisoners.

The debate between Islamists and secularists over Turkey's Islamic identity is far from being resolved. In May 2001 the debate shifted to the presidency. Ecevit had proposed a change in the Constitution to allow Suleyman Demirel, the incumbent, to run for a second term but to reduce his term to five years rather than seven. Demirel's election was seen as a sure thing, once the GNA had accepted the proposed changes. However, a majority of deputies rejected the proposal. Their candidate, Ahmet Cevdet Sezer, chief judge of the Constitutional Court, was elected to the largely ceremonial post on the third ballot by a 60 percent margin.

Sezer's election was a bitter blow to Ecevit, and when the president refused to sign a controversial measure that would cause thousands of government employees to lose their jobs if they were suspected of separatist or Islamic fundamentalist activities, there was open warfare between the two leaders. Sezer's support for the repeal of the restrictive press laws, an end to the ban on use of the Kurdish language in schools and on official documents, and civilian control over the military leadership has put him at odds with military leaders as well, although Turkey's acceptance as a member of the European Union depends on the implementation of such reforms.

One EU requirement is that of a reduction in the powers of the National Security Council. The 10-member body, composed of the president, four cabinet ministers, and the five top military commanders, sets the agenda for all important issues, even laws, before they may be debated by the GNA. The order for dismissal of government employees for their "Islamist" beliefs was originally issued as a directive to the GNA by the council. It did not go into effect because Sezer refused to sign it, not as a council member but in his capacity as president.

The November 2002 elections for the 550-member GNA resulted in another flip-flop in Turkey's seesawing political fortunes. AKP won a clear majority, 363 seats to 178 for the RPP; the remainder were spread among several minor parties. AKP leader Abdullah Gul was named prime minister of Turkey's first single-party majority government in 15 years. The GNA subsequently amended the constitution to allow Erdogan to run in a special by-election. In February, the ex-mayor took his seat in the GNA and was then named prime minister.[12]

THE "KURDISH PROBLEM"

Ataturk's suppression of Kurdish political aspirations and a separate Kurdish identity

within the nation effectively removed all traces of a "Kurdish problem" from national consciousness during the first decades of the republic.

However, the general breakdown in law and order in Turkey in the late 1970s led to a revival of Kurdish nationalism. The Workers' Party of Kurdistan (PKK), founded as a Marxist-Leninist organization, was the first left-wing Kurdish group to advocate a separate Kurdish state. It was outlawed after the 1980 military coup; some 1,500 of its members were given jail sentences, and several leaders were executed for treason.

The PKK then went underground. In 1984 it began a campaign of guerrilla warfare. Its leader, Abdullah ("Apo") Ocalan, had won a scholarship in political science at Ankara University. While there, he became influenced by Marxist ideology and went into exile in Syria. From his Syrian base, and with Syrian support and financing, he called for a "war of national liberation" for the Kurds. Prior to the 1991 Gulf War, PKK guerrillas mounted mostly cross-border attacks into Turkey from bases in northern Lebanon, where they came under Syrian protection. But with Iraq's defeat and the establishment of an autonomous Kurdish region in northern Iraq, the PKK set up bases there to supplement their Lebanese bases.

ACHIEVEMENTS

The ancient Silk Road, which ran eastward from Turkey through Iran, Central Asia, and Afghanistan into China, was once one of the main routes of east-west trade and vice versa. Today it is more likely to be carrying "black gold," oil and gas from Iran and Central Asian sources through pipelines to the West, including those that follow the road through Turkey.

The PKK then resumed the conflict, which by 2000 had claimed 40,000 lives, the majority of them villagers caught between security forces and the guerrillas. Some 3,000 villages had been destroyed and 2 million Kurds made refugees.

Yet despite Turkey's huge military superiority, its struggle with the PKK remained a stalemate until 1999.

After evading capture by Turkey for many years, Ocalan was eventually apprehended and found guilty. He was sentenced to death, but the sentence has since been commuted to life in prison. During his trial Ocalan testified that he had learned his lesson. He renounced violence as a "mistaken policy" and asserted that he would work as a loyal citizen toward the goal of peace and brotherhood.

For its part, the PKK said that it would obey its imprisoned leader's direction and end the armed struggle. Its leader stated: "The Kurdish and Turkish people are as inseparable as flesh and blood."[13]

Violence in the southeast lessened significantly in 2000–2001. As a result the government lifted martial law, ending the state of emergency and enabling Kurds to travel freely and even return to their native villages. The PKK itself morphed into a new political party, Dehap (Democratic Peoples' Party), and registered for the next national election. However, in June 2004 the PKK renewed intermittent attacks on Turkish troops.

FOREIGN POLICY

For the most part, Turkey has been consistently a Western ally in its foreign policy. Turkey's relations with Iraq have always been complex and have had a negative effect on the Turkish economy, with an estimated loss of $40 billion from the cutoff in Iraqi oil exports. The UN sanctions limit Turkey to 75,000 barrels per day (b/pd), insufficient to meet domestic needs. A large, illegal cross-border trade developed in 2000–2001, with Iraqi oil trucked to the Kurdish border and smuggled into Turkey. With the overthrow of Saddam Hussein in March 2003, the pipeline from Kirkuk to the Turkish port of Ceyhan was reopened briefly but then closed due to sabotage.

Turkey's long-established friendship with the United States as its major ally, maintained through two world wars and many minor conflicts, underwent a severe strain when U.S. forces invaded Iraq in 2003. During the countdown to the invasion, the GNA refused permission for American troops to enter Iraq from its territory. Despite threats that the Bush administration would reduce U.S. aid, the Turks held firm, preferring to work through the UN to force Saddam Hussein to expose and remove his presumed weapons of mass destruction. As things turned out, the aid was maintained at the same level, but Turkish troops have yet to take part in the occupation of Iraq.

Turkey's relatively independent posture in foreign policy has been marked by agreements with Iran and Israel for training of its air-force pilots. The country reached agreement with Israel in April 2001 for water deliveries, as a part of its "water for peace" program for the Middle East. Under the terms of the agreement, Israel would receive 50 million cubic meters annually of water from the Tigris and Euphrates Rivers, both of which rise in Turkey.

The Cyprus issue, which has divided Turkey and Greece ever since Turkish troops occupied the northern part of the island republic in 1974, moved toward a solution in 2004 as Greek and Turkish Cypriot leaders began serious negotiations under UN sponsorship. The Turkish government on its part threw its official support toward Cypriot unity.

The country has also improved its links with the newly independent Turkish-speaking nations of Central Asia. Turkey was the first country to recognize the independence of Kazakhstan and Azerbaijan. In 2000 the government signed a 15-year agreement with Azerbaijan for imports of natural gas from the Shaykh Deniz field, offshore in the Caspian Sea. Another important agreement, among Turkey, Georgia, Azerbaijan, and Kazakhstan, has initiated construction of the thousand-mile oil pipeline from Baku, Azerbaijan, to Ceyhan (Adana) on Turkey's Mediterranean coast.

THE ECONOMY

Turkey has a relatively diversified economy, with a productive agriculture and considerable mineral resources. Cotton is the major export crop, but the country is the world's largest producer of sultana raisins and hazelnuts. Other important crops are tobacco, wheat, sunflower seeds, sesame and linseed oils, and cotton-oil seeds.

Mineral resources include bauxite, chromium, copper, and iron ore, and there are large deposits of lignite. Turkey is one of the world's largest producers of chromite (chromium ore). Another important mineral resource is meerschaum, used for pipes and cigarette holders. Turkey supplies 80 percent of the world market for emery, and there are rich deposits of tungsten, perlite, boron, and cinnabar, all important rare metals.

Turkey signed a customs agreement with the European Union in 1996. The agreement eliminated import quotas on Turkish textiles and slashed customs duties and excise taxes on Turkish imports of manufactured iron and steel products from the European Union.

The agreement was intended as a first step toward full membership in the EU. However, the country's poor human-rights record, its political instability, and more recently, its financial crisis of 2000–2001 have delayed the process.

The "liquidity crisis" that nearly overwhelmed the Turkish economy in 2001 resulted from a combination of factors. Ironically, one of them was the economic reform program introduced by the Ecevit government to meet EU requirements. Corruption in economic and fiscal management was another factor, while a third grew from a dispute over privatization of state-owned enterprises. The slow pace of privatization led to a fiscal crisis in November 2000. The liquidity crisis followed, with a run on foreign-currency reserves in the Central Bank as worried Turks and foreign investors rushed to retrieve their funds. The bank lost $7.5 billion in reserves in a two-day period. The government's stopgap decision to end currency controls and allow the Turkish lira to float caused it to lose nearly 50 percent of its value. In December 10 banks collapsed; they included Ihlas Finans, the country's largest Islamic bank. (Under Turkish banking laws, deposits in such banks, which are interest-free under Islamic prohibitions against usury, are not covered by federal deposit guarantees. Consequently, 200,000 depositors lost their life savings.)

Timeline: PAST

330
The founding of Constantinople as the Roman Christian capital, on the site of ancient Byzantium

1453
The capture of Constantinople by Sultan Mehmed II; the city becomes the capital of the Islamic Ottoman Empire

1683
The Ottoman Empire expands deep into Europe; the high-water mark is the siege of Vienna

1918–1920
The defeat of Ottomans and division of territories into foreign protectorates

1923
Turkey proclaims its independence

1960
The first military coup

1980s
Military coup; civilian rule later returns; the government imposes emergency rules

1990s
The Kurdish problem intensifies; Alawi and Kurdish social unrest; thousands die as earthquakes devastate Turkey

PRESENT

2000s
Serious financial crises threaten the nation; Turkey continues to try to meet requirements for EU membership

The crisis was averted temporarily when the International Monetary Fund agreed "in principle" to provide $5 billion in emergency aid. However, the IMF's insistence on fiscal reform as a precondition brought on another crisis in March–April 2001.

NOTES

1. The New York Life Insurance Company agreed recently to pay $10 million to the heirs or relatives of Armenians killed during the deportations in claims on policies issued before 1915. The agreement resulted from a bill passed by the California state legislature that extends the statute of limitations on such claims. California has a large Armenian community, and the company chose to pay the claims rather than incur numerous lawsuits.

2. Martin van Bruinessen, "Kurds, Turks and the Alevi Revival in Turkey," *Middle East Report* (July–Sept 1996), p. 7.

3. John Noble Wilford, "The Secrets of Croesus' Gold," *The New York Times* (August 15, 2000). Another Asia Minor ruler, King Midas of Phrygia, was said to have the "golden touch," because everything he touched (including his daughter) turned to gold; he had angered the gods, it seemed.

4. Cf. Lord Kinross, *The Ottoman Centuries: The Rise and Fall of the Turkish Empire* (New York: William Morrow, 1977).

5. *Ibid.*, p. 25.

6. An American astronomer, Kevin Pang, advanced the proposal that the fall of the Byzantine 'skies' and other portents of doom related to the eruption of the volcano Kuwae, in the New Hebrides, in 1453. See Lynn Teo Simarski, "Constantinople's Volcanic Twilight," *Aramco World* (November/December 1996), pp. 8–13.

7. The marching bands at football games and parades in our society apparently derive from Janissary bands of drummers and cymbal players who marched ahead of invading Ottoman armies, striking terror in their enemies with their loud sounds.

8. V. A. Danilov, "Kemalism and World Peace," in A. Kazancigil and E. Ozbudun, eds., *Ataturk, Founder of a Modern State* (Hamden, CT: Archon Books, 1981), p. 110.

9. Maurice Duverger, *Political Parties* (New York: John Wiley, 1959), p. 277.

10. C. H. Dodd, *Democracy and Development in Turkey* (North Humberside, England: Eothen Press, 1979), p. 135.

11. One reason for its success at the polls was due the fact that AKP was viewed by the electorate as "clean." (AK, in Turkish, means "white" or "clean.")

12. Stephen Kinzer, in *The New York Times* (June 1, 1999).

13. *Ibid.*

Turkmenistan

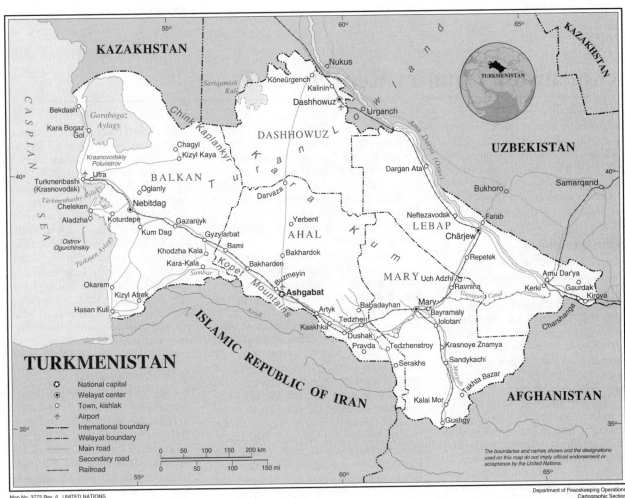

Map No. 3772 Rev. 6 UNITED NATIONS
January 2004

Department of Peacekeeping Operations
Cartographic Section

Turkmenistan Statistics

GEOGRAPHY

Area in Square Miles (Kilometers): 188,407
(488,100) (about the size of California)
Capital (Population): Ashkhabad
(Ashgabat) (536,000)

PEOPLE

Population

Total: 4,604,000
Annual Growth Rate: 1.85%

Major Languages: Turkmen; Russian;
Uzbek
Ethnic Makeup: 85% Turkmen; 4%
Russian; 5% Uzbek; 6% others

Religions: 87% Muslim; 11% Eastern
  Orthodox; 2% unknown

Health

Life Expectancy at Birth: 57 years (male);
  65 years (female)
Infant Mortality Rate (Ratio): 73/1,000

Education

Adult Literacy Rate: 98%

GOVERNMENT

Type: republic

Head of State/Government: President
  Saparmurad Niyazov is both head of
  state and head of government

Political Parties: Democratic Party of
  Turkmenistan; opposition parties are
  outlawed

ECONOMY

Currency ($ U.S. Equivalent): 5,350
  manats = $1
Per Capita Income/GDP: $4,300/$19.6
  billion
Inflation Rate: 14%
Exports: $2.4 billion
Imports: $1.65 billion

Turkmenistan Country Report

Turkmenistan is one of the least populated of the Central Asian republics. Its Islamic culture has become a prominent aspect of daily life, now that communist-inspired atheism no longer exists. It is relatively well endowed with mineral resources and has a fairly homogeneous population.

Turkmenistan and Russia

To the satisfaction of the Kremlin, Turkmenistan's president, Saparmurad Niyazov, is keenly aware of the need to have good relations with Russia. It is on that relationship that Turkmenistan depends for the bulk of its foreign trade, the export of its natural gas and oil, its transportation and communications infrastructure, and its national security. Relations between the two countries are good, with Turkmenistan closely aligning itself in political, economic, and military matters with Russia.

Conversely, with the renewal of interest in Islamic traditions accompanied by the growth of an ethnoculturally based nationalism, Turkmen citizens are likely to become increasingly intolerant of a situation that contributes to their poverty—that is, the highly visible Russian presence in and management of the country's economic life, which the Niyazov regime has tolerated for reasons of expediency. Another problem stems from Russia's control of Turkmenistan's oil and natural-gas pipelines. President Niyazov once promised "to put a Mercedes automobile in the driveway of every newlywed couple." Instead, Turkmenistan's economy has encountered hard times. The era of good earnings from exports of natural gas and oil came to an end

after 1993, when Russia closed down Turkmenistan's pipeline to lucrative markets in Central/Eastern Europe. Instead, they sold most of Turkmenistan's energy to cash-strapped neighbors in Central Asia, which have had difficulty paying for what they bought. By late 1997 these countries owed Turkmenistan about $1 billion for past deliveries.

At the end of 1997, Niyazov took a major step toward increasing Turkmenistan's export revenue by opening a pipeline to Iran that could eventually link up with other pipelines to let gas from the Caspian Sea reach Europe through Turkey. It was a problematical move because it annoyed the United States, which wanted any new routes for Caspian gas to avoid Iran. Indeed, Turkmenistan's developing ties to Iran as well as to other neighboring Muslim states unsettled the equilibrium of interstate relations within Central Asia, though the growing ties were understandable. Turkmenistan shares a border with Iran, and there are significant cultural and tribal connections between Turkmen and Iranians. Moreover, there is a large Turkmen minority of more than 1 million people in northern Iran, a very significant number given the fact that there are only about 4 million Turkmen in Turkmenistan itself. Religious differences exist between Turkmen and Iranians (the Iranians are Shi'a Muslims, while the Turkmen are Sunni) but are not productive of conflict.

Turkmenistan and the United States

In the aftermath of the September 11, 2001, terrorist attacks, the George W. Bush administration sought the cooperation of

Niyazov in the war against terrorism; Niyazov cited his repression of political critics and opponents as his version of the war on terrorism.

The Bush administration pursued military cooperation with Turkmenistan. In August 2002 General Tommy Franks, commander of American forces in the Central Asian region, met with Niyazov to formalize arrangements for the United States to train and equip Turkmenistan's small military establishment and to play a larger role in border security and policing. This put some U.S. forces in areas in which Russia had been helping not only Turkmenistan but other ex-Soviet Central Asian republics throughout the 1990s.

Recent Developments

In early April 2003 the Kremlin concluded a lucrative oil deal with Turkmenistan. The Kremlin also wanted good relations with the Nayazov regime because of the construction of a pipeline from Turkmenistan westward through Afghanistan and Pakistan which would benefit Russian oil companies. The Karzai government in Kabul and the Musharraf government in Islamabad were interested in this proposed project and willing to talk about it. Karzai visited Niyazov in Ashgabad in early March 2002, and the two leaders concluded several agreements, including an energy cooperation deal. Turkmenistan also pledged to help the Karzai government revive Afghanistan's broken-down health care sector.

Uganda (Republic of Uganda)

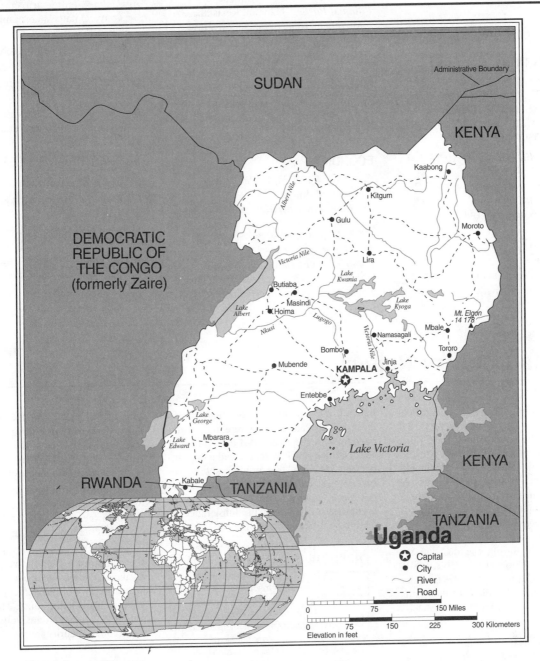

Uganda Statistics

GEOGRAPHY

Area in Square Miles (Kilometers): 91,076 (235,885) (about the size of Oregon)

Capital (Population): Kampala (1,274,000)

Environmental Concerns: draining of wetlands; deforestation; overgrazing; soil erosion; widespread poaching

Geographical Features: mostly plateau, with a rim of mountains

Climate: generally tropical, but semiarid in the northeast

PEOPLE

Population

Total: 26,404,543

Annual Growth Rate: 2.94%

Rural/Urban Population Ratio: 87/13

Major Languages: English; Swahili; Bantu languages; Nilotic languages

Ethnic Makeup: Bantu; Nilotic; Nilo-Hamitic; Sudanic

Religions: 66% Christian; 18% indigenous beliefs; 16% Muslim

Health

Life Expectancy at Birth: 39 years (male); 40 years (female)

Infant Mortality: 89.3/1,000 live births
Physicians Available: 1/20,700 people
HIV/AIDS Rate in Adults: 6.1%

Education

Adult Literacy Rate: 62%

COMMUNICATION

Telephones: 81,000 main lines
Televisions: 27 per 1,000 people
Internet Users: 125,000 (2003)

TRANSPORTATION

Highways in Miles (Kilometers): 16,200
 (27,000)
Railroads in Miles (Kilometers): 745 (1,241)
Usable Airfields: 27
Motor Vehicles in Use: 51,000

GOVERNMENT

Type: republic
Independence Date: October 9, 1962
 (from the United Kingdom)

Head of State/Government: President
 Yoweri Kaguta Museveni is both head of
 state and head of government
Political Parties: National Resistance
 Movement (only organization allowed to
 operate unfettered)
Suffrage: universal at 18

MILITARY

Military Expenditures (% of GDP): 2.1%
Current Disputes: continuing ethnic strife
 in the region

ECONOMY

Currency ($ U.S. Equivalent): 1,963
 Uganda shillings = $1
Per Capita Income/GDP: $1,400/$36
 billion
GDP Growth Rate: 4.4%
Inflation Rate: 7.9%
Labor Force by Occupation: 82%
 agriculture; 13% services; 5% industry
Population Below Poverty Line: 35%

Natural Resources: copper; cobalt; salt;
 limestone; hydropower; arable land
Agriculture: coffee; tea; cotton; tobacco;
 cassava; potatoes; corn; millet; pulses;
 livestock
Industry: sugar; brewing; tobacco; textiles;
 cement
Exports: $367 million (primary partner
 Europe)
Imports: $1.26 billion (primary partners
 Kenya, United States, India)

SUGGESTED WEB SITES

http://www.ugandaweb.com
http://www.government.go.ug
http://www.monitor.co.ug
http://www.mbendi.co.za/
 cyugcy.htm
http://www.uganda.co.ug/
http://www.cia.gov/cia/
 publications/factbook/geos/
 ug.html

Uganda Country Report

Uganda's foreign and domestic conflicts pose a potential threat to the very real progress that the country has made since the coming to power of Yoweri Museveni's National Resistance Movement (NRM). In 1985 after years of repressive rule accompanied by massive interethnic violence, Uganda is still struggling for peace and reconciliation. A land rich in natural and human resources, Uganda suffered dreadfully during the despotic regimes of Milton Obote (1962–1971, 1980–1985) and Idi Amin (1971–1979). Under these two dictators, hundreds of thousands of Ugandans were murdered by the state.

DEVELOPMENT

In the past few years, Uganda's economy has been growing at an average annual rate of about 5%, boosted by increased investment. Foreign economic assistance nonetheless accounts for approximately 29% of government spending.

The country had reached a state of general social and political collapse by 1986, when the NRM seized power. The new government soon made considerable progress in restoring a sense of normalcy in most of the country, except for the north. In May 1996 Museveni officially received 74 percent of the vote in a contested presiden-

tial poll. Despite charges of fraud by his closest rival, Paul Ssemogerere, most independent observers accepted the poll as an endorsement of Museveni's leadership, including his view that politics should remain organized on a nonparty basis. There has since, however, emerged growing international criticism of his intolerance of genuine political pluralism.

FREEDOM

The human-rights situation in Uganda remains poor, with government security forces linked to torture, extra-judicial executions, and other atrocities. Freedom of speech and association are curtailed. Insurgent groups are also associated with atrocities; the Lord's Resistance Army continues to kill, torture, maim, and abduct large numbers of civilians, enslaving numerous children.

HISTORIC GEOGRAPHY

The breakdown of Uganda is an extreme example of the disruptive role of ethnic and sectarian competition, which was fostered by policies of both its colonial and postcolonial governments. Uganda consists of two major zones: the plains of the northeast and the southern highlands. It has been said that you can drop anything into the rich volcanic

soils of the well-watered south and it will grow. Until the 1960s the area was divided into four kingdoms—Buganda, Bunyoro, Ankole, and Toro—populated by peoples using related Bantu languages.

Cash-crop farming, especially of cotton, by local peasants spurred an economic boom in the south. The Bugandan ruling class benefited in particular.

The south's growing economy stood in sharp contrast to the relative neglect of the northeast. Forced to earn money to pay taxes, many northeasterners became migrant workers in the south. They were also recruited, almost exclusively, to serve in the colonial security forces.

THE REIGN OF TERROR

In 1966, in the name of abolishing "tribalism," Obote established a one-party state and ruled in an increasingly dictatorial fashion. However, in 1971 he was overthrown by his army chief, Idi Amin. Amin began his regime with widespread public support but alienated himself by favoring fellow Muslims and Kakwa. He expelled the 40,000-member Asian community and distributed their property to his cronies. The Langi, suspected of being pro-Obote, were also early targets of his persecution, but his attacks soon spread to other members of Uganda's Christian community, at the time about 80 percent of the total population. Educated people in particular were purged. The number of Ugandans murdered by Amin's death squads is unknown; the most commonly cited figure is 300,000, but estimates range from 50,000 to 1 million. Many others went into exile.

HEALTH/WELFARE

Millions of Ugandans live below the poverty line. Uganda's traditionally strong school system was damaged but not completely destroyed under Amin and Obote. In 1986 some 70% of primary-school children attended classes. The killing and exiling of teachers has resulted in a serious drop of standards at all levels of the education system, but progress is under way. The adult literacy rate has risen to 62%.

A Ugandan military incursion into Tanzania led to war between the two countries in 1979. Many Ugandans joined with the Tanzanians in defeating Amin's army and its Libyan allies.

Unfortunately, the overthrow of Amin, who fled into exile, did not lead to better times. In 1980 Obote was returned to power through a fraudulent vote count. His second administration was characterized by a continuation of the violence of the Amin years. Obote's security forces massacred an estimated 300,000 people, mostly southerners, while an equal number fled the country. Much of the killing occurred in the Bugandan area known as the Luwero triangle, which was completely depopulated; its fields are still full of skeletons today. As the killings escalated, so did the resistance of Museveni's NRM guerrillas, who had taken to the bush in the aftermath of the failed election. In 1985 a split between Ancholi

and Langi officers led to Obote's overthrow and yet another pattern of interethnic recrimination. Finally, in 1986 the NRM gained the upper hand.

ACHIEVEMENTS

The Ugandan government was one of the first countries in Africa (and the world) to acknowledge the seriousness of the HIV/AIDS epidemic within its borders. It has instituted public-information campaigns and welcomed outside support.

Thereafter a new political order began to emerge based on Museveni's vision of a "no-party government." His position was strengthened in March 1994, when elections to a Constituent Assembly resulted in his supporters' capturing more than two-thirds of the seats.

THE STRUGGLE CONTINUES

The restoration of peace to most of the country has promoted economic growth. Western-backed economic reforms produced an annual growth rate of 13 percent between 1990 and 1998. The rate of inflation also improved, falling from 200 to 7 percent in the same period. On the regional level, Museveni has championed the formation of a new "East African Community" (EAC), which is intended to lay the groundwork for economic and ultimately monetary integration with Tanzania and Kenya.

While rebuilding their shattered country, Ugandans have had to cope with an especially severe outbreak of HIV/AIDS. Thousands have died of the disease in the last decade; it is believed that literally hundreds of thousands of Ugandans are HIV-positive. The government's bold acknowl-

edgment and proactive efforts to address the crisis, however, have been credited with helping to contain the pandemic.

United Arab Emirates

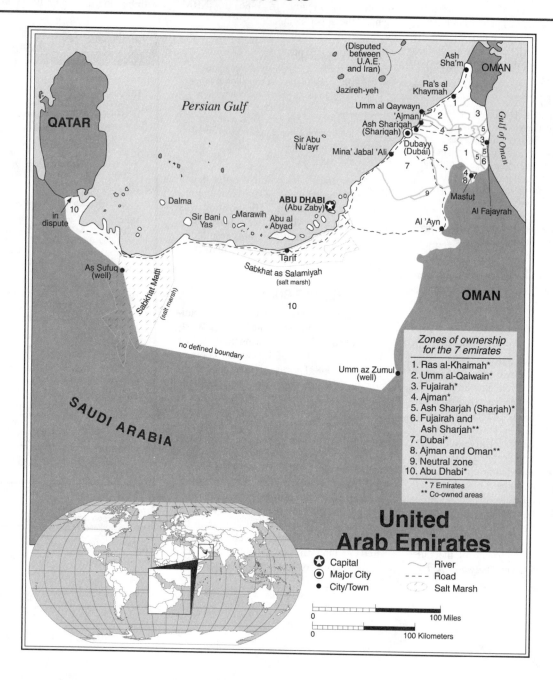

Zones of ownership for the 7 emirates
1. Ras al-Khaimah*
2. Umm al-Qaiwain*
3. Fujairah*
4. Ajman*
5. Ash Sharjah (Sharjah)*
6. Fujairah and Ash Sharjah**
7. Dubai*
8. Ajman and Oman**
9. Neutral zone
10. Abu Dhabi*

* 7 Emirates
** Co-owned areas

United Arab Emirates

★ Capital
◉ Major City
● City/Town

〜 River
- - - Road
Salt Marsh

0   100 Miles
0   100 Kilometers

United Arab Emirates Statistics

GEOGRAPHY

Area in Square Miles (Kilometers): 31,992 (82,880) (about the size of Maine)

Capital (Population): Abu Dhabi (799,000)

Environmental Concerns: lack of natural freshwater; desertification; oil pollution of beaches and coastal waters

Geographical Features: flat, barren coastal plain merging into rolling sand dunes of vast desert; mountains in the east

Climate: hot, dry desert; cooler in the eastern mountains

PEOPLE

Population

Total: 2,563,212 (including 1,606,079 nonnationals)

Annual Growth Rate: 1.54%

Rural/Urban Population Ratio: 16/84

Major Languages: Arabic; Persian (Farsi); English; Hindi

Ethnic Makeup: 19% Emirati; 23% other Arab and Iranian; 50% South Asian; 8% East Asian and Westerner

Religions: 96% Muslim (80% Sunni, 16% Shi'a); 4% Hindu, Christian, and others

Health

Life Expectancy at Birth: 72 years (male);
77 years (female)
Infant Mortality Rate: 14.5/1,000 live births
Physicians Available (Ratio): 1/545 people

Education

Adult Literacy Rate: 77.9%

COMMUNICATION

Telephones: 1,135,800 main lines
Daily Newspaper Circulation: 135 per
1,000 people
Televisions: 18 per 1,000 people
Internet Users: 1,110,200 (2000)

TRANSPORTATION

Highways in Miles (Kilometers): 3,002
(1,088)
Railroads in Miles (Kilometers): none
Usable Airfields: 35
Motor Vehicles in Use: 400,000

GOVERNMENT

Type: federation of emirates

Independence Date: December 2, 1971
(from the United Kingdom)

Head of State/Government: Supreme
Council of Rulers of the 7 emirates:
President Sheikh Khalifa bin Zayid Al
Nuhayyan; Prime Minister Maktum bin
Rashid al-Maktoum

Political Parties: none

Suffrage: none

MILITARY

Military Expenditures (% of GDP): 3.1%

Current Disputes: Iranian occupation of
Greater and Lesser Tunbs Islands
contested by U.A.E.; boundary with
Oman formally demarcated and ratified
in 2003

ECONOMY

Currency ($ U.S. equivalent): 3.673
dirhams = $1
Per Capita Income/GDP: $25,200/$63.67
billion
GDP Growth Rate: 5.7%
Inflation Rate: 3.2%
Labor Force: 2,360,000 (74% of those in
age group 15–64 are nonnationals)
Natural Resources: petroleum; natural gas
Agriculture: dates; vegetables;
watermelons; poultry; dairy products; fish
Industry: petroleum; fishing;
petrochemicals; construction materials;
boat building; handicrafts; pearling
Exports: $69.48 billion (primary partners
Japan, India, Singapore)
Imports: $45.66 billion (primary partners
Japan, United States, United Kingdom)

SUGGESTED WEB SITES

http://lcweb2.loc.gov/frd/cs/
aetoc.html

United Arba Emirates Country Report

The United Arab Emirates (U.A.E.) is a
federation of seven independent states with
a central governing council located on the
northeast coast of the Arabian Peninsula.
The states—called emirates, from the title
of their rulers—are Abu Dhabi, Ajman,
Dubai, Fujairah, Ras al-Khaimah, Sharjah,
and Umm al-Qaiwain. They came under
British "protection" in the 1800s and were
given their independence from Great Britain by treaty in 1971. At that time, they
joined in the federal union. From its modest beginnings, the U.A.E. has come to
play an important role in Middle East Arab
affairs because of its oil wealth.

Abu Dhabi, the largest emirate, contains
87 percent of the U.A.E.'s total land area.
The federal capital is also named Abu
Dhabi, but Dubai, capital of the second
largest emirate, is a larger city, with a population of approximately 1 million. Dubai
has the U.A.E.'s only natural harbor, which
has been enlarged to accommodate supertankers, Abu Dhabi, Dubai, and Sharjah
produce oil; Sharjah also has important
natural-gas reserves and cement. Fujairah
port is a major entrepôt for shipping. The
other emirates have little in the way of resources and have yet to find oil in commercial quantities.

The early inhabitants of the area were
fishermen and nomads. They were converted to Islam in the seventh century A.D.,
but little is known of their history before

the sixteenth century. By that time, European nations, notably Portugal, had taken
an active interest in trade with India and the
Far East. Gradually, other European countries, particularly the Netherlands, France,
and Britain, challenged Portuguese supremacy. As more and more European
ships appeared in Arabian coastal waters or
fought over trade, the coastal Arabs felt
threatened with loss of their territory.
Meanwhile, the Wahhabis, militant Islamic
missionaries, spread over Arabia in the
eighteenth century. Wahhabi agents incited
the most powerful coastal group, the Qawasim, to interfere with European shipping. European ships were seized along
with their cargoes and their crews held for
ransom. To the European countries, this
was piracy; to the Qawasim, however, it
was defense of Islamic territory against the
infidels. Ras al-Khaimah was their chief
port, but soon the whole coast of the
present-day U.A.E. became known as the
Pirate Coast.

Piracy lasted until 1820, when the British, who now controlled India and thus
dominated Eastern trade, convinced the
principal chiefs of the coast to sign a treaty
ending pirate activities.

Then, in the 1960s, the British decided—
for economic and political reasons—to give
up most of their overseas colonies, including those in the Arabian Peninsula, which
were technically protectorates rather than

DEVELOPMENT

The U.A.E.'s huge oil revenues
(33 percent of GDP) have
enabled it overall to maintain a
high per capita income and
accumulate an annual trade surplus despite
the uneven distribution of wealth among the
emirates. With oil and gas reserves estimated
to last no more than a century, Abu Dhabi and
Dubai in particular have pushed non-oil sector
development through such projects as
Aluminium Dubai and the world's largest
drydock.

colonies. Thus, the United Arab Emirates,
when it became independent in 1971, included only six emirates. Ras al-Khaimah
joined in 1972.

PROBLEMS OF INTEGRATION

Differences in size, wealth, resources, and
population have hampered U.A.E. integration since it was formed. Another problem
is poor communications. Until recently,
one could travel from emirate to emirate
only by boat, and telephone service was
nonexistent. A combination of economic
growth and technology (for example the
Internet and cell phones), have produced
full integration and rapid communication
between the seven emirates.

The U.A.E. federal system is defined in
the 1971 Constitution. The government

consists of a Supreme Council of Rulers of the seven emirates; a Council of Ministers (cabinet), appointed by the president of the Council; and a unicameral Federal National Assembly of 40 members appointed by the ruling emirs on a proportional basis, according to size and population.

One of the strengths of the system is that Shaykh Zayed, the ruler of Abu Dhabi, has served as president of the Council of Rulers since its inception. Other unifying features of the U.A.E. are a common commercial-law code, currency, and defense structure. The sharing of revenues by the wealthy emirates with the less prosperous ones has also helped to foster U.A.E. unity.

The September 11, 2001, terrorist attacks on the United States intensified the importance of increased security for oil operations on the part of Abu Dhabi and Dubai, the chief oil-producing U.A.E. states. Also, during this time, prior to the U.S. invasion of Iraq, another Arab satellite all-news TV channel, Al-Arabiya, began operating in the U.A.E. to supplement Qator's Al-Jazeera station.

The governments of the emirates themselves are best described as patriarchal. Each emir is head of his own large "family" as well as head of his emirate. The ruling emirs gained their power a long time ago from various sources—through foreign trade, pearl fishing, or ownership of lands. In recent years, they have profited from oil royalties to confirm their positions as heads of state. Disagreements within the ruling families have sometimes led to violence or "palace coups," there being no rule or law of primogeniture.

FREEDOM

The Supreme Council of the U.A.E. exercises overall federal authority, but rulers of the emirates have full control over their territories. Although the patriarchal system of government and Arab tradition preclude the introduction of a Western-model democratic system, with checks and balances, the custom of weekly majlises (public assemblies) provides an outlet for citizen concerns.

Ajman and Umm al-Qaiwain are coastal ports with agricultural hinterlands. Ras al-Khaimah has continually disappointed oil seekers; its only natural resource is aggregate, which is used in making cement. Fujairah, although lacking in energy resources, has become a major oil-bunkering and -refining center. In 1996 the new bunkering terminal in its port went into operation. Built

by the Dutch-owned Van Ommeren Tank Company, the world's largest independent operator, the facilities will eventually double the millions of tons of cargo now being handled by the port.

AN OIL-DRIVEN ECONOMY

In the past, the people made a meager living from breeding racing camels, some farming, and pearl fishing. Pearls were the main cash crop. But twentieth-century competition from Japanese cultured pearls ruined the Arabian pearl-fishing industry.

HEALTH/WELFARE

The first all-female taxi service in the Gulf went into operation in the U.A.E. June 2000, as participation by women in the labor force increased. Also in 2000, U.A.E. banks set a quota system for employment of nationals to replace departed foreign workers. The quota is to be increased by 4% a year until the banks are fully staffed by U.A.E. nationals.

Oil exports began in 1962, and from then on the fortunes of the Gulf Arabs improved dramatically. Production was 14,200 barrels per day (b/d) in 1962; by 1982, it was 1.1 million b/d, indicating how far the country's oil-driven economy had moved in just two decades. Oil reserves are approximately 98 billion barrels, while gas reserves are 205 trillion cubic feet—10 percent of global reserves. They are expected to last well into the twenty-first century at current rates of extraction.

ACHIEVEMENTS

Nearly 2 million acres of desert have been reclaimed for cultivation. In 1997 Shaykh Zayed, the moving spirit behind the U.A.E. drive for self-sufficiency in food and the "greening" of the desert, received the Gold Panda award from the Worldwide Fund for Nature for his services to global conservation—the first head of state to be so honored. In 2000 the U.A.E.'s first satellite went into orbit, another first for the Gulf region.

The bulk of hydrocarbon production and reserves is in Abu Dhabi. Dubai, not content with second place in U.A.E. development, launched a Strategic Development Plan in 1998, intended to increase its non-oil income to $20,000 per capita by 2010. Its government earlier had established a free-trade zone in the port of Jebel Ali. It provides 100 percent foreign ownership, full repatriation of capital and profits, and

a 15-year exemption from corporate and other taxes. By 1996 more than 1,000 companies had located in the zone. In October 2000 the Dubai City Internet free-trade zone opened for business. The zone is in the process of creating a "wired economy" for the emirates, to link them with global markets and the media. Companies such as Microsoft, Compaq, and IBM are helping to establish Dubai as the marketing hub of the region.[1]

The U.A.E.'s dependence on expatriate workers, who comprise approximately 80 percent of the labor force, has been an obstacle to self-sufficiency and diversification. Elsewhere in Dubai skyscraper hotels, beachfront resorts and free-trade zones have encouraged foreign trade, investment, and tourism on a grand scale.

NOTES

1. 1. Steve Krettman, "Oil Realm Embraces a Wired Economy," *The New York Times* (June 10, 2001).

2. Ken Ringle, "The Best-Kept Secret in the Middle East," *Smithsonian Magazine* (October 2003), pp. 42–46.

Timeline: PAST

1853, 1866
Peace treaties between Great Britain and Arab shaykhs establishing the Trucial States

1952
Establishment of the Trucial Council under British advisers, the forerunner of federation

1971
Independence

1973
The U.A.E. becomes the first Arab oil producer to ban exports to the U.S. after the Yom Kippur War

979
Balanced federal Assembly and cabinet are established

1990s
The U.A.E. reduces its dependence on oil revenues; the free-trade zone proves a success

PRESENT

2000s
The U.A.E. joins with other GCC members in a mutual-defense pact; the U.A.E. supports the international coalition against terrorism; Khalifa bin Zayed bin Sultan Al Nahayan becomes president

Uzbekistan

Map No. 3777 Rev. 6   UNITED NATIONS
January 2004

Department of Peacekeeping Operations
Cartographic Section

Uzbekistan Statistics

GEOGRAPHY

Area in Square Miles (Kilometers): 172,696
(447,440) (about the size of California)

Capital (Population): Tashkent
(2,282,000)

PEOPLE

Population

Total: 25,156,000

Annual Growth Rate: 1.6%

Major Languages: Uzbek; Russian

Ethnic Makeup: 80% Uzbek; 5% Russian;
5% Tajik; 3% Kazakh; 2% Tartar; 2%
Karakalpak; 3% others

Religions: 88% Muslim (mostly Sunni);
9% Eastern Orthodox; 3% others

Health

Life Expectancy at Birth: 60 years (male);
68 years (female)

Infant Mortality Rate (Ratio): 72/1,000

Education

Adult Literacy Rate: 99%

GOVERNMENT

Type: republic

Head of State/Government: President
Islom Karimov; Prime Minister Otkir
Sultonov

Political Parties: People's Democratic
Party (formerly the Communist Party);
Fatherland Progress Party; Social
Democratic Party; others

ECONOMY

Currency ($ U.S. Equivalent): 111.9 soms
= $1

Per Capita Income/GDP: $2,400/$60
billion

Inflation Rate: 40%

Exports: $2.9 billion

Imports: $2.6 billion

Uzbekistan Country Report

Uzbekistan is run by a neo-communist dictator with a tight grip over the country. President Islam Karimov's leadership suits the Kremlin at the moment, assuring Uzbekistan's respect for and determination to cooperate with Russia.

The Kremlin has welcomed Karimov's stern effort to quarantine his country from Islamic fundamentalism. Uzbek security police keep a close watch on the local Islamic clergy and severely punish anyone suspected of trying to disseminate fundamentalist ideas. Karimov's government also has carefully watched

signs of an Islamic revival in the northeastern part of Uzbekistan known as Fergama, not far from the border with Tajikistan. But Karimov has shrewdly refrained from repressing this revival or attacking religion as his Communist predecessors did. Indeed, he has gone out of his way to convince Uzbeks that he is not an atheist.

Uzbekistan's interest has also been to cooperate with Russia in preserving the secular government of Tajik president Rakhmanov.

In particular, Karimov worries about a spillover of the seemingly endless civil strife in Tajikistan into neighboring Central Asian republics, especially Uzbekistan.

UZBEKISTAN'S RUSSIAN MINORITY

Karimov, like other Central Asian leaders, has proceeded carefully in matters pertaining to his country's small Russian minority, to avoid antagonizing the Kremlin and giving strength to nationalists in the Russian Parliament.

Roya Marefat, 1987, Courtesy of the Aga Khan Visual Archive, M.I.T. (UZB87MA)

The Façade of the Ulugh Beg Madrassah in Samarqand, Uzbekistan. Ulugh Beg was Mongol Emperor Tamerlane's grandson and Samarqand, which is one of the oldest cities in the world, was Tamerlane's capital. Like most Central Asian Islamic seminaries, this one has a *pishtaq* (monumental gateway) decorated with beautifully colored tiles. It was also famous for its advanced study in astronomy.

UPSWING IN RUSSIAN-UZBEK RELATIONS

Despite these problems, Russian-Uzbek relations have remained stable. To the Kremlin's satisfaction, Karimov has acknowledged the importance of military cooperation between Uzbekistan and Russia, saying in 1996 that Russia has been and will remain Uzbekistan's "strategic partner," especially in the face of danger of fundamentalism's onslaught from the south. Other evidence that Russian relations with Uzbekistan are on a sound footing is Russia's willingness to accommodate the hypersensitivity of Uzbek leaders to their newly won independence and sovereignty. Moscow now sees Uzbekistan, despite its short existence as an independent state, as a partner, and is willing to relate to it as an equal.

UZBEKISTAN AND THE UNITED STATES

When the American government requested that Uzbekistan help deal with the September 11, 2001, terrorist attacks, President Islam Karimov did not hesitate. Karimov was deeply disturbed by the reach of Islamic fundamentalist terrorism, given Uzbekistan's proximity to its source in Afghanistan and the vulnerability of its poor Muslim population to extremist fundamentalist ideas and practices. Karimov also saw in an alliance with the United States a means of strengthening its hand in dealing with an occasionally overbearing Kremlin. Uzbekistan also stood to gain materially. Uzbekistan was now in line for a substantial program of American economic and financial aid, a direct consequence of the new strategic situation in Afghanistan.

By the end of 2001, the U.S. military commander for the Afghan theater, General Tommy Franks, had established his Central Command headquarters in Uzbekistan, and the United States had begun to deploy several thousand uniformed military personnel there.

Yemen (Republic of Yemen)

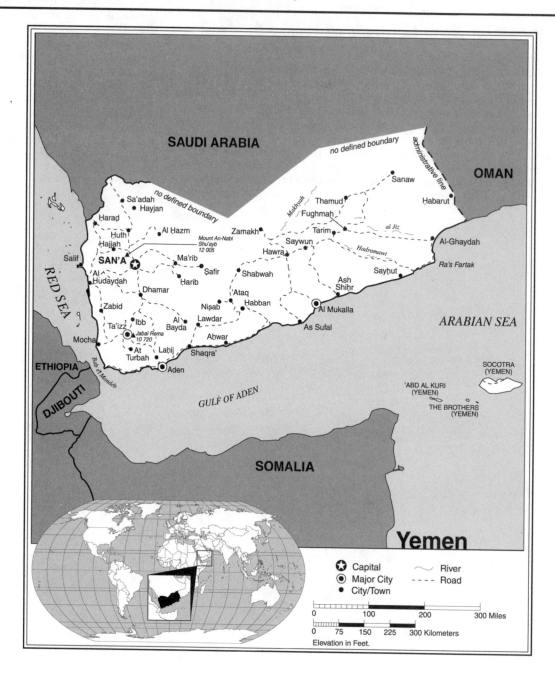

Yemen Statistics

GEOGRAPHY

Area in Square Miles (Kilometers): 203,796 (527,970) (about twice the size of Wyoming)

Capital (Population): San'a (political capital) (972,000); Aden (economic capital) (562,000)

Environmental Concerns: limited freshwater supplies; inadequate potable water; overgrazing; soil erosion; desertification

Geographical Features: a narrow coastal plain backed by hills and mountains; dissected upland desert plains in the center slope into desert

Climate: mostly desert; hot, with minimal rainfall except in mountain zones

PEOPLE

Population

Total: 20,727,063

Annual Growth Rate: 3.45%

Rural/Urban Population Ratio: 66/34

Major Language: Arabic

Ethnic Makeup: predominantly Arab; small Afro-Arab, South Asian, and European communities

Religions: nearly 100% Muslim; small numbers of Christians, Jews, and Hindus

Health

Life Expectancy at Birth: 59 years (male); 63 years (female)

Infant Mortality Rate: 61/1,000 live births

Physicians Available (Ratio): 1/4,530 people

Education

Adult Literacy Rate: 50.2%

Compulsory (Ages): 6–15

COMMUNICATION

Telephones: 542,200 main lines

Televisions: 6.5 per 1,000 people

Internet Users: 100,000 (2002)

TRANSPORTATION

Highways in Miles (Kilometers): 37,557 (67,000)

Railroads in Miles (Kilometers): none

Usable Airfields: 44

Motor Vehicles in Use: 510,000

GOVERNMENT

Type: republic, formed by merger of former Yemen Arab Republic and People's Democratic Republic of Yemen

Independence Date: formally united May 22, 1990 (date of merger)

Head of State/Government: President Ali Abdullah Salih (elected 1999); Prime Minister Abd al-Qadir Bajammal

Political Parties: 12 active; General Peoples' Congress serves as the majority party; main opposition parties are Islamic Reform Grouping (Islah) and Yemeni Socialist Party

Suffrage: universal at 18

MILITARY

Military Expenditures (% of GDP): 7.8%

Current Disputes: final boundary with Saudi Arabia remains to be resolved; Yemen protests Saudi erection of a

concrete-filled pipe as a security barrier in 2004 to stem illegal cross-border activities in sections of the boundary

ECONOMY

Currency ($ U.S. Equivalent): 184.78 rials = $1

Per Capita Income/GDP: $800/$16.25 billion

GDP Growth Rate: 1.9%

Inflation Rate: 12.2%

Unemployment Rate: 35%

Natural Resources: petroleum; fish; rock salt; marble; small deposits of coal, gold, lead, nickel, and copper; fertile soil in west

Agriculture: grain, fruits; vegetables; qat; coffee; cotton; livestock; fish

Industry: petroleum; cotton textiles and leather goods; food processing; handicrafts; aluminum products; cement

Exports: $4.46 billion (primary partners Thailand, China, South Korea)

Imports: $3.73 billion (primary partners Saudi Arabia, United Arab Emirates; United States)

Yemen Country Report

The Republic of Yemen occupies the extreme southwest corner of the Arabian Peninsula. It consists of three distinct regions, which until 1990 had been separated geographically for centuries and divided politically into two states: the Yemen Arab Republic (North Yemen, or Y.A.R.) and the People's Democratic Republic of Yemen (South Yemen, or P.D.R.Y.). The former Y.A.R.'s territory consists of two distinct regions: a hot, humid coastal strip, the Tihama, along the Red Sea, and an interior region of mountains and high plains that shade off gradually into the bleak, waterless South Arabian Desert.

Yemeni territory also includes Socotra, a remote island 550 miles from Aden, and two other small islands, Abd al-Khuri and the Brothers, which lie off the African coast of Somalia. Socotra is the only world habitat for Dragon's Blood trees, which produce cinnabar resin, and of some 850 other plants that exist nowhere else.

The Yemeni interior is very different not only from the Tihama but also from other parts of the Arabian Peninsula. It consists of highlands and rugged mountains ranging up to 12,000 feet. At the higher elevations, the mountain ridges are separated by deep, narrow valleys, usually with swift-flowing streams at the bottom. The ample rainfall allows extensive use of

terracing for agriculture. The main crops are coffee, cereals, vegetables, and qat (a shrub whose leaves are chewed as a mildly intoxicating narcotic).

This part of Yemen has been for centuries the home of warlike but sedentary peoples who have formed a stable, stratified society living in villages or small cities. These groups have been the principal support for the Shi'a Zaidi Imams, whose rule was the political nucleus of Yemen from the ninth century A.D. to the establishment of the republic in 1962. The Yemeni political capital, San'a, is located in these northern highlands.

The former P.D.R.Y., almost twice the size of its neighbor but less favored geographically, consists of the port and hinterland of Aden (today Yemen's economic capital); the Hadhramaut, a broad valley edged by desert and extending eastward along the Arabian Sea coast; the Perim and Kamaran Islands, at the south end of the Red Sea; and Socotra Island. Until the recent discoveries of oil, South Yemen was believed to have no natural resources. The dominant physical feature is the Wadi Hadhramaut. It is one of the few regions of the country with enough water for irrigation. Except for Aden, the area has little rainfall; in some sections, rain may fall

only once every 10 years. Less than 2 percent of the land is cultivable.

In ancient times, the whole of Yemen was known to the Greeks, Romans, and other peoples as Arabia Felix ("Happy Arabia"), a remote land that they believed to be fabulously wealthy. They knew it as the source of frankincense, myrrh, and other spices as well as other exotic products brought to Mediterranean and Middle Eastern markets from the East. In Yemen itself, several powerful kingdoms grew up from profits earned in this trade. One kingdom in particular, the Sabaeans, also had a productive agriculture based on irrigation. The water for irrigation came from the great Marib Dam, built around 500 B.C. Marib was a marvel of engineering, built across a deep river valley. The Sabaean economy supported a population estimated at 300,000 in a region that today supports only a few thousand herders.

The Sabaeans were followed by the Himyarites. Himyarite rulers were converted to Christianity by wandering monks in the second century A.D.

Sabaeans and Himyarites ruled long ago, but they are still important to Yemenis as symbols of their long and rich historical past. The Imams of Yemen, who ruled until 1962, used a red dye to sign their official documents in token of their relationship to

Himyarite kings. (The word *Himyar* comes from the same root as *hamra*, "red.")

The domestication of the camel and development of an underground irrigation system of channels (*falaj*) made this civilization possible.

Yemenis were among the first converts to Islam. The separation of the Yemenis into mutually hostile Sunni and Shi'a Muslims took place relatively early in Islamic history. Those living in the Tihama, which was easily accessible to missionaries and warriors expanding the borders of the new Islamic state, became Sunnis, obedient to the caliphs (the elected "successors" of Muhammad). The Yemeni mountaineers were more difficult to reach; and when they were converted to the new religion, it was through the teachings of a follower of the Shi'at Ali, "Party of Ali," those who felt that Muhammad's son-in-law Ali and his descendants should have been chosen as the rightful leaders of the Islamic community. Yemenis in Aden and the Hadhramaut, as well as those in the Tihama, became Sunni, creating the basis for an intra-Yemeni conflict, which still exists.

THE ZAIDI IMAMATE

In the late ninth century A.D., a feud among certain nominally Muslim groups in inland Yemen led to the invitation to a religious scholar living in Makkah to come and mediate in their dispute. This scholar brought with him a number of families of Ali's descendants who sought to escape persecution from the Sunnis. He himself was a disciple of Zaid, Ali's great-grandson. He settled the feud, and, in return for his services, he was accepted by both sides of the conflict as their religious leader, or Imam. His followers received lands and were given a protected status, so that in time they became a sort of theocratic aristocracy. This was the beginning of the Zaidi Imamate, a theocratic state that lasted for a thousand years (until 1962).

The Zaidi Imams continued to rule inland Yemen until the nineteenth century, when the Ottoman Turks, who controlled the Tihama, sent an army to conquer all of Yemen (except for Aden, which remained under British protection for their establishment of rule there in 1839). The Turks installed an Ottoman governor in San'a and made Yemen a province (*vilayet*) of the empire. But this action did not sit well with the mountain peoples. The Turkish occupation sparked a revolt. Turkish forces were unable to defeat the mountain peoples, and in 1911 they signed a treaty that recognized Imam Yahya as ruler in the highlands. In return, the Imam recognized Turkish rule in the Tihama. At the end of

World War I, the Turks left Yemen for good. The British, who now controlled most of the Middle East, signed a treaty with Imam Yahya, recognizing his rule in all Yemen.

The two Yemens followed divergent paths in the twentieth century, accounting in large measure for the difficulties that they faced in incorporating into a single state. North Yemen remained largely uninvolved in the political turmoil that engulfed the Middle East after World War II. Imam Yahya ruled his feudal country as an absolute monarch with a handful of advisers, mostly tribal leaders, religious scholars, and members of his family.

DEVELOPMENT

Yemen's modest growth has been affected periodically by fluctuating world oil prices. Oil is its only significant exportable resource. The bombing of the U.S. destroyer *USS Cole* and an attack on the French tanker *Limburg* in 2002 have adversely affected commerce in Aden port, due particularly to high-risk insurance premiums. The last container line based there moved to Salalah, Oman, after the *Limburg* attack.

Yahya was determined to keep foreign influences out of Yemen and to resist change in any form. Although Yemen was poor by the industrial world's standards, it was self-sufficient, free, and fully recognized as an independent state. Yahya hoped to keep it that way. He even refused foreign aid because he felt that it would lead to foreign occupation. In 1948 Imam Yahya was murdered in an attempted coup.

Crown Prince Ahmad, the Imam's eldest son and heir, was as tough and resourceful as his 80-year-old father had been.[4] He gathered support from leaders of other clans and nipped the rebellion in the bud. Imam Ahmad (1948–1962) ruled as despotically as his father had ruled.

In 1955 the Imam foiled an attempted coup. Other attempts, in 1958 and 1961, were also unsuccessful. The old Imam finally died of emphysema in 1962, leaving his son, Crown Prince Muhammad al-Badr, to succeed him.

THE MARCH TO INDEPENDENCE

In Aden, a strong anti-British nationalist movement developed in the trade unions among dock workers and refinery employees. This movement organized a political party, the People's Socialist Party, strongly influenced by the socialist, anti-Western, Arab nationalist programs of President Gamal Abdel Nasser in Egypt.

The party had two branches: the moderate Front for the Liberation of Occupied South Yemen (FLOSY) and the leftist Marxist National Liberation Front (NLF). About all they had in common was their opposition to the British and the South Arabian sultans, whom they called "lackeys of imperialism." FLOSY and the NLF joined forces in 1965–1967 to force the British to leave Aden. British troops were murdered; bombs damaged the refinery. By 1967, Britain had had enough. British forces were evacuated, and Britain signed a treaty granting independence to South Yemen under a coalition government made up of members of both FLOSY and the NLF.

Muhammad al-Badr held office for a week and then was overthrown by a military coup. Yemen's new military leaders formed a Revolution Command Council and announced that the Imam was dead. Henceforth, they said, Yemen would be a republic. It would give up its self-imposed isolation and would become part of the Arab world. But the Revolution proved to be more difficult to carry out than the military officers had expected. The Imam was not dead, as it turned out, but had escaped to the mountains. The mountain peoples rallied to his support, helping him to launch a counterrevolution. About 85,000 Egyptian troops arrived in Yemen to help the republican army. The coup leaders had been trained in Egypt, and the Egyptian government had not only financed the Revolution but also had encouraged it against the "reactionary" Imam.

For the next eight years, Yemen was a battleground. The Egyptians bombed villages and even used poison gas against civilians in trying to defeat the Imam's forces. But they were unable to crush the people hidden in the mountains of the interior. Saudi Arabia also backed the Imam with arms and kept the border open. The Saudi rulers did not particularly like the Imam, but he seemed preferable to an Egyptian-backed republican regime next door.

After Egypt's defeat by Israel in the 1967 Six-Day War, the Egyptian position in Yemen became untenable, and Egyptian troops were withdrawn. It appeared that the royalists would have a clear field. But they were even more disunited than the republicans. A royalist force surrounded San'a in 1968 but failed to capture the city. The Saudis then decided that the Imam had no future. They worked out a reconciliation of royalists and republicans that would reunite the country. The only restriction was that neither the Imam nor any of his relatives would be allowed to return to Yemen.

Thus, as of 1970, two "republics" had come into existence side by side. The Yemen Arab Republic was more of a tribal state than a republic in the modern political sense of the term. Prior to 1978, its first three presidents either went into exile or were murdered, victims of rivalry within the army. Colonel Ali Abdullah Saleh, a career army officer, seized power in that year and was subsequently chosen as the republic's first elected president. He was reelected in 1983 and again in 1988 for consecutive five-year terms. (With unification, he became the first head of state of all Yemen.)

FREEDOM

The 1991 Constitution established a parliamentary republic in unified Yemen. Elections in 1997 for the national legislature resulted in a two-party division of power, with majority (GPC) and minority (Islah) parties represented. The press is free, and women enjoy full civil rights and may run for public office. Yemen's legal code, based on Islamic law and approved by referendum in 1994, is also unusual in outlawing the death penalty for juvenile offenders under age 18. However, tribal law makes the ban difficult to enforce in the country's rural areas.

Saleh provided internal stability and allowed some broadening of the political process in North Yemen. A General People's Congress (GPC) was established in 1982. A Consultative Council, elected by popular vote, was established in 1988 to provide some citizen input into legislation. Saleh displayed great skill in balancing tribal and army factions and used foreign aid to develop economic projects such as dams for irrigation to benefit highland and Tihama Yemenis alike.

SOUTH YEMEN: A MARXIST STATE

With the British departure, the South Arabian Federation collapsed. The main problem was political. A power struggle developed between FLOSY and the NLF. The former favored moderate policies, good relations with other Arab states, and continued ties with Britain. The NLF were leftist Marxists. By 1970 the Marxists had won. FLOSY leaders were killed or went into exile. The new government set its objectives as state ownership of lands, state management of all business and industry, a single political organization with all other political parties prohibited, and support for antigovernment revolutionary movements in other Arab states, particularly Oman and Saudi Arabia.

UNIFICATION

Despite their natural urge to unite in a single Yemeni nation, the two Yemens were more

often at odds with each other than united in pursuing common goals. This was due in part to the age-old highland-lowland, Sunni-Shi'a conflict that cut across Yemeni society. But it was also due to their very different systems of government.

Improved economic circumstances and internal political stability in both Yemens revived interest in unity in the 1980s, especially after oil and natural-gas discoveries in border areas promised advantages to both governments through joint exploitation. In May 1988 President Saleh and Prime Minister al-Attas of the P.D.R.Y. signed the May Unity Pact, which ended travel restrictions and set up a Supreme Yemeni Council of national leaders to prepare a constitution for the proposed unitary state.

From then on, the unity process snowballed. In 1989 the P.D.R.Y. regime freed supporters of former president Ali Nasir Muhammad. Early in 1990 the banks, postal services, ports administration, and customs of the two republics were merged, followed by the merger under joint command of their armed forces.

Formal unification took place on May 22, 1990, with approval by both governments and ratification of instruments by their legislative bodies. Ali Abdullah Saleh was unanimously chosen as the republic's first president, with a four-member Presidential Council formed to oversee the transition. A draft constitution of the new republic established a 39-member Council of Ministers headed by P.D.R.Y. Prime Minister al-Attas, with ministries divided equally between North and South. In a national referendum in May 1991, voters approved the new all-Yemen Constitution. The Constitution provides for elections to a 301-member Parliament.

HEALTH/WELFARE

Yemenis spend many hours chewing qat, the leaves of a shrub that are mildly narcotic. Arguing that qat-chewing was an obstacle to development, President Saleh launched a nationwide campaign to "kick the habit" in 1999. But because qat provides 30% of GDP, farmers have been reluctant to plant other crops such as coffee and sorghum, which bring them less than 1/5 of the return from their qat crop.

After a short civil war disrupted the unification process, with its conclusion coming out more or less on North Yemen's terms, Saleh was offered another opportunity to unify the nation. The first step would be the restoration of representative government.

The election was held on April 27, 1993. Some 2,300 candidates vied for the 301

Timeline: PAST

A.D. 500
Collapse of the Marib Dam, destroying the flourishing Himyarite civilization

890
Establishment of the Zaidi Imamate in highland Yemen

1517, 1872
Yemen is occupied by the Ottoman Turks; it eventually becomes an Ottoman province

1839
The capture of Aden by a British naval expedition

1882–1914
South Arabian protectorates are established by the British

1934
Yemen is recognized as an independent nation under Imam Yahya

1962
A revolution overthrows Imam al-Badr; a military group proclaims a republic in North Yemen

1962–1969
Civil war between supporters of Badr and Egyptian backed republicans; protectorates merge with Aden Crown Colony

1967
British forces withdraw from Aden; the National Liberation Front proclaims South Yemen an independent republic

1980s
Major oil and natural-gas discoveries

1990s
The two Yemens unite on May 22, 1990; free elections are held on April 27, 1993; civil war in 1994

PRESENT

2000s
The U.S. destroyer *Cole* is attacked in Aden harbor; Yemen states willingness to join international coalition against terrorism

seats in the unicameral Yemeni national Legislature. As expected, the GPC won a large majority, 239 seats to 62 for Islah, the main opposition party. The Yemen Socialist Party, which boycotted the elections, was shut out of legislative participation entirely.

What struck outside observers about the election was its faithful adherence to political democracy. The entire process was supervised by the Supreme Election Commission, established by law as an independent body with balanced political representation. Despite having one of the lowest literacy rates in the world, Yemenis participated with enthusiasm and in great numbers, illiterate voters being assisted by literate volunteers to mark their ballots inside the curtained polling booths.

In September 1999 Yemen's first direct presidential election marked a milestone in the slow progress of the state—and Arab states in general—toward Western-style representative government. Prior to the election, the Constitution was amended to allow an incumbent to serve for two consecutive five-year terms. He was nominated by both his own party and the opposition Islah Party, and President Ali Abdullah Saleh easily defeated his opposition in the presidential election.

Although on the surface Yemen seems to offer fertile ground for Islamic fundamentalism due to its poverty, its high unemployment rate, and its divisions between a tribal north and a Marxist south, until recently no homegrown Islamic fundamentalist movement existed there. Following the withdrawal of Soviet troops from Afghanistan in 1989, a large number of Afghan resistance fighters (*mujahideen*) and Muslim volunteers from other countries who had gone to Afghanistan to defend Islam against atheistic Communists fled to Yemen. At the end of 1994, one mujahideen group, Aden-Abyan Islamic Jihad, carried out a number of bombings and kidnappings of foreign tourists and oil company employees. Its objectives were unclear, but it was said that the group was seeking to enforce the strict observance of Islamic law in Yemen. The group was subdued by government forces in 1999, and in January 2000, the Yemen high court convicted 10 of its members of terrorism. Three were sentenced to death, and the leader was immediately executed.

THE ECONOMY

Discoveries of significant oil deposits in the 1980s should have augured well for Yemen's economic future. Reserves are estimated at 1 billion barrels in the Marib basin and 3.3 billion in the Shabwa field northeast of Aden, with an additional 5.5 billion in the former neutral zone shared by the two Yemens and now administered by the central government. Yemen also has large deposits of natural gas, with reserves estimated at 5.5 trillion cubic feet.

Unfortunately, the political conflicts of the 1990s had a negative effect on these rosy prospects. The Gulf War, in which Yemen supported Iraq against the UN-U.S.-Saudi coalition, caused Saudi Arabia to deport some 850,000 Yemeni workers. And the civil war in 1994 seriously damaged the infrastructure, requiring some $200 million in repairs to schools, hospitals, roads, and power stations.

ACHIEVEMENTS

 Although Yemen's connections with international terrorism have caused some friction with the United States nonpolitical cooperation has yielded some positive dividends. Apart from military aid, U.S. Peace Corps volunteers teach English in a number of rural villages, and American specialists have been brought in to help remove the thousands of land mines left over from the civil war.

FOREIGN RELATIONS

The range of anti-U.S. terrorism reached Yemen in October 2000, when the U.S. Navy destroyer *Cole* was attacked while it was in Aden Harbor for refueling. Seventeen Americans were killed in the attack, which was carried out by several men in a small boat packed with explosives. After a lengthy investigation, some 10 militants, who were all connected with or members of al-Qaeda, were arrested and held for trial. In 2003 they all escaped from prison but were recaptured early in 2004. They included the alleged mastermind of the attack, Jamal Badawi, described as Yemen's most-wanted terrorist.

The intensified global hunt for al-Qaeda terrorists has made President Saleh's job more tenuous. The murders of the American medical missionaries and of an Islah Party official in January 2003 marked the widening rift of anti-Americanism of the Yemeni people.

NOTES

1. Robin Bidwell, *The Two Yemens* (Boulder, CO: Westview Press, 1983), p. 10.

2. Quoted in Robert Stookey, *Yemen: The Politics of the Yemen Arab Republic* (Boulder, CO: Westview Press, 1978), p. 168.

3. John Peterson, "Nation-Building and Political Development in the Two Yemens," in B. R. Pridham, ed., *Contemporary Yemen: Politics and Historical Background* (New York: St. Martin's Press, 1985), p. 86.

4. Yemenis believed that he slept with a rope around his neck to terrify visitors, that he could turn twigs into snakes, and that he once outwrestled the devil. Bidwell, *op. cit.*, p. 121.

5. William A. Rugh, "A (Successful) Test of Democracy in Yemen," *The Christian Science Monitor* (May 28, 1997), p. 19.

The Holy Book

IN THE KORAN, WORDS FOR LIVING A RIGHTEOUS LIFE

BY LINDA KULMAN

The Koran is the ultimate authority in Islam. For centuries, the holy book has guided Muslims on weighty issues like faith and ethics and such practical matters as marriage and inheritance. Like the Scriptures of Judaism and Christianity, the Koran is considered a revelation from the same God who revealed himself to Abraham, Moses, and Jesus. Many of the prophets revered by Christians and Jews are also honored in the Koran. And first-time readers of the Koran may be surprised to find Noah and his ark, Joseph's brothers, and Mary's Immaculate Conception.

And yet, despite the similarities, the Koran is not the Muslim Bible. And it is the differences in the ways that the Koran and Jewish and Christian Scriptures developed that illuminate the most critical distinctions in Islam.

Unlike the Bible, the Koran was not written by men; it was revealed by God through the angel Gabriel to Muhammad over little more than two decades. The Bible, for its part, was written by many men, in multiple languages, and compiled over several centuries. Says Jane Dam-men McAuliffe, dean of the College of Georgetown University and general editor of the *Encyclopaedia of the Qur'an:* "There's a whole process of collection and redaction."

According to Islamic tradition, the Prophet Muhammad received divine revelations, starting around the year 610, and recited them in the public square. But since he was illiterate, he wrote nothing down. (*Koran* itself means "recitation.") At the time of Muhammad's death in 632, therefore, the Koran existed not as a written book but only as a memorized document, alive in the hearts of those who had heard the Prophet speak and as random notes they had jotted on bones or parchment. Compiling the text became the job of Muhammad's secretary, Zaid ibn Thabit, who completed the task between 644 and 656. The reigning caliph at the time, Uthman, declared Zaid's work the official version of the Koran and ordered all other copies destroyed. Since then, Zaid's text has been off limits to additions or subtractions of any kind. "There could be no Koranic equivalent of the elevation to scriptural status of the letters of St. Paul," writes Thomas Lippman in his book *Understanding Islam.*

The timing of the revelations is also crucial to understanding the Koran. Muslims believe that Muhammad is the "seal of the prophets," the last prophet God has sent to humankind. The Koran, consequently, serves to complete—or, in some views, to correct—the Jewish and Christian Scriptures. Islamic tradition, which derives from both the Koran and the Sunna, the narratives of Muhammad's life, holds that in. their original form; God's revelations to Moses and to Jesus were completely compatible with the Koran but that they were later corrupted—either inadvertently or deliberately.

"Historically, the idea is that at some undefined time, Jews and Christians collaborated to delete references to the coming of Muhammad," says David Cook, assistant professor of religious studies at Rice University. "The idea came from the fact that certain verses and ideas in the Koran are incompatible with those in the Bible, which is chronologically earlier, and therefore the answer to this incompatibility must be a malevolent process of deletion or suppression." Omid Safi, an associate professor of religion at Colgate University, sees it differently; "My reading of early Islamic history is that Jews were criticized for coming up with a legal tradition that was more strict than that which God had required of them originally, whereas Christians are criticized for the doctrine of the Trinity."

While there is overlap with the Jewish and Christian: Scriptures, the Koran often differs significantly. Islamic tradition holds that Jesus was neither God nor the Son of God but "no more than God's apostle ... God is but one God. God forbid that he should have a son!" the Koran reads. Muhammad is on an equal footing with Jesus—and indeed Muslims are instructed to respect all of God's prophets equally. Christians "expect some Christ figure to stand at the center of the [Koranic] text," Safi says, but for Muslims, "there is no God incarnate, no salvific figure, nor a need for one."

Rather than being a chronology, the Koran's 114 suras, or chapters, are generally laid out according to length, from longest (286 verses) to shortest (three verses). Believed by Muslims to have been arranged by Muhammad according to divine instruction, the Koran opens with a brief invocation that is traditionally followed by a sura known as "The Cow"—which delivers a miscellany of unrelated information including the saga of Adam and Eve, God's warnings to the children of Israel, fasting during Ramadan, and the rules governing divorce.

The order can be a challenge to non-Muslims. "People who start out from the Bible expect that every Scripture should begin with Genesis and should end with a book of Revelation," says Safi. "They expect Page 1, Chapter 1 of the Koran to state, 'In the beginning God created the heavens and the earth.'"

Compounding the difficulty for beginners, the Koran assumes that readers are already familiar with the stories of the Hebrew Bible and the New Testament, at least in the broad sense. "What in the Jewish and Christian Scriptures is often prolonged narrative is, in the Koran, short, alluding to [well-known] stories," McAuliffe says.

The language of the Islamic holy book is also of terrific importance: All of God's revelations were delivered to Muhammad in Arabic, and the Koran is the first book in the Arabic tongue. Whereas missionaries have translated the New Testament into hundreds of languages to extend its reach while never questioning its authenticity, traditional Muslims treat all translations of the Koran as merely interpretations. What is lost in translation, they believe, is not only the original meaning but also the literal and lyrical power of the language of God. "We can read the Bible in English and feel that we are reading the Bible," McAuliffe says, "but Muslims cannot pick up an Indonesian version and think that they're reading the Koran."

Indeed, for Muslims, Arabic is the sale language of ritual prayer. Going back to the tradition of recitation begun by Muhammad, the Koran is primarily an aural experience—"something you hear rather than something you read," McAuliffe notes—and something that even the youngest children are taught to memorize. "Their experience is of beautiful sounds in Arabic recited by people who are very accomplished. An analogy would be if our experience of the Bible were through Gregorian chants." Recitation is not only an art form but also a lucrative career for the most accomplished reciters, who speak in public and on television and audiotape.

But while the words of the Koran never vary, their meanings are open to interpretation, in part because Arabic originally contained no vowels. In this sense, the Koran is similar to other scriptures, which have also generated controversies about interpretation. Over the centuries, the Koran has spawned countless commentaries, including the first guidance from Muhammad, to help explain the text.

Furthermore, "the Koran speaks with a number of different voices," Cook says. For instance, the Koran's degree of tolerance for Christians and Jews seems to change from one verse to another. The portrayal of God is another example of the Koran's variations. He is all transcendent in some verses and intimate—closer than the "jugular vein"—in others.

Some scholars attribute the changes in message to differences in the times at which Muhammad's recitations were revealed. During the first, or Meccan, period of Muhammad's life, the language was one of peace, stressing monotheism. After Muhammad left for Medina, under attack from polytheistic Mecca, the recitations became increasingly political; the Muslim community was looking to God's guidance through the Koran to help orient it. That's why "it's fruitless to engage in debates about is Islam inherently *x* or *y*," says Roxanne Euben, an associate professor of political science at Wellesley College. "The Koran is indeterminate of what it means to be a good Muslim."

The arguments among Muslims today are not over whether the Koran represents divine guidance, says Safi, but rather how the Koran is to be interpreted—whether some verses are to be highlighted over others—and the processes of interpretation that are brought to the text. People turn to different verses of the Koran to justify their own agendas, says McAuliffe. One such debate turns on whether men and women are created with equal rights and dignity or whether men are inherently superior to women. Another is whether warfare is a natural state or something people resort to when attacked. Nonetheless, Safi concludes, it is in this text—"magical and mystical, historical and divine"—that Muslims continue to confront reality and existence, seeking to conform to God's will.

Journey of a Lifetime

The Pilgrimage to Mecca Is Dangerous but Exhilarating

Linda L. Creighton

It is a voyage to the heart of Islam. The hajj, or the pilgrimage to Mecca, is the central event in the religious life of every devout Muslim, an epic quest on a scale beyond any other on Earth. Spiritually and physically, it is an experience that binds the entire Islamic world.

The fifth and final "pillar of faith," the hajj is asked of every able-bodied Muslim just once in a lifetime. But the scope of it—the size, the diversity, the history—strengthens both the individuals and the whole of Islam. Few Muslims return the same. "It was the journey of my soul," says Sohel Ahmed, a pilgrim from Northern Virginia. "I had been searching for purpose in this life, and hajj shows we are all connected to one another"

Through 14 centuries of war and natural disaster, pilgrims have sought salvation in the five days of ritual commemorating the life of Abraham and following in the footsteps of Muhammad. This year the hajj drew more than 2.5 million pilgrims to Saudi Arabia—the largest single gathering on the face of the planet.

The hardship of the trip is legendary; in the past, it took months, years, or decades to complete. "The land routes were often littered with the remains of caravans ravaged by raiding tribes, stricken by disease, short of water, or just plain lost," writes scholar David Tschanz in *Journeys of Faith, Roads of Civilization*. Even in recent years, thousands of pilgrims have been trampled, suffocated, or burned alive, including 250 deaths in a 2004 stampede, 343 in a fire in 1977, and almost 1,500 in a crowded tunnel in 1990.

Although Mecca is a modern city, and the Saudis spend billions on tourist services, it is strictly Muslim, and entry controls, including roadblocks, keep Muslim pretenders away. Yet non-Muslims have gone to great lengths to witness the hajj firsthand. British explorer Richard Burton made it to Mecca by ship and caravan, but only after satisfying Muslim custom by having himself circumcised.

To prepare for the hajj, the Koran instructs pilgrims to enter a state of consecration called the *ihram:* A pilgrim must avoid angry words, sexual intercourse, and the cutting of hair or nails. In a symbolic purification, each pilgrim bathes and discards regular clothes. Men wear two unstitched lengths of white cloth, and women wear simple versions of their normal dress with no veil or gloves. Clad in identica1 50-cent sandals, pilgrims embark on the hajj as equals before God.

Travelers go first to the vast Haram Mosque. With 4 acres of floor space, it is five times larger than the world's largest stadium, yet pilgrims still spill out onto the streets. Each day, a billion Muslims turn to face this spot. Centered in its expanse of white marble is the Kaaba—literally, the "cube"—representing the one God. Said to have been built by Adam and rebuilt by Abraham, the Kaaba is draped at all times with a black curtain on which the words of the Koran are embroidered in gold.

Inside the Kaaba is the legendary Black Stone, said by some to be a meteorite from heaven, by others the surviving piece of Abraham's original building. In a ritual known as the Turning, pilgrims circle the Kaaba seven times, trying to touch or gesture as they pass the Black Stone. As they do, they can be literally lifted off their feet, swept into a maelstrom of hundreds of thousands. At the outer edges of the circle, the weak or elderly are carried aloft on litters.

Beneath the Kaaba flows the origin of Mecca: the Zamzam well In Islamic history, Hagar, mother of Abraham's child Ishmael, was exiled with her child to the desert. Desperate for water, she ran between two nearby hills until miraculously a well appeared. Now, 1,400 years later, the well still gushes, and pilgrims drink from tin cups and fill bottles to take home. Retracing Hagar's quest for water, the pilgrims then make seven runs between the hills, although today they do it in an air-conditioned arcade.

On the second day of hajj, over 2 million pilgrims stream by bus, by car, and on foot into the 10-mile-long valley of Mina. Normally empty, Mina is transformed during hajj into a 618-acre tent city. Pilgrims are grouped by country, the men segregated from the women. Some tents are air conditioned, but poorer pilgrims or those wishing to experience the hajj as Muhammad did sleep under the stars in 100 degree heat. The goal of the gatherings is to enhance the spirit of brotherhood and foster discussion among different communities; the result has been some of the great works of Islamic theology.

On Day 3, the entire community moves east to the Plain of Arafat for the most important ritual of the hajj. Known as the Standing, this event is the spiritual climax. From noon until sunset, the old and young, healthy and well, rich and poor spread across the wide plain to pray, read the Koran, and meditate. As millions of gallons of water are misted from overhead poles, all of it evaporating before it hits ground, many of the pilgrims are moved to tears, feeling spiritually renewed.

When the sun has set below the barren hillsides, the travelers turn their course back toward Mecca. Along the way, they stop at the plain of Muzdalifah. Under a crescent moon, the pilgrims gather 49 pebbles, each no smaller than a chickpea or larger than a hazelnut. At dawn, they will re-enact an episode in which Abraham is said to have driven away Satan by throwing stones. This ritual is the most dangerous part of the hajj—scores-deep rows of pilgrims jockeying for spots and hurling stones-and it is here that most of the deaths have occurred.

The return to Mina marks the start of a three-day feast, Eid al-Adha, which is the greatest celebration of the year. Islamic tradition holds that when Abraham obeyed God's command to kill his own son, God substituted a ram at the last moment. Today, a goat, sheep, or camel is sacrificed in remembrance of Abraham's devotion; this year more than a million animals were slain for the feast. The hajj completed, the pilgrims ride a wave of euphoria and exhaustion back to Mecca. There, many of the men shave their heads, and women clip their nails and a short length of hair.

Batul Al-Saigh, 32, of Northern Virginia made the hajj this year for the first time. "To stand before the Kaaba, to see the footprints where Abraham stood, to realize that the Prophet was here—and now I am here where he stood," she says, her voice breaking. She looks down at her daughter, whose small pigtails fall against her mother's dark robe. "I will someday take my children," she says as her tears fall.

Jesus in the Quran

Jamal Badawi, Ph.D.

1. JESUS [P]¹ AS A COMMON LINK BETWEEN MUSLIMS AND CHRISTIANS

Islam is an Arabic term, which is derived from the Arabic root [S-L-M] meaning peace, submission and commitment. The three meanings are interrelated as Islam means to attain peace through submission to Allah [God]² and committing one's life to His service. This willing, conscious, loving and trusting submission is seen as the only way to attain true peace; with God; with oneself; with other humans and with the universe created by Allah.

As a generic and universal faith, Islam was the common "religion" and message of all prophets and messengers sent by Allah to guide humankind throughout history. Likewise, all prophets were "Muslims"; literally submitters to the will of Allah. As such, an article of faith for the Muslim is to believe in and honor all prophets of Allah. Of the many prophets honored, five stand out as the greatest; Noah, Abraham, Moses, Jesus and Muhammad [peace be upon them all]³. It is in that sense that Jesus [p] is a common link between Christians and Muslims, even though they believe in him in different, yet positive ways.

Muslims base their understanding of Jesus [p] on the Qur'an which, to them, is Allah's final holy book revealed to His last and final prophet Muhammad [p]. Echoing what Allah says in the Qur'an, prophet Muhammad [p] said: "I am the closest (in love) to Jesus, son of Mary in this life and in the life to come. Prophets are but [one] brotherhood. Their mothers are different [but] their father is one. There has been no prophet [sent] between us."⁴

Following the instructions of Allah and His final messenger; Muhammad [p], a true Muslim must believe in, respect, love and honor all of Muhammad's prophetic predecessors including Jesus [p]. This is to be observed, not as a matter of "political correctness" or goodwill gesture towards his/her fellow Christians, but as an article of faith without which a person cannot remain a Muslim.

The purpose of this essay is to familiarize the reader with a concise and documented profile of Jesus [p] as a common link between Muslims and Christians from an Islamic perspective. The Qur'an is the primary source for this essay.⁵

2. PRAISES OF THE FAMILY OF JESUS [P]

Mention of Jesus [p] and about him appear in over ninety verses distributed among more than ten chapters in the Qur'an. The titles of three chapters relate to Jesus [p], the family of 'Imran [possibly biblical Amram], the Table Spread and Mary [chapters # 3, 5, and 19].

Praises of Jesus [p] in the Qur'an begins with his family, particularly his mother "Indeed, Allah chose Adam and Noah, and the House of Abraham, and the House of 'Imran above all humankind, in one line of descent and Allah is all-hearing and all-knowing." [3:33-34]⁶

When Mary's mother became pregnant she vowed to dedicate what is in her womb to the service of Allah. It appears that Mary's mother was hoping to give birth to a male child, who would be eligible to serve the temple or become a priest "Behold; when a woman [of the House of] 'Imran said: O my Lord! I dedicate to Your service [the child] that is in my womb, so accept this from me for You alone are the all-hearing, all-knowing. When she had given birth to the child, she said: 'O my Lord! Behold, I have given birth to a female child'!—and Allah knew best what she gave birth to—and I have named her Maryam [Mary], and, verily, I seek Your protection for her and her offspring from Satan the accursed." 3:35-36⁷

The mother's earnest prayers to Allah on behalf of her daughter and her future progeny were answered. Young Mary was placed under the care of her relative, Prophet Zakariyya [Zachariah] who noted unusual occurrences about that young lady. As Qur'an puts it:

"And so her lord graciously accepted her and caused her to grow up in a goodly manner, and placed her in the care of Zakariyya. Whenever Zakariyya entered the sanctuary where she was, he found her supplied with food. He said: 'O Mary! Where is [this food] from?.' She said: 'It is from Allah, for Allah provides sustenance to who He pleases, without measure.'" [3:37]

It was this obvious blessing of Mary which inspired Zakariyya [p], who was old and whose wife was old and barren, to pray to Allah to grant him a pious progeny of his own: "There did Zakariyya pray to his Lord [saying] 'O my Lord! Bestow upon me [too], out of Your grace, the gift of goodly offspring; for You, indeed, hear all prayer.'" [3:38]. Like Mary's mother, Zakariyya's prayer was also answered. His old barren wife gave birth to a son: "While he was standing in prayer in the sanctuary, the angels called unto him: 'Allah gives you the glad tidings of [a forthcoming birth of] a son whose name shall be Yahya [John the Baptist], who [will come] to confirm the truth of a word from Allah [Jesus], noble, chaste, and a prophet of the righteous.' [3:39][8].

With a mixture of pleasure and surprise, Zakariyya responded: 'O my Lord! How shall I have a son, seeing I am very old, and my wife is a barren"? [3:40]. The angel's response: "So [it will be], Allah does what he wills." [3:40]

This section of Surah 3 in the Qur'an describes the righteous environments in which Jesus [p] was to be born. It describes also the "miraculous" birth of John the Baptist as a precursor to an even greater miracle yet to come: the birth of Jesus [p]. "The virgin birth" of Jesus [p], while a debatable issue among some Christians, is decisive and explicit in the Qur'an.

3. CONCEPTION OF JESUS [P]

The glad tiding began with an angelic praise and exhortation: "Behold! The angels said: 'O Mary! Allah has chosen you and purified you and chosen you above the women of all nations. O Mary! Be obedient to your Lord, prostrate yourself and bow down [in prayer] with those who bow down." [3:42-43]. It is in the midst of such purity and devotion that a surprising news was communicated to Mary:

"Behold! The angels said: 'O Mary! Allah gives you glad tidings of a word from Him, whose name will be the Anointed [Christ] Jesus, son of Mary, held in honor in this world and the Hereafter and of those nearest to Allah". Qur'an 3:45

A more detailed account of this episode is given to Surah 19:16-19:

"Relate in the Book [the story of] Mary, when she withdrew from her family to a solitary place in the East. Then We sent to her Our spirit [Gabriel] and it assumed for her the likeness of a perfect man. She said: 'Verily, I seek refuge from you with the Most Gracious [Allah]! [come not near me] if you do fear Allah'. He said 'I am only a messenger from your Lord [to announce to you] the gift of a son endowed with purity'". [19:16-19][9]

Like prophet Zakariyya and his wife, Mary was also surprised and puzzled: "She said: 'how shall I have a son, seeing that no man has touched me, and I am not unchaste'"? [19:20]. The angel answered: "so [it will be], your Lord says, 'it is Easy for Me, and that We might make him a sign unto humankind and a Mercy from Us': It is a matter [so] decreed." [19:21]. In another verse

[66:12], the Qur'an calls both Jesus [p] and his mother as a "sign unto humankind". That decree of Allah was one more manifestation of His inconceivable and absolute powers to create whoever He wishes in whichever way He wills. Creation of the human make takes place through what we call natural laws; creation of a fetus through man-woman union [as the case with all readers, I suppose!]; without the intervention of either man or woman [Adam], from a male without the intervention of a female [Eve]; or from a female without intervention of a male [Jesus]. In fact, the Qur'an makes an analogy between the creation of Adam [p] and that of Jesus [p]:

"The similitude of Jesus before Allah is as that of Adam; He created him [Adam] from dust, then said to him: 'Be': and he was" [3:59].

4. BIRTH OF JESUS

After receiving the news, Mary conceived Jesus [p]. There is no indication in the Qur'an that her pregnancy was different from other mothers. As the moment of birth drew nearer she withdrew to a remote place: "So she conceived him, and she retired with him to remote place. And the pains of childbirth drove her to the trunk of a date palm-tree: she cried [in her anguish] 'Ah! Would that I had died before this! Would that I had been a thing forgotten, utterly forgotten'" [19:22-23]. In her agony and anxiety, she heard a voice from beneath her assuring her and instructing her not to engage in any discourse with anyone for that day:

"Thereupon [a voice] called out to her from below her: 'grieve not! Your Lord has provided a rivulet [running] underneath you, and shake the trunk of the palm-tree towards you: it will drop fresh, ripe dates upon you. Eat, then, and drink and let your eyes be gladdened! Should you see any mortal, say 'I have vowed a fast [from talking] unto the Beneficent [Allah], and will speak this day to any mortal'" [19:25-26].[10]

Sooner or later, Mary had to go back to her people and face a humiliating accusation: "Then she brought him [Jesus] to her own folk, carrying him. They said: O Mary! You have surely done something strange! O sister of Harun [Aaron]! Your father was not a wicked man nor was your mother unchaste" [19:27-28].[11]

Following the instructions received upon the birth of Jesus [p], Mary said nothing but pointed to her infant. While her people were arguing with her as to how they can speak to an infant in the cradle, Jesus [P] summed up his nature and mission:

"Behold!, I am the servant of Allah. He has [decreed to] give me the book and to make me a prophet and made me blessed wherever I may be; and He has enjoined upon me prayer and prayers and charity as long as I live. He made me kind to my mother, and has not made me arrogant, unblest. Hence, peace be upon me on the day I was born, and the day I die and the day I shall be raised to life [again]" [19:30-33].[12]

5. NATURE OF JESUS [P]

According to the Qur'an Jesus [p] was an honored creature of Allah, sent as a prophet and messenger to "the children of Israel". He is called 'Eesa [which is probably an Arabized form of the] Syriac "Yeshu'". This name appears in the Qur'an 25 times; in 16 of which it is followed by Ibn Maryam [son of Mary]. Like Prophet Muhammad [p], Jesus is given more than one name. According to the Qur'an, Jesus [p] is also called Al-Masih [11 times], commonly translated as Christ [the anointed], literally it means "one who is rubbed" or "one who rubs". He is also called "son of Mary" 23 times, 16 of which are in conjuction with the name 'Eesa or al-Masih 'Eesa.

Among the other honorific names/titles of Jesus [p] in the Qur'an are: a servant of Allah [Abdullah], a prophet [Nabi], a messenger [Rasool], a blessed one [Mubarak], Al-Masih [the anointed one] and son of Mary, Ayah, literally a sign [of Allah's power and mercy]; a title which he shares with his mother, a mercy from Allah, one who is honored in this life and in the next life and among those nearest to Allah, one who is among the righteous, an example [role model] to the children of Israel. The exclusive humanity of Jesus [p], like other prophets, is repeated in the Qur'an.[13] It is in this Qur'anic context, that Jesus is called a word from Allah; the word "kun" or "be" [36:82]. In fact, Allah's words [18:109] are beyond count. Likewise, the Qur'an uses expression that Jesus [p] a spirit from Allah. The meaning of "spirit" in the context of Allah's creation of humans is explained in other Suras of the Qur'an. Allah breathed something of His "rooh" or spirit into every human being [32:6-9]. This Qur'anic expression symbolizes the pure innate nature [fitrah] endowed to humans; the inner call to believe in Allah, to seek His protection to relate to Him. It is also in that sense that Allah "breathed into Mary's womb something of His spirit" [66:12].

6. THE MISSION OF JESUS (P)

As one of the Major Prophets of Allah, Jesus' basic mission was no different from that of prophets before him or the mission of prophet Muhammad [p] after him; to believe in and worship the One and Only Universal God of all. The Qur'an quotes Jesus [p] as telling his people "Verily Allah is my Lord and your Lord; so worship Him alone. This [alone] is the straight way" [19:36]. Like other great prophets, Jesus [p] was supported by a number of "miracles". "Miracles", in themselves, do not constitute the core of prophetic teachings. They may help, however, to persuade the skeptics who, instead of evaluating the character of the prophet and reflect on the validity of his teaching, are looking for physical proofs "miracles". Yet, some never accepted their prophets, no matter what "miracles" were performed by them.

Besides the "Virgin birth" which was discussed earlier, the Qur'an mentions other miracles of Jesus [p] including healing the leper and blind and bringing the dead to life.

In all cases, the Qur'an quotes Jesus [p] to say that all such miracles were done "by the leave of Allah".

"As one of the major prophets of Allah, Jesus' (p) basic mission was no different from that of prophets before him or the mission of prophet Muhammad (p) after him; to believe in and worship the only one, the universal God of all."

7. THE END OF JESUS' MISSION

In spite of all signs, the majority of the Israelites rejected Jesus [p]. The Qur'an alludes to a conspiracy to kill him which did not succeed. Instead, Allah raised him up and it only "appeared to them" that they crucified him. [4:157]. The Arabic term used in this verse "Shubbiha Iahum", can be translated "it so appeared to them" or "it was made to appear to them as such". No further detail is given in the Qur'an itself as to how was Jesus [p] saved from crucifixion or precisely what happened. This is not unusual for the style of the Qur'an regarding history. Unlike the Bible, the Qur'an does not always deal with detailed histories. Narrations are rather suited to the main message of a given surah or passage. While the question of the "historicity" of the common story of crucifixion is at the heart of the "church" ad its interpretation of the real "mission" of Jesus [p], it is not so in the Qur'an as there is no parallel in the Qur'an to the notion of "original sin", the necessity of bloodshed for forgiveness. Furthermore, the Qur'an clearly confirms the humanity of Jesus [p] as a human being and a creature of Allah. As such, the specificity of what happened that made it "appear to them" that Jesus [p] was crucified and the identity of the person actually crucified are issued of no theological implication from the Qur'anic perspective. It should be noted, however, that some explanations given by some Muslim commentators on the Qur'an represent their own views and are not part of the text of the Qur'an.

8. RETURN OF JESUS

Whatever events marked the end of the prophetic career of Jesus [p], Hadeeth literature indicates his second coming towards the end of life on earth; that is when all Muslims and Christians will become one Ummah; community of believers in the pure longstanding Abrahamic ethical Monotheism taught by all the prophets from Noah [p] to Abraham [p] to Moses [p] to Jesus [p] and finally Muhammad [p]. the second return of Jesus, according to Hadeeth literature will be in his capacity as a servant of Allah even as he was and as he claimed himself to be more than 2000 years ago.

Theological "disputes" should not stand in the way of mutual respectful dialogue and more importantly, the over-arching human brotherhood and co-operation for the common good of all.

9. CONCLUSION

There are certainly some elements of the Qur'anic profile of Jesus [p] on which Muslims and their Christian brethren differ. Some of such differences may be significant and lie at the core of the beliefs of both faith communities. The fact remains, however, that both believe in Jesus [p], revere him, love him and look forward for his second coming. Allah alone is the Ultimate Judge of the extent of "theological correctness" as seen by one community or the other. As the Qur'an explains "If you Lord had so willed, He could have made humankind one people: but they will not cease to dispute" [11:118]. Such theological "disputes", however, should not stand in the way of mutual respectful dialogue and more importantly, the over-arching human brotherhood and co-operation for the common good of all.

NOTES

1. [P] stands for "peace be upon him", a formula used by Muslims to express respect and love of all the prophets whenever their names are mentioned. Some utter that formula in secret as well.
2. The term "Allah" will be used, as it is not subject to gender or plurality unlike the term "god"; which is more accurate when referring to "God".
3. These five great prophets are referred to the Qur'an as the ones with great determination.
4. Narrated by Muslim. See Al-Montheri, Mukhtasar Sahih Muslim, Al-Maktab Al-Islami, Damascus, 1977, Hadeeth# 1618, P. 429.
5. A combination of translations of the Qur'an were used jointly for greater accuracy and clarity in the opinion of the author. These include A. Usuf Ali, Mhuammad Asad and Muhammad M. Pickthall.
6. 'Imran may be the same as the Biblical Amram.
7. Some commentators on the Qur'an understand "the male is not like the female" to mean that the male that Mary's mother hoped for would not have been as important as this female [Mary] who was especially chosen by Allah to give birth to Jesus [p].
8. The expression "word" may refer to the divine command "Be" or to "a word of promise", like saying "I give you my word".
9. In Muslim belief, every child is born pure and free of sin. John the Baptist [Yahya] is referred to in the Qur'an as "purity" [19:13].
10. Some commentator in the Qur'an interpret this "voice" to be that of Jesus [p], others interpret it as referring to Gabriel.
11. The expression "Sister of Aaron" means "you belong to the house of Aaron; the priestly family of the descendents of Aaron". Similar expressions are found in the Bible as well. For example, Elisabeth, Wife of Prophet Zachariah is referred to as one of the "daughters of Aaron" [Luke 1:5]. This does not mean that Elizabeth was a contemporary of Aaron.
12. Consistent with other verses in the Qur'an, also with numerous sayings of Prophet Muhammad [p], Prophet Jesus [p] will die after his second coming and will be resurrected like all humans on the Day of Judgement. That is the contextual explanation of "...the Day I die and the Day I will be raised to life again".

   In spite of theological differences between Muslims and Christians, they do share a significant common ground which are easily forgotten by those who sow division and animosity and find nothing to dwell upon but differences. In fact, some forms of unity may occur even before that day though.

13. See for example: "Christ the son of Mary was no more than a Messenger; many were the Messengers that passed away before him. His mother was a women of truth. They had both to eat their [daily] food [like other mortals]...." [5:75], also "Say: 'will you worship, besides Allah, something which has no power either to harm or benefit you—when Allah alone is the all-hearing, all-knowing" [5:76] The Qur'an does not only negate what most Christians considered as heresies, such as physical sonship of Jesus [p] to Allah or the deification of Mary or crude "Tritheism", but also the notion of "Trinity". See for example 4:171; 5:75-80. It is noted that when the Qur'an uses the term "three", it does not say "three gods". This led some translators of the meaning of the Qur'an, such as Abdullah Usuf Ali and Muhammad Asad to translate it "Trinity", which is a more accurate rendering of the Qur'anic Arabic expression.

Dr. Jamal Badawi is a leading Islamic scholar of North America. He is a professor of Management at Saint Mary's University, Halifax, Canada.

From *The Message International*, vol. 27/28, no. 12/1, December 2002/January 2003. Copyright © 2002 by The Message International. Reprinted by permission.

Islam's Medieval Outposts

For centuries, young men have gathered at Islamic seminaries to escape Western influences and quietly study Islamic texts that have been handed down unchanged through the ages. But over the last two decades, revolution, Great Power politics, and poverty have combined to give the fundamentalist teachings at some of these *Madrasas* a violent twist. And now, in one of globalization's deadlier ironies, these "universities of jihad" are spreading their medieval theology worldwide.

by Husain Haqqani

As a 9-year-old boy, I knelt on the bare floor of the neighborhood *madrasa* (religious school) in Karachi, Pakistan, repeating the Koranic verse, "Of all the communities raised among men you are the best, enjoining the good, forbidding the wrong, and believing in God."

Hafiz Gul-Mohamed, the Koran teacher, made each of the 13 boys in our class memorize the verse in its original Arabic. Some of us also memorized the translation in our own language, Urdu. "This is the word of God that defines the Muslim *umma* [community of believers]," he told us repeatedly. "It tells Muslims their mission in life." He himself bore the title *hafiz* (the memorizer) because he could recite all 114 chapters and 6,346 verses of the Koran.

Most students in Gul-Mohamed's class joined the *madrasa* to learn basic Islamic teachings and to be able to read the Koran. Only a handful of people in Pakistan spoke Arabic, but everyone wanted to learn to read the holy book. I completed my first reading of the Koran by age seven. I was enrolled part time at the *madrasa* to learn to read the Koran better and to understand the basic teachings of Islam.

Gul-Mohamed carried a cane, as all *madrasa* teachers do, but I don't recall him ever using it. He liked my curiosity about religion and had been angry with me only once: I had come to his class straight from my English-language school, dressed in the school's uniform—white shirt, red tie, and beige trousers. "Today you have dressed like a *farangi* [European]. Tomor-

row you will start thinking and behaving like one," he said. "And that will be the beginning of your journey to hell."

Hafiz Gul-Mohamed read no newspapers and did not listen to the radio. He owned few books. "You don't need too many books to learn Islam," he once explained to me when I brought him his evening meal. "There is the straight path, which is described in the Koran and one or two commentaries, and there are numerous paths to confusion. I have the books I need to keep me on the straight path." He had never seen a movie and advised me never to see one either. The only time he had allowed himself to be photographed was to obtain a passport for the obligatory pilgrimage to Mecca, known as the hajj. Television was about to be introduced in Pakistan, and Gul-Mohamed found that prospect quite disturbing. One *hadith* (or saying attributed to the Prophet Mohammed) describes "song and dance by women lacking in virtue" coming to every home as one of the signs of apocalypse. Television, Gul-Mohamed believed, would fulfill that prophecy, as it would bring moving images of singing and dancing women into every home.

The *madrasa* I attended, and its headmaster, opposed the West but in an apolitical way. He knew the communists were evil because they denied the existence of God. The West, however, was also immoral. Westerners drank alcohol and engaged in sex outside of marriage. Western women did not cover themselves. Western

culture encouraged a mad race for making money. Song and dance, rather than prayer and meditation, characterized life in the West. Gul-Mohamed's solution was isolation. "The *umma* should keep away from the West and its ways."

But these were the 1960s. Although religion was important in the lives of Pakistanis, pursuit of material success rather than the search for religious knowledge determined students' career choices. Everyone in my *madrasa* class dropped out after learning the essential rituals. I remained a part-time student for almost six years but eventually needed to devote more time to regular studies that would take me through to college. Gul-Mohamed was disappointed that I did not seek a *sanad* (diploma) in theology, but he grudgingly understood why I might not want a degree in theology from a parallel education system: "You don't want to be a mullah like me, with little pay and no respect in the eyes of the rich and powerful."

And so it was for much of the four decades before the terrorist attacks of September 11, 2001, a period when policymakers were more interested in the thoughts of Western-educated Muslims responsible for energy policy in Arab countries than those of half-literate mullahs trained at obscure seminaries. But Taliban leaders, who had ruled Afghanistan since the mid-1990s, were the products of *Madrasas* in Pakistan, and their role as protectors of al Qaeda terrorists has generated keen interest in their alma maters. A few weeks after September 11, I visited Darul Uloom Haqqania (Center of Righteous Knowledge), situated on the main highway between Islamabad and Peshawar, in the small town of Akora Khattak. Taliban leader Mullah Omar had been a student at Haqqania, and the *madrasa*, with 2,500 students aged 5 to 21 from all over the world, has been called "the University of Jihad." The texture of life in the *madrasa* still has elements that represent a continuum not over decades but over centuries. But at Haqqania, I saw that the world of the *madrasa* had changed since I last bowed my head in front of Hafiz Gul-Mohamed.

In a basement room with plasterless walls adorned by a clock inscribed with "God is Great" in Arabic, 9-year-old Mohammed Tahir rocked back and forth and recited the same verse of the Koran that had been instilled into my memory at the same age: "Of all the communities raised among men you are the best, enjoining the good, forbidding the wrong, and believing in God." But when I asked him to explain how he understands the passage, Tahir's interpretation was quite different from the quietist version taught to me. "The Muslim community of believers is the best in the eyes of God, and we must make it the same in the eyes of men by force," he said. "We must fight the unbelievers and that includes those who carry Muslim names but have adopted the ways of unbelievers. When I grow up I intend to carry out jihad in every possible way." Tahir does not believe that al Qaeda is responsible for September 11 because his teachers have told him that the attacks were a conspiracy by Jews against the Taliban. He also considers Mullah Omar and Osama bin Laden great Muslims, "for challenging the might of the unbelievers."

The remarkable transformation and global spread of *Madrasas* during the 1980s and 1990s owes much to geopolitics, sectarian struggles, and technology, but the schools' influence and staying power derive from deep-rooted socioeconomic conditions that have so far proved resistant to change. Now, with the prospect of *Madrasas* churning out tens of thousands of would-be militant graduates each year calls for reform are growing. But anyone who hopes for change in the schools' curriculum, approach, or mind-set is likely to be disappointed. In some ways, *Madrasas* are at the center of a civil war of ideas in the Islamic world. Westernized and usually affluent Muslims lack an interest in religious matters, but religious scholars, marginalized by modernization, seek to as-

sert their own relevance by insisting on orthodoxy. A regular education costs money and is often inaccessible to the poor, but *Madrasas* are generally free. Poor students attending *Madrasas* find it easy to believe that the West, loyal to uncaring and aloof leaders, is responsible for their misery and that Islam as practiced in its earliest form can deliver them.

The *madrasa* Boom

Madrasas have been around since the 11th century, when the Seljuk Vizier Nizam ul-Mulk Hassan bin Ali Tusi founded a seminary in Baghdad to train experts in Islamic law. Islam had become the religion of a large community, stretching from North Africa to Central Asia. But apart from the Koran, which Muslims believe to be the word of God revealed through Prophet Mohammed, no definitive theological texts existed. The dominant Muslim sect, the Sunnis, did not have a clerical class, leaving groups of believers to follow whomever inspired them in religious matters. But Sunni Muslim rulers legitimated their rule through religion, depending primarily on an injunction in the Koran binding believers to obey the righteous ruler. Over time, it became important to seek religious conformity and to define dogma to ensure obedience of subjects and to protect rulers from rebellion. Nizam ul-Mulk's *madrasa* was intended to create a class of ulema, muftis, and *qazis* (judges) who would administer the Muslim empire, legitimize its rulers as righteous, and define an unalterable version of Islam.

Abul Hassan al-Ashari, a ninth-century theologian, defined the dogma adopted for this new *madrasa* (and the tens of thousands that would follow) in several polemical texts, including *The Detailed Explanation in Refutation of the People of Perdition and The Sparks: Refutation of Heretics and Innovators*. This canon rejected any significant role for reason in religious matters and dictated that religion be the focus of a Muslim's existence. The *Madrasas* adopted a core curriculum that divided knowledge between "revealed sciences" and "rational sciences." The revealed sciences included study of the Koran, *hadith*, Koranic commentary, and Islamic jurisprudence. The rational sciences included Arabic language and grammar to help understand the Koran, logic, rhetoric, and philosophy.

Largely unchanged and unchallenged, this approach to education dominated the Islamic world for centuries, until the advent of colonial rule, when Western education

penetrated countries previously ruled by Muslims. Throughout the Middle East, as well as in British India and Dutch-ruled Indonesia, modernization marginalized *Madrasas*. Their graduates were no longer employable as judges or administrators as the Islamic legal system gave way to Western jurisprudence. Muslim societies became polarized between *madrasa*-educated mullahs and the economically prosperous, Western-educated individuals attending modern schools and colleges.

But the poor remained faithful. The failings of the post-colonial elite in most Muslim countries paved the way for Islamic political movements such as al-Ikhwan al-Muslimin (the Muslim Brotherhood) in the Arab world, Jamaat-e-Islami (the Islamic Party) in South Asia, and the Nahdatul Ulema (the Movement for Religious Scholars) in Indonesia. These movements questioned the legitimacy of the Westernized elite, created reminders of Islam's past glory, and played on hopes for an Islamic utopia. In most cases, the founders of Islamic political movements were religiously inclined politicians with a modern education. *Madrasas* provided the rank and file.

The Iranian Revolution and the Soviet occupation of Afghanistan, both in 1979, inspired a profound shift in the Muslim world—and in the *Madrasas*. Iran's mullahs had managed to overthrow the shah and take power, undermining the idea that religious education was useless in worldly matters. Although Iranians belong to the minority Shiite sect of Islam, and their *Madrasas* have always had a more political character than Sunni seminaries, the image of men in turbans and robes running a country provided a powerful demonstration effect and politicized *Madrasas* everywhere.

Ayatollah Khomeini's revolutionary regime promised to export its revolutionary Shiite ideas to other Muslim states. Khomeini invited teachers and students from *Madrasas* in other countries to Tehran for conferences and parades, and he offered money and military training to radical Islamic movements. Iranians argued that the corrupt Arab monarchies must be overthrown just as Iranians had overthrown the shah. Iran's Arab rivals decided to fight revolutionary Shiite fundamentalism with their own version of Sunni fundamentalism. Saudi Arabia and other gulf countries began to pour money into Sunni *Madrasas* that rejected the Shiite theology of Iran, fund ulema who declared the Shiite Iranian model unacceptable to Sunnis, and call for a fight against Western decadence rather than Muslim rulers.

In the midst of this conflict, and the *madrasa* boom it spawned, the United States helped create an Islamic resistance to communism in Afghanistan, encouraging Saudi Arabia and other oil-rich states to fund the Afghan resistance and its supporters throughout the Muslim world. Pakistan's military ruler at the time, Gen. Mohammed Zia ul-Haq, decided to establish *Madrasas* instead of modern schools in Afghan refugee camps, where 5 million displaced Afghans provided a natural supply of recruits for the resistance. The refugees needed schools; the resistance needed mujahideen. *Madrasas* would provide an education of sorts, but they would also serve as a center of indoctrination and motivation.

General Zia's model spread throughout the Muslim world. Maulana Samiul Haq, headmaster of the Haqqania *madrasa*, is a firebrand orator who led anti-U.S. demonstrations soon after the beginning of the war in Afghanistan. When I asked if he thought it appropriate to involve his 5- and 6-year-old charges in political demonstrations, Haq remarked, "No one is too young to do the right thing." Later, he added, "Young minds are not for thinking. We catch them for the *Madrasas* when they are young, and by the time they are old enough to think, they know what to think." Students and teachers carried militant Islamic ideology from one *madrasa* to another. On one of the walls of the *madrasa* of my youth, someone had written the *hadith* "Seek knowledge even if it takes you as far as China." Across the road from the *madrasa* at Haqqania, some of Tahir's classmates have written a different *hadith*: "Paradise lies under the shade of swords."

The success of General Zia's experiment led to the creation of similar free schools in places as diverse as Morocco, Algeria, Indonesia, and the Philippines. Muslim immigrants in Europe and North America established *Madrasas* alongside their mosques, ostensibly to teach religion to their children. Islam requires Muslims to set aside 2.5 percent of their annual savings as *zakat* (charity), and religious education is one area on which *zakat* can be spent. *Madrasas* do not need huge funds to run, though. Teachers' salaries are low, the schools need no funding for research, and books are handed down from one generation to the next.

Madrasas have proliferated with *zakat* and financial assistance from the Gulf states. (Some classrooms at Haqqania have a small inscription informing visitors that Saudi Arabia donated the building materials for the classroom.) Modern technology has also played a role, whether by creating international financing networks or new methods of spreading the message, such as through online *Madrasas*. Pakistan had 244 *Madrasas* in 1956. By the end of last year, the number had risen to 10,000. As many as 1 million students study in *Madrasas* in Pakistan, compared with primary-school enrollment of 1.9 million. Most Muslim countries allocate insignificant portions of their budgets for education, leaving large segments of their growing populations without schooling. *Madrasas* fill that gap, especially for the poor. The poorest countries, such as Pakistan, Bangladesh, Somalia, Yemen, and Indonesia, boast the largest *madrasa* enrollment.

Classes at Haqqania are free, as are meals, which are quite basic. Tahir, the seventh of nine children, likes being at the *madrasa* because it provides him an education without costing his parents anything. He lives in a crowded dormitory of 40 to 50 students, sleeping on rugs and mattresses on the floor. He spends most of the day memorizing texts, squatting in front of a teacher who memorized them in a similar fashion as a child. "God has blessed me as I am learning His word and the teaching of His Prophet," Tahir told me. "I could have been like others in the refugee camp, with no clothes and no food."

Tahir's teacher carries a cane and can often be brutal. One *madrasa* in Pakistan has resorted to the practice of chaining students to pillars until they memorize the day's lesson. But compared with life in a squalid refugee camp, the harshness of the *madrasa* probably is a blessing. Tahir's day begins with the predawn prayer and a breakfast comprising bread and tea; it ends with the night prayer and a dinner of rice and mutton. And if Tahir does well at the *madrasa* and earns a diploma, he can expect to find a job as a preacher in a mosque.

No Turning Back

An estimated 6 million Muslims study in *Madrasas* around the world, and twice that number attend *maktabs* or *kuttabs* (small

Koranic schools attached to village mosques). An overwhelming majority of these *Madrasas* follow the quietist tradition, teaching rejection for Western ways without calling upon believers to fight unbelievers. The few that teach violence, however, drill in those beliefs firmly. The militant *madrasa* is a relatively new phenomenon, the product of mistakes committed in fighting communism in Afghanistan. But even the quietist *madrasa* teaches a rejection of modernity while emphasizing conformity and a medieval mind-set. The Muslim world is divided between the rich and powerful, who are aligned with the West, and the impoverished masses, who turn to religion in the absence of adequate means of livelihood. This social reality makes it difficult for the *Madrasas* to remain unaffected by radical ideas, even after the militancy introduced during the last two decades disappears. Cutting off outside funding might help, but because of their modest expenses, *Madrasas* can survive without assistance from oil-producing states.

Legitimizing secular power structures through democracy might reduce the political influence of *Madrasas*. But that influence is unlikely to wane dramatically as long as *Madrasas* are home to a theological class popular with poor Muslims. And the fruits of modernity will need to spread widely before dual education systems in the Muslim world will come to an end.

Muslim states are now calling upon Western governments to support *madrasa* reform through financial aid. The proposed recipe for reform is to add contemporary subjects alongside the traditional religious sciences in *madrasa* curriculum. But *Madrasas* will probably survive these reform efforts, just as they survived the introduction of Western education during colonial rule. Can learning science and math, for example, change the worldview shaped by a theology of conformity? I asked Tahir if he is interested in learning math. He said, "In *hadith* there are many references to how many times Allah has multiplied the reward of jihad. If I knew how to multiply, I would be able to calculate the reward I will earn in the hereafter."

Husain Haqqani is a Pakistani columnist and a visiting scholar at the Carnegie Endowment for International Peace.

Islam and the middle way: Extremism is a betrayal of Islam's essence, states Imam Abduljalil Sajid

Imam Abduljalil Sajid

Most people treat Islam and Muslims as synonymous and mutually interchangeable terms. In my opinion the word 'Islam' should be used exclusively for the way of life based upon the Qu'ran, the word of God, and Sunnah, the proven practices of the Prophet. 'Muslims', as human beings, are free to abide or deviate from Divine Guidance.

Islam has never claimed to be a new faith, it is the same faith that God ordained with the creation of the first man sent to earth. The only difference is in theology, concepts and practices.

In the Constitution of Medina (Sahifat al-Madinah), the Prophet Muhammad legislated for a multi-religious society, based on tolerance, equality and justice, many centuries before such an idea existed anywhere else in the world. Under the terms of this document each religious group enjoyed cultural and legal autonomy. The Jews and Christians were equal with Muslims before the law, in what Murad Hoffman calls the 'true Islamic model of religious pluralism'.

INTERFAITH DIALOGUE

The Qur'an not only conveys a message of peace, tolerance and compassion; it provides mankind with a global framework for cooperation and a charter for interfaith dialogue. It repeatedly stresses that all peoples have had their prophets and messengers, and that multiplicity of every kind is part of God's magnificent design: 'Among his wonders is … the diversity of your tongues and colours.'

This means that prophetic guidance is not limited to any one community, period or civilization. So Muslims—if they are true to their faith—do not claim a monopoly of the truth or of revelation.

The actions of a few Muslim fanatics have been interpreted as vindicating the old idea that Islam promotes violence. All too often in the media the word 'terrorism' is coupled with the adjective 'Islamic'. If Islam were really,

as some suppose, a religion of fire and sword, why would 'the true servants of the Most Merciful' be defined in the Qur'an as 'those who walk gently on the earth and who, when the ignorant address them, say "peace"'?

According to the Qur'an, 'God does not love aggressors' and war is only permitted in self-defence, or in defence of religion. When the opportunity for peace arises, Muslims are encouraged to be forgiving and to seek reconciliation, for mercy and compassion are God's chief attributes. War in itself is never holy, and if the lesser jihad of war is not accompanied by what the Prophet Muhammad called 'the greater jihad', the struggle to control the lower instincts and the whims of the ego, then war may be diabolical.

The following principles may be derived from the Qur'an:

- Muslims should not ridicule the beliefs of others.
- Muslims should not associate with those who ridicule our faith.
- When Muslims address those who do not share our beliefs, we should speak with courtesy.
- Muslims should invite people to use their reason, appealing to the intellect to interpret God's words, because there is no contradiction between faith and reason.

Above all, there must be freedom of opinion and discussion both with those who hold other religious views and with those who share our faith—for if we cannot appreciate diversity within our own community, we will certainly not be able to value religious diversity.

If Muslims were to follow these principles, they would become once again a 'community of the middle way' (Qur'an 2:143), exercising moderation and avoiding all extremes.

However, before one can begin to apply these principles there has to be the willingness to listen and to engage in dialogue, and there has to be some degree of mutual respect and equality between the two parties. When there is a gross disparity of wealth, power and privilege, such as exists between Israel and Palestine, dialogue is very difficult. The arrogance and selfishness of the rich nations, and the ever-widening gap between them and the rest of the world, generate feelings of resentment and discontent. In Islam a rich man does not merely have a duty to distribute some of his wealth to the poor, but the poor have a right to share in his wealth.

TREATED UNJUSTLY

We have to make a choice—individually and collectively—between confrontation and dialogue, destruction and construction, war and diplomacy. True global cooperation will not be possible until we recover an awareness of the ecumenical, ecological and ethical principles which are at the heart of every spiritual tradition. In most of the world's trouble spots, Muslims have been massacred and tortured and denied their most basic rights. Thousands of innocent people have died in Afghanistan and in the Iraq War. Not unnaturally Muslims feel that they have been treated unjustly by what is euphemistically called 'the world community'.

As the British Chief Rabbi Jonathan Sacks has written, 'No one creed has a monopoly of spiritual truth; no one civilization encompasses all the spiritual, ethical and artistic expressions of mankind'. Those who share this view, and see religious, cultural and ethnic diversity as a blessing, must find the middle way between religious fanaticism and fanatical secularism.

It is essential, as Prince Hassan of Jordan has said, that we promote a dialogue of civilizations, and that we should not allow extremists to hijack Islam or any other religion. It is vitally important to refute those shallow secularists who regard religion itself as inevitably divisive, and to rediscover the ethical principles upon which all the great spiritual traditions are based. It is not simply a matter of respecting religious differences; we have to recover the practical spiritual wisdom which unites us and makes us human.

The Holy Qur'an commands believers 'to come to common grounds' (3:64) for interfaith cooperation. Can we find a common ground on which Muslims and non-Muslims stand comfortably in a democratic and pluralistic society? My answer is a resounding yes.

Religious conflict, particularly between Islam and Christianity in the past, or the more recent conflict between Israel and Palestine, more often than not rose out of human excesses and the desire to stir religious passion to support political goals. Muslims, Jews and Christians share similar core values of respect for human life and dignity and profound commitment to charity and the common good. In fact all religions cherish honesty and sincerity, compassion and love, sacrifice and selflessness, justice and fairness, patience and perseverence. There is no religion that does not regard human dignity and mutual respect as vital aspects of a flourishing civilization.

Islam is a religion of peace. The terms 'Islam' and 'peace' have the same root, 'salaam'. Whenever Muslims meet they exchange the greeting, 'Peace be unto you'. The Muslim also utters this statement at the end of every ritual prayer.

In history, whenever Muslim armies entered a country they would give guarantees of life, property and honour to all the non-belligerents. Even in war Muslims are not allowed to kill an old person, a woman, children, or those who are crippled or disabled. Not even trees and crops may be destroyed.

AMNESTY

When the Holy Prophet entered Mecca as victor, everyone was offered amnesty. When Caliph Umar entered Jerusalem he was not even prepared to pray in a Church for fear that those who came after him might treat the place as a mosque and take it away from the Christians. But when the Crusaders took Jerusalem, there was a total massacre of the population.

Islam condemns and rejects all forms of terror. I feel ashamed when I hear that Muslims are breaking the Law of Islam. I sincerely apologize to those who have suffered due to any senseless actions of so-called Muslims.

Islam is firm in asserting that the end cannot justify the means. 'Good and bad are not equal,' states the Qur'an (41:34). 'Replace evil by good.' If you fight falsehood with falsehood it is falsehood which prevails. If you change evil by evil, it is evil which is victorious. Islam says that evil is to be eliminated by good. This strikes at the roots of fanaticism.

We must address the root causes of terrorism, hatred and hurt. Unless we do this, irrational people will continue to commit heinous crimes against humanity. We must eliminate injustice and exploitation, pray to overcome hatred and violence in ourselves, and rededicate ourselves to peace, human dignity and the eradication of injustice.

There is a famous saying in Islam: 'Remember, remember, remember. Evil is not in the body. Evil is in the mind. therefore harm nobody. Just change the mind.'

Imam Abdujalil Sajid is the Chairman of the Muslim Council for Religious and Racial Harmony, UK.s

How Islam Won, and Lost, the Lead in Science

DENNIS OVERBYE

Nasir al-Din al-Tusi was still a young man when the Assassins made him an offer he couldn't refuse.

His hometown had been devastated by Mongol armies, and so, early in the 13th century, al-Tusi, a promising astronomer and philosopher, came to dwell in the legendary fortress city of Alamut in the mountains of northern Persia.

He lived among a heretical and secretive sect of Shiite Muslims, whose members practiced political murder as a tactic and were dubbed hashishinn, legend has it, because of their use of hashish.

Although al-Tusi later said he had been held in Alamut against his will, the library there was renowned for its excellence, and al-Tusi thrived there, publishing works on astronomy, ethics, mathematics and philosophy that marked him as one of the great intellectuals of his age.

But when the armies of Halagu, the grandson of Genghis Khan, massed outside the city in 1256, al-Tusi had little trouble deciding where his loyalties lay. He joined Halagu and accompanied him to Baghdad, which fell in 1258. The grateful Halagu built him an observatory at Maragha, in what is now northwestern Iran.

Al-Tusi's deftness and ideological flexibility in pursuit of the resources to do science paid off. The road to modern astronomy, scholars say, leads through the work that he and his followers performed at Maragha and Alamut in the 13th and 14th centuries. It is a road that winds from Athens to Alexandria, Baghdad, Damascus and Cordoba, through the palaces of caliphs and the basement laboratories of alchemists, and it was traveled not just by astronomy but by all science.

Commanded by the Koran to seek knowledge and read nature for signs of the Creator, and inspired by a treasure trove of ancient Greek learning, Muslims created a society that in the Middle Ages was the scientific center of the world. The Arabic language was synonymous with learning and science for 500 years, a golden age that can count among its credits the precursors to modern universities, algebra, the names of the stars and even the notion of science as an empirical inquiry.

"Nothing in Europe could hold a candle to what was going on in the Islamic world until about 1600," said Dr. Jamil Ragep, a professor of the history of science at the University of Oklahoma.

It was the infusion of this knowledge into Western Europe, historians say, that fueled the Renaissance and the scientific revolution.

"Civilizations don't just clash," said Dr. Abdelhamid Sabra, a retired professor of the history of Arabic science who taught at Harvard. "They can learn from each other. Islam is a good example of that." The intellectual meeting of Arabia and Greece was one of the greatest events in history, he said. "Its scale and consequences are enormous, not just for Islam but for Europe and the world."

But historians say they still know very little about this golden age. Few of the major scientific works from that era have been translated from Arabic, and thousands of manuscripts have never even been read by modern scholars. Dr. Sabra characterizes the history of Islamic science as a field that "hasn't even begun yet."

Islam's rich intellectual history, scholars are at pains and seem saddened and embarrassed to point out, belies the image cast by recent world events. Traditionally, Islam has encouraged science and learning. "There is no conflict between Islam and science," said Dr. Osman Bakar of the Center for Muslim-Christian Understanding at Georgetown.

"Knowledge is part of the creed," added Dr. Farouk El-Baz, a geologist at Boston University, who was science adviser to President Anwar el-Sadat of Egypt. "When you know more, you see more evidence of God."

So the notion that modern Islamic science is now considered "abysmal," as Abdus Salam, the first Muslim to win a Nobel Prize in Physics, once put it, haunts Eastern scholars. "Muslims have a kind of nostalgia for the past, when they could contend that they were the dominant cultivators of science," Dr. Bakar said. The relation between science and religion has generated much debate in the Islamic world, he and other scholars said. Some scientists and historians call for an "Islamic science" informed by spiritual values they say Western science ignores, but others argue that a religious conservatism in the East has dampened the skeptical spirit necessary for good science.

The Golden Age

When Muhammad's armies swept out from the Arabian peninsula in the seventh and eighth centuries, annexing territory from Spain to Persia, they also annexed the works of Plato, Aristotle, Democritus, Pythagoras, Archimedes, Hippocrates and other Greek thinkers.

Hellenistic culture had been spread eastward by the armies of Alexander the Great and by religious minorities, including various Christian sects, according to Dr. David Lindberg, a medieval science historian at the University of Wisconsin.

The largely illiterate Muslim conquerors turned to the local intelligentsia to help them govern, Dr. Lindberg said. In the process, he said, they absorbed Greek learning that had yet to be transmitted to the West in a serious way, or even translated into Latin. "The West had a thin version of Greek knowledge," Dr. Lindberg said. "The East had it all."

In ninth-century Baghdad the Caliph Abu al-Abbas al-Mamun set up an institute, the House of Wisdom, to translate manuscripts. Among the first works rendered into Arabic was the Alexandrian astronomer Ptolemy's "Great Work," which described a universe in which the Sun, Moon, planets and stars revolved around Earth; Al-Magest, as the work was known to Arabic scholars, became the basis for cosmology for the next 500 years.

Jews, Christians and Muslims all participated in this flowering of science, art, medicine and philosophy, which endured for at least 500 years and spread from Spain to Persia. Its height, historians say, was in the 10th and 11th centuries when three great thinkers strode the East: Abu Ali al-Hasan ibn al-Haytham, also known as Alhazen; Abu Rayham Muhammad al-Biruni; and Abu Ali al-Hussein Ibn Sina, also known as Avicenna.

Al-Haytham, born in Iraq in 965, experimented with light and vision, laying the foundation for modern optics and for the notion that science should be based on experiment as well as on philosophical arguments. "He ranks with Archimedes, Kepler and Newton as a great mathematical scientist," said Dr. Lindberg.

The mathematician, astronomer and geographer al-Biruni, born in what is now part of Uzbekistan in 973, wrote some 146 works totaling 13,000 pages, including a vast sociological and geographical study of India.

Ibn Sina was a physician and philosopher born near Bukhara (now in Uzbekistan) in 981. He compiled a million-word medical encyclopedia, the Canons of Medicine, that was used as a textbook in parts of the West until the 17th century.

Scholars say science found such favor in medieval Islam for several reasons. Part of the allure was mystical; it was another way to experience the unity of creation that was the central message of Islam.

"Anyone who studies anatomy will increase his faith in the omnipotence and oneness of God the Almighty," goes a saying often attributed to Abul-Walid Muhammad Ibn Rushd, also known as Averroes, a 13th-century anatomist and philosopher.

Knocking on Heaven's Door

Another reason is that Islam is one of the few religions in human history in which scientific procedures are necessary for religious ritual, Dr. David King, a historian of science at Johann Wolfgang Goethe University in Frankfurt, pointed out in his book "Astronomy in the Service of Islam," published in 1993. Arabs had always been knowledgeable about the stars and used them to navigate the desert, but Islam raised the stakes for astronomy.

The requirement that Muslims face in the direction of Mecca when they pray, for example, required knowledge of the size and shape of the Earth. The best astronomical minds of the Muslim world tackled the job of producing tables or diagrams by which the qibla, or sacred directions, could be found from any point in the Islamic world. Their efforts rose to a precision far beyond the needs of the peasants who would use them, noted Dr. King.

Astronomers at the Samarkand observatory, which was founded about 1420 by the ruler Ulugh Beg, measured star positions to a fraction of a degree, said Dr. El-Baz.

Islamic astronomy reached its zenith, at least from the Western perspective, in the 13th and 14th centuries, when al-Tusi and his successors pushed against the limits of the Ptolemaic world view that had ruled for a millennium.

According to the philosophers, celestial bodies were supposed to move in circles at uniform speeds. But the beauty of Ptolemy's attempt to explain the very ununiform motions of planets and the Sun as seen from Earth was marred by corrections like orbits within orbits, known as epicycles, and geometrical modifications.

Al-Tusi found a way to restore most of the symmetry to Ptolemy's model by adding pairs of cleverly designed epicycles to each orbit. Following in al-Tusi's footsteps, the 14th-century astronomer Ala al-Din Abul-Hasan ibn al-Shatir had managed to go further and construct a completely symmetrical model.

Copernicus, who overturned the Ptolemaic universe in 1530 by proposing that the planets revolved around the Sun, expressed ideas similar to the Muslim astronomers in his early writings. This has led some historians to suggest that there is a previously unknown link between Copernicus and the Islamic astronomers, even though neither ibn al-Shatir's nor al-Tusi's work is known to have ever been translated into Latin, and therefore was presumably unknown in the West.

Dr. Owen Gingerich, an astronomer and historian of astronomy at Harvard, said he believed that Copernicus could have developed the ideas independently, but wrote in Scientific American that the whole idea of criticizing Ptolemy and reforming his model was part of "the climate of opinion inherited by the Latin West from Islam."

The Decline of the East

Despite their awareness of Ptolemy's flaws, Islamic astronomers were a long ways from throwing out his model: dismissing it would have required a philosophical as well as cosmological revolution. "In some ways it was beginning to happen," said Dr. Ragep of the University of Oklahoma. But the East had no need of heliocentric models of the universe, said Dr. King of Frankfurt. All motion being relative, he said, it was irrelevant for the purposes of Muslim rituals whether the sun went around the Earth or vice versa.

From the 10th to the 13th century Europeans, especially in Spain, were translating Arabic works into Hebrew and Latin "as fast as they could," said Dr. King. The result was a rebirth of learning that ultimately transformed Western civilization.

Why didn't Eastern science go forward as well? "Nobody has answered that question satisfactorily," said Dr. Sabra of Harvard. Pressed, historians offer up a constellation of reasons. Among other things, the Islamic empire began to be whittled away in the 13th century by Crusaders from the West and Mongols from the East.

Christians reconquered Spain and its magnificent libraries in Cordoba and Toledo, full of Arab learning. As a result, Islamic centers of learning began to lose touch with one another and with the West, leading to a gradual erosion in two of the main pillars of science—communication and financial support.

In the West, science was able to pay for itself in new technology like the steam engine and to attract financing from industry, but in the East it remained dependent on the patronage and curiosity of sultans and caliphs. Further, the Ottomans, who took over the Arabic lands in the 16th century, were builders and conquerors, not thinkers, said Dr. El-Baz of Boston University, and support waned. "You cannot expect the science to be excellent while the society is not," he said.

Others argue, however, that Islamic science seems to decline only when viewed through Western, secular eyes. "It's possible to live without an industrial revolution if you have enough camels and food," Dr. King said.

"Why did Muslim science decline?" he said. "That's a very Western question. It flourished for a thousand years—no civilization on Earth has flourished that long in that way."

Islamic Science Wars

Humiliating encounters with Western colonial powers in the 19th century produced a hunger for Western science and technology, or at least the economic and military power they could produce, scholars say. Reformers bent on modernizing Eastern educational systems to include Western science could argue that Muslims would only be reclaiming their own, since the West had inherited science from the Islamic world to begin with.

In some ways these efforts have been very successful. "In particular countries the science syllabus is quite modern," said Dr. Bakar of Georgetown, citing Malaysia, Jordan and Pakistan, in particular. Even in Saudi Arabia, one of the most conservative Muslim states, science classes are conducted in English, Dr. Sabra said.

Nevertheless, science still lags in the Muslim world, according to Dr. Pervez Hoodbhoy, a Pakistani physicist and professor at Quaid-e-Azam University in Islamabad, who has written on Islam and science. According to his own informal survey, included in his 1991 book "Islam and Science, Religious Orthodoxy and the Battle for Rationality," Muslims are seriously underrepresented in science, accounting for fewer than 1 percent of the world's scientists while they account for almost a fifth of the world's population. Israel, he reports, has almost twice as many scientists as the Muslim countries put together.

Among other sociological and economic factors, like the lack of a middle class, Dr. Hoodbhoy attributes the malaise of Muslim science to an increasing emphasis over the last millennium on rote learning based on the Koran.

"The notion that all knowledge is in the Great Text is a great disincentive to learning," he said. "It's destructive if we want to create a thinking person, someone who can analyze, question and create." Dr. Bruno Guideroni, a Muslim who is an astrophysicist at the National Center for Scientific Research in Paris, said, "The fundamentalists criticize science simply because it is Western."

Other scholars said the attitude of conservative Muslims to science was not so much hostile as schizophrenic, wanting its benefits but not its world view. "They may use modern technology, but they don't deal with issues of religion and science," said Dr. Bakar.

One response to the invasion of Western science, said the scientists, has been an effort to "Islamicize" science by portraying the Koran as a source of scientific knowledge.

Dr. Hoodbhoy said such groups had criticized the concept of cause and effect. Educational guidelines once issued by the Institute for Policy Studies in Pakistan, for example, included the recommendation that physical effects not be related to causes.

For example, it was not Islamic to say that combining hydrogen and oxygen makes water. "You were supposed to say," Dr. Hoodbhoy recounted, "that when you bring hydrogen and oxygen together then by the will of Allah water was created."

Even Muslims who reject fundamentalism, however, have expressed doubts about the desirability of following the Western style of science, saying that it subverts traditional spiritual values and promotes materialism and alienation.

"No science is created in a vacuum," said Dr. Seyyed Hossein Nasr, a science historian, author, philosopher and professor of Islamic studies at George Washington University, during a speech at the Massachusetts Institute of Technology a few years ago. "Science arose under particular circumstances in the West with certain philosophical presumptions about the nature of reality."

Dr. Muzaffar Iqbal, a chemist and the president and founder of the Center for Islam and Science in Alberta, Canada, explained: "Modern science doesn't claim to address the purpose of life; that is outside the domain. In the Islamic world, purpose is integral, part of that life."

Most working scientists tend to scoff at the notion that science can be divided into ethnic, religious or any other kind of flavor. There is only one universe. The process of asking and answering questions about nature, they say, eventually erases the particular circumstances from which those questions arise.

In his book, Dr. Hoodbhoy recounts how Dr. Salam, Dr. Steven Weinberg, now at the University of Texas, and Dr. Sheldon Glashow at Harvard, shared the Nobel Prize for showing that electromagnetism and the so-called weak nuclear force are different manifestations of a single force.

Dr. Salam and Dr. Weinberg had devised the same contribution to that theory independently, he wrote, despite the fact that Dr. Weinberg is an atheist while Dr. Salam was a Muslim who prayed regularly and quoted from the Koran. Dr. Salam confirmed the account in his introduction to the book, describing himself as "geographically and ideologically remote" from Dr. Weinberg.

"Science is international," said Dr. El-Baz. "There is no such thing as Islamic science. Science is like building a big building, a pyramid. Each person puts up a block. These blocks have never had a religion. It's irrelevant, the color of the guy who put up the block."

How to take Islam back to reason: Far from being anti-science, as George Carey suggests, the Koran demands scientific study. Now Muslim leaders are planning its revival and hope to restore a golden age, reports Ziauddin Sardar.

Ziauddin Sardar

Science and Islam are intimately linked. This sounds odd. First, because we normally think of religion as harmfully hostile to science. Wasn't there a long and protracted war between science and Christianity? Did the Church not prosecute Galileo? But this "war" between science and religion was purely a western affair. There is no counterpart in Islam of such mutual hostilities. Second, science and technology are conspicuous in Muslim societies largely by their absence. It is this state of affairs that has led many—including at a recent seminar in Rome, George Carey, the former archbishop of Canterbury—to conclude that Islam is anti-science.

But nothing could be further from the truth. Islam not only places a high premium on science, but positively encourages its pursuit. Indeed, Islam considers it as essential for human survival.

The Koran devotes almost one-third of its contents to singing the praises of scientific knowledge, objective inquiry and serious study of the material world. The first Koranic word revealed to the Prophet Muhammad is: "Read." It refers to reading the "signs of God" or the systematic study of nature. It is a basic tenet of Muslim belief that the material world is full of signs of God; and these signs can be deciphered only through rational and objective inquiry. "Acquire the knowledge of all things," the Koran advises its readers; "…say: 'O my Lord! increase me in knowledge'. One of the most frequently cited verses of the Koran reads:

Surely in the heavens and earth, there are signs for the believers;

And in your creation, and the crawling things He has scattered abroad, there are signs for a people having sure faith;

And in the alternation of night and day, and the provision God sends down from heaven, and therewith revives the earth after it is dead, and the turning about of the winds, there are signs for a people who understand. (45:3-5)

The sayings of the Prophet Muhammad reinforce these teachings. Islamic culture, he insisted, was a knowledge-based culture. He valued science over extensive worship and declared: "An hour's study of nature is better than a year's prayer." This is why he directed his followers to "listen to the words of the scientist and instil unto others the lessons of science".

The religious impulse propelled science in Muslim civilisation during the classical period, from the eighth to the 15th centuries. The need to determine accurate times for daily prayers and the direction of Mecca from anywhere in the Muslim world, and to establish the correct date for the start of the fasting month of Ramadan as well as the demands of the lunar Islamic calendar (which required seeing the new moon clearly), led to intense interest in celestial mechanics, optical and atmospheric physics, and spherical trigonometry. Muslim inheritance laws led to the development of algebra. The religious requirement of the annual pilgrimage to Mecca generated intense interest in geography, map-making and navigational tools.

Given the special emphasis that Islam placed on learning and inquiry, and the great responsibility that Muslim states took on themselves to assist in this endeavour, it was natural for Muslims to master ancient knowledge. At the instigation of powerful patrons, teams of translators lovingly translated Greek thought and learning into Arabic. But Muslims were not content with slavishly copying Greek knowledge; they tried to assimilate Greek teachings and applied Greek principles to their own problems, discovering new principles and methods. Scholars such as al-Kindi, al-Farabi, Ibn Sina, Ibn Tufayl and Ibn Rushd subjected Greek philosophy to detailed critical scrutiny.

At the same time, serious attention was given to the empirical study of nature. Experimental science, as we understand it today, began in the Muslim civilisation. "Scientific method" evolved out of the work of such scientists as Jabir Ibn Hayyan, who laid the foundations of chemistry in the late eighth century, and Ibn al-Haytham, who established optics as an experimental science in the tenth century. Medicine and surgery, as we know them today, evolved in the Muslim civilisation. Ibn Sina's Canons of Medicine was a standard text in Europe until the 19th century. Many surgical instruments, such as scalpels, midwifery hooks for pulling out foetuses and instruments for eye surgery, were first developed by Muslims. From astronomy to zoology, there was hardly a field of study that Muslim scientists did not pursue vigorously or make an original contribution to.

The nature and extent of this scientific enterprise can be illustrated with four institutions considered typical of "the Golden Age of Islam': scientific libraries, universities, hospitals and instruments for scientific observation (particularly astronomical instruments such as celestial globes, astrolabes, sundials and observatories). The most famous library was the 'House of Science', founded in Baghdad by the Abbasid ruler Caliph al-Mamun, which played a decisive role in spreading scientific knowledge throughout the Islamic empire. In Spain, the library of Caliph Hakam II of Cordoba had a stock of 400,000 volumes. Similar libraries existed from Cairo and Damascus to places as far off as Samarkand and Bukhara.

The first university in the world was established at al-Azhar Mosque in Cairo in 970. It was followed by a host of other universities in such cities as Fez and Timbuktu. Like universities, hospitals—where treatment was mostly provided free of charge—were institutions for training and for theoretical and empirical research. The Abodi hospital in Baghdad and the al-Kabir al-Nuri hospital in Damascus acquired worldwide reputations for their research output.

Similarly, there was a string of observatories dotted throughout the Muslim world; the most influential one was established by the celebrated astronomer Nasir al-Din al-Tusi, who developed the "Tusi couple"—a mathematical device that helped Copernicus to formulate his theory that the earth moved around the sun—at Maragha in Azerbaijan.

All this is, sadly, in stark contrast to the standing of science and technology in the Muslim world today. Apart from the notable exceptions of Abdus Salam, the Pakistani Nobel laureate, and Ahmed Zewail, the Egyptian scientist who won the Nobel prize in chemistry in 1999, modern Muslim societies have produced hardly any scientists of international repute. Scientific research has a very low priority in most Muslim states. The little that is undertaken is usually associated with defence and confined to developing nuclear or other weapons. Not a single university of international renown can be found in any Muslim country.

But things are about to change. A new movement is emerging dedicated to bringing science back to Islam. And these efforts begin with a frank admission: we cannot blame everything on colonialism and the west. As Building a Knowledge Society, the UN's 2003 Arab Human Development Report, makes clear, a great deal of responsibility for the lack of science and technology in contemporary Islamic societies lies with Muslims themselves. The ground-breaking report blames authoritarian thinking, lack of autonomy in universities, the sorry state of libraries and laboratories, and underfunding in the Arab world. "The time has come," it declares, "to proclaim those positive religious texts that cope with current realities." In particular, the report calls for "reviving ijtihad and the protection of the right to differ".

Ijtihad, or systematic original thinking, is a fundamental concept of Islam. It was the driving force behind the scientific spirit of Muslim civilisation. But the religious scholars, a dominant class in Muslim society, feared that continuous and perpetual ijtihad would undermine their power. They were also concerned that scientists and philosophers enjoyed a higher prestige in society than religious scholars. So they banded together—around the 14th and 15th centuries—and closed "the gates of ijtihad". The way forward, they suggested, was taqlid, or imitation of the thought and work of earlier generations of scholars. Ostensibly, this was a religious move. But given that, in Islam, everything is connected to everything else, it had a hugely damaging impact on all forms of inquiry. The religious scholars thus buried scientific inquiry to preserve their hold on society.

It is now widely thought that science itself can play an important role in reopening the gates of ijtihad. So the revival of science in Muslim societies and the reform of Islam itself can proceed hand in hand. Similar thoughts are being echoed by the Organisation of the Islamic Conference's standing commission on scientific and technological co-operation. The commission has argued that substantial increases in scientific expenditure and original work would not only improve Muslim societies, but would have a catalytic effect on Islamic thought. "Science played a key role in transforming Muslim societies in history; it can play the same role in transforming Islamic thought today," says Dr Anwar Nasim, an adviser to the commission.

Dr Gamal Serour, professor and consultant in obstetrics and gynaecology at al-Azhar University in Cairo, agrees. "It was the neglect of science that plunged the contemporary Muslim world into poverty and underdevelopment," he says.

During a recent visit to al-Azhar to make a Radio 4 documentary, I spoke to several scientists who expressed similar sentiments. Traditionally, the university concentrated on religious subjects. But now science is emphasised as much as religion. And the atmosphere of scientific inquiry and criticism in its classes and laboratories is bound to find its way into religious discourse.

Muslim societies have an emotional attachment to Islamic history. But their grasp of the true achievements of Muslim scientists is rather limited. Efforts are now under way in Turkey, Malaysia and Pakistan, as well as in some Arab countries, to introduce the history of Islamic science into school and university textbooks. In Britain, similar efforts are being made by the recently formed Foundation for Science, Technology and Civilisation. The foundation, which aims to popularise, disseminate and promote an accurate account of Islamic scientific heritage, has generated tremendous interest in the subject among Muslim students. Based in Manchester, and managed by a volunteer force of young Muslims, it maintains the popular website www.muslimheritage.com. The website, which claims to present a thousand years of missing history of science and technology, has become an invaluable educational forum for the Muslim community.

The wide-ranging Science and Religion in Schools Project (www.srsp.net), based at the Ian Ramsey Centre at Oxford University, aims to produce educational materials on Islam and science for GCSE and A-level students. The initial output of the project, which is led by John Hedley Brooke, professor of science and religion at Oxford, is being tested in a number of schools in Britain. Once its initial phase is over, the project will spread to other countries.

To be faithful to their scientific heritage, Muslims need to do much more than simply preserve the ashes of its fire; they need to transmit its flame. "The best way to appreciate the scientific heritage of Islam," says Nasim, "is by building the scientific capacity of Muslim societies." Muslims are now moving in the right direction. "We are beginning to realise that conscious efforts to reopen the gates of ijtihad and return to systematic, original thinking mean placing science where it belongs: at the very centre of Islamic culture," Nasim declares.

Beyond the Headlines
Changing Perceptions of Islamic Movements

John Esposito

Despite the failures political Islam has confronted when governing Afghanistan, Sudan, Pakistan, and Iran, Islamic movements in the 21st century continue to be a significant force in mainstream Muslim politics, from Morocco to Indonesia. The September 11 attacks against the World Trade Center and the Pentagon in Washington, DC; suicide bombers' slaughter of noncombatants in Israel and Palestine; bombings in Bali, Indonesia; and the arrests of suspected terrorist cells in Europe and the United States reinforce fears of radical Islamic movements. Muslim rulers in Tunisia, Algeria, Egypt, Turkey, Indonesia, and the Central Asian Republics, as well as the governments of Israel, India, China, and the Philippines, have exploited the danger of Islamic radicalism and global terrorism to deflect from the failures of their governments. They focus on the Islamist threat to divert criticism from their indiscriminate suppression of opposition movements, both mainstream and extremist, as well as to attract US and European aid.

A War on Terrorism?

After September 11, 2001, US President George Bush and many other policy makers emphasized that the United States was waging a war against global terrorism, not against Islam. However, in the Muslim world, a contrasting viewpoint prevails. The US international and domestic prosecution of its broad-based war against terrorism, and the rhetoric that has accompanied it, have made commonplace the belief in the Muslim world that the war is indeed against Islam and Muslims.

Several factors have reinforced this perception, contributing significantly to a widespread anti-US sentiment that cuts across Muslim societies as well as countries in Europe and elsewhere. The United States is increasingly seen as an "imperial" state whose overwhelming military and political power is used unilaterally, disproportionately, and indiscriminately in a war not just against global terrorism and religious extremists but also against Islam itself. The broadening of the US-led military campaign beyond Afghanistan, its "axis of evil" policy, the war against Saddam Hussein and Iraq, and the failure of the Bush administration to establish parity in rhetoric and policies in the conflicts between Palestine and Israel, India and Pakistan, and Russia and Chechnya fuels anti-US sentiment in the Islamic mainstream as well as hatred of the United States among militant extremists. Across the political spectrum there are those who believe that a clash of civilizations is on the horizon, fostered by the United States as well as by Al Qaeda and other extremists. Osama bin Laden grows in popularity among many of the younger generation as a cultural hero. In countries and societies whose leaders and elites are often seen as authoritarian and corrupt, bin Laden is a "Robin Hood," willing to forgo a life of privilege to live simply and wage a *jihad* against injustice, whether that injustice takes the form of Soviet occupation of Afghanistan or US hegemony in the Muslim world.

The Other Face

While the events of September 11 and the period following have reinforced the threat of the dark side of political Islam, with its extremists and their theologies of hate, forces of democratization and the diversity of Islamic movements remain important in electoral politics. Elections in late 2001 in Pakistan, Turkey, Bahrain, and Morocco reinforced the continued saliency of Islam in Muslim politics in the 21st century. Islamic candidates and Muslim parties increased their influence threefold in Morocco and tenfold in Pakistan. In Turkey, the AK (Justice and Development Party) came to power, and in Bahrain, Islamic candidates won 19 of 40 parliamentary seats.

These examples of Islamic candidates and movements urging a turn toward ballots not bullets are not new. If much of the 1980s was dominated by fears of Iran's export of revolutionary Islam, in the late 1980s and early 1990s, Islamically oriented candidates were elected as mayors and parliamentarians in countries as diverse as Morocco, Egypt, Turkey, Lebanon, Kuwait, Bahrain, Pakistan, Malaysia, and Indonesia. They served in cabinet-level positions and as speakers of national assemblies, Prime Ministers in Turkey and Pakistan, Deputy Prime Ministers in Malaysia, and as the first democratically elected president in Indonesia. The general response of many governments to Islam's political power was to retreat from open elections, identifying their Islamic opposition as extremist, or simply falling back on their "time-honored tradition" of canceling or manipulating elections, as occurred in Tunisia, Algeria, Egypt, and Jordan.

The most remarkable demonstration of Islam's prominence in mainstream politics was the victory of Turkey's AK, which won a parliamentary majority in a secular state with a predominantly Muslim population. The party's victory followed similarly important performances by Islamic candidates in Morocco, Bahrain, and Pakistan as well as the persistent strength of religious currents in countries like Egypt, Jordan, Lebanon, Kuwait, Malaysia, and Indonesia, all key US allies.

Turkey, an important US ally in NATO, elected AK, a party with Islamist roots originating from the former Welfare and Virtue parties; AK is mainstream, not extremist. Islamist success in Turkey indicates the way mainstream Islamic parties approach politics. More often than not, voters vote based on their interests and concerns. One should not necessarily conclude that AK exploited the situation just because it responds effectively to economic problems. AK simply responded as any political party would. Mainstream Islamist and Muslim parties have learned to adapt to the ways that modern politics are played. The AK-led Turkish government has indicated its willingness to work with Europe, the United States, and the international community while retaining Turkey's independence. The example of Turkey's AK Party shows that experience and the realities of politics can lead to change. Though its roots were Islamist, the founders of AK chose to create a more broad-based party, much as Christian Democrats once did in Europe.

Bahrain's monarchy attempted a top-down reformation, as part of a promised move toward democratization. In the October 2002 elections in Bahrain, the first in 30 years, Islamic candidates, representing Sunni and Shi'a Islamic parties, won 19 of 40 seats in Parliament. Bahrain's parliament has a total of 80 seats, of which half are elected and the remaining are filled by members of a consultative council, appointed by the king, Sheikh Hamad bin Isa al-Khalifa. Moreover, Bahrain is the only Gulf country where women are allowed to vote in national elections and to run for office; however, no women were elected.

Democracy fared less well in Morocco's parliamentary elections in September 2002. The Justice and Development Party (PJD) was a major gainer, jumping from 14 to 42 seats, tripling its vote, and winning 10 percent of the seats in Parliament. The largest Islamist opposition group, the banned Al-Adl Wal Ihsan (Justice and Charity), boycotted the elections, although it had a strong chance of victory if it had been allowed to run. However, despite the performance of the PJD, reformist King Mohammed VI refused to name an Islamist to any of 31 Cabinet posts. This failure reinforced critics who charge that though his rhetoric and style seem different, he is ultimately little different from his father, King Hassan II, who last held elections in 1997 amid allegations of vote-rigging and rampant fraud.

Many observers were shocked in Pakistan when an Islamic bloc—The Joint Action Forum, Muttahida Majlis-e-Amal, (MMA)

which included the more moderate Jamaat-e-Islami and hardline religious parties-placed third with 30 seats in the October 10, 2002, elections. Running on a platform critical of President Pervez Musharraf, the MMA denounced his control of elections, failure to democratize, backing of the US military campaign in Afghanistan, and the continued US military presence in the region. In addition to Parliament, some of Pakistan's Islamic parties now govern the Northwest Frontier Province and extended a helping hand to Afghan and Pakistani extremists. Some observers charge that the Pakistani army willingly played into their hands, rigging last October's general elections. Thus, the surprising success of Islamic parties at the polls enabled General Musharraf to claim greater need for US support for his government now "threatened by fundamentalists."

> # The leadership of most Islamic movements continues to be lay rather than clergy, graduates of modern educational systems rather than *madrasa*, and trained in science ... rather than religious disciplines.

Islamic candidates and parties share some common issues but also reflect significant differences. All were critics of the status quo political and economic establishments. Most cast themselves as reformers and emphasized justice and development. Importantly, most of their supporters were not just the downtrodden but also the aspiring middle class. The leadership of most Islamic movements continues to be lay rather than clergy, graduates of modern educational systems rather than *madrasa*, and trained in science, engineering, or education rather than religious disciplines. Their attitudes toward the West vary considerably from Pakistan's Joint Action Forum's denunciation of US presence to the Turkish AK's care to demonstrate that it was not anti-US or anti-European as it considered the placement and deployment of US-led military forces in Turkey.

The continued performance and relative success of Islamic movements in

many countries reflect the failures of their governments and the extent to which mainstream Islamic movements are prepared to participate in the electoral process. At the same time, their performance is a reminder that Islam remains a potent force in mainstream Muslim politics. Policy makers have been challenged to refocus on the implications of the Bush administration's decision in 2002 to support the promotion of democratization. The Bush administration has spoken in far more ambitious terms than its predecessors about encouraging democracy in the Muslim world. In an interview, US Secretary of State Colin Powell went out of his way not to rule out US support for Islamic parties, noting that "the fact that the party has an Islamic base to it in and of itself does not mean that it will be anti-[United States] in any way." A major test for US policy on democracy will be Iran, where a majority of the population, especially students and women, has twice voted overwhelmingly for reform by backing President Mohammad Khatami. Opposition voices and student protests have sent a clear message to hardline clerics. However, US President Bush's axis of evil policy set back democratic reformers in Iran. Moreover, continued pressure from neoconservatives to "get tough" with Iran plays into the hands of Ayatollah Khamenei and the hardliners.

A more open attitude toward both Islamic and non-Islamic mainstream opposition parties and other policies that support broader political participation and democratization could improve the US image abroad, while strengthening democratic institutions and civil society in countries where decades of authoritarian rule have all but extinguished them.

The Christian Right

Western perceptions of Islam and Islamic movements remain a sensitive and explosive issue in Muslim countries. In the United States, denunciations of Islam as an evil religion, Muhammad as a terrorist and pedophile, and other inflammatory statements by US televangelists like Pat Robertson, Jerry Falwell, and Franklin Graham—who gave the prayer at President Bush's inauguration—have reinforced the belief that despite his public statements, President Bush is swayed by the Christian Right. The association of the President, other members of his administration, and members of Congress with the Christian Right strengthens the conviction that US foreign policy is anti-Islamic.

The unholy alliance between the Christian Right and many Republican neoconservatives, who espouse a theological and ideological right-wing US agenda—including support for hardline Israeli policies, the "axis of evil" paradigm, military action against Iraq, and regime change in other Muslim states—seems to confirm the fears of those who claim there is a widespread "conspiracy" against Islam.

Authoritarian Muslim regimes from North Africa to Southeast Asia have also taken the war against global terrorism as a green light to further limit the rule of law and civil society and to repress both secular and Islamic opposition. To excuse their authoritarianism, they use the label "Wahhabi" or "terrorist" for all Islamic movements, including mainstream ones, who are characterized as wolves in sheep's clothing. As a result, many Western governments have overtly or quietly pursued a "double standard" in their promotion of democratization and human rights, fearing that Islamic candidates' participation in the democratic process would necessarily lead to the hijacking of elections. These fears often obscure the fact that many, if not most, rulers in the Muslim world, secular as well as religious, have non-democratic, authoritarian track records themselves.

Ongoing Tensions

The continued tendency since September 11 to see Islam, Islamic movements, and events in the Muslim world through explosive headlines hinders the public's ability to distinguish between the religion of Islam and the actions of extremists who hijack Islamic discourse and belief to justify their acts of terrorism. It reinforces the tendency to equate all Islamic movements—political and social, mainstream and extremists, non-violent and violent—with terrorism.

Yet, a deadly radical minority continues to exist. Osama bin Laden, Al Qaeda, and other extremist groups are a threat to Muslim societies and to the West. Appealing to real as well as imagined injustices, they prey on the oppressed, alienated, and marginalized sectors of society. Thus, the short-term military response to bring the terrorists to justice must also be balanced by long-term policy that focuses on the core political, economic, and educational issues that contribute to conditions that breed radicalism and extremism.

> The continued tendency since September 11 to see Islam ... through explosive headlines hinders the public's ability to distinguish between the religion of Islam and the actions of extremists.

The US-led war in Iraq has increased anti-US sentiment exponentially in the Muslim world as well as in European countries and elsewhere. In the Arab and Muslim world, it is seen as part of a new US empire's war against Islam and the Muslim world, an attempt to redraw the map of the Middle East. The rage and alienation of a minority toward the United States, coupled with the authoritarianism, repression, and corruption of regimes and failed economies of many Muslim states, will produce new Osama bin Ladens and new al Qaeda-like movements.

The occupation of Iraq and establishment of a client state with a strong military presence coupled with stated goals to deal with Syria and Iran and reform allies like Egypt and Saudi Arabia plays directly into the hands of militant extremists. However much many Arabs and Muslims want reform and democratization, they do not want Western-imposed reform and control in order to implement a New American Century.

In the 21st century, given the political and socioeconomic realities of the Muslim world, religion will continue to be an important presence and force. Islamic movements, mainstream and extremist, will be pivotal players. Relations between the Muslim world and the West will require a cooperative effort to eradicate or contain global terrorism while at the same time supporting mainstream Muslim efforts to democratize their societies.

The process will entail constructive engagement, dialogue, self-criticism, and change on both sides. The extremists aside, the bulk of criticism of Western, and particularly US foreign policy, from Islamic movements and Muslim populations in general comes from a mainstream majority that judges the West by whether its policies and actions reflect principles and values that are admired: self-determination, political participation, freedom, human rights, a desire for economic prosperity, peace, and security. In the end, the ability to communicate these values to Islamic movements and cooperate on policy initiatives will prove the coming years' greatest cooperative challenge, both to Muslim and Western governments.

JOHN ESPOSITO is Professor of Religion and International Affairs and of Islamic Studies at Georgetown University.

From *Harvard International Review*, vol. 25, no. 2, Summer 2003. Copyright © 2003 by Harvard International Review. Reprinted by permission.

A Debate on Cultural Conflicts

The Coming Clash of Civilizations—Or, the West Against the Rest

Samuel P. Huntington

World politics is entering a new phase in which the fundamental source of conflict will be neither ideological or economic. The great divisions among mankind and the dominating source of conflict will be cultural. The principal conflicts of global politics will occur between nations and groups of different civilizations. The clash of civilizations will dominate global politics.

During the cold war, the world was divided into the first, second and third worlds. Those divisions are no longer relevant. It is far more meaningful to group countries not in terms of their political or economic systems or their level of economic development but in terms of their culture and civilization.

A civilization is the highest cultural grouping of people and the broadest level of cultural identity people have short of that which distinguishes humans from other species.

Civilizations obviously blend and overlap and may include sub-civilizations. Western civilization has two major variants, European and North American, and Islam has its Arab, Turkic and Malay subdivisions. But while the lines between them are seldom sharp, civilizations are real. They rise and fall; they divide and merge. And as any student of history knows, civilizations disappear.

Global conflict will be cultural.

Westerners tend to think of nation-states as the principal actors in global affairs. They have been that for only a few centuries. The broader reaches of history have been the history of civilizations. It is to this pattern that the world returns.

Civilization identity will be increasingly important and the world will be shaped in large measure by the interactions among seven or eight major civilizations. These include the Western, Confucian, Japanese, Islamic, Hindu, Slavic-Orthodox, Latin American and possibly African civilizations. The most important and bloody conflicts will occur along the borders separating these cultures. The fault lines between civilizations will be the battle lines of the future.

Why? First, differences among civilizations are basic, involving history, language, culture, tradition and, most importantly, religion. Different civilizations have different views on the relations between God and man, the citizen and the state, parents and children, liberty and authority, equality and hierarchy. These differences are the product of centuries. They will not soon disappear.

Second, the world is becoming smaller. The interactions between peoples of different civilizations are increasing. These interactions intensify civilization consciousness: awareness of differences between civilizations and commonalities within civilizations. For example, Americans react far more negatively to Japanese investment than to larger investments from Canada and European countries.

Third, economic and social changes are separating people from long standing local identities. In much of the world, religion has moved in to fill this gap, often in the form of movements labeled fundamentalist. Such movements are found in Western Christianity, Judaism, Buddhism, Hinduism and Islam. The "unsecularization of the world," George Weigel has remarked, "is one of the dominant social facts of life in the late 20th century."

Fourth, the growth of civilization consciousness is enhanced by the fact that at the moment that the West is at the peak of its power a return-to-the-roots phenomenon is occurring among non-Western civilizations—the "Asianization" in Japan, the end of the Nehru legacy and the "Hinduization" of India, the failure of Western ideas of socialism and nationalism and, hence, the "re-Islamization" of the Middle East, and now a debate over Westernization versus Russianization in Boris Yeltsin's country.

More importantly, the efforts of the West to promote its values of democracy and liberalism as universal values, to maintain its military predominance and to advance its economic interests engender countering responses from other civilizations.

The central axis of world politics is likely to be the conflict between "the West and the rest" and the responses of non-Western civilizations to Western power and values. The most prominent example of anti-Western cooperation is the connection between Confucian and Islamic states that are challenging Western values and power.

Fifth, cultural characteristics and differences are less mutable and hence less easily compromised and resolved than political and economic ones. In the former Soviet Union, Communists can become democrats, the rich can become poor and the poor rich, but Russians cannot become Estonians. A person can be half-French and half-Arab and even a citizen of two countries. It is more difficult to be half Catholic and half Muslim.

Finally, economic regionalism is increasing. Successful economic regionalism will reinforce civilization consciousness.

On the other hand, economic regionalism may succeed only when it is rooted in common civilization. The European Community rests on the shared foundation of European culture and Western Christianity. Japan, in contrast, faces difficulties in creating a comparable economic entity in East Asia because it is a society and civilization unique to itself.

As the ideological division of Europe has disappeared, the cultural division of Europe between Western Christianity and Orthodox Christianity and Islam has re-emerged. Conflict along the fault line between Western and Islamic civilizations has been going on for 1,300 years. This centuries-old military interaction is unlikely to decline. Historically, the other great antagonistic interaction of Arab Islamic civilization has been with the pagan, animist and now, increasingly, Christian black peoples to the south. On the northern border of Islam, conflict has increasingly erupted between Orthodox and Muslim peoples, including the carnage of Bosnia and Sarajevo, the simmering violence between Serbs and Albanians, the tenuous relations between Bulgarians and their Turkish minority, the violence between Ossetians and Ingush, the unremitting slaughter of each other by Armenians and Azeris and the tense relations between Russians and Muslims in Central Asia.

The historic clash between Muslims and Hindus in the Subcontinent manifests itself not only in the rivalry between Pakistan and India but also in intensifying religious strife in India between increasingly militant Hindu groups and the substantial Muslim minority.

Groups or states belonging to one civilization that become involved in war with people from a different civilization naturally try to rally support from other members of their own civilization.

Decreasingly able to mobilize support and form coalitions on the basis of ideology, governments and groups will increasingly attempt to mobilize support by appealing to common religion and civilization identity. As the conflicts in the Persian Gulf, the Caucasus and Bosnia continued, the positions of nations and the cleavages between them increasingly were along civilizational lines. Populist politicians, religious leaders and the media have found it a potent means of arousing mass support and of pressuring hesitant governments. In the coming years, the local conflicts most likely to escalate into major wars will be those, as in Bosnia and the Caucasus, along the fault lines between civilizations. The next world war, if there is one, will be a war between civilizations.

Only Japan is non-Western and modern.

If these hypotheses are plausible, it is necessary to consider their implications for Western policy. These implications should be divided between short-term advantage and long-term accommodation. In the short term, it is clearly in the interest of the West to promote greater cooperation and unity in its own civilization, particularly between its European and North American components; to incorporate into the West those societies in Eastern Europe and Latin America whose cultures are close to those of the West; to maintain close relations with Russia and Japan; to support in other civilizations groups sympathetic to Western values and interests; and to strengthen international institutions that reflect and legitimate Western interests and values. The West must also limit the expansion of the military strength of potentially hostile civilizations, principally Confucian and Islamic civilizations, and exploit differences

and conflicts among Confucian and Islamic states. This will require a moderation in the reduction of Western military capabilities, and, in particular, the maintenance of American military superiority in East and Southwest Asia.

In the longer term, other measures would be called for. Western civilization is modern. Non-Western civilizations have attempted to become modern without becoming Western. To date, only Japan has fully succeeded in this quest. Non-Western civilizations will continue to attempt to acquire the wealth, technology, skills, machines and weapons that are part of being modern. They will attempt to reconcile this modernity with their traditional culture and values. Their economic and military strength relative to the West will increase.

Hence, the West will increasingly have to accommodate to those non-Western modern civilizations, whose power approaches that of the West but whose values and interests differ significantly from those of the West. This will require the West to develop a much more profound understanding of the basic religious and philosophical assumptions underlying other civilizations and the ways in which people in those civilizations see their interests. It will require an effort to identify elements of commonality among Western and other civilizations. For the relevant future, there will be no universal civilization but instead a world of different civilizations, each of which will have to learn to co-exist with others.

Samuel P. Huntington is professor of government and director of the Olin Institute for Strategic Studies at Harvard. This article is adapted from the lead essay in the summer issue of *Foreign Affairs*.

Global Debate on a Controversial Thesis

A Clash Between Civilizations—or Within Them?

A recent essay by Harvard professor Samuel P. Huntington in "Foreign Affairs" magazine—"The Clash of Civilizations?"—has attracted a good deal of attention not only in the U.S. but abroad, as well. Huntington is attempting to establish a new model for examining the post-cold-war world, a central theme around which events will turn, as the ideological clash of the cold war governed the past 40 years. He finds it in cultures. "Faith and family, blood and belief," he has written, "are what people identify with and what they will fight and die for." But in the following article, Josef Joffe, foreign-affairs specialist at the independent "Süddeutsche Zeitung" of Munich, argues that "kulturkampf"—cultural warfare—is not a primary threat to world security. And in a more radical view, Malaysian political scientist Chandra Muzaffar writes for the Third World Network Features agency of Penang, Malaysia, that Western dominance—economic and otherwise—continues to be the overriding factor in world politics.

SüddeutscheZeitung

A ghost is walking in the West: cultural warfare, total and international. Scarcely had we banished the 40-year-long cold war to history's shelves, scarcely had we begun to deal with the seductive phrase "the end of history," when violence broke out on all sides. But this time it was not nations that were behind the savagery but peoples and ethnic groups, religions and races—from the Serbs and Bosnians in the Balkans to the Tiv and Jukun in Nigeria. Working from such observations, one of the best brains in America, Harvard professor Samuel Huntington, produced a prophecy, perhaps even a philosophy of history. His essay "The Clash of Civilizations?" has caused a furor. For centuries, it was the nations that made history; then, in the 20th century, it was the totalitarian ideologies. Today, at the threshold of the 21st century, "the clash of civilizations will dominate global politics." No longer will "Which side are you on?" be the fateful question but "What are you?" Identity will no longer be defined by passport or party membership card but by faith and history, language and customs—culture, in short. Huntington argues that "conflicts between cultures" will push the old disputes between nations and ideologies off center stage. Or put more apocalyptically: "The next world war, if there is one, will be a war between civilizations."

Between which? Huntington has made a list of more than half a dozen civilizations, including the West (the U.S. plus Europe), the Slavic-Orthodox, the Islamic, the Confucian (China), the Japanese, and the Hindu. At first glance, he seems to be right. Are not Catholic Croats fighting Orthodox Serbs—and both of them opposing Muslim Bosnians? And recently, the ruthless struggle between the Hindus and Muslims of India has re-erupted. Even such a darling of the West as King Hussein of Jordan announced during the Persian Gulf war: "This is a war against all Arabs and all Muslims and not against Iraq alone." The long trade conflict pitting Japan against the United States (and against Europe) has been called a "war"—and not only by the chauvinists. Russian Orthodox nationalists see themselves in a two-front struggle: against the Islamic Turkic peoples in the south and the soulless modernists of the West. And even worse: The future could mean "the West against the rest."

But this first look is deceptive; after a closer look, the apocalypse dissolves, to be replaced by a more complex tableau. This second look shows us a world that is neither new nor simple. First of all, conflicts between civilizations are as old as history itself. Look at the struggle of the Jews against the Turks in the 19th century, or the revolt of the Greeks against the Turks in the 19th century. The Occident and Orient have been in conflict, off and on, for the last 1,300 years. Second, the disputes with China, Japan, or North Korea are not really nourished by conflicts among civilizations. They are the results of palpable national interests at work. Third, if we look only at the conflicts between cultures, we will miss the more important truth: Within each camp, divisions and rivalries are far more significant than unifying forces.

Reprinted with permission from *World Press Review*, February 1994, pp. 24-26. Originally from Süddeutsche Zeitung.

The idea of cultural war seems to work best when we examine Islam. The demonization of the West is a part of the standard rhetoric of Islamic fundamentalists. The Arab-Islamic world is one of the major sources of terrorism, and most armed conflicts since World War II have involved Western states against Muslim countries. But if we look more closely, the Islamic monolith fractures into many pieces that cannot be reassembled. There is the history of internecine conflicts, coups, and rebellions: a 15-year-long civil war of each against all in Lebanon (not simply Muslims against Maronite Christians), the Palestine Liberation Organization against Jordan, and Syria against the PLO. Then consider the wars among states in the Arab world: Egypt versus Yemen, Syria against Jordan, Egypt versus Libya, and finally Iraq versus Kuwait. Then the wars of ideologies and finally, the religiously tinted struggles for dominance within the faith—between Sunnis and Shiites, Iraq and Iran.

But more important: What does the term "Islam" really mean? What does a Malay Muslim have in common with a Bosnian? Or an Indonesian with a Saudi? And what are we to understand by "fundamentalism"? The Saudi variety is passive and inward-looking, while the expansive Iranian variety arouses fear. It is true that, from Gaza to Giza, fundamentalists are shedding innocent blood. But most of the Arab world sided with the West during the Gulf war. And, beyond this, only 10 percent of the trade of the Middle East takes place within the region; most of it flows westward. Economic interdependence, a good index of a common civilization, is virtually nonexistent in the Islamic world.

The real issue is not a cultural war but actually another two-fold problem. Several Islamic nations are importing too many weapons, and some are exporting too many people. The first demands containment and denial, calling for continued military strength and readiness in the West. And what of the "human exports"? They are not just a product of the Islamic world but of the entire poor and overpopulated world—no matter what culture they are part of. Along with the spread of nuclear weapons and missiles, this is the major challenge of the coming century, because massive migrations of people will inevitably bring cultural, territorial, and political struggles in their wake. No one has an answer to this. But a narrow vision produced by the "West-against-the-rest" notion is surely the worst way to look for answers.

—*Josef Joffe*

The West's Hidden Agenda

Third World Network
FEATURES

Like Francis Fukuyama's essay "The End of History?" published in 1989, Samuel Huntington's "The Clash of Civilizations?" has received a lot of publicity in the mainstream Western media. The reason is not difficult to fathom. Both articles serve U.S. and Western foreign-policy goals. Huntington's thesis is simple enough: "The clash of civilizations will dominate global politics. The fault lines between civilizations will be the battle lines of the future."

The truth, however, is that cultural, religious, or other civilizational differences are only some of the many factors responsible for conflict. Territory and resources, wealth and property, power and status, and individual personalities and group interests are others. Indeed, religion, culture, and other elements are symbols of what Huntington would regard as "civilization identity" are sometimes manipulated to camouflage the naked pursuit of wealth or power—the real source of many conflicts.

But the problem is even more serious. By overplaying the "clash of civilizations" dimension, Huntington has ignored the creative constructive interaction and engagement between civilizations. This is a much more constant feature of civilization than conflict per se. Islam, for instance, through centuries of exchange with the West, laid the foundation for the growth of mathematics, science, medicine, agriculture, industry, and architecture in medieval Europe. Today, some of the leading ideas and institutions that have gained currency within the Muslim world, whether in politics or in economics, are imports from the West.

That different civilizations are not inherently prone to conflict is borne out by another salient feature that Huntington fails to highlight. Civilizations embody many similar values and ideals. At the philosophical level at least, Buddhism, Christianity, Hinduism, Islam, Judaism, Sikhism, and Taoism, among other world religions, share certain common perspectives on the relationship between the human being and his environment, the integrity of the community, the importance of the family, the significance of moral leadership, and indeed, the meaning and purpose of life. Civilizations, however different in certain respects, are quite capable of forging common interests and aspirations. For example, the Association of Southeast Asian Nations encompasses at least four "civilization identities," to use Huntington's term—Buddhist (Thailand), Confucian (Singapore), Christian (the Philippines), and Muslim (Brunei, Indonesia, and Malaysia). Yet it has been able to evolve an identity of its own through 25 years of trials.

"U.S. and Western dominance is at the root of global conflict."

It is U.S. and Western dominance, not the clash of civilizations, that is at the root of global conflict. By magnifying the so-called clash of civilizations, Huntington tries to divert attention from Western dominance and control even as he strives to preserve, protect, and perpetuate that dominance. He sees a compelling reason for embarking on this mission. Western dominance is under threat from a "Confucian-Islamic connection that has emerged to challenge Western interests, values, and power," he writes. This is the most mischievous—and most dangerous—implication of his "clash of civilizations."

By evoking this fear of a Confucian-Islamic connection, he hopes to persuade the Western public, buffeted by unemployment and recession, to acquiesce to huge military budgets in the post-cold-war era. He argues that China and some Islamic nations are acquiring weapons on a massive scale. Generally, it is the Islamic states that are buying weapons from China, which in turn "is rapidly increasing its military spending." Huntington observes that "a Confucian-Islamic military connection has thus come into being, designed to promote acquisition by its members of the weapons and weapons technologies needed to counter the military power of the West." This is why the West, and the U.S. in particular, should not, in Huntington's view, be "reducing its own military capabilities."

There are serious flaws in this argument. One, it is not true that the U.S. has reduced its military capability; in fact, it has enhanced its range of sophisticated weaponry. Two, though China is an important producer and exporter of arms, it is the only major power whose military expenditures consistently declined throughout the 1980s. Three, most Muslim countries buy their weapons not from China but from the U.S. Four, China has failed to endorse the Muslim position on many global issues. Therefore, the Confucian-Islamic connection is a myth propagated to justify increased U.S. military spending.

It is conceivable that Huntington has chosen to target the Confucian and Islamic civilizations for reasons that are not explicitly stated in his article. Like many other Western academics, commentators, and policy analysts, Huntington, it appears, is also concerned about the economic ascendancy of so-called Confucian communities such as China, Hong Kong, Taiwan, Singapore, and overseas Chinese communities in other Asian countries. He is of the view that "if cultural commonality is a prerequisite for economic integration, the principal East Asian economic bloc of the future is likely to be centered on China." The dynamism and future potential of these "Confucian" economies have already set alarm bells ringing in various Western capitals. Huntington's warning to the West about the threat that China poses should be seen in that context—as yet another attempt to curb the rise of yet another non-Western economic competitor.

As far as the "Islamic threat" is concerned, it is something that Huntington and his kind have no difficulty selling in the West. Antagonism toward Islam and Muslims is deeply embedded in the psyche of mainstream Western society. The rise of Islamic movements has provoked a new, powerful wave of negative emotions against the religion and its practitioners. Most Western academics and journalists, in concert with Western policy makers, grant no legitimacy to the Muslim resistance to Western domination and control. When Huntington says, "Islam has bloody borders," the implication is that Islam and Muslims are responsible for the spilling of blood. Yet anyone who has an elementary knowledge of many current conflicts will readily admit that, more often than not, it is the Muslims who have been bullied, bludgeoned, and butchered.

The truth, however, means very little to Huntington. The title of his article "The Clash of Civilizations?" is quoted from [British educator] Bernard Lewis's "The Roots of Muslim Rage," an essay that depicts the Islamic resurgence as an irrational threat to Western heritage. Both Huntington and Lewis are "Islam baiters" whose role is to camouflage the suffering of and the injustice done to the victims of U.S. and Western domination by concocting theories about the conflict of cultures and the clash of civilizations. Huntington's "The Clash of Civilizations?" will not conceal the real nature of the conflict: The victims—or at least some of them—know the truth.

—Chandra Muzaffar

Reprinted with permission from *World Press Review*, February 1994, pp. 25-26. Originally from *Third World Network Features*.

THE CLASH OF IGNORANCE

EDWARD W. SAID

Samuel Huntington's article "The Clash of Civilizations?" appeared in the Summer 1993 issue of *Foreign Affairs*, where it immediately attracted a surprising amount of attention and reaction. Because the article was intended to supply Americans with an original thesis about "a new phase" in world politics after the end of the cold war, Huntington's terms of argument seemed compellingly large, bold, even visionary. He very clearly had his eye on rivals in the policy-making ranks, theorists such as Francis Fukuyama and his "end of history" ideas, as well as the legions who had celebrated the onset of globalism, tribalism and the dissipation of the state. But they, he allowed, had understood only some aspects of this new period. He was about to announce the "crucial, indeed a central, aspect" of what "global politics is likely to be in the coming years." Unhesitatingly he pressed on:

"It is my hypothesis that the fundamental source of conflict in this new world will not be primarily ideological or primarily economic. The great divisions among humankind and the dominating source of conflict will be cultural. Nation states will remain the most powerful actors in world affairs, but the principal conflicts of global politics will occur between nations and groups of different civilizations. The clash of civilizations will dominate global politics. The fault lines between civilizations will be the battle lines of the future."

Most of the argument in the pages that followed relied on a vague notion of something Huntington called "civilization identity" and "the interactions among seven or eight [sic] major civilizations," of which the conflict between two of them, Islam and the West, gets the lion's share of his attention. In this belligerent kind of thought, he relies heavily on a 1990 article by the veteran Orientalist Bernard Lewis, whose ideological colors are manifest in its title, "The Roots of Muslim Rage." In both articles, the personification of enormous entities called "the West" and "Islam" is recklessly affirmed, as if hugely complicated matters like identity and culture existed in a cartoonlike world where Popeye and Bluto bash each other mercilessly, with one always more virtuous pugilist getting the upper hand over his adversary. Certainly neither Huntington nor Lewis has much time to spare for the internal dynamics and plurality of every civilization, or for the fact that the major contest in most modern cultures concerns the definition or interpretation of each culture, or for the unattractive possibility that a great deal of demagogy and downright ignorance is involved in presuming to speak for a whole religion or civilization. No, the West is the West, and Islam Islam.

The challenge for Western policy-makers, says Huntington, is to make sure that the West gets stronger and fends off all the others, Islam in particular. More troubling is Huntington's assumption that his perspective, which is to survey the entire world from a perch outside all ordinary attachments and hidden loyalties, is the correct one, as if everyone else were scurrying around looking for the answers that he has already found. In fact, Huntington is an ideologist, someone who wants to make "civilizations" and "identities" into what they are not: shut-down, sealed-off entities that have been purged of the myriad currents and counter-currents that animate human history, and that over centuries have made it possible for that history not only to contain wars of religion and imperial conquest but also to be one of exchange, cross-fertilization and sharing. This far less visible history is ignored in the rush to highlight the ludicrously compressed and constricted warfare that "the clash of civilizations" argues is the reality. When he published his book by the same title in 1996, Huntington tried to give his argument a little more subtlety and many, many more footnotes; all he did, however, was confuse himself and demonstrate what a clumsy writer and inelegant thinker he was.

The basic paradigm of West versus the rest (the cold war opposition reformulated) remained untouched, and this is what has persisted, often insidiously and implicitly, in discussion since the terrible events of September 11. The carefully planned and horrendous, pathologically motivated suicide attack and mass slaughter by a small group of deranged militants has been turned into proof of Huntington's thesis. Instead of seeing it for what it is—the capture of big ideas (I use the word loosely) by a tiny band of crazed fanatics for criminal purposes—international luminaries from former Pakistani Prime Minister Benazir Bhutto to Italian Prime Minister Silvio Berlusconi have pontificated about Islam's troubles, and in the latter's case have used Huntington's ideas to rant on about the West's superiority, how "we" have Mozart and Michelangelo and they don't. (Berlusconi has since made a half-hearted apology for his insult to "Islam.")

Labels like Islam and the West mislead and confuse the mind, which is trying to make sense of a disorderly reality.

But why not instead see parallels, admittedly less spectacular in their destructiveness, for Osama bin Laden and his followers in cults like the Branch Davidians or the disciples of the Rev. Jim Jones at Guyana or the Japanese Aum Shinrikyo? Even the normally sober British weekly *The Economist*, in its issue of September 22–28, can't resist reaching for the vast generalization, praising Huntington extravagantly for his "cruel and sweeping, but nonetheless acute" observations about Islam. "Today," the journal says with unseemly solemnity, Huntington writes that "the world's billion or so Muslims are 'convinced of the superiority of their culture, and obsessed with the inferiority of their power.'" Did he canvas 100 Indonesians, 200 Moroccans, 500 Egyptians and fifty Bosnians? Even if he did, what sort of sample is that?

Uncountable are the editorials in every American and European newspaper and magazine of note adding to this vocabulary of gigantism and apocalypse, each use of which is plainly designed not to edify but to inflame the reader's indignant passion as a member of the "West," and what we need to do. Churchillian rhetoric is used inappropriately by self-appointed combatants in the West's, and especially America's, war against its haters, despoilers, destroyers, with scant attention to complex histories that defy such reductiveness and have seeped from one territory into another, in the process overriding the boundaries that are supposed to separate us all into divided armed camps.

This is the problem with unedifying labels like Islam and the West: They mislead and confuse the mind, which is trying to make sense of a disorderly reality that won't be pigeonholed or strapped down as easily as all that. I remember interrupting a man who, after a lecture I had given at a West Bank university in 1994, rose from the audience and started to attack my ideas as "Western," as opposed to the strict Islamic ones he espoused. "Why are you wearing a suit and tie?" was the first retort that came to mind. "They're Western too." He sat down with an embarrassed smile on his face, but I recalled the incident when information on the September 11 terrorists started to come in: how they had mastered all the technical details required to inflict their homicidal evil on the World Trade Center, the Pentagon and the aircraft they had commandeered. Where does one draw the line between "Western" technology and, as Berlusconi declared, "Islam's" inability to be a part of "modernity"?

One cannot easily do so, of course. How finally inadequate are the labels, generalizations and cultural assertions. At some level, for instance, primitive passions and sophisticated know-how converge in ways that give the lie to a fortified boundary not only between "West" and "Islam" but also between past and present, us and them, to say nothing of the very concepts of identity and nationality about which there is unending disagreement and debate. A unilateral decision made to draw lines in the sand, to undertake crusades, to oppose their evil with our good, to extirpate terrorism and, in Paul Wolfowitz's nihilistic vocabulary, to end nations entirely, doesn't make the supposed entities any easier to see; rather, it speaks to how much simpler it is to make bellicose statements for the purpose of mobilizing collective passions than to reflect, examine, sort out what it is we are dealing with in reality, the interconnectedness of innumerable lives, "ours" as well as "theirs."

In a remarkable series of three articles published between January and March 1999 in *Dawn*, Pakistan's most respected weekly, the late Eqbal Ahmad, writing for a Muslim audience, analyzed what he called the roots of the religious right, coming down very harshly on the mutilations of Islam by absolutists and fanatical tyrants whose obsession with regulating personal behavior promotes "an Islamic order reduced to a penal code, stripped of its humanism, aesthetics, intellectual quests, and spiritual devotion." And this "entails an absolute assertion of one, generally de-contextualized, aspect of religion and a total disregard of another. The phenomenon distorts religion, debases tradition, and twists the political process wherever it unfolds." As a timely instance of this debasement, Ahmad proceeds first to present the rich, complex, pluralist meaning of the word *jihad* and then goes on to show that in the word's current confinement to indiscriminate war against presumed enemies, it is impossible "to recognize the Islamic—religion, society, culture, history or politics—as lived and experienced by Muslims through the ages." The modern Islamists, Ahmad concludes, are "concerned with power, not with the soul; with the mobilization of people for political purposes rather than with sharing and alleviating their sufferings and aspirations. Theirs is a very limited and time-bound political agenda." What has made matters worse is that similar distortions and zealotry occur in the "Jewish" and "Christian" universes of discourse.

The 'Clash of Civilizations' thesis is better for reinforcing self-pride than for a critical understanding of the interdependence of our time.

It was Conrad, more powerfully than any of his readers at the end of the nineteenth century could have imagined, who understood that the distinctions between civilized London and "the heart of darkness" quickly collapsed in extreme situations, and that the heights of European civilization could instantaneously fall into the most barbarous practices without preparation or transition. And it was Conrad also, in *The Secret Agent* (1907), who described terrorism's affinity for abstractions like "pure science" (and by extension for "Islam" or "the West"), as well as the terrorist's ultimate moral degradation.

For there are closer ties between apparently warring civilizations than most of us would like to believe; both Freud and Nietzsche showed how the traffic across carefully maintained, even policed boundaries moves with often terrifying ease. But then such fluid ideas, full of ambiguity and skepticism about notions that we hold on to, scarcely furnish us with suitable, practical guidelines for situations such as the one we face now. Hence the altogether more reassuring battle orders (a crusade, good versus evil, freedom against fear, etc.) drawn out of Huntington's alleged opposition between Islam and the West, from which official discourse drew its vocabulary in the first days after the September 11 attacks. There's since been a noticeable de-escalation in that discourse, but to judge from the steady amount of hate speech and actions, plus reports of law enforcement efforts directed against Arabs, Muslims and Indians all over the country, the paradigm stays on.

One further reason for its persistence is the increased presence of Muslims all over Europe and the United States. Think of the populations today of France, Italy, Germany, Spain, Britain, America, even Sweden, and you must concede that Islam is no longer on the fringes of the West but at its center. But what is so threatening about that presence? Buried in the collective culture are memories of the first great Arab-Islamic conquests, which began in the seventh century and which, as the celebrated Belgian historian Henri Pirenne wrote in his landmark book *Mohammed and Charlemagne* (1939), shattered once and for all the ancient unity of the Mediterranean, destroyed the Christian-Roman synthesis and gave rise to a new civilization dominated by northern powers (Germany and Carolingian France) whose mission, he seemed to be saying, is to resume defense of the "West" against its historical-cultural enemies. What Pierenne left out, alas, is that in the creation of this new line of defense the West drew on the humanism, science, philosophy, sociology and historiography of Islam, which had already interposed itself between Charlemagne's world and classical antiquity. Islam is inside from the start, as even Dante, great enemy of Mohammed, had to concede when he placed the Prophet at the very heart of his *Inferno*.

Then there is the persisting legacy of monotheism itself, the Abrahamic religions, as Louis Massignon aptly called them. Beginning with Judaism and Christianity, each is a successor haunted by what came before; for Muslims, Islam fulfills and ends the line of prophecy. There is still no decent history or demystification of the many-sided contest among these three followers—not one of them by any means a monolithic, unified camp—of the most jealous of all gods, even though the bloody modern convergence on Palestine furnishes a rich secular instance of what has been so tragically irreconcilable about them. Not surprisingly, then, Muslims and Christians speak readily of crusades and *jihads*, both of them eliding the Judaic presence with often sublime insouciance. Such an agenda, says Eqbal Ahmad, is "very reassuring to the men and women who are stranded in the middle of the ford, between the deep waters of tradition and modernity."

But we are all swimming in those waters, Westerners and Muslims and others alike. And since the waters are part of the ocean of history, trying to plow or divide them with barriers is futile. These are tense times, but it is better to think in terms of powerful and powerless communities, the secular politics of reason and ignorance, and universal principles of justice and injustice, than to wander off in search of vast abstractions that may give momentary satisfaction but little self-knowledge or informed analysis. "The Clash of Civilizations" thesis is a gimmick like "The War of the Worlds," better for reinforcing defensive self-pride than for critical understanding of the bewildering interdependence of our time.

Edward W. Said, University Professor of English and Comparative Literature at Columbia University, is the author of more than twenty books, the most recent of which is Power, Politics, and Culture (Pantheon). *Copyright Edward W. Said, 2001.*

Islam's tensions:

Enemies within, enemies without

Islam remains a tolerant faith, despite its apparent new ferocity

CAIRO

Like every great religion, Islam is, and has been for all but the first of its 1,400 years, a varied and fractious faith. Muslims do not differ on essentials such as the oneness of God, the literalness of his word as voiced by Muhammad, or the duty to perform prayer, charity, fasting, pilgrimage and *jihad*, which means something like "struggle". There is not much debate over the first four of these duties, though quite a few Muslims choose to ignore them. But the last, which embraces everything from resisting temptation to attacking Islam's perceived enemies, is a much more contentious term.

Nearly all Muslims, almost all the time, lean to the softer meaning. They think of *jihad* as striving to perfect oneself, or to give hope to others by good example. In short, they get on with their lives much like anyone else. When the faith is under threat, however, some may be inspired to go further—to fight to expel crusaders from Palestine, say, as Muslims did in the 13th century, or to kick Russians out of Afghanistan, as they did in the 1980s. A few may go to greater extremes. Some, for example, follow the teachings of a 14th-century firebrand, Ibn Taymiyya, who stated unequivocally, "*jihad* against the disbelievers is the most noble of actions." And some of these, a tiny radical minority, may go so far as to plot carefully, and execute fearlessly,

a suicidal slaughter of thousands of innocents in the name of Allah.

Yet such a calamitous misdirection of energy can occur only under certain conditions. The sense that the faith is under threat must be strong enough, and widely enough perceived, to provoke real fear and anger. Leaders—men with the charisma and credibility to warp the words of Islam's founding texts to suit their own convictions—are needed to channel noble thoughts into ghastly deeds. There must be a pool of recruits who are so frustrated by, or so blinded to, the other options of this world that their minds remain concentrated on the next. And there must be proper logistical underpinnings: easy access to transport, communications and information, and skill at using them.

Tragically for America, and just as tragically for Islam, the modern age has generated all these conditions at once. A modicum of money and education can now provide anyone with the means of rapid movement, organisation and proselytising, as well as the capacity to cause immense destruction. A sense of being under threat is now shared, to some degree, by many sects in many religions. From Buddhist monks to Jewish Hasidim to left-wing Luddites, there is no shortage of voices decrying such alleged ills as materialism, secularisation, sexual permissiveness, or the drowning of cultural variety in the tide of globalisation.

Because most such groups are marginal, their Utopian yearnings are diluted. In the case of Muslims, however, history and numbers combine to magnify the grudge many hold against their present fate. The judgment of Samuel Huntington, the Harvard scholar who ignited controversy with a 1993 article entitled "The Clash of Civilisations", was cruel and sweeping, but nonetheless acute. Today, he wrote, the world's billion or so Muslims are "convinced of the superiority of their culture, and obsessed with the inferiority of their power."

Post-colonial wounds

European colonialism was not entirely a bad thing. It created nations where there were none before, in America and Africa. It shocked the resilient old cultures of Asia into modernity, and ended up freeing India's Hindus from centuries of Muslim overlordship. But colonialism and its aftermath fractured the Islamic world both horizontally and vertically. Rival states replaced its congenially porous old empires. Impatient, western-minded governments dropped Islamic law in favour of imported systems. This brought genuine progress, yet it also cut the chain of rich tradition that linked present to past, and ruptured the old Islamic notion of unity between religion and state which, in theory at least, tied the temporal to the eternal. To the pious, Islam seemed to have been cast adrift from its own history.

Modern Islamism, a term that describes a broad range of political movements, most of them peaceable, some aggressive, is a product of this sensibility. From Egypt's venerable Muslim Brotherhood, founded in 1928, to the brutal *maquisards* of present-day Algeria, what unites these groups is a determination to save Islam, to recapture the reins of its history. Like the religious right in the United States, or for that matter in Israel, Islamists seek to return religion to centrality, to make faith the determining component of identity and behaviour.

The past three decades have provided fertile ground for these ideas. Nearly every Muslim country has experienced the kind of social stress that generates severe doubt, discontent and despair. Populations have exploded. Cities, once the abode of the privileged, have been overrun by impoverished, disoriented provincials. The authoritarian nature of many post-colonial governments, the frequent failure of their great plans, and their continued dependence on western money, arms and science have discredited their brand of secularism. The intrusion of increasingly liberal western ways, brought by radio, films, television, the Internet and tourism, has engendered schism by seducing some and alienating others. Growing gaps in wealth, both within Muslim societies and between the poor nations of the Islamic world and the oil-rich Arabian Gulf, have spawned resentment, too.

Islam has also suffered external stresses. Although the post-colonial fires troubling much of the globe have now subsided, the Muslim world's wounds continue to fester. In the past decade alone a score of conflicts have simmered on its borders. These range from ethnic war in the Balkans, to militant insurgency in the Philippines, to what sometimes looks like anti-colonial revolts in Chechnya, Kashmir and the Palestinian territories.

The Palestinian struggle, in particular, has stoked rage against not only Israel and its backers, pre-eminently the United States, but also the feebleness of Arab and Muslim governments in the face of them. Even conflicts that did not at first involve religious adversaries have, in the minds of many, taken on religious overtones. America's continuing strikes against Iraq and, in particular, the persistence of sanctions, have aroused widespread anger.

This sudden accumulation of woes has reinforced the notion that Islam itself is somehow in danger. For the first time in the modern world, a sense of Islam as a whole, as a nation or a polity, has marched back upon the stage.

A stiffening orthodoxy

In response to all these pressures, the outward nature of the faith has changed. A religion that once included diverse strands of mysticism, and even of mild paganism—especially in countries like Indonesia, whither Islam was borne by traders, not conquerors—has begun to harden around a very rigid textualism. Money, migrant labour and the pilgrimage to Mecca have spread far and wide the Saudis' bleak desert version of Islam. To the dismay of many Muslims, this doctrine, one stripped of subtlety, nuance and compromise, is being presented as a new orthodoxy.

This hard-edged modern Islam has produced a new kind of preacher. As the clerics of the Ottoman empire foresaw five centuries ago when they banned printing, the spread of literacy has ended the professional scholars' monopoly on interpreting religion. Their hold, already undermined by their association with unpopular regimes, is further weakened by the dispersion of Muslims in small communities around the globe, communities that are often isolated among non-believers. Amid the general dislocation, staid supporters of the older tolerant ways are often shouted down. The increasingly dominant voice is an angry one that sees Islam as a beleaguered faith, surrounded by enemies without and within.

And yet the emotionally charged, electronically amplified tone of today's mosque sermons still has only limited influence. Islam remains a diverse and broadly tolerant faith. A growing number of Muslims, better educated than their forebears and far more exposed to alternative ways of life through television and the Internet, rather like much that is on offer. They want a chance, naturally, to have a bigger share in the modern world's material comforts. More important, many of them are attracted by the idea of individual responsibility, the notion that each person has the right to think his or her own way through life's problems. The Muslim world, in short, may be starting to grope its way towards its own Reformation.

At the same time, the painful experience of countries such as Iran, Algeria and Egypt has convinced many that excessive zeal is misguided. The Taliban's blinkered atavism, for example, is abhorrent to nearly everyone else. Its destruction of ancient Buddhist monuments earlier this year was condemned by virtually every Muslim authority in the rest of the world.

In Arab countries generally, the ultra-radical fringe has seemed to be shrinking. Most Arab governments have long since recognised the threat it poses. Concerted and often brutal policing has decapitated most of the extreme groups. Some organisations that were once considered dangerously radical, such as Lebanon's Shia militia, Hizbullah, have moved into the mainstream. Even Egypt's Gamaa Islamiya, an organisation that wrought havoc in the early 1990s, has renounced violence, although its jailed leader has since wavered. To most Muslims, the contention of Osama bin Laden and his followers that God has ordered Muslims to kill Americans is not only silly, but presumption bordering on heresy.

In all but a few cases, the inroads made by Islamism are reflected not in violent extremism, but in an increased religious consciousness. Muslims today are in general more knowledgeable about their faith, more attuned to its demands, and more assertive about their identity.

But which direction does this assertiveness take? Does it tend to inward *jihad*, or offensive *jihad*? This is a question that must be settled, in the long run, by the people of the Muslim world themselves, and by their success or failure at making their societies better ones to live in. If they succeed, there will be no place for the bin Ladens of this world. Historically, Islam has reserved its greatest wrath not for outsiders, but for heretics.

GHOSTS OF OUR PAST

To win the war on terrorism, we first need to understand its roots

BY KAREN ARMSTRONG

ABOUT A HUNDRED YEARS AGO, almost every leading Muslim intellectual was in love with the West, which at that time meant Europe. America was still an unknown quantity. Politicians and journalists in India, Egypt, and Iran wanted their countries to be just like Britain or France; philosophers, poets, and even some of the *ulama* (religious scholars) tried to find ways of reforming Islam according to the democratic model of the West. They called for a nation state, for representational government, for the disestablishment of religion, and for constitutional rights. Some even claimed that the Europeans were better Muslims than their own fellow countrymen since the Koran teaches that the resources of a society must be shared as fairly as possible, and in the European nations there was beginning to be a more equitable sharing of wealth.

So what happened in the intervening years to transform all of that admiration and respect into the hatred that incited the acts of terror that we witnessed on September 11? It is not only terrorists who feel this anger and resentment, although they do so to an extreme degree. Throughout the Muslim world there is widespread bitterness against America, even among pragmatic and well-educated businessmen and professionals, who may sincerely deplore the recent atrocities, condemn them as evil, and feel sympathy with the victims, but who still resent the way the Western powers have behaved in their countries. This atmosphere is highly conducive to extremism, especially now that potential terrorists have seen the catastrophe that it is possible to inflict using only the simplest of weapons.

Even if President Bush and our allies succeed in eliminating Osama bin Laden and his network, hundreds more terrorists will rise up to take their place unless we in the West address the root cause of this hatred. This task must be an essential part of the war against terrorism.

We cannot understand the present crisis without taking into account the painful process of modernization. In the 16th century, the countries of Western Europe and, later, the American colonies embarked on what historians have called "the Great Western Transformation." Until then, all the great societies were based upon a surplus of agriculture and so were economically vulnerable; they soon found that they had grown beyond their limited resources. The new Western societies, though, were based upon technology and the constant reinvestment of capital. They found that they could reproduce their resources indefinitely, and so could afford to experiment with new ideas and products. In Western cultures today, when a new kind of computer is invented, all the old office equipment is thrown out. In the old agrarian societies, any project that required such frequent change of the basic infrastructure was likely to be shelved. Originality was not encouraged; instead people had to concentrate on preserving what had been achieved.

So while the Great Western Transformation was exciting and gave the people of the West more freedom, it demanded fundamental change at every level: social, political, intellectual, and religious. Not surprisingly, the period of transition was traumatic and violent. As the early modern states became more centralized and efficient, draconian measures were often required to weld hitherto disparate kingdoms together. Some minority groups, such as the Catholics in England and the Jews in Spain, were persecuted or deported. There were acts of genocide, terrible wars of religion, the exploitation of workers in factories, the despoliation of the countryside, and anomie and spiritual malaise in the newly industrialized mega-cities.

Successful modern societies found, by trial and error, that they had to be democratic. The reasons were many. In order to preserve the momentum of the continually expanding economy, more people had to be involved—even in a humble capacity as printers, clerks, or factory workers. To do these jobs, they needed to be educated, and once they became educated, they began to demand political rights. In order to draw upon all of a society's resources, modern countries also found they had to bring outgroups, such as the Jews and women, into the mainstream. Countries like those in Eastern Europe that did not become secular, tolerant, and democratic fell behind. But those that did fulfill these norms, including Britain and France, became so powerful that no agrarian, traditional society, such as those of the Islamic countries, could stand against them.

In the West, we have completed the modernizing process and have forgotten what we had to go through. We view the Islamic countries as inherently backward and do not realize we're seeing imperfectly modernized societies.

Today we are witnessing similar upheaval in developing countries, including those in the Islamic world, that are making their own painful journey to modernity. In the Middle East, we see constant political turmoil. There have been revolutions, such as the 1952 coup of the Free Officers in Egypt and the Islamic Revolution in Iran in 1979. Autocratic rulers predominate in this region because the modernizing process is not yet sufficiently advanced to provide the conditions for a fully developed democracy.

In the West, we have completed the modernizing process and have forgotten what we had to go through, so we do not always understand the difficulty of this transition. We tend to imagine that we have always been in the van of progress, and we see the Islamic countries as inherently backward. We have imagined that they are held back by their religion, and do not realize that what we are actually seeing is an imperfectly modernized society.

The Muslim world has had an especially problematic experience with modernity because its people have had to modernize so rapidly, in 50 years instead of the 300 years that it took the Western world. Nevertheless, this in itself would not have been an insuperable obstacle. Japan, for example, has created its own

highly successful version of modernity. But Japan had one huge advantage over most of the Islamic countries: It had never been colonized. In the Muslim world, modernity did not bring freedom and independence; it came in a context of political subjection.

Modern society is of its very nature progressive, and by the 19th century the new economies of Western Europe needed a constantly expanding market for the goods that funded their cultural enterprises. Once the home countries were saturated, new markets were sought abroad. In 1798, Napoleon defeated the Mamelukes, Egypt's military rulers, in the Battle of the Pyramids near Cairo. Between 1830 and 1915, the European powers also occupied Algeria, Aden, Tunisia, the Sudan, Libya, and Morocco—all Muslim countries. These new colonies provided raw materials for export, which were fed into European industry. In return, they received cheap manufactured goods, which naturally destroyed local industry.

This new impotence was extremely disturbing for the Muslim countries. Until this point, Islam had been a religion of success. Within a hundred years of the death of the Prophet Muhammad in 632, the Muslims ruled an empire that stretched from the Himalayas to the Pyrenees. By the 15th century, Islam was the greatest world power—not dissimilar to the United States today. When Europeans began to explore the rest of the globe at the beginning of the Great Western Transformation, they found an Islamic presence almost everywhere they went: in the Middle East, India, Persia, Southeast Asia, China, and Japan. In the 16th century, when Europe was in the early stages of its rise to power, the Ottoman Empire [which ruled Turkey, the Middle East, and North Africa] was probably the most powerful state in the world. But once the great powers of Europe had reformed their military, economic, and political structures according to the modern norm, the Islamic countries could put up no effective resistance.

Muslims would not be human if they did not resent being subjugated this way. The colonial powers treated the natives with contempt, and it was not long before Muslims discovered that their new rulers despised their religious traditions. True, the Europeans brought many improvements to their colonies, such as modern medicine, education, and technology, but these were sometimes a mixed blessing.

Thus, the Suez Canal, initiated by the French consul Ferdinand de Lesseps, was a disaster for Egypt, which had to provide all the money, labor, and materials as well as donate 200 square miles of Egyptian territory gratis, and yet the shares of the Canal Company were all held by Europeans. The immense outlay helped to bankrupt Egypt, and this gave Britain a pretext to set up a military occupation there in 1882.

Railways were installed in the colonies, but they rarely benefited the local people. Instead they were designed to further the colonialists' own projects. And the missionary schools often taught the children to despise their own culture, with the result that many felt they belonged neither to the West nor to the Islamic world. One of the most scarring effects of colonialism is the rift that still exists between those who have had a Western education and those who have not and remain perforce stuck in the premodern ethos. To this day, the Westernized elites of these countries and the more traditional classes simply cannot understand one another.

After World War II, Britain and France became secondary powers and the United States became the leader of the Western world. Even though the Islamic countries were no longer colonies but were nominally independent, America still controlled their destinies. During the Cold War, the United States sought allies in the region by supporting unsavory governments and unpopular leaders, largely to protect its oil interests. For example, in 1953, after Shah Muhammad Reza Pahlavi had been deposed and forced to leave Iran, he was put back on the throne in a coup engineered by British Intelligence and the CIA. The United States continued to support the Shah, even though he denied Iranians human rights that most Americans take for granted.

Fundamentalists are convinced that modern, secular society is trying to wipe out the true faith and religious values. When people feel that they are fighting for their very survival, they often lash out violently.

Saddam Hussein, who became the president of Iraq in 1979, was also a protégé of the United States, which literally allowed him to get away with murder, most notably the chemical attack against the Kurdish population. It was only after the invasion in 1990 of Kuwait, a critical oil-producing state, that Hussein incurred the enmity of America and its allies. Many Muslims resent the way America has continued to support unpopular rulers, such as President Hosni Mubarak of Egypt and the Saudi royal family. Indeed, Osama bin Laden was himself a protégé of the West, which was happy to support and fund his fighters in the struggle for Afghanistan against Soviet Russia. Too often, the Western powers have not considered the long-term consequences of their actions. After the Soviets had pulled out of Afghanistan, for example, no help was forthcoming for the devastated country, whose ensuing chaos made it possible for the Taliban to come to power.

When the United States supports autocratic rulers, its proud assertion of democratic values has at best a hollow ring. What America seemed to be saying to Muslims was: "Yes, we have freedom and democracy, but you have to live under tyrannical governments." The creation of the state of Israel, the chief ally of the United States in the Middle East, has become a symbol of Muslim impotence before the Western powers, which seemed to feel no qualm about the hundreds of thousands of Palestinians who lost their homeland and either went into exile or lived under Israeli occupation. Rightly or wrongly, America's strong support for Israel is seen as proof that as far as the United States is concerned, Muslims are of no importance.

In their frustration, many have turned to Islam. The secularist and nationalist ideologies, which many Muslims had imported from the West, seemed to have failed them, and by the late 1960s Muslims throughout the Islamic world had begun to develop what we call fundamentalist movements.

Fundamentalism is a complex phenomenon and is by no means confined to the Islamic world. During the 20th century, most major religions developed this type of militant piety. Fundamentalism represents a rebellion against the secularist ethos of modernity. Wherever a Western-style society has established itself, a fundamentalist movement has developed alongside it. Fundamentalism is, therefore, a part of the modern scene. Although fundamentalists often claim that they are returning to a golden age of the past, these movements could have taken root in no time other than our own.

Fundamentalists believe that they are under threat. Every fundamentalist movement—in Judaism, Christianity, and Islam—is convinced that modern, secular society is trying to wipe out the true faith and religious values. Fundamentalists believe that they are fighting for survival, and when people feel their backs are to the wall, they often lash out violently. This is especially the case when there is conflict in the region.

The vast majority of fundamentalists do not take part in acts of violence, of course. But those who do utterly distort the faith that they purport to defend. In their fear and anxiety about the encroachments of the secular world, fundamentalists—be they Jewish, Christian, or Muslim—tend to downplay the compassionate teachings of their scripture and overemphasize the more belligerent passages. In so doing, they often fall into moral nihilism, as is the case of the suicide bomber or hijacker. To kill even one person in the name of God is blasphemy; to massacre thousands of innocent men, women, and children is an obscene perversion of religion itself.

Osama bin Laden subscribes roughly to the fundamentalist vision of the Egyptian ideologue Sayyid Qutb, who was executed by President Nasser in 1966. Qutb developed his militant ideology in the concentration camps in which he, and thousands of other members of the Muslim Brotherhood, were imprisoned by Nasser. After 15 years of torture in these prisons, Qutb became convinced that secularism was a great evil and that it was a Muslim's first duty to overthrow rulers such as Nasser, who paid only lip service to Islam.

Bin Laden's first target was the government of Saudi Arabia; he has also vowed to overthrow the secularist governments of Egypt and Jordan and the Shiite Republic of Iran. Fundamentalism, in every faith, always begins as an intra-religious movement; it is directed at first against one's own countrymen or co-religionists. Only at a later stage do fundamentalists take on a foreign enemy, whom they feel to lie behind the ills of their own people. Thus in 1998 bin Laden issued his fatwa against the United States. But bin Laden holds no official position in the Islamic world; he simply is not entitled to issue such a fatwa, and has, like other fundamentalists, completely distorted the essential teachings of his faith.

The Koran insists that the only just war is one of self-defense, but the terrorists would claim that it is America which is the aggressor. They would point out that during the past year, hundreds of Palestinians have died in the conflict with Israel, America's ally; that Britain and America are still bombing Iraq; and that thousands of Iraqi civilians, many of them children, have died as a result of the American-led sanctions.

None of this, of course, excuses the September atrocities. These were evil actions, and it is essential that all those implicated in any way be brought to justice. But what can we do to prevent a repetition of this tragedy? As the towers of the World Trade Center crumbled, our world changed forever, and that means that we can never see things in the same way again. These events were an "apocalypse," a "revelation"—words that literally mean an "unveiling." They laid bare a reality that we had not seen clearly before. Part of that reality was Muslim rage, but the catastrophe showed us something else as well.

In Britain, until September 11, the main news story was the problem of asylum seekers. Every night, more than 90 refugees from the developing world make desperate attempts to get into Britain. There is now a strong armed presence in England's ports. The United States and other Western countries also have a problem with illegal immigrants. It is almost as though we in the First World have been trying to keep the "other" world at bay. But as the September Apocalypse showed, if we try to ignore the plight of that other world, it will come to us in devastating ways.

So we in the First World must develop a "one world" mentality in the coming years. Americans have often assumed that they were protected by the great oceans surrounding the United States. As a result, they have not always been very well-informed about other parts of the globe. But the September Apocalypse and the events that followed have shown that this isolation has come to an end, and revealed America's terrifying vulnerability. This is deeply frightening, and it will have a profound effect upon the American psyche. But this tragedy could be turned to good, if we in the First World cultivate a new sympathy with other peoples who have experienced a similar helplessness: in Rwanda, in Lebanon, or in Srebrenica.

We cannot leave the fight against terrorism solely to our politicians or to our armies. In Europe and America, ordinary citizens must find out more about the rest of the world. We must make ourselves understand, at a deep level, that it is not only Muslims who resent America and the West; that many people in non-Muslim countries, while not condoning these atrocities, may be dry-eyed about the collapse of those giant towers, which represented a power, wealth, and security to which they could never hope to aspire.

We must find out about foreign ideologies and other religions like Islam. And we must also acquire a full knowledge of our own governments' foreign policies, using our democratic rights to oppose them, should we deem this to be necessary. We have been warned that the war against terror may take years, and so will the development of this "one world" mentality, which could do as much, if not more, than our fighter planes to create a safer and more just world.

Karen Armstrong is the author of The Battle for God: A History of Fundamentalism *and* Islam: A Brief History.

Lifting the Veil
Understanding the Roots of Islamic Militancy

Henry Munson

In the wake of the attacks of September 11, 2001, many intellectuals have argued that Muslim extremists like Osama bin Laden despise the United States primarily because of its foreign policy. Conversely, US President George Bush's administration and its supporters have insisted that extremists loathe the United States simply because they are religious fanatics who "hate our freedoms." These conflicting views of the roots of militant Islamic hostility toward the United States lead to very different policy prescriptions. If US policies have caused much of this hostility, it would make sense to change those policies, if possible, to dilute the rage that fuels Islamic militancy. If, on the other hand, the hostility is the result of religious fanaticism, then the use of brute force to suppress fanaticism would appear to be a sensible course of action.

Groundings for Animosity

Public opinion polls taken in the Islamic world in recent years provide considerable insight into the roots of Muslim hostility toward the United States, indicating that for the most part, this hostility has less to do with cultural or religious differences than with US policies in the Arab world. In February and March 2003, Zogby International conducted a survey on behalf of Professor Shibley Telhami of the University of Maryland involving 2,620 men and women in Egypt, Jordan, Lebanon, Morocco, and Saudi Arabia. Most of those surveyed had "unfavorable attitudes" toward the United States and said that their hostility to the United States was based primarily on US policy rather than on their values. This was true of 67 percent of the Saudis surveyed. In Egypt, however, only 46 percent said their hostility resulted from US policy, while 43 percent attributed their attitudes to their values as Arabs. This is surprising given that the prevailing religious values in Saudi Arabia are more conservative than in Egypt. Be that as it may, a plurality of people in all the countries surveyed said that their hostility toward the United States was primarily based on their opposition to US policy.

The issue that arouses the most hostility in the Middle East toward the United States is the Israeli-Palestinian conflict and what Muslims perceive as US responsibility for the suffering of the Palestinians. A similar Zogby International survey from the summer of 2001 found that more than 80 percent of the respondents in Egypt, Kuwait, Lebanon, and Saudi Arabia ranked the Palestinian issue as one of the three issues of greatest importance to them. A survey of Muslim "opinion leaders" released by the Pew Research Center for the People and the Press in December 2001 also found that the US position on the Israeli-Palestinian conflict was the main source of hostility toward the United States.

It is true that Muslim hostility toward Israel is often expressed in terms of anti-Semitic stereotypes and conspiracy theories—think, for example, of the belief widely-held in the Islamic world that Jews were responsible for the terrorists attacks of September 11, 2001. Muslim governments and educators need to further eliminate anti-Semitic bias in the Islamic world. However, it would be a serious mistake to dismiss Muslim and Arab hostility toward Israel as simply a matter of anti-Semitism. In the context of Jewish history, Israel represents liberation. In the context of Palestinian history, it represents subjugation. There will always be a gap between how the West and how the Muslim societies perceive Israel. There will also always be some Muslims (like Osama bin Laden) who will refuse to accept any solution to the Israeli-Palestinian conflict other than the destruction of the state of Israel. That said, if the United States is serious about winning the so-called "war on terror," then resolution of the Israeli-Palestinian conflict should be among its top priorities in the Middle East.

Eradicating, or at least curbing, Palestinian terrorism entails reducing the humiliation, despair, and rage that drive many Palestinians to support militant Islamic groups like Hamas and Islamic Jihad. When soldiers at an Israeli checkpoint prevented Ahmad Qurei (Abu al Ala), one of the principal negotiators of the Oslo accords and president of the Palestinian Authority's parliament, from traveling from Gaza to his home on the West Bank, he declared, "Soon, I too will join Hamas." Qurei's words reflected his outrage at the subjugation of his people and the humiliation that Palestinians experience every day at the checkpoints that surround their homes. Defeating groups like Hamas requires diluting the rage that fuels them. Relying on force alone tends to increase rather than weaken their appeal. This is demonstrated by some of the unintended consequences of the US-led invasion and occupation of Iraq in the spring of 2003.

On June 3, 2003, the Pew Research Center for the People and the Press released a report entitled *Views of a*

Changing World June 2003. This study was primarily based on a survey of nearly 16,000 people in 21 countries (including the Palestinian Authority) from April 28 to May 15, 2003, shortly after the fall of Saddam Hussein's regime. The survey results were supplemented by data from earlier polls, especially a survey of 38,000 people in 44 countries in 2002. The study found a marked increase in Muslim hostility toward the United States from 2002 to 2003. In the summer of 2002, 61 percent of Indonesians held a favorable view of the United States. By May of 2003, only 15 percent did. During the same period of time, the decline in Turkey was from 30 percent to 15 percent, and in Jordan it was from 25 percent to one percent.

Indeed, the Bush administration's war on terror has been a major reason for the increased hostility toward the United States. The Pew Center's 2003 survey found that few Muslims support this war. Only 23 percent of Indonesians did so in May of 2003, down from 31 percent in the summer of 2002. In Turkey, support dropped from 30 percent to 22 percent. In Pakistan, support dropped from 30 percent to 16 percent, and in Jordan from 13 percent to two percent. These decreases reflect overwhelming Muslim opposition to the war in Iraq, which most Muslims saw as yet another act of imperial subjugation of Muslims by the West.

The 2003 Zogby International poll found that most Arabs believe that the United States attacked Iraq to gain control of Iraqi oil and to help Israel. Over three-fourths of all those surveyed felt that oil was a major reason for the war. More than three-fourths of the Saudis and Jordanians said that helping Israel was a major reason, as did 72 percent of the Moroccans and over 50 percent of the Egyptians and Lebanese. Most Arabs clearly do not believe that the United States overthrew Saddam Hussein out of humanitarian motives. Even in Iraq itself, where there was considerable support for the war, most people attribute the war to the US desire to gain control of Iraqi oil and help Israel.

Not only has the Bush administration failed to win much Muslim support for its war on terrorism, its conduct of the war has generated a dangerous backlash. Most Muslims see the US fight against terror as a war against the Islamic world. The 2003 Pew survey found that over 70 percent of Indonesians, Pakistanis, and Turks were either somewhat or very worried about a potential US threat to their countries, as were over half of Jordanians and Kuwaitis.

This sense of a US threat is linked to the 2003 Pew report's finding of widespread support for Osama bin Laden. The survey of April and May 2003 found that over half those surveyed in Indonesia, Jordan, and the Palestinian Authority, and almost half those surveyed in Morocco and Pakistan, listed bin Laden as one of the three world figures in whom they had the most confidence "to do the right thing." For most US citizens, this admiration for the man responsible for the attacks of September 11, 2001, is incomprehensible. But no matter how outrageous this widespread belief may be, it is vitally important to understand its origins. If one does not understand why people think the way they do, one cannot induce them to think differently. Similarly, if one does not understand why people act as they do, one cannot hope to induce them to act differently.

The Appeal of Osama bin Laden

Osama bin Laden first engaged in violence because of the occupation of a Muslim country by an "infidel" superpower. He did not fight the Russians in Afghanistan because he hated their values or their freedoms, but because they had occupied a Muslim land. He participated in and supported the Afghan resistance to the Soviet occupation from 1979 to 1989, which ended with the withdrawal of the Russians. Bin Laden saw this war as legitimate resistance to foreign occupation. At the same time, he saw it as a *jihad*, or holy war, on behalf of Muslims oppressed by infidels.

When Saddam Hussein invaded Kuwait in August 1990, bin Laden offered to lead an army to defend Saudi Arabia. The Saudis rejected this offer and instead allowed the United States to establish bases in their kingdom, leading to bin Laden's active opposition to the United States. One can only speculate what bin Laden would have done for the rest of his life if the United States had not stationed hundreds of thousands of US troops in Saudi Arabia in 1990. Conceivably, bin Laden's hostility toward the United States might have remained passive and verbal instead of active and violent. All we can say with certainty is that the presence of US troops in Saudi Arabia did trigger bin Laden's holy war against the United States. It was no accident that the bombing of two US embassies in Africa on August 7, 1998, marked the eighth anniversary of the introduction of US forces into Saudi Arabia as part of Operation Desert Storm.

Part of bin Laden's opposition to the presence of US military presence in Saudi Arabia resulted from the fact that US troops were infidels on or near holy Islamic ground. Non-Muslims are not allowed to enter Mecca and Medina, the two holiest places in Islam, and they are allowed to live in Saudi Arabia only as temporary residents. Bin Laden is a reactionary Wahhabi Muslim who undoubtedly does hate all non-Muslims. But that hatred was not in itself enough to trigger his *jihad* against the United States.

Indeed, bin Laden's opposition to the presence of US troops in Saudi Arabia had a nationalistic and anti-imperialist tone. In 1996, he declared that Saudi Arabia had become an American colony. There is nothing specifically religious or fundamentalist about this assertion. In his book *Chronique d'une Guerre d'Orient*, Gilles Kepel describes a wealthy whiskey-drinking Saudi who left part of his fortune to bin Laden because he alone "was defending the honor of the country, reduced in his eyes to a simple American protectorate."

In 1996, bin Laden issued his first major manifesto, entitled a "Declaration of Jihad against the Americans Occupying the Land of the Two Holy Places." The very title focuses on the presence of US troops in Saudi Arabia, which bin Laden calls an "occupation." But this manifesto also refers to other examples of what bin Laden sees as the oppression of Muslims by infidels. "It is no secret that the people of Islam have suffered from the oppression, injustice, and aggression of the alliance of Jews and Christians and their collaborators to the point that the blood of the Muslims became the cheapest and their wealth was loot in the hands of the enemies," he writes. "Their blood was spilled in Palestine and Iraq."

Bin Laden has referred to the suffering of the Palestinians and the Iraqis (especially with respect to the deaths caused by sanctions) in all of his public statements since at least the mid-1990s. His 1996 "Declaration of Jihad" is no exception. Nonetheless, it primarily focuses on the idea that the Saudi regime has "lost all legitimacy" because it "has permitted the enemies of the Islamic community, the Crusader American forces, to occupy our land for many years." In this 1996 text, bin Laden even contends that the members of the Saudi royal family are apostates because they helped infidels fight the Muslim Iraqis in the Persian Gulf War of 1991.

A number of neo-conservatives have advocated the overthrow of the Saudi regime because of its support for terrorism. It is true that the Saudis have funded militant Islamic movements. It is also true that Saudi textbooks and teachers often encourage hatred of infidels and allow the extremist views of bin Laden to thrive. It is also probably true that members of the Saudi royal family have financially supported terrorist groups. The fact remains, however, that bin Laden and his followers in Al Qaeda have themselves repeatedly called for the overthrow of the Saudi regime, saying that it has turned Saudi Arabia into "an American colony."

If the United States were to send troops to Saudi Arabia once again, this time to overthrow the Saudi regime itself, the main beneficiaries would be bin Laden and those who think like him. On January 27, 2002, a *New York Times* article referenced a Saudi intelligence survey conducted in October 2001 that showed that 95 percent of educated Saudis between the ages of 25 and 41 supported bin Laden. If the United States were to overthrow the Saudi regime, such people would lead a guerrilla war that US forces would inevitably find themselves fighting. This war would attract recruits from all over the Islamic world outraged by the desecration of "the land of the two holy places." Given that US forces are already fighting protracted guerrilla wars in Iraq and Afghanistan, starting a third one in Saudi Arabia would not be the most effective way of eradicating terror in the Middle East.

Those who would advocate the overthrow of the Saudi regime by US troops seem to forget why bin Laden began his holy war against the United States in the first place. They also seem to forget that no one is more committed to the overthrow of the Saudi regime than bin Laden himself. Saudi Arabia is in dire need of reform, but yet another US occupation of a Muslim country is not the way to make it happen.

In December 1998, Palestinian journalist Jamal Abd al Latif Isma'il asked bin Laden, "Who is Osama bin Laden, and what does he want?" After providing a brief history of his life, bin Laden responded to the second part of the question, "We demand that our land be liberated from the enemies, that our land be liberated from the Americans. God almighty, may He be praised, gave all living beings a natural desire to reject external intruders. Take chickens, for example. If an armed soldier enters a chicken's home wanting to attack it, it fights him even though it is just a chicken." For bin Laden and millions of other Muslims, the Afghans, the Chechens, the Iraqis, the Kashmiris, and the Palestinians are all just "chickens" defending their homes against the attacks of foreign soldiers.

In his videotaped message of October 7, 2001, after the attacks of September 11, 2001, bin Laden declared, "What America is tasting now is nothing compared to what we have been tasting for decades. For over 80 years our *umma* has been tasting this humiliation and this degradation. Its sons are killed, its blood is shed, its holy places are violated, and it is ruled by other than that which God has revealed. Yet no one hears. No one responds."

Bin Laden's defiance of the United States and his criticism of Muslim governments who ignore what most Muslims see as the oppression of the Palestinians, Iraqis, Chechens, and others, have made him a hero of Muslims who do not agree with his goal of a strictly Islamic state and society. Even young Arab girls in tight jeans praise bin Laden as an anti-imperialist hero. A young Iraqi woman and her Palestinian friends told Gilles Kepel in the fall of 2001, "He stood up to defend us. He is the only one."

Looking ahead

Feelings of impotence, humiliation, and rage currently pervade the Islamic world, especially the Muslim Middle East. The invasion and occupation of Iraq has exacerbated Muslim concerns about the United States. In this context, bin Laden is seen as a heroic Osama Maccabeus descending from his mountain cave to fight the infidel oppressors to whom the worldly rulers of the Islamic world bow and scrape.

The violent actions of Osama bin Laden and those who share his views are not simply caused by "hatred of Western freedoms." They result, in part at least, from US policies that have enraged the Muslim world. Certainly, Islamic zealots like bin Laden do despise many aspects of Western culture. They do hate "infidels" in general, and Jews in particular. Muslims do need to seriously examine the existence and perpetuation of such hatred in their societies and cultures. But invading and occupying their countries simply exacerbates the sense of impotence, humiliation, and rage that induce them to support people like bin Laden. Defeating terror entails diluting the rage that fuels it.

Henry Munson is Chair of the Department of Anthropology at the University of Maine.

Glossary of Terms and Abbreviations

(A) = Arabic word; (P) = Persian word; (U) = Urdu word; (T) = Turkish word; sing. = singular; pl. = plural; d = died; r = reign.

Abbasids Descendants of Prophet Muhammad's uncle, Al-Abbas ibn-Abd al-Mutalib. The Arab Abbasid dynasty came to power after the collapse of the Umayyad dynasty (661–750 CE) and reigned over the Islamic Empire from 750 to 1258 CE.

Abd (A) Literally "slave" or "servant"; in the Islamic context, it is the slave or servant of God; commonly used in personal names such as Gamal Abd al-Nasser.

Abraham In Islam, Abraham is revered as one of the most important prophets sent by God, and as the common patriarch of Judaism, Christianity, and Islam.

Abu (A) Literally, "the father of"; commonly used in proper names such as Abu Abbas which means "the father of Abbas."

Abu Bakr One of the earliest coverts to Islam, Prophet Muhammad's close companion, and the first Caliph of Islam (r. 632–639 CE).

Abu Hanifa The Iraqi-born *alim* (Islamic scholar) who founded the Hanafi *madhab* (sect) of Sunni Islam. His religious worldview was promoted by a number of Abbasid and Ottoman rulers. A majority of Sunni Muslims in Turkey, Afghanistan, Egypt, Central Asia, China, and South Asia belong to the Hanafi sect.

Abu Sayyaf Group (ASG) A Muslim extremist terrorist group formed in 1991 in the Philippines. It separated from the Moro National Liberation Front that was fighting against the Philippines government on the island of Mindanao

A.D. Abbreviation for *Anno Domini* or Year of our Lord, namely, Jesus Christ.

Adab Muslim etiquette, manners, and proper behavior.

Adhan (A) "The call" to prayer made by a *muezzin* (prayer-caller)

Adl (A) Equity, fairness, justice, balance, and equilibrium. In Islam, it is often interpreted as justice, an attempt to give everyone his due, and the hallmark of a devout Muslim. It is the fundamental value governing all social behaviour and forming the basis of all social dealings and the Islamic legal framework.

A.H. The abbreviation for the numbering of years in the Islamic calendar; it literally means "After the *Hijra*" (migration) of Prophet Muhammad from Makkah to Madina in 622 CE. The Islamic calendar starts on this date.

Ahad (A) The oneness of God. The denial that God has any partner or companion associated with Him.

Ahkam (A) Literally, principles, directives, rules, regulations, or judgments. It often applies to the numerous principles, directives, and rules embodied in the Qur'an and *shariah*, that Muslims should observe.

Ahadith (A) sing. Hadith Prophet Muhammad's Sayings; these sayings do not appear in the Qur'an and are recorded for posterity by his extended family and *sahabah* (close companions).

Ahl al-Bayt (A) Prophet Muhammad's extended family. Shi'as restrict the term to Prophet Muhammad's daughter, Fatimah; Prophet Muhammad's son-in-law and Fatimah's husband, Ali ibn Abi Talib; and select members of the couple's descendants.

Ahl al-Kitab (A) Literally, "People of the Book," the Qur'anic term for Jews and Christians who adhered to God's earlier revelations/scriptures.

Ahl-i-Hadith (U) From the Arabic term *ahl al-hadith* (partisans of the *hadith*); those belonging to this group are Sunni Muslims who, besides the Qur'an, prefer the authority of the *hadith* over

that of a conflicting legal ruling accepted by one of the four Sunni schools of jurisprudence.

Ahl-i-Sunnah (U) Literally, "followers of the *sunnah*"; often refers to Sunnis, although Shi'as believe in Prophet Muhammad's *sunnah* (sayings and deeds) too. See SUNNAH, SUNNI, and SHI'A.

Ahmadis An offshoot of Sunni Islam that was founded by Mirza Ghulam Ahmad (1837–1908 CE), who was born in a village in the Indian Punjab called Qadian. Thus Ahmadis are also called Qadianis. Other Muslims view them as having moved beyond the pale of Islam because of some of their beliefs.

Ajami (A) Those Arabs, who during Prophet Muhammad's life, exhibited strong linguistic nationalism, and chauvinistically considered non-Arabic speaking foreigners (especially Persians) as "dumb."

Akhbari Those Twelver Shi'as in Iran who relied primarily on the traditions of the Imams as a source of religious knowledge, in contrast to the Usuli school, which advocated greater speculative reasoning in Islamic theology and law. See USULI.

Al (A) Literally, "the" (in an article form) or "the clan."

Alawites (Nusayri) A subsect of the Shi'a Muslim minority in the Muslim world; have been in power in Syria since 1970 when Hafiz al-Assad, an Alawite air force general came to power through a coup d'etat. Bashar al-Assad assumed Syria's presidency after his father died in 2000.

Al-Akhira (A) The life in the hereafter; the other life/world. See YAUM AL-AKHIR

A'mal (A) Good deeds or good works.

Aqidah (A) Profession or declaration of the Islamic faith.

Al-Aqsa Mosque Also called *Masjid al-Aqsa* (The Furthest Mosque), one of the holiest mosques in Islam and the Muslim world because it is located at the south end of Haram al-Sharif (The Noble Sanctuary) or the Temple Mount in Jerusalem's Old City. It was the mosque that Prophet Muhammad went to in his night journey from Makkah before ascending to Heaven from the Foundation Rock, which is housed in the Dome of the Rock.

Al-Asthma Al-Husna Literally, "the most beautiful names"; in Islam, it refers to the ninety-nine names of God, through which Muslims understand the major attributes of God. Many Muslims repeat these names, using ninety-nine rosary beads that are threaded together.

Al-Bayt Al-Haram Literally, "the holy house"; refers to the cube-shaped shrine that is situated at the center of the Grand Mosque in Makkah. See GRAND MOSQUE, HARAM AL-SHARIF, and KHANA-I-KA'ABAH.

Al-Dunya (A) Literally, "this world"; life in this world as opposed to life in al-akhira (hereafter or next world).

Alawite Offshoot of the Twelver Shi'a sect who glorify Ali ibn Abu Talib to such an extent that its members consider him an incarnation of divinity; also called Nusayri because the sect was founded by Ibn-Nusair (d. 873 CE), who was the follower and emissary of the eleventh apostolic Shi'a Imam, Hasan al-Askari.

Al-Azhar First built as a mosque in Cairo, Egypt, on the orders of the Fatimid Caliph Al-Muizz in 970 CE; it is one of the oldest and most prestigious Islamic centers of learning in the world. It was formally organized as an Islamic university by 988 CE.

Al-Qaeda (A) Literally, "the Base"; name of the Islamic terrorist organization founded by Osama bin Laden as Soviet troops began withdrawing from Afghanistan in 1988.

Alhmadu Lillah Literally, "Glory be to God."

Ali ibn Abi Talib Abu Talib's son, Prophet Muhammad's cousin and son-in-law, one of the first converts to Islam, Islam's fourth caliph (r. 656-661 CE), and the first Shi'a Imam.

Alids A term used for the recognized descendants of Ali ibn Abi Talib. Those claiming descent from Ali are numerous and spread all over the world. They are distinguished from other Muslims by the title of Sayyid, Sharif, or Mir.

Alim, pl. ulama (A) Literally, "one possessing *ilm* (knowledge)," hence a learned person. It refers to a Muslim who is immensely learned in Islam and is also used for muftis, imams, maulvis, mullahs, and maulanas.

Allah The Arabic-Islamic term referring to the one and only omnipotent, omnipresent, just, and merciful God, who is the Creator and Lord of the universe. Derives from the Arabic word "Illah," which means "the one deserving of all worship," the One to Whom all human beings submit in love, fear, and veneration. Belief in Allah is the first and most essential tenet of Islam.

Allahu Akbar (A) Literally, "God is Great"; many Muslims interpret it as "God is Most Great" or "God is the Greatest."

Amal (A) Good deeds or good works; also an influential Shi'a Muslim guerrilla group in Lebanon.

Amin (A) Literally, "trustworthy"; Arabs referred to Prophet Muhammad as al-Amin even before he began to propagate Islam.

Amir/Emir (A) It is the title given to military commanders, governors, and princes. It is used by a number of present-day Muslim rulers and leaders of some Islamic political parties.

Amir Al-Mu'minin (A) The honorific title of "Supreme Commander of the Faithful," given to the first four rightly-guided caliphs.

Amr Bil Mahroof Literally means "promote what is proper." The Taliban's religious police in Afghanistan. The Taliban's Ministry for the Promotion of Virtue and Prevention of Vice (1996–2001).

Anjuman (P) Assembly, association, or political organization.

Ansar (A) Plural of naseer, which means "helper" or "supporter." In Islamic history the *ansar* were residents of Madina who gave asylum to Prophet Muhammad and actively supported him when he emigrated from Makkah in 622 CE.

Aqaid, sing. aqidah (A) Islamic beliefs and doctrines.

Aql (A) Reason, intellect.

Arab A Semite who most often speaks Arabic and identifies with Arab culture. A majority of the 300 million Arabs are Muslims and live in twenty-one Arabic-speaking countries in the Middle East. Thousands of Arabs also live in non-Arabic-speaking countries worldwide.

Arab League Regional organization designed to promote political military, and economic cooperation among the Arab states. It was established in 1945 and currently comprises 22 member states in the Middle East (Southwest Asia and North Africa).

Arabic A Semitic language originating in the Arabian Peninsula. Written from right to left, it is spoken by 300 million people living in at least 21 countries of the Middle East, but also by millions of Arabic-speaking Palestinians, Arab minorities, and non-Arabs located all over the world. It is the language in which formal/ritual prayers are offered by Muslims the world over.

Arkan ad-Din The five pillars of Islam, consisting of the declaration of faith, prayer, fasting, charity, and pilgrimage to Makkah. See FARAIDH, SHAHADAH, SALAT, SAWM, ZAKAT, HAJJ, MAKKAH.

Aryamehr (P) The title of "Sun of the Aryans" assumed by Muhammad Reza Shah Pahlavi in the mid-1960s.

Ashab (A) Companions of Prophet Muhammad.

Asharite The followers of the Iraqi-born *alim* Abul Hassan al-Ashari (873–935 CE), who spearheaded a traditionalist Islamic movement. Abbasid rulers (833–942 CE) used al-Ashari's theological arguments to silence the liberal rationalism of the Mutazilites and thereby played a role in capping Islam's dynamism.

Ashraf (A) People who trace their lineage to Prophet Muhammad or his close companions and thus are highly respected.

Ashura (A) The tenth day in the first Islamic month of Muharram when Muslims commemorate the anniversary of the martyrdom of Prophet Muhammad's grandson, Hussein ibn Ali.

Aslaf (A) Refers to the pious companions of Prophet Muhammad who are considered to have had special insight into the requirements of the faith because of their close association with Prophet Muhammad.

As-Salamu Alaikum Literally, "peace be with/upon you." This is an Islamic greeting made by a Muslim who meets other Muslim(s).

ASEAN (Association of Southeast Asian Nations) Established in 1967 to promote economic cooperation among the countries of Indonesia, Malaysia, the Philippines, Singapore, Thailand, and Brunei.

Auliya, sing. Wali (A) Literally, "favorites of Allah"; often applied to prophets, imams, and mujaddids.

Auqaf, sing. waqf (A) Charitable organizations operated by the government and/or private organizations that help mosques, *madrassahs*, orphanages, as well as the poor and needy.

Ayah (A) pl. Ayat Literally, "sign," "symbol," "mark," or "token"; in Islam the term is used to refer to the "sign" or "miracle" of God's existence and power that can be seen in any of the 6,200 verses in the Qur'an. See QUR'AN and SURAH.

Ayatollah (P) The term *ayat*, literally means the sign, token, miracle, such as a verse in the Qur'an. Since *Allah* is the Islamic term for God, *ayatollah* literally means the "miraculous sign of Allah" on earth. An Ayatollah is a revered Shi'a theologian and jurist who studies and interprets God's directives embodied in the Qur'an.

Ba'ath (A) Literally, "rebirth" or "renaissance." The Ba'ath ideology or Ba'athism initially emphasized nationalism, pan-Arabism, Arab socialism, anti-Western imperialism, secularism, and democracy.

Babism In 1884, a thousand years after the disappearance of the twelfth Shi'a Imam, Mirza Ali Muhammad (1819–1950) a young Shi'a merchant in Shiraz, Persia/Iran, proclaimed himself "the Bab" (the Gate) to the Hidden Imam/Mahdi, then the Hidden Imam himself, and finally God's messiah. The Bab claimed that the *shariah* could not remedy the contemporary problems facing humankind and, therefore, had to be superseded by his teachings, summarized in the *Bayan* (Sayings). In venerating the Bab as a prophet and the Bayan as God's message, the Babis violate two fundamental Islamic principles, namely, that Prophet Muhammad was God's last messenger, who came with His last message, embodied in the Qur'an.

Bahaism Around 1863, a leading disciple of the Bab, Mirza Husain Ali Nuri, known as Bahaullah (1817–1892) or "splendor of God" proclaimed himself the "messiah" (Promised One or savior) in Persia/Iran. Bahaullah recognized the Bab as Prophet Muhammad's successor and the Bayan as a sacred book. However, claimed that he was the "promised one" whom the Bab had said "God shall make manifest." His persuasive skills won over the majority of Babis, who came to be known as Bahais or the adherents of Bahaism.

Bait-ul-Mal Islamic charitable/welfare fund raised from a progressive taxation system in an Islamic state.

Bai'ya (A) An "oath of allegiance" that is taken pledging one's total loyalty and obedience to a religiopolitical leader.

Banu Adam (A) Adam's descendents.

Banu Hashim Prophet Muhammad's clan in the Quraysh tribe.

Glossary of Terms and Abbreviations

Barakah (A) The "gift of God's blessing"; spiritual influence emanating from a holy man, a charismatic leader, a place, or a thing, making the person, place, or a thing worthy of reverence or veneration.

Basij (A) Literally, "mobilization"; In Iran *basij* is the auxiliary force of the Islamic Revolutionary Guards called the *Pasdaran* (Guardians of the Islamic Revolution).

Basij-i-Mustazafin (P) Literally, "mobilization of the oppressed"; an organization that was established in Iran in early 1980 by Ayatollah Khomeini's Islamic government.

Bay'a (A) Oath of fealty, pledge, or pact.

Bayt (A) House or household.

Bazaar (P) Market or marketplace.

Bazaari (P) A merchant who sells produce and other goods in the market. The Iranian *bazaaris* largely financed Iran's Islamic Revolution in the late 1970s.

Bedouins Nomadic Arabs who originally inhabited desert areas of the Middle East. Less than 2 percent of the Arab world today is inhabited by bedouins (most of whom are Muslims).

B.C.E. Abbreviation for "Before the Common Era"; Christians refer to it as "Before the Christian Era."

Bey (T) A commander in the Ottoman army; also used for the heads of the Ottoman Regency of Algiers and Tunisia prior to the French conquests.

Bid'ah (A) Literally, "innovation"; some Sunni Revolutionary Islamists consider any "innovation" in the purity of Islamic beliefs and practices of the *aslaf* as *bid'ah*, or an "unworthy innovation," and thus reprehensible.

Bilad al-Makhzan (A) In the Maghrib (North Africa), it is land under the control of a central authority (e.g. the sultans of Morocco).

Bismillah (A) Literally, "In the name of Allah," a statement with which Muslims ought to begin any undertaking.

Bismillah ir-Rahman-ir-Rahim (A) "In the name of Allah, the Most Merciful and Most Kind."

Blowback A term that the CIA invented to refer to the unintended consequences of U.S. policies overseas that were in many cases kept secret from the American public. In his book entitled *Blowback The Costs and Consequences of the American Empire*, Chalmers Johnson lays out the perils involved with such activities.

Burqa Veil worn by conservative Muslim women in traditional Muslim societies. The burqa is a voluminous head-to-toe covering with a mesh grid over the eyes.

Caliph The Anglicized term for *khalifah* or the religiopolitical leader of the ummah who assumed power after Prophet Muhammad's death.

Caliphate The Anglicized term for *khilafat* (caliphate) or rule by a *khalifah* (caliph). See KHALIFAH, CALIPH.

C.E. Abbreviation for Common Era.

Chador (P) The long garment or cloak worn by conservative Iranian Muslim women. The garment covers a woman's head and entire body, but not her face. See HIJAB.

Civilization A society that has a high level of culture and social organization. See CULTURE.

Clash of Civilizations According to Professor Samuel P. Huntington, cultural identity or civilization (defined primarily in terms of religion) is becoming the central force shaping the patterns of integration, conflict, and disintegration in the post-Cold War international relations. Although Huntington discusses the clashes between at least eight competing civilizations—Western, Confucian, Japanese, Islamic, Hindu, Slavic-Orthodox Christian, Latin American, and African (Sub-Sahara Black Africa)—he is particularly concerned about an "intercivilizational war" between the Islamic and non-Islamic civilizations.

Crusades The two-centuries-long (1097–1291 CE) military encounters between Latin Christians from central and western Europe and Muslims in the Holy Land of Palestine in the eastern Mediterranean coastal strip.

Culture A pattern of values, attitudes, beliefs, behaviors, customs, traditions, and expectations that are learned and shared by a group of people. Culture tells people what they should consider important, defines what is considered good or bad, right or wrong, and delineates the roles people are expected to play in life.

Dar (A) House, abode, tribal territory.

Dar al-Harb (A) Literally, "abode of war"; refers to a land ruled by non Muslims where non Islamic laws prevail. Until modern times, there was a widespread feeling among Traditionalist and Revolutionary Islamists that in these lands Muslims were not allowed to freely practice their religion, felt insecure, and suffered discrimination. Thus, a state of conflict prevailed between the non Muslim rulers and their Muslim subjects and between the *dar al-harb* and the *dar al-Islam* (abode of Islam or the Muslim world).

Dar al-Islam (A) Literally, "abode of Islam"; refers to a land where Muslim regimes govern and where, ideally Islamic laws are practiced and Islamic institutions exist.

Dar al-Ulum (A) An institution where Islamic instruction is imparted. In Egypt it often refers to *Al-Azhar* in Cairo.

Dars-i-Nizamiyya The Islamic curriculum developed by Mullah Nizamuddin (d.1748 CE) of Oudh, India, and popularized by the Traditionalist *ulama* of Farangi Mahall in Lucknow, India, during the eighteenth and nineteenth centuries. It still exerts influence over *madrassah* education in the South Asian subcontinent.

Da'wa (A) The call, invitation, or summons to acknowledge religious truth and join a religious community, missionary movement, or religiopolitical organization; missionary activity; and propagation of Islam.

Dhikr (A) Literally, "remembrance"; in Islam, it is used for the repetition of certain words or phrases in praise of God and/or Prophet Muhammad. Sufis often chant God's name as a mantra to induce a heightened state of consciousness.

Dhimmis (A) Derives from the Arabic term *dhimma* (an agreement of protection); often applied to free non-Muslims (especially "people of the Book," namely, Christians and Jews) who lived in Muslim countries and were guaranteed freedom of worship and government protection. *Dhimmis* paid no *zakat* or *ushr* taxes, but paid a capitation tax called *jizya* for the state protection guaranteed them and for not bearing the responsibility of defending the *dar al-Islam* in times of war. See ZAKAT; USHR; JIZYA; DAR AL-ISLAM.

Diaspora From the Greek word meaning "dispersion," it often refers to the protracted exile of the Jewish people after the Romans conquered Israel over 2,000 years ago. The term is also often used by those sympathetic to the plight of the Palestinians after the creation of Israel in 1948 and the four Arab-Israeli wars.

Din (A) Literally, "religion"; In Islam, it is the sum total of a Muslim's faith.

Din-i-Ellahi (U) The eclectic "Religion of the Supreme Being" initiated by India's Moghul Emperor Jalal-ud-din Muhammad Akbar (r.1556–1605 CE) and combining the best features of the major religions in India. It was accepted by only a few Moghul courtiers and faded away soon after Akbar's death.

Druze (or Druse) An offshoot of Islam that has developed its own beliefs, rituals, and practices as well as a close-knit community structure; the Druze are to be found in Lebanon, Jordan, Syria, and Israel.

Dua A prayer, blessing, or plea offered by Muslims at any time, any where, and for a broad spectrum of reasons. It should not be confused with the obligatory ritual prayer service. However, Muslims do thank God, praise Him, and request His assistance in the form of a brief *dua* after their ritual prayer is over.

Eid/Id (A) Literally, "festival" or a "holiday"; Muslims celebrate two eids annually: *Eid al-Fitr*, literally "the festival breaking the fast," which celebrates the completion of a month of fasting, and *Eid al-Adha*, which celebrates the completion of the *hajj*. See EID AL-FITR, EID AL-ADHA.

Eid al-Adha (A) The festival of sacrifice, the feast of sacrifice, the Feast of Abraham, or simply the Great Feast, is the climactic event (when animals are slaughtered) that is held at the close of the *hajj* season (on the tenth day of the Islamic calendar month of Dhul Hijj and after three days of *hajj* rituals). It commemorates Abraham's willingness to sacrifice his son Ishmael as commanded by God in a dream to test his faith.

Eid al-Fitr (A) One of the most joyous holidays in the Islamic lunar calendar. It is celebrated on the first day of the Islamic calendar month of Shawal or one day after the month of Ramadan (during which time Muslims fasted from dawn to dusk). See RAMADAN

Eid-i-Milad-un-Nabi (U) Called *Maulid* or *Maulud* in Arabic, it is a festival commemorating Prophet Muhammad's birthday. See MAULID/MAULUD.

Emir (or Amir) A title of rank, denoting either a patriarchal ruler, provincial governor, or military commander. Today it is used exclusively for rulers of certain Arabian Peninsula states.

Emirate A country ruled by an Emir (monarch or king).

End of History This concept is based on German philosopher Frederich Hegel's idea of the dialectical method—thesis, antithesis, and synthesis—that contributes to progress of history in the world. Francis Fukuyama promoted the controversial thesis that with the triumph of Western capitalist democracies over totalitarian fascism in 1945 and totalitarian communism in 1988, liberal capitalist democracy was the final synthesis of historical processes and the ideal form of human government. According to Muslims, Islam is the final and ideal synthesis in terms of the Hegelian dialectic and will be embraced by the majority of humankind at the "end of history" or the end of the world as we know it.

Ethnic Cleansing The expulsion, imprisonment, or killing of ethnic minorities by a dominant majority group.

Ethnocentrism Belief in the inherent superiority of one's own cultural or ethnic group.

Fallah (pl. fallahun; A) Peasant or small farmer.

Falsafah (A) Literally, "philosophy"; an esoteric philosophical movement which tried to reconcile the revealed religion of the Qur'an with the Greek rationalism of Plato and Aristotle. Ayatollah Khomeini taught *falsafah*, and his idea of the *Velayat-e-Faqih* was influenced by his study of Plato.

Faqih (A) An expert in Islamic jurisprudence and law.

Faraidh, sing. Fardh (A) Literally, "compulsory duties" or "obligations." In Islam, omission of these duties will be punished and the commission of them will be rewarded. The five obligatory *faraidh* are: (a) the *shahadah* (proclamation of one's faith in Islam); (b) *salat* (prayers); (c) *sawm* (fasting during Ramadan); (d) *zakat* (alms to the poor); and (e) *haj* (pilgrimage to Makkah).

Farangi Mahall The name of a mansion in Lucknow, India, that was built by a French indigo merchant. It came to be the home of an extended family of Traditionalist Sunni *ulama*—popularly known as the Farangi Mahallis because they lived in Farangi Mahall—in the late seventeenth century.

Farsi (P) The Persian language spoken by Persians/Iranians.

Fatah (A) Literally, "conquest" or "victory."

Fatimah bint Muhammad Daughter of Prophet Muhammad, wife of Ali, mother of Hasan and Hussein, and regarded by all Muslims as a paragon of virtue, piety, and compassion. Many Muslims add the honorific title *Al-Zahra* (The Shining One) to her name.

Fatwa (A) A formal and authoritative Islamic legal decree on a civil or religious issue that is often formulated and promulgated by a mufti or a qualified and respected Islamic theologian-jurist. It is based on the Qur'an, *Hadith, Shariah,* and *Fiqh* (Islamic jurisprudence).

Fedayeen (A) Those Muslims who are willing to sacrifice themselves in a *jihad* (holy struggle).

Fellaheen (A) Arab peasants and laborers.

Fertile Crescent The geographical and political term for the crescent-shaped region stretching along the Mediterranean coast from Asia to southern Palestine. It includes parts of what are now Iraq, Syria, Lebanon, Israel, and Jordan.

Fida'i (A) plural Fia'iyun, also Fedayeen, cf. Mujahideen) Literally, "sacrificer"; a Muslim warrior who engages in *jihad* against the enemies of Islam and the *ummah*.

Fiqh (A) Islamic jurisprudence, which covers all aspects of religious, political, economic, and social life. While a *fiqh* is not as comprehensive, divine, eternal, and immutable as the shariah, each *madhab* within the "House of Islam" has its own *fiqh*.

Fiqh-i-Jafariyyah (A) The Shi'a school of jurisprudence that was codified by the sixth Shi'a Imam, Ja'far al-Sadiq (d. 765 CE).

Fitna Civil disorder within the *ummah*; fighting between Muslims

Fitrah (A) Literally, "primordial nature." Islam posits that the original nature of human beings is good, disagreeing with the Christian view of "Original Sin." See ORIGINAL SIN.

Fundamentalism A term initially used for 19th century American Protestants who emphasized the literal interpretation and absolute inerrancy of the Bible as fundamental to Christianity. In the second half of the twentieth century, the Western mass media and scholarly community popularized the term *fundamentalism* to signify a religiopolitical movement of any religious group that is traditionalist, orthodox, conservative, radical, revolutionary, or zealous in its orientation. However, the term was originally coined by white American Christians about American Protestant Christians in the 19th century. Furthermore, since the term has come to imply religious extremism, fanaticism, bigotry, and even violence and terrorism, many devout Muslims—who firmly believe in the fundamentals of their faith and actively practice them—strongly object to the term being used for Islam and/or Muslims. In this book, the term *Revolutionary Islamism* has been used instead of *Fundamentalism*. See REVOLUTIONARY ISLAMISM.

Fundamentalist The term has been popularized in the West to imply a member belonging to any religion who believes in the literal interpretation of his/her infallible or inerrant scriptures. A Fundamentalist believes that his faith is God-given, pure, and right. Thus, those who share his dogmatic, doctrinaire, and often narrow-minded beliefs, are favored by God/Supreme Being and destined to a better life after death, while those who do not share his religious convictions, are wrong, misled, and destined to a miserable life in the hereafter. Fundamentalists often come across as very pious, exceedingly moralistic, messianic, autocratic, exclusivist, closed-minded, fanatical, zealous, and assertively or aggressively political. Most fundamentalists believe that secularization, secularism, materialism, hedonism, and Godless ideologies have corrupted the world and humankind. See REVOLUTIONARY ISLAMIST.

Glossary of Terms and Abbreviations

Ghair-Muqallid (P) A Muslim who does not want to be restricted to only one school of Islamic jurisprudence (such as Ahl-i-Hadith).

Ghayba (A) The condition of anyone who has been physically withdrawn by God from the sight of human beings and whose life during that period of disappearance may have been miraculously prolonged. Shi'a doctrine says the twelfth Imam disappeared and will reappear at a foreordained time to lead people back to "true" Islam. In the meantime, supreme *mujtahids* have the authority to interpret the twelfth Imam's will in his absence.

Ghazi (A) A Muslim who fights in a *jihad* to defend his faith, his community, and/or his Islamic state/Muslim homeland. The Ottoman sultans conferred this title upon those generals and warriors who distinguished themselves in the battlefield.

Globalization The global interdependence of all states in the world due to the revolution in communications, transportation, trade, and finance. The increasing integration of states contributes to a holistic and single global system in which the process of change increasingly binds people together in a common fate.

Grand Mosque See HARAM AL-SHARIF.

GCC (Gulf Cooperation Council) The Arab Gulf states established the GCC in 1981 as mutual defense organization. Members include Bahrain, Kuwait, Oman, Qatar, Saudi Arabia, and the United Arab Emirates. It is headquartered in Riyadh, Saudi Arabia.

GDP (Gross Domestic Product) It is the money value of all the goods and services produced in a particular country in a year. When it is divided by the population of the country, it gives us the GDP per capita. GDP equals GNP minus the "net factor incomes" (profits, salaries, and wages) repatriated from abroad.

GNP (Gross National Product) The money value of all the goods and services produced by a country's residents in any given year.

Group of 77 Established in 1964 by 77 developing countries. It functions as a caucus on economic matters for the developing counries.

Hadd The punishment prescribed by the *shariah* for crimes.

Hadith (A) Prophet Muhammad's recorded saying(s) or statement(s) that were memorized and written down by members of his extended family and *sahabah* (close companions), and later compiled into various collections. The most authentic and popular of these compilations are the Sahih Bukhari and Sahih Muslim. See AHADITH.

Hadith Al-Sahih An authoritative statement of Prophet Muhammad.

Hafiz-i-Qur'an One who has memorized the entire Qur'an in Arabic.

Hajar Al-Aswad (A) Literally, "black stone"; on the wall and near the door at the northeast corner of the *Haram al-Sharif* is embedded the holy "Black Stone," which was given to Abraham by God. Muslim pilgrims, in imitation of Prophet Muhammad, try to kiss this black stone during the *hajj* and/or *umrah*. See HARAM AL-SHARIF

Hajj (A) Literally, "pilgrimage." Adult Muslims of sound mind and body have been enjoined by their faith to undertake the *hajj*, the spiritual journey to Mecca, once in their lifetime, if they can afford it. *Hajj* is the fifth pillar of Islam and it is formally undertaken between the seventh and tenth of *Dhul-Hijj*, the last month in the Islamic calender. See FARAIDH.

Hajji (A) A pilgrim to Makkah who has performed the *hajj* during the annual *hajj* season, and also a title assumed by someone who has successfully completed the pilgrimage.

Halal That which is lawful. It is often used to refer to meat from animals slaughtered according to Islamic laws and customs (*zabiha*). *Zabiha* (*halal*) meat is very similar to kosher meat in Judaism; the opposite of *haram*.

Hamas (A) Literally, "zeal"; also an Arabic acronym for the Arabic terms *Harkat al-Muqawwamma al-Islamiyya* (literally meaning "the Islamic movement"). It is a militant anti-Israeli organization based in the Gaza Strip and the West Bank.

Hanafis The Hanafis are Sunni Muslims who follow the teachings of the Iraqi-born *Imam* Abu Hanifa al-Nu'man ibn-Thabit (699–569 CE), actively promoted by a number of Abbasid and Ottoman rulers and widely prevalent in Turkey, Afghanistan, Egypt, Central Asia, China, and South Asia.

Hanbalis Those Sunnis who follow the teachings of the Iraqi-born theologian and jurist Ahmad ibn-Hanbal (780–855 CE). The puritanism of the Hanbalis combined with the promotion of the Hanafi *madhab* by the Ottoman rulers who crushed the Wahhabis (adherents of the Hanbali *madhab*) resulted in the Hanbalis being the smallest of the four Sunni *madhabs*. Hanbalis are concentrated in Saudi Arabia and Qatar.

Haq (A) That which is true or the absolute truth; for example, the Qur'an and Islam itself. In Islamic law it is the legal rights, shares, claims, or obligation of an individual. For Sufis the term refers to the "Divine Essence," or Allah.

Haram Literally, "restricted" or "forbidden"; that which is unlawful in Islam (like alcohol or pork). By extension, it also applies to that which is sacred, such as religious sanctuaries or holy places where some otherwise lawful activities are prohibited.

Haram Al-Sharif In Islam it refers to "the sacred ground" of the Grand Mosque in Mecca, which houses the *Al-Bayt al-Haram, Bayt-Allah* or the *Khana-i-Ka'abah*. The *Ka'abah* was first built by Prophet Abraham and his son Ishmael for worship of one God. It was later rebuilt and consecrated by Prophet Muhammad in 605 CE for the worship of Allah. Muslims turn to the *Ka'abah* when they pray and have been enjoined by their faith to come to the *Ka'abah* once in their lifetime to perform the *hajj*.

Haramain (A) Refers to two of the holiest cities in the Muslim world, namely, Makkah and Madina. It also refers to the holy mosques, mausoleums, and shrines in those cities.

Hazrat (A) A title of respect that is the equivalent of "your reverence" or "his reverence" when applied to eminent spiritual leaders. It is also indiscriminately used for any intellectual.

Hezbollah (P) /Hizb Allah (A) Literally, "Party of Allah," the name was adopted by radical Shi'a organizations in Iran and Lebanon.

Hijab The "veil" or headscarf worn by Muslim women when they are in public. The basic reason for the *hijab* is Islam's emphasis on modesty in dress for both women and men.

Hijaz A mountainous region of the Arabian Peninsula adjacent to the Red Sea coast, which includes the holy cities of Makkah and Madina, where Islam originated.

Hijra (A) Literally, migration, emigration, or flight; In Islam, it refers to the "migration" of Prophet Muhammad and his close companions from Makkah to Madina in 622 CE. The Islamic calendar begins with this migration and the establishment of the first Islamic state in Madina.

Hijrat (A) Literally, "migration," "emigration," or "flight"; In Islam, some devout Muslims have from time to time emigrated from areas ruled by *kafirs* or "wayward Muslims" to areas where "true" Islam was practiced or would be practiced. See HIJRA.

Hilal Refers to the "new moon" or "crescent." The new moon is important in Islam because of the Islamic lunar calendar. The crescent, analogous to the Christian "cross," the Jewish "star of David," and other religious symbols, is found on the flags of a number of Muslim countries.

Hizb (A) Party

Hizb-i-Islami (A) The name literally means "party of Islam." Led by Gulbuddin Hekmatiyar, it was one of the Afghan *mujahideen*

organizations that fought against the Soviet colonialists in Afghanistan during the 1980s.

Hosayniyyeh (P) Religious center for the commemoration of the martyrdom of Imam Hussein and the performance of related ceremonies.

Hujjati (P) Member of the clerical faction in Iran that opposed clerical rule.

Hukumat (P) Centralized government.

Hussein ibn Ali The son of Ali ibn Abi Talib and Fatimah bint Muhammad, the grandson of Prophet Muhammad, and the third Shi'a Imam, who was martyred at Karbala in 680 CE. See ALI IBN ABU TALIB, FATIMAH BINT MUHAMMAD, SHI'A, KARBALA.

Ibadat (A) Performance of ritual religious worship/practices or religious obligations, including prayer, fasting, giving alms to the poor, and making the pilgrimage to Mecca.

Ibadi A militant early Islamic group that split with the majority (Sunni) over the question of succession to Muhammad. Their descendants form majorities of the population in Oman and Yemen.

Iblis (A) The Quranic term for Satan or the Devil.

Ibn (A) Literally, "son of"; corresponds to "ben" in Hebrew.

Ibn Taymiyyah, Taqi Al-Din (1263–1328 CE) A Syrian-born theologian-jurist who spent his life elaborating upon Hanbali teachings in puritanical writings and sermons. He rejected *taqlid*(leagal conformity) and *ijma*(consensus), insisting on the literal interpretation of the Qur'an and sunnah. He condemned *bid'ah*, and crusaded against the influences of Greek philosophy, denounced Sufism, and censured the cult of Prophet Muhammad and the practice of saint worship.

Ihram (A) The two white seamless cotton garments worn by Muslim pilgrims going to perform the hajj during the twelfth Islamic lunar month of *Dhul Hidj*.

Ihsan Mercy, kindness, and compassion.

Ijma (A) "Agreement," "unanimity," or "consensus"; considered to be the third *usul* or source of Islamic law. The consensus can be that of the first generation of Muslims, the great theologian-jurists of the medieval era of Islam, the *ummah* scattered all over the world, or even an entire nation.

Ijtihad (A) The word *ijtihad* derives from the same Arabic root as *jihad* and literally means "to exert oneself." Technically, *ijtihad* implies a Muslim jurist exercising his personal, independent reasoning, knowledge, and judgment to give his opinion on a legal issue where there is no specific order in the Qur'an. The term now commonly implies the independent interpretation or reinterpretation of Islamic laws.

Ikhwan (A) Literally, "brotherhood" or "brethren."

Ikhwan Al-Muslimun (A) Muslim   Brotherhood   or   Muslim Brethren. Hassan al-Banna founded an Islamic political party by this name in Egypt in 1928, which in due course, spread to other Arab countries.

Ilm (A) Literally, "to know," "knowledge," and "learning." It is often used by Muslims for the knowledge of Islam that is regarded as all-encompassing. One possessing *ilm* is called an *alim*.

Imam (A) A prayer leader or officiating cleric in a mosque or a very learned and competent *alim*. In the Shi'a sect, the title of Imam is also used for the divinely-guided and rightful religiopolitical successors of Prophet Muhammad starting with Imam Ali, the Prophet's cousin and son-in-law. The Twelver Shi'as believe that first Imam, Ali, and eleven of his lineal descendants held that position.

Imamat (A) The divine right of Ali ibn Abu Talib and his male descendents to lead the *ummah* (brotherhood of believers).

Iman (A) Refers to the five articles of the Islamic creed, which are: (a) belief in Allah; (b) belief in angels; (c) belief in the prophets of Allah with Adam as the first prophet and Muhammad as the last; (d) belief in the holy books revealed by Allah, i.e., the Torah, the Bible, and the Quran; and (e) belief in the Day of Judgment.

Infitah (A) Literally, "opening up"; In 1972, Egypt's President Muhammad Anwar al-Sadat inaugurated an "open door policy" that opened Egypt up to foreign investment and initiated a policy of economic liberalization or capitalism. Attractive tax breaks and duty-free zones lured foreign multinational corporations to a country that had gone through nearly two decades of socialism.

Injil (A) The Qur'anic term for God's revelations to Jesus, son of Mary, embodied in the Bible, which is the holy book of the Christians. Muslims believe in the Old Testament, but not in the New Testament. This is because in the latter Jesus Christ is mentioned as the son of God, which in Islam is *shirk* (polytheistic, and therefore sinful). See SHIRK.

Insaf (A) Literally, "impartiality," "objectivity," "integrity," and "equity"; refers to a code of ethics and morality becoming of a devout Muslim.

Insan (A) Human being.

Insan-i-Kamil (A) Literally, the perfect human being. Often used for Prophet Muhammad.

Intifadah (A) Literally, "shaking-off"; it has come to imply a popular grassroots "uprising" or "revolt." The first Palestinian *intifadah* began in Israeli-controlled Gaza (followed soon thereafter in the West Bank) on December 9, 1987, and ended in 1993. The second al-Aqsa *intifadah* began in Gaza and the West Bank on September 28, 2000.

Inshallah (A) Literally, "God willing." Devout Muslims often use this Arabic term when they say they are going to do something later.

Isa Arabic term for Jesus Christ.

Ishmael The first son of Abraham from his wife's handmaiden, Hagar. Muslims believe that Ishmael, not Isaac, was the son of God's promise to Abraham, and the one he was asked to sacrifice.

Islah (A) In Islam, the term for reform, purification, and revitalization of the Muslim community based on Islamic principles. The *islah* movement, or the movement of Islamic reformism, represented by such Islamic scholars and thinkers as Muhammad Abduh and Muhammad Rashid Rida of Egypt, who attempted to address contemporary problems with the help of the Qur'an and *sunnah*.

Islam (A) Derived from the Arabic root "s,l,m" and literally means submission or surrender. Those who believe in Islam are called Muslims. For Muslims, Islam is the final and perfect religion of God. They also believe that only by surrendering to the Will of Allah and by obeying His laws can one achieve true peace and happiness in this world and in the hereafter.

Islamdom The lands where Muslim communities are present; the Muslim world.

Islamic Calendar The Islamic lunar calendar begins with Prophet Muhammad's migration from Makkah to Madina and the establishment of the first Islamic state. The twelve months of the Islamic calendar in proper sequence are: (1) *Muharram*, (2) *Safar*, (3) *Rabi al-Awwal*, (4) *Rabi al-Thani*, (5) *Jumadi al-Awwal*, (6) *Jamadi al-Thani*, (7) *Rajab*, (8) *Shaban*, (9) *Ramadan*, (10) *Shawwal*, (11) *Dhul-Qadah* and (12) *Dhul-Hijj*.

Islamic Revival The renewal of heightened interest in Islamic symbols, ideas, and ideals subsequent to a period of relative dormancy of interest.

Islamism It can be viewed as the ideologization of Islam, whereby Islam becomes a comprehensive political ideology; the generic term for the phenomenon of Islamic revivals occurring around the world. It incorporates the dynamic action, reaction, and interaction of three types of Islamists or Islamic revivalists, namely, the Revolutionary Islamists, the Traditionalist Islamists, and the Progressive Islamists.

Islamist A term used generically in the literature on Islamic revivalism to refer to any participant in an Islamic revival. However, it is more specifically used for prominent Islamic revivalists who make a significant contribution to bringing about an Islamic revival at crucial moments in history. In propagating their perception of the "true" Islam, all Islamic revivalists frequently, but not necessarily, promote the creation of an Islamic state by teaching, preaching, and/or writing, and on rare occasions even by the force of arms. There are three types of Islamists or Islamic revivalists: the Revolutionary Islamists, the Traditionalist Islamists, and the Progressive Islamists.

Isma'ilis A branch of Shi'ism which follows the religiopolitical leadership of Isma'il, a son of Ja'far al-Sadiq and his descendants. The two largest Isma'ili branches in existence are the Dawoodi Bohra and the Agha Khan sects.

Isnad, sing. sanad (A) Literally, "a chain of authorities." In Islam, it refers to the chain of people responsible for transmitting the *hadith*. The validity of the *hadith* depends on the transmitters being perceived as men of honesty and integrity in Islamic history.

Isthna Ashari (A) The Twelver Shi'ah sect, which believes that Ali ibn Abi Talib should have been Islam's first caliph because Prophet Muhammad had nominated him. They follow twelve infallible Imams beginning with Ali and ending with Muhammad Mahdi, who disappeared in 873 CE and is promised to reappear as "true" Islam's savior.

Jahannam (A) "Hell"; where sinners will go after death.

Jahiliyyah (A) Derived from the Arabic word *jahila*, "to be ignorant." Muslims claim that the pre-Islamic period in Arabia was the "Age of Ignorance" and a state of primitive savagery.

Jama'at (A) A group, an association, an assembly, a congregation, an organization, or a political party.

Jamahiriyyah Literally, "popular democracy." Libya claims to have one, but it is actually an autocratic state that has been governed by Muammar Gaddafi since 1969.

Jannah (A) In Islam it means Heaven or Paradise.

Jihad (A) Literally, "to strive" or "struggle"; in Islam it means "to struggle in the way of God." A *jihad* is a "holy struggle" sanctioned by the *ulama* and fought against aggressors and tyrants. It also refers to the spiritual struggle waged against one's own baser instincts.

Jihad-i-Akbar (A) The greatest "holy struggle"; a peaceful, spiritual struggle against one's baser instincts.

Jihad-i-Asghar (A) The smaller "holy struggle"; the military campaign waged against aggressors and tyrants.

Jirga A tribal council of respected elders at which major political, economic, social, and legal issues are discussed and decisions made; it plays an important role in Afghanistan and Northern Pakistan.

Jizya (A) The poll tax or capitation tax levied on *dhimmis* or non-Muslims for protection, exemption from military duty, and full rights of citizenship given to them in an Islamic state.

Ka'abah This cube-shaped Islamic shrine in the holy city of Mecca (present-day Saudi Arabia) is the most sacred place in the Muslim world. According to Muslims, Abraham and his son, Ishmael, first built it to worship God, and then Muhammad cleansed it of idols and rededicated it to the worship of God. It is the direction in which Muslims all over the world turn to offer their ritual prayers. See AL-BAYT AL-HARAM, HARAM AL-SHARIF.

Kafir (A) The term was first applied to "unbelieving" Makkans who rejected Prophet Muhammad's message and denounced

him. The term has also been used for non-Muslim enemies of Islam and Muslims as well as for apostates, polytheists, infidels, hypocrites, and "wayward" or non-practicing Muslims. See MUSHRIKEEN.

Kalam (A) Literally, "speech," or "dialectic"; in Islam, it is applied to Islamic theology, which is the study of God's Words, the subject that attempts to give rational proofs for religious beliefs, deals with the problems of God's oneness, His attributes, and human free will and self-determination, among other philosophical issues.

Kalimah A defining statement or declaration of faith in one God and His last Prophet.

Karbala A town in southeastern Iraq where in A.D. 680 a historic battle took place between the armies of Yazid ibn Mu'awiyah, who had become the ruler of the Islamic empire, and Hussein ibn Ali, the grandson of Prophet Muhammad, who refused to endorse Yazid as the new caliph. In the ensuing battle Hussein and his male relatives and followers were killed on the tenth of Muharram. Annually, Muslims all over the world commemorate Hussein's martyrdom, over 1,300 years ago and vow to struggle against corruption, injustice, and tyranny even if it means giving up their lives. Shi'ahs make every effort to visit the tombs and shrines of the martyrs in Karbala once in their lifetime.

Kemalist Adherent of the secularist principles of Kemal Ataturk, the founder of modern Turkey, who was against Islamism and advocated secularism, Turkish nationalism, and modernization instead.

Khadijah bint Khuwaylid The daughter of a respected chieftain of the Makkan Qureish tribe. After her father's death, she managed his thriving business. One of her business agents was Muhammad, who had a reputation for being honest and trustworthy. She subsequently married Muhammad. Khadijah was the first to accept Islam and was her husband's staunchest supporter.

Khalifah (A) Caliph; Prophet Muhammad's religiopolitical successors and leaders of the worldwide *ummah*.

Khan A title given to military, clan, or tribal leaders in some Muslim regions. Mongol and Tartar chieftains and tribal leaders were referred to as khans, as were the Ottoman sultans and provincial governors in Safavid Persia. In India under the Turkish kings of Delhi, khan was the title of the principal nobles, especially those of Persian or Afghan heritage. Today it is a common surname of Muslims.

Khedive Viceroy, the title of rulers of Egypt in the nineteenth and twentieth centuries who ruled as regents of the Ottoman sultan.

Khulafah-i-Rashidun Also referred to as Khulafah-i-Rashidin; Most Muslims only revere the first four rightly-guided caliphs—Abu Bakr, Umar, Uthman, and Ali—and consider all caliphs thereafter as political rulers, lacking the mantle of spiritual leadership.

Khana-i-Ka'abah (U) See HARAM AL-SHARIF, HAJR AL-ASWAD.

Kharijites (singular: khariji; plural: khawarij) (A) Derived from the Arabic term *khuruj*, which means "to rebel" and "secede." Another possible derivation is the Arabic word *kharij*, which means "to go out." In Islamic history, the Kharijites or the Khawarij were one of the earliest Muslim dissidents and revolutionary Islamists who opposed Caliph Ali and started a civil war in the Islamic empire.

Khatam al-Ambiya/Khatam-un-Nabiyin (A) Literally, seal of the Prophets; the title is reserved by Muslims for Prophet Muhammad, who was the last of God's prophets and brought His last message. See PROPHET MUHAMMAD; QUR'AN.

Khilafat Literally, "Caliphate"; refers to the religiopolitical rule by a *khalifah*. Most Muslims look up to the caliphate of the first four rightly guided caliphs, namely Abu Bakr, Umar, Uthman, and Ali. However, many scholars have broadened the term to include the regimes of many Muslim rulers in Islamic history. Mustafa Kemal Ataturk abolished the institution of the *khilafat* in 1924.

Khulafah-i-Rashidin/Khulafah-i-Rashidun Literally, "rightly guided *khalifahs*." The Caliphate (religiopolitical rule) of the first four righteous *khalifahs* of Islam, namely Abu Bakr, Umar, Uthman, and Ali. Also see Khilafat

Khums (A) Besides the voluntary donation of *zakat*, Shi'as have been enjoined by their faith to give *khums*, which is a donation of one fifth of their savings to provide maintenance for and support the work of needy *sayyids*, who are Prophet Muhammad's descendants.

Khutbah (A) In Islam, it is a sermon delivered by a Muslim cleric or a mosque imam to a congregation, usually at the Friday congregational prayers and during Eid congregational prayers.

Kismet The idea that evolved in the *ummah* that their fate has been preordained and predestined. It is more a tradition than a principle of faith.

Kufr (A) In Islam it means blasphemy, hypocrisy, lies, and disbelief. A person guilty of *kufr* is a *kafir*.

Lailat al-Qadr (A) Literally, "the night of power"; Muslims believe that Prophet Muhammad received the first divine revelation on one of the last ten nights of the month of Ramadan. Muslim commemorate it most often on the 27th night of Ramadan.

Levant Literally, "lands of the rising sun." Originally designated the entire East, as seen from southern Europe, but particularly the eastern coast of the Mediterranean, from Greece to Egypt. The use of the term gradually changed to mean only the Asia Minor, Syria-Lebanon, and Palestine. Recent usage limits the term to only Syria and Lebanon.

Loya Jirga Literally, the "great council" in the Pashtun language or Pushto. In Afghanistan, it is the traditional meeting of tribal chieftains, clan leaders, respected elders, and the *ulama* to choose a new Afghan king or president. Such a council was convened in June 2002 under United States auspices in Kabul to create a provisional government to restore civil order to the war-ravaged country of Afghanistan. *Loya jirga* is also the principal legislative body in the country.

Madhab (A) Literally, "a direction"; in Islam, it applies to the four recognized Sunni schools or rites of jurisprudence, namely the Hanafi, Hanbali, Maliki, and Shafi'i sects. There is also one major school of Shi'a jurisprudence called *Fiqh-i-Jafariyyah*.

Madina A city in Saudi Arabia. In Islamic history, Prophet Muhammad and a few of his close companions migrated to Madina in 622 CE and set up the first Islamic state. It was in Madina that Prophet Muhammad died (632 CE) and where his tomb can be found.

Madrassah (A) A school, college, seminary, or academy where the primary emphasis is on a broad spectrum of classical Islamic disciplines, which are taught by the *ulama*. Students also learn such subjects as Arabic, astronomy, logic, mathematics, medicine, literature, philosophy, and metaphysics.

Maghreb (A) Literally, "West" or "land of the setting sun"; at one time, it was used to refer to the former Arabic-speaking colonies of France in Northwest Africa, namely, Morocco, Algeria, and Tunisia. After the 1970s, the term was extended to include Mauritania and Libya.

Mahdi (A) Literally, "the divinely guided one," "the expected deliverer," "the redeemer," or "the savior." The doctrine of the Mahdi in Islamic history first originated in the Shi'a sect with their belief in the hidden twelfth Imam who will be sent by God to establish "true Islam". In due course, the appealing Mahdist hope also came to be held by many Sunnis and non-Muslims.

Majlis (A) Literally, "session," "meeting," "assembly," or "council"; in Shi'a Islam, a majlis is a religious session in which a knowledgeable Muslim discusses the life and works of the *Ahl al-Bayt*. It is also the term used for the national legislature in some Muslim countries.

Majlis-i-Shura (A) Literally, a "consultative body" or an "elected council" to make recommendations to the ruler of an Islamic state or a Muslim homeland; it is also a term used for the national legislature in some Muslim countries.

Makkah A major city in Saudi Arabia; it is the holiest city in the world of Islam because it is the birthplace of Prophet Muhammad (570 CE), the city where Muhammad received the first revelations from God and began to propagate Islam. It is the site of the *Ka'abah*, to which Muslims from all over the world come to perform the *hajj* and the direction in which all Muslims say their daily prayers.

Maktab (A) An elementary school for teaching children recitation of the Qur'an, the *hadith*, and Arabic.

Maktabi (P) A student or graduate of a *maktab* or Qur'anic school. In Iran, it refers to the doctrinaire and dogmatic revolutionary Islamists (Muslim fundamentalists) and those faithful to the principles of Ayatollah Ruhollah Khomeini that clerics should play a leading role in the governance of societies.

Malikis Sunnis who follow the Islamic jurisprudence of jurist Abu Abd Allah Malik ibn Anas (716–795 CE). The Maliki sect spread in Muslim Spain and Africa.

Marabout A Sufi Muslim leader in Africa believed to have supernatural power.

Marja-i-Taqlid (P) Literally, "source of emulation"; in the Ithna Ashari Shi'a sect, any *mujtahid* who has reached the position of Ayatollah can be *marja-i-taqlid*.

Mashallah (A) A phrase occurring in the Qur'an and widely used by Muslims generally meaning "what God does, is well done."

Masjid (A) Derived from the word *sajdah*, meaning "to prostrate oneself." It is the place for (ritual) prostration or a Muslim house of worship, also called a mosque.

Masjid al-Aqsa (A) Also called the *Al-Aqsa* mosque, *Bayt al-Muqaddas* (The Holy House), or "The Dome of the Rock." It is located in Jerusalem and is the site from where Prophet Muhammad is said to have gone on his miraculous nocturnal journey to the seventh heaven and returned. It was also the direction in which Muslims prayed before Prophet Muhammad directed Muslims to pray in the direction of the *Ka'abah*.

Masjid al-Haram (A) The Grand Mosque in Makkah where the Ka'abah is located.

Masjid an-Nabawi (A) Another name for the *Masjid ar-Rasool* (Prophet Muhammad's Mosque) in Madina. It is the second most revered mosque in Islam, the first being the *Masjid al-Haram* in Makkah, and the third being the *Masjid al-Aqsa* in Jerusalem.

Ma'sum (A) A sinless and infallible person.

Maulana (A) Derived from the Arabic root, *maula*, which means "lord," "patron," "master," and "tutor"; the title is applied to scholars of Islamic theology, jurisprudence, and history.

Maulid/Maulud (A) A celebration commemorating the birth of Prophet Muhammad. It is celebrated on the twelfth day of the third Islamic calendar month of *Rabi al-Awwal* with speeches, writings, and qawwalis (poems and hymns praising God, Prophet Muhammad, or a Muslim saint). Muslims regard the birth date (12th *Rabi al-Awwal* in 570 CE) as one of the most important events in the history of the world. The term could also denote the birth of a religious or Sufi saint.

Maulvi Another term for an Islamic teacher or preacher. See MULLAH, MAULANA.

Meelad-un-Nabi (U) Birthday of the Prophet Muhammad. See MAULID, MAULUD.

Mehram A blood relative who should accompany a woman to the *hajj* and even outside the home if the Islamic *shariah*, as interpreted by some sects, is to be followed rigorously (as it was under the Taliban in Afghanistan).

Messiah (A) Literally, "the anointed one," the religiopolitical leader who is sent by God to lead people back to the straight path. Jews, Christians, and Muslims believe that it is he who will establish the Kingdom of God on earth.

Middle East The term Middle East is said to have been coined around 1900 by Captain Alfred T. Mahan, the noted American naval historian/strategist. Most Middle East scholars include all the Arabic-speaking countries, Turkey, Iran, and Israel in the region.

Mihrab A recess in the wall of a *masjid* to indicate the *qibla*, i.e. the direction of Mecca, for the correct orientation of ritual prayer. See MASJID, QIBLA, and SALAT.

Millet A religious community in the Ottoman empire; it is usually used for the *dhimmi* (non-Muslim) communities which had some measure of autonomy in the Ottoman empire.

Minaret Steeple or tower of a *masjid*, from which the Muslim call to prayer is sounded five times a day.

Minbar The pulpit in a *masjid*, from which the imam of the *masjid* delivers the *khutbah* (sermon).

Miraj Literally, "ladder" or "way of ascent"; in Islam, it refers to Prophet Muhammad's *Laylat ul-Miraj* or "night journey." According to the Qur'an, on this night (probably the 27th of Ramadan), angel Gabriel took Prophet Muhammad from the Mosque in Mecca to Mount Moriah in Jerusalem. Muhammad was taken to Jerusalem, then ascended to heaven, meeting the prophets and ultimately, God, Himself. The latter told him that Muslims should pray five times a day. Progressive Islamists consider this experience to be a dream that Prophet Muhammad had instead of having physically made this time. In several Arab countries, there is a holiday entitled *al-Isra Wal Miraj* marking this miraculous event.

Moghuls The longest ruling Muslim dynasties in the Indian subcontinent (1526-1857 CE) that created a sophisticated civilization. It was established by Zahiruddin Muhammad Babur (r. 1526–1530), a Muslim warrior and descendant of Mongol warrior Tamerlane. Its last emperor was Bahadur Shah II (1837–1857 CE) who was exiled by the British to Rangoon (Burma) after the beginning of the Indian Mutiny (1857). The term "Moghul" is simply "Mongol" in a phonetic form adapted to the Persian language and the Arabic script.

Mu'amalat Worldly transactions; mutual relations.

Muezzin (A) The person at the mosque who calls people to prayer.

Mufassirin (A) The interpreters of the Qur'an.

Mufti A learned, competent, and respected expert on Islamic theology and jurisprudence; the mufti has the authority to not only interpret Islamic law but also to issue *fatwas*.

Muhaddith (A) A scholar of the *hadith*.

Muhajir Literally, "migrant" or "refugee"; In South Asia, many Urdu-speaking Indian Muslims migrated or fled to the new-born Islamic country of Pakistan when India was partitioned in mid-August 1947.

Muhajirun (A) Literally, "the emigrants"; it is the name given to the earliest converts to Islam from the Makkan tribe of Qureish, who went with Prophet Muhammad to Madina. Also called *muhajirs* in Urdu.

Muhammadanism (A) A term that is incorrectly given by non-Muslims to Islam. Prophet Muhammad did not create or start the religion nor is he worshiped by Muslims. The creator of Islam as well as of everything else according to Muslims is Allah.

Muharram (A) The name of the first month in the Islamic calendar; it was the month in which Hussein, son of fourth Caliph and first Shi'a Imam Ali ibn Abu Talib, and his 71 male followers were martyred on the battlefield of Karbala in 680 CE.

Mujaddid (A) Literally, "renewer," "restorer," or "regenerater" of Islam; Muslims believe that *mujaddids* are sent by God in times of spiritual crisis to set the world on the right path again.

Mujaddid Alf-i-Thani (U) The renewer of Islam in the second millenium of Islamic history.

Mujahideen sing. Mujahid (A) Those Muslims who fight in a *jihad*.

Mujtahid (A) An *alim* (especially, an expert in Islamic jurisprudence) who practices *ijtihad* or interpretive reasoning, to inquire into and clarify the intent of the law; one who has the right to give *fatwas* or Islamic decrees. See ALIM, IJTIHAD, FATWA.

Mulhid (A) In the Islamic context, it is a Muslim who has deviated from Islam, hence becoming a heretic, infidel, or kafir.

Mullah Formerly another term for *alim*; hence someone to be revered; now it is commonly used for a Muslim clergyman of the lower ranks who serves as an Islamic teacher, preacher, or imam in the *masjid*. See MAULANA, ALIM.

Mu'min Literally, "a true believer"; a practicing Muslim who has tried to get as close to the ideal human being as possible.

Munafiqun (A) Literally, "doubters," "waverers," "dissemblers," and "hypocrites." In Islamic history it was a term first used by Prophet Muhammad for those residents of Madina who, during his first stay in that city ostensibly joined Islam, but were secretly doubting the Word of Allah and were critical of His messenger.

Muqallid (A) A Muslim who considers himself bound by the principle of *taqlid*. Also called "imitators."

Murid (A) Literally, "one who is desirous of knowledge"; a student; in the Islamic context, it applies to the disciple of a *pir* or Sufi teacher.

Murtadd (A) One who renounces Islam; an "apostate."

Musa The Arabic term used for Prophet Moses in the Qur'an.

Musawaat-i-Muhammadi (U) Literally, "Prophet Muhammad's egalitarianism"; it refers to the socioeconomic equity and justice of the ideal Islamic system.

Mushrikeen or Mushrikun (A): Literally, "unbelievers," "infidels," "polytheists," or "heretics" who believe in and worship many gods and are perceived as the enemies of Islam and Muslims. See KAFIR.

Muslihun (A) Those who work for *islah* (reform).

Muslim, pl. Muslimun (A) Literally, "one who submits or surrenders to the will of God." Muslim worship the same God as do Jews and Christians, and share many of the same prophets and ethnical traditions, including respect for innocent life. It was a term that came to apply to those who followed the religion of Islam that Prophet Muhammad preached.

Muslim Secularists Muslims by name and birth who cherish Islamic ideals, identify with the Muslim community and culture, and are perceived as Muslims by non-Muslims. Most are non-practicing Muslims; view the classical and medieval Islamic doctrines and practices as anachronistic, reactionary, and impractical in the modern age; and look to a broad spectrum of ages and philosophies for their models of political and socioeconomic progress. Despite their secular worldview and commitment to promote secularization and secularism, some Muslim secularists opportunistically engage in the politics of Islam to enhance their legitimacy; to integrate and unite their fragmented citizenry; and to inspire, mobilize, and galvanize Muslims.

Mustakbirin (A) Literally, "the rich and exploitative elite."

Mut'ah (A) A temporary marriage for a stipulated period of time. Mut'ah is still practiced by some Shi'a sects when special circumstances prevail. According to the *Ithna Ashari* Shi'a sect, Imam Ali allowed the practice, which was common in Arabia and had even been condoned by Prophet Muhammad. The practice is denounced by Sunnis because Caliph Umar I prohibited it.

Mutazilites A school of Islamic theologians and jurists advocating rationalism and free will. It was founded by Wasil ibn Ata, who separated from the conservative and literalist school of Hasan al-Basri around 732 CE. The school's reasoned arguments were a criticism of those Muslims who read the Qur'an literally. The Mutazilites influenced the intellectual environment in the eighth and ninth centuries.

Muttaqi (A) A devout and "God-conscious" (God-loving and God-fearing Muslim). See *TAQWA*.

Muwahiddun, sing. muwahid (A) Literally, "monotheists" or "unitarians" who are staunch believers in "the unity and oneness of God"; Wahhabis preferred to be known as *Al-Muwahidun*.

Muztazafin (A) A Qur'anic term for the poor, oppressed, and exploited people; a term popularized during the Iranian Revolution.

Nabi (A) Literally, "prophet," whose mission lies within the framework of an existing religion. Muslims believe that Adam was the first prophet, Muhammad the last, and that there were 124,000 prophets in between.

Nabuwat (A) The office or work of a *Nabi* who has been directly inspired by Allah and to whom a special mission has been entrusted.

Nafs Literally, "soul."

Al-Nakba Literally, "the catastrophe"; use by Palestinians, and almost all Muslims, to characterize the Palestinian fate as a result of the creation of Israel in 1948.

Nahda Literally, rebirth or renaissance; Arab revival.

NAM (Non-Aligned Movement) A loose association of mostly non-Western developing states, many of which had been colonies of Western powers, but during the Cold War chose not to be politically or militarily associated with either the West or the former Communist bloc.

Namaz (P) See *SALAT*.

Nation of Islam An African-American pseudo-Islamic group that Wallace Fard Muhammad founded in the United States in 1931. Fard said that blacks were members of the ancient Muslim tribe of Shabazz and that redemption through self-knowledge would free blacks from their oppression by blue-eyed "white devils" and bring them Allah's favor. Fard made Elijah Poole (renamed Elijah Muhammad) his successor and disappeared three years later. Elijah Muhammad developed and popularized the organization among African Americans until he died in 1975. On Elijah Muhammad's death, his son, Wallace D. Muhammad, became the leader of the organization. Assuming the name Warith Deen Muhammad, he called his father an enlightened teacher instead of a prophet; rejected the organization's racist philosophy; removed all racial restrictions on membership; did away with the rigid dress code; allowed members to participate in American politics and join the U.S. armed forces; renamed the organization the American Muslim Mission; and in 1985, encouraged his followers to join Sunni Islam. Louis Farrakhan, with a relatively small percentage of the former Nation of Islam's followers, has continued to espouse many of Elijah Muhammad's ideas.

Nazr (A) Literally, an "offering," "gift," or "present."

Nizam (P) Literally, "system" or "order."

Nizam-i-Mustafa (U) Literally, "the Islamic Order of Prophet Muhammad." It was the rallying cry of the nine opposition parties in the three-month Islamic mass movement in Pakistan just after the "rigged" election of 1977.

Nur Literally, "light"; in Shi'a Islam it is the light that resides in Prophet Muhammad and the Imams. See *SHI'A*; *IMAM*.

OAPEC Acronym for Organization of Arab Petroleum Exporting Countries. Established in January 1968, OAPEC soon included Algeria, Bahrain, Egypt, Iraq, Kuwait, Libya, Qatar, Saudi Arabia, Syria, and the United Arab Emirates (UAE).

OIC Acronym for the Organization of the Islamic Conference; it was established in 1969 after the arson attack at the Al-Aqsa Mosque in Jerusalem at the initiative of Saudi King Faisal ibn Abdul Aziz. The first meeting of the OIC, attended by twenty-four predominantly Muslim countries, took place in Rabat, Morocco. Currently fifty-seven countries with majority Muslim populations make up the OIC.

OPEC Acronym for Organization of Petroleum Exporting Countries. Formed by Iran, Iraq, Kuwait, Saudi Arabia, and Venezuela at the Baghdad Conference (September 1960) to serve as a united bloc for oil producers to achieve their economic objectives. The five founding members were later joined by Libya, Algeria, Qatar, Indonesia, Nigeria, and the United Arab Emirates (UAE).

Orientalists Non-Muslim Western scholars who have studied, researched, interpreted, and written about the Orient (the East), and non-Western cultures in general in an ethnocentric, patronizing, and/or disparaging manner. Islamists believe that the Orientalists have undermined the Qur'an's integrity, Prophet Muhammad's personal character and personality, and the authenticity of the last Prophet's Hadith. Islamists also believe that Orientalists have distorted the concept of *jihad* to mean only an aggressive "holy war"; have over-emphasized Islam's conditional permission of polygamy, the veiling and segregation of women, and the second-class status of women in the Muslim world; exaggerated the medievalism and barbarity of *shariah* (Islamic law) punishments; overstated the schisms, heresies, and fanaticism in Islamdom; and denigrated the backwardness of Islamic culture. Finally, Islamists accuse Orientalists of downplaying or marginalizing the achievements of Islamic civilization to humankind and dwelling instead on its weaknesses and problems.

Original Sin The Christian belief in the sinful state of human nature deriving from the disobedience of Adam and Eve. In Islam, Adam and Eve did disobey God when they ate from the Tree of Knowledge–but they repented, and God who is famous for His mercy, forgave them. Therefore, unlike Christians, Muslims do not believe that human beings are born into sin or that Jesus came to wash away their sins.

Ottoman The name given to a member of the Turkish ruling dynasty, descended from Uthman (d. 1324 CE) that ruled over a multinational empire from the fourteenth century. At its height in the early sixteenth century, the Ottoman Empire ruled much of the Middle East, the Balkan Peninsula, and a large part of the Caucasus region. Defeated at Vienna in 1529, the Ottoman Empire slowly declined in power until, allied with Germany, it was defeated in World War I, and carved up by the League of Nations in 1919. Mustafa Kemal Ataturk formally ended the Ottoman Empire and Ottoman Caliphate in 1922, after assuming power and proclaiming a Turkish Republic. Ottoman also refers to any member of the ruling class in the Ottoman Empire or a subject of the Ottoman Empire.

Glossary of Terms and Abbreviations

Pahlavi The language of ancient Persia. It was also the name that Reza Khan—a commander of the Cossack Brigade who assumed power in Persia in 1921—gave his dynasty. Reza Khan was deposed and exiled by the British in 1941 for his pro-Nazi sympathies and replaced by his nineteen-year-old son, Muhammad Reza Pahlavi (r. 1941–1979).

Palestinians Called *Filistini* in Arabic because they belong to *Filistin* (Palestine), which in 1948 became the Zionist State of Israel. While most of the 9 million Arabic-speaking Palestinians scattered all over the world (including Israel and the Israeli-occupied West Bank and Gaza) are Muslims, there is a significant and influential Christian minority among them.

Palestinian Authority (PA) The Palestinians call it the Palestinian National Authority (PNA), while Israel and the West often refer to it simply as the Palestinian Authority. The PNA is the first Palestinian self-governing authority or government to be established inside historic Palestine. It was the result of the secret negotiations between Israeli and PLO representatives in Oslo, Norway, and the Declaration of Principles (DOP) formally signed by PLO Chairman Arafat and Israel's Prime Minister Yitzhak Rabin on the White House lawn in Washington, D.C. on September 13, 1993.

Pasdaran (P) Literally, "security guard"; in Iran, the *Pasdaran-i-Inqelab-i-Islami* (Guardians of the Islamic Revolution) was a paramilitary force that was created by Khomeini's Islamic regime immediately after assuming power in Iran in February 1979.

Persia The name given to Iran by the ancient Greeks. Iran was called Persia until 1935, when the name was changed by Reza Khan (r.1921–1941, named Reza Shah Pahlavi I in 1925).

Persian The name given to the national language of Persia, written in a modified Arabic script from right to left. The Persian language is also called *Farsi* by native Persians or Iranians. A Persian is also an inhabitant of Persia (called Iran since 1935) and a member of the majority ethnic group of Iran.

Persian Gulf The body of water separating Iran from the Arabian Peninsula and connecting the *Shatt al-Arab* waterway to the Arabian Sea. Also called the Arabian Gulf or just "the Gulf."

Pir (P) A spiritual leader, guide, and teacher; in South Asia, it refers to a sufi or a religiopolitical leader of a tribe.

Progressive Islamists Knowledgeable and religiously devout Muslims who vehemently criticize *taqlid*, pursuasively advocate *ijtihad*, and make a dedicated effort to reconcile the differences between traditional religious doctrine and secular scientific rationalism. Modernists advocate the incorporation of numerous "modern-day" ideas and emphasize major revisions in Islamic laws.

Purdah (A) The term applies to the veiling, segregation, and seclusion of women in the Muslim world.

Qadhi (A) An Islamic judge who administers justice under the *shariah*.

Qawwali Devotional poems or hymns praising God, Prophet Muhammad, or a Muslim saint.

Qiblah (A) In Islam, it is the direction (facing the *Ka'abah* in Makkah) in which a Muslim must turn to perform his daily prayers.

Qir'at (A) Literally, reading or recitation; In Islam, it often refers to the reading or recitation of the Qur'an.

Qiyas (A) Literally, "analogical reasoning." Technically, the fourth *usul* or founding principle of the *shariah* after the Qur'an, the *sunnah*, and *ijma*. An Islamic theologian-jurist may use analogical reasoning with situations that are covered in the Qur'an and the *sunnah* to arrive at an Islamic solution.

Qom (A) A world-renowned center of Shi'a learning in Iran.

Quaid-i-Azam (U) Literally, "Great Leader"; it is the reverential title used by Pakistanis for Muhammad Ali Jinnah, the founding father of Pakistan.

Al-Quds (A) Literally, "the holy"; Muslims reverentially call Jerusalem, Al-Quds, because it has sacred sites associated with such biblical prophets as Abraham, David, Solomon, Moses, and Jesus.

Qur'an (A) Literally, "recitation"; according to Muslims the Qur'an is the collection of revelations sent by God to Prophet Muhammad through the agency of Archangel Gabriel (who recited them to Prophet Muhammad in Arabic). Prophet Muhammad in turn recited these revelations to his companions, who wrote them down and recited them to others. The name *Qur'an* was later given to the holy book containing these revelations. According to Muslims the Qur'an is the last of all holy books.

Quraysh The group of clans that made up Prophet Muhammad's community in Makkah.

Rabb (A) Literally, "Allah," "God," or "Lord," who created the universe and all that exists in it. See ALLAH.

Rahman (A) Literally, "the Merciful"; in Islam, God is always referred to as "The Merciful" and "The Compassionate".

Ra'i (A) Literally, "opinion" or "personal judgment" of the *faqih* in interpreting the Qur'an, the *hadith*, and the *shariah*.

Ramadan (A) The ninth month of the Islamic calendar. The name "Ramadan" is derived from *ramz*, which means "to burn." Therefore, fasting from dawn to dusk during the month of Ramadan is said to burn away one's sins. It was in the month of Ramadan that God revealed the Qur'an to Prophet Muhammad through the agency of Archangel Gabriel. See SAWM.

Rasul/Rasul Allah (A) A term used for God's Prophet or messenger of God who brings His message or revelation. See NABI.

Revolutionary Islamists Muslims who are often revolutionary and puritanical in their religiopolitical orientation. They usually believe in *ijtihad* and are extremely critical of *taqlid* and Western ideas. They often have a passionate desire to establish an Islamic state based on the comprehensive and rigorous application of the *shariah*.

Riba (A) The term used for "usury" or charging "excessive" interest on loans, it has been prohibited in Islam.

Rukn, pl. Arkan (A) Literally, "pillar," "principle," or "tenet" of faith. In Islam there are five pillars or tenets of faith called the *faraidh*. See FARAIDH.

Sabbath The seventh day of the week that is often observed as a day of worship by Jews and some Christians. The Sabbath or "day of rest," in Judaism and Christianity, is premised on the idea that God rested on the seventh day after completing the creation of the universe in six days. Therefore, man ought to also have a day's much-deserved rest from work in which he can revitalize himself and thank His creator for his blessings. Non-Muslims often refer to Fridays as the Islamic Sabbath because Muslims have been enjoined by their faith to perform their midday Zohar prayers on Fridays in a congregation (at a mosque, an Islamic community center, or in a public place). However, there is no concept of a Sabbath in Islam because Muslims do not believe that the omnipotent God in whom they believe needs rest. Muslims, therefore, carry on their activities before and after their Friday prayer services.

Sadaqah (A) The voluntary charitable contribution of money or food for the sake of acquiring merit with Allah and the saints. It is often criticized by Sunni Fundamentalists.

Sahaba (A) Literally, "companions'; in Islamic history, it specifically refers to the companions of Prophet Muhammad.

Salaf (A) A pious companion of Prophet Muhammad. See ASLAF.

Salafi (A) Those who closely emulate the pious companions of Prophet Muhammad. Two Modernist Islamists of Egypt—Muhammad Abduh (1849–1905) and Muhammad Rashid Rida (1865–1935)—called their Islamic reform movement: "the salafiyyah movement."

Salat (A) See NAMAZ.

Salla Allah Alayhi wa-Sallam (S.A.W.) Literally, "God's peace and blessing be upon him" (P.B.U.H.) or the Arabic expression Alayhis Salaam (peace be upon him or A.S.). Devout English-speaking Muslims use the aforementioned words in speech and abbreviations in writing as a sign of reverence after the name of one of God's prophets in the Qur'an, especially Prophet Muhammad.

SAVAK Persian acronym for Sazeman-i-Ettelaat-va-Amniyat-i-Kashvar (State Organization for Intelligence and Security). SAVAK was the feared secret police of the Shah of Iran established in 1955 to combat anti-government activities and cited by Amnesty International in the mid-1970s for the torture and murder of political prisoners. It was disbanded by the Islamic revolutionary government of Iran in 1979.

Sawm (A) The term for fasting from dawn till dusk during the month of Ramadan which is required of all healthy adult Muslims. Exemption is given to travellers, the ill, and to women who are pregnant, nursing a baby, or having their menstrual cycle. See FARAIDH, RAMADAN.

Sayyid/Sayed A title reserved for the descendants of Prophet Muhammad. In some countries, they wear a black (as in Iran) or green turban to show their honorable heritage.

Secular The civil, non-religious, or temporal realm in contradistinction to the ecclesiastical, religious, sacred, or spiritual realm.

Secularism A government that promotes secularism clearly separates the Church/Mosque from the State, refuses to act as the promoter and defender of a particular faith, and rejects religious ideas as the basis of its political legitimacy.

Secularists Those who believe that religion should not enter into the conduct of governmental affairs and promote secularization.

Secularization The separation of religion from politics; the government's promotion of secularism; the gradually transformation of people's values from the strict adherence of religious beliefs and practices to an increasingly secular, rational and pragmatic orientation; and the gradual decline in the influence of religious leaders and groups in the society.

Seerah Literally, "biography"; in Islam, the term is often used to refer to the life, deeds, and accomplishments of Prophet Muhammad. It is studied as an example of how to lead a fully actualized life.

Semite In antiquity, they included the Ammonites, Amorites, Assyrians, Babylonians, Canaanites, and Phoenicians. Some believe that it was used for those who descended from Noah's son Shem; today it is used for people who speak a Semitic language (Jews and Arabs).

Shafi'is Those who follow the teachings of Muhammad ibn Idris ash-Shafi'i (767–820 CE) who tried to reconcile the Maliki and Hanafi schools of Islamic jurisprudence.

Shagird (P) A term that refers to a student, apprentice, or novice.

Shah (P) A title that has often been used for Iranian monarchs.

Shahadah (A) A declaration of faith in God and in the Prophethood of Muhammad which reads: "*La ilaha illa Llah, Muhammad ar Rasulu Llah*" ("There is no God but Allah and Muhammad is His Prophet"). It is the first pillar of the Islamic faith.

Shaheed (A) A Muslim who dies fighting in a *jihad* is a martyr who is destined to go to Heaven because he died in "the path of Allah."

Shariah (A) The comprehensive, eternal and immutable body of law that governs the individual and community life of Muslims.

Sharif, pl. Ashraf (A) Literally, "noble," "high-born" or "exalted." Initially applied to a descendant of Prophet Muhammad's family, but now includes a member of a prominent family or a descendant of illustrious ancestors.

Shaykh (A) Literally, "an elder," and therefore "wise man." It is often used for tribal chieftains, members of the *ulama*, Sufi teachers in religious brotherhoods, and generally for men enjoying positions of authority in a Muslim society. Also written as *sheikh* and *shaikh*.

Shaykhdom A country ruled by a shaykh or sheikh (monarch or king).

Shaykh al-Islam (A) The highest religious office in Sunni Islam.

Shaytan (A) Satan or the Devil, is God's principal enemy and mankind's biggest tempter to commit evil deeds.

Sherwani (U) The long coat made of cotton or wool worn by Muslims of the Indian subcontinent.

Shi'a (A) Members of this minority sect of Islam are "partisans" or "followers" of Ali ibn-i-Abu Talib and believe that God and Prophet Muhammad wanted Ali to be Islam's first caliph. They, like the Sunnis, believe in the fundamentals of Islam, the Qur'an, the five *faraidh*, the Prophet Muhammad's *hadith* and *seerah*. Islamic *shariah* are very similar to the Sunnis.

Shirk (A) From the Arabic verb *shirika* (to associate). This often occurs when more than one God is worshiped (polytheism) and/or when anyone or anything other than Allah is assigned divine attributes and powers (idolatry). Those guilty of *shirk* are called *mushrikeen*. See MUSHRIKEEN.

Shura (A) Often referes to a group, assembly, or council of knowledgeable and pious Muslims who are consulted by leaders. The Qur'an has recommended "consultation" with erudite and pious Muslims in matters where there is no specific guidance in the Qur'an and the *sunnah*.

Silsilas See TARIQAHS.

Sirat al-Mustaqim (A) Literally, "the right path," and "the path pursued by righteous Muslims."

Suffrage The right to vote in political matters.

Sufis The term Sufi has been derived from early Muslim ascetics and pious mystics who wore simple clothes made out of *suf* (coarse wool). *Sufis* became lax in their observance of the *shariah* and devoted their lives to meditation and proselytization. They emphasize the spirit rather than the literal interpretation of the Qur'an and the *sunnah*, and a search for eternal Truth and Goodness.

Sufism That body of Islamic beliefs and practices which tends to promote the spiritual union between self and God through religious discipline and mystical experience. See SUFIS.

Sultan The title of some Muslim monarchs.

Sultanate The office of and territory ruled by a Sultan.

Sunnah (A) In Islam it is understood as Prophet Muhammad's "trodden path," "way," "custom," or "tradition." The *sunnah* comprising Prophet Muhammad's sayings and deeds complements the Qur'an as the major source of Islamic faith and practice.

Sunni (A) Refers to the majority Islamic sect (approximately 80 percent of the Muslim world) as well as to the member of that sect. Sunnis follow the *sunnah* or "the way, the path or the road shown by Prophet Muhammad." However, Shi'as follow the *sunnah* too. See SUNNAH, MADHABS, FIQH.

Surah (A) Literally, a "step-up or gate"; in Islam the term is used exclusively for each of the 114 chapters of the Qur'an, comprising a "series" of revelations.

Glossary of Terms and Abbreviations

Tabarruk (A) Literally, "that which brings a blessing." In Islam it refers to food, flowers, etc., offered at a saint's shrine.

Tabligh (A) Islamic missionary activity and proselytization directed at Muslims and non-Muslims.

Tafsir The commentary, explanation, and interpretation of Qur'anic verses and chapters.

Taghut (P) A pre-Islamic idol at Makkah; therefore, its literal meaning is a "false god." Figuratively, it refers to all those individuals and governments that have been corrupted by power. Ayatollah Khomeini often referred to the Shah of Iran as a *taqhuti*.

Tajdid (A) Literally, "revival" or "renewal"; a revolutionary Islamic movement that calls for a return to the Qur'an and *sunnah*, a return to Islamic piety and purity practiced in the classical period of Islamic history, and a rejection of all legislation, customs, and traditions after the Khulafah-i-Rashidun.

Takbir (A) Praising God by saying Allahu Akbar ("God is the Greatest")

Talib (pl. Tulaba or Taliban) A student in an Islamic madrassah school. See MADRASSAH, TALIBAN.

Taliban Students or graduates of *madrassah* schools. The Revolutionary Islamist Afghan regime (made up of Pashtuns) that ruled Afghanistan from 1996 till the end of December 2001.

Taqdir (A) Literally, "destiny," "predestination" or "fate."

Taqiyyah (A) From the Arabic word *wagha*, which means to safeguard or to protect oneself. The concealment of one's religious beliefs and not to practice some external religious rituals in order to avoid imminent harm. Though permitted in Islam, Shi'as have had to resort to dissimulation far more often because Sunnis have dominated the Muslim world for most of Islamic history, and persecuted Shi'as who practiced their rituals openly.

Taqlid (A) "Following without inquiry"; in Islam, it means "legal conformity"; Traditionalist Sunni Islamists require rigid and unquestioning adherence to the legal rulings of one or more of the Sunni schools of jurisprudence compiled during Islam's medieval period. See *Fiqh*.

Taqveeat-ul-Iman (U) From an Arabic term, *taqveeat al-Imam*, literally meaning "strengthening of the faith."

Taqwa (A) Literally, "fear of God" and "piety." Since God is omnipresent and is aware of our innermost thoughts, it not only refers to doing good deeds, but also avoiding evil thoughts.

Tariqah (A) The term refers to the path or method of mysticism and spiritualism promoted by Sufi teachers, and, the social groups (like Sufi brotherhoods) formed by followers of such Sufi teachers.

Tatbiq (A) Accommodation, harmonization and integration.

Tawaaf (A) The ritual of going around a shrine; often used for going around the *Ka'abah* seven times during the *hajj* and *umrah*.

Tawba (A) Repentance; asking forgiveness for one's sins and transgressions and a commitment to follow the "true" path.

Tawhid (A) In Islam it signifies the unity and oneness of God and His sovereignty. This is the most important tenet of Islam.

Taziyah (A) In Islam, Shi'as commemorate the martyrdom of Imam Hussein on the tenth of Muharram by taking out mourning processions with replicas of tombs (made of paper, wood or metal) of the martyrs of Karbala. Some Sunnis also take out *taziyah* processions.

Theocracy A country ruled by religious leaders. In a theocracy, there is no separation of church/mosque and state or religion and politics. Iran is the classic example of an Islamic state based on the *shariah* and run by Shi'a clerics. In this state, the full power of the state is used to assure mass compliance with a particular set of religious doctrines. See SHARIAH.

Traditionalist Islamists Muslims (often Islamic scholars) who tend to conserve and preserve not only the Islamic laws, customs, and traditions practiced in the classical period of Islam but in the medieval period as well. The major hallmark of Traditionalists is their rejection of *ijtihad* and belief in the dogma of *taqlid*. Though often apolitical, passive, and status-quo oriented, these scholarly minded custodians of Islam do get involved in politics when they perceive Islam and/or the *ummah* to be in imminent danger.

Trinity In the Christian doctrine of the Trinity, God is actually three entities—Father, Son, and Holy Spirit—in one Godhead. Islam, being an uncompromisingly monotheistic faith, is opposed to the concept of the Trinity.

Ulama/Ulema (A) Learned scholars of Islamic theology and jurisprudence.

Ummah (A) In Islam it refers to the Muslim "nation" or the Brotherhood of Believers (Muslims).

Umayyads Descendants of Umayyah within the Quraish tribe. They were one of the most influential families at the time of Muhammad and established the first hereditary caliphate in 661 CE.

Ummi (A) Literally, "uneducated" or "unlettered". Muhammad is referred to in the Qur'an as *al-Nabi al-Ummi* (the unlettered Prophet). This simply means that he did not attend any school and receive formal education in reading, writing, and arithmetic. However, being an intelligent, curious, reflective person, he learnt from the numerous people he came into contact with throughout his life.

Umrah: The pilgrimage to Makkah and Madina undertaken by a Muslim at any time other than during the *hajj* period. It is also called "the lesser pilgrimage." See HAJJ.

Urs (A) In Islam, it is the graveside celebration of the death of a saint's death, often at his tomb. The popular belief is that the saint goes and meets God upon his death.

Ushr (A) In Islam, a ten percent voluntary tax is expected annually from farmers owning irrigated farm land. The levy is payable in money or kind by each landholder to the poor or to charitable institutions.

Ustad (U) Literally, "teacher" or "instructor."

Usul (A) Literally, source, foundation, or fundamentals. In the Islamic context, it applies to the fundamentals of Islam. The four *usul* of Islam are the Qur'an, the *sunnah, ijma* and *qiyas*. Some *ulama* include *ijtihad* as a fifth *usul*.

Usul al-Fiqh (A) Literally, "principles," "roots," "sources," or "foundations" or Islamic jurisprudence.

Usuli (A) From the root *usul,* or principles (of jurisprudence). A Twelver Shi'ah movement that became influential in Iran at the end of the eighteenth century. In contrast to the Akhbari school, the Usuli school advocated greater speculative reasoning in the principles of theology and Islamic law.

Uthman ibn Affan A wealthy Meccan merchant in the Qureish tribe, among the first converts to Islam, Prophet Muhammad's son-in-law, and the third caliph of Islam (r. 644–656 CE).

Velayat-i-Faqih (P) Literally, Guardianship or Government of the Islamic Jurist. Ayatollah Ruhollah Khomeini's idea that a devout, learned, and just Islamic jurist ought to be the supreme guardian of the Islamic state during the absence of the awaited twelfth Imam. In Iran, Khomeini was the *velayat-i-faqih* for much of the 1980's.

Wa' Alaykum as-Salaam (A) Literally, "peace be upon/with you too." When a Muslim greets another Muslim with "*as-salaamu alaykum,*" the response should be "*wa' alaykum as-salaam.*"

Wahhabis Followers of Muhammad ibn Abd al-Wahhab (1703–1792 CE). They belong to the Hanbali school of Islamic jurisprudence and are concentrated in contemporary Saudi Arabia and Qatar, where royal families in both kingdoms have adopted and propagated Wahhabism. Wahhabis initially disliked the term assigned to them by Westerners, claiming the term *Wahhabi* implied that they venerated Muhammad ibn Abd al-Wahhab; in actuality, though, they venerated no one but God. They prefer to be known as al-Muwahhidun, which literally means "montheists" or "Unitarians." The term *monotheists*, though, encompassed both Muslims and many non-Muslims, while the term *unitarians* had strong Christian overtones. Thus, for want of a more appropriate term and because the term *Wahhabis* had been popularized, they grudgingly came to accept it. Wahhabis are Revolutionary Islamists who revert back to the Qur'an and *sunnah* to establish an Islamic state on the *shariah* and classical Islamic principles; draw on Taqi al-Din ibn Taimiyyah's puritanical writings; are critical of the Traditionalist *ulama* for failing to be competent, dynamic, and assertive standard-bearers of the Islamic faith and *ummah*; live an ascetic and pious life; condemn ornamentation, music, dancing, and singing; denounce accretions that have crept into Islam since the classical era; and engage in a perpetual *jihad* as their principal means of winning converts and redirecting "wayward" Muslims to what they considered "the righteous path."

Wahid Literally, "the one". In Islam, it often refers to the absolute "oneness" of God and to the uncompromising monotheism of the Islamic faith.

Wahy Revelation or inspiration from God given to chosen men and women; God revealed the Qur'an to Muhammad over a 22 year period (610–632 CE).

Wajib (A) Literally, that which is "obligatory," "mandatory," "incumbent," or "binding."

Wali (A) In Islam, it denotes a learned pir, Sufi, cleric or saint who enjoys God's favor and consequently possesses significant powers. In Islamic law, the *wali* is the guardian or legal representative of an individual. It is also one to whom a ruler delegates authority. Shi'as believe that Prophet Muhammad made Ali the *wali* or Imam over the *ummah*, a point disputed by the Sunnis.

Waqf (pl. Auqaf) An Arabic term for an Islamic endowment (usually of landed property) established for pious charitable purposes. See *Auqaf*.

Wasi (A) Literally, "legatee," an "appointed guardian," or "executor of a will." In Islam, a *wasi* is the vice-regent of Prophet Muhammad; in popular Islam, he is a holy man.

Watan (A) Literally, "homeland" or "nation"; a concept borrowed from Western nationalism.

Wisaya (A) Literally, the appointment or designation of someone to assume specified responsibilities. Among Shi'as the term refers to Prophet Muhammad's designation of Ali as his successor as the religiopolitical leader of the entire Muslim world.

Wudhu The Islamic practice of washing the face, hands, arms, and feet with clean water to achieve a ritually pure state before standing in front of God in prayer.

Yaum al-Akhira (A) Literally, the Day of Judgment; The Qur'an clearly informs Muslims that the world will come to an end someday. On that Day of Judgment, the dead will be resurrected in order to be judged by an all-knowing, totally just, and immensely merciful God. Righteous human beings, who believed in God and have done good deeds in this world, will be rewarded with an eternal life of happiness in Heaven/Paradise. Those human beings, however, who have refused to follow God's guidance and done evil deeds in this world, will be sent to Hell.

Yaum ul-Jumah (A) Literally, the "Day of Assembly"; in Islam, it refers to the "assembly" or "congregation" of the *ummah* on Fridays when Muslims have been recommended to perform their midday prayers along with their brethren at the nearest mosque or Islamic community center. The Qur'an states: "O ye who believe! When the call is proclaimed for prayer on Friday, hasten earnestly to the remembrance of God, and leave off business; that is best for you if you but knew" (62:9). These congregational prayer services often include a sermon by a respected Islamic cleric called *Imam-i-Jum'ah wa Jama'at* (Friday congregational prayer leader).

Yazid ibn Mu'awiya The son of Mu'awiya and the second Ummayad ruler (r. 680–683 CE). He is notorious in Islamic history because he was responsible for the deaths of Imam Hussein and 71 of his male relatives and followers on the battlefield of *Karbala*.

Zakat (A) The fourth pillar of Islam in which Muslims are enjoined by their faith to donate two-and-a-half percent of their wealth to the poor or to charitable causes and institutions.

Zamindar A wealthy and powerful landlord who owns large tracts of land and has many peasants working on his farmland.

Zawiya (A) In North Africa it is a small room in a mosque or in a saints shrine where members of a tribe or a Sufi order gather and engage in religious discussions. It may also comprise a building complex that includes a mosque, a *madrassah*, and living quarters.

Zina Muslims guilty of fornication (premarital and adultery) according to the *shariah*.

Zionism The Jewish nationalist movement advocating the migration of Jews from all over the world to Palestine. Theodor Herzl, an Austrian Jewish journalist, was primarily responsible for launching the Zionist movement with the publication of his pamphlet entitled *Der Judenstaat* (The Jewish State) in 1896, and with his establishment of the World Zionist Organization (WZO) in Basel, Switzerland, in 1897. The WZO was instrumental in establishing the sovereign Jewish State of Israel in Palestine on May 14, 1948.

Ziyarat (A) The visit or pilgrimage that Muslims make to the grave, tomb, mausoleum, or shrine of a venerated Muslim.

Zulm (A) Oppression.

Index

Index

Moghul Dynasty, of Pakistan, 215
Mohammad, Prophet, 23, 34
monarchy, of Iraq, 151
Mongol invasion, 8
Monnet, Jean, 157
Morocco: foreign relations of, 197–198; history of, 195–196; overview of, 194–199
mosques, influential role of, 34
Mozambique Liberation Front (Frelimo), 201, 202
Mozambique, overview of, 200–202
Mubarak, Hosni, 34, 120, 121, 162
Muhammad VI, crown prince of Morocco, 198, 199
Muhammad, Elijah, 58–61
Muhammad, Wallace Fard, 58
mujahideen, 35, 38, 53, 66, 76, 289
multipartyism, Senegal and, 238
Museveni, Yoweri, 277
Musharraf, Pervez, 219
Muslim Brotherhood, 22, 34, 162, 255
Muslim League, 216–217
Muslim secularists, 21, 23, 27–31

N

Nano, Fatos, 80, 81
Nasr al-Din, nineteenth century ruler of Iran, 143–144
Nasser, Gamal Abdel, 36, 68, 118, 119, 120, 287
National Action Plan, 199
National Liberation Front (FLN), 84
National Pact, Lebanese politics and, 174
National Progressive Front, 255
National Resistance Movement (NRM), 277
natural diasters, Bangladesh and, 92
natural resources, Bangladesh and, 93
Nazarbayev, Nursultan, 165
Neo-Destour Party, 264
Netanyahu, Benjamin, 36, 225
"New Economic Policy" (NEP), 184
Niger, overview of, 203–205
Nigeria: Cameroon and, 104; overview of, 206–209
Nimeiri, Jaafar, 247
Niyazov, Saparmurad, 275
no-fly zones, 39
nomads, 179, 211, 268, 280
Nuclear Non-Proliferation Treaty, 181
nuclear weapons, Kazakhstan and, 165

O

Obote, Milton, 277, 278
"offshore Banking Units" (OBUs), 90
oil, importance of, 39, 90, 107, 124, 146–147, 151, 169, 180, 208–209, 231, 233, 247, 255, 265, 275; in Islam, 90, 98; in United Arab Emirates, 281
Old Testament, 15, 52, 64–65
Oma: foreign relations of, 213; geography of, 211; history of, 211–212; and Islam and Muslim World overview, 1–73; overview of, 210–213; society of, 212
Operation Anfal, 152
Operation Restore Hope, 244
"Organic Law," 234, 235

Organization of Petroleum Exporting Countries (OPEC), 36–37, 208
Organization of the Islamic Conference (OIC), 37, 73
Orthodox ulama, 9
Oslo accords, 120, 224, 225
Ottoman Empire, 7, 151, 232, 267, 268–269

P

Pahlavi, Raza Shah, 144
Pakistan, 92; and Islam and Muslim World overview, 1–73; overview of, 214–220
Palestine Liberation Organization (PLO), 161, 168, 174, 175, 213, 255
Palestine: and Islam and Muslim World overview, 1–73; overview of, 221–226
paper mill, Muslims and, 3
Parliamentary elections, in Albania, 80
participation crisis, 33
Pashtun people, of Afghanistan, 75
Peel Commission, 223
penetration crisis, 32
People's Socialist Party, 287
Peres, Shimon, 36
petroleum. *See* oil
philosophy, Arabs and, 5
Phoenicia. *See* Lebanon
phosphates, 162–163
plantation economy, 250
political system, Islamic, as second manifestation of Islamism, 22
politics, 270; Benin and, 96; Cote d'Ivoire and, 112; Egypt and, 120; Gambia and, 126; in Indonesia, 139–140; in Iran, 145–146; in Iraq, 150; Morocco and, 197; of Qatar, 229; Pakistan and, 216–218; Senegal and, 238; of Suriname, 250;
population: Egypt and, 118; Kuwait and, 168 of Mauritania, 193; of Morocco, 195; of Mozambique, 202
Portugal, Guinea-Bissau and, 132
Pragmatists, 32, 34
Preaching of Islam, The (Arnold), 54
Progressive Islamists, 23, 25–28, 32
Prophet Muhammad, 1, 13–14, 52, 53, 57, 58, 61, 83, 196; Jesus and, 48–52
prophets, 10
Provisional Constitution of 1970, 152

Q

Qaddafi, Mu'ammar, 36, 68
Qadhafi, Muammar Muhammad al-, 179–180, 181
Qatar, 236; foreign relations of, 228–229; history of, 228; and Islam and Muslim World overview, 1–73; overview of, 227–229
Qualifying Industrial Zones (Q.I.Z.s), 122
Qu'ran, 10, 11–12, 14–16, 23, 24, 34, 53, 54, 61, 64–65; verses from, 47, 52, 54–57
Qutb, Syyid, 120

R

Rabin, Yitzhak, 36, 225–226

Rahman, Abdul, 183
Rahman, Mujibar, 92
Ramadan, 13
raw materials, Malaysia and, 184
Reagan, Ronald, 64, 66
refugees: in Djibouti, 115; in Guinea, 129
"relative deprivation," 32
religion: Benin and, 96; Cameroon and, 104; Iran and, 142. *See also* specific religions
Resolution 153, 153
Resolution 687, 153
Resolution 713, 153
Resolution 799, 224
Resolution 986, 153
Revolution of 1958, 151–152
Revolution of 1969, Libya and, 179
Revolutionary Command Council (RCC), 152
Revolutionary Islamists, 23, 24, 32; comparison table between Muslim secularists and, 26–27; comparison table between Progressive Islamists and, 29–31
Reza, Muhammad, Crown Prince of Iran, 144–145
"road map to peace," 226
Robertson, Pat, 67
Rome, Tunisia and, 263
Rubinstein, Alvin Z., on anti-Americanism, 63–69
Russia, 22, 66, 87, 165, 269; Iran and, 146; Kyrgyzstan and, 171; Tajikistan and, 258; Turkmenistan and, 275; Uzbekistan and, 284

S

Sabaean people, 286–287
Sabahs, paternalistic rule of the, 167
sacred struggle, as type of jihad, 53
Sadat, Muhammad Anwar al-, 36
Said, Qabus ibn, sultan of Oman, 212
sakk, credit system based on, 4
salat, as second pillar of Islam, 12–13, 16
Saleh, Ali Abdullah, 288, 289
Sanusiya Movement, 178–179
Saudi Arabia, 160, 178; Islam and Muslim World overview, 1–73; overview of, 230–236
sawm, as fourth pillar of Islam, 13, 16
Schuman, Robert, 157
secular ideologies, failure of, 31
secular nationalism, 9
secularists, 32
Security Council, 153
seerah, 1
Senegal, overview of, 237–239; Islam and, 238
Sezer, Ahmet Cevdet, 271
shahadah, as first pillar of Islam, 12, 16
shariah, 1, 10, 15, 16, 21, 23, 24, 38, 186, 235
Sharif, Mian Nawaz, 218–219
Sharon, Ariel, 225
Shatt al-Arab, 149
Shia Muslims, 10, 15–16, 35, 37, 38, 53, 75, 83, 89, 143, 150, 151, 153, 173, 175, 287; comparison table between Sunni Muslims and, 17–21